THE TABLETS AND THEIR SCRIBES

THE PALAEOGRAPHY OF HITTITE CUNEIFORM AND WRITING PRACTICES IN HITTITE ANATOLIA

Studien zu den Boğazköy-Texten

Herausgegeben im Auftrag
der Akademie der Wissenschaften und der Literatur, Mainz,
von Elisabeth Rieken und Daniel Schwemer
Band 73

The Tablets and Their Scribes

The Palaeography of Hittite Cuneiform and Writing Practices in Hittite Anatolia

Proceedings of the Second International HFR Symposium, Mainz, 2–4 May 2024

Edited by
Susanne Görke, Adam Kryszeń,
Gerfrid G. W. Müller, and Charles W. Steitler

2025

Harrassowitz Verlag · Wiesbaden

Gefördert durch die Akademie der Wissenschaften und der Literatur, Mainz, im Rahmen des vom Bundesministerium für Bildung und Forschung, Bonn/Berlin, dem Ministerium für Bildung, Wissenschaft, Weiterbildung und Kultur Rheinland-Pfalz, Mainz, dem Hessischen Ministerium für Wissenschaft und Kunst, Wiesbaden, und dem Bayerischen Staatsministerium für Wissenschaft und Kunst, München, finanzierten Akademienprogramms.

Bibliografische Information der Deutschen Nationalbibliothek
Die Deutsche Nationalbibliothek verzeichnet diese Publikation in der Deutschen Nationalbibliografie; detaillierte bibliografische Daten sind im Internet über https://dnb.de/ abrufbar.

Bibliographic information published by the Deutsche Nationalbibliothek
The Deutsche Nationalbibliothek lists this publication in the Deutsche Nationalbibliografie; detailed bibliographic data are available on the Internet at https://dnb.de/.

For further information about our publishing program consult our website https://www.harrassowitz-verlag.de/

Printed on permanent/durable paper.
Printing and binding: Memminger MedienCentrum AG
Printed in Germany

ISSN 0585-5853 eISSN 2702-0002
ISBN 978-3-447-12382-2 eISBN 978-3-447-39695-0

CONTENTS

ABBREVIATIONS

Bibliographical Abbreviations

AA	*Archäologischer Anzeiger*
ABoT	*Ankara Arkeoloji Müzesinde bulunan Boğazköy Tabletleri / Boğazköy Tablets in the Archaeological Museum of Ankara*
ÄAT	Ägypten und Altes Testament
AION	*Annali dell'Istituto Universitario Orientale di Napoli*
AMD	Ancient Magic and Divination
AnSt	*Anatolian Studies*
AOAT	Alter Orient und Altes Testament
AoF	*Altorientalische Forschungen*
BBVO	Berliner Beiträge zum Vorderen Orient
BiOr	*Bibliotheca Orientalis*
BoHa	Boğazköy-Ḫattuša. Ergebnisse der Ausgrabungen
BSIEL	Brill's Studies in Indo-European Languages and Linguistics
CAD	*The Assyrian Dictionary of the Oriental Institute of the University of Chicago*. Chicago: Oriental Institute, 1956–2010.
CHANE	Culture and History of the Ancient Near East
CHD	*The Hittite Dictionary of the Oriental Institute of the University of Chicago*. Chicago: Oriental Institute, 1980–.
CHDS	Chicago Hittite Dictionary. Supplements
ChS	Corpus der hurritischen Sprachdenkmäler
CollAnat	*Colloquium Anatolicum*
CTH	Emmanuel Laroche. *Catalogue des textes hittites*. Paris: Klincksieck, 1971 (with supplements in *RHA* 30 [1972]: 94–133 and *RHA* 33 [1973]: 68–71; now extensively expanded and revised in the online *Catalog der Texte der Hethiter* of the *Hethitologie-Portal Mainz*: Silvin Košak, Gerfrid G.W. Müller, Susanne Görke, and Charles W. Steitler (eds.). hethiter.net/*CTH* – last accessed 09.09.2024).
DAAM	Documenta Antiqua Asiae Minoris
DBH	Dresdner Beiträge zur Hethitologie
DBH 43/2	İlknur Taş. *Hethitische Texte in Transkription. Bo 8264 – Bo 8485. Teil 2: Autographien*. DBH 43/2. Wiesbaden: Harrassowitz, 2017.
DBH 46/2	Rukiye Akdoğan. *Hethitische Texte. Bo 4658 – Bo 5000. Teil 2: Autographien*. DBH 46/2. Wiesbaden: Harrassowitz, 2016.
DMOA	Documenta et Monumenta Orientis Antiqui
HANEM	History of the Ancient Near East. Monographs
HbOr	Handbuch der Orientalistik / Handbook of Oriental Studies

HED	Jaan Puhvel. *Hittite Etymological Dictionary.* Trends in Linguistics. Documentation. Berlin et al.: de Gruyter, 1984–.
HEG	Johann Tischler. *Hethitisches etymologisches Glossar.* Innsbrucker Beiträge zur Sprachwissenschaft 20. Innsbruck: Institut für Sprachwissenschaft, 1977–2016.
hethiter.net/: *CTH* … :	online text editions on the *Hethitologie-Portal Mainz*
HKM	Hethitische Keilschrifttafeln aus Maşat Höyük
HT	Hittite Texts in the Cuneiform Character from the Tablets in the British Museum. Autographed by Leonard William King – London 1920.
HW^2	*Hethitisches Wörterbuch. Zweite, völlig neubearbeitete Auflage auf der Grundlage der edierten hethitischen Texte.* Indogermanische Bibliothek, zweite Reihe: Wörterbücher. Heidelberg: Winter, 1975–.
HZL	Christel Rüster and Erich Neu. Hethitisches Zeichenlexikon. Inventar und Interpretation der Keilschriftzeichen aus den Boğazköy-Texten. StBoTB 2. Wiesbaden: Harrassowitz, 1989.
IBoT	İstanbul Arkeoloji Müzelerinde bulunan Boğazköy Tabletleri(nden seçme metinler)
IM	*Istanbuler Mitteilungen*
JANER	*Journal of Ancient Near Eastern Religions*
JAOS	*Journal of the American Oriental Society*
JCS	*Journal of Cuneiform Studies*
JEOL	*Jaarbericht van het Vooraziatisch-Egyptisch Genootschap "Ex Oriente Lux"*
JNES	*Journal of Near Eastern Studies*
KBo	Keilschrifttexte aus Boghazköy
KIM	*Kültepe Internation Meetings…*
KUB	Keilschrifturkunden aus Boghazköy
KuSa 1/1	Gernot Wilhelm. *Keilschrifttexte aus Gebäude A.* Kuşaklı–Šarišša. Band 1/1. Rahden: Leidorf, 1997.
MDOG	*Mitteilungen der Deutschen Orient-Gesellschaft zu Berlin*
MTK	Materiale Textkulturen
MVAeG	Mitteilungen der Vorderasiatisch-Ägyptischen Gesellschaft
NABU	*N. A. B. U. Nouvelles Assyriologiques Brèves et Utilitaires*
OA	*Oriens Antiquus*
OAM	*Orientis Antiqui Miscellanea*
OLZ	*Orientalistische Literaturzeitung*
OrNS	*Orientalia. Nova Series*
PIHANS	Publications de l'Institut historique et archéologique néerlandais de Stamboul = Uitgaven van het Nederlands Historisch-Archaeologisch Instituut te Istanbul
RANT	*Res Antiquae*
RlA	*Reallexikon der Assyriologie (und Vorderasiatischen Archäologie)*
SAA	State Archives of Assyria
SAMR	Studies in Ancient Mediterranean Religions

SANER	Studies in Ancient Near Eastern Records
SMEA	*Studi micenei ed egeo-anatolici*
StAs	Studia Asiana
StBoT	Studien zu den Boğazköy-Texten
StBoTB	Studien zu den Boğazköy-Texten. Beihefte
StMed	Studia Mediterranea
THeth	Texte der Hethiter
TLH^{dig}	Thesaurus Linguarum Hethaeorum digitalis
TTKY	Türk Tarih Kurumu Yayınları
TUAT	Texte aus der Umwelt des Alten Testaments
TUAT NF	Texte aus der Umwelt des Alten Testaments. Neue Folge
TÜBA-AR	*Türkiye Bilimler Akademisi Arkeoloji Dergisi*
UAVA	Untersuchungen zur Assyriologie und Vorderasiatischen Archäologie
VSNF	Vorderasiatische Schriftdenkmäler der Staatlichen Museen zu Berlin. Neue Folge
WAW	Society of Biblical Literature Writings from the Ancient World
WdO	*Die Welt des Orients*
ZA	*Zeitschrift für Assyriologie und Vorderasiatische Archäologie*
ZVS	Zeitschrift für vergleichende Sprachforschung

General Abbreviations

.../a to .../z	Inventory number of Boğazköy tablets excavated 1931–1967
ah.	Althethitisch
BCS	Büklükale Cuneiform Seal
BHS	Büklükale Hieroglyphic Seal
BKT	Büklükale Text
Bo	Inventory number of tablets found at Boğazköy
DN	divine name
ENS	Early New Script
HFR	Hethitische Festrituale
Kp	Inventory number of tablets found at Kayalıpınar
KpT	= DAAM 1
KuT	Text number of texts found at Kuşaklı
l.e.	left edge
lo.e.	lower edge
LMS	Late Middle Script
LNH	Late New Hittite
LNS	Late New Script
MH	Middle Hittite
mh.	Mittelhethitisch
MS	Middle Hittite Script
ms.	manuscript
NH	New Hittite
NS	New Hittite Script
obv.	obverse
OH	Old Hittite
Or.	Inventory number of tablets found at Ortaköy
OS	Old Hittite Script
PN	personal name
p.	page
rev.	reverse
SZM	Inventory number of the Szépművészeti Múzeum Budapest
u.e.	upper edge
viz.	namely

Symbols

?	reading of a sign is doubtful
(?)	reading of sign string is doubtful
!	abnormal or mistaken sign; designation of column or side of tablet varies from hand copy
[ ]	encloses lost text
[( )]	encloses restorations according to duplicate text
⸢ ⸣	encloses damaged but legible signs
⟨ ⟩	omitted by scribal error
⟨⟨ ⟩⟩	sign to be omitted
x	illegible sign (in transliteration
[x x]	indicates amount of space in gaps; each x = space for one sign
...	encloses signs over erasure
*	reconstructed form
+	fragments join directly; after reference to a single fragment adjoining other fragment(s) (listed elsewhere)
(+)	fragments join indirectly
//	duplicate/parallel text
/	line break (in transliteration)
𒀹	*Glossenkeil* (single)
𒑱	*Glossenkeil* (double)
=	separates morphological elements within words
=	for division of logograms at the end of printed lines

Cursive text in translations indicates uncertain meanings or restorations.

PREFACE

This volume presents the contributions of the Second International HFR Symposium that took place at the Academy of Sciences and Literature | Mainz, May 2–4, 2024. It thereby constitutes the second in a series of symposia of the long-term project "Das Corpus der hethitischen Festrituale: Staatliche Verwaltung des Kultwesens im spätbronzezeitlichen Anatolien" (HFR) that are intended to foster regular interaction within the scholarly community of Hittitologists. The first symposium "Cult, Temple, Sacred Spaces. Cult practices and Cult spaces in Hittite Anatolia and Neighbouring Cultures" took place in Mainz in June 2019 and its proceedings were published as StBoT 66 (2020). Further symposia devoted to linguistic, economic, political, social and historical religious perspectives of the Hittite cult are planned for the future.

The topic of this second HFR symposium was chosen – in accordance with the research objectives planned for the various phases of HFR – to provide a palaeographic study concluding the first third of the entire project. This entails various approaches to writing practices, including the development of automatic tools to recognize and analyze sign forms and handwriting of individual scribes, a task undertaken mainly by Gerfrid G.W. Müller. Since the online publication of the HFR *Basiscorpus* in 2021, the festival texts serve as a perfect departure point for answering questions regarding the organization and realization of the writing process in Hittite Anatolia. The aim of the Second International Symposium was thus to discuss recent developments and approaches to numerous questions: In which way can methods of digital humanities contribute to understanding ancient writing practices? What kind of automatic tools are at our disposal? In which way and to which degree can traditional, macroscopic methods be useful? How many scribes were active in producing a well-defined corpus? Which writing practices and scribal customs are recognizable in various text genres? How do palaeographic conventions differ in different Hittite sites? These questions have been explored in more detail in the following introduction to the symposium's proceedings by Gerfrid G.W. Müller.

It was a special honour for us that the director of the Ankara Museum of Anatolian Civilizations, Yusuf Kıraç, was able to attend our symposium. His museum hosts a huge quantity of the tablets discovered at the Hittite capital of Ḫattuša and the Hittitological community is grateful that he and his team welcome visitors from abroad to study the original tablets in a stimulant and friendly environment.

We want to express our thanks to the primary organizers of the symposium, Elisabeth Rieken (Marburg) and Daniel Schwemer (Würzburg), who encouraged us to publish the proceedings in the series *Studien zu den Boğazköy-Texten,* and – as editors of this series – provided us with generous feedback. We were fortunate to have been able to use the facilities of the Academy of Sciences and Literatur | Mainz as an extremely suitable conference venue. The Academy is the primary organizational and financial supporter of the HFR project and simultaneously houses the *Hethitologie-Archiv*, which is one of three research sites (alongside Würzburg University and Marburg University) where indispensable analog and digital tools for ancient Anatolian studies have been developed over the last decades. The HFR team is very grateful to the administration and staff of the Academy for their support.

As editors, we would like to express our gratitude to all the contributors whom we asked to spend their summer finishing their contributions to make this volume available within less than a year after the conference. We are grateful to Valentin Gusev for the work on the typesetting of this volume. Finally, we express our gratitude to the staff of the Harrassowitz Verlag for their technical support during the process of forming this volume into a print publication.

Marburg / Mainz, December 2024

Susanne Görke

Adam Kryszeń

Gerfrid G.W. Müller

Charles W. Steitler

Yusuf Kıraç (left), Director of the Museum of Anatolian Civilisations at Ankara, receiving from Daniel Schwemer (right) an original drawing by Heinrich Otten for *Keilschrifttexte aus Boghazköi* 27 (1982), the first volume produced at the Academy of Sciences and Literature | Mainz within the framework of the research programme of the German Academies: KBo 27. 42 obv. ii, Hittite KI.LAM Festival.

ANADOLU MEDİNİYETLERİ MÜZESİ DİREKTÖRÜN KUNUŞMASI

Yusuf Kıraç

Anadolu Mediniyetleri Müzesi, Ankara

Ankara'da ilk müze, Atatürk'ün telkinleriyle merkezde bir "Eti Müzesi" kurma fikrinden hareket edilerek Kültür Müdürü Mübarek Galip Bey tarafından 1921 yılında Ankara Kalesinin Akkale burcunda kurulmuştur. Yine Cumhuriyetin ilk yıllarından itibaren Ankara'ya gelen eserler Augustus Mabedi ile Roma Hamamında da toplanmıştır.

1938 yılında Kültür Müdürü Hamit Zübeyr Koşay tarafından, metruk halde bulunan Mahmut Paşa Bedesteni ve Kurşunlu Hanın onarılarak müze binası olarak kullanılması fikri kabul edilerek, 1938 yılından 1968'e kadar devam eden bir restorasyon çalışması başlatılmıştır. Bedestenin orta bölümünde yer alan 10 kubbeli mekânın büyük bir kısmının onarımının 1943 yılında bitirilmesi ile eserler, Alman Hititolog Prof. Dr. Hans Gustav Güterbock başkanlığındaki bir heyet tarafından yerleştirilmiş ve ziyarete açılmıştır.

Müze yapısı 1968 yılında son şeklini almıştır. Bugün idari bina olarak kullanılan Kurşunlu Han'da araştırmacı odaları, kütüphane, konferans salonu, eser depoları, laboratuvar ve iş atölyeleri yer almakta, Mahmut Paşa Bedesteni ise teşhir salonu ve eğitim ve deneyim alanı olarak kullanılmaktadır.

Konuşmamın bu bölümünde bir parantez açarak Sayın Prof. Dr. Hans Gustav Güterbock'dan bahsetmeden geçemeyeceğim. Güterbock 27 Mayıs 1908' yılında Berlin'de doğmuş ve genç yaşlardan itibaren Eski Yakındoğu dillerine, tarihine ilgi duymaya başlamıştır. Eğitim ve öğrenimini Hititoloji, Sumeroloji-Assirioloji dillerinde döneminin en ünlü bilginlerinin yanında tamamlamış ve Berlin Müzesinde ilk görevine başlamıştır.

1936–1948 yılları arasında ülkemizin ilk Hititoloji disiplininin kurucusu olarak, eski Anadolu Tarihi ve kültürleri için çok önemli olan bu bilim dalının kurulup gelişmesinde, uzmanların yetişmesinde, öğretim ve araştırma alanında gerçekleştirilmesinde gerekenlerin en çoğunu başarmış ve öğrencilerinin orijinal Hitit tabletlerini yayımlamaya başlamalarını sağlamıştır.

Uppsala Üniversitesi'nde misafir profesör olarak görev aldıktan sonra, 1949 yılında Şikago Üniversitesi "The Oriental Institute"de göreve başlayan H. G. Güterbock 1976 yılında seçkin emeritus profesör oldu.

Ankara Üniversitesi Dil ve Tarih-Coğrafya Fakültesi'nde Hititoloji'nin müstakil bir disiplin olarak gelişmesini, ilk Hititoloji kütüphanesinin kurulmasını sağlamıştır. Öğrencileri üniversitede, müzelerde görevlendirilmişler, çivi yazılı tablet arşivlerinin sorumluluğunu üstlenmişlerdir. Anadolu Medeniyetleri Müzesi büyük salonunun tertip ve tanzimi de yine onun eseridir.

Boğazköy kazılarına Hititolog olarak katılmış, Hitit çivi yazılı metinlerini, hiyeroglif yazıtlı Hitit kral mühürlerini ayrı ciltler halinde yayımlamış, hiyerogliflerin okunmasına, anlaşılmasına büyük katkılarda bulunmuş, bu konuda çalışan bilginler arasında seçkin ve saygın yerin sahibi olmuştur. TTK kazılarında keşfedilmiş hiyeroglifli belgeleri, tam zamanında, bilim dünyasına sunmuştur.

O, Hitit kültürünün her alanında yoğunlaştırdığı araştırmalarını, yani tarihini, dilini, edebiyatını, dinini, mitolojisini, gramerini, kanunlarını, devlet yönetimini, sosyal yapısını, etnik ayrılıkları bütün detay ve özellikleriyle aydınlatan ve yazılı belgelerin ışığında sanat eserlerini yorumlayan ender hititologların başında yerini almıştır. Onun Hititoloji alanında aydınlatmaya çalışmadığı, üzerinde durmadığı bir konu, bir problem yoktur. Meslektaşları Hititoloji disiplinine H.G. Güterbock kadar katkıda bulunmuş bilginlerin az olduğunu, yerinin hititologlar listesinde çok özel olduğunu, haklı olarak, vurgulamaktadırlar.

O, üstün araştırıcılığının yanında, kendisini Hititolojiye adamış bir hoca olarak, yaşamının sonuna kadar kendisiyle ilişki kurmuş olan zamanın bütün hititologlarına yaptığı yardımlarını, tavsiyelerini, öneri ve tenkitlerini hiç azaltmamış ve bugün ondan yararlanma şansına sahip olmuş bilginlerin sayısı azımsanamayacak bir seviyeye gelmiştir.

Güterbock yaşamının son yıllarını büyük bir projenin gerçekleşmesine "Şikago Üniversitesi Hitit Lügati Projesine" adamıştır. Proje üzerinde çalışan meslektaşları onun katılım ve katkılarından övgüyle söz etmektedirler; bu lügat onun en önemli eserlerinden biri olacaktır.

Güterbock'a ithaf edilen iki armağan kitabı 1974 ve 1986 yılında iki ciltte derlenmiştir. "Kumarbi Efsanesi" hakkındaki kitabı ayrı olarak, değişik konulardaki makaleleri de Türk Tarih Kurumu dergisi Belleten'de de yayımlanmıştır.

Akademi üyelikleri, şeref doktorluklarıyla ödüllendirilmiş olan Güterbock, Türkiye Bilimler Akademisi'nin şeref üyesi; The British Academy'nin, The American Academy of Arts and Sciences'ın, Bayerische Akademie der Wissenschaften'in üyesi; Uppsala ve Ankara Üniversitelerinin şeref doktorudur.

Dil ve Tarih-Coğrafya Fakültesi'nin ilk Hititoloji profesörü ve aynı zamanda Türk Tarih Kurumu'nun şeref üyesi olan Güterbock 24 Mart 2000 yılında 91 yaşında Şikago'da vefat etmiştir. Kendisini bilime Hititoloji'ye ve ülkemize yaptığı katkılarından dolayı şükranla anıyoruz.

Bugün kendine özgü koleksiyonları ile dünyanın sayılı müzeleri arasında yer alan Anadolu Medeniyetleri Müzesi 1997 yılında Avrupa'da yılın müzesi ödülünü almıştır. Anadolu Arkeolojisi, Paleolitik Çağdan başlayarak günümüze kadar Osmanlı devrinin bu tarihi mekânlarında kronolojik bir sırayla sergilenmekte olup daha da önemlisi müzenin teşhir ve depolarında yer alan eserlerden hiçbirisi başka bir ülkeden kaçırılmış değil, sadece Anadolu eserleri olup, herhangi bir kaçakçılığa konu olmamıştır.

Müzemiz Ayrıca Dünya Miras Listesine dahil edilmiş olan Ankara'ya yaklaşık 90 km. mesafede yer alan Friglerin Başkenti Gordion'da bulunan Gordion Müzesini, Ankara'nın içinde yer alan Roma Dönemi Caracalla Hamamını, Augustus Mabedini ve Ankyra Tiyatrosu ve Arkeoloparkını da bünyesinde barındırmaktadır.

Anadolu Medeniyetleri Müzesi Mahmut Paşa Bedesteni, teşhir salonlarında Paleolitik Dönem, Kalkolitik Dönem, Erken Tunç Dönemi, Asur Ticaret Kolonileri Dönemi, Hitit Dönemi, Geç Hitit Dönemi, Frig Dönemi, Urartu Dönemi, Pers Dönemi, Hellenistik Dönem, Grek ve Roma Dönemi ile Selçuklu ve Osmanlı Dönemine ait eserler kronolojik olarak teşhir edilmektedir.

Müzenin farklı kategorilerde oluşturulmuş toplam 35 deposunda 200.000 civarında eser bulunmaktadır. Bahis konusu depolardan Tablet ve Bulla Deposunda ise 39.447 Tablet ve 3.551 adet Bulla yer almaktadır. Söz konusu tabletlerden 18.955 adedini Kültepe Kaniş Karum Asur Tabletleri oluştururken, büyük bir kısmını Boğazköy Hitit Tabletleri, oluşturmaktadır.

Boğazköy'de bulunan Hitit tabletlerinin sayısı bugüne kadar yaklaşık 32.000'e ulaşmış ve bunların çoğu çivi yazılı el kopyaları olarak yayınlanmıştır. Oldukça hızlı ve yoğun bir yayın sürecine rağmen, Boğazköy kazılarından kaynaklanan ve hala yayınlanmamış tablet parçaları bulunmaktadır. "Bo" simgesini taşıyan bu tabletler, 1906–1912 yılları arasındaki erken dönem Osmanlı-Alman kazılarında ortaya çıkmış ve sonradan konservasyon amacıyla Berlin'deki *Staatliche Museen* Devlet Müzesine gönderilmiştir. Uzun yıllar bürokratik ve idari girişimlerden sonra söz konusu tabletlerin son kısmı 1987 yılında Türkiye'ye iade edilmiştir.

Doğu Berlin'e gönderilen ve daha sonra Bakanlığımızın girişimleriyle 1987 yılında müzemize getirilen 7.308 adet tablet 1988 yılında Türk Hititologlardan oluşan bilimsel yeterliliği olan akademisyenlere araştırma ve yayımlama görevi ile verilmiştir. Ancak yaklaşık 25 yıllık bir dönemden sonra, ekibin bazı üyeleri vefat etmiş, bazıları emekli olmuş veya ekip içindeki görevlerinden ayrılmışlardır. Bu nedenle Türkiye Cumhuriyeti Kültür Bakanlığı'nın 2010 yılında aldığı bir karara dayanarak, yayınlanmamış Bo-metinleri üzerinde çalışmaya devam etmek üzere yeni bir Türk Hititolog ekibi oluşturulmuştur. Bunlar kısmen eski çalışma grubundan bilim insanları ve Ankara, İstanbul, Çorum, Kocaeli, Adana ve Şikago'daki çeşitli üniversiteler ve müzelerden 21 genç Hititolog arasında tekrar paylaştırılmıştır. Her ekip üyesi sorumluluğuna 170, 190 ya da 250 parça olmak üzere bir tablet grubu almıştır.

2020 yılında ise araştırmacılar arasında yaşanan telif hakları ile ilgili mahkeme ve teftiş soruşturmaları sonucunda Kültür ve Turizm Bakanlığı tarafından daha önce verilmiş olan araştırma, inceleme ve yayım haklarının bakanlığa geçtiği tüm araştırmacılara resmi olarak bildirilmiştir. Alınan cevaplara göre yayımlanmamış tabletlerle ilgili yıllık 50 adet olmak üzere Bakanlığımıza veya müzemize başvuru yapan akademisyenlere imzalanacak protokol kapsamında bir yıl içinde araştırma, ikinci yıl uzatma ve üçüncü yılda yayımlama hakkı tanınmış, 3 yıl içinde yayım yapmayan akademisyenin haklarının tekrar bakanlığa geçeceği şeklinde mevzuat düzenlemesi yapılmıştır.

Bilimsel literatürde "yayımlanmamış Bo-metinleri" olarak bilinen yazım eserleri, yüksek tarihi ve kültürel değere sahip orijinal antik belgeler kategorisine aittir. Bo-metinleri fiziksel bakımdan çoğunlukla küçük ve kötü korunmuş yapıya sahip olsa da, yeni kopya ve join metinlerin keşfedilmesi ve bunun sayesinde Boğazköy'den iyi bilinen ve daha iyi korunmuş kompozisyonlara doğrudan bağlantılar yapılması potansiyeli her zaman mevcuttur ve bu da mevcut Hitit yazım malzemesini kesinlikle zenginleştirecektir. Bo-metinleri araştırmasının uzun vadeli amacı, daha fazla epigrafik malzemeyi kullanarak Hitit dili, tarihi ve kültürüne ilişkin sonuçları gelecekteki yayımlar aracılığıyla beşerî bilimlerdeki akademisyenler topluluğuna erişilebilir kılmaktır. Yayımlanmamış Bo-metinlerinin edisyonu, son otuz yılda Hititoloji'nin önemli bir görevi haline gelmiştir ve Hititoloji dünyası tarafından uzun zamandır beklenmektedir. Bu anlamda, epigrafik malzemenin hem kitap olarak hem de elektronik ortamda (fotoğraflar ve özellikle 3D taramalar) basılması ve yayımlanması, uluslararası bilimsel çabalarının beklenen ve sevindirici bir sonucu olacaktır.

Ben bu duygu ve düşüncelerle Anadolu'nun Kadim Tarihinin, Medeniyetlerinin, geçmiş uygarlıklarının yaşantısının ve en önemlisi kültür varlığı olarak günümüze kadar gelen tabletlerin yani Hitit Dilinin araştırılmasında, bilimsel olarak çalışılıp yayımlanmasında emeği geçen tüm akademisyenlere, bu sempozyumun hazırlanmasında emeği geçenlere müzem adına ve ülkem adına teşekkür ediyor şükranlarımı sunuyorum.

GREETINGS FROM THE DIRECTOR OF THE MUSEUM OF ANATOLIAN CIVILIZATIONS

Yusuf Kıraç
Museum of Anatolian Civilizations, Ankara

The first museum in Ankara was established in 1921 by Mübarek Galip Bey, Director of Culture, in the *Akkale Tower* of *Ankara Castle*, based on the idea of establishing an "*Eti Museum*" in the city center of Ankara, following a suggestion of Atatürk. In the first years of the Republic, artefacts coming to Ankara were collected in the *Augustus Temple* and the *Roman Baths*.

In 1938, the Director of Culture Hamit Zübeyr Koşay accepted the idea of repairing both the abandoned *Mahmut Pasha Bedesten* and *Kurşunlu Han* and of using them jointly as a museum building. Restoration work was executed from 1938 to 1968. After the restoration of a large part of the 10-domed space in the central part of the *Bedesten* was completed in 1943, the artefacts were put on display by a committee headed by the German Hittitologist Prof. Dr. Hans Gustav Güterbock and opened to visitors.

The museum building took on its final shape in 1968. Today, the *Kurşunlu Han* serves as an administrative building, with research rooms, a library, a conference hall, artefact storage rooms, laboratories, and workshops, while the *Mahmut Pasha Bedesten* is used as an exhibition hall and an educational area.

At this point in my speech, I would like to focus our attention on Prof. Dr. Hans Gustav Güterbock. Güterbock was born in Berlin on May 27, 1908; he was interested in ancient Near Eastern languages and history from his youth on. He completed his education and training in Hittitology, Sumerology and Assyriology under the most famous scholars of his time and his first position was at the Berlin Museum.

Between 1936 and 1948, as the founder of the discipline of Hittitology in Turkey, he was able to establish and develop this discipline, which is very important for ancient Anatolian history and cultures. He trained experts, undertook research and taught students, which thus enabled them to publish original Hittite tablets.

After spending time as a visiting professor at Uppsala University, Güterbock joined the Oriental Institute (now Institute for the Study of Ancient Cultures [ISAC]) at the University of Chicago in 1949 and became a distinguished emeritus professor in 1976.

He ensured the formation of Hittitology as an independent discipline at the Faculty of Language, History and Geography of Ankara University and the establishment of the first Hittitological library in Turkey. His students were employed at the university and museums and took responsibility for the archives of cuneiform tablets. The layout and arrangement of the great hall of the Museum of Anatolian Civilizations is also his work.

Güterbock participated in excavations at Boğazköy as a Hittitologist: he published Hittite cuneiform texts and Hittite royal seals with hieroglyphic inscriptions in multiple volumes. His work enlarged our knowledge of deciphering and understanding hieroglyphs. On the whole, he became distinguished and respected among scholars in his field. He promptly presented the hieroglyphic documents that were discovered during the excavations of the *Türk Tarih Kurumu* to the world of science.

He has been one of the rare Hittitologists who focused their research on every field of Hittite culture, i. e. history, language, literature, religion, mythology, grammar, laws, state administration, and social structure. He interpreted the artworks in light of the written documents. There is hardly a subject or problem in the field of Hittitology that he did not endeavor to elucidate. Few scholars have contributed to the discipline of Hittitology as much as Hans Gustav Güterbock.

In addition to his outstanding research and his devotion to Hittitology, Güterbock was a teacher who never withheld his help, advice, suggestions and criticisms to all the Hittitologists who were in contact with him until the end of his life. Until today the number of scholars who have had the chance to benefit from him has reached a level that cannot be underestimated.

Güterbock devoted the last years of his life to the realization of a major project, the *Hittite Dictionary* project of the University of Chicago. His colleagues working on the project speak highly of his participation and contribution; this dictionary is one of his most important contributions to the field.

Two publications were presented to him in his honor, 1974 and 1986. Apart from his book on the "Legend of Kumarbi", his articles on various subjects were published also in *Belleten*, the journal of the *Türk Tarih Kurumu.*

He was an honorary member of the Turkish Academy of Sciences, a member of the *British Academy*, the *American Academy of Arts and Sciences*, the *Bayerische Akademie der Wissenschaften*, and he held honorary doctorates from Uppsala and Ankara Universities.

Güterbock, the first professor of Hittitology at the Faculty of Language, History and Geography at Ankara University and also an honorary member of the Turkish Historical Society, died in Chicago on March 24, 2000 at the age of 91. We remember him with gratitude for his contributions to science, Hittitology, and our country.

Today, the Museum of Anatolian Civilizations with its unique collections is one of the world's leading museums. For its achievements, it received the European Museum of the Year award in 1997. Its exhibition of Anatolian Archaeology covers the entire timeline from the Paleolithic Age to the present day, while the setting in the buildings of the Ottoman period adds a special historic flair. More importantly, none of the artefacts in the museum's exhibitions and depots have been smuggled from another country.

Our museum also includes the *Gordion Museum* in Gordion, the capital of the Phrygians, which is included in the World Heritage List and located about 90 km west of Ankara, as well as the *Roman Baths of Caracalla*, the *Temple of Augustus*, and the *Ankyra Theatre* and *Archaeopark* in Ankara.

The exhibition halls of the Museum of Anatolian Civilizations in the *Mahmut Pasha Bedesteni* display artefacts in chronological order from the Paleolithic and Chalcolithic Periods, through the Early Bronze Age, the period of the Assyrian Trade Colonies, the Hittite Period, the Late Hittite Period, the Phrygian and Urartian Period, the Persian, Hellenistic, Greek and Roman Periods, and up to the Seljuk and Ottoman Periods.

There are around 200,000 artefacts in a total of 35 depots of the museum. Among these, the Tablet and Bulla storerooms contain 39,447 tablets and 3,551 bullae. While 18,955 of these tablets are Assyrian tablets from Kültepe Karum Kaniş, the majority are Hittite tablets from Boğazköy.

Up to now, the number of Hittite tablets found at Boğazköy has reached approximately 32,000, most of which have been published as cuneiform hand copies. Despite a very rapid and intensive publication process, there are still unpublished fragments of tablets from the Boğazköy excavations. These tablets, bearing the abbreviation "Bo", were unearthed during the early Ottoman-German excavations between 1906 and 1912 and later sent to the *Staatliche Museen* in Berlin for conservation. After many years of bureaucratic and administrative attempts, the last part of the tablets was returned to Turkey in 1987.

The 7,308 tablets, which were sent to East Berlin and then brought to our museum in 1987 with the initiatives of our Ministry, were handed over to a team of scientifically qualified Turkish Hittitologists for research and publication in 1988. However, after a period of approximately 25 years, some members of the team had passed away, and some retired or left their positions. Therefore, based on a decision taken by the Turkish Ministry of Culture in 2010, a new team of Turkish Hittitologists was formed to continue work on the unpublished Bo-texts. These were partly redistributed between the scientists from the former working group and 21 young Hittitologists from various universities and museums in Ankara, Istanbul, Çorum, Kocaeli, Adana, and Chicago. Each team member took responsibility for a group of 170, 190, or 250 tablets.

In 2020, all researchers were officially notified that the research, examination, and publication rights previously granted by the Ministry of Culture and Tourism were transferred to the Ministry as a result of court and inspection investigations regarding copyrights between researchers. Then, academics who applied to our Ministry or our museum with an annual number of 50 unpublished tablets were given the right to do research in year one, with a possible extension to year two, and then publish in the third year within the scope of the signed protocol. According to a legislative arrangement, the rights of an academic who does not publish within three years will be given back to the ministry.

The fragments, known in the scientific literature as "(un)published Bo-texts", are original ancient documents of high historical and cultural value. Although the Bo-texts are often physically small and poorly preserved, there is always the potential for the discovery of new copies and joining texts, with direct connections to well-known and better-preserved compositions from Boğazköy, which would certainly enrich the existing Hittite scribal material. The long-term goal of the Bo-texts research is to publish more epigraphic material to offer conclusions about Hittite language, history, and culture and to make them accessible to the community of scholars in the humanities through future publications. The edition of unpublished Bo-texts has become an important task of Hittitology in the last thirty years and has been long awaited by the world of Hittitology. In this sense, the publication and dissemination of the epigraphic material, both in printed and in electronic forms (photographs and especially 3D scans) will be an anticipated and well-received outcome of this international scholarly endeavor.

With these feelings and thoughts, I hope that the information that comes out of this symposium will be a resource for future generations that will contribute to the understanding of the Ancient History of Anatolia, the Hittite tablets, and the Hittite language. I would like to thank and express my gratitude to the Academy of Sciences and Literature in Mainz, the University of Würzburg, and all who contributed to the symposium.

INTRODUCTION

Gerfrid G.W. Müller
Julius-Maximilians-Universität Würzburg
Akademie der Wissenschaften und der Literatur | Mainz

What appearance do Hittite clay tablets, their layout and their characters have over time, in geographical space and in the individual design of their scribes? How can the countless individual observations be reliably used, classified and compared?

The symposium discussed a variety of phenomena related to scribal habits and practices in the Hittite kingdom. This includes both systematic changes that the cuneiform script has undergone throughout its history in Anatolia, as well as handwriting and idiosyncrasies of individual scribes, and the habits to prepare and arrange tablets, text, sealings and space. By studying the overall appearance of the tablet and sign shapes it is, in principle, not only possible to date the text, but also to attribute it to a particular scribe or a scribal circle. There was a broad exchange of experience on palaeographical questions and practical ways to answer them.

The title "The Tablets and Their Scribes" opens up the possibility for a wide variety of questions. As it turned out, however, the majority of the participants were primarily concerned with the question of dating tablets and assigning them to scribes.

In 1938 Hans Gustav Güterbock wrote that "our possession of texts about the Old Kingdom is due to the historical interest of the later Hittites. For the few texts about that period are probably all in late copies, i. e. those of the Empire period, at least according to their paleographic correspondence with the texts of this period." (Güterbock 1938: 97; original citation in German, translated by the author).

Fifteen years later, Heinrich Otten described the newly found Zukraši text as Old Hittite according to its language, and noted that the writing is closely set, but the ductus corresponds completely to Neo-Hittite forms (Otten 1953). He saw its value above all in the fact that this tablet fragment clearly came from an ancient Hittite layer, i. e. it was an old original, not a later copy.

The idea of the Old Hittite script only emerged slowly and with further new discoveries. There are indications that the idea originated with Güterbock (Klinger 2022: 263f.), but by the early 1960's it had become consensus. Hittite palaeography flourished, the sign forms became reliable dating criteria and young Hittitologists were primed on the dating criteria of writing. Nearly a quarter of a century after the launch of the Hittitology Portal Mainz we have almost forgotten that in the last millennium only very few people had access to photos and the original clay tablets and that the perception of Hittite cuneiform tablets and signs was shaped primarily by the autographs. Since the 1970s, a method of dating based on diagnostic sign-forms has been developed, culminating in the *Hethitisches Zeichenlexikon* (Rüster and Neu 1989) with the signs tentatively arranged in chronological order. Efforts were made to obtain more precise datings (e. g. Starke 1985, Klinger 1996).

At that time, distinctive handwriting of individual scribes was not the main focus of palaeographic analysis. If my intuition is correct, and some remarks in the papers point to this, we are only slowly learning to recognize the individual scribe, even if some milestones have already been reached along the way (e. g. Gordin 2015). It is of course easier and probably necessary to orient oneself according to standard forms and to assess the deviations, but for a successful classification of manuscripts, we will have to learn to concentrate more on the individual characteristics of the signs and also use deep learning and AI to handle the large amounts of information required. It is no coincidence that in traditional forensic handwriting analysis, usually only one document is compared to others. We are dealing with a gigantic game of 'Memory'.

In his contribution to this volume, Yusuf Kıraç, the director of the Museum of Anatolian Civilizations in Ankara, discusses the history of the museum, which has the largest collection of Hittite clay tablets, and he pays tribute to the role of Hans Gustav Güterbock. In doing so, he also reminds us of the context in which Güterbock developed his ideas, and of the importance of the conservation and provision of the cuneiform texts by our colleagues in the museums.

1. Text basis

The selection of texts for the individual studies was based mainly on the criteria of content. The festival rituals, which are the subject of the HFR project, naturally represent a much larger group.

The *nuntarriyašḫa-* festival comprises around 200 text fragments, but Kryszeń confined himself to the 17 outline tablets. Each of these provides a complete overview of the festival and it is assumed that they are all originals and not copies, and can therefore be dated with greater certainty. Steitler uses the 16th day of the AN.DAḪ.ŠUM festival, which is heterogeneous with regard to content and palaeography, and Doğan-Alparslan examines the *ḫišuwa-* festival.

Görke devotes herself to the texts with passages in Palaic or the mention of Palaic gods in Old Script (OS) as well as the Ziparwa festivals within the itinerant state festivals of AN.DAḪ.ŠUM and *nuntarriyašḫa-*, some of which can be dated by the names of the scribes.

The 15 "Intake and Storage" records, a subset of the Palace-Temple Administrative Corpus (Burgin), the cult inventories (Cammarosano) as well as the oracle texts (Trameri) are of a completely different nature. These are usually written hastily and with less care.

Another group selected according to content are the surviving Hittite votive texts, mainly records of vows made by Queen Puduḫepa, which show her concern for the welfare of her family and the country (Schwemer).

Some ensembles of texts are defined by the circumstances of their discovery at excavation sites outside Ḫattuša, such as the text finds from the site of Büklükale on the western Kızılırmak, which continue to come to light after the first text discovery there in 2009 (Weeden), or the 121 fragments from the "archive excavation" in Kayalıpınar (Lorenz and Rieken).

The 36 Middle Hittite texts from Maşat Höyük (Tapikka), examined by Leonard on the basis of photographs and 3D models, also come from outside Ḫattuša. This corpus consists of letters that my have been sent there from Ḫattuša or Šapinuwa.

The contribution by Soysal focuses on the important "Zukraši Text" mentioned above and, in addition to philological questions on the understanding of the text, also deals with the characteristics of Old Hittite texts.

The scope of Waal's contribution is cross-corpus in comparing the practice of writing Luwian hieroglyphs with writing the cuneiform script.

In the more technical investigations, Gordin uses the xml data of HFR as the basis for his stylometric experiments, and Müller uses 3D models of tablets with scribal names and the collection of photographs in the Mainz Photo Archive for the development of analytical methods.

2. Questions

Waal approaches the question of which writing habits were adopted by the Hittites along with the cuneiform script and which are of internal Anatolian origin by examining sealing practices and the use of determinatives.

Kryszeń's investigation of how the *nuntarriyašḫa-* festival changed over time focuses primarily on text dating. He uses the outline tablets, tablets written at the time of editing the text that were not copied, to determine the **relative chronology** of the **festival's development**. Steitler's focus is also on the palaeographic strata represented in the texts and the comparison of the **relative dating** of the texts with the aim of observing the **development of the festival** over time and, in particular, clarifying the changing role of the king and crown prince. Görke poses several questions concerning the two-part Palaic corpus: for the group of Old Hittite texts, she investigates whether one of the **scribes** of the **Palaic texts** also wrote **other Old Hittite** texts and, based on this, **how many scribes** we can assumed to have been active in the Old Hittite period. For the second group, written in New Script, she also searches for **scribes who wrote several** texts and attempts an **internal chronology**. The study by Doğan-Alparslan on the *ḫišuwa-* festival also focuses on chronological aspects of the writing, in particular the Middle Hittite fragments and their implications for the history of the text tradition.

The study by Burgin begins with an attempt to use palaeography to determine how many scribal hands were present in the administrative texts examined, and thus to estimate the **total number of scribes** in the administration. This approach is aimed more at **differentiating between handwritings**. Cammarosano's study of the cult inventories also focuses on the **question of authorship**.

Trameri searches for specific writing practices and writing habits in Hittite oracle tablets and under what circumstances handwritings with different appearances occur on oracle reports.

Schwemer asks whether the votive texts were written by **specialists** or by **scribes of the royal administration**.

Soysal discusses the archaic features and peculiarities of the Zukraši text after an intensive autopsy of this important Old Hittite manuscript.

Lorenz and Rieken's research on the Kayalıpınar texts goes beyond an attempt to identify scribal hands on the basis of visual appearance of the sign forms and determining the number of scribes. Their paper also addresses the question of **joining** tablet fragments on the basis of palaeographic and physical characteristics, the unity of the scattered archive and its function.

For the tablets from Büklükale, Weeden's aims to **date** of the tablets and **classify unusual sign-forms** (local inventions, localization of specific sign-forms).

Leonard examines the **chronological features** of the syllabary of the Maşat texts, finding some NS sign forms, and examining the signs of three scribes more carefully. However, considering the small basis of data, he refrains from ascribing anonymous tablets to any particular scribe.

Gordin experiments with the operationalization of the xml files of HFR to transform abstract writing habits into explorable latent features. Thes can be used to describe the proximity of texts and text groups for the purpose of identifying genre, authorship and textual traditions, especially on the basis of Luwian and Hurrian festival rituals.

Finally, Müller asks how handwritings can be distinguished using technical means, and which tools can be used to assist with palaeographic examinations.

3. Methods

Prior to the online publication of photographs on HPM, most Hittite cuneiform texts were only available in the form of hand-copies. For a long time, it has been common practice in Hittitology to reproduce the signs in the autographs as closely as possible to the original. Inevitably, however, copyists tend to typify the sign in both their conception of as well as rendering of the signs. This sign typification aids in dating the texts, which is considered perhaps the most important task of palaeography. However, it also artificially conceals individual differences in handwriting.

Since photos are now available for most of the texts on HPM, their use as a basis for handwriting comparison and join suggestions has gradually become established. The starting point for examining a document's handwriting is usually a comparison of the signs with established dating criteria and, in addition, individual observations of writing idiosyncrasies. Ideally, the examination includes an entire inventory of signs. But due to the great effort involved, this is only possible for small text ensembles, so a selection is usually made.

To simplify matters, groups of characters with similar design elements can also be described summarily (Kryszeń). The characterization of the signs can also be done by a detailed description of the properties and peculiarities, as perceived by an experienced copyist (Schwemer).

Two contributions attempted to apply the method described by Yakubovich and Mouton (2023: 29–46). The procedure first classifies all the larger fragments by handwriting and then examines those with similar handwriting for further characteristics such as slanted verticals, use of space, shape and depth of column dividers, shape of the tablet, etc. In this way, it is often possible to show that the fragments with the same handwriting belonged to the same text series. This process alone orders the tablet series in distinct categories based on the different handwritings identified. Small fragments could be assigned to these. Parallel passages and colophons helped to confirm that two tablets could not belong to the same hand.

Burgin first tried to distinguish handwritings using a list of possible diagnostic signs. The failure of this method was demonstrated when he attempted to separate the handwritings based on the individual signs of a large number of texts of different genres. This was due to the arbitrary classification of variants as belonging to the same or to different handwritings. In a second attempt, he created complete character tables for each tablet of a small, thematically similar group. This resulted in more precise observations and comparable text passages, which had also proved helpful with Yakubovich and Mouton's approach.

Lorenz and Rieken also used this method to prepare their investigation, which should clarify the character of the find ensemble of 121 fragments from Kayalıpınar. First, as many fragments as possible should be joined, or at least their affiliation should be determined on the basis of writing characteristics. It proved difficult to find sign forms in small fragments that could be compared, and also the range of variation in the shapes of individual sign forms, so that the relevance of sign forms for or against a join remained uncertain.

Statements such as "signs useful for dating texts and the set of signs useful for distinguishing scribal hands are not the same" (Burgin) or "the sign forms relevant for the dating are not necessarily the same as those significant for identifying the handwriting" (Kryszeń) indicate that the analysis process is determined by the approach to dating through diagnostic signs. But the process of handwriting identification is much more complex, since both the signs and their features can vary (as showed the experience of Burgin). So, e. g., in one context a simple sign like BI consistently written with the same indentation of a horizontal wedge can be a distinguishing criterion, but within another context, the indentation of the upper and lower horizontal wedge can alternate.

Macroscopic analysis without digital methods for metric and microscopic examination limits the possibilities for identifying subtle differences between handwriting. But even with digital tools, the range of variation in the handwriting – even of one and the same scribe – can be an obstacle. Furthermore, it is often possible to identify fragments that share a significant number of handwriting and cursive writing characteristics. If these fragments are comparatively small, it is difficult to make a final decision as to whether they were written by the same hand, even if the sign forms and types on the respective fragments largely match.

Weeden argues for a distinction between cuneiform palaeography and material handwriting studies. From a systematic point of view, this is plausible. In practice, however, it should be considered that in a palaeographic database, all character forms should be available without pre-classification.

4. The case of Hieratic

The remarks above show that a digital, interoperable syllabary is needed for Hittitology. In order to look beyond our own discipline, Svenja A. Gülden was invited to speak about an Egyptological project that investigates cursive writing. The project *Altägyp-*

Fig. 1. AKU-PAL homepage (image courtesy of S. Gülden).

tische Kursivschriften. Digitale Paläographie und systematische Analyse des Hieratischen und der Kursivhieroglyphen (AKU-Projekt) is funded by the Union of the German Academies of Sciences and Humanities and is also located at the Academy of Sciences and Literature | Mainz (Gülden et al. 2020).

In her explanation of the objects and aims of the project, Gülden noted that ancient Egyptian has several cursive scripts. Of these, cursive hieroglyphs and hieratic were in use from time immemorial and represented the handwritten variant of monumental hieroglyphs. In the first millennium BC, highly abbreviated variants were developed in addition to these, namely cursive hieratic and demotic. Each of these scripts has its own sign repertoire, which differs from that of hieroglyphics.

The aim of the project is to set up a sign repertoire of Hieratic and to store digitized hieratograms in a dynamic repository. The annotated metadata allows the characters to be selected according to dating, place of discovery, and other criteria. The digitized Hieratograms in AKU-PAL – the online palaeography of Hieratic – have been available on an open-access platform since 2022 (https://aku-pal.uni-mainz.de). The AKU project stores the digitized files in SVG 1.1 (vector-based) and TIF 6.0 (pixel-based). Both data formats are suitable for digital analysis and archiving. In addition to the digitization of printed palaeographs, text photographs are digitized in high resolution so that the individual strokes can be accurately recognized and traced. This opens up the potential

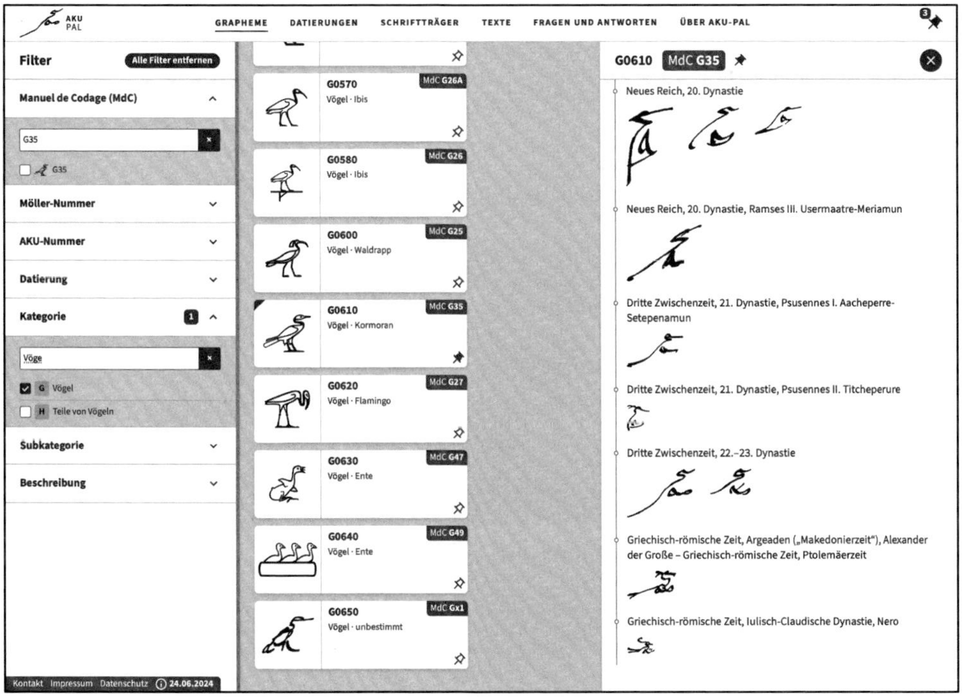

Fig.2. An exemplary search for the cormorant (with the phonetic value Aq), the logo of the AKU project (image courtesy of S. Gülden).

for new insights, but also makes the procedure very labor intensive. Therefore, only certain text groups can be incorporated, which are selected according to strict criteria. These include dating according to non-palaeographic information, type of writing material (much broader than with clay tablets), the genre. The texts must also be published, edited and accessible for the creation of high-resolution photos.

Another goal of the project is digital analysis. For this purpose, experiments were carried out with a tool for visualizing cultural collections (VIKUS) (https://vikusviewer.fh-potsdam.de). This web tool not only allows for selected objects to be displayed in a timeline, but also the option of displaying visually similar image data in groups, which is particularly interesting for the shape analysis of the hieratograms. The similarity calculation in this view is based on a pre-trained model of image data from ImageNet (https://image-net.org/) (Gerhards and Konrad 2022). For the visualization, the VIKUS Viewer uses an algorithm to sort the image data according to similarity. This makes it possible to visualize a large amount of data with little computing power; such analytical instruments could also be implemented for cuneiform research.

5. Requirements for digital palaeography

This shows the close connection between content and palaeographic issues; therefore, a comprehensive palaeography cannot be a self-contained, authoritative and monumental work, but, in the modern sense, only a complex, extensive work tool that provides signs and sign forms (enriched with metadata like source and date) enables visual comparisons and, in addition, allows for geometric and statistical categorizations that flexibly enable and offer content-based interpretations. To do this, enormous amounts of data must be considered, and the analytical basis of interpretations must at all times be comprehensible and capable of being expanded and modified by new material.

Bibliography

Gerhards, Simone and Tobias Konrad

2022 Von Bildern und Bienen – Methodenreflexionen zur digitalen paläografischen Analyse des Hieratischen. In: Svenja A. Gülden, Tobias Konrad, and Ursula Verhoeven (eds.), *Ägyptologische „Binsen"-Weisheiten IV. Hieratisch des Neuen Reiches: Akteure, Formen und Funktionen. Akten der internationalen Tagung in der Akademie der Wissenschaften und der Literatur | Mainz im Dezember 2019.* Abhandlungen der Geistes- und Sozialwissenschaftlichen Klasse – Einzelveröffentlichungen 17. Stuttgart: Franz Steiner Verlag, 183–219. http://doi.org/10.25358/openscience-9257.

Gordin, Shai

2015 *Hittite Scribal Circles. Scholarly Tradition and Writing Habits.* StBoT 59. Wiesbaden: Harrassowitz.

Gülden, Svenja A.

2022 Materialität, Textsorten, Schreiberhände – eine experimentelle digitale Analyse zu Schriftzeichen der 18. Dynastie. In: Svenja A. Gülden, Tobias Konrad, and Ursula Verhoeven (eds.), *Ägyptologische „Binsen"-Weisheiten IV. Hieratisch des Neuen Reiches: Akteure, Formen und Funktionen. Akten der internationalen Tagung in der Akademie der Wissenschaften und der Literatur | Mainz im Dezember 2019.* Abhandlungen der Geistes- und Sozialwissenschaftlichen Klasse – Einzelveröffentlichungen 17. Stuttgart: Franz Steiner Verlag, 221–78. http://doi.org/10.25358/openscience-9264.

Gülden, Svenja A., Celia Krause, and Ursula Verhoeven.

2020 Digital Palaeography of Hieratic. In: Vanessa Davies and Dimitri Laboury (eds.), *The Oxford Handbook of Egyptian Epigraphy and Paleography.* Oxford: Oxford University Press, 634–46. https://doi.org/10.1093/oxfordhb/9780190604653.013.42.

Güterbock, Hans Gustav

1938 Die historische Tradition und ihre literarische Gestaltung bei Babyloniern und Hethitern bis 1200 (2. Teil: Hethiter). *ZA* 44: 45–149.

Klinger, Jörg

1996 *Untersuchungen zur Rekonstruktion der hattischen Kultschicht.* StBoT 37. Wiesbaden: Harrassowitz.

2022 Zu den Anfängen der hethitischen Überlieferung überhaupt und zur Methode der paläographischen Textdatierung. In: Eva Cancik-Kirschbaum and Ingo Schrakamp (eds.), *Transfer, Adaption und Neukonfigurierung von Schrift- und Sprachwissen im Alten Orient.* Episteme in Bewegung 25. Wiesbaden: Harrassowitz, 255–340.

Otten, Heinrich

1953 Vorläufiger Bericht über die Ausgrabungen in Boğazköy im Jahre 1952. Die inschriftlichen Funde. *MDOG* 86: 59–64.

Rüster, Christel and Erich Neu

1989 *Hethitisches Zeichenlexikon. Inventar und Interpretation der Keilschriftzeichen aus den Boğazköy-Texten.* StBoTB 2. Wiesbaden: Harrassowitz.

Starke, Frank

1985 *Die keilschrift-luwischen Texte in Umschrift.* StBoT 30. Wiesbaden: Harrassowitz.

Yakubovich, Ilya and Alice Mouton

2023 *Luwili. Hittite-Luwian Ritual Texts Attributed to Puriyanni, Kuwatalla and Šilalluḫi (CTH 758–763). Volume II: Discussion and Glossary.* StBoT 72,2. Wiesbaden: Harrassowitz.

HOW MANY HANDS?

Collaboration and Accountability in Hittite Administrative Texts

James M. Burgin
Julius-Maximilians-Universität Würzburg

Abstract

This article investigates the "Intake and Storage" records, a subset of the Palace-Temple Administrative Corpus, to determine how many scribal hands were present. Using a methodology of side-by-side comparison of comprehensive sign lists for each of the fifteen texts, it is proposed that at least ten of the "Intake and Storage" texts were composed by one of two hands. Analysis of the duplicate passages in the group shows that in spite the absence of a text-internal system of metadata, scribes working economic administration had access to each other's records, copying and working from each other's tablets. In one instance, it is even demonstrated that a single tablet was composed by two scribes. This provides evidence for the first time that a "four-eyes principle" was in effect for Hittite economic administration, whereby scribes worked at a minimum in pairs, presumably for reasons of accountability.

1. Introduction

The Palace-Temple Administrative Corpus (PTAC) is a group of some 255 texts and text fragments concerning the administration of luxury objects and durable goods at Ḫattuša.[1] Judging by the ductus and the prosopography, almost every text from the PTAC comes from a narrow period at the end of the reign of Ḫattušili III and beginning of the reign of Tudḫaliya IV (Siegelová 1986: 535–46; Burgin 2022a: 110). The combination of a thematically focused corpus from a short time period should offer the chance to investigate the economic administrative techniques of the late Hittite New Kingdom. However, the administrative "Sitz im Leben" of the PTAC remains elusive. "Metadata," such as responsible institution, dating, tablet series, etc., are almost completely lacking in the corpus. For example, one might reasonably assume that the PTAC was produced by a limited number of scribes, but this cannot be proven because the texts are anonymous: colophons are sparse to begin with, and colophons with scribal signatures are non-existent.[2] When I began work on this contribution, it was my intention

1 These texts were most recently edited in my *Studies in Hittite Economic Administration* (Burgin 2022a, 2022b). Note that I will be referring to tablets here by their edition number in that work (see concordance of edition and publication numbers at the end of this contribution), prefixed by the abbreviation *SHEA* where necessary for clarity.

2 Only one tablet, VBoT 87 (*SHEA* 9.1.9), has a "signature" scratched into the tablet with Anatolian hieroglyphs. The use of hieroglyphs presumably indicates that the named individual was cuneiform illiterate, and therefore was not the scribe who wrote the text.

to use paleography as a way to indirectly estimate the number of scribes involved in the PTAC. A corpus written by a large number of hands would imply a large bureaucracy, more in-line with the administrations of contemporary cuneiform cultures. A smaller number of hands would imply a smaller, more "artisanal" bureaucracy, as I had favored in my recent book.[3] As will be seen, the task of evaluating the number of hands in entire PTAC proved beyond me. Nevertheless, the results I obtained from a subset of the corpus yielded some fascinating and, for me, completely unexpected results.

2. Methodology

2.1 Problems and premises

To prepare for this paper I familiarized myself with the methodology for constructing paleographic charts demonstrated in Yakubovich and Mouton 2023: 29–46. Their method had demonstrated great success for their corpus of Luwian ritual texts, but I was cognizant that there were crucial differences between their corpus and the PTAC. Most significantly, Yakubovich and Mouton were able to assume that one hand could be assigned to one tablet series, and that each tablet series had a distinct hand (Yakubovich and Mouton 2023: 29f.). In effect, this drastically reduced the number of compositions they dealt with, since each tablet series was in effect a single, extended composition that was written by a single scribe over a circumscribed period of time. This meant that on the not infrequent occasions they had duplicate or parallel passages, they could confirm that two tablets could not belong to the same tablet series and hence to the same hand. They also had colophons with scribal signatures and versions in Middle and New Script. The nature of the PTAC meant that I had the opposite: almost all of the texts were NS *unica*, and it was safe to assume that multiple unrelated texts had probably been composed by the same person, maybe even years apart.

In essence, the scribes of the PTAC could only be distinguished by handwriting alone. But how to do this? It was my initial thought to simply read through the corpus starting with "1. Texts Concerning Sales, Purchases, and Exchange" and attempted to classify the hands of the tablets into groups. I resolved to look for every syllabic sign plus a few select Sumerograms. Over the first few texts it became apparent that not every sign would be useful for classification. Some syllabic signs did not appear in the texts. Others were so simple to be non-diagnostic. In the end, AŠ, BE (*pát*), and U were removed for being non-diagnostic; IA was covered by I and A; UK and AZ were combined into a single category; PIRIG+, GU, IL, GEŠTIN, UZ, and NE were excluded for being too rare in the texts considered. I thus settled on the following signs for classification:

Vowels	A, E, I, Ú
B series	BA, BI, BU, PA, AB, E/IB, UB
D series	DA, DE/I, DU, TA, TE, TI, TU, AD, E/ID, UD
G series	GA, GE/I, KA, KE/I, KU, QA, AG, E/IG

3 See Burgin 2022a: 97–104. An alternative picture of Hittite bureaucracy that argues for a larger, more professionalized institution, can be found in Klinger 2022.

Ḫ series	ḪA, ḪE/I, ḪU, VḪ
R series	RA, RE/I, RU, AR, E/IR, UR
L series	LA, LE/I, LU, AL, EL, UL
M series	MA, ME, MI, MU, AM, E/IM, UM
N series	NA, NI, NU, AN, EN, IN, UN
W series	WA
Š series	ŠA, ŠE, ŠI, ŠU, EŠ, IŠ, UŠ
Z series	ZA, ZE/I, ZU (GÍN), E/IZ
CVC signs	TAR, KÁN, ḪUR
Sumerograms	PIRIG+, URU, LÚ, URUDU, KÚ, TÚG, KUŠ, PISAN, NA$_4$

It must be stressed: the set of signs useful for dating texts and the set of signs useful for distinguishing scribal hands are not the same. As will be seen in the appendices at the end of this contribution, there is no single sign or group of signs that is distinct for each hand. It is impossible to predict which signs will be decisive for classifying a hand, so full tables need to be created in every instance.

2.2 Methodology (first attempt)

My first attempt at creating scribal tables failed, but I include it here because perhaps it will be instructive for those embarking on similar analyses. I started with *SHEA* 1.1 (KUB 31.65++) and proceeded through every published "Sales Text" with photographs. I began by creating a table of the above-listed signs and inserted a picture of each sign I encountered in 1.1. This I called "Hand 1." I moved on to 1.4, the next published text. To my judgment, the signs look very similar to 1.1, so I also classified it as "Hand 1." I added in any signs missing from 1.1 to the table, and noted further attestations. I moved on to 1.5. The hand of this tablet was very close to 1.1 and 1.4, but different enough to raise suspicions. I started a new table, "Hand 2," with a note that it could just be a variant of Hand 1. The next tablet, 1.6, was also different, so I created "Hand 3." So far, so good.

I then began with the next group of texts, the "2. Inventory Records Concerned with Intake and Storage." There was a total of 16 published texts, including two sets of tablets containing partial duplicate text. The first one, 2.1.A, looked like another example of "Hand 1," so I updated the table. 2.1.B, a single-column tablet, the text of which is duplicated in the multi-column 2.1.A, was highly interesting. Most of the signs, perhaps 80%, seemed very similar to Hand 1. The remaining were highly ornate, inserting extra wedges wherever possible.

Fig. 1. "Ornate" sign variants of *SHEA* 2.1.B. From left to right: ḪI, LA, TA.

Since 2.1.A and 2.1.B contained duplicate text, and since most of the sign variants were similar between the texts, I assumed that 2.1.B was written by the same scribe as 2.1.A, just with an extra level of care and ornateness. I created an extra column in the "Hand 1" table for these "ornate" variants and added in all of the examples from 2.1.B. I then continued with the "Intake and Storage" records.

Here is where the problems began. Every tablet in the "Intake and Storage" category looked to me like they belonged to "Hand 1". There would occasionally be minor differences, but most of the signs looked identical to "Hand 1", at least in the context of the tablet. I would methodically go through the list of signs and compare what I had already with the photos of the new tablet. Sometimes, a tablet that was otherwise solidly "Hand 1" would contain a particular sign or string of signs that would stand out as slightly odd. In some instances, it was difficult not to think that the scribe had made a slip of the stylus. This was indubitably true in instances where the "normal" form of the same sign appeared in the same tablet a few lines later:

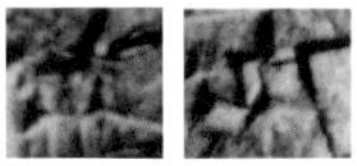

Fig. 2. TA-variants in *SHEA* 2.13.

In other instances, entire passages would be systematically affected. For example, a tablet might look like a normal "Hand 1," just written at a slight slant falling from left to right. Some passages would have words or entire lines slightly compressed, affecting every sign in the text. In more than once instance, a passage was written over a large erasure or what seemed to be partially dried clay:

Fig. 3. Passage from *SHEA* 2.5 rev. 9′–11′ written over partially dried clay?

I mostly ignored the "one-off mistakes" and systematic variations for the purposes of identifying scribal hands.

Yet there were also variants I could not ignore. It was also not uncommon to find different variants of the same sign within a text. Not just the expected ones, like the "old" and "young" variants of the LI, but also multiple variants of DU, GI, KÙ, and others.

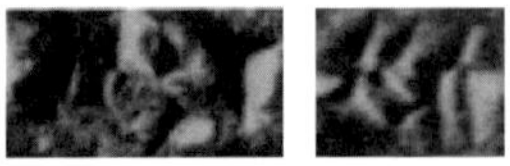

Fig. 4.1. LI-variants (*SHEA* 2.2).

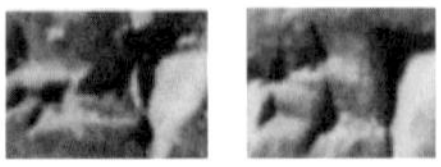

Fig. 4.2. DU-variants (*SHEA* 2.9).

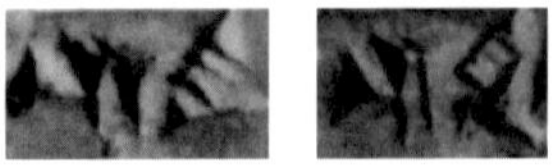

Fig. 4.3. GI-variants (*SHEA* 2.7.A).

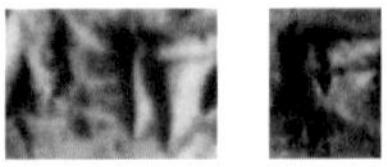

Fig. 4.4. KÚ-variants (*SHEA* 2.16).

The arrangement of the UD-group within signs (see UD, NA, WA, NA_4) in particular was often highly variable within a text.[4] One could also find stacked and stepped examples of BI signs, the signs ŠU and TÚG with squared-off and receding horizontal groups, etc., all in a single text. These I added as legitimate variants into the table of "Hand 1" when I came across them and a note that they occurred in the same text. But this made the boundaries of "Hand 1" ever fuzzier. In fact, the variation I was seeing within a tablet seemed often as great or greater than that between tablets, or between a given tablet and the hand that was growing in my table. As "Hand 1" grew, when I came to a new text, I could almost always find a variation that had appeared at least once in another text alongside a "normal" version of the sign. Every sign variant could be chained together, and everything was on a spectrum.

It seemed to me highly improbable that one scribe should have written all the tablets of the "Intake and Storage" group, and two of the "Sales Text" group. The decisive moment was when I came to *SHEA* 2.17 (KUB 42.81+). All of the previous texts with known findspots came from Büyükkale (2.3, 2.5, 2.7.B, 2.12, 2.16), but 2.17 was found at Temple 1. I thought that, under the (admittedly unprovable) assumption that scribes tended to work in one location, here we would surely find a different hand. Unfortunately, the text also looked like the "Hand 1" that I had developed, albeit an edge case. It was obvious that my methodology had failed. I had produced a pastiche of a "hand" that at this point I was certain did not belong to a single scribe. The identified result was something between a hand and a ductus, the uniformity of which only proved that the cuneiform-literate economic-administrative staff in mid-13th century Ḫattuša shared a common education and probably remained in regular contact with each other.

At this point I had processed twenty-two texts, less than a twelfth of the corpus, using the above method. I had gone through the transliterations of each text searching for each of the 84 signs, downloaded photos of each tablet from the *Konkordanz*, and compared the signs against the tables of hands I was developing. I found that was not enough to stop at the first example of a particular sign in a text, since there were often variants of the same sign hidden later in the text. It was always a judgement call which example to pick as the "standard" for a given tablet, as well as how different a variant had to be to warrant its inclusion. I had spent longer than I care to admit on these twenty-two texts, and it became obvious I was never going to get through the entire PTAC.

2.3 *Methodology (second attempt)*

I resolved to try a new approach. More precision was needed, so I decided that I would only focus on the "Intake and Storage" records. I started a new table using the method of Yakubovich and Mouton. This entailed creating a full sign table for every tablet. I retained the set of signs established in the first attempt. Even though my texts were on average much shorter, and even though I could not fall back on the same the extra-textual classificatory aides, I hoped that I could "brute force" the problem by placing all of the signs of all of the texts next to each other.

4 See the contribution of Adam Kryszeń in this volume for the methodological observation that sign subcomponents are often the more efficient *loci* of comparison between texts.

The results were striking. I started with a pair of texts, 2.7.A and 2.7.B, that had duplicate passages. I had previously seen these texts as written by the same hand. When the signs were placed side-by-side in isolation, however, subtle differences emerged. The heads of the inscribed verticals of the TA, GA, KÁN, and ŠA signs in 2.7.B were consistently placed above the horizontals, whereas in 2.7.A this was only occasionally so. One of the ZU (GÍN) signs in 2.7.B had a middle horizontal that was nearly in-line with the top horizontal. The MA of 2.7.B was long, but not nearly as long as those in 2.7.A. I was not yet ready to call them separate hands, but they were more different than I had originally thought.

I repeated the process for the remaining texts of the "Intake and Storage" texts. The more texts I added, the more apparent the differences became. A number of other texts reflected the same differences as found between 2.7.A and 2.7.B, leading me to assign them to separate hands. In the end, I was able to distinguish two distinct hands that accounted for more than half of the "Intake and Storage" Texts. These, along with the texts I could not assign to a particular hand, are presented in the *3. Results* below. Moreover, the recognition of these hands led to some interesting observations, including the fact that other texts with duplicate passages, 2.1.A and 2.1.B, as well paragraphs within a single text, 2.2, were also written by different hands. The implications of this will be discussed under *4. Analysis.*

3. Results

3.1 Hand 1 (see Appendix 1)

What I am naming here Hand 1 in the "Intake and Storage" texts is distinguished by its penchant for ornate variants. These ornate variants are marked by a profusion of filler wedges, as was shown already in Figure 2 above. Some texts, above all 2.1.B and to a lesser extent 2.9, consistently use the ornate variants. But almost all of the texts of Hand 1 include an occasional ornate variant (cf. the four inscribed verticals in the KÁN and the extra top horizontal of the RA [HZL 233/27] in 2.16, or the LÚ with inscribed vertical [HZL 78/12] in 2.2). The texts of Hand 1 also tend towards including the older and newer configurations of sign forms, having texts showing both forms of DU (HZL 128/A, 128/B) in 2.9; GI (HZL 30/A or 30/1, 30/B) in 2.7.A and 2.14; LI (HZL 343/8, 343/17) in 2.2; and KÁN (HZL 69/A, 69/B) in 2.7.A and 2.16. The preference for older signs is not consistent, since only the young AG-variant (HZL 81/B) is attested (2.2 r. 6–19, possibly 2.14). Other distinguishing features of Hand 1 are the highly variable configuration of the UD-group within signs (see UD, NA, WA, NA_4), inscribed verticals that tend not break the top horizontals (see TA, KÁN, ŠA), and an elongated MA.

2.9 is included here as an uncertain example of Hand 1. The text is in general an extremely close match, displaying the ornate signs, variability, and a number of exact matches with other signs in Hand 1. The only reason for caution is that the BI sign in 2.9 is non-stepped, whereas those in 2.2 r. 6–19 and 2.7.A are stepped. There is admittedly only one BI in 2.9, so it is possible that this was an exception. Since 2.9 is an omnibus of chest descriptions, it is possible that one of its forerunners was a text with non-stepped BI-s.

2.14 is another uncertain example of Hand 1. It is kept with this hand based on the configuration of the UD-group and the shape of the two GI and the old LI, which are similar to those in 2.7.A. The EN in 2.14 written with a near-horizontal, broken diagonal (similar to HZL 40/3, but without an apparent inscribed vertical) instead of *Winkelhaken* gives one pause.

3.2 Hand 2 (see Appendix 2)

Hand 2 tends to be blockier and more consistent than Hand 1, with all signs slightly more horizontally compressed. Distinguishing features include inscribed verticals that sometimes break the top horizontal, a more consistent UD-group, and AN-variants in which the tail of the horizontal often, but not always, transects the vertical. The NA can be distinct, with the lower *Winkelhaken* below the tail of the horizontal (HZL 15/5) as in 2.7.B and 2.15, although a "normal" NA (HZL 15/1) is attested in 2.2 r. 1–5. Sign variants tend to be of the older variety, with the older AG (81/A) in 2.2 r. 1–5 and 2.6; older DU (HZL 128/A) in 2.2 r. 1–5 and 2.15; older LI (HZL 343/8) in 2.7.B; and older KÙ in 2.2 r. 1–5. A single older URU variant (HZL 229/A) without the protruding middle horizontal is attested in 2.7.B. Younger sign forms are also encountered, such as the young LI (HZL 343/B) in 2.7.B and the younger AL with inscribed horizontal (HZL 183/10) in 2.1.A. Old and new sign variants are so far consistent within texts, but this is probably a result of preservation.

3.3 Unclassified texts (see Appendix 3)

I could not confidently assign the remaining "Intake and Storage" texts to a particular hand. Of the unclassified texts, 2.4 is set apart by highly distinctive TA and ŠA signs, which have the initial horizontals and inscribed verticals almost written as a separate group from the subsequent *Winkelhaken* and vertical. ZI is also highly distinctive, with the top left *Winkelhaken* of the ŠE-group conspicuously lower than usual. The most distinctive feature, however, is the consistently high placement of the first *Winkelhaken* of the UD-group in all signs containing one (UD, NA, WA, NA_4), such that the first *Winkelhaken* is in-line with second.

2.5 is very similar to Hand 2, such that I almost placed it there. The unique shape of DA (HZL 214/C, the youngest form, but with the middle horizontal and *Winkelhaken* placed unusually high) and DU (HZL 128/A, the older form, but with the second head of the broken lower horizontal placed far to the right), and the use of the young AG (HZL 81/B) suggest that it should be kept apart.

2.12 and 2.13 possibly belong to the same hand, but there are not enough overlapping signs to be sure. The distinguishing features of 2.12 are horizontally compressed signs and a slight downward slant to most horizontals. 2.13 could be the same hand, with the low-set horizontal of GI being the most convincing shared feature with 2.12. The fact that the horizontal of GI in 2.12 does not transect the verticals, whereas in 2.13 it does, is probably not probative: cf. ZI in 2.12, where the horizontal transects the verticals. The positioning of the *Winkelhaken* in ḪA are also similar between 2.12 and 2.13.

2.17 was recovered from Temple 1, making it *a priori* almost certain that it was written in a different hand from Hands 1 and 2, since at least one text in each of the other hands was found at Büyükkale. Visually, 2.17 is most similar to the style of Hand 1 (cf. especially the shape of NA), and it is possible that some texts assigned to Hand 1 actually belong to the same hand as 2.17. The sign that most distinguishes 2.17 from Hand 1 is LA, which has the first lower horizontal in-line with the main lower horizontal (this form is not recognized in the HZL). The fact that the inscribed vertical of GA and ŠA in 2.17 break above the top horizontal also strongly suggests that 2.17 should be kept separate from Hand 1. Finally, one instance of KUŠ in 2.17 has a late form with the top horizontal somewhat below with what should be the first inset horizontal (*quasi* HZL 213/6), which is not encountered in any of the other hands.

4. Analysis

The first surprising result for me concerned the texts with duplicate passages. Not only were the two sets of texts copied by different hands, but apparently it was the same pair of hands: 2.1.B and 2.7.A were written by Hand 1, whereas 2.1.A and 2.7.B were written by Hand 2. No previous edition of these texts, including my own, had caught this. It also did not correspond to my model of how the administrative work-flow operated in the PTAC. Given the paucity of metadata, I had assumed that scribes had maintained exclusive control of the texts. Now, with clear evidence that different scribes worked from each other's tablets, this assumption is shattered. This makes the lack of metadata if anything even more acute.

The two text-sets with duplicated passages seemingly arose from different scenarios. In 2.7, it was clearly an instance of one administrative matter being extended to the next session. As discussed in the edition (Burgin 2022b: 37–47), 2.7.B is probably a "scrap" tablet, since it combines thematically unrelated administrative actions. The obverse of 2.7.B is a list of wool allotments (edited separately as *SHEA* 4.1.3.5.A), and is itself duplicated by another text. The reverse of 2.7.B is a list of chests that have not yet been systematically inventoried (*nawi ḫatiwitan*). 2.7.B rev. ends with no indication that it should be continued. 2.7.A picks up by duplicating the final three lines of 2.7.B rev., and then continuing with EGIR-*anda=ya* "and later ...," recording how the queen adds in a number of items to the chest that the 2.7.B rev. ended with. I had already thought in my edition that the scribe had begun a new tablet with 2.7.A and linked it to 2.7.B by repeating the last lines.[5] I had assumed it was the same scribe, who had finished a day's work on the chests one day and then started back in at a later date. Now it seems it was a team of scribes who had access to each other's records. They must have worked closely together, since again there is no metadata internal to the texts that would have kept the tablets organized. Were there baskets or labelled shelves that allowed them to coordinate their work? Did the scribe of 2.7.B physically hand his tablet over to the scribe of 2.7.A so he could carry on with the inventorying process after the queen intervened?

5 J. Klinger is at the moment preparing a study on these "tail–head" linking tablets in the context of the Hittite Laws.

The pair 2.1.A and 2.1.B represent a different administrative scenario. The tablets duplicate about seven lines of text between them. The duplicated passage begins and ends with breaks, so it does not seem that one tablet continued where the other left off. Instead, 2.1.A is a two-column tablet whereas 2.1.B is probably a one-column tablet. Since tablets share roughly the same lineation, 2.1.A was almost certainly the larger tablet, probably being an omnibus record compiled from multiple single-column tablets. It can be interpreted that the scribe of 2.1.B prepared a first draft of incoming chests, which the scribe of 2.1.A then copied into a combined document. Interestingly, the scribe of 2.1.B used Hand 1, which as noted above, contains many ornate forms. I had assumed that the scribe of Hand 1 was a sophisticated, highly trained scribe, who perhaps served as a supervisor to the scribe of Hand 2. The fact that the scribe of Hand 1 was also the scribe who worked directly with the queen in 2.7.A supported this assumption. Yet here, the scribe of Hand 1 is found making the single-column "first draft" tablets (as they are usually assumed: see Siegelová 1986: 4, 567f.; Waal 2015: 90), while the scribe of Hand 2 assembled the omnibus text. Also, 2.9, which is written in an ornate version of Hand 1, contains a large uncorrected erasure in 2.9.A_2 obv. i 5″–6″. It seems clear that the scribe of Hand 1 did not solely work on final drafts.

The two duplicate passages in 2.1 and 2.7 led me to reevaluate my "analysis" of the scribes behind Hands 1 and 2. I had thought that the scribe with the penchant for ornate handwriting and diversity of sign forms was the more experienced scribe, perhaps wanting to show off his erudition. But now I think the regular "printed" look of Hand 2, combined with the preference for older forms, makes Hand 2 the more experienced scribe. Whether the use of older forms indicates that he was from an older generation, or, more likely, that he regularly worked with older texts and/or was educated in a scribal circle that worked with older texts, is unclear.

The second and far more surprising result for me was the discovery that one of the texts, 2.2, was apparently written by two scribes. I must confess that when I was editing this text for my book, I did not realize that the two hands were different. It in fact did not enter my mind that a tablet would be written on by more than one scribe.[6]

6 At the moment, only a few tablets possibly written by more than one scribe are known. A short list of texts with different scripts was presented by Berman (1982: 94 n. 5), although whether these are multi-scribe tablets is an open question. The contribution of Andrea Trameri in this volume discusses a number of further possible examples among the oracle texts. One of these, KUB 49.39, was seemingly prepared with pre-ruled paragraphs in which only the first line of a paragraph was written out; the rest was left uninscribed, which was intended for another scribe to fill out later. An example of a similar arrangement might be found in the PTAC, in *SHEA* 3.17.A_2 (KBo 7.24), where a number of paragraphs appear with only two or three words entered and the rest left blank. One can easily imagine this resulted from coordination between two scribes, which in this case failed.
A further example of what seems almost certainly to be a multi-scribe tablet was cordially provided to me by Tomoki Kitazumi. KBo 23.1 (edited Strauß 2006: 253–71) contains a colophon that indicates that one scribe wrote the text "first" (*ḫantezziya*), but that "later" (EGIR-*az*) another scribe completed it. Strauß (2006: 254f.) noted that the statement in the colophon is supported by the conspicuous change in handwriting and orthography after obv. ii 22. The agreement between colophon and hands in the text is, for me at least, the "smoking gun" that proves that multi-scribe tablets were, under certain circumstances, possible at Ḫattuša.

And indeed, without having systematically identified the hands of the two main scribes of the "Intake and Storage" texts, one could easily misinterpret the change as a single scribe writing more hurriedly or sloppily after a hiatus. However, with the advantage of the sign tables, the result is unambiguous: The reverse of 2.2 shows Hand 2 in rev. 1–5, and then Hand 1 in rev. 6–19 (see Fig. 5).[7] The change of hands can be easily seen by comparing, e. g. AN in rev. 2 and 7, BI in rev. 3 and 10, DU in rev. 2 and 18, AG in rev. 5 and 18, and KÙ in rev. 5 and in 7, 10, and 11 (although cf. the old KÙ in rev. 8).

Fig. 5. *SHEA* 2.2 (VSNF 12.116) rev.

Transliteration of *SHEA* 2.2 rev. [8]

rev.

1 [n ^{GIŠ}*tu*]*p-pa* TUR.TUR 2 *a-*⸢*šu-ša-an-zi*$^{(?)}$⸣ [

2 [n ^{GI}PI]SAN SA$_5$ *ŠUL-MAN-TI* KUR *kar*$^{!}$(text: A)-^{D}*du-*⸢*ni*⸣*-a*[*š*

3 [n ^{G}]^{IŠ}*ḫu-up-pár-liš* SA$_5$ *ka-pí-nu-uš* *MA-LU-*⸢*Ú*⸣ [

7 The photo of 2.2 obv. is unavailable. Judging by the handcopy, it seems more likely than not that the obverse was written in the same hand as rev. 1–5, i. e. Hand 2.

8 This transliteration follows that of Burgin 2022b: 26–28, but with improvements in rev. 1–3 and 15.

4 [n+]1 GAL KÙ.BABBAR ŠÀ ^{GIŠ}PISAN *A-NA* $^{\text{LÚ.MEŠ}}$KÙ.D[ÍM

---

5 [n GÍ]N KÙ.BABBAR *A-NA* GAL$^{\text{ḪI.A}}$ *wa-ak-ši-ia-a*[*t*

---

lines rev. 6–13 can be restored from 4.1.1.1.A_1 rev. 3′–9′//4.1.1.1.B_1 obv. ii 7′–18′

6 [n *ku-r*]*u-up-ši-ni-iš* KÙ.BABBAR 4 *a-ra-an-te-eš* 2 UR.M[AḪ KÙ.BABBAR 4 *a-ra-an-te-eš*]
7 [n] ˹*a*˺*-pu-pí-iš* KÙ.BABBAR 4 *a-ra-an-te-eš* 2 ˹GU$_4$˺.M[AḪ KÙ.BABBAR 4 *a-ra-an-te-eš*]
8 [^{m}x.L]Ú$^{(?)}$*-aš-kán A-NA* $^{\text{LÚ.MEŠ}}$KÙ.DÍM ŠÀ ^{É}*ḫa-l*[*i-in-tu-wa-aš* ^{URU}*ḫa-ad-du-ši-kán ar-ḫa da-a-aš*]
9 [*k*]*a-ru-ú kán-ga-an nu-uš-ma-ša-at* EGIR [*ḫa-liš-šu-wa-an-zi pí-i-e-er*/*pi-ia-an-zi*]

---

10 ˹30˺ GÍN KÙ.BABBAR-*ma A-NA BI-IB-RI*$^{\text{ḪI.A}}$ *wa-ak-*[*ši-ia-at* EGIR-*an-da* 1$^{?}$ GAL DÙ-*zi*]
11 ˹29˺ GÍN KÙ.BABBAR 1 ˹KI˺.LÁ TI$_8$^{MUŠEN} ŠU ^{m}*eḫ-l*[*i*-^{D}30 17 GÍN KÙ.SI$_{22}$ *ŠA* KUR *kar-*^{D}*du-ni-aš*]
12 ŠU ^{m}˹*eḫ*˺*-li-*˹^{D}˺30 ˹ḪAR˺$^{\text{ḪI.A}}$ DÙ-*zi* 𒑱 [
13 *⟨⟨*k*[*i*$^{?}$]-⟩⟩* erasure [

end restoration from 4.1.1.1

---

14 1 *ME* 7 ŠUL.PÁT KÙ.BABBAR *GÁM-RU* Š[À
15 [Š]U ˹^{m}*eḫ-li-*˹*ia*˺[9] 12 GÍN KÙ.SI$_{22}$ [
16 [x x x] 2 ^{GIŠ}*tup-pa-aš* ŠU $^{\text{m.D}}$10-˹PAB˺ x[

---

17 [n $^{\text{(GIŠ)}}$GA.ZUM] SÍG ZU$_9$ AM.SI BABBAR 1 x[
18 [n *pé-ra-a*]*n pé-e-du-ma-aš* x[
19 [n GAM-*an ti-i*]*a-u-wa-aš* ˹ZU$_9$˺ A[M.SI
tablet breaks off

What motivated the change in hands on the reverse of 2.2 is a mystery. The change of hands takes place exactly where information from another text, in this case from KBo 18.153(+) (*SHEA* 4.1.1.1.A_1) 3′–9′//KUB 26.66(+) (*SHEA* 4.1.1.1.B_1) obv. ii 7′–18′, a production text, is inserted. The obverse of the text contains short descriptions of chests. This continues on the reverse up to rev. 4, at which point the text adopts the language of the production texts, noting that certain silver objects have been sent to the smiths. The change in hand occurs two lines later, with the aforementioned insertion from the production text *SHEA* 4.1.1.1. The reason for the shared tablet must remain speculation, but it looks very much like the scenario in 2.7, where one scribe picked up the work of another scribe. The handover occurred right after the first scribe started working on objects that had been sent to the smiths for repair. It could be imagined that the second scribe had a special expertise of connection to the matter at hand. In fact, I would say that the hands of 2.2 rev. 6–19 and 4.1.1.1.B are probably the same, i. e. both Hand 1. Moreover, 2.2 rev. 6–19 and 4.1.1.1.B are different from 4.1.1.1.A, which is probably not

9 Eḫliya is probably a diminutive or *Kurzform* of the name Eḫli-^{D}30 (Eḫli-Kusuḫ) encountered in rev. 12.

written in Hand 2. It seems that the scribe of Hand 2 called over the scribe of Hand 1 to enter information about an administrative matter he knew his colleague working on.[10] In this case, the scribe of Hand 1 did not bother to start a new tablet, but just took over where his colleague left off.

The existence of texts with duplicated passages, and indeed a text written by more than one scribe, answers a question that had bothered me while working on the texts of the PTAC. In the absence of metadata, and with the interpretation of a text dependent on the scribe who wrote it, what prevented the scribes from concealing potential misdeeds by falsifying inventories? The fact that the scribes at a minimum apparently worked in pairs, and that their tablets were openly available to each other, suggests that administration operated under the "four-eyes principle", where administrative activity was not conducted alone.

Preliminary analysis of other tablets with duplicate passages in the PTAC shows mixed results for the "four-eyes principle": the pair 4.1.1.1.A, 4.1.1.1.B and the pair 4.1.1.2.A, 4.1.1.2.B, both of which involve the weighing of precious metals, were clearly written in different hands, whereas 3.1.8.A rev. and 3.1.8.B, a list of incoming domestic tribute, and 3.1.11.A and 3.1.11.B, a list of incoming domestic silver destined for various deities, seem each to have been written in only one hand. The vast majority of texts in the PTAC are of course *unica* showing only one hand. This does not mean that a supervisor or co-administrator was not standing by while the texts were being composed, only that the second person did not usually need to interact with the tablet. The hieroglyphic "counter-signature" of Pupuli at the end of *SHEA* 9.1.9 (VBoT 87), a tablet from the "Inventory of Arnuwanda," might represent another, exceptional, form of supervisory interaction.

5. Conclusions

The recognition that most of the texts in the "Intake and Storage" records were written by two scribes, and that these scribes worked together and must have to some extent monitored each other, was an unexpected and rewarding discovery. It answers a longstanding question on how scribes were kept accountable in the absence of text-internal metadata. Analysis of the scribal hands in the rest of the PTAC would be no doubt equally rewarding. However, I have concluded that such an endeavor is not feasible at the moment. I would estimate that it would take me six to eight months, working on nothing else, to process the rest of the corpus. Even then, in the absence of the "guiderails" of tablet series, extensive duplicates, scribal signatures, etc., many of the text would not be assignable to hands. Moreover, those that could be assigned would always have an element of uncertainty. I am fairly confident in my division of the texts from the "Intake and Storage" records analyzed here, but I would not be surprised if

10 The alternative scenario, that there was no change in scribe, but that the script of the tablet was affected by the scribe of Hand 2 copying from a tablet written in Hand 1 seems unlikely. The change in script is too stark, and in any event, we have seen in 2.1 and 2.7 that duplicate passages could be copied without affecting the normal script of a hand.

one or two of the fragments assigned to Hand 1 and Hand 2 turned out to belong elsewhere. Vice-versa, it is possible that some of texts that I could not classify belong to Hands 1 and 2.

This research exercise proved for me an important methodological point, namely that it is in most cases impossible to distinguish scribal hands with the naked eye. This problem is all the more acute in texts of the same period, written by scribes working side-by-side on the same topics, and copying each other's texts. Simply comparing texts side-by-side, or signs *in situ* within a text against a consolidated chart, is usually insufficient to distinguish hands. At least, I could not do it. Instead, complete sign charts must be created for each text and compared as a group. Even then, the fragments must be large and the sign charts must have extensive overlaps if any level of certainty is to be achieved.

The larger problem, which I addressed only tangentially in observing the variability of Hand 1, is that we have no objective data on how much an individual hand can vary, neither within a tablet, nor between tablets, nor over a person's career. A person's handwriting changes over time, and I think we can all recognize that our own handwriting varies, sometimes inexplicably, within a composition and between compositions. Before computer-aided techniques that can distinguish subtleties such as wedge angle and depth (see the contribution of Gerfrid Müller this volume), and before the establishment of a statistical baseline for variation within a text and then between texts using tablets known to be composed by the same scribe, we should reserve judgment on the hands of most corpora. We must simply be content for now that for ephemeral corpora such as the PTAC, and, I would guess, the oracle texts and some of the letters, we will not be able to distinguish scribal hands in most texts. Success can be achieved in limited instances, especially in texts with duplicate passages, but even then, a fundamental degree of uncertainty is present. The methodology of Yakubovich and Mouton is more promising for larger corpora with colophons and tablet series. For other corpora, the paleographical sub-discipline of hand-writing identification awaits the next era of digital humanities.

Concordance

2.1.A	KUB 42.18
2.1.B	KUB 42.20
2.2	VSNF 12.116 (photo of obv. unavailable)
2.4	CHDS 5.55
2.5	KBo 18.180
2.6	CHDS 4.54
2.7.A	IBoT 1.31
2.7.B	KUB 42.65 (+) KBo 42.23
2.9	KUB 42.27 (A_1), KUB 42.23 (A_2), KUB 42.22 (A_3)
2.12	KBo 18.179

2.13	KUB 42.19
2.14	DBH 43/2.73
2.15	KUB 42.25
2.16	KBo 18.176
2.17	KUB 42.81 + Col. Univ. Lib. + KBo 69.331 + Bo 7477

Notes on excluded texts: 2.3 (KBo 14.72) and 2.10 (Bo 7236) each preserve too few signs to be considered. 2.11 (Bo 7290) remains unpublished. The surface of 2.18 (IBoT 4.4) was highly damaged and contained too little available text to evaluate.

Appendices

Appendix 1: Hand 1

	Probable				Uncertain	
Sign	2.1.B	2.2 r. 6-19	2.7.A	2.16	2.9	2.14
A	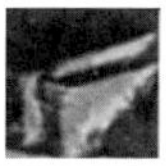					
E						
I			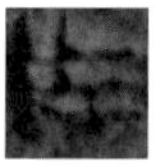		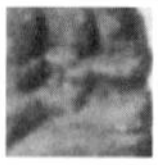	
Ú			 			
BA						
BE/I						
BU				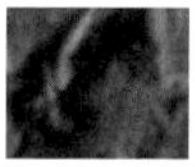		

	Probable				Uncertain	
Sign	2.1.B	2.2 r. 6-19	2.7.A	2.16	2.9	2.14
PA			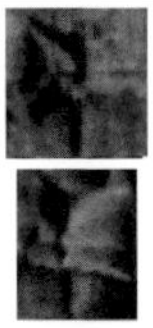			
AB						
E/IB			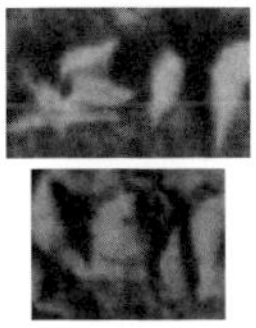			
UB						
DA			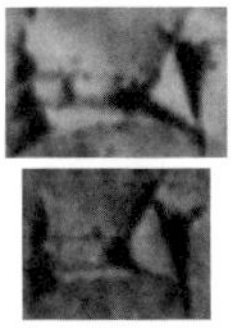	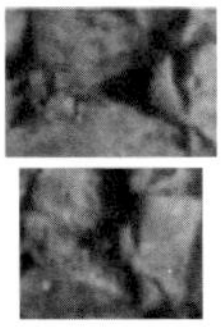		
DE/I			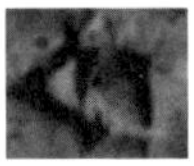			
DU						
TA	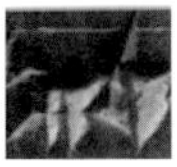		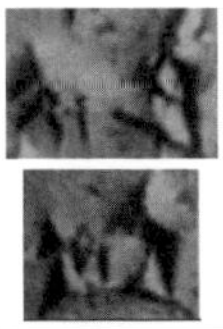		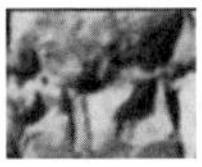	
TE		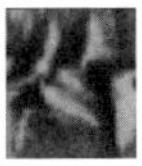		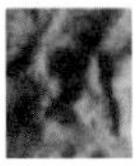		

	Probable				Uncertain	
Sign	2.1.B	2.2 r. 6-19	2.7.A	2.16	2.9	2.14
TI	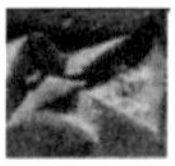		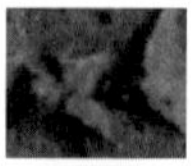 			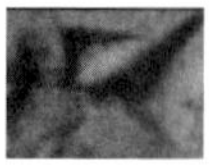
TU						
AD			 		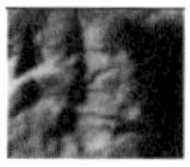	
E/ID						
UD		 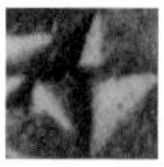	 			
GA		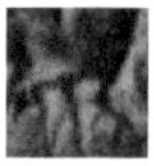				
GE/I			 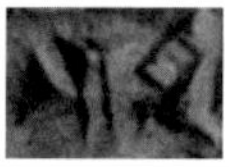	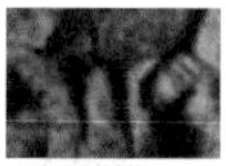 	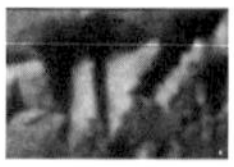	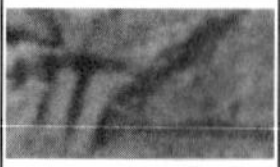 
KA			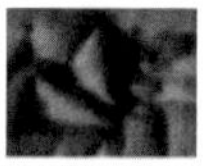 	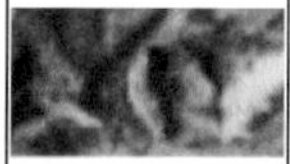		
KE/I			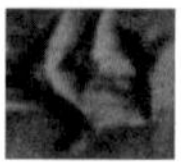			

	Probable				Uncertain	
Sign	2.1.B	2.2 r. 6-19	2.7.A	2.16	2.9	2.14
KU						
QA						
AG						
E/IG						
ḪA	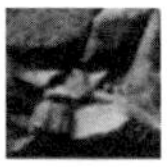			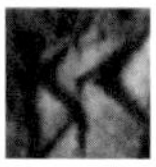	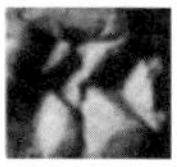	
ḪE/I						
ḪU						
VḪ			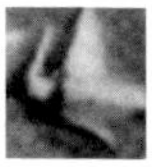			
RA			 			
RE/I			 	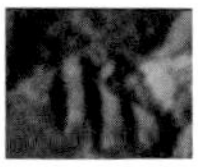		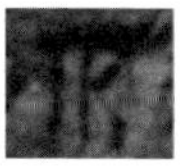
RU		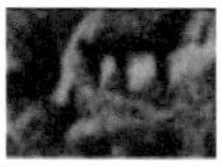			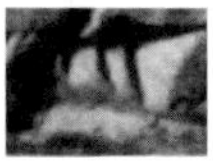	
AR						
E/IR						

	Probable				Uncertain	
Sign	2.1.B	2.2 r. 6-19	2.7.A	2.16	2.9	2.14
UR				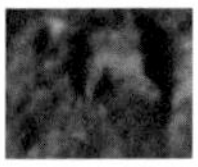		
LA				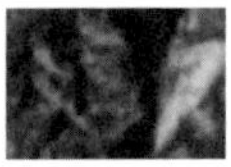		
LE/I		 				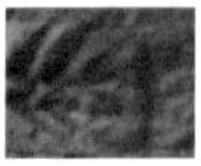
LU						
AL				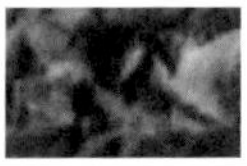		
EL						
UL						
MA			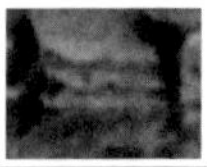 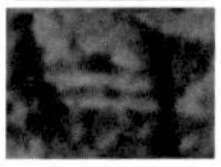	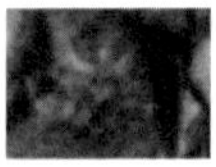		
ME					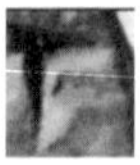	
MI						
MU						
AM				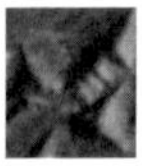		
E/IM						
UM			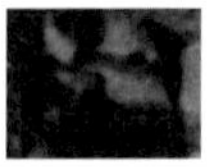			

	Probable				Uncertain	
Sign	2.1.B	2.2 r. 6-19	2.7.A	2.16	2.9	2.14
NA			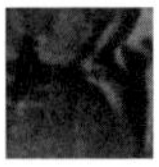		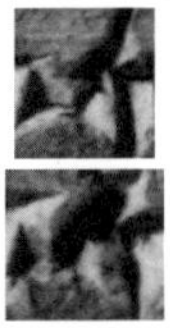	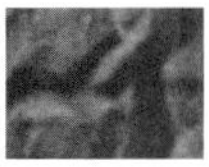
NI		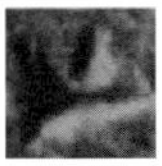			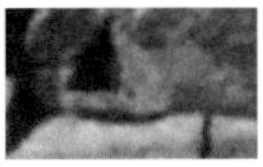	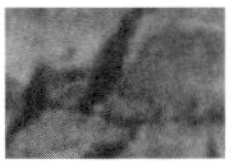
NU		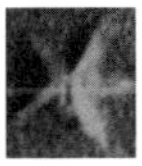		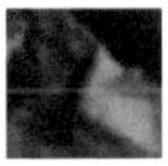		
AN		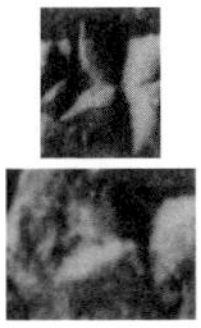	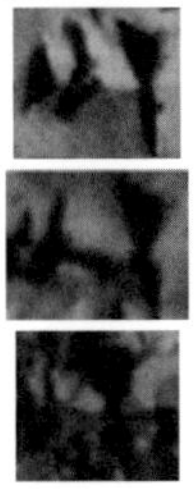	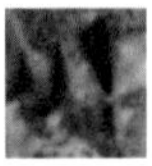		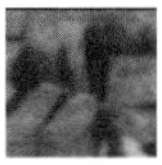
EN			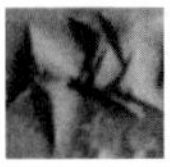			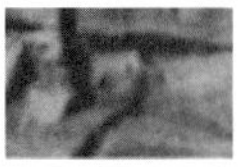
IN						
UN						
WA						
ŠA			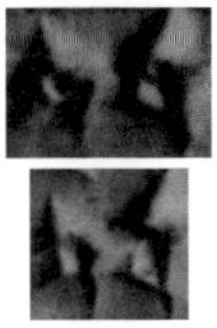			
ŠE						
ŠI		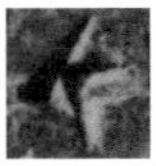	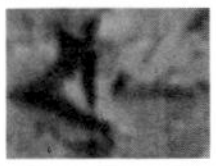			

	Probable				Uncertain	
Sign	2.1.B	2.2 r. 6-19	2.7.A	2.16	2.9	2.14
ŠU			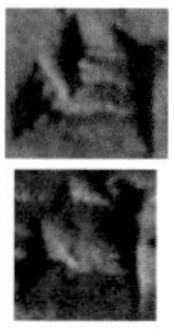	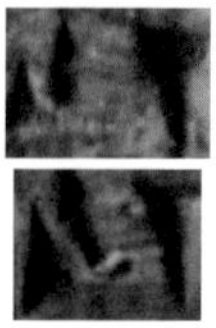		
EŠ			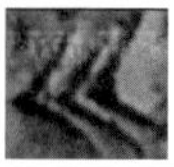			
IŠ		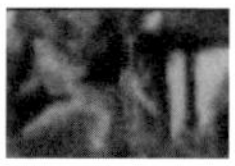	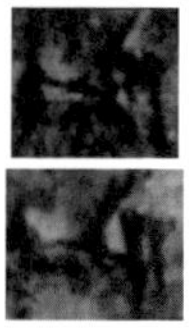	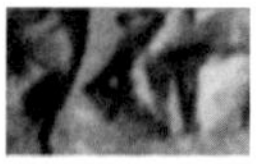		
UŠ		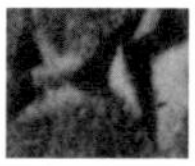	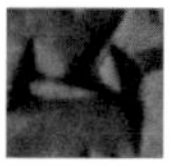			
ZA						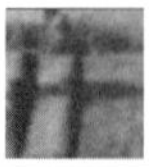
ZE/I				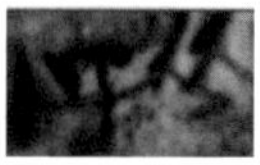		
ZU (GÍN)		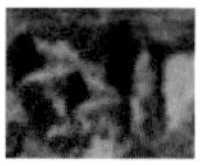		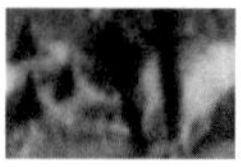		
E/IZ		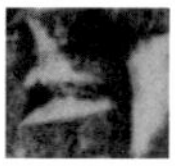	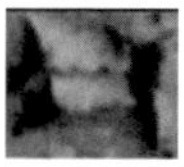	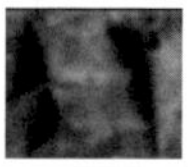		
TAR						
KÁN			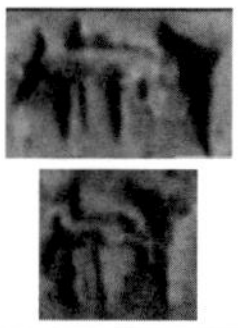	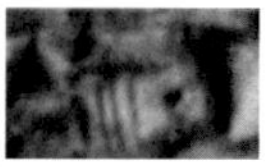		

	Probable				Uncertain	
Sign	2.1.B	2.2 r. 6-19	2.7.A	2.16	2.9	2.14
ḪUR		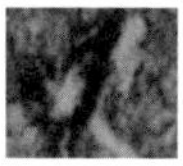				
PIRIG+			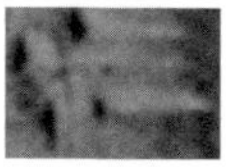			
URU			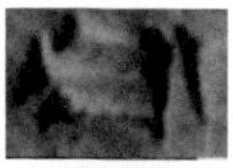 			
LÚ						
URUDU			 			
KÙ		 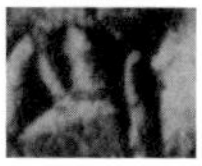	 	 		
TÚG			 			
KUŠ			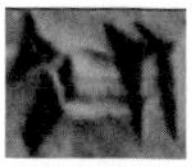			
PISAN				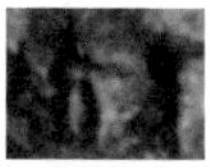		
NA_4	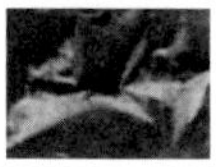			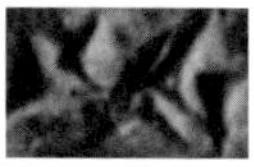		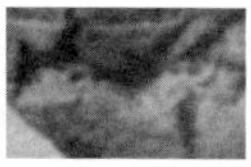

Appendix 2: Hand 2

Sign	2.1.A	2.2 r. 1-5	2.6	2.7.B	2.15
A					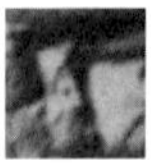
E					
I					
Ú					
BA					
BE/I		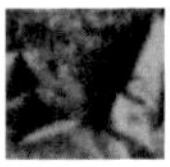			
BU					
PA		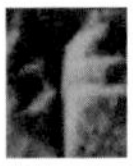			
AB					
E/IB					
UB					
DA			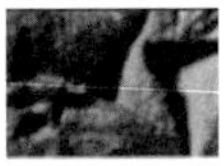		
DE/I					
DU					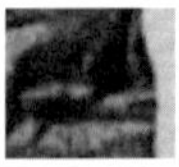
TA					
TE					
TI		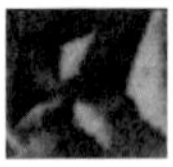			

Sign	2.1.A	2.2 r. 1-5	2.6	2.7.B	2.15
TU					
AD					
E/ID					
UD					
GA					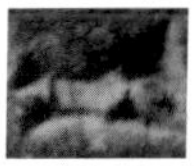
GE/I					
KA					
KE/I					
KU					
QA	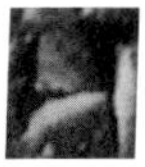				
AG					
E/IG					
ḪA					
ḪE/I				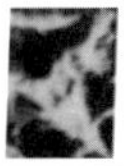	
ḪU					
VḪ			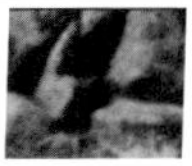		

Sign	2.1.A	2.2 r. 1-5	2.6	2.7.B	2.15
RA					
RE/I					
RU	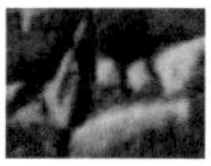			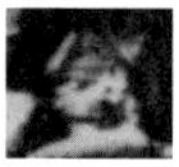	
AR					
E/IR					
UR					
LA					
LE/I			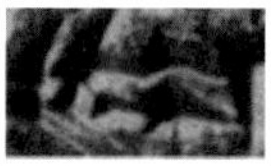	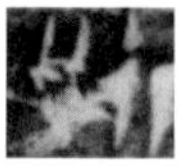 	
LU					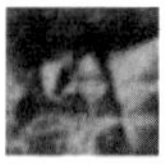
AL				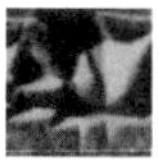	
EL					
UL					
MA		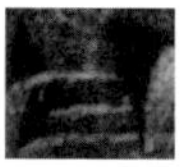			 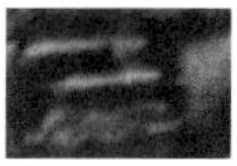
ME					
MI					
MU					

Sign	2.1.A	2.2 r. 1-5	2.6	2.7.B	2.15
AM					
E/IM					
UM					
NA				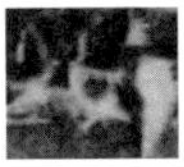	
NI					
NU					
AN		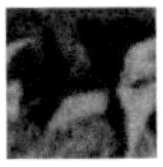		 	
EN					
IN					
UN					
WA	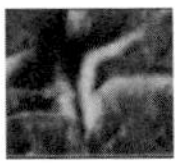				
ŠA					
ŠE					
ŠI		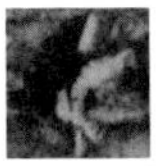			
ŠU					
EŠ				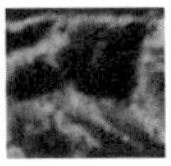	

Sign	2.1.A	2.2 r. 1-5	2.6	2.7.B	2.15
IŠ				 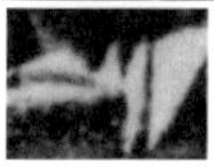	
UŠ		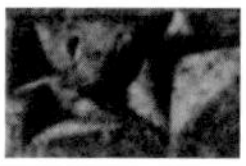			
ZA					
ZE/I					
ZU (GÍN)		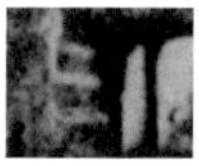			
E/IZ				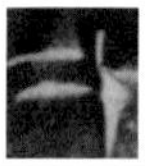	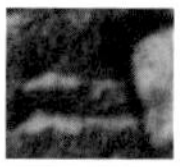
TAR					
KÁN		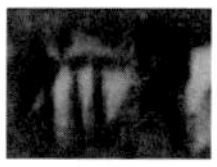			
ḪUR				 	
PIRIG+					
URU					
LÚ					
URUDU					
KÙ		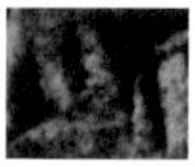			

Sign	2.1.A	2.2 r. 1-5	2.6	2.7.B	2.15
TÚG					
KUŠ					
PISAN	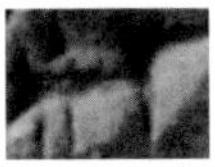				
NA_4	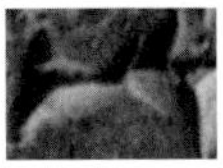				

Appendix 3: Texts that could not be assigned to a particular hand

Sign	2.4	2.5	2.12	2.13	2.17
A					
E			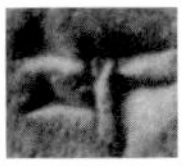		
I					
Ú					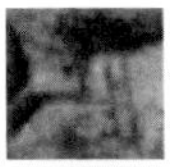 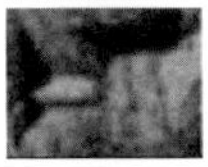
BA					
BE/I					
BU					
PA					
AB					
E/IB					

Sign	2.4	2.5	2.12	2.13	2.17
UB					
DA					 
DE/I					
DU		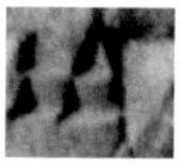	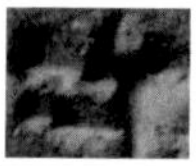		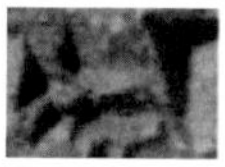
TA				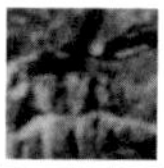 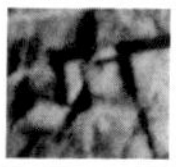	
TE					
TI					
TU					
AD			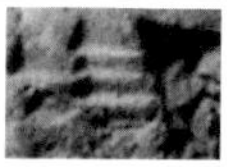		
E/ID					
UD					
GA					
GE/I					 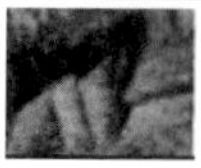
KA					

Sign	2.4	2.5	2.12	2.13	2.17
KE/I			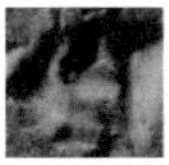		
KU					
QA					
AG					
E/IG					
ḪA			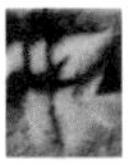		
ḪE/I		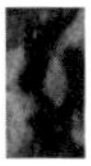			
ḪU					
VḪ					
RA		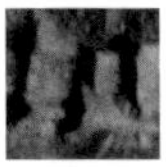			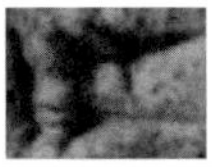
RE/I					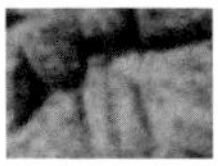
RU					
AR					
E/IR					
UR					
LA					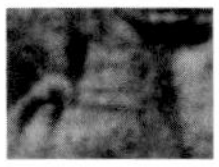
LE/I					

Sign	2.4	2.5	2.12	2.13	2.17
LU					
AL					
EL					
UL					
MA					
ME					
MI				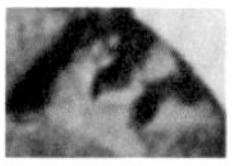	
MU					
AM		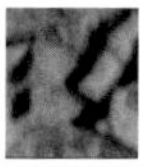			
E/IM					
UM					
NA			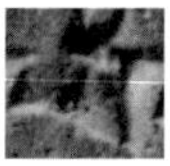		 
NI					
NU			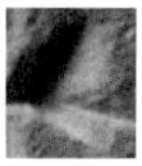		
AN	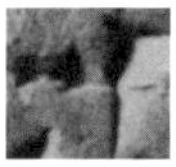	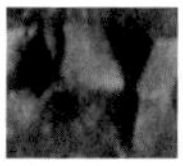			
EN					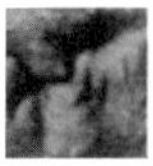

Sign	2.4	2.5	2.12	2.13	2.17
IN					
UN					
WA		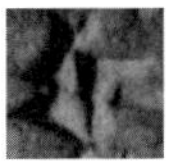			
ŠA			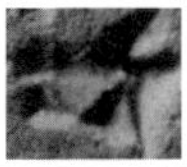		
ŠE			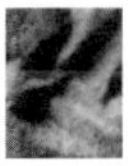		
ŠI		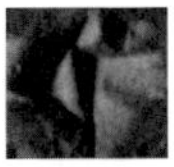			
ŠU			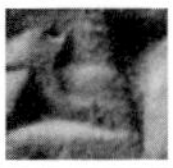		
EŠ		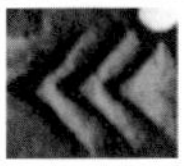	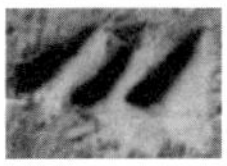		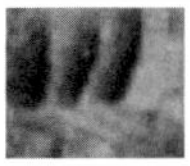
IŠ		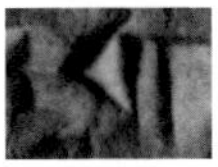			
UŠ					
ZA		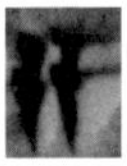			
ZE/I			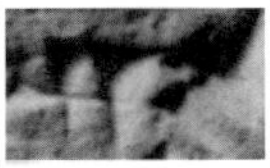		
ZU (GÍN)		 			
E/IZ		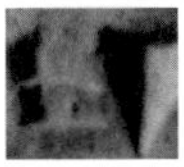			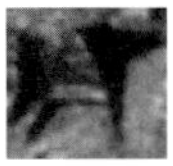
TAR					

Sign	2.4	2.5	2.12	2.13	2.17
KÁN					
ḪUR			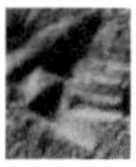		
PIRIG+					
URU					
LÚ					
URUDU		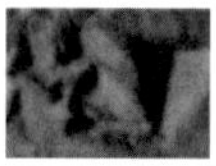	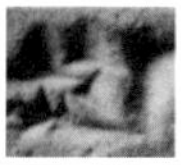		
KÙ					
TÚG		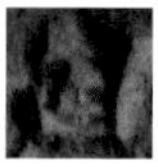	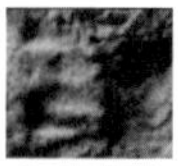 		
KUŠ					 
PISAN			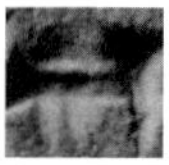		
NA_4					

Bibliography

Berman, Howard

1982 Some Hittite Oracle Fragments. *JCS* 34: 94–98.

Burgin, James M.

2022a *Studies in Hittite Economic Administration. A New Edition of the Hittite Palace-Temple Administrative Corpus and Research on Allied Texts Found at Ḫattuša. Volume I: Background, Corpus Overview, Case Studies, Lexical Commentary, and Glossary*. StBoT 70. Wiesbaden: Harrassowitz.

2022b *Studies in Hittite Economic Administration. A New Edition of the Hittite Palace-Temple Administrative Corpus and Research on Allied Texts Found at Ḫattuša. Volume II: Text Editions and Philological Commentary*. StBoT 71. Wiesbaden: Harrassowitz.

Klinger, Jörg

2022 Hittite Economics. In: Stefano de Martino (ed.), *Handbook Hittite Empire. Power Structures*. Empires through the Ages in Global Perspective 1. Berlin / Boston: de Gruyter Oldenburg, 605–47.

Siegelová, Jana

1986 *Hethitische Verwaltungspraxis im Lichte der Wirtschafts- und Inventardokumente*. 3 vols. Praha: Naìrodniì muzeum v Praze.

Strauß, Rita

2006 *Reinigungsrituale aus Kizzuwatna. Ein Beitrag zur Erforschung hethitischer Ritualtradition und Kulturgeschichte*. Berlin / Boston: de Gruyter.

Waal, Willemijn

2015 *Hittite Diplomatics. Studies in Ancient Document Format and Record Management*. StBoT 57. Wiesbaden: Harrassowitz.

Yakubovich, Ilya and Alice Mouton

2023 *Luwili: Hittite-Luwian Ritual Texts Attributed to Puriyanni, Kuwattalla and Šilalluḫi (CTH 758–763). Volume II: Discussion and Glossary*. StBoT 72,2. Wiesbaden: Harrassowitz.

WHO WROTE THE HITTITE CULT INVENTORIES?

Looking at Cuneiform Tablets through a Combined Appraisal of Paleographic and Orthographic Features

*Michele Cammarosano**
University of Naples 'L'Orientale'

Abstract

The paper explores the authorship of the Hittite cult inventories by combining a systematic evaluation of selected paleographic and orthographic features with a comparison with festival texts, in particular the two groups of festival tablets from the time of Tudḫaliya IV recently studied by Charles Steitler and produced by the schools traceable to Anuwanza and Palluwaraziti-Piḫawalwi respectively. The first section concerns material handwriting analysis, discussing 'cursive script' in cuneiform writing and identifying a specific slant in vertical and horizontal wedges arguably connected to writing speed. The second section presents a quantitative study of sign forms typical of the paleographic 'facies' customarily labeled 'IIIc'. The analysis reveals a remarkable analogy between the use of IIIc forms in the cult inventories and in the tablets of the Palluwaraziti-Piḫawalwi school, in contrast to the Anuwanza school, with the sign QA emerging as a key marker. The distribution patterns observed in the target corpora suggest that some of the inventories are older than the reign of Tudḫaliya IV. The third section compares phonographic vs logographic spellings for the expressions 'he offers' and 'altar' in the cult inventories vs (Late) New Script festival texts, showing that logographic spelling is almost exclusive in cult inventories, while festival texts prefer the phonographic form, yet with a sizable minority using logographic forms. This minority is concentrated in a few *CTH* numbers, particularly those having affinities of various kind with the cult inventories, and seems to be associated with the circle of Palluwaraziti and Piḫawalwi. These findings support the working hypothesis that the cult inventories were written from Ḫattušili III onwards, with Tudḫaliya IV-period inventories produced by scribes using graphic habits similar to those of the circle of Palluwaraziti and Piḫawalwi, if not by those very scribes. By holistically integrating the analysis of material handwriting features, sign forms, and orthographic patterns, the study advances our understanding of the IIIc paleographic 'facies' and highlights key dynamics of Hittite writing practices in the Late Empire.

1. Wedges

This study aims to address questions related to the authorship of Hittite cuneiform tablets by looking at them through combined angles, those of paleography and ortho-

* I would like to thank the organizers of the symposium for their invitation and hospitality in Mainz, all the participants for the most stimulating discussions, and Susanne Görke and Adam Kryszeń for their patience and effort in curating this contribution. A special word of thanks goes to Charles Steitler, who generously shared with me the analytical data on which his 2019 study is based, and to Gerfrid G.W. Müller who kindly provided photographs of Hittite tablets from the *Mainzer Fotoarchiv*. Last but not least, I am deeply indebted to Jörg Klinger for his insightful comments on a draft version of this paper.

graphy. In doing so, it hopes to shed light on selected aspects of the materiality of writing in ancient Anatolia, which may be of relevance for other areas of the cuneiform world as well. The analysis focuses on two corpora, namely cult inventories and festival texts. The former are a corpus of about 500 cuneiform tablets and fragments of tablets containing reports written by the central Hittite bureaucracy on the status of local cults in the central areas of the Hittite kingdom in the Late Empire period. The latter are a major corpus of about 10,000 cuneiform tablets and fragments of tablets containing protocols related to state cult festivals, spanning the entire life of the Hittite archives.[1]

In studying cuneiform tablets, it is useful to distinguish the three different elements that constitute the unity of a manuscript: the codicological element, which concerns the materiality of the medium apart from the writing, the paleographic element, which concerns the writing itself in the materiality of the written sign, and the philological element, which concerns the content of the written text. While across different writing traditions the primary aim of paleography has been to investigate the diachronic development of sign forms, thus to date manuscripts based on them, the term is used here in its broad sense, thus encompassing what Mark Weeden (this volume) aptly labels 'material handwriting studies', in particular aspects related to individual handwriting (cf. the term chirography) and writing process (cf. the term graphology).[2]

The present paper addresses selected aspects in the (broadly intended) paleographic sphere and a single aspect in the philological sphere, namely the distribution of certain orthographic patterns. The study is divided into three parts. The first part sets out the basic methodological assumptions for the study of individual handwriting and explores issues of writing speed and wedge execution. The second part focuses on an analytical study of sign forms across two case studies, the corpus of cult inventories and a group of late festival texts. The third part addresses aspects related to spelling patterns across cult inventories and festival texts.

1.1 Exploring the relationship between stylus and wedge components

In the realm of writing, the cuneiform scribe engages in a markedly different process compared to their Egyptian or medieval counterparts. Cuneiform signs do not emerge through the smooth gliding of a quill or pen across a surface. Rather, they are meticulously crafted by 'poking' the moist clay with a stylus, each stroke of which forms the fundamental elements known as wedges. The stylus impresses into the soft clay, never sliding over it, lest the sign become illegible. This action resembles more of a piercing motion, a fact underscored by the etymological roots of the verbs used in ancient Near Eastern languages to describe cuneiform writing ('to pierce, to prick'), contrasting with the verbs associated with linear writing, such as 'to trace' or 'to draw' (Fig. 1).

1 See https://www.hethport.uni-wuerzburg.de/txhet_kultinv/projekt.php and https://www.hethport.uni-wuerzburg.de/HFR/ for compact web presentations of the two corpora. More detailed overviews can be found in Cammarosano 2022 and Schwemer 2016 respectively.

2 Refer to Weeden (this volume) for a thoughtful methodological insight into key concepts of analysis in cuneiform paleography. For an in-depth insight into methodological issues and pitfalls in Hittite paleography, see the masterful study on the so-called Old Script and the dating of Hittite tablets by Klinger 2022.

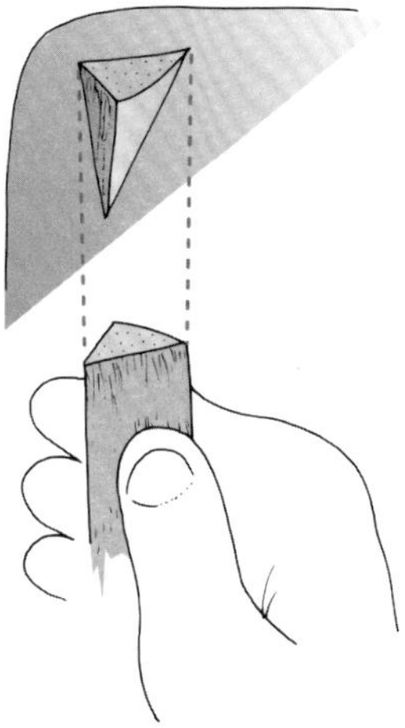

Fig. 1. Schematic representation of the relationship between stylus and wedge on the example of a classic reed stylus (note, however, that in Hittite Anatolia, styluses were not made using reeds and therefore the characteristic pattern of fibrous imprints and curvature of the right inner face of the wedge that is so typical of Mesopotamian tablets is never observed).

From a geometric standpoint, the wedge essentially embodies a tetrahedron, while the writing tip – responsible for physically shaping the wedge – is akin to a polyhedral cone. It is worth noting that whether the stylus section is triangular, square, or otherwise does not impact the wedge's geometry. The distinctive three-dimensional shape of the wedge depends not only on the geometry of the tip of the stylus, but also on the trajectory it follows during impression and any subsequent changes the wedge undergoes after impression. These changes include slight shifts in clay caused by adjacent wedge impressions, which offer valuable insights into the stroke sequence.

This seemingly trivial aspect often fails to garner the full appreciation it deserves in paleographic investigations centered on cuneiform tablets. While extensively discussed in prior studies (Cammarosano 2014, 2015), its key implications will be briefly outlined here. The shape of the wedge hinges upon multiple factors, first and foremost the angles of all three edges of the stylus at the writing tip and the relative positions of the stylus and writing surface throughout the impression process. Assuming a linear trajectory for the former as it presses into the clay, the inner angles of the wedge will align with those of the stylus' edges at the writing tip only if the trajectory falls within the polyhedral cone originating from the projection of its three edges. Should the stylus deviate outside this cone during its trajectory, a discrepancy between the inner angles of the wedge and those of the stylus' edges at the writing tip will arise.[3]

Thus, certain configurations of the stylus' edges are predisposed to produce wedges with stable inner angles, while others tend to yield less stable angles. This phenomenon is readily verified through empirical experiments.[4] Notably, it elucidates why wedges

3 Cammarosano 2014: 80 with Fig. 18.

4 Cammarosano 2014: 80–82.

with slanted heads can be achieved using a stylus whose 'top' has a right-angled right edge.[5] This phenomenon also accounts for variations in wedge slopes observed in certain tablets. Coupled with the orientation of the stylus edges at the writing tip, variation of the stylus' lateral tilt can significantly influence the inner and outer angles of the wedges.

Of particular interest are instances where scribes slightly rotated the stylus on its axis when transitioning between vertical and horizontal wedges (and *vice versa*). In such cases, horizontal wedges do not merely appear as verticals rotated 90° (and *vice versa*); rather, each wedge type exhibits distinct characteristics corresponding to varying inclinations of the aperture angle (Fig. 2).[6] This phenomenon is precisely observable in various corpora, including Hittite cult inventories (see below).

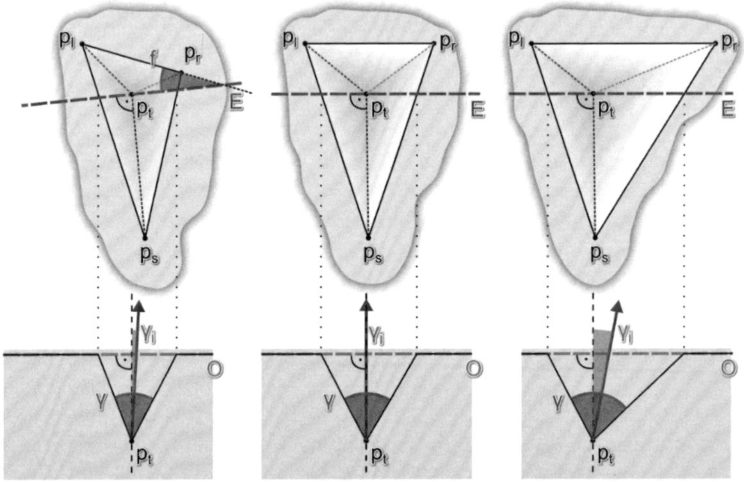

Fig. 2. Terminology for secondary wedge components, after Cammarosano 2015: 154 Fig. 4 (drawing by Denis Fisseler). Y aperture angle; Y_i aperture angle inclination; O tablet surface; E cross-sectional plane; f wedge head slope.

In general, deviating from linear movements of the stylus during the impression process is typically unnecessary and tends to compromise the cleanliness and legibility of the wedges. However, a notable exception arises in the form of a slight rotation of the stylus along its main axis, termed the 'stylus twist'. This maneuver results in an increase in both the top inner angle and aperture angle of the wedge. Moreover, when executed in a particular manner, it causes the right-hand face of the wedge to adopt a convex shape rather than remaining flat. Intriguingly, evidence suggests that certain

5 Cammarosano 2014: 82f. The slope of the wedge head refers to the angle between the top outer edge and the cross-sectional plane perpendicular to the spine, determining the extent to which the wedge head 'leans' towards one side relative to the spine. For further wedge terminology, refer to Cammarosano 2015: 151–53.

6 The 'aperture angle' is calculated on the cross-sectional plane perpendicular to the spine's projection on the tablet's surface, defining the wedge's width. The inclination of the aperture angle denotes the angle between the bisector of the aperture angle and the perpendicular to the tablet surface, determining how much a wedge 'leans' towards one side. See Cammarosano 2015: 152f.

scribes consistently employed the 'stylus twist' technique for a specific type of wedge, namely the *Winkelhaken*.[7]

1.2 On individual handwriting

The aforementioned observations substantially impact the examination of individual scribal hands. Given that the shape of the wedge greatly hinges on the particular stylus (tip) used for impressing it, mere measurements of its components prove useful in characterizing the script of a particular fragment and identifying joins, but fall short in characterizing specific scribal hands. To achieve this, one must explore the variation of these values across various types and arrangements of wedges.

This approach underwent quantitative testing in a case study centered on the tablets inscribed by two scribes documented in the corpus of letters from Maşat Höyük: Šuriḫili and Tarḫunmiya.[8] It was revealed that, despite significant variability in both the geometry of individual wedges (varying depths of impression, differing inclinations relative to the tablet's surface, etc.) and the execution of a sign across different tablets, and even to a certain extent within the same tablet, a discernible pattern emerged in the orientation of wedges within the constellation forming a specific sign (in this instance, the sign NA). This pattern can be deemed a hallmark of a scribal hand, and is independent both of the geometric characteristics of the stylus (tip) employed for a specific tablet and of factors such as the depth of wedge impressions, which, as Mark Weeden (2020: 326) rightly noted in his comprehensive paleographic examination of the letter of Tawagalawa, can be influenced by external circumstances unrelated to individual calligraphy, such as the composition and moisture content of the clay at the time of inscription.

Therefore, an element like the wedge heads' slope, taken in itself, can be considered a characteristic element of a specific scribal hand only under the assumption that this hand consistently used the same stylus throughout its activity – an assumption that is not guaranteed at all but rather seems extremely unlikely. An example may be drawn from Charles Steitler's recent study of 34 festival tablets written at the time of Tudḫaliya IV by scribes of two distinct circles, namely that of Anuwanza and of Palluwaraziti-Piḫawalwi (Steitler 2019). Steitler was able to demonstrate that specific aspects related to sign forms and wedge positioning within a sign constellation show a consistent distribution and contribute to the characterization of the writing style across the two circles.[9] The wedges heads' slope however, on the contrary, does not show any consistent correlation with the individual scribal hands (Fig. 3): indeed, as per the above assumption, this particular feature is heavily dependent on the geometrical configuration of the writing implement, rather than on personal handwriting. All this does not mean that an element like the inclination of the heads of the wedges cannot emerge as characteristic of a specific scribal hand or a group of scribes, or even an entire scribal tradition, for example, in a certain historical period. However, this can only be established through an extensive and sophisticated analysis of a large number of tablets, taking into account all factors at play.

7 Cammarosano et al. 2014: 27–29.

8 Cammarosano 2015: 162–67.

9 Steitler 2019: 422, 425, Fig. 14, Fig. 23; see further below.

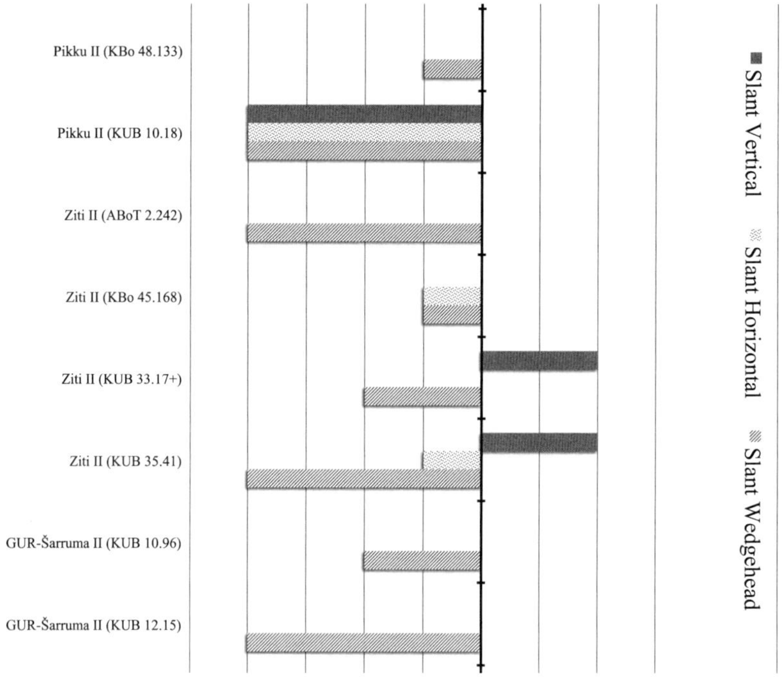

Fig. 3. Close-up from Steitler 2019: 441 Fig. 14, highlighting the absence of correlation between wedge head slope and personal handwriting in scribal hands.

1.3 On writing speed and cursive script

How does writing speed influence individual handwriting and what impact does it have on the identification of individual scribal hands? This issue is directly related to that concerning 'cursive' script, a term that is rarely defined with explicit criteria in cuneiform studies and is generally used to characterize a script with a less polished appearance, often associated with features such as the presence of simplified graphic forms (i. e. with less wedges than in the contemporary standard forms), frequent erasures, and shallow impression of the wedges.[10]

It is important to keep in mind that in Latin paleography, where the concept of cursive writing originated, writing speed is an additional aspect and not intrinsic to the 'set' vs 'cursive' polarity, although it usually correlates with it (set: low writing speed, cursive: high writing speed). The two writing modes, set and cursive, are fundamentally independent from each other within the writing system, reflecting two different ways of forming letters, and do not represent two distinct tendencies within one graphic system (Casamassima 1988). In the case of cuneiform though, there is no opposition between two distinct graphic sets as in the Latin script: the basic configuration of the signs is basically constant, irrespective of the 'elegance' or presumed speed with which they are executed, and the same arguably applies to the order of execution of

10 Cammarosano 2015: 167 with literature in n. 40.

the wedges (notwithstanding possible isolated exceptions, see Weeden 2020: 326). Simplified forms are indeed observed in administrative tablets for which a 'speedy' execution can be reasonably assumed, such as in cult inventories. However, this phenomenon remains limited, and in these same types of documents, quantitatively more elaborate forms than the standard ones are also observed (i. e. featuring more wedges than the standard forms; see Section 2.1 below). In sum, the characterization of cuneiform tablets as displaying 'cursive' script remains subject to evaluation based on the external appearance (or 'Gestalt') of the wedges, the criteria for which should be explicitly specified whenever this concept is invoked.

Identifying correlations between writing speed and certain graphic aspects of the written sign would provide an additional tool for analyzing handwriting. In a previous study, I hypothesized that one of these correlations is constituted by a structural asymmetry in the inclination of the aperture angle of the vertical wedges compared to the horizontal ones.[11] According to this theory, as the writing speed increases, the asymmetry also increases: the higher speed required when transitioning between horizontal and vertical wedges and *vice versa* would cause the scribe to develop a tendency to impress the horizontal wedges as symmetrical to the writing surface, while the vertical ones are 'resting' on the right side. This difference is reflected in a different inclination of the aperture angle, minimal in the case of horizontals and pronounced in the case of verticals (Fig. 4).

Fig. 4. Close-up of KUB 57.108 obv. ii; note the different inclination of the aperture angle in verticals vs horizontals (hethiter.net/: fotarch BoFN02416).

A test on a pilot sample of tablets provided encouraging results regarding the possibility of considering this aspect as characteristic of an 'accelerated' writing style. In order to corroborate or refute the theory, it will be necessary to refine the method and extend the analysis to larger samples. Above all, it would be important to conduct an in-depth study on groups of tablets for which the scribes are known, in order to verify whether this aspect is indeed likely to be related to writing speed rather than to individual scribal hands or writing habits other than speed.

11 Cammarosano 2015: 167–69.

In the frame of another study (Cammarosano 2021: 15), I also argued that

> cursive script correlates with a nonstandard placement of wedges in certain configurations, determined by the higher writing speed: in particular, the *Winkelhaken* at the end of a sign tend to 'slide up,' and the oblique wedge in signs like NI or GAG tends to be impressed almost parallel to the horizontal. When a vertical is followed by a horizontal at the end of a sign, as in ŠI and WA, the latter sometimes has the appearance of a shallow 'dash,' i.e. it lacks a proper 'head,' apparently because its spine was impressed using the right edge of the stylus.

Both features can be observed, among other corpora, in the letters from Maşat Höyük and in cult inventories (Fig. 5).

Fig. 5. Close-up from DAAM 1.39 obv. i; note the difference in the appearance of the horizontal, e. g. in ŠI in line 2 vs e. g. in AŠ in line 6 (hethiter.net/: fotarch BF02874).

Yet another factor that seems to be associated with writing speed pertains to the inclination (or 'slope') of both vertical and horizontal wedges in respect to the writing line, as proposed in Cammarosano 2021: 16 (referencing specific tablets). According to this thesis, an increase in writing speed would naturally lead the hand to minimize the angle of movement required for the wrist when transitioning between horizontals and verticals (and *vice versa*), following the principle of least effort. Consequently, vertical wedges would lean towards the left (slope to the upper left), while horizontals would slope downward (slope to the lower right). This results in a smaller angle between verticals and horizontals than the standard 90° (Fig. 6).

While the validity of the proposed correlation with writing speed requires further investigation and experimentation for validation or refutation, the observed slope of verticals and horizontals is noticeable in several tablets that also exhibit features previously argued to be indicative of potentially hurried writing. Notably, it is intriguing that the only two known cult inventory fragments displaying verticals sloping to the upper right (KUB 46.31 and DBH 43/2.109) exhibit handwriting markedly distinct from the 'cursive' style, characterized by deeply and clearly impressed wedges, and absence of asymmetry in the inclination of the aperture angle discussed above.

Fig. 6. Close-up of KBo 34.106(+) rev. iv; note the verticals' slope to the upper left, and the horizontals' slope to the lower right (hethiter.net/: fotarch BoFN04686b).

In light of the above considerations, it is interesting that precisely the tendency to impress vertical wedges sloping to the upper left and horizontals downward is the main graphological characteristic that, in the aforementioned analysis conducted by Charles Steitler on a group of late Hittite festival texts, characterizes the script of the circle of Palluwaraziti and Piḫawalwi as opposed to that associated with Anuwanza.[12] The significance of this fact appears even greater as the Palluwaraziti-Piḫawalwi circle shares with the corpus of cult inventories another paleographic element of a different nature, namely the relatively frequent use of IIIc sign forms (see Section 2.3 below). The corpus investigated by Steitler, being composed of 'signed' tablets, provides an opportunity that is lacking in the case of cult inventories, namely to investigate in-depth how certain graphic aspects are likely to be linked to the individual scribal hands or to other factors, including writing speed. A study of this kind, combined with appropriate practical experimentation, can answer the question of how the inclination of horizontal and vertical wedges, discussed now, can be considered a characteristic element of a specific writing style or rather specific scribal hands or circles. Steitler (2019: 425f.) observes that "another peculiar aspect of the handwriting of the Palluwaraziti and Piḫawalwi tablets is a tendency to employ relatively narrow horizontal wedges in comparison to the verticals. This gives the impression of a hastily (or, in German, *flüchtig*) written script, distinct from the more common deeper impressions of the horizontals" in the handwriting typical of the circle of Anuwanza.

If the correlation suggested independently by Steitler and myself is validated, the joint inclination of verticals to the upper left and horizontals to the lower right would stand out as an indicator of increased writing speed rather than an element characterizing individual handwriting. It is worth noting that verticals leaning towards the *right* – hence not at all related to writing speed, unless horizontals lean toward the bottom which to my knowledge never happens – seems to be characteristic of the Old Script, warranting a separate investigation.

12 Steitler 2019: 421f., 425.

2. Signs

2.1 General considerations on the paleography of cult inventories

The paleography of the cult inventories has been discussed in general terms in Cammarosano 2021: 17f. (with reference to specific studies and previous bibliography), while the commentaries to the 450 texts presented in digital edition on the *Hethitologie Portal Mainz* (accessible from the *Textcorpora* section, not directly from the *Konkordanz*)[13] provide specific observations on the paleography of individual manuscripts. Here, it will be sufficient to recap the overall picture and then expand the study on a particular aspect, namely, the use of forms typical for the paleographic *facies* traditionally defined as IIIc and considered characteristic of the final phase of scribal activity in Ḫattuša (see Section 2.2 below).[14]

The sign height exhibits a range from approximately 1–2 mm (e. g. in KBo 13.250, KBo 13.252, KBo 26.151, KBo 26.160, KBo 49.111, KUB 7.24+) to around 4–5 mm (e. g. in KBo 19.131, KBo 26.182, KUB 38.14, KUB 46.32), with the majority of tablets showcasing a sign height of around 3 mm (colophons, as usual, consistently feature larger script sizes compared to the rest of the tablet). Indeed, based on provisional observations, 3 mm seems to be the standard in Hittite tablets.[15]

The paleography of the cult inventories consistently aligns with their contextual dating to the Empire period (see Section 2.2 for details). Specifically, a number of tablets exhibit sign forms that are characteristic of the IIIc *facies*, including QA (HZL 21/6–9), EN (HZL 40/11), UN (HZL 197/8), KU (HZL 206/4–8), URU (HZL 229/11), DI (HZL 312/8–10), and KI (HZL 313/19–25). While some tablets display a consistent choice for a specific form of one or more of these (and other) signs, most present a coexistence of different forms for the same sign(s). In this case, while the distribution of such forms on the tablet is usually random, occasionally a pattern emerges. The most conspicuous example is the large tablet KBo 12.53+, where the sign LI is inscribed in the older form on the obverse (obv. 20′, 26′, 42′) and in the later form on the reverse (rev. 15, 16, 20, 28, 35, 41, 43). Furthermore, the verbal form "(the king) instituted" is represented logographically (ME-*iš*) up to obv. 37′ (with one exception in obv. 16′) and phonographically (*daiš*) from obv. 38′ onwards. Without any indication of multiple scribes at work on the tablet, it is reasonable to conclude that this observed pattern reflects a unique quirk of the scribe. Analogous examples in the Tawagalawa letter are discussed in Weeden 2020: 326 where he notes that "it is often observable that scribes adopt particular sign-forms in clusters over certain stretches of a text, while choosing other forms of the same sign for other stretches of the same text. The reasons underlying such distribution are not entirely clear, but it never occurs to my knowledge with the rigour we have before us on this tablet". KBo 12.53+ seems to me to provide precisely another case.

---

13 https://www.hethport.uni-wuerzburg.de/txhet_kultinv/textindex.php?l=x.

14 The term 'facies' (Latin for 'face') is used here instead of 'phase' to prevent misunderstandings. This is because, strictly speaking, 'facies' defines a typological category, not a chronological one.

15 See already Steitler 2019: 414 and Fig. 2.

'Reduced' sign forms, characterized by fewer wedges than standard forms, are well-documented within the corpus; particularly relevant is the 'halved' ALAM (not booked in the HZL), which seems to be attested in the corpus of the cult inventories only (KBo 2.1, KUB 17.35, KUB 38.23, KUB 38.34, and KUB 56.40); a new, reduced form of GUL appears in DAAM 1.36 obv. i 33. While the adoption of reduced forms aligns with the expectation that the criterion of least effort is in play, it is crucial to emphasize that cult inventories, even those displaying features of 'cursive' script and reduced sign forms, frequently incorporate forms with 'superfluous' wedges. This is evident in signs such as KÁN, GAL, MEŠ, and others, as is also observable in other corpora (e. g. Steitler 2019: 420). This phenomenon, not unique to this corpus, echoes practices found in other manuscript cultures, underscoring that the principles governing the graphic elements of these texts cannot be simplistically defined solely as 'least effort' in terms of minimizing the number of impressed wedges. Instead, these principles encompass a complex interplay of factors, notably including the writing habits and specific training to which individual scribes have been exposed.

2.2 A quantitative study of IIIc sign forms in cult inventories

This section expands on a particular aspect, namely, the use of forms typical for the paleographic *facies* traditionally defined as IIIc and considered characteristic of the final phase of scribal activity in Ḫattuša.[16] It is important to emphasize from the outset that, with multiplying numbers of in-depth studies on specific groups of tablets whose likely dating and scribes are known, it becomes increasingly clear that the paleographic dating method must operate cumulatively. In particular, two circumstances are now established: IIIc forms were already in circulation in Ḫattuša long before becoming widespread in scribal practice (Weeden 2020: 327–30), and contemporaneous scribes (and scribal circles) happened to use different sets of graphic forms, arguably dependent on factors such as training, personal preferences, and possibly also genre (Gordin 2015; Steitler 2019). The more paleographic studies on the Late Empire period progress, the more it will be possible to understand the dynamics and timing of appearance and usage of specific sign forms. At present, it is advisable to consider the label IIIc, as proposed by Mark Weeden and others, as a primarily typological rather than a chronological classification, with its distinctive characteristics being continuously fine-tuned. However, while primarily typological, the IIIc *facies* also holds value for dating, since despite the uncertainty about the precise inception of its individual sign forms, it clearly proliferates during the Late Empire period (hence, for simplicity, the typical pre-IIIc forms are referred to as 'older' forms). Although competing paleographic habits persisted concurrently, the IIIc *facies* can therefore be used as one of several features to support the dating of Late Empire tablets and corpora.

The IIIc sign forms that have been systematically reviewed throughout the corpus for the purpose of the present study (Fig. 7) are those related to the signs QA (HZL 21/6–9), EN (HZL 40/11), UN (HZL 197/8), KU (HZL 206/4–8), and DI/KI (HZL 312/8–10

16 See the discussion in van den Hout 1989: 326–43; see now also Goedegebuure 2014: 9f.; Klinger 1996: 32–39; Giorgieri and Mora 2004: 30–37; Weeden 2011: 49–52; 2020: 327–30 with further literature.

and 313/19–25). Further IIIc-related forms, such as for the signs URU (HZL 229/11), SAR (HZL 353/11–18), and ḪA (HZL 367/B) are also present in the corpus, but have not been systematically surveyed. In general, it can be stated that both the 'older' and the 'later' forms are amply attested and sometimes both are present on the same tablet: taking as an example the sign ḪA, some tablets show a coherent picture of using either the form with two *Winkelhaken* (e. g. VSNF 12.111, KBo 21.81+, KUB 17.35) or with one *Winkelhaken* (e. g. KUB 57.108+, KUB 25.22, KUB 7.24+), while others attest both forms (e. g. KBo 12.53+, DAAM 1.39, KUB 53.21). In the group of tablets attesting IIIc forms of the signs EN, UN, KU, DI, KI, and QA, the presence vs absence of the IIIc form of the sign ḪA (i. e. the one with a single *Winkelhaken*) has also been systematically recorded.

Fig. 7. IIIc sign forms relevant to the present study (redrawn from HZL). Upper row: systematically reviewed IIIc forms for QA, EN, UN, KU, and DI/KI; bottom row: IIIc forms for URU, SAR, and ḪA.

Table 1 lists all tablets where at least one IIIc form of the systematically investigated signs EN, UN, KU, DI, KI, and QA is present; for these tablets, the attested form of ḪA is also noted.[17]

Leitfragment	Systematically surveyed signs					ḪA
	EN	UN	KU	DI, KI	QA	
KBo 22.222	+					+
KuSa 1/1.3		+		+		+
KuSa 1/1.5		+				+
VSNF 12.111		+				-
KBo 21.81			+	+		-
KBo 39.48			+	+		-
KUB 38.2			+			-
KUB 41.34			+			-
KUB 54.67			+			+
KUB 38.1				+	+	-
KUB 56.39				+	+	-
KBo 12.53				+	+	+
KUB 57.108				+	+	+
DAAM 1.39				+		+

17 As stressed above, scribes not infrequently used both pre-IIIc forms and IIIc forms of diagnostic signs on the same tablet, so the recorded presence of a IIIc form in a certain tablet does not necessarily imply that no pre-IIIc form is present there as well.

Leitfragment	Systematically surveyed signs					ḪA
	EN	UN	KU	DI, KI	QA	
KUB 38.21				+		+
KBo 2.13					+	+
KBo 70.109					+	+
KUB 25.23					+	+
KUB 38.25					+	+
KUB 38.12					+	-
KUB 38.6					+	-
KBo 26.182					+	-
KBo 26.211					+	n/a
KBo 58.73					+	n/a
KUB 13.32					+	+
KUB 17.35					+	-
KUB 17.36					+	n/a
KUB 25.21					+	-
KUB 25.22					+	+
KUB 25.24					+	+
KUB 42.105					+	+
KUB 42.92					+	?
KUB 44.21					+	-
KUB 46.27					+	-
KUB 46.28					+	+?
KUB 53.21					+	+
KUB 55.48					+	+
KUB 57.97					+	+?
KUB 58.7					+	+
KUB 7.24					+	+
VBoT 26					+	+
VBoT 37					+	n/a
VBoT 122					+	n/a
Total (43 tablets)	**1**	**3**	**5**	**9**	**32**	

Table 1. Target IIIc sign forms in the cult inventories, sorted by diagnostic sign, with the relevant form of ḪA noted (+: IIIc form present, -: pre-IIIc form present; n/a: sign not attested).

The significance of these numbers lies primarily in the fact that they reflect a systematic survey of a significantly large corpus (450 fragments), that is relatively confined in time (see section 2.4 below), self-contained and coherent as a genre.[18]

18 On the internal coherency of the corpus see the most recent discussion in Cammarosano 2022: 70–75. Admittedly, a certain number of occurrences of diagnostic signs might have escaped scrutiny, but it seems reasonable to assume that this does not affect the substance of the analysis presented here.

The first takeaway from these raw data is the relative scarcity of fragments exhibiting typical IIIc forms of the selected diagnostic signs. Out of 450 fragments constituting the corpus, only 43, just under 10%, present at least one IIIc form of the six diagnostic signs considered (Table 2).[19]

The second takeaway concerns the predominance of QA in the group of signs under consideration: in about three-quarters of the fragments where at least one occurrence of the surveyed diagnostic forms is recorded, it concerns the QA sign, followed at a great distance by DI or KI (9 fragments, approximately one-fifth of the pool), and finally by very few occurrences for KU, UN, and EN.

	No. of IIIc tablets	Proportion within the IIIc tablets	Proportion within the corpus
EN	1	2.3%	0.2%
UN	3	7.0%	0.7%
KU	5	11.6%	1.1%
DI, KI	9	20.9%	2.0%
QA	32	74.4%	7.1%
IIIc tablets	43	100.0%	9.6%

Table 2. Selected IIIc forms in the cult inventories corpus (450 tablets and fragments): raw figures. The label 'IIIc tablets' refers to the group of tablets in which at least one instance of a IIIc form is attested. Note that the total of 43 'IIIc tablets' is smaller than the sum of the individual groups of tablets with IIIc forms for each sign, since several tablets display IIIc forms of multiple signs, as recorded in Table 1.

However, the impression given by these raw data changes when corrective measures are applied to refine the analysis and make the impression given by the absolute percentages less misleading. In fact, the percentages given do not take into account a fundamental element, namely that a number of fragments do not show any of the diagnostic signs. Therefore, in order to assess the real weight of IIIc forms in a corpus, it is necessary first to assess the number of fragments in which the diagnostic signs are attested.[20]

The number of fragments containing at least one occurrence of the diagnostic signs (irrespective of the attested forms), and the resulting percentages regarding the frequency of attestation of IIIc forms, are presented in Table 3.

19 It must be emphasized, however, that this and the following figures refer to the signs systematically surveyed. If IIIc ḪA had been included, the number of tablets with IIIc ḪA would undoubtedly exceed the number of tablets with IIIc QA, and the overall proportion of 'IIIc tablets' within the corpus would be higher.

20 What would be an extremely long and laborious analysis if carried out with traditional criteria can be easily performed thank to the availability of digital transliterations of all corpus fragments, produced in the frame of the 'Hittite Local Cults' project, and is greatly facilitated by the efficient search tool provided by the 'Thesaurus Linguarum Hethaeorum digitalis' project. While it is obvious that a certain number of occurrences may escape analysis in this way, this is greatly compensated by the efficiency in obtaining substantially reliable data for the aspects of interest here.

	No. of IIIc tablets	No. of tablets preserving the sign	Proportion of IIIc tablets
EN	1	35	2.9%
UN	3	73	4.1%
KU	5	151	3.3%
DI, KI	9	124	7.3%
QA	32	85	37.6%
IIIc tablets	43	261	16.5%

Table 3. Selected IIIc forms in the cult inventories corpus (450 tablets and fragments): calibrated figures, taking into account the number of tablets on which the relevant signs are present (irrespective of the attested forms) and the resulting proportion of tablets showing at least one instance of the corresponding IIIc forms. For the label 'IIIc tablets', see caption to Table 2 above.

The refined analysis brings to light two crucial aspects. By excluding fragments that do not preserve any of the diagnostic signs from the count, the percentage of fragments in which at least one IIIc form of the diagnostic signs is attested rises significantly, reaching 16.5% of the total. It is interesting to compare these numbers with the paleographic characterization of the corpus in the invaluable *Konkordanz der hethitischen Texte* by Silvin Košak (2002–). Out of 662 fragments catalogued as cult inventories, 413 are dated to the 'jh.' (*junghethitisch*) *facies* and 190 to the 'sjh.' (*spätjunghethitisch*) *facies* (of the remaining, 49 are undated and ten are dated to *facies* preceding the jh. one).[21] The group of 190 fragments dated to the 'sjh.' paleographic *facies* corresponds to a share of 28.7% (31.5% if calculated on the subtotal of 603 jh./sjh. fragments). This proportion, double compared to the share of IIIc fragments resulting from the criteria outlined above, likely reflects the adoption of more inclusive criteria for classification in the 'sjh.' *facies* compared to those adopted above for classification in the IIIc *facies*, in particular, the probable inclusion among the diagnostic forms of ḪA with one *Winkelhaken.*

The second pivotal point concerns the relevance of the IIIc form of the QA sign: in over one-third of the fragments in which the sign is attested, the IIIc form is present (on how to interpret this feature, see further below). Once again, the significance of this finding lies not in merely observing the presence of the form within the corpus, as its circulation in the IIIc paleographic *facies* is well known, but rather in the ability to quantify the specific weight of the form within a vast and internally consistent corpus.

The refined analysis also reveals the non-negligible weight of the IIIc form of the DI and KI signs, and the 'surpassing' of the KU sign by UN in terms of overall percentage weight compared to absolute numbers.

Finally, it is worth considering the use of ḪA in those tablets where IIIc forms of the systematically studied signs occur. While this does not eliminate the desideratum of a corpus-wide survey, it does provide a welcome insight into the degree of correlation with the other signs. The survey shows that of 37 tablets in which specific forms of ḪA

21 'Jh.' corresponds to NS (New Script) and 'sjh.' to LNS (Late New Script) in the CHD terminology.

are preserved, 14 (38%) have the conservative form, while 23 (62%) have the IIIc form. Restricting the survey to the sub-sample of tablets with IIIc QA gives similar figures. Out of 26 tablets with both IIIc QA and any form of ḪA, 9 (35%) have the conservative form and 17 (65%) have the IIIc form of ḪA. In other words, the IIIc form of ḪA is predominant within the sample, but by no means exclusive, as over a third of these tablets use the conservative form. Importantly, this usage contrasts with the picture that emerges from both the tablet authored by the Palluwaraziti and Piḫawalwi circle and the cult inventories that can be securely dated to Tudḫaliya IV, as will be seen in section 2.4 below.

2.3 IIIc forms in late festival texts, and their relation to cult inventories

Once again, it is instructive to compare the picture emerging from the examination of cult inventories with the meticulous analysis conducted by Charles Steitler on the group of festival tablets written by scribes from two scribal circles active during the time of Tudḫaliya IV – thus presumably contemporary with the bulk, or at least a portion, of the cult inventory corpus – which were associated respectively with Anuwanza and Palluwaraziti-Piḫawalwi.[22] The sample comprises 34 tablets, with 13 attributable to the Anuwanza circle and 21 to the Palluwaraziti-Piḫawalwi circle. The signs considered by Steitler to be diagnostic for the IIIc *facies* are ḪA, EN, QA, KI, DI, UN. The paleographic analysis conducted by Steitler highlights the adoption of two distinct graphic habits by the two contemporary scribal circles. The IIIc forms are absent in tablets written by scribes of the Anuwanza circle, being limited to occurrences of late QA in the colophon of only two tablets, which otherwise use the older form; they are instead frequent in tablets written by scribes of the Palluwaraziti-Piḫawalwi circle.[23]

In light of the analysis conducted on the cult inventories presented above, it is significant to delve deeper into Steitler's outcome through the appreciation of the analytical data regarding the individual investigated signs, which were not presented in the 2019 study and which he kindly provided for the purpose of the present study (Table 4). These reveal that the most frequently encountered IIIc form is ḪA with one *Winkelhaken*, observed in 11 out of the 21 tablets of the Palluwaraziti-Piḫawalwi circle, followed by the late form of QA, observed in 7 tablets of the Palluwaraziti-Piḫawalwi circle in addition to the two already mentioned for the Anuwanza circle; the third most attested form is late KI, with 4 tablets (plus one with late DI), while the late forms of EN and UN come last.

22 Below, for simplicity, the two scribal circles will be referred to as the Anuwanza and Palluwaraziti-Piḫawalwi circles, but the reference is always to the two groups of festival tablets written by the scribes belonging to those circles as investigated by Steitler. Note that the relevant scribes are active two generations after Anuwanza; refer to the detailed study by Gordin 2015 with previous literature. The two groups of festival tablets include compositions booked under the following *CTH* numbers: 263, 330, 594, 670, 679, 691, 700, 706, 720, 759, 763, 825 (circle of Anuwanza); 529, 597, 598, 608, 615, 617, 620, 625, 626, 627, 628, 639, 666, 670, 685, 705, 750 (circle of Palluwaraziti-Piḫawalwi).

23 Steitler 2019: 421 and Fig. 9–10, 425 and Fig. 17–21; see already Gordin 2015: 333.

Scribe	*Leitfragment*	*CTH*	ḪA	EN	QA	KI	DI	UN	Notes
Circle of Anuwanza									
Angulli	KUB 56.35	679							
GUR-Šarruma II	KUB 10.96	825							
GUR-Šarruma II	KUB 12.15	720			-				
GUR-Šarruma II	KUB 51.12	670	-			-			
Ḫanikkuili II	KBo 10.34	700	-	-	-				
Pikku II	KBo 48.133	670			-				
Pikku II	KUB 10.18	594			+/-				IIIc QA: in colophon
Šakkapi	KBo 5.11+	263	-		+/-				IIIc QA: in colophon
ZA.ḪUM-ZA	KUB 55.59	706							
Ziti II	ABoT 2.242	763							
Ziti II	KBo 45.168	691	-	-	-	-		-	
Ziti II	KUB 33.17+	330	-			-			
Ziti II	KUB 35.41	759							
Total IIIc forms, circle of Anuwanza			**0**	**0**	**2**	**0**	**0**	**0**	
Circle of Palluwaraziti-Piḫawalwi									
Alalimi	KUB 11.21a	598	-		-	-			
Alalimi (Piḫawalwi)	KBo 22.214	620	-		+				
Armaziti	KBo 19.128	625				+			
Ḫešni	KUB 25.10	626			+	-			
Ḫešni (Palluwaraziti, Piḫawalwi, Ḫulla)	KUB 44.24	685					-		
Palluwaraziti, Piḫawalwi	İzmir 1270+	627	+			+		-	
Palluwaraziti, Piḫawalwi	İzmir 1274	627							
Palluwaraziti, Piḫawalwi	KBo 23.62	670	+						
Palluwaraziti, Piḫawalwi	KBo 30.15	627	+						
Palluwaraziti, Piḫawalwi	KBo 35.144	705	+			-			
Palluwaraziti, Piḫawalwi	KBo 45.11	597	+						
Palluwaraziti, Piḫawalwi	KBo 45.34	608	+		+				
Palluwaraziti, Piḫawalwi	KBo 46.102	615	+			+/-		+	Both IIIc and pre-IIIc KI
Palluwaraziti, Piḫawalwi	KUB 2.8	617		+	+	+/-	+		Both IIIc and pre-IIIc KI
Palluwaraziti, Piḫawalwi	KUB 41.26+	750	+	+	+			+	
Palluwaraziti, Piḫawalwi	KUB 51.77	666	+						
Palluwaraziti, Piḫawalwi	KUB 55.13	627	+						
Palluwaraziti, Piḫawalwi	KUB 60.28	529			+	-			
Šandaruntiya	KBo 26.178	529	-						
Talmi-Šarruma	KBo 35.260	628	-						
Zuwa	KBo 23.97	639	+/-		+				IIIc QA: in colophon
Total IIIc forms, circle of Palluwaraziti-Pihawalwi			**11**	**2**	**7**	**4**	**1**	**2**	

Table 4. Selected IIIc forms in the late festival texts written by scribes of the circles of Anuwanza and Palluwaraziti-Piḫawalwi, based on data kindly provided by Charles Steitler. "+": IIIc form attested; "-": pre-IIIc form attested; "+/-": both forms attested. Scribal supervisors are given in brackets.

As with the cult inventories, the figures on the proportion of IIIc forms relative to the tablets where the diagnostic signs are actually attested are more indicative than the absolute numbers. The 'calibrated' figures further highlight the consistency in the two graphic habits. The scribes of the Anuwanza circle appear, as mentioned, completely consistent in avoiding the use of IIIc forms, confined to the colophons (two tablets attesting both QA forms, IIIc in the colophon and the older one in the main text). On the other hand, the scribes of the Palluwaraziti-Piḫawalwi circle embraced the IIIc forms, while continuing to some extent to use older forms alongside them. Specifically, and with reference to this scribal circle alone, for ḪA there are 10 tablets attesting the IIIc form as opposed to four attesting the older form (and one, KBo 23.27, attesting both); for QA, we have six tablets exclusively with the IIIc form, one with the older form, and one with both forms, the older one in the main text and the IIIc one in the colophon (as also occurs in two additional tablets belonging to the Anuwanza circle); for KI, we have four tablets with the IIIc form and 7 with the older form (though two of these also display the IIIc form); for DI, it is one against one; for UN, two with the IIIc form and one with the older form; for EN, two tablets with the IIIc form. Zooming in on the sign form distribution within each of the two circles further highlights the coherence in usage. For the two best-attested signs, ḪA and QA, these signs are consistently IIIc in tablets 'signed' by Palluwaraziti and Piḫawalwi, while conservative forms of ḪA and QA appear only in tablets 'signed' by others within their circle (Alalimi, Šandaruntiya, and Talmi-Šarruma).

At this point, it is important to address a significant *caveat* relevant to both this discussion and the one that will follow regarding orthographic patterns (see Section 3 below). The conclusions drawn here, based on observable patterns in the numerical distribution of specific elements, are meaningful only under the assumption that these patterns are not influenced by external factors beyond those explicitly considered. Such factors could, in principle, obscure the true significance of the numbers presented. Specifically, the sample of festival tablets under consideration is treated as if it were a fundamentally homogeneous group in terms of content and textual tradition, particularly regarding the presence of models (*Vorlagen*) and the nature of the textual tradition behind each composition. The interpretation of the numerical data proposed here is a working hypothesis based on the assumption of a fundamental comparability between the tablets from the Anuwanza circle and those from the Palluwaraziti-Piḫawalwi circle. Therefore, this interpretation is subject to revision if an analysis considering the *Sitz im Leben* and the textual tradition of the individual compositions reveals elements that invalidate such comparability. The same applies to the corpus of cult inventories, insofar as its treatment as a whole is based on the assumption that it can be considered a fundamentally coherent corpus in itself (as argued in Cammarosano 2022).

The picture emerging from the considered group(s) of festival tablets – two consistently diverging graphic styles, one avoiding, the other embracing IIIc forms – can be compared to the findings from the cult inventories presented above. It is expected that the cult inventories constitute a corpus originating from multiple scribes (possibly from multiple circles), and this would exhibit both conservative and innovative forms. These scribes, unlike those of the festival texts considered by Steitler, remain anonymous to us. Importantly, the coexistence of the IIIc form of QA with the conservative form of ḪA in several cult inventories suggests that this mixed usage might be diachronically conditioned rather than merely a reflection of synchronic variance. This issue will be further explored in section 2.4 below.

Steitler's case study, itself expanding and complementing previous work by Shai Gordin, Jörg Klinger, Theo van den Hout and others, confirms what was already observed by Mark Weeden:[24]

> While Kammenhuber's essential view that these were 'just' matters of hand-writing (i.e. graphology) is certainly too far in the wrong direction … the process of fine-dating on the basis of sign-forms alone has also led to anomalies which are in need of review. We are most certainly dealing with contemporary scribes who have been exposed to different traditions and educational experiences. These are reflected in their work.

Of course, this conclusion does not mean that we cannot use the IIIc *facies* for dating purposes. Especially when used in a 'cumulative' manner, in light of meaningful patterns, and under consideration of the textual tradition of the involved tablets, the presence vs absence of diagnostic forms definitely has an intrinsic value as a dating criterion.[25]

Despite the small sample size requiring caution in interpreting the statistical significance of these numbers, the comparison with the picture emerging from the analysis of cult inventories is enlightening in several respects. One of the most significant results concerns the confirmation of the importance of the IIIc form of the QA sign for characterizing the IIIc *facies*: while in the corpus of cult inventories this form is present in one-third of the tablets attesting the sign, in the group of tablets from the two circles of Anuwanza and Palluwaraziti-Piḫawalwi we have 6 tablets exclusively with the IIIc form (all in the Palluwaraziti-Piḫawalwi circle), 5 tablets exclusively with the older form (four in the Anuwanza circle, one in the Palluwaraziti-Piḫawalwi circle), and three with both forms, the older one in the main text and the IIIc one in the colophon (of these, two belong to the Anuwanza circle, one to the Palluwaraziti-Piḫawalwi circle): the IIIc form is thus present in 9 out of 14 tablets attesting the sign, corresponding to a proportion of 64%, roughly double that observed in the cult inventories, and rising to almost 90% if we consider the Palluwaraziti-Piḫawalwi circle alone (7 tablets out of 8, with one of these using it in the colophon while using the older form in the main text). Analogous conclusions can be drawn from the evidence of the attested forms of the sign ḪA, as seen above.

As noted above, textual genre and tradition are certainly among the factors that influence the choice of paleographic forms, and since these aspects have not yet been addressed in detail, the conclusions drawn by Steitler and extended here are significant only under the assumption of a fundamental comparability between the two groups of tablets. If this assumption is correct, the observed divergent graphic patterns show that the difference in the use or non-use of IIIc forms is not due to textual genre or tradition, but rather reflects the different background of their training: scribes of the Palluwaraziti-

24 Weeden 2011: 50, also quoted in Steitler 2019: 430; see also Weeden's contribution to this volume.

25 As already observed in the seminal study by van den Hout 1989: 342; on the methodology of paleographic dating see now Klinger 2022.

Piḫawalwi circle had been taught, so to say, to embrace 'modern' graphic forms, while those of the Anuwanza circle had been taught to avoid them apart for colophons.[26]

2.4 Relevance of the above evidence for dating the cult inventories

What are the implications of this state of affairs for interpreting the evidence of the cult inventories, particularly for two crucial questions: the dating of the corpus and whether it is the product of a group of scribes specifically devoted to this textual genre or of the same scribes responsible for other types of texts, in particular of festival texts? The variety of options hypothesized a priori may be reduced to three main scenarios:

(a) The cult inventories may all date back to Tudḫaliya IV, and may originate from at least two distinct scribal circles: one producing tablets without IIIc variants (à la Anuwanza), and the other with IIIc variants (à la Palluwaraziti-Piḫawalwi).

(b) The cult inventories may all date back to Tudḫaliya IV, but they may originate from one single scribal circle, which would display a graphic style different from the Palluwaraziti-Piḫawalwi school, with a 'mixed' usage of IIIc and pre-IIIc variants.

(c) The cult inventories may span beyond Tudḫaliya IV's reign, with variations in sign usage possibly indicating diachronic developments. Some tablets, particularly those showing consistency in IIIc usage akin to the Palluwaraziti-Piḫawalwi circle, could be contemporary (and in principle could even have been written by them), while others lacking such patterns might be older.

The anonymous nature of the cult inventories, which are not 'signed' by their scribes as in the case of festival texts, makes it seemingly impossible to choose between these scenarios, at least based solely on paleographic data. However, an attempt can be made. Within the corpus, a group of 20 tablets can be reasonably dated to the reign of Tudḫaliya IV based on internal textual references, the foremost being the mention of the sovereign himself (Cammarosano 2012: 21f.). Therefore, it is worth examining in detail the paleography of this group of tablets, particularly the distribution of IIIc sign forms, and compare it with the general picture presented above. The results of the analysis are illustrated in Table 5.

The evidence of these securely datable tablets reveals interesting patterns of paleographic distribution. Regarding the QA sign, out of eight tablets preserving it, six exhibit the IIIc form, while only two use the conservative form. Notably, all six tablets with IIIc QA also display IIIc ḪA. Among the two tablets with the conservative QA, one also features the conservative ḪA and the other the IIIc ḪA. As for the ḪA sign, out of 16 tablets, 13 show the IIIc form and only three the conservative form.

The comparison of these figures with the overall cult inventories and the festival tablets from the Anuwanza and Palluwaraziti-Piḫawalwi circles reveals a clear pattern. Paleographically, the cult inventories securely dateable to Tudḫaliya IV align closely with the Palluwaraziti-Piḫawalwi circle, where the IIIc forms of QA and ḪA overwhelmingly prevail. This contrasts significantly with the overall cult inventories, where the IIIc QA appears in about one-third of the corpus and the IIIc ḪA in about

26 A circumstance which confirms they did know these forms. Indeed, colophons represent 'special' scribal spaces, where non-standard behaviors find expression – both towards a conservative, or even archaizing, and a 'modernist' attitude; see e. g. Gordin 2015: 333, 341.

Leitfragment	Grounds for the dating	QA	Other signs
KBo 12.57	explicit reference to Tudḫaliya	n/a	IIIc ḪA
KBo 26.179	explicit reference to Tudḫaliya	n/a	n/a
KBo 26.188	explicit reference to Tudḫaliya	n/a	IIIc ḪA
KUB 7.24+	explicit reference to Tudḫaliya	IIIc	IIIc ḪA
KUB 13.32	explicit reference to Tudḫaliya	IIIc	IIIc ḪA
KUB 25.22	explicit reference to "Tud(ḫaliya)"	IIIc	IIIc ḪA
KUB 25.23	explicit reference to Tudḫaliya	IIIc	IIIc ḪA
KUB 25.24	explicit reference to Tudḫaliya	IIIc	IIIc ḪA
KUB 38.23	likely reference to Tudḫaliya	n/a	IIIc ḪA
KUB 38.35	explicit reference to Tudḫaliya	n/a	IIIc ḪA
KUB 42.100	content; reference to the "father of My Sun"	pre-IIIc	pre-IIIc UN and ḪA
KUB 46.34	explicit reference to "Tudḫali(ya)" (draft)	n/a	IIIc ḪA
KUB 56.56	content	n/a	pre-IIIc ḪA
KUB 58.7	explicit reference to Tudḫaliya	IIIc	QA IIIc most likely, IIIc ḪA
IBoT 2.131	reference to Urḫi-Teššob and the "father of My Sun"	n/a	pre-IIIc ḪA
KuSa 1/1.3	reference to the "father of My Sun"	n/a	IIIc DI/KI and ḪA
KuSa 1/1.5	reference to the "father of My Sun"	pre-IIIc	IIIc UN and ḪA
KuSa 1/1.39	reference to the "father of My Sun"	n/a	n/a
Bo 3998	explicit reference to Tudḫaliya	?	?

Table 5. Selected paleographic features of the cult inventories securely attributable to Tudḫaliya IV.

two-thirds of the 'IIIc tablets' (those with at least one instance of IIIc EN, UN, KU, DI, KI, or QA).

The picture, including the converging evidence from QA and ḪA, has important implications. If there were reasons to suspect that the group of securely dateable cult inventories came from a specific scribe or scribal circle, the evidence could still be compatible with the hypothesis that the entire corpus dates back to Tudḫaliya IV's reign. It would then suffice to assume that the (bulk of) non-securely datable tablets were written by contemporary scribes with more conservative habits. However, there is no apparent reason to assume a particular scribe or scribal circle for the dateable group. These 20 tablets do not form a homogeneous cluster within the corpus but are analogous to the other tablets, aside from their mentions of the ruler or content-based arguments that allow them to be confidently dated. Therefore, if the entire corpus is dated to Tudḫaliya IV's reign, one would expect the distribution of QA forms in the dateable tablets to mirror that of the whole corpus. The fact that it does not suggests that the corpus spans a greater chronological range, with a significant portion arguably dating back to his predecessor's reign.

In a previous study, I proposed that the fact that Tudḫaliya IV is the only sovereign to whose era some cult inventories can be securely dated does not automatically justify extending this dating to the entire corpus. Specifically, I argued that the statistical predominance of tablets securely attributable to Tudḫaliya IV compared to those of other sovereigns (20 vs 0) should not be taken as a compelling argument for dating of the entire corpus to Tudḫaliya's reign, provided there are reasons to suspect that this sovereign is disproportionately mentioned by name compared to others, and argued that such grounds for 'overexposure' are indeed identifiable (Cammarosano 2012: 24–27). At that time, my concern was primarily methodological: I was keen to avoid that hasty and, in my opinion, mistaken logical leap that led to the repetition in literature of the assumption according to which, since Tudḫaliya IV was the only sovereign to whom cult inventories could securely be attributed, the entire corpus was likely to date back to his reign. Having not discovered elements to substantiate the dating of particular tablets to other sovereigns, I underscored that my argument was directed solely at refuting a flawed reasoning, and did not imply that the hypothesis suggesting the entire corpus originated from Tudḫaliya IV was inherently implausible or improbable.

The systematic analysis of the paleography of the corpus, and in particular the distribution of forms of the QA sign, combined with the case study on festival texts from the time of Tudḫaliya IV examined by Steitler, now allows us to enrich the discussion with new data. Steitler's examination of the paleography of tablets by two groups of scribes active during the reign of Tudḫaliya IV showcases the presence of two distinct and consistent graphic styles (more, of course, certainly existed). The IIIc form of the QA sign emerges as an important marker in distinguishing between these two styles, being restricted to colophons in one group and most widely employed throughout the other. The analysis of the paleography of cult inventories indicates that the usage of the QA sign closely mirrors the latter style among tablets securely attributable to Tudḫaliya IV, while a different distribution is observed when considering the corpus as a whole. Analogous considerations hold true for the sign ḪA. The most plausible interpretation of this finding, albeit with the *caveat* of a limited sample size, suggests that a significant portion of the cult inventory corpus may date to the period preceding Tudḫaliya IV's reign. The paleographic characteristics exhibited by the Palluwaraziti-Piḫawalwi circle and the group of inventories linked to Tudḫaliya IV can be regarded as representative of one among multiple established graphic styles during this sovereign's era, one that embraced the use of 'innovative' sign forms. Conversely, the paleography of tablets from the Anuwanza circle reflects a 'conservative' style.

To further specify, correct, or refute this hypothesis, it will be necessary to broaden the analysis to encompass additional tablet groups with secure or probable dating. Furthermore, a more detailed and systematic tallying of sign forms employed is necessary in order to highlight significant patterns for the identification of graphical specificities both at the synchronic and diachronic level.

3. Words

3.1 Orthographic patterns in late festival texts and cult inventories: the case of the spellings for the expressions "he offers" and "altar"

In a previous study, an initial overview of the orthographic distribution of selected forms across cult inventories and festival texts was provided, arguing that the observable distribution cannot be explained solely by the criteria of minimal effort and genre-specific jargon, and may even be interpreted in the sense that the two groups of texts derive from two different groups of scribes (Cammarosano 2021: 20–25). The main argument on the latter point concerned a seeming incongruity of the observed distributions for certain forms compared to the hypothesis that the two groups of texts originated from the same group of scribes. Here, I would like to revisit that discussion by analyzing in more detail the spellings attested for two specific expressions.[27]

The analysis is facilitated by the availability of two new powerful research tools, which had not yet been released at the time of that study: the *HFR Basiscorpus* comprising all festival texts (with the *HFR-Suche* search engine) and the *Thesaurus Linguarum Hethaeorum digitalis* (with similar search engine), where the transliterations prepared within the framework of the *Hittite Local Cults* project have been incorporated.[28]

The two cases analyzed here are represented by the spellings BAL-(*an*)-*ti* vs *šipanti* 'he offers' and ^{GIŠ}ZAG.GAR.RA(-) vs *ištanan...* 'altar', taking into consideration the paleographic dating as recorded in the *Konkordanz* (jh. vs sjh.), the absolute number of occurrences (including restored ones), and the number of manuscripts (tablets) in which at least one occurrence of these forms is attested. In considering the paleographic dating according to the *Konkordanz*, it should be recalled that the indications 'jh.' and 'sjh.', strictly speaking, are not to be taken as referring to two chronologically distinct phases but rather as pertaining to two distinct graphic *facies*, which may appear in manuscripts contemporary to each other (see Section 2.1 above; on the criteria for this classification see further below).

Table 6 presents the results of this analysis for the expression 'he offers' in the considered spellings. The interpretation of the numbers is straightforward: cult inventories almost exclusively use the logographic form, while festival texts show a strong preference for the phonographic form. Within this general framework, the percentage

	Occurrences				Tablets				Tablets, jh.+sjh.	
	jh.		sjh.		jh.		sjh.			
	cult inv.	festivals	cult inv.	festivals	cult inv.	festivals	cult inv.	festivals	cult inv.	festivals
BAL#-*ti*	40	205	25	63	17	121	12	28	29	149
ši-#pa-an-ti	3	1784	1	223	3	767	1	97	4	864
Total	**43**	**1989**	**26**	**286**	**20**	**888**	**13**	**125**	**33**	**1013**
BAL#-*ti*, %	*93.0*	*10.3*	*96.2*	*22.0*	*85.0*	*13.6*	*92.3*	*22.4*	*87.9*	*14.7*
ši-#pa-an-ti, %	*7.0*	*89.7*	*3.8*	*78.0*	*15.0*	*86.4*	*7.7*	*77.6*	*12.1*	*85.3*

Table 6. Spellings for the verbal form 'he offers' in cult inventories vs festival texts. The special character '#' reflects the use of the corresponding search operator in the *HFR-Suche* search engine (any text except space). The figures in the two bottom rows refer to percentages.

27 This also provides an opportunity to rectify an error present in that study: the occurrence numbers related to festival texts reported in Table 2.4 on page 21 referred to the sum of NS + LNS manuscripts and not, as erroneously stated, to LNS manuscripts alone.

28 Currently the corpus is entirely classified there under the number 530 of the *CTH*, a circumstance that further facilitated data retrieval for the present study.

of festival texts using the logographic form is significantly higher in manuscripts classified as 'sjh.' compared to those classified as 'jh.'

The distribution of forms for the term 'altar' (Table 7) reveals a more complex picture. The overall pattern is similar: here too, cult inventories almost exclusively use the logographic form (only seven occurrences of the phonographic form, four of which are in KBo 2.13), while festival texts, despite the preference for the phonographic form, reveal a significant number of manuscripts using the logographic form. The consistency of this latter group is even greater than in the previous case, consisting of a fifth of the manuscripts classified as 'jh.' and even half of those classified as 'sjh.' (the average is thus 25%).

	Occurrences				Tablets				Tablets, jh.+sjh.	
	jh.		sjh.		jh.		sjh.			
	cult inv.	festivals	cult inv.	festivals	cult inv.	festivals	cult inv.	festivals	cult inv.	festivals
^{GIŠ}ZAG.GAR.RA	99	61	97	73	34	48	29	30	63	78
iš-ta-na-n	7	297	0	56	4	188	0	30	4	218
Total	**106**	**358**	**97**	**129**	**38**	**236**	**29**	**60**	**67**	**296**
^{GIŠ}ZAG.GAR.RA, %	*93*	*17*	*100*	*57*	*89.5*	*20*	*100*	*50*	*94*	*26*
iš-ta-na-n, %	*7*	*83*	*0*	*43*	*10.5*	*80*	*0*	*50*	*6*	*74*

Table 7. Spellings for the noun 'altar' in cult inventories vs festival texts. The provided forms reflect those used in performing the query in the *HFR-Suche* search engine. The figures in the two bottom rows refer to percentages.

3.2 Interpretation of the observed distribution

The refined analysis, which distinguishes between NS and LNS festival fragments, dispels the arguments I put forward in Cammarosano 2021: 24f. regarding the alleged absence of "any apparent rationale to explain the distribution of the observed spellings". At first sight, the evidence presented above could simply be interpreted in the light of the fact that cult inventories are all *unica*, never copies of older manuscripts as is often the case with festival texts. The overwhelming prevalence of the logographic form in cult inventories would thus more directly reflect the graphic practice of the period in which they were presumably written, a period which, as is well known, tends to increasingly use logographic forms against phonographic ones.[29] Secondly, the logographic form in most cases offers an advantage over the phonographic form in terms of the least amount of mechanical effort and space required, and it is therefore natural to assume that it would be favored in the context of manuscripts with a highly formulaic content and an administrative, relatively ephemeral nature, such as the cult inventories.[30] Late festival texts, on the other hand, which have a much more complex textual tradition and are often copies (albeit with variants) of older models, would contain a proportionally greater number of phonographic forms because they may tend to reproduce the spellings of

29 For literature on this point, see Cammarosano 2021: 20 with n. 62.

30 As for the mechanical effort involved in the use of logograms vs phonographic spellings, consider also the *caveat* argued in Cammarosano 2021: 23 with n. 71.

the older manuscripts they are based on, may be less standardized than the cult inventories and may use partly different strategies for encoding and decoding meaning.[31]

While the role of individual factors, especially of issues of textual tradition, are still to be clarified, a closer look at the manuscripts in question allows us to formulate a more nuanced working hypothesis. If we look at which festival texts attest to the logographic spelling, it emerges that, apart from occurrences related to manuscripts not yet classified (*CTH* 670), the majority of manuscripts that use the logographic form are concentrated in a few groups of texts (Table 8), namely the *nuntarriyašḫa-* festival (*CTH* 626, four manuscripts), a few manuscripts related to the AN.DAḪ.ŠUM festival (*CTH* 612, 617, 618, 625, totaling six manuscripts), and especially two groups of festival texts that have significant affinities with the cult inventories, namely (a) the festive protocols related to the cults of Nerik restored by Ḫattušili III and Tudḫaliya IV (*CTH* 672, 678, 679) and (b) the festival protocols related to the Stag god cults around Karaḫna (*CTH* 681–685).[32] The case for suspecting an affinity between cult inventories and these groups of festival texts becomes even stronger when looking at the identity of the scribes known for these tablets: in addition to two tablets signed respectively by Piḫami, a pupil of Ḫalwaziti, and a certain Kuniya (perhaps also from the Ḫalwaziti circle), all four tablets for which the scribe is known are signed by Palluwaraziti (and Piḫawalwi), thus precisely by those scribes who, as seen in the previous sections, exhibit graphic habits similar to those observable in cult inventories.

The combination of these circumstances does not seem to be attributable to chance and suggests a different hypothesis than the one proposed in my 2021 study, namely that a specific group of scribes active in the genre of festival texts was also responsible for the cult inventories – more specifically, if the hypotheses reached in the previous part of this study are correct, for those cult inventories that exhibit the graphic habit attested by them. If true, this scenario would also be more in line with the assumption that the writing of cuneiform tablets at Ḫattuša was probably managed by a relatively small number of professional scribes.[33] Extending the analysis to as many orthographic forms as possible and considering as detailed as possible all the paleographic and content aspects of the manuscripts involved will allow to corroborate, further specify, or refute this hypothesis.

---

31 This general explanation is not intended to minimize the complexity of the concept of 'economy' in writing practices. While fewer signs may reduce the physical effort of writing, they increase the cognitive load required for encoding and decoding meaning, so that the use of logograms does not necessarily mean less effort, as the workload is simply shifted to another level. This dynamic is particularly relevant when the degree of standardization and formulaic content of certain passages, as well as the textual tradition of the texts studied, are taken into account, which considerably complicates the analysis. Cord Kühne's study of the graphic realization of the Hittite reflexive particle (1988) provides an excellent, compelling demonstration of the complex, interacting factors that determine spelling habits. Statistical comparisons between logographic and phonographic spellings in different genres, while providing valuable data and allowing the formulation of new working hypotheses, necessarily fail to capture these nuances, making it essential to consider a wider range of factors in any future discussion of the scenario tentatively proposed here.

32 The affinities with cult inventories concern both form and content, and have been discussed in Cammarosano 2021: 5f.

33 See most recently van den Hout 2020, with ample discussion of all involved aspects and competing scenarios; for the distinction between 'scribal craftsmen' and 'scholar-scribes' see van den Hout 2015.

Content	Ms.	(s)jh.	Scribe
CTH 500 Fragments of Kizzuwatnaean festival and magical rituals	KBo 38.277	jh.	
CTH 597 Winter festival	KBo 45.11	jh.	Palluwaraziti
CTH 612 AN.DAḪ.ŠUM, day 16: temple of Zababa; Sun-goddess of the earth	IBoT 4.76	jh.	
CTH 617 AN.DAḪ.ŠUM, day 32: for the protective deity of Tauriš	KUB 2.8	sjh.	Palluwaraziti
CTH 618 AN.DAḪ.ŠUM, day 33–34: on Mt. Puškurunuwa	KUB 57.99+	sjh.	
CTH 625 Fragments of the AN.DAḪ.ŠUM festival	IBoT 2.4	sjh.	
CTH 625 Fragments of the AN.DAḪ.ŠUM festival	KBo 9.138	jh.	
CTH 625 Fragments of the AN.DAḪ.ŠUM festival	KUB 10.82+	sjh.	
CTH 626 Festival of haste (EZEN$_4$ *nuntarriyašḫaš*)	Bo 5549	sjh.	Palluwaraziti & Piḫawalwi
CTH 626 Festival of haste (EZEN$_4$ *nuntarriyašḫaš*)	KBo 30.77	sjh.	
CTH 626 Festival of haste (EZEN$_4$ *nuntarriyašḫaš*)	KBo 66.287+	jh.	
CTH 626 Festival of haste (EZEN$_4$ *nuntarriyašḫaš*)	KUB 20.70	sjh.	
CTH 628 *(ḫ)išuwa-* festival	KBo 15.64+	jh.	
CTH 628 *(ḫ)išuwa-* festival	KUB 51.4	jh.	
CTH 635 Fragments of the festival of Zippalanda and Mt. Daḫa	KUB 20.92	sjh.	
CTH 647 Festivals celebrated by the Prince	KBo 45.69	sjh.	Piḫami (pupil of Ḫalwaziti)
CTH 647 Festivals celebrated by the Prince	KUB 20.7	sjh.	
CTH 647 Festivals celebrated by the Prince	KUB 55.41	sjh.	Kuniya?
CTH 652 Festival fragments referring to the "Man of the Storm-god"	KBo 63.79	sjh.	
CTH 662 Offerings for local cults	KBo 55.263+	jh.	
CTH 665 Festival fragments referring to the *ašuša(tal)la-* men	KBo 45.199+	sjh.	
CTH 667 Texts from the cult of Zalpuwa	CHDS 5.183	sjh.	
CTH 669 Larger festival fragments	KBo 24.93+	sjh.	
CTH 670 Festival fragments	Bo 4343	jh.	
CTH 670 Festival fragments	Bo 5065	sjh.	
CTH 670 Festival fragments	Bo 5444	sjh.	
CTH 670 Festival fragments	Bo 5854	jh.	
CTH 670 Festival fragments	Bo 8015	sjh.	
CTH 670 Festival fragments	Bo 9377	sjh.	
CTH 670 Festival fragments	CHDS 3.10	jh.	
CTH 670 Festival fragments	CHDS 4.48	jh.	
CTH 670 Festival fragments	CHDS 4.73	jh.	
CTH 670 Festival fragments	IBoT 4.137	jh.	
CTH 670 Festival fragments	IBoT 4.317	jh.	

Content	Ms.	(s)jh.	Scribe
CTH 670 Festival fragments	KBo 11.26	sjh.	
CTH 670 Festival fragments	KBo 46.200	jh.	
CTH 670 Festival fragments	KBo 49.45	jh.	
CTH 670 Festival fragments	KBo 51.133	jh.	
CTH 670 Festival fragments	KBo 51.167	sjh.	
CTH 670 Festival fragments	KBo 52.144	jh.	
CTH 670 Festival fragments	KBo 53.168	jh.	
CTH 670 Festival fragments	KBo 54.183	jh.	
CTH 670 Festival fragments	KBo 56.158	jh.	
CTH 670 Festival fragments	KBo 57.165	jh.	
CTH 670 Festival fragments	KBo 57.167	jh.	
CTH 670 Festival fragments	KBo 59.159	jh.	
CTH 670 Festival fragments	KBo 60.191	jh.	
CTH 670 Festival fragments	KBo 63.109	jh.	
CTH 670 Festival fragments	KBo 64.334	jh.	
CTH 670 Festival fragments	KUB 20.5	jh.	
CTH 670 Festival fragments	KUB 44.19	jh.	
CTH 672 Monthly festival at Nerik	KBo 2.4	jh.	
CTH 672 Monthly festival at Nerik	KBo 23.95	jh.	
CTH 672 Monthly festival at Nerik	KUB 56.48	jh.	
CTH 672 Monthly festival at Nerik	KUB 56.49	sjh.	
CTH 678 Festival fragments on the cult of Nerik	KBo 11.60	jh.	
CTH 678 Festival fragments on the cult of Nerik	KBo 64.163+	sjh.	
CTH 678 Festival fragments on the cult of Nerik	KUB 42.85	jh.	
CTH 678 Festival fragments on the cult of Nerik	KUB 56.54	jh.	
CTH 678 Festival fragments on the cult of Nerik	KUB 58.31+	sjh.	
CTH 679 unassigned	KUB 53.16	jh.	
CTH 681 Festival of Karaḫna	KBo 39.154+	sjh.	
CTH 682 Festival for the protective deities	Bo 3306+	sjh.	
CTH 682 Festival for the protective deities	KUB 11.21	jh.	
CTH 682 Festival for the protective deities	KUB 44.16+	jh.	
CTH 682 Festival for the protective deities	KUB 54.71	jh.	
CTH 682 Festival for the protective deities	KUB 55.12	jh.	
CTH 683 Renewal of the hunting bag for the protective deities	KBo 24.95	jh.	
CTH 683 Renewal of the hunting bag for the protective deities	KBo 43.85+	jh.	
CTH 684 Festival for the protective deities of the river	KBo 45.25+	sjh.	
CTH 685 Fragments of festivals for the protective deities	KUB 9.17	jh.	
CTH 701 Drink offering for the throne of Ḫebat	KUB 32.42+	jh.	

Content	Ms.	(s)jh.	Scribe
CTH 714 Festival for Ištar of Nineveh	KBo 52.208	jh.	
CTH 738 Festival for the goddess Tetešḫapi	KBo 37.51+	sjh.	
CTH 738 Festival for the goddess Tetešḫapi	KBo 45.129	jh.	
CTH 744 Festival fragments with Hattian recitations	KBo 71.89	jh.	
CTH 750 Festival for Ziparwa	KBo 43.218	sjh.	
CTH 750 Festival for Ziparwa	KUB 41.26+	sjh.	Palluwaraziti & Piḫawalwi

Table 8. Festival texts classified in the *Konkordanz* as 'jh.' or 'sjh.' attesting the spelling GIŠZAG.GAR.RA, sorted by *CTH* number. Background shading aims to highlight specific groups of texts as discussed in the paper.

4. Summary and outlook

This study investigated the authorship of the Hittite cult inventories by combining a systematic evaluation of selected paleographic and orthographic features with a comparison with festival texts, in particular the two groups of festival tablets from the time of Tudḫaliya IV recently studied by Charles Steitler, produced by the school traceable to Anuwanza and the school of Palluwaraziti and Piḫawalwi respectively.

The comparison between these groups of tablets is particularly useful in shedding light on certain dynamics of Hittite writing practice in the Late Empire, because these festival texts highlight two contemporary but distinct graphic habits, which must also have been contemporary with at least part of the cult inventories.

The study began by considering the materiality of the wedges, noting that a specific slant of the verticals and horizontals, typical of the school of Palluwaraziti-Piḫawalwi and many cult inventories but absent in the school of Anuwanza, is plausibly an indicator connected with a greater writing speed.

At the level of the sign forms used, a non-trivial analogy between the use of IIIc forms in the cult inventories and in the tablets of the school of Palluwaraziti and Piḫawalwi was identified, unlike in the school of Anuwanza. The sign QA emerged as a key element for the characterization of the IIIc graphic *facies*.

In the group of cult inventories securely datable to Tudḫaliya IV, the distribution of the sign forms of QA and ḪA is the same as that observed in the tablets of the Palluwaraziti and Piḫawalwi school. In the corpus of the cult inventories as a whole, however, the frequency is significantly lower, suggesting that a portion of the inventories are older, plausibly dating back to Ḫattušili III.

Finally, orthographic analysis was conducted through the case study represented by the phonographic vs logographic spellings for the expression 'he offers' and the term 'altar' in the cult inventories vs the jh./sjh. festival texts.

The use of the logographic spelling is overwhelmingly prevalent in the cult inventories; the festival texts prefer instead the phonographic form, but a sizable minority uses the logographic form. By looking at which texts constitute this minority, it emerges that they are especially concentrated in a few *CTH* numbers, particularly those that have a special affinity with the cult inventories. In the cases in which the scribe is known, this is related to the circle of Palluwaraziti and Piḫawalwi.

With all due caution, these findings converge on the working hypothesis that the extant cult inventories were written (1) probably from the time of Ḫattušili III onwards, and (2) as far as the age of Tudḫaliya IV is concerned, by a group (or groups) of scribes who used the same graphic habits observed in the circle of Palluwaraziti and Piḫawalwi, and possibly by these very scribes. Confirmation or refutation of these hypotheses requires further study and extension of the paleographic and orthographic analyses now presented, and remains work for the future.

Bibliography

Cammarosano, Michele

2012 Hittite Cult Inventories. Part Two: The Dating of the Texts and the Alleged 'Cult Reorganization' of Tudḫaliya IV. *AoF* 39: 3–37.

2014 The Cuneiform Stylus. *Mesopotamia* XLIX: 53–90.

2015 3D-Joins und Schriftmetrologie. A Quantitative Approach to Cuneiform Palaeography. In: Elena Devecchi, Gerfrid G.W. Müller, and Jana Mynářová (eds.), *Current Research in Cuneiform Palaeography. Proceedings of the Workshop held at the 60th Rencontre Assyriologique Internationale, Warsaw 2014.* Gladbeck: PeWe, 145–86.

2019 Kultinventare aus Kayalıpınar (Šamuḫa). In: Elisabeth Rieken (ed.), *Keilschrifttafeln aus Kayalıpınar 1 (1999–2017).* DAAM 1. Wiesbaden: Harrassowitz, 47–110.

2021 *At the Interface of Religion and Administration: The Hittite Cult Inventories. With a contribution by Adam Kryszeń.* StBoT 68. Wiesbaden: Harrassowitz.

2022 A Quantitative Analysis of Theonyms and Panthea in the Hittite Cult Inventories. In: Livio Warbinek and Federico Giusfredi (eds.), *Theonyms, Panthea and Syncretisms in Hittite Anatolia and Northern Syria. Proceedings of the TeAI Workshop Held in Verona, March 25–26, 2022.* Firenze: Firenze University Press, 69–88.

Cammarosano, Michele, Gerfrid G.W. Müller, Denis Fisseler, and Frank Weichert

2014 Schriftmetrologie des Keils. Dreidimensionale Analyse von Keileindrücken und Handschriften. *WdO* 44: 2–36.

Casamassima, Emanuele

1988 *Tradizione corsiva e tradizione libraria nella scrittura latina del Medioevo.* Roma: Gela.

Giorgieri, Mauro and Clelia Mora

2004 *Le lettere tra i re ittiti e i re assiri ritrovate a Ḫattuša.* HANEM 7. Padova: Sargon.

Goedegebuure, Petra

2014 *The Hittite Demonstratives: Studies in Deixis, Topics and Focus.* StBoT 55. Wiesbaden: Harrassowitz.

Gordin, Shai

2015 *Hittite Scribal Circles. Scholarly Tradition and Writing Habits.* StBoT 59. Wiesbaden: Harrassowitz.

Klinger, Jörg

1996 *Untersuchungen zur Rekonstruktion der hattischen Kultschicht.* StBoT 37. Wiesbaden: Harrassowitz.

2022 Zu den Anfängen der hethitischen Überlieferung überhaupt und zur Methode der paläographischen Textdatierung. In: Eva Cancik-Kirschbaum and Ingo Schrakamp (eds.), *Transfer, Adaption und Neukonfigurierung von Schrift- und Sprachwissen im Alten Orient.* Episteme in Bewegung 25. Wiesbaden: Harrassowitz, 255–340.

Košak, Silvin

2002– *Konkordanz der hethitischen Keilschrifttafeln, Online-Datenbank Version.* https://www.hethport.uni-wuerzburg.de/hetkonk (2.plus) – last accessed 10.08.2024.

Kühne, Cord

1988 Über die Darstellung der hethitischen Reflexivpartikel *-z*, besonders in postvokalischer Position. In: Erich Neu und Christel Rüster (eds.), *Documentum Asiae minoris antiquae. Festschrift für Heinrich Otten zum 75. Geburtstag.* Wiesbaden: Harrassowitz, 203–33.

Schwemer, Daniel

2016 Quality Assurance Managers at Work: The Hittite Festival Tradition. In: Gerfrid G.W. Müller (ed.), *Liturgie oder Literatur? Die Kultrituale der Hethiter im transkulturellen Vergleich: Akten eines Werkstattgesprächs an der Akademie der Wissenschaften und der Literatur Mainz, 2.–3. Dezember 2010.* StBoT 60. Wiesbaden: Harrassowitz, 1–29.

Steitler, Charles

2019 Festival Tablets from the Final Decades of the Hittite Empire: Scribes and Writing Conventions. In: Stefano de Martino and Elena Devecchi (eds.), *Anatolia Between the 13th and the 12th Century BCE.* Eothen 23. Firenze: Logisma, 411–55.

van den Hout, Theo P.J.

1989 *KBo IV 10+ (CTH 106). Studien zum Spätjunghethitischen, Texte der Zeit Tudhalijas IV.* PhD dissertation, University of Amsterdam.

2015 In Royal Circles: The Nature of Hittite Scholarship. *JANER* 2: 203–27.

2020 *A History of Hittite Literacy: Writing and Reading in Late Bronze-Age Anatolia (1650–1200 BC).* Cambridge: Cambridge University Press.

Weeden, Mark
2011 *Hittite Logograms and Hittite Scholarship*. StBoT 54. Wiesbaden: Harrassowitz.
2020 Palaeography, Handwriting and Spelling of VAT 6692. In: Susanne Heinhold-Kramer and Elisabeth Rieken (eds.), *Der 'Tawagalawa-Brief'. Beschwerden über Piyamaradu. Eine Neuedition*. UAVA 13. Berlin / Boston: de Gruyter, 317–37.

THE RECORDING OF THE *ḪIŠUWA*- FESTIVAL

*Meltem Doğan-Alparslan**
Istanbul University

Abstract

The paper discusses some of the fragments of the *ḫišuwa*- festival (*CTH* 628), with a focus on their scribes, scribal habits and practices. The *ḫišuwa*- festival corpus, which contains approximately 500 fragments, including those identified by the latest research and excavations, is known best through its Empire Period manuscripts. The fact that most of the copies of the festival date back to this period is undoubtedly connected to queen Puduḫeba who emphasized the importance of this cathartic festival and promoted it by assigning scribes to copy the texts describing it. This paper offers a new approach to the interpretation of this festival based on the Middle Hittite Period copies of the *ḫišuwa*- festival.

1. Introduction

The *ḫišuwa*- festival, whose existence was first discovered during the excavations in Boğazköy in 1951, occupies a special place among Hittite festivals due to its cathartic nature. The *ḫišuwa*- festival currently comprises 492 fragments and the size of this corpus has increased thanks to newly published texts. In 2022, Torri (2022: 192f.) listed the number of fragments as 266.

Fragments of the *ḫišuwa*- festival that were found in the excavations of Ḫattuša are kept in the museums in Ankara, Istanbul and Çorum. New fragments belonging to the festival have been found in excavations carried out in Ḫattuša in recent years. Several additional texts have been identified in the archives of Ortaköy/Šapinuwa and Kayalıpınar/Šamuḫa (Rieken 2009: 210f.; Groddek 2011: 112). Among the Bo fragments published in recent years, many have been identified as fragments of the *ḫišuwa* festival (see Table 2 and 3).

2. The classification of the *ḫišuwa*- festival fragments

Most of the fragments came to light in the excavations on Büyükkale (Table 1). According to Gordin (2015: 176f.), Building A of the Palace may have been the scriptorium in which a group of scribes worked during the Hittite Empire under the direction of the

* This article is a result of the project "(H)išuwa Bayramı; Bir Hurri-Hitit Bayramı'nın Metin Rekonstrüksiyonu: Çivi Yazılı Metnin Transkripsiyonu, Hititçeden Çevirisi ve Filolojik/Kültürel Yorumu" supported by The Scientific and Technological Research Council of Turkey (TÜBİTAK; Project number 108K332).

Location	Dating	Number of texts
Büyükkale Building A	jh./sjh./mh.	190
Büyükkale other than Building A	jh.	86
Temple 1	jh.	24
Haus am Hang	jh.	5
unknown	jh./sjh./mh.	176
other	jh.	14

Table 1. Distribution of *CTH* 628 fragments according to their find spots in Ḫattuša (Košak 2002–).

chief scribe Walwaziti in drafting the festival texts. Thus, the majority of the fragments are written in New Script (NS). The tablets' colophons show that the *ḫišuwa-* festival was carried out in Ḫattuša by order of the queen Puduḫeba, who assigned to Walwaziti and his team the task of collecting, organizing and drafting the festival text from Kizzuwatnean tablets. The *ḫišuwa-* festival stood out as a group of texts originating from Kizzuwatna, the region from which Puduḫeba herself hailed.

KBo 15.60 rev.[1]

3′ [MUN]US.LUGAL ^{f}*pu-d*[*u-ḫé-pa-aš-kán ku-wa-pí*]
4′ [^{m}]UR.MAḪ-LÚ-*in* [GAL DUB.SAR^{MEŠ}]
5′ [^{UR}]^{U}*ḫa-at-tu-š*[*i* *A-NA TUP-PA*$^{ḪI.A}$]
6′ [^{UR}]^{U}*ki-iz-zu-wa-*[*at-na*]
7′ [*š*]*a-an-ḫu-u-wa-an-*⸢*zi*⸣ [*ú-e-ri-ia-at*]
8′ [*n*]*a-aš-ta ke-e* *TUP*-[*PA*$^{ḪI.A}$]
9′ [*ŠA*] EZEN₄ *i-*⸢*šu*⸣-[*wa-a-aš* UD-*at*]
10′ [*ar-ḫa a-n*]*i*$^{?}$*-i*[*a*$^{?}$*-at*]

[When qu]een Pud[uḫeba commanded] Walwaziti, [chief of the scribes,] in Ḫattuša to look [for tablets] of Kizzuwa[tna, on that day he co]pi[ed$^{?}$ out] these tab[lets of] the (*ḫ*)*išu*[*wa-*] festival.

However, the *ḫišuwa-* festival was not only preserved in New Script copies. In recent years, several examples of the *ḫišuwa-* festival in Middle Script were published in CHDS volumes 4–6 (Table 2) and in other publications of Bo fragments (Table 3). The discovery of fragments of the *ḫišuwa-* festival in recent excavations in Ḫattuša (published by Daniel Schwemer, Table 4) raises hope that the corpus will continue to grow.

Inventory No.	*CTH* No.	Dating and Script
Bo 6099	*CTH* 628	NS
Bo 6107 + KUB 40.103	*CTH* 628	NS
Bo 6111	*CTH* 628	NS
Bo 6141	*CTH* 628.Tf08.D	NS
Bo 6145	*CTH* 628.Tf13.O	NS

1 Thesaurus Linguarum Hethaeorum digitalis, hethiter.net/: TLHdig KBo 15.60 (2021-12-31); Gordin 2015: 41.

Bo 6258	*CTH* 628	NS
Bo 6299	*CTH* 628	NS
Bo 6360	*CTH* 628.II	NS
Bo 6377	*CTH* 628.Tf10.N	NS
Bo 6401	*CTH* 628	(E)NS$^{?}$
Bo 4907 + KUB 40.102	*CTH* 628	NS
Bo 5351	*CTH* 628.Tf02.F	NS
Bo 5434	*CTH* 628$^{?}$ (CTH 670)	MS
Bo 5453	*CTH* 628	NS
Bo 5490 + Bo 7029	*CTH* 628	LMS
Bo 5519	*CTH* 628	MH/NS
Bo 5523 + Bo 7287	*CTH* 628	NS
Bo 5540	*CTH* 628	NS
Bo 5593	*CTH* 628	MH/NS
Bo 5601 + KUB 47.72	*CTH* 628	(L)MS
Bo 5624	*CTH* 628	NS
Bo 4485	*CTH* 628	NS
Bo 5248	*CTH* 628	MS

Table 2. Newly published Bo fragments of the *ḫišuwa-* festival in CHDS 4, 5 and 6, among them four in MS.

Inventory No.	*CTH* No.	Dating and Script
Bo 7890	*CTH* 628.Tf08.Y	NS
Bo 7090	*CTH* 628	NS
Bo 7857	*CTH* 628	NS
Bo 7850	*CTH* 628	NS

Table 3. Newly published Bo fragments of the *ḫišuwa-* festival in Sir Gavaz and Keçeci 2024 and Sir Gavaz and Masalcı Şahin 2021.

Text	*CTH* No.	Dating and Script
KBo 71.88	*CTH* 628	NS
KBo 71.151	*CTH* 628	NS
Bo 2024/9	*CTH* 628	NS

Table 4. Fragments of the *ḫišuwa-* festival recently discovered in Ḫattuša, already or soon to be published in KBo 71.

As mentioned above, fragments related to the *ḫišuwa-* festival have also been found in centers other than the Hittite capital of Ḫattuša. The five fragments found in Šamuḫa have been dated paleographically to the Middle Hittite period:[2]

2 See DAAM 1, XV–XVI, Tafel II, Tafel V, Tafel VII; Košak 2002–.

Text	*CTH* No.	Dating and Script
DAAM 1.5	CTH 628.Var77	MS
DAAM 1.16	CTH 628.Tf08.V	MS
DAAM 1.17	CTH 628.Tf07	MS
DAAM 1.20	CTH 628	MS?
DAAM 1.80	CTH 628	MS?

Table 5. Fragments of the *ḫišuwa-* festival found in Šamuḫa.

3. The dating of the *ḫišuwa-* festival

The following section discusses the fragments of the *ḫišuwa-* festival from a paleographic perspective, focusing on the Middle Script copies of the festival and their characteristics. In order to understand the development of the *ḫišuwa-* festival and to answer questions about the period in which the festival was practiced or celebrated as a purification ritual,[3] it is necessary to review its colophons and scribes.

According to Wegner and Salvini (1991: 3–6), the *ḫišuwa-* festival consisted of a "standard series version", written in six columns; moreover, a two-column and a single-column version seemingly existed as well. When we look at the colophons of the festival, those of the 6th and 8th tablets especially stand out, since they are more extensive than the standard colophons.[4] These mentioned that chief scribe Walwaziti was appointed by Puduḫeba to collect the Kizzuwatna tablets. Also, like other colophons, these contain the scribe's signature and even includes his genealogy. More tablets of this festival have been written by the scribes Ḫulanabi and Talmi-Teššup, the sons of Walwaziti (Wegner and Salvini 1991: 3f.; de Martino 2017: 157). Hints within the festival, such as in KUB 40.102, point to connections of the festival and its scribes with Kizzuwatna.[5] Additionally, the mountain and river names listed in the text are mostly associated with Kizzuwatna.

The importance of the *ḫišuwa-* festival can be demonstrated already prior to the reign of Ḫattušili III. The new materials added to the festival celebrations during the reign of Muwatalli II are the best indication of this. An example is the mention of his

3 See Doğan-Alparslan 2020a: 124; 2020b: 372.

4 KBo 15.37 rev. VI 3–15″: (3) [DUB n+]2^{KAM} (4) [*ŠA* EZE]N$_4$ [*ḫ*]*i-šu-wa-a-aš QA-TI* (ca. 5 unbeschriebene Zeilen) (5′) [MUNUS.LUGAL ^{f}*pu-du-ḫé-pa-aš-kán*] (6′) [*ku-wa-pí* ^{m}UR.MAḪ-LÚ-*in* GAL DUB.SAR$^{\text{M]EŠ}}$ (7′) [^{URU}*ḫa-at-tu-ši A-NA TUP-PA*$^{\text{ḪI.A}}$] (8′) [^{URU}*ki-iz-zu-wa-at-na ša-an-ḫu-wa-an-zi ú-e-ri-ia-a*]*t* (9′) [*na-aš-ta ke-e TUP-PA*$^{\text{ḪI.A}}$ *ŠA* EZEN$_4$ *i-šu-wa-a-aš*] (10′) [UD-*at a-ni-ia-at*] (Text bricht ab; Platz für ca. 12 unbeschriebene Zeilen) (10″) [ŠU$^{?}$ ^{m}*ta*]*l*$^{?}$-*m*[*e*$^{?}$]-⸢^{D}⸣IŠKUR-*up* (11″) [DUMU] ⸢^{m}⸣UR.MAḪ-LÚ GAL DUB.SAR^{MEŠ} (12″) [DUMU.DU]MU-⸢*ŠU*⸣ *ŠA* ^{m}*mi-it-ta-an-na-mu-u-wa* (13″) [G]ÁB.ZU.ZU *ŠA* ^{m}MAḪ-DINGIR^{MEŠ}-*na* (14″) *PA-NI* ^{m}UR.MAḪ-LÚ GAL DUB.SAR^{MEŠ} (15″) *IŠ-ṬUR*; Thesaurus Linguarum Hethaeorum digitalis, hethiter.net/: TLHdig KBo 15.37 (2021-12-31).

5 KUB 40.102 rev. VI 1′–5′: (1′) [ ] ⸢*nu*⸣ ^{D}⸢IŠKUR EN-*IA*⸣ (2′) [^{D}*le-el-lu-ri-iš-ša w*]*a-ar-ši-an-te-eš* (3′) [*a-ša-an-du* LUGA]L-*un-na* MUNUS.LUGAL-*an* DUMU^{MEŠ}.LUGAL (4′) [KUR ^{URU}*ḪA-AT-T*]*I* *x* KUR ^{URU}*ki-iz-zu-wa-at-na-ia* (5′) [ŠÀ-*aš-ša*] *ar-nu-uš-ki*; Thesaurus Linguarum Hethaeorum digitalis, hethiter.net/: TLHdig KUB 40.102 (2021-12-31).

name on the 8th tablet in relation to a formerly unknown rite (Dinçol 1989: 6; Haas 1994: 848):[6]

KUB 40.102 rev. V

4′ EGIR-*an-*⌜*da* 1?⌝ *za-am-*⌜*mu*⌝*-ri-in* *ŠA* 1 *SA*20*-A-TI ti-*[*a*]*n-zi*
5′ *ka-a-aš za-am-mu-ri-iš an-na-al-la-aš* *A-NA TUP-PA*ḪI.⌜A⌝
6′ *Ú-UL e-eš-ta na-an-kán* mNIR.GÁL LUGAL GAL
7′ EGIR-*an-da ne-ia-a*[*t*]

Afterwards they place one? *zammuri*-bread of one seah. This *zammuri*-bread was not mentioned in the old tablets; Muwattalli, the Great King, added it.

As mentioned, it is clear that the *ḫišuwa-* festival texts were written by a certain family of scribes. Most members of this family were close to the kings of the period and held critical and important political positions.[7] This family almost formed a school, and perhaps the most important tablets of this school that have survived to the present day belong to the *ḫišuwa-* festival. According to Gordin (2015: 84), the festival was recorded by an expert team of scribes. The distinct style of the three scribes (DUB.SAR) of the Walwaziti school can be identified in the text fragments: Ḫulanabi, Talmi-Tešub and Kuruntaili used distinct forms of the NI, IR and KÁN signs.

Text	Composition	Findspot	Scribe
Bo 10293	3rd tablet	–	Ḫulanabi (?)
KBo 39.43	2 columned tablet, tablet unknown	Bk. A	[Kuwalanaziti]
KBo 46.145	standard version, tablet unknown	Bk. F	Ana[...]
KBo 33.177	standard version, tablet unknown	Bk. A	–
KBo 33.178	standard version, tablet unknown	Bk. D	–
KBo 33.179	standard version, tablet unknown	Bk. A	–
KBo 33.180	standard version, tablet unknown	Bk. A	–
KBo 40.65	standard version, tablet unknown	–	–
KBo 41.66	standard version, tablet unknown	–	–
Bo 5921	standard version, tablet unknown	–	–
KBo 33.182 + KBo 35.262 + KUB 32.100	standard version, tablet unknown	Bk. A	–
KBo 15.52 + KUB 34.116 + KBo 41.67 + VBoT 116	standard version, 10th tablet	Bk. A	Kuruntaili
KBo 35.260 + SZM 51.2401	2 columned tablet, 12th tablet	Bk. M	Talm[i-Šar]ruma

6 Thesaurus Linguarum Hethaeorum digitalis, hethiter.net/: TLHdig KUB 40.102 (2021-12-31).
7 For detailed information on DUB.SAR Mitannamuwa and his family members, see Doğan-Alparslan 2007.

KUB 32.128 + KUB 32.99	standard version, 5th tablet	Bk. A	Ḫulanabi
KBo 15.60	standard version, 5th tablet	Bk. H	–
KBo 33.175 + ABoT 1.2	standard version, 5th tablet	Bk. A	[Talmi-Teššub]
KBo 7.45 + KBo 35.253 + KBo 38.19 + KBo 20.114 + KBo 34.178 + KBo 20.118	standard version, 5th tablet	Bk. A	–
KUB 20.74	standard version, 6th tablet	–	–
KUB 40.102	standard version, 8th tablet	–	–
KBo 15.37	standard version, 13th tablet	Bk. A	[Talmi]-Teššub
KBo 23.28 + KUB 32.65 + KUB 32.61 + KBo 33.191	standard version, 2nd tablet	Bk. A	[Talmi-Teššub]
KUB 12.12	standard version, 3rd tablet	–	Ḫulanabi
KBo 33.173 + KBo 33.194 + KBo 14.131 + KBo 30.159	standard version, 3rd tablet	Bk. A, C	Ḫu[lanabi]
KBo 15.58	standard version, 8th tablet	Bk. H	–

Table 6. Colophons and names of scribes of the *ḫišuwa-* festival (according to Gordin 2015: 63–66).

Important observations have been made about the sections written in Hurrian. As stated by Wegner and Salvini (1991: 1), Hurrian recitations are only found in the first four tablets of the festival, a distinguishing feature helping in tablet reconstruction. While the scribes included Hurrian recitations at length in the first parts of the festival, they preferred to include Hittite recitations and Hurrian words in some places, starting from the 5th tablet.

As mentioned before, a few Middle Script fragments of the festival have been found in the archives of Ḫattuša: KBo 46.143, KBo 33.131, KUB 54.48, IBoT 2.45, KUB 55.29, KUB 47.72, KUB 45.56 (all MS according to the *Konkordanz*). For several fragments, a dating as MS or NS is uncertain, as shown in Table 7.

Text	Dating	Characteristic Signs		
KBo 24.64+ KBo 43.200	MS?	ḪAR 	TA? 	
KBo 23.11	MS?	DA? 	TA 	AḪ 
KBo 8.84	MS?	DA 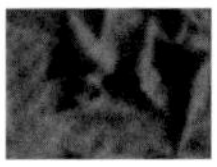	ŠA 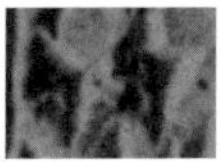	

KBo 53.125	MS?	DA 	TA 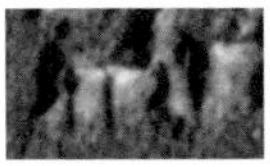	AḪ? 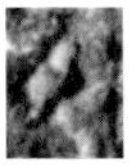
KUB 47.74	MS?	ḪAR 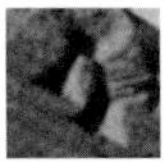	TA 	
IBoT 3.55	MS?	DA 	ŠA 	AḪ 
KUB 25.43	MS?	DA 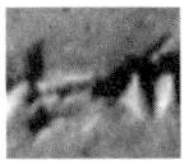	E 	AḪ? 
VSNF 12.22	MS?	ḪAR 	E 	TA 
KUB 45.52	MS?	DA 	ŠA 	

Table 7. Characteristic signs of the possibly Middle Script *ḫišuwa-* fragments.

When we re-examine the fragments whose dating as Middle Script is uncertain, it can be suggested that a few fragments, such as KBo 24.64 + KBo 43.200, KBo 23.11, KBo 53.125, KUB 47.74, IBoT 3.55, KUB 25.43 and VSNF 12.22 may be Middle Script copies (Table 7) because of the shape of the signs AḪ, E, DA, ḪAR, ŠA and TA.

Considering the connection of the *ḫišuwa-* festival with the 13th century BCE royal family and its scribes, its association with the Empire Period is undeniably clear. However, the point we wish to emphasize in this paper is the relationship between the *ḫišuwa-* festival and the Middle Hittite period. Identified or still-debated Middle Script copies assist us in this regard. The Middle Script fragments provide only a few examples of the festival. These few fragments do not show significant differences in content compared to the Empire Period ones.

There are only a few fragments related to the *ḫišuwa-* festival within the Šapinuwa tablet corpus. Numerous festivals related to Hurrian culture were recorded by the scribes of Šapinuwa (de Martino and Süel 2017: 11f.). Among these, a colophon fragment belonging to the 6th tablet of the *ḫišuwa-* festival, found during the 2007 excavations, stands out (Fig. 1).[8]

8 I would like to thank Prof. Dr. Aygül Süel for providing the opportunity to analyze and publish the Šapinuwa fragments of the *ḫišuwa-* festival.

Or. 07/124 rev. IV?[9]

1′ [ ]x[

2′ [*lu-u*]*k-kat-ta-ma* x[
3′ [ ]-*uš-ša* UDU$^{\text{ḪI.A}}$ G[U$_4$$^{\text{HI.A}}$
4′ [ ]x-*aš* $^{\text{LÚ.MEŠ}}$*tap-ri-e-eš š*[*i*?-
5′ [*ta*]-*ma-iš-ma* *Ú-UL* *ku-i*[*š*?-*ki*?

6′ DUB 6^{KAM} *QA-T*[*I*
7′ EZEN$_4$ *i-šu-*[*wa-a-aš*
8′ ⸢KA×U⸣-[*a*]*z* x[
9′ x x[

[...] but the [ne]xt day [...]... sheeps [and] catt[les ...]... *tapri-* men [...] but another [...] nobo[dy? ...]

Sixth tablet; finish[ed.] (Of) the (*ḫ*)*išu*[*wa-*] festival [...] from the mouth ...[...]

It is known that the sixth tablet of the *ḫišuwa-* festival is documented in KUB 20.74 (NS, from Ḫattuša). However, the Šapinuwa fragment is very different from the Ḫattuša version.[10]

Despite its fragmentary state, the Šapinuwa fragment provides some information. The mention of the *tapri-* men in the fragment is noteworthy since there are only three other references within the *ḫišuwa-* festival texts (HT 24, KUB 55.49, Bo 7858). However, in all these examples, ^{LÚ}*tapri-* occurs in the singular, not in the plural as in the Šapinuwa example. Therefore, no parallel can be established with the Šapinuwa fragment. On the other hand, a ^{MUNUS}*tapri-* is frequently documented within the *ḫišuwa-* texts.

In comparison to other texts, a similar order of expressions within the colophon is observable in one colophon of the *itkalzi* ritual found in Šapinuwa (Or. 90/1473; de Martino and Süel 2017: 13). This parallel suggests that the Šapinuwa scribal school wrote the tablet colophons according to a specific template.

It has often been stated by Prof. Süel that most or all of the tablets found in Šapinuwa were written in Middle Hittite ductus (Süel 1998: 556f.). It is clearly seen that the three signs E, TA, KAD/T in the fragment Or. 07/124, which contains a colophon related to the *ḫišuwa-* festival, also reflect Middle Script characteristics (Fig.2).

9 The text KUB 20.74 contains the 6th tablet of the *ḫišuwa-* festival and consists of six columns. Considering the example of Ḫattuša, we can also suggest that the 6th tablet from Šapinuwa was written in six columns.

10 KUB 20.74 Rev. VI 8′–16′: (8′) [DUB 6^{KAM} *ŠA* EZEN$_4$ *ḫi-š*]*u-wa-a-aš* (9′) [*nu-uš-ša-an i*]*r-ḫa-at-ta-an-za* (10′) [*zi-in-na-an-za* E]ZEN$_4$-*ma-aš-ša-an* (11′) [*Ú-UL*] *QA-TI* (12′) [MUNUS.LUGAL ^{f}*pu-d*]*u-ḫé-pa-aš-kán ku-wa-pí* (13′) [^{m}UR.MAḪ-LÚ-*i*]*n* GAL DUB.SAR^{MEŠ} (14′) [^{URU}*ḫa-at-tu-š*]*i A-NA TUP-PA*$^{\text{ḪI.A}}$ (15′) [^{URU}*ki-iz-zu-w*]*a-at-na* (16′) [*ša-an-ḫu-wa-an-z*]*i* ⸢*ú-e-ri-at*⸣ “[Sixth tablet of the (*ḫ*)*iš*]*uwa-* festival, finished, but the festival [is not] finished. When [the queen Pud]uḫeba charged [Walwaziti], chief of the scribes, t[o look] in [Ḫattuš]a for tablets of [Kizzuw]atna.”

Fig. 1. An example of a *ḫišuwa-* festival fragment from the Šapinuwa archive (photograph: Ortaköy Excavation Archive).

KAD/T		TA	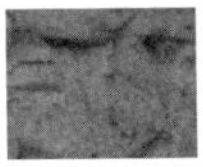	E	

Fig. 2. The signs KAD/T, TA, and E in Or. 07/124.

4. Conclusions

As can be seen, the oldest copies of the *ḫišuwa-* festival date back to the Middle Hittite Period. The festival was developed with various completions during the Empire Period and became one of the most comprehensive Hittite religious events. The paleographic features of the festival indicate a tradition of approximately 200–250 years.[11]

We can state that the *ḫišuwa-* festival has been celebrated since the Middle Hittite Period in three different centers. In all of them, Ḫattuša, Šapinuwa, and Šamuḫa (see Table 5), Middle Script fragments came to light. The colophon fragment found in Šapinuwa clearly demonstrates that the *ḫišuwa-* festival was celebrated during the Middle Hittite Period, raising numerous questions: Was the *ḫišuwa-* festival, which comes from the Kizzuwatnean tradition, copied by scribes in Šamuḫa or Šapinuwa earlier than in Ḫattuša? Did the festival celebration come to the capital after it was known in these cities, and was it during the reign of King Muwatalli II and the subsequent period that it developed into a traditional festival in the capital? Is this the reason why the festival was reassembled at the order of queen Puduḫeba? How can one explain the MS tablets from Ḫattuša?

There is undoubtedly Hurrian influence upon the tradition of the *ḫišuwa-* festival. Hurrian influence, which became widespread during the Middle Hittite Period, likely played a role in the practice of the festival. The widespread celebration of the festival can be understood through the fragments coming from three important centers.

The *ḫišuwa-* festival includes purification rituals aimed at the cathartic cleansing of the Hittite kings and the royal family. Therefore, it is directly related to the king. It is known that Šamuḫa and Šapinuwa were cities inhabited by the Hittite kings.[12] Thus, during the periods when the kings occasionally resided for some time in these important cities, the celebrations of the *ḫišuwa-* festival had to take place wherever the king was located. For this reason, it is not surprising that copies related to the festival have been found in the archives of Šapinuwa and Šamuḫa.

Bibliography

de Martino, Stefano

2017 The Hurrian Language in Anatolia in the Late Bronze Age. In: Alice Mouton (ed.), *Hittitology Today: Studies on Hittite and Neo-Hittite Anatolia in Honor of Emmanuel Laroche's 100th Birthday / L'Hittitologie Aujourd'hui: Études sur l'Anatolie Hittite et Néo-hittite à l'occasion du cente-*

11 However, Wegner and Salvini believed that this festival was created by combining the older Kizzuwatna festivals that served as building blocks for a new festival celebrated in the Empire Period (Wegner and Salvini 1991: 3).

12 For detailed information on the subject see: Doğan-Alparslan 2012: 118–22; Doğan-Alparslan and Alparslan 2011.

naire de la naissance d'Emmanuel Laroche – 5èmes Rencontres d'Archéologie de l'IFÉA 2014. İstanbul: Zero, 151–62.

de Martino, Stefano and Aygül Süel

2017 *The "Great itkalzi Ritual".* Eothen 22. Firenze: LoGisma.

Dinçol, Ali M.

1989 Ein hurro-hethitisches Festritual: (H)išuwaš, *Belleten* 53/206: 1–50.

Doğan-Alparslan, Meltem

2007 Drei Schreiber, zwei Könige. In: Alfonso Archi and Rita Francia (eds.), *VI Congresso Internazionale di Ittitologia, Roma,* 5–9 Settembre 2005. *Parte I. SMEA* 49: 247–57.

2012 *Hitit Kralı II. Muwatalli: Kişiliği ve İcraatı, Filolojik Belgeler Işığında (mit deutscher Zusammenfassung).* Turkish Institute of Archaeology, Studia ad Orientem Antiquum. İstanbul: Ege Yayınları.

2020a The Hišuwa Festival As a Political Instrument. In: Stefano de Martino and Elena Devecchi (eds.), *Anatolia Between the 13th and the 12th Century BCE.* Eothen 23. Firenze: LoGisma, 117–27.

2020b The Hittite *ḫišuwa-* Festival and Its Terminology. In: Susanne Görke and Charles W. Steitler (eds.), *Cult, Temple, Sacred Spaces. Cult Practices and Cult Spaces in Hittite Anatolia and Neighbouring Cultures. Proceedings of the First International HFR Symposium, Mainz, 3–5 June 2019.* StBoT 66. Wiesbaden: Harrassowitz, 363–75.

Doğan-Alparslan, Meltem and Metin Alparslan

2011 Wohnsitze und Hauptstädte der hethitischen Könige. *IM* 61: 85–103.

Gordin, Shai

2015 *Hittite Scribal Circles, Scholarly Tradition and Writing Habits.* StBoT 59. Wiesbaden: Harrassowitz.

Groddek, Detlev

2011 Die 11. und 12. Tafel des *ḫišuu̯a-* Festes. *RANT* 8: 111–50.

Haas, Volkert

1994 *Geschichte der hethitischen Religion.* HbOr 1/15. Leiden / New York / Köln: Brill.

Košak, Silvin

2002– *Konkordanz der hethitischen Keilschrifttafeln, Online-Datenbank Version.* hethiter.net/: hetkonk (2.plus) – last accessed 20.10.2024.

Rieken, Elisabeth

2009 Tontafelfunde in Kayalıpınar 2006–2009. *MDOG* 141: 208–14.

Sir Gavaz, Özlem and Gülgüney Masalcı Şahin

2021 Boğazkale Arşivinden Hišuwa Bayramını Konu Alan Yeni Bir Fragman (Bo 7850). *Archivum Anatolicum* 15: 171–92.

Sir Gavaz, Özlem and Melih Salih Keçeci
2024 Boğazkale Arşivinden Hišuwa Bayramı İçerikli Üç Yeni Hititçe Tablet Fragmanı / Three New Hittite Tablet Fragments from Boğazkale Archives with Content of Hišuwa Festival (Bo 7860-Bo 7909-Bo 7957). *Türk Arkeoloji ve Etnografya Dergisi* 87: 13–28.

Süel, Aygül
1998 Ortaköy – Šapinuwa Tabletlerinin Tarihlendirilmesi. In: Sedat Alp and Aygül Süel (eds.), *Acts of the IIIrd International Congress of Hittitology* (Çorum 1996). Ankara: Norol Matbacılık: 551–58.

Torri, Giulia
2022 *The* Haus am Hang *at Hattuša. A Late Hittite State Scriptorium and Its Tablet Collections.* StBoT 67. Wiesbaden: Harrassowitz.

Wegner, Ilse and Mirjo Salvini
1991 *Die hethitisch-hurritischen Ritualtafeln des (ḫ)išuwa-Festes.* ChS I/4. Roma: Multigrafica.

THE PALEOGRAPHY OF THE PALAIC TEXTS FROM ḪATTUŠA

Susanne Görke
Philipps-Universität Marburg

Abstract

This article analyzes the paleography of the Palaic texts from Ḫattuša from two perspectives: on the one hand, it seeks to discover whether one or more OH texts, including other festival and historical texts, were written by the same scribes and whether it is possible to propose how many scribes were active during OH times. On the other hand, the question is raised concerning the NS manuscripts of the Ziparwa festivities within the AN.DAḪ.ŠUM and *nuntarriyašḫa-* festivals, in relation to a possible chronological order of these manuscripts. Even if the results in both cases are rather meager and disappointing, it is hoped that the following discussion of procedure and methodology will contribute to further studies in this field.

Introduction

The corpus of the Palaic texts found in the archives of the Hittite capital, Ḫattuša, is comprised of around 200 fragments, which belong to 130 individual tablets at most. These fragments either indicate that parts of the respective texts were in the Palaic language or mention one of the Palaic gods. The group of Palaic gods met in these materials is rather fixed, with only very minor aberrations. They are, for example, mentioned with their Palaic names in a Palaic recitation spoken during offerings of meat in given festivals: Zaparwa, Kataḫzipuri, the Sun-god Tiyaz, the Ilaliyantiki deities, Ḫašamili, Ḫašauwanza Kamama, Šaušḫalla, Ḫilanzipa, the Fate-deities, and the Uliliyantiki deities.[1] In Hittite texts, Palaic gods are also mentioned in the context of offerings to them. One example relates how the chief of the palace servants hands one sour and one sweet loaf of bread to the king, who then breaks it, while another palace servant takes it and deposits it before a god or goddess.[2] The list begins with the loaves being placed on the altar 'for the deity' (*A-NA* DINGIR-*LIM*) which refers to the main god Ziparwa, in its Hittite name form. The following gods receiving offerings are Kataḫzipuri, the Sun-god, the Ilaliyant deities, Ḫašameli, Ḫašawanza Kammama, Šawašḫila, Ḫilašši, the Fate-deities, and the Aššanuwant deities. Some of these show name variants or name forms different from their Palaic counterparts mentioned above, as can be seen for example in Palaic Ilaliyantiki vs Hittite Ilaliyant gods.

1 See for example KUB 35.165 rev. 11′–18′ (*CTH* 751.1); see Görke and Sasseville 2024c: cola 78–93.
2 KUB 2.4+ obv. II 14 – obv. III 19′ with duplicates KBo 48.65(+), KBo 58.220+, and KBo 51.219+. See Görke 2024a: cola 34–71.

Deviations of this order can be seen in a few texts; the Old Hittite KBo 17.35+ (*CTH* 750.1), for example, mentions the Storm-god (ᴰIŠKUR) instead of Ziparwa, providing thereby a clue to the nature of the main Palaic god. Moreover, it cites the god Inar instead of Ḫašawanza Kammama and omits Šawašḫila and the Aššanuwant deities.[3] The Late New Script text CHDS 4.240 (*CTH* 750.11),[4] presumably a text in Hittite rather than Palaic, exhibits some of the gods' names in their Palaic version, a feature it shares with two other texts (see DBH 46/2.121 – *CTH* 750.6, KBo 42.218 – *CTH* 750.7): *pašḫu-lati*?-, likely connected to Palaic *pašḫullašaš* used in combination with the Sun-god Tiyaz,[5] and Ḫilanzipa in place of Hittite Ḫilašši, which in HT 26: 5 (*CTH* 750.9) is attested as Ḫellazipa. As these texts demonstrate the above-mentioned deviations in the list of Palaic gods, they were grouped neither with the texts in Palaic language (*CTH* 751) or festival fragments with Palaic recitations (*CTH* 753), nor with Ziparwa's veneration during the AN.DAḪ.ŠUM (*CTH* 610) or the *nuntarriyašḫa-* festivals (*CTH* 626);[6] rather, they appear to reflect actual versions of Ziparwa's festival (*CTH* 750). Most of the fragments are rather small, and not much can be said concerning their content, their relationship to each other, or to the other Ziparwa texts.

The Ziparwa sections of the AN.DAḪ.ŠUM and *nuntarriyašḫa-* state festivals

The outline tablets of the two itinerant festivals AN.DAḪ.ŠUM and *nuntarriyašḫa-* hint at the veneration of the god Ziparwa and his circle during two and three days respectively. For the AN.DAḪ.ŠUM festival we find the following passage on the outline tablet KBo 10.20:

Day 12:

KBo 10.20 obv. II 14:

lukkatti=ma LUGAL-*uš I-NA* É ᴰ*ziparwā paizzi nu* EZEN$_4$

On the next day, the king goes to the temple of Ziparwa, and the festival (takes place).

Day 13:

KBo 10.20 obv. II 25:

lukkatti=ma LUGAL-*uš I-NA* É ᴰ*ziparwā* [*na*]*mma paizzi nu* EZEN$_4$-*ŠU*

3 KBo 17.35+ rev.? III 6′–15′. The second column of the same text (KBo 38.70 obv. (II) 4′ – KBo 31.219+ obv. II 31′) gives a second list, which seems to write ᴰ*ḫal-ki* instead of Kataḫzipuri and Inar for Ḫašawanza Kammama, and which also omits Šawašḫila and the Aššanuwant deities. See Görke and Sasseville 2024a.

4 This dating of the *Konkordanz* (Košak 2002–) was presumably made because of the existence of the sign ḪA with just one *Winkelhaken*. For the validity of this sign, see below.

5 See Steitler 2023: 162–65 on this epithet.

6 They neither belong to the Palaic festival including the myth of a disappearing deity (*CTH* 752) nor to fragments in Palaic language (*CTH* 754).

On the next day, the king goes [ag]ain to the temple of Ziparwa and his (i. e. Ziparwa's) festival (takes place).[7]

Ziparwa is not mentioned in any other outline tablet of AN.DAḪ.ŠUM.

During the *nuntarriyašḫa-* festival, festivities for the god Ziparwa lasted three days, including one preparatory day on which the *parā uwanza* 'supervisor' goes into the temple of Ziparwa, whereas the king is present only on the second and third day. As the outline tablets of the *nuntarriyašḫa-* festival always represent different versions, the exact day of the Ziparwa festivities varies:[8]

Day 8:[9]

KBo 22.228+ 7′f.:

> *[l]u[kkatt]i=ma [p]arā uwanza I-NA* É ^{D}*[ziparwā] pai[zz]i*
>
> On [t]he nex[t day], a [s]upervisor go[e]s to the temple of the god [Ziparwa].

Day 9:

KBo 22.228+ 13′:

> *lukkatt[i=m]a* LUGAL-*uš I-NA* É ^{D}*zip[arwā paizzi]*
>
> On the next d[ay], the king [goes] into the temple of Zip[arwa].

Day 10:

KBo 14.76 obv. I 15′:

> *[lukkatti=ma* LUGAL-*uš I-NA* É] ^{D}*z[iparwā] paizzi*
>
> [On the next day, the king] goes [into the temple of] Z[iparwa].

Among the few colophons that mention the festivals of Ziparwa, instances of festivals in the spring were attributed to the AN.DAḪ.ŠUM festival, whereas tablets mentioning a festival for Ziparwa in the autumn were counted as belonging to *nuntarriyašḫa-*. The following colophons refer to a first day of a spring festival:

DBH 46/2.170+ (*CTH* 610.1.A) rev. VI:[10]

1′ [DU]B 1^{KAM} *ŠA* ^{D}⌈*zi*⌉*-pár-[wa$_{a}$-a]*
2′ *[m]a-a-an* LUGAL-*uš ḫa-m[e-eš-ḫi]*
3′ *[I]-NA* É ^{D}*zi-pár-w[a$_{a}$-a]*
4′ *[pa]-iz-zi Ú-UL [QA-TI]*

> First [tabl]et of Zipar[wa. W]hen the king [g]oes [in]to the temple of Ziparwa in spri[ng]. Not [finished].

---

7 See the upcoming edition of AN.DAḪ.ŠUM by Ch. Steitler which will be found on https://www.hethport.uni-wuerzburg.de/txhet_festrit/textindex.php?g=festrit&l=x.

8 See Kryszeń in press and his upcoming online edition on https://www.hethport.uni-wuerzburg.de/txhet_festrit/textindex.php?g=festrit&l=x.

9 Cf. IBoT 4.71+ obv. 10′f., on day 7; Bo 9159+ 8′f., on day 8; KBo 14.76 i 10′f., on day 9. The following days are mentioned later in these texts. KUB 55.5+ obv. also mentions Ziparwa's festival, but without preserving the concrete day numbering.

10 Cf. HT 83+ 1′–4′ (*CTH* 610.1.B) for a duplicate with minor aberrations of this colophon.

KUB 41.26+ (*CTH* 750.2) rev. IV:

26 DUB 1⸢^{KAM} *Ú*⸣-*UL QA-TI*
27 EZEN$_4$ *ḫa-*[*m*]*e-iš-ḫa-an-da-aš ŠA* ^{D}*zi-pár-wa$_a$*
28 ⸢*iš-tar*⸣-[*ni-i*]*a-aš* EGIR-*an tar-nu-um-ma-aš*
29 [*A-N*]*A* [GIŠ.ḪUR]-*kán ḫa-a-an-ta-a*-⸢*an*⸣
30 [KASKAL$^{?\ \mathrm{m}}$]*pí-ḫa*-UR.MAḪ DUB.SAR.⸢GIŠ⸣
31 [... ^{m}*pa*]*l-lu-wa-ra*-LÚ DUB.⸢SAR⸣

First tablet, not finished. Sp[r]ing festival of Ziparwa. Pr[e]-final version. Collated [again]st [the original]. [Task force$^{?}$ of] Piḫawalwi, scribe of wood tablets, [Pa]lluwaraziti, scribe.

Despite its mention of a spring festival of Ziparwa, this last text is not a version of the AN.DAḪ.ŠUM festival. This is based on several points. First, this text exhibits two Palaic – i. e. not Hittite – names of the Palaic gods; this relates to the texts mentioned above, which were counted as festivals of their own. Second, it also combines in one day both rites of offering bread (written on its obverse) and the libation of wine (on its reverse); comparable offering descriptions in the AN.DAḪ.ŠUM rites, however, belong to different days, day 1 and day 2. Third, the text mentions foods, such as the *tuni-* mush, or an *išnuri-* vessel, which are not attested in other fragments that can be attributed to the Ziparwa days of AN.DAḪ.ŠUM or *nuntarriyašḫa-*. Nevertheless, *tuni-* and *išnuri-* are mentioned in texts that were kept separate from the itinerant state festivals, as they are considered to be independent festivals (*CTH* 750). This demonstrates the difficulty of attributing a text with its colophon mentioning solely a spring or autumn festival to the itinerant state festivals. Nevertheless, the first text, DBH 46/2.170+, represents the first tablet of Ziparwa's festival during the AN.DAḪ.ŠUM festival.[11]

The following colophons testify to autumn festivals for Ziparwa and his gods:

KBo 34.162 (*CTH* 626-Ziparwa.0.C) rev. IV?:

1′ DUB 1^{KAM} *QA-TI*
2′ [*Š*]*A* UD^{KAM} *MAḪ-RI-I*
3′ [^{LÚ}*p*]*a-ra-a ú-wa-an-za*
4′ [*ma-a*]*ḫ-ḫa-an zé-e-ni*
5′ [*I-NA*] É ^{D}*zi-pár-wa$_a$-a*
6′ [*pa-i*]*z-zi*

First tablet. Finished. [O]f the first day. [Wh]en the [su]pervisor [go]es [into] the temple of Ziparwa in autumn.

VSNF 12.20+ (*CTH* 626-Ziparwa.1.A) rev. VI:

1′ [D]UB ⸢2^{KAM} *ŠA* UD 2$^{?\mathrm{KAM}}$⸣
2′ *ŠA* EZEN$_4$ ^{D}*zi-pár-wa$_a$-a* NU [TI]L
3′ *ma-a-an* LUGAL-*uš zé-e-ni*
4′ *I-NA* É ^{D}*zi-pár-wa$_a$-a*
5′ *pa-iz-zi*

11 The colophon of KUB 20.8 (*CTH* 610.8) refers to the end of the AN.DAḪ.ŠUM festival of Ziparwa and the beginning of the following festival, the AN.DAḪ.ŠUM of the Sun-goddess of the Earth.

Second [t]ablet.[12] Of the second day of Ziparwa's festival. Not [finish]ed. When the king goes into the temple of Ziparwa in autumn.

One tablet thus belongs to the first or preparatory day, while a second tablet describes rites of the second day, presumably the first day with the king attending the ceremonies. On these tablets one also finds fragmentary descriptions of rites that help to reconstruct Ziparwa's festivals during the itinerant state festivals. Additional colophons, some of them very fragmentary, are preserved, but do not reveal any ritual descriptions.[13]

On the whole it appears as if the first day of the AN.DAḪ.ŠUM festivities for Ziparwa and his group in spring was dedicated to offerings of bread, more precisely to sour and sweet bread loaves that were offered in a certain way for every Palaic god (cf. above), while a ^{MUNUS}ŠU.GI ritual expert recited the 'words of the loaves' in Palaic. Moreover, groats and wine were offered similarly to every god, while the 'words of groats' and the 'words of groats and wine' were recited (see *CTH* 610.1 in the online edition). The second day included various meat offerings, among them cut liver parts on broken sour and sweet loaves, meat from sheeps and goats, liver, wine offerings out of animal-shaped rhyta in combination with liver and sour bread, often noted for each Palaic god separately (see *CTH* 610.2 in the online edition).[14]

The *nuntarriyašḫa-* festival in the autumn added a preparatory day without the presence of the king. On this day, cultic personnel prepared for the festival by cleaning themselves, bringing in various materials, or cooking meat. Offerings to the Palaic gods already took place, among them offerings of loaves and libations. After a cultic meal, pieces of meat were also donated to the gods. More food was brought from several administrative institutions (see *CTH* 626-Ziparwa.0 in the online edition). On the first day of the *nuntarriyašḫa-* festival, with the king attending, more meat offerings took place, including meat from a ram and a bull, the raw meat of which was afterwards presented to the Palaic gods.[15] These gods also received liver on bread as *canapés* (see *CTH* 626-Ziparwa.1 in the online edition). For the second day of the king's attendance, corresponding to the festival's last day, one finds descriptions of drinking rites out of animal-shaped rhyta, partly in combination with bread offerings (see *CTH* 626-Ziparwa.2 in the online edition).[16]

On the whole, the corpus of the festivals of the Palaic gods that take place during the itinerant Hittite state festivals comprises around 100 fragments that stem from about 70 tablets (see Appendices 1–2), which provide us with different versions of these festivals. It has to be kept in mind, however, that a number of these fragments are very small, preventing a full reconstruction of even one of the tablets, so that some of these conclusions must remain provisional.

12 KUB 20.82 rev. VI 2′ and Lewis 2 rev. 1′ read: DUB 4^{KAM} "forth tablet".

13 KBo 58.222+ l.col. 1′–4′ (*CTH* 610.2.A); KUB 20.8 rev. VI 1′–10′ (*CTH* 610.8); KBo 22.177 rev. 1′–8′ (*CTH* 626-Ziparwa.2.C); Bo 6057 rev. 1′–5′ (*CTH* 626-Ziparwa.7); KUB 7.28+ rev. IV 1′–4′ (*CTH* 750.4.B).

14 This sequence of offerings, first bread and then meat, seem to coincide with the same order in the older Palaic festivals in Palaic language *CTH* 751; see Görke and Sasseville 2024b. For texts belonging to Ziparwa's festivities during the AN.DAḪ.ŠUM festival, see Appendix 1.

15 During this day, only the first five gods of the list are mentioned: Ziparwa, Kataḫzipuri, the Sun-god, the Ilaliyant deities, and Ḫašameli.

16 Görke 2024b. For texts belonging to Ziparwa's festivities during the *nuntarriyašḫa-* festival see Appendix 2.

Remarks on the paleography of the Palaic text corpus

The Palaic corpus consists, on one side, of both of old festivals, partly in Palaic language, and of some individual festivals (*CTH* 750–754); on the other side, the corpus is also comprised of younger texts belonging to the itinerant state festivals created during the Empire period (*CTH* 610 and *CTH* 626-Ziparwa). The corpus was written during all periods of Hittite history. Only two tablets within the corpus mention scribal names, of which one, the independent festival *CTH* 750.2 (cf. above), names Piḫawalwi and Palluwaraziti, while the second one, a part of the AN.DAḪ.ŠUM festival, contains the name of the scribe Ḫapatiwalwi, son of Tuwaziti.[17] Only one tablet mentions someone, named Ḫantili (II), as a possible historical character in a fragmentary Palaic context (KBo 19.155+ 3′ – *CTH* 751.2). The dating of the tablets therefore needs to rely, among other things, on the paleographic methods that have been developed in Hittitology in the last decades.[18] In the past ten years, questions of handwriting and the possibility of recognizing scribal hands by the forms of their signs have also come into discussion, especially thanks to the digital analyses undertaken by G. G. W. Müller.[19] With the help of (digital) tools, the search for joins – which had long been done by the comparison of sign forms or shapes of tablets' breaks, with the aid of hand copies and photos – should be simplified, but this will take additional time before it can be successfully employed in general use. Recently, Yakubovich and Mouton (2023: 29–239) have proposed a more mechanical method to establish which tablets and fragments were written by the same hand.

The following analysis has two goals: first, it examines the texts in Old Script that are part of the Palaic corpus. By comparing sign forms with other, better-preserved texts in Old Script, it strives to determine whether the Palaic texts were written by the scribe who also wrote other Old Hittite texts and whether it is possible to propose how many Old Hittite scribes can be differentiated. The second part of this study turns to the manuscripts of the Ziparwa festivals within the AN.DAḪ.ŠUM and *nuntarriyašḫa*-festivals, so as to examine whether it is possible to identify the same scribe responsible for multiple tablets and whether it is possible to establish an internal chronological order of the manuscripts.

The OH Palaic texts in comparison with other OH texts

The Palaic corpus includes three compositions bearing Old Hittite Script (OS). The first is comprised of both major manuscripts of *CTH* 752, the festival that includes a Palaic myth about a disappearing deity, A: KUB 32.117+ and B: KBo 25.139+. These were written down at the end of the 16th century BC.[20] In addtion, KBo 17.35+, which consti-

17 KUB 20.8 (*CTH* 610.8); cf. below.

18 See Klinger 2022; Gordin 2015: 83–94; Weeden 2011: 42–52; each with references to older literature.

19 See Cammarosano et al. 2014; Müller 2014; 2016; Müller and Pirngruber 2019; Devecchi et al. 2015; 2019.

20 Neu 1980: XVIf. n. 11, excluded KBo 25.139+ from his corpus of OS texts, even if it "besitzt zwar Eigenschaften, die für ein altes Schriftbild mehr oder weniger charakteristisch sein können, jedoch sind

tutes an independent festival for Ziparwa (*CTH* 750.1), exhibits features comparable to the texts of *CTH* 752. Although none of the three texts is completely preserved, each contains sufficient written text to enable reliable statements about OS sign forms. Old Script texts show specific features, among them "eine schwer wiegende Handschrift", "enge Zeichensetzung", "geringe Wortabstände", "Zeichenligaturen", and "leicht nach rechts hin schräge Neigung der Köpfe senkrechter Keile",[21] which are all recognizable to a greater or lesser extent in the three texts. All three are two-columned, a feature they share with some other OH texts.[22] It can be stated that the three Palaic texts are indeed Old Hittite. This allows for the next steps outlined above, namely, an establishment of a plausible internal chronological order for the texts as well as an assessment of the number of scribes who wrote them. For these purposes a table for internal use was created that included some 40 signs. Among them were diagnostic signs for dating Old Hittite texts, like TA, GA, A+NA, I+NA, KAT+TA,[23] and also DA, Á, IG, UG, AZ, and Ù, which all show specific variants for Middle Hittite scripture.[24] Additional signs, like BI, EL, GAL, GIŠ, ḪU, IŠ, LÚ, NÍG, RU, and ŠU – some of which are important for dating or distinguishing hand writings in NS texts[25] – turned out to be insignificant for these matters in OS texts. Signs such as NA and KI, on the other hand, are included in the discussion, because these show variants with only one *Winkelhaken*, which are also present in other OS texts (see below). On the whole, the approach presented here chose specific signs and thus refrained from creating a table with all signs (and also all sign variants within one text). This has to be kept in mind when considering its results.

It becomes clear on the basis of the analysis of the collected signs that the handwriting of the three OS Palaic texts is not the same. The signs Á, DA, E, GA, RA, and ŠA, for example, differ in several ways, especially concerning the arrangement of the small inscribed wedges (see Fig. 1).

Moreover, the forms of some diagnostic signs, A+NA, AḪ, GA, TA (see Fig. 2), suggest that text *CTH* 752.1.B (KBo 25.139+) is younger than *CTH* 752.1.A (KUB 32.117+): the spaces between the inscribed verticals and the upper horizontal in the signs GA and TA, for example, are smaller in *CTH* 752.1.A than those appearing in *CTH* 752.1.B. Furthermore, the paleographic dating of *CTH* 750.1 (KBo 17.35+) appears similar to that of *CTH* 752.1.A (KUB 32.117+).

---

die Zeichenformen (vgl. besonders TA) nicht immer einheitlich, was uns bewogen hat, diesen Text mit seinen hethitischen Passagen nicht in die Umschriftausgabe aufzunehmen." Moreover, KUB 32.117+ (referred to as KUB 35.168) shows "Duktustyp II" within the "Alter Duktus". Note van den Hout's (2012: 152f.) remarks on the use of "Duktus" and "Zeichenform" in Hittitology with respect to general works on paleography and manuscript terminology.

21 See Weeden 2011: 43 with references to previous literature.

22 See Soysal's contribution to this volume.

23 Cf. Weeden 2011: 43 with n. 189 for a list of characteristic Old Script signs according to HZL: GA, TA, ŠA, E, URU, LI, ḪAR, AḪ, NA, UD, KI, SAR, AK, IG, AL, and DA. See also the list in Gordin 2015: 90, who names the signs NA, IK, AK, ŠA, GA, TA, AL, E, URU, DI, KI, UD, AḪ, ḪAR, LI, SAR, and MEŠ in their specific form.

24 This follows Starke according to Gordin: 2011, 90, who counts the following signs in their specific MS form: TA, ŠA, AZ, UK, DA, Á, and AR. Weeden 2011: 44 lists TA, UK, AZ, AR, DA, Á, ŠA, E, URU, AḪ, ḪAR, SAR, and AL in their specific form.

25 On the relevance of the sign BI, see, e. g. the contributions to this volume by Schwemer and Kryszeń.

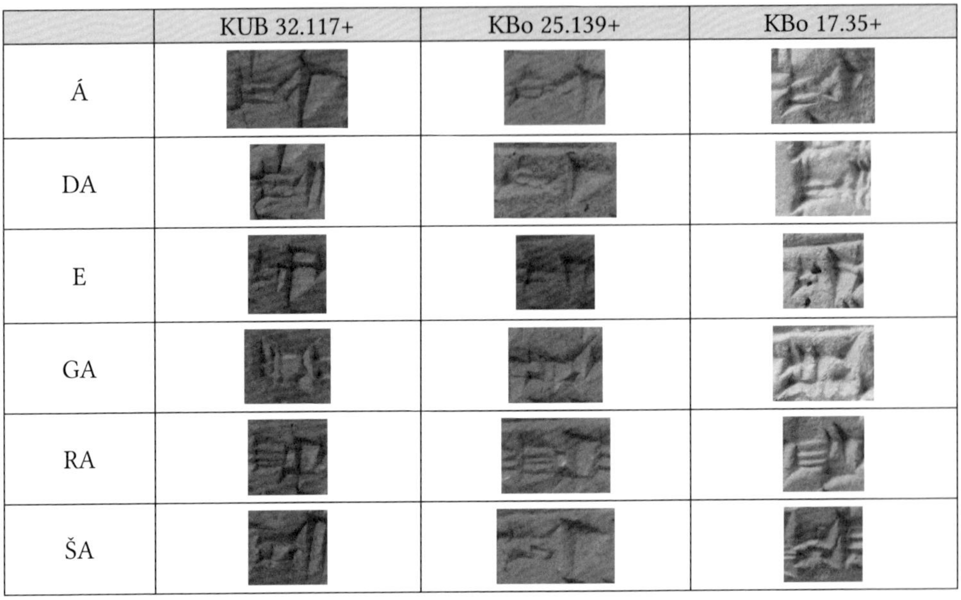

Fig. 1. The signs Á, DA, E, GA, RA, and ŠA in the OS Palaic texts.

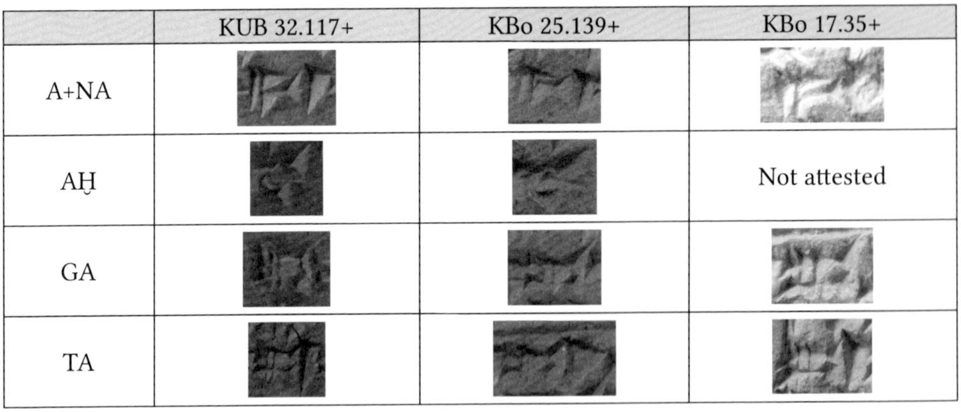

Fig.2. Diagnostic signs of the OS Palaic texts.

Having established that the three OS copies of the Palaic festivals were not written by the same scribe, a question that arises is whether one of these OS Palaic texts was written by the same scribe who is responsible for any other OS festival or historical texts. In order to address this, those manuscripts dated by the *Konkordanz* as "ah." were selected that were large enough so as to provide the same sign inventory as the OH Palaic texts.[26] Table 1 presents the texts complying with these requirements:

26 Included are also a few texts outside this range, e. g. the laws (*CTH* 291 and 292) and the Royal edict (*CTH* 272), that was mentioned by Klinger 2022: 297 with n. 118, 307, 316, 321f.

	Text	Text Title
1	KUB 32.117+ (*CTH* 752)	Myth in Palaic and Ritual
2	KBo 25.139+ (*CTH* 752)	Myth in Palaic and Ritual
3	KBo 17.35+ (*CTH* 750.1)	Festival for Ziparwa in Hittite
4	KBo 25.68+ (*CTH* 668)	Texts from the cult of Ḫanḫana
5	KBo 25.56+ (*CTH* 665)	Festival fragments referring to the *ašuša(tal)la-* men
6	KBo 25.54+ (*CTH* 665)	Festival fragments referring to the *ašuša(tal)la-* men
7	KBo 25.33+ (*CTH* 649)	Festival fragments referring to a NIN.DINGIR priestess
8	KBo 25.31 (*CTH* 649)	Festival fragments referring to a NIN.DINGIR priestess
9	KBo 17.14+ (*CTH* 635)	Fragments of the festival of Zippalanda and Mt. Daḫa
10	KBo 25.86+ (*CTH* 635)	Fragments of the festival of Zippalanda and Mt. Daḫa
11	KBo 30.29+ (*CTH* 631)	Thunder festival
12	KBo 25.12+ (*CTH* 627)	KI.LAM festival
13	KBo 17.21+ (*CTH* 627)	KI.LAM festival
14	KBo 3.22 (*CTH* 1)	Proclamation of Anitta
15	KBo 22.2 (*CTH* 3)	Zalpa tale
16	KUB 36.104 (*CTH* 8)	Palace Chronicle
17	KBo 8.42 (*CTH* 9)	Fragments of palace chronicles
18	KUB 36.100+ (*CTH* 14)	*Res gestae* of Ḫattušili I – the so-called Zukraši Text
19	KBo 22.62+ (*CTH* 291)	Laws, first series: "If a Man"
20	KBo 25.85+ (*CTH* 292)	Laws, second series: "If a Grapevine"
21	KUB 36.108 (*CTH* 25)	Treaty of Zidanza II with Pilliya of Kizzuwatna[27]
22	KBo 22.1 (*CTH* 272)	Royal edict

Table 1. List of OS texts chosen for comparison.

Texts 1–3 in Table 1 are the OS Palaic texts already mentioned above; texts 4–13 and 14–22 represent OH festival and historical texts, respectively. Since a comparison of the massive sign tables is difficult, a different approach was undertaken by the author, though still with the purpose of establishing whether two or more texts may have been written by the same scribe. Fifteen signs which show sufficient differences (Á, DA, A+NA, IGI, AḪ, ḪAR, GA, TA, KI, NA, ḪA, RA, URU, TE, and MEŠ) were selected so as to enable their arrangement into two (or, in the case of DA and Á, three) distinguishable groups.

The first sign presented here is DA (Fig. 3). It exhibits, like the sign Á, three major variants: (1) with three horizontal wedges that are vertically aligned (left column, nos. 1, 3, 5, 8, 12, 17, 19, and 20); (2) with the indented (broken) middle horizontal (right column, nos. 4, 7, 9, 10, 13, 15, 16, and 21); (3) with an at least slightly stressed and protruding lower horizontal wedge (left column, nr. 2, 11, 14, 18, and 22; see below for the reasoning of this grouping). Likewise, the sign Á (Fig. 4) can be arranged into three groups according to variants: (1) with the heads of the three horizontals vertically aligned (upper left column); (2) with an indented middle horizontal in the right column; and (3) with the lower wedge protruding and stressed (lower left column). The ligature A+NA (Fig. 5)

27 This MS text was included in this list as it was considered OS in older research articles. It indeed shares some features with other texts presented here; cf. Klinger 2022: 264 n. 24, 269, 289 n. 92, 318.

Fig. 3. DA in OH texts. Text numbers according to Table 1.

Fig. 4. Á in OH texts. Text numbers according to Table 1.

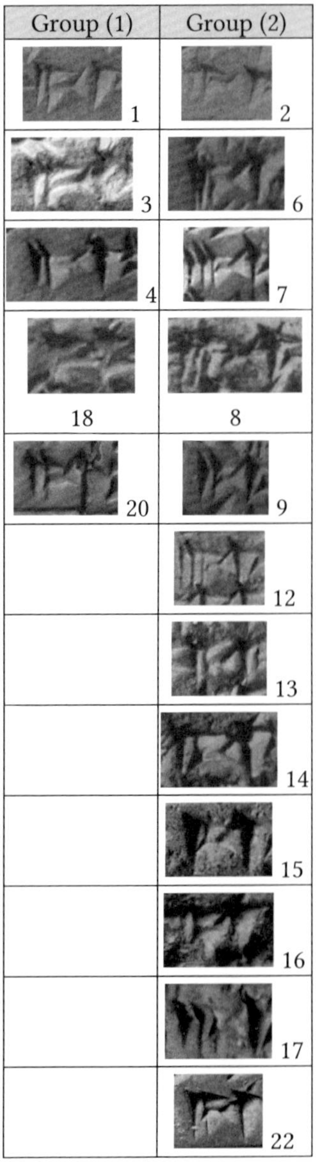

Fig. 5. *A+NA* in OH texts. Text numbers according to Table 1.

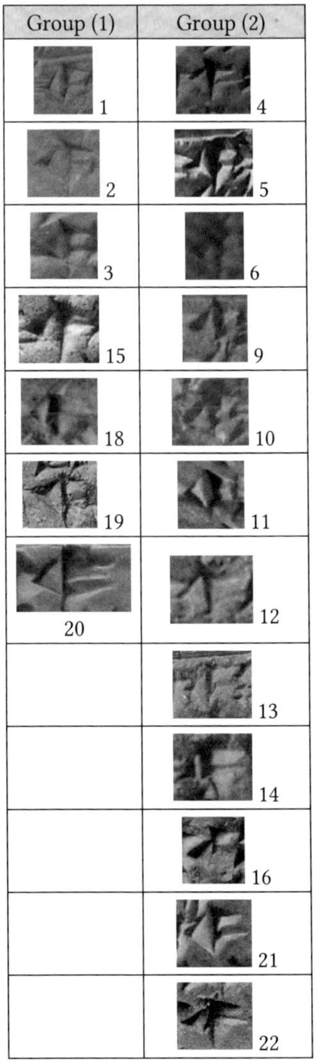

Fig. 6. IGI in OH texts. Text numbers according to Table 1.

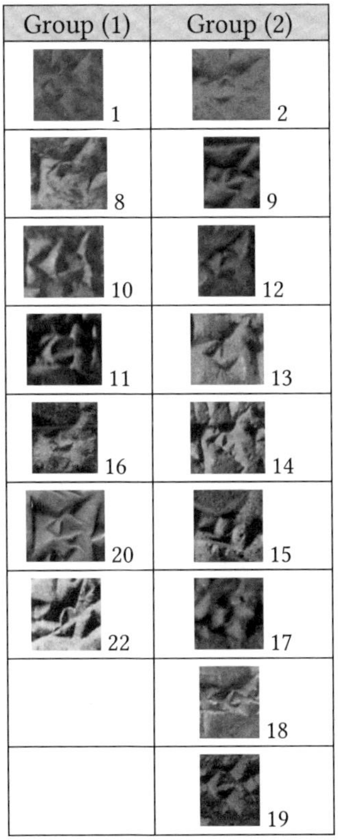

Fig. 7. AḪ in OH texts. Text numbers according to Table 1.

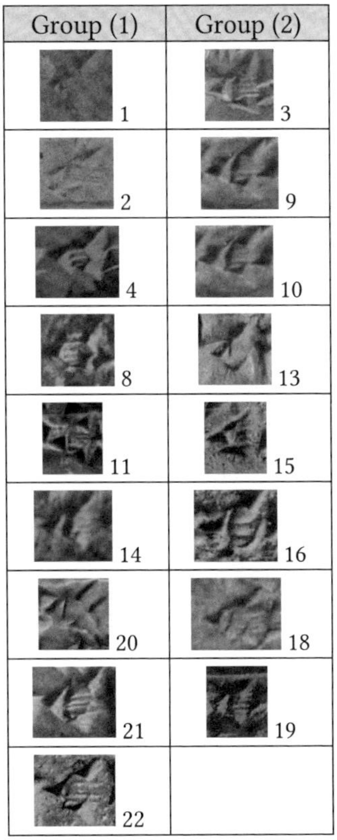

Fig. 8. HAR in OH texts. Text numbers according to Table 1.

exhibits two variants: (1) the beginning of the horizontal of NA merges with the second vertical of A (left column); (2) the horizontal of NA starts after A and/or has a clearly visible head (right column). The sign IGI (Fig. 6), like A+NA, exhibits variations where (1) the horizontal merges with the vertical (left column), or (2) the horizontal's wedge is clearly visible (right column). The sign AḪ, too, can be broken down according to variants (Fig. 7): (1) the horizontal starts immediately after the first *Winkelhaken* (left column); (2) the horizontal does not start before the beginning of the second and third *Winkelhaken* (right column). Variants of the sign ḪAR exhibit a similar breakdown (Fig. 8).

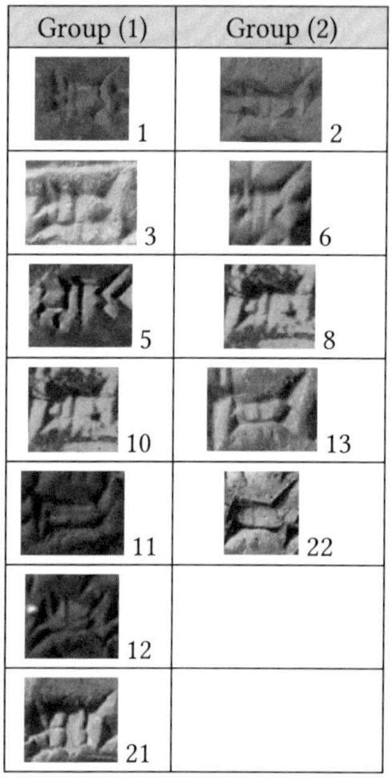

Fig. 9. GA in OH texts. Text numbers according to Table 1.

Fig. 10. TA in OH texts. Text numbers according to Table 1.

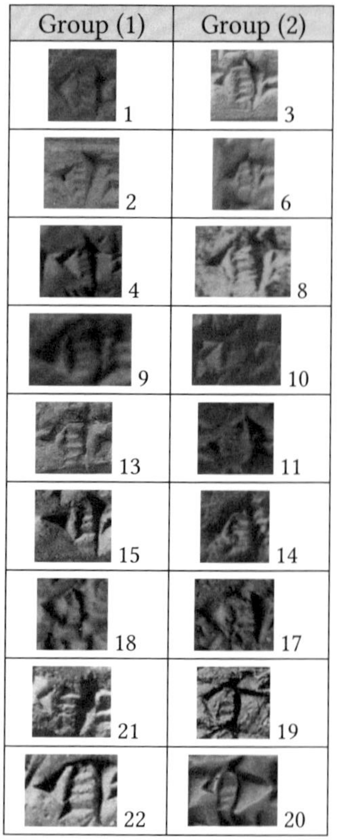

Fig. 11. KI in OH texts. Text numbers according to Table 1.

For the sign GA (Fig. 9) a difference appears in the position of the two inscribed verticals: (1) either clearly above the upper horizontal (left column); or (2) immediately on top of the upper horizontal (right column). This also applies to TA (Fig. 10), which shows two variants regarding the distance between the inscribed verticals and the upper horizontal wedge: (1) greater distance (left column); and (2) smaller distance (right column). The sign KI (Fig. 11) also appears to have two variants: (1) with apparently only one *Winkelhaken* (left column); and (2) with clearly two *Winkelhaken* (right column). The sign NA (Fig. 12) also appears to exhibit variations: (1) where the second *Winkelhaken* is barely visible (left column); (2) with two *Winkelhaken*, which follow each other, with the second one written higher than the first (right column). Most of the ḪA signs (Fig. 13) can be separated into two categories, in which: (1) the two *Winkelhaken* appear one after the other, only slightly diverging in height (left column); or (2) the second

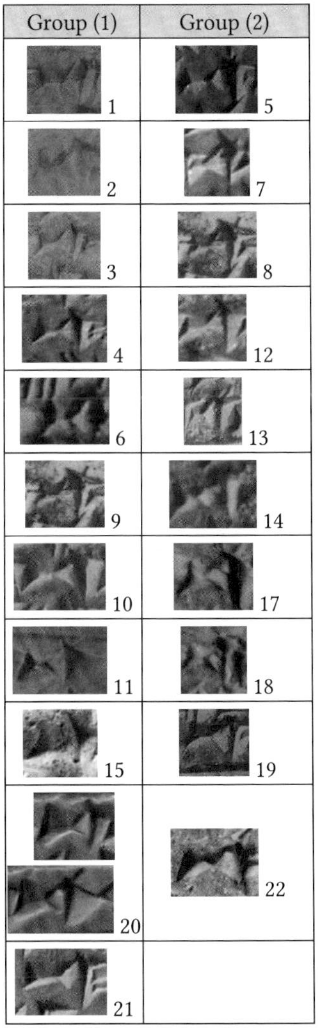

Fig. 12. NA in OH texts. Text numbers according to Table 1.

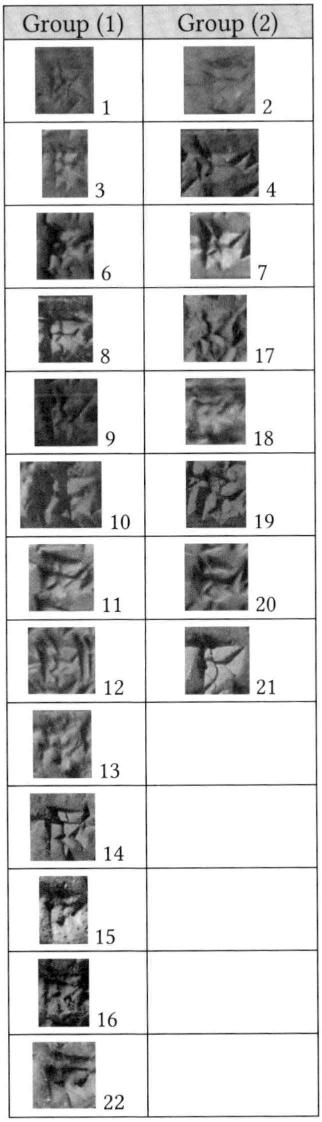

Fig. 13. ḪA in OH texts. Text numbers according to Table 1.

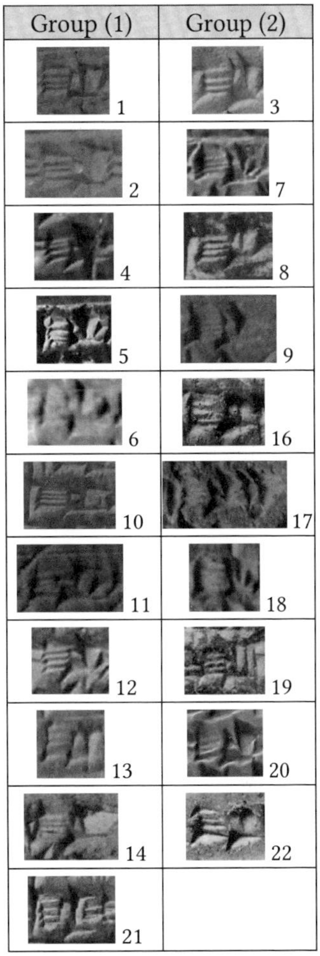

Fig. 14. RA in OH texts. Text numbers according to Table 1.

Winkelhaken is placed more to the right, almost out of the sign and thus separated from the rest of the sign (right column). The variations of RA (Fig. 14) differ in shapes with: (1) a very small first vertical (left column); and (2) the two verticals almost identical in size (right column). The sign URU (Fig. 15), like RA, has two variants: (1) one with a very small first vertical (left column); (2) the other with a slightly taller first vertical, though still smaller than the second (right column). The sign TE (Fig. 16) has two variations: (1) one with four horizontals before the vertical (left column); and

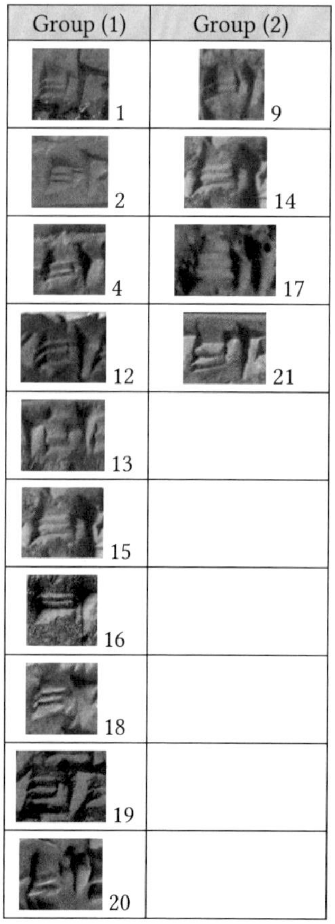

Fig. 15. URU in OH texts. Text numbers according to Table 1.

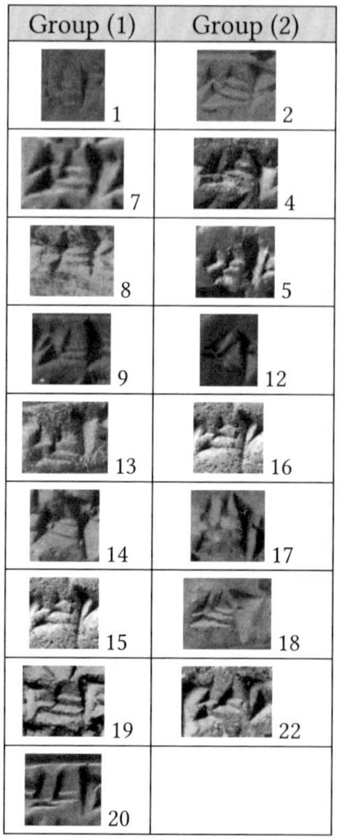

Fig. 16. TE in OH texts. Text numbers according to Table 1.

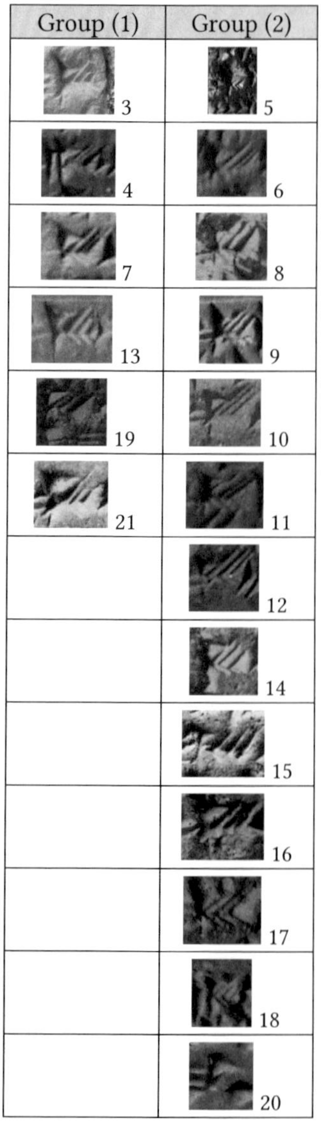

Fig. 17. MEŠ in OH texts. Text numbers according to Table 1.

(2) the other with four *Winkelhaken* (right column). Two variations of the sign MEŠ are shown in Fig. 17: (1) with the form ME.EŠ (left column); (2) as MEŠ (right column).

After describing the most important variations of sign shapes in OS texts, the question of whether some of these texts were possibly written by the same scribe will now be addressed. The forms of the sign Á in the texts 1, 4, 12, and 20, for example, look rather alike (Fig. 4); these also all appear on the left column. For the sign DA (Fig. 3), texts 1, 12, and 20 belong to part of one group (left), while text 4 is part of the other (right). The shape of the sign A+NA (Fig. 5) on the other hand, clearly distinguishes text 12 from the others, according to the writing of the horizontal behind the second vertical. According to Fig. 6, the sign variations of IGI in texts 1 and 20 in the left column differ from the ones of 4 and 12, right column. Signs of texts 1 and 20 appear in the left column ten out of fifteen times; in two cases, neither text attests the signs; text 20 is listed three times in the right column (Fig. 11: KI; Fig. 13: ḪA; Fig. 17: MEŠ). Given major differences in writing, as in the case of KI and MEŠ especially, it is unlikely that texts 1 and 20 were written by the same scribe. Far more notably, however, is the overall picture, which cannot make a clear case for the same scribe for any two texts out of the twenty-two under consideration.

Out of the fifteen signs selected for the analysis of the handwriting, eleven are also interesting with respect to their potential for ordering the texts chronologically; these are: DA, Á, AḪ, A+NA, ḪAR, GA, TA, KI, NA, URU, and MEŠ.[28] A tally of how often a given text exhibits sign variants belonging to either the first (1) or second (2) group of the figures above, is shown in Table 2.

To the foregoing discussion several remarks should be added:

- The groups were established using photographs provided by the *Konkordanz*, though these are of varying quality. Thus the classification could differ upon examination of the original tablet or better photos.
- Not every text contains every sign. Texts with fewer than nine of the eleven signs attested (nos. 3, 4, 21, 10, 5, 6, 16, 17, 7), among them the last six of Table 2, should perhaps be given less weight if taken into consideration.
- Table 2 presents a possible chronological order based only on sign forms. It does not take into consideration other features of the tablet, such as the appearance of the writing (e. g. "schwer wiegende Handschrift", "geringe Wortabstände")[29] or the shape of the tablet (e. g. "cushion-shape")[30].
- The assumption that the signs in group 1 are older than those of group 2 is mainly based on the consideration that sign variants that can be more distinctly differentiated from MS and NS forms are older than those that are more similar in their appearance.[31] Some of the considered signs, such as AḪ and ḪAR, only manifest smaller nuances in their variation, which may not justify their division into two groups.
- In the tables above, several signs exhibit clear variants. This concerns, for example, the ligature A+NA, which has one variant (1) with the horizontal of NA di-

28 See Weeden 2011: 43 and Gordin 2015: 90 for lists of signs with specific OS variants (see also above note 23). For the sign DA and Á (Fig. 3 and 4) see Klinger 2022: 302–7, who declares the variant with stressed protruding lowest horizontal as oldest (here DA and Á group (3)), followed by the one where the three horizontals are vertically aligned (DA and Á groups (1) in Fig. 3 and 4). The signs E, LI, ŠA, SAR, AK, and AL, significant in their OS form as mentioned by Weeden and Gordin, were either too uniformly written to be valuable for a comparison of handwriting or too seldom attested within the chosen corpus of Table 2.

29 See Weeden 2011: 43 with reference to the original literature.

30 See Klinger 2022: 312–15 with reference to previous literature. Cf. also the contribution by O. Soysal to this volume.

31 But cf. the remarks on the form of DA in Klinger 2022: 202–7; see here note 28.

Text	Features of group (1)	Features of group (2)	
20	8	2	KBo 25.85+ (*CTH* 292)
1	8	1	KUB 32.117+ (*CTH* 752)
2	7	3	KBo 25.139+ (*CTH* 752)
3	7	1	KBo 17.35+ (*CTH* 750.1)
4	7	-	KBo 25.68+ (*CTH* 668)
11	6	3	KBo 30.29+ (*CTH* 631)
12	5	4	KBo 25.12+ (*CTH* 627)
18	5	4	KUB 36.100+ (*CTH* 14)
22	5	4	KBo 22.1 (*CTH* 272)
8	4	6	KBo 25.31 (*CTH* 649)
9	4	6	KBo 17.14+ (*CTH* 635)
14	4	6	KBo 3.22 (*CTH* 1)
19	4	5	KBo 22.62+ (*CTH* 291)
21	4	2	KUB 36.108 (*CTH* 25)
13	3	8	KBo 17.21+ (*CTH* 627)
15	3	7	KBo 22.2 (*CTH* 3)
10	3	5	KBo 25.86+ (*CTH* 635)
5	3	1	KBo 25.56+ (*CTH* 665)
6	2	4	KBo 25.54+ (*CTH* 665)
16	2	3	KUB 36.104 (*CTH* 8)
17	1	7	KBo 8.42 (*CTH* 9)
7	1	5	KBo 25.33+ (*CTH* 649)

Table 2. OS texts sorted according to the number of features of group 1 and 2.

rectly pressed on the second vertical of A rendering the head invisible, and another variant (2) in which the horizontal starts a bit further to the right and therefore shows a wedge's head (cf. Fig. 5). The same difference can be pointed out for the sign IGI (above, Fig. 6). It remains unclear whether this is to be interpreted as a chronological difference.[32] Moreover, in some of the OS texts one finds variants of KI and NA with only one *Winkelhaken* (see Fig. 11 and 12). Here, too, a chronological sequence remains either uncertain or alternatively has not yet been discussed. Likewise, the variations of the signs URU and RA along with those of TE and MEŠ[33] have not been considered for their chronological value, although there is no reason to exclude them from the discussion.

– It is interesting to see that the Anitta text, often declared to be the oldest known written Hittite document,[34] does not fill one of the first ranks of this list.[35]

32 Weeden and Gordin simply mention the ligature as an OS feature.

33 Gordin 2015: 90 mentions this sign written ME.EŠ as an OS feature but does not discern between the two variants listed here.

34 See Klinger 2022, 319f. with n. 171–73 and further references.

35 In his recent paper, Klinger, considers KBo 3.22, KBo 22.1 and the Zukraši text (KBo 7.14+ resp. KUB 36.100+) as "besonders frühe Texte" (Klinger 2022: 307) based on "inhaltliche" or: internal (Klinger 2022:

On the whole, the present investigation of the paleography of OS texts has raised more questions than it has solved. For example, the fact that it was not possible to attribute two texts to the same scribe raises new questions about scribal life in Ḫattuša. In light of this, one would expect a greater number of scribes from the beginning of the Hittite Empire onwards; or else it may be the case that future scholarship on Hittite scribal practice will have to revise the length of written transmission in Anatolia upwards; and it is not impossible that revisions in terms of both will eventually be called for. Moreover, it became clear that only a systematic examination of all Old Hittite texts, including the forms of (all) signs, visual aspects of the tablets, spelling conventions, tradition, genre and possible artistic license, will shed light on their paleography and internal sequence.

Remarks on the paleography of the NS Palaic texts

The last part of this paper deals with the paleography of the New Script texts of the Ziparwa festivals within the state festivals AN.DAḪ.ŠUM (*CTH* 610) and *nuntarriyašḫa-* (*CTH* 626). Since only one text reveals the name of its scribe,[36] the focus of the following discussion concerns itself with the question of how many scribes wrote the tablets with the Ziparwa festivals. The basis of this analysis are NS texts that are preserved well enough to deliver a reliable presentation of sign forms. For *CTH* 610, the parts of the AN.DAḪ.ŠUM festival devoted to Ziparwa, nine texts fulfilled this requirement, also including *CTH* 750.2, which describes an independent Ziparwa festival but is closely related to the texts of *CTH* 610 (see above). A table for internal use was created that contains 38 signs,[37] among them diagnostic signs like DA, LI, and URU, but also signs that exhibit specific forms, including É, EGIR, LUGAL or Ú. The diagnostic signs taken from this table[38] (Fig. 18) indicate that KUB 41.26+ (*CTH* 750.2) presents the youngest of the chosen texts (see DA, EN, ḪA, and UN): it does not yet show the youngest variant of KI with two verticals, which is not attested in any of the Palaic texts. With additional help offered by the names of Piḫawalwi and Palluwaraziti, the scribes mentioned in its colophon, KUB 41.26+ can be dated to the realm of Tutḫaliya IV (Gordin 2015: 209–13, esp. 212). KUB 20.8 also exhibits the youngest variants of DA and ḪA, but it does not provide

282) criteria. See also Kloekhorst and Waal 2019: 189, who understood the texts KBo 3.22, KBo 22.1, KBo 22.2, and KBo 17.21+ as comprising a specific group of texts owing to their "physical features (notably their 'cushion-shape'), paleography and spelling conventions", which "may originally stem from elsewhere, predating the establishment of Ḫattuša as the Hittite capital". Klinger 2022: 312–15, on the other side, points to more heterogeneity of this "group". I was not able to see a difference in sign forms of KBo 3.22 or KBo 22.2 (cf. de Martino 2022: 206f.) to other texts found at Ḫattuša. Cf. also Neu 1980: XV–XVII concerning arguments for his text compilation in StBoT 25.

36 KUB 20.8 (*CTH* 610.8), a very fragmentary text that reports the end of the AN.DAḪ.ŠUM festival of Ziparwa and the following AN.DAḪ.ŠUM festival of the Sun-goddess of the Earth, contains the name of the scribe Ḫapatiwalwi, son of Tuwatziti. Cf. below.

37 Because of its size, the table is not printed here.

38 See Weeden 2011: 44 and Gordin 2015: 91 for diagnostic signs of Hittite Empire times and further literature. Not all signs are attested in the Palaic texts of *CTH* 610.

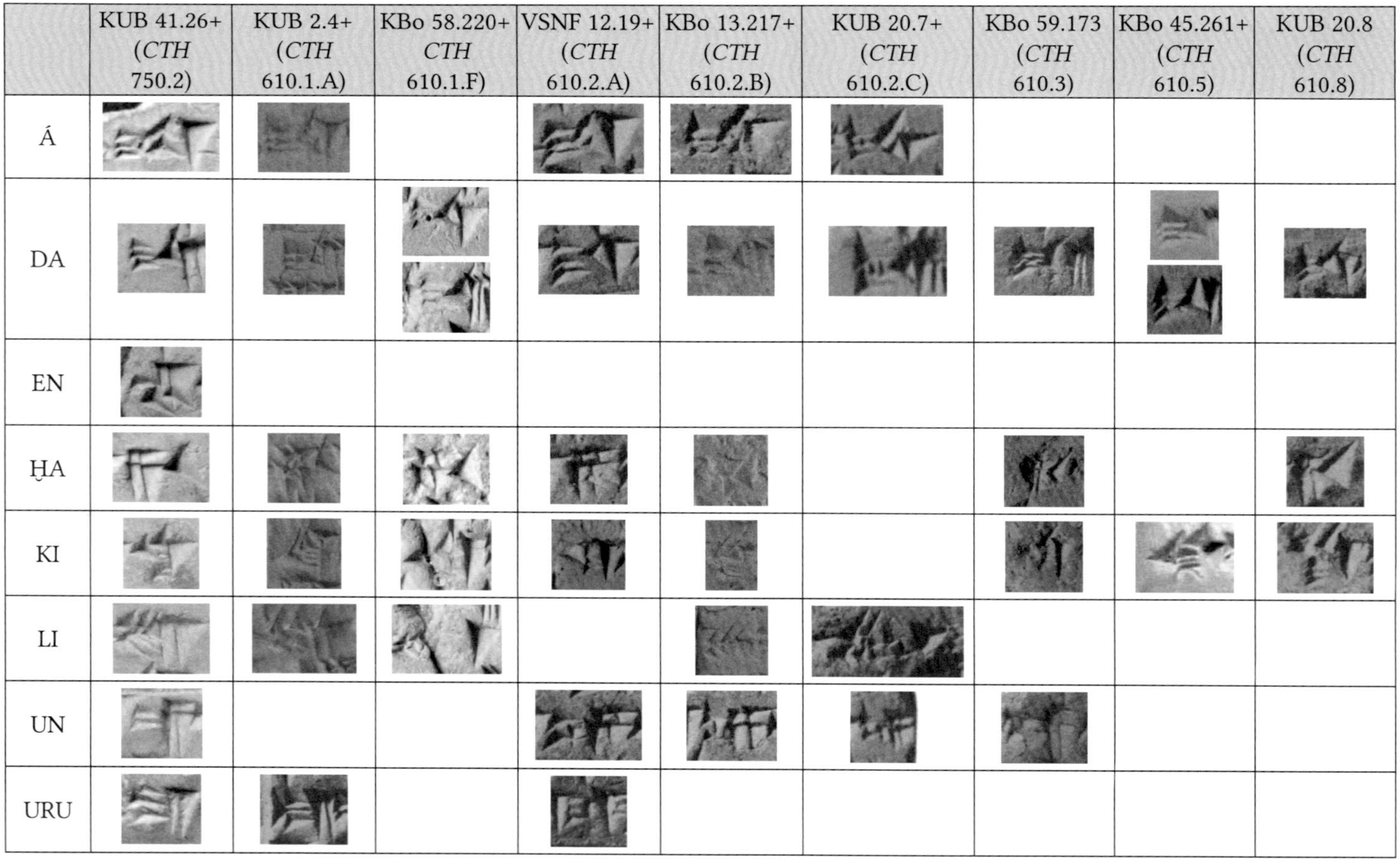

Fig. 18. Diagnostic signs of *CTH* 610.

more diagnostic signs. Here, too, the name of the scribe, Ḫapatiwalwi, son of Tuwatziti, who wrote under the supervision of Anuwanza, hints at a date of the writing of this text at some point from the later reign of Ḫattušili III and through the reign of Tutḫaliya IV (Gordin 2015: 193). It also becomes clear that the existence of a young ḪA does not necessarily label a text as LNS, as demonstrated by the texts KUB 41.26+ (*CTH* 750.2) and KUB 20.8 (*CTH* 610.8), which both exhibit the youngest form of ḪA, but not of KI. The other texts of Fig. 18 all show NS IIIb signs, with only KBo 58.220+, KUB 20.7+ and VSNF 12.19 + KBo 58.222 showing IIIa variants of LI, respectively URU. These three texts therefore may be slightly older than the others, though all still belong to the NS IIIb phase, which means a later NS, but not yet the latest phase, LNS. By comparing the diagnostic signs one can propose the following chronological order of the nine texts within NS IIIb: The three texts *CTH* 610.1.F, *CTH* 610.2.A, and *CTH* 610.2.C seem to be paleographically older than the four texts *CTH* 610.1.A, *CTH* 610.2.B, *CTH* 610.3, and *CTH* 610.5. The texts *CTH* 610.8 and *CTH* 750.2 are presumably the youngest of the nine texts.

A second list selected from the large internal *CTH* 610 table collects signs, also from smaller fragments, which include a significant form that may allow to attribute fragments to one scribe. Particularly noteworthy in this regard is a comparison of the signs É, LUGAL, and RA (Fig. 19), which reveals the possibility of distinguishing individual handwritings. Such an undertaking reveals similar forms of the sign É in *CTH* 610.1.A and *CTH* 610.2.B or in *CTH* 610.1.C, *CTH* 610.2.A, and *CTH* 610.2.R; or comparable variants of the sign RA in *CTH* 610.1.C and *CTH* 610.1.O or in *CTH* 610.1.D and *CTH* 610.1.G. It thus seems likely that a couple of scribes wrote more than one manuscript of the spring Ziparwa festival.

A similar examination was undertaken for the festivities for the god Ziparwa during the *nuntarriyašḫa-* festival in fall. The texts of this festival are not as well preserved as those of the spring festival, so that the internal sign list with the most important signs, for analyzing both dating and handwriting, consists only of six texts. The paleographic analysis is thus based on fewer texts and signs, which may compromise the reliability of the following statements. The table of the diagnostic signs selected from the internal table (Fig. 21) demonstrates that KBo 66.287+ (*CTH* 626-Ziparwa.0.A) seems to be the youngest manuscript, still not showing the youngest form of KI, but already the younger LI, ḪA, DA, and Á;[39] the other manuscripts still exhibit an older LI, ḪA, DA, and Á and therefore may be slightly older.

A broader comparison of the signs LUGAL and RA (Fig. 20) suggests that one scribe wrote Lewis 2 (*CTH* 626-Ziparwa.1.I) and KBo 59.172+ (*CTH* 626-Ziparwa.2.A). The variants of RA and É in *CTH* 626-Ziparwa.4 and *CTH* 626-Ziparwa.5 may also originate from the same hand. *CTH* 626-Ziparwa.0.B, *CTH* 626-Ziparwa.1.A, and *CTH* 626-Ziparwa.1.E – and maybe *CTH* 626-Ziparwa.9 – show a similar variant of É, which was also found in two texts from the AN.DAḪ.ŠUM festival, *CTH* 610.1.A and *CTH* 610.2.B. For the Ziparwa parts of the *nuntarriyašḫa-* festival, too, some tablets appear to have been written by the same scribe, and one of these likely also wrote some of the Ziparwa parts of the spring festival. For both festivals, the comparison of the signs É, LUGAL, and RA

39 Another text of comparable dating seems to be CHDS 6.194 (*CTH* 626-Ziparwa.4) which shows young DA, Á, KI and ḪA, but also not the youngest variant of KI.

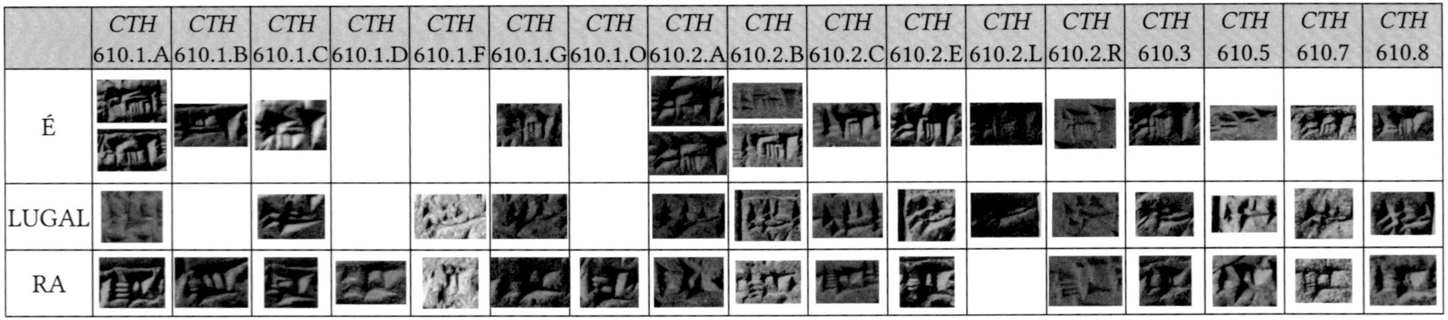

Fig. 19. Selected signs of *CTH* 610. See Appendix 1 for the texts of each *CTH* number.

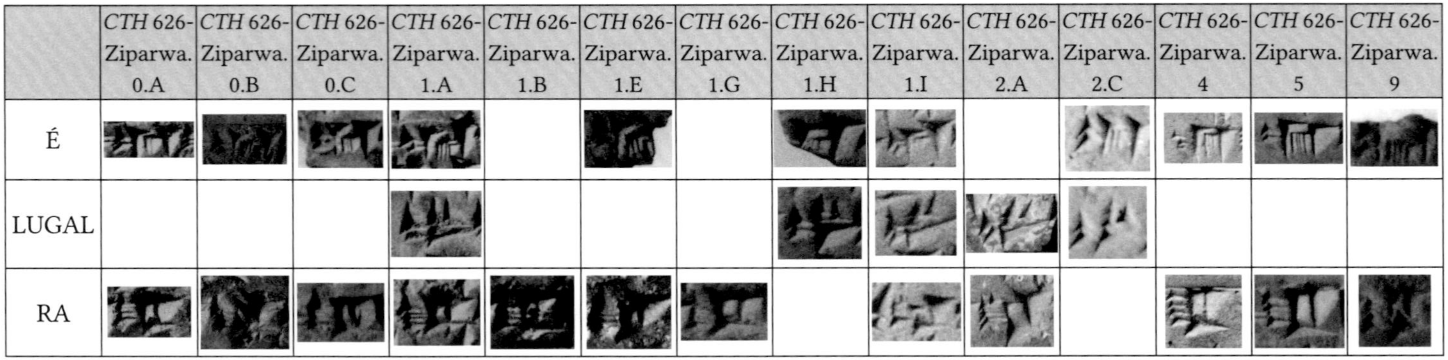

Fig. 20. Selected signs of the Ziparwa texts of *CTH* 626-Ziparwa. See Appendix 2 for the texts of each *CTH* number.

	KBo 66.287+ (*CTH* 626-Ziparwa.0.A)	KBo 59.176 (*CTH* 626-Ziparwa.0.B)	KBo 34.162 (*CTH* 626-Ziparwa.0.C)	IBoT 2.71+ (*CTH* 626-Ziparwa.1.A)	KBo 59.172+ (*CTH* 626-Ziparwa.2.A)	KBo 22.177 (*CTH* 626-Ziparwa.2.C)
Á						
DA						
EN						
ḪA	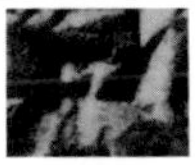					
KI						
LI	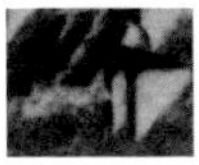			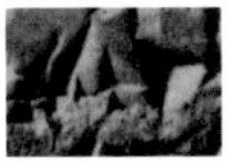		
UN						

Fig. 21. Diagnostic signs of the Ziparwa texts of *CTH* 626-Ziparwa.

in combination with other diagnostic features was fruitful for the detection of common scribal hands. Nevertheless, it also became clear that several contemporaneous scribes were in charge of Ziparwa's AN.DAḪ.ŠUM and *nuntarriyašḫa-* festivals.[40]

Conclusions

In sum, the analysis of the paleography of the Palaic texts was meager. For the roughly twenty OH texts selected, which represent different text genres (mainly religious and historical texts), no attribution of two texts to the same scribe was possible. The procedure presented here also demonstrated that the question of an internal sequence of the OH texts appears difficult to answer; at the very least, a much more systematic examination is needed, not only of sign forms but also of visual aspects of the tablets, spelling conventions, tradition, genre and other considerations. One also has to keep in mind that only one OH fragment, the so-called Zukraši text, was found in an archaeologically defined OH layer. All other texts were attributed to this period for more or less obvious reasons: their similar appearance, shape, or the like. The previously undertaken

40 See already Gordin 2015: 352f. with a conclusion of the work of scribal circles on festivals and chapter 6 with sections on manuscripts that can be attributed to a specific scribe.

chronological ordering of texts according to physical features, spelling conventions, or criteria of content (cf. note 35 above) as well as the assumption of the development of sign forms should thus be critically reviewed. Such a review should also include all OS manuscripts. Moreover, considerations of influence of other written traditions, text genre, and scribal habits must play a role in future investigations of these matters.

Concerning the Ziparwa fragments of the itinerant state festivals AN.DAḪ.ŠUM and *nuntarriyašḫa-*, the results are likewise meager. Some signs, especially É, LUGAL and RA, seem to be useful in identifying similar handwritings. A special form of É, which occurs in texts belonging to the AN.DAḪ.ŠUM and *nuntarriyašḫa-* festivals, may hint at common scribes of both festivals. This is not surprising, since the scribes Palluwaraziti and Piḫawalwi were responsible for several festivals, among them the Ziparwa text *CTH* 750.2.[41]

The work with the tablets' photos and especially the fragmentary state of most tablets also factors in the limit of reliable conclusions. An example of which is KBo 13.217+ (*CTH* 610.2.B), which reveals two shapes of the sign NA: one variant shows one *Winkelhaken* above the other (Fig. 22), the other one exhibits the two *Winkelhaken* following each other (Fig. 23).

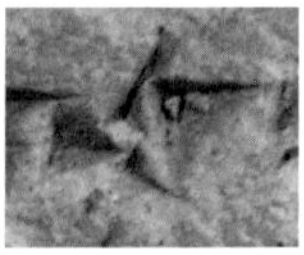

Fig. 22. The sign NA with the two *Winkelhaken* one upon the other.

Fig. 23. The sign NA with the two *Winkelhaken* following each other.

Whereas on the preserved parts of the obverse only the first version of NA appears, the reverse attests this version only in *A+NA* and *šu-un-na-a-i*; for all other evidence the second version appears (see Fig. 24). Different versions of signs are therefore used by one scribe on one tablet, which complicates the classification of fragments to one tablet.

Fig. 24. KBo 13.217+ rev. (section) with two different NA signs marked by circle and rectangle.

41 Gordin 2015: 209 mentions, among others, AN.DAḪ.ŠUM, KI.LAM, a winter festival, and a listing of Hurrian deities in festivals.

A paleographic study of a corpus like the Palaic festivals by the mere examination of signs, devoid of almost any historical hint and comprised of a very fragmented inventory leads to unsatisfying results. It is hoped that a computer-based analysis will be able to recognize and arrange signs in a superior manner, providing a larger basis for sign forms. This then may lead to a more reliable statement in the future on whether or not two or more texts were composed by the same scribe.

Appendices

Appendix 1. Texts belonging to Ziparwa's festivities during the AN.DAḪ.ŠUM *festival (CTH 610).*

CTH 610.1:

A	KUB 2.4 (+) KUB 51.24 + DBH 46/2.170 + DBH 46/2.168
B	KBo 44.197 + IBoT 2.38 (+) HT 83 (+) IBoT 2.37 (+) Bo 5273
C	KBo 51.219 + Bo 3398
D	KBo 54.228
E	KBo 59.174
F	KBo 58.220 + KUB 41.39
G	KBo 48.65 (+) KBo 64.177 (+) KBo 27.48
H	KBo 53.220
I	IBoT 4.299
J	Bo 9302
K	KBo 53.163
L	KBo 48.161
M	KBo 58.221
N	CHDS 5.152
O	KUB 58.44
P	KBo 56.195
Q	KBo 61.74

CTH 610.2:

A	KBo 58.222 (+) KBo 59.175 (+) VSNF 12.19
B	KBo 13.217 + KBo 45.262 (+) KBo 45.116 (+) VSNF 12.21 + KUB 10.64 + KUB 10.34
C	IBoT 4.114 + KUB 20.72 + CHDS 4.232 + Bo 8893
D	Bo 5043
E	CHDS 4.53
F	KBo 60.220
G	KBo 67.122
H	KBo 61.223
I	ABoT 2.73
J	HT 62
K	KBo 43.126

	L	KUB 10.46
	M	KBo 66.142
	O	KBo 63.103
	P	Bo 6042
	Q	Bo 6733
	R	KBo 59.171 + KBo 67.270
	S	Bo 5952
CTH 610.3:		
	A	KBo 59.173
CTH 610.4:		
	A	KBo 60.219
CTH 610.5		
	A	KBo 45.261 + KBo 13.215
CTH 610.6:		
	A	Bo 4258
CTH 610.7:		
	A	KUB 44.40
CTH 610.8:		
	A	KUB 20.8

Appendix 2. Text belonging to Ziparwa's festivities during the nuntarriyašḫa- *festival (CTH 626-Ziparwa).*

CTH 626-Ziparwa.0:		
	A	KBo 66.287 + Bo 5139
	B	KBo 59.176
	C	KBo 34.162
CTH 626-Ziparwa.1:		
	A	IBoT 2.71 + VSNF 12.20
	B	KUB 25.33
	C	KBo 67.299 + ABoT 2.144
	D	KBo 45.260
	E	KBo 45.259 + KUB 20.56
	F	KBo 60.189
	G	IBoT 4.113
	H	KUB 20.82
	I	Lewis 2
	J	KBo 14.78
CTH 626-Ziparwa.2:		
	A	KBo 59.172 + KBo 64.178 + KBo 59.177
	B	KBo 49.296

C	KBo 22.177
D	Bo 3434

CTH 626-Ziparwa.3:

A	KUB 10.36
B	KBo 61.192
C	Bo 4163

CTH 626-Ziparwa.4:

A	CHDS 6.194

CTH 626-Ziparwa.5:

A	VSNF 12.114

CTH 626-Ziparwa.6:

A	KBo 13.266 + KBo 56.92
B	Bo 9099

CTH 626-Ziparwa.7:

A	Bo 6057

CTH 626-Ziparwa.8:

A	KBo 71.160

CTH 626-Ziparwa.9:

A	KBo 53.129

CTH 626-Ziparwa.10:

A	KBo 44.159

Bibliography

Cammarosano, Michele, Gerfrid G.W. Müller, Denis Fisseler, and Frank Weichert
2014 Schriftmetrologie des Keils. Dreidimensionale Analyse von Keileindrücken und Handschriften. *WdO* 44: 2–36.

de Martino, Stefano
2022 Hatti: From Regional Polity ot Empire. In: Stefano de Martino (ed.), *Handbook Hittite Empire. Power Structures.* Empires through the Ages in Global Perspective 1. Berlin / Boston: de Gruyter Oldenburg, 205–270.

Devecchi, Elena, Gerfrid G.W. Müller, and Jana Mynářová (eds.)
2015 *Current Research in Cuneiform Palaeography. Proceedings of the Workshop organised at the 60th Rencontre Assyriologique Internationale, Warsaw 2014.* Gladbeck: PeWe.
2019 *Current Research in Cuneiform Palaeography 2. Proceedings of the Workshop organised at the 64th Rencontre Assyriologique Internationale, Innsbruck 2018.* Gladbeck: PeWe.

Görke, Susanne

2024a AN.DAḪ.ŠUM: Tag 12, der erste Tag des Festes für Ziparwa und seinen Kreis. hethiter.net/: CTH 610.1 (INTR 2024-12-17) – last accessed 07.01.2025.

2024b *nuntarriyašḫa-*: Festbeschreibungen für Ziparwa und seinen Kreis. hethiter.net/: CTH 626-Ziparwa (INTR 2024-10-01) – last accessed 07.01.2025.

Görke, Susanne and David Sasseville (eds.)

2024a Ein althethitisches Festritual für das palaische Pantheon. hethiter.net/: *CTH* 750.1 (TX 2024-01-14; TRde 2023-11-03) – last accessed 01.07.2024.

2024b Tafeln mit palaischen Rezitationen für Brot-, Fleisch- und Getränkeopferungen an palaische Götter. hethiter.net/: *CTH* 751 (INTR 2024-02-05) – last accessed 01.07.2024.

2024c Palaische Rezitationen anlässlich der Opferung von Brot, Fleisch und Getränken. hethiter.net/: *CTH* 751.1 (TX 2024-01-16; TRde 2024-01-24) – last accessed 01.07.2024.

Gordin, Shai

2015 *Hittite Scribal Circles. Scholarly Tradition and Writing Habits.* StBoT 59. Wiesbaden: Harrassowitz.

Klinger, Jörg

2022 Zu den Anfängen der hethitischen Überlieferung überhaupt und zur Methode der paläographischen Textdatierung In: Eva Cancik-Kirschbaum and Ingo Schrakamp (eds.), *Transfer, Adaption und Neukonfigurierung von Schrift- und Sprachwissen im Alten Orient.* Episteme in Bewegung 25. Wiesbaden: Harrassowitz, 255–340.

Kloekhorst, Alwin and Willemijn Waal

2019 A Hittite Scribal Tradition Predating the Tablet Collections of Ḫattuša? The origin of the 'cushion-shaped' tablets KBo 3.22, KBo 17.21+, KBo 22.1, and KBo 22.2. *ZA* 109: 189–203.

Košak, Silvin

2002– *Konkordanz der hethitischen Keilschrifttafeln, Online-Datenbank Version.* hethiter.net/: hetkonk (2.plus) – last accessed 01.02.2024.

Kryszeń, Adam

in press The Outline Tablets of the *nuntarriyašḫa-* Festival. A Reappraisal. *ZA*.

Müller, Gerfrid G.W.

2014 Forensik und Fragmente. In: Piotr Taracha (ed.), *Proceedings of the Eighth International Congress of Hittitology. Warsaw, 5–9 September 2011.* Warsaw: Agade, 588–600.

2016 Auf der Suche nach dem Schreiberprofil. In: Šárka Velhartická (ed.), *Audias fabulas veteres. Anatolian Studies in Honor of Jana Součková-Siegelová.* CHANE 79. Leiden / Boston: Brill, 257–75.

Müller, Gerfrid G.W. and Reinhard Pirngruber
2019 Identifying Cuneiform Handwritings: a Case Study from the Late Babylonian Eanna Archive from Uruk. In: Elena Devecchi, Gerfrid G.W. Müller, and Jana Mynářová (eds.), *Current Research in Cuneiform Palaeography 2. Proceedings of the Workshop organised at the 64th Rencontre Assyriologique Internationale, Innsbruck 2018.* Gladbeck: PeWe, 177–210.

Neu, Erich
1980 *Althethitische Ritualtexte in Umschrift.* StBoT 25. Wiesbaden: Harrassowitz.

Steitler, Charles W.
2023 Solar and Chthonic Deities in Ancient Anatolia: The Evolution of the Chthonic Solar Deity in Hittite Religion. In: Livio Varbinek and Federico Giusfredi (eds.), *Theonyms, Panthea and Syncretisms in Hittite Anatolia and Northern Syria.* StAs 14. Firenze: Firenze University Press, 149–79.

van den Hout, Theo P.J.
2012 The Ductus of the Alalaḫ VII Texts and the Origin of Hittite Cuneiform. In: Elena Devecchi (ed.), *Palaeography and Scribal Practices in Syro-Palestine and Anatolia in the Late Bronze Age. Papers read at a Symposium in Leiden, 17–18 December 2009.* PIHANS 119. Leiden: Nederlands Instituut voor het Nabije Oosten, 147–70.

Weeden, Mark
2011 *Hittite Logograms and Hittite Scholarship.* StBoT 54. Wiesbaden: Harrassowitz.

Yakubovich, Ilya and Alice Mouton
2023 *Luwili. Hittite-Luwian Ritual Texts Attributed to Puriyanni, Kuwatalla and Šilalluḫi (CTH 758–763). Volume II: Discussion and Glossary.* StBoT 72,2. Wiesbaden: Harrassowitz.

MATTERS OF GENRE, STYLE, AND ORTHOGRAPHY

Hittite Scribal Habits through the Stylometric Lens

*Shai Gordin**
Ariel University / Open University of Israel

Emma Yavasan
Ariel University

Avital Romach
Yale University

Abstract

This paper explores the application of stylometric methods to analyze authorship and textual traditions in the Hittite festival ritual corpus, specifically focusing on Hurrian and Luwian festival texts. Using a dataset of approximately 1,000 texts from 27 *CTH* (Catalogue of Hittite Texts) groups, we employed computational methods, particularly *tf-idf* (term frequency-inverse document frequency) and t-SNE visualization, to measure textual similarities and relationships. A detailed case study of *CTH* 701 (rituals performed by the AZU priest) demonstrated how computational analysis can complement traditional philological work. By examining shared tokens between manuscripts, we identified patterns in scribal practices and textual transmission. The study showcases how quantitative methods can provide new perspectives on ancient texts, allowing scholars to test hypotheses about style and authorship on both macro and micro scales. This approach, combining philological and data science methods, opens new possibilities for understanding textual relationships and scribal practices in ancient Anatolia. The research benefited from the machine-readable corpus provided by the *Hethitische Festrituale* (HFR) project, demonstrating the value of digital humanities initiatives in ancient studies.

1. Translating textual criticism into measurable metrics?

The issue of authorship and textual tradition in cuneiform texts is a complex matter of contention (Foster 1991; 2019; Helle 2019). We wish to lay out the potential of applying stylometry, a series of established mathematical and statistical metrics (Juola 2008), to address these issues in the Hittite cuneiform corpus. The main application of this

* The authors contributed to this work as follows: *Sh.G.* designed the study, analysed and interpreted the results of the computational analysis, and wrote the text; *E.Y.* pre-processed the texts for computational analysis and wrote the code; *A.R.* designed the experiments, wrote the code of the machine learning analysis, and wrote the methodological sections. The code for stylometric analysis of ancient cuneiform texts (and ancient Egyptian) written by *A.R.* is available at the GitHub of the *Ancient Language Processing* course of Shai Gordin and Eliese-Sophia Lincke at https://github.com/DigitalPasts/ALP-course/tree/master/course_notebooks under “05_Vector_Space_Model.”. Data is available on Zenodo, see Yavasan and Gordin 2024.

method will be through *telescopic* and *microscopic* readings of meaningful clusters of the text corpus, teased out using statistical and probabilistic methods. We focus on the Hittite festival ritual texts, now fully machine readable as part of the HFR *Basiscorpus* (https://www.hethport.uni-wuerzburg.de/HFR/). These provide a unique opportunity to create a baseline for a hypothesis testing open questions of authorship by using quantifiable measures.[1] This type of operationalization (Moretti 2013) is one way to transform abstract writing habits (*Schreibgewohnheiten*) into a set of quantitatively and qualitatively explorable latent features. Could these features reveal new patterns of style, scribal voice, or even authorship?

Consider the classification of the Hurrian-Hittite festival ritual traditions, which are known to have derived from a large geographical area: mostly Kizzuwatna in southeastern Anatolia, but also northern Syria and upper Mesopotamia (Klinger 2001; Miller 2006; Gilan 2019; Trameri 2020; Görke 2022; Bastici 2024). In a recent article, Susanne Görke analysed the admixture of Hurrian and Luwian elements in rituals and festivals of the Kizzuwatnean tradition, and concluded that at least for the case of the festivals, Hurrian was dominant (Görke 2022: 155). Searching for this hybrid Kizzuwatna cultic tradition, her study laid out a good definition of the division between two festival groups, the larger Hurrian one and the one from Luwian cultic centres. While the particularities of the former are only beginning to be better understood (Kaynar 2019; Trameri 2020; Bastici 2024), the characteristics of the latter group were elucidated thanks to the identification of four different Luwian dialects. One of the main dialects in this group, the Luwian of Kizzuwatna and the Lower Land, shows evidence of a strong Hurrian influence, but also of the Luwian dialect of Empire Period Ḫattuša (Giusfredi et al. 2023: 377–80; Yakubovich and Mouton 2023: 1–28; Yakubovich in Giusfredi et al. 2023: 284–312).

We witness a similar situation in Ḫattuša, in which two large scribal circles, one led by a supervisor named Anuwanza and the other by a chief scribe known as Walwaziti, alongside smaller related scribal families, show invested interest in different Hurrian and Luwian cultic and ritual traditions. Partly perpetuated by the royal court, these scribes exhibit a mix of writing habits incorporating both contemporary and earlier scribal traditions, some of which can be traced back to the 15th and 14th centuries BCE (Gordin 2014; 2015: 109–15, 351–55). By the mid-13th century, the compositions themselves were already a fusion of different traditions, and unlike most cuneiform writing centres across Syro-Mesopotamia, Hittite scribes attempt to systematically record the named authors of many compositions, especially rituals and festivals, adding their title, and often geographical designation (Miller 2004: 488–92; Dardano 2006: 358–62; Gordin 2015: 113–22).

It would, therefore, make good sense to look into the question of authorship of the Hurrian-Luwian festival tradition, since a coherent corpus can be ascertained and linked to different scribal circles and authorial voices.

1 We wish to thank Daniel Schwemer and Gerfrid Müller who provided early access to the XML files, and also express our appreciation to all the contributors to the project whose work allowed this study (https://www.hethport.uni-wuerzburg.de/HFR/bascorp_intro.php). All texts in the HFR corpus and the larger *Thesaurus Linguarum Hethaeorum digitalis* (TLH[dig]: https://www.hethport.uni-wuerzburg.de/TLHdig/) are made available under a CC BY-SA 4.0 license (https://creativecommons.org/licenses/by-sa/4.0/).

2. Measuring the degree of similarity between Hurrian and Luwian festivals

This paper presents our work in progress to view this corpus from a quantitative perspective. We measured the degree of similarity between the two festival groups, made up of a thousand texts in 27 of Laroche's *CTH* groups, categorised in the online *Catalogue of Hittite Texts* (*CTH*; Košak et al. 2022) under five different overarching designations:

- Various festivals – two *CTH* groups: the large Kizzuwatna *ḫišuwa*- festival (*CTH* 628) and festivals involving the *ašuša(tal)la*- men (*CTH* 665);
- Cult of Ḫuwaššanna of Ḫubešna in the Lower Land (*CTH* 690–694);
- Cults concerning Teššub and Ḫebat (*CTH* 698–701, 704–706);
- Cults of Ištar/Šawuška (*CTH* 711–715, 719–722);
- Luwian festival texts related to Ištanuwa and Lallupiya (*CTH* 770–773).

Fig. 1 shows the relative distances between Hurrian and Luwian festivals. These distances were calculated based on ca. 90,000 words that appear in this textual corpus – the more words two *CTH* groups have in common, the closer together they appear. Imagine this as a galaxy of the Hurrian and Luwian Festival texts, where there are three clear "constellations" of textual groups, marked with different colours and trend lines. On the left hand side (constellation **L** in red), mostly the Hurrian cultic festivals of Teššub and Ḫebat, derived from Syria and Kizzuwatna; in the middle (constellation **M** in orange), primarily Luwian cult including Ḫuwaššanna texts and the festivals involving the *ašuša(tal)la*- men; and on the right (constellation **R** in yellow), primarily the Kizzuwatnean and Syro-Mesopotamian cult of Ištar, but also the large group of rituals

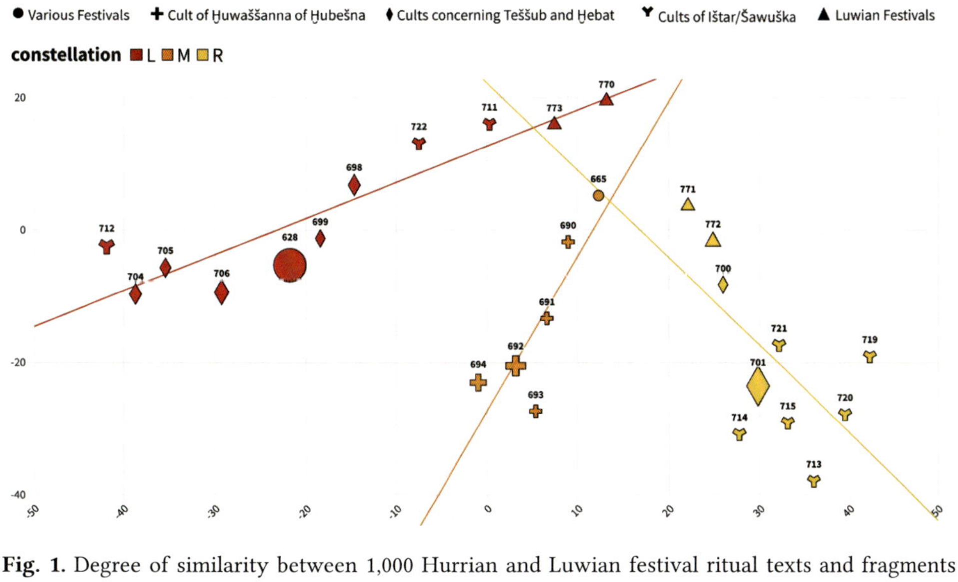

Fig. 1. Degree of similarity between 1,000 Hurrian and Luwian festival ritual texts and fragments measured on word's *tf-idf* score using cosine similarity. Visualisation method is a t-SNE in which each point is a *CTH* group.

performed by the AZU priest. Each dot is sized according to the number of words which appear in all of its *CTH* manuscripts combined.

In what follows, we first introduce the methods used to create these visualisations. Then, we bring some examples on how such visualisations can be used as a guide for exploring the corpus. The main benefit we currently see from this approach is the ability to start from a telescopic view of the entire corpus at once, and then look at the specific details through the microscope, instead of starting from the details without knowing your surroundings and without the ability to know which details will be most indicative as you continue your exploration.

3. On methodology, or, is there text in my data?

The key to using quantifiable metrics on texts is transforming the texts into meaningful numbers. In the approach presented here, we use a method called *tf-idf*, short for 'term frequency-inverse document frequency', which is common in computational textual studies (Eder 2015; Piasecki et al. 2018; Hay et al. 2020). Simply put, it calculates each term's frequency in a document and in the corpus at large, resulting in a unique number for each term in each document (see Fig. 2). Then, each document is represented by the sequence of *tf-idf* frequencies of the terms it contains (Table 1). Once each document is represented in numerical form, a form that preserves the textual information within it, we can calculate distances between the numerical sequences, and identify which specific terms in the sequences make a pair of documents similar or dissimilar.

$$\mathrm{TF} = \frac{\text{Number of times term A appears in a document}}{\text{Number of words in the document}}$$

$$\mathrm{IDF} = \log\left(\frac{\text{Number of documents in the corpus}}{\text{Number of documents in which term A appears}}\right)$$

$$\text{TF-IDF} = \mathrm{TF} \times \mathrm{IDF}$$

Fig. 2. Term frequency-inverse document frequency (*tf-idf*) formula.

txtid	SIR-*RU*	NINDA.GUR$_4$.RA	GEŠTIN	EGIR-*ŠU-ma*	*našta*
KBo 55.237	0.04131930081	0.1625620516	0.0771293682	0.04124245115	0
KBo 38.23	0	0.1331010182	0	0.6753620773	0.1113998389
KBo 38.22	0	0.09621348785	0.09129911264	0.09763853331	0
KBo 35.262+	0.02219653527	0	0.04143353609	0.04431050398	0.01827235778

Table 1. Sample of term (e. g. word) frequencies within a set of documents in the corpus. The terms are left unparsed to represent how they are processed in our algorithms.

We purposefully say terms and not words, because terms can be either words, or sequences of characters – in our case, sequences of Unicode cuneiform characters, of a length of our choosing – one, two, three, or more characters (Table 2).[2]

2 A sequence of *n* adjacent symbols in a particular order is also known as *n*-grams, made popular through Google Ngram Viewer (https://books.google.com/ngrams/) and their potential for looking into large cultural trends over time (Michel et al. 2011).

txtid	[illegible]	[illegible]	[illegible]	[illegible]
KUB 32.128+	0.04277045364	0	0.01999039089	0.02223670433
KUB 10.63	0.02248340921	0.01162908942	0.0180145244	0
KUB 27.6	0.005318284137	0	0.01597950934	0.03318022658
KBo 29.204+	0.02091267571	0.009013882695	0.01047249728	0

Table 2. Sample of n-grams (e. g. Unicode) frequencies within a set of documents in the corpus.

For our present purposes, however, we focus on using words as tokens. The tokenization process employed the normalizations of Hittite words, as much as possible, and as many normalizations as were available in the HFR Basic Corpus. We also removed texts that had less than 17 words preserved before tokenization, as such fragmented texts are hard to attribute stylistically with or without algorithms. The number 17 was chosen based on the average length of the texts.

After tokenization, there are several ways to visualise relationships between texts. First, we can measure the distance between each text and all the other texts, and visualise it as a matrix (Fig. 3). This, however, is not very helpful in order to explore the corpus from a new perspective. For that we further use t-SNE (t-distributed Stochastic Neighbour Embedding). This is a probabilistic method for taking high-dimensional data and reducing it to 2 or 3 dimensions, so that it can more easily be assessed visually (Leclercq and Kestemont 2021). In our case, each column of the matrix is a dimension – a representation of the distance between a given text and all the other texts – and we can reduce the information from all of those dimensions into two.

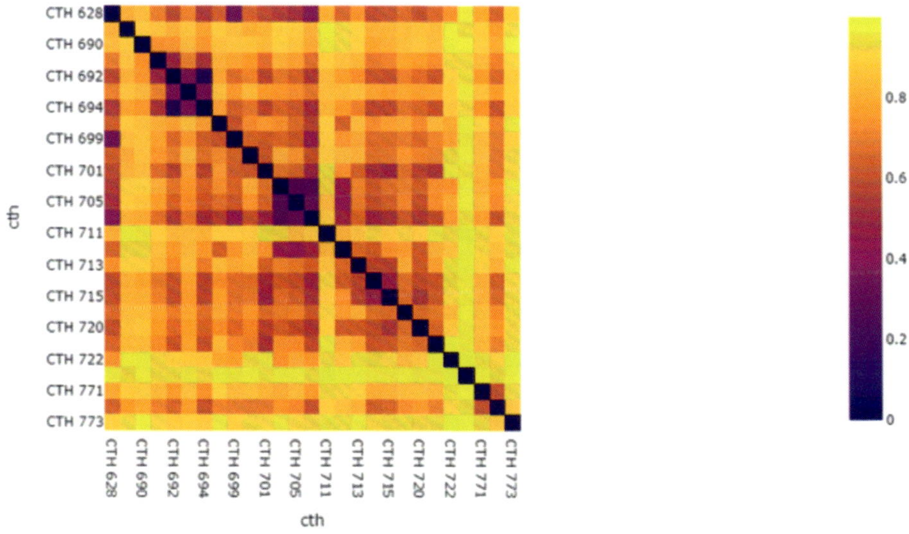

Fig. 3. Distance matrix between the *CTH* groups in our corpus. The lower the score (i. e. in a darker colour), the more similar the two *CTH* groups are. Note that not all *CTH* numbers can be accounted for in this static visualisation.

This is how we created Fig. 1. Before tokenization, we combined the texts of all manuscripts according to their *CTH* number. In essence, we created a big bag-of-words for each *CTH* made up of all its known constituent parts. We then measured the distances between the *CTH* groups by creating a similarity matrix and then running the t-SNE algorithm. This gives a synthesised view of all the textual information each text group contains, as well as its relationship to all of the other texts in the corpus, in one concise visual representation.

4. Quantitative scribal habits at scale: A distant reading of Hurrian and Luwian style

Let us look again at the three constellations. This is a distant view or distant reading of our sources, which is useful for identifying overarching patterns in a corpus. How does it compare with broad Hurrian and/or Luwian textual elements already discussed in previous literature on these hybrid festival traditions? Already Fig. 1 shows that not all the *CTH* categories fall neatly together, but rather some are split across the different constellations. But perhaps the constellations represent the underlying Hurrian and Luwian traditions that have been hard to pinpoint.

Kizzuwatna-Lower Land (Hurrian)	Syro-Mesopotamia (Hurrian)	Luwian cult centres	Mixed (Hurrian, Syrian, Luwian)
CTH 628	*CTH* 698	*CTH* 665	*CTH* 704
CTH 699	*CTH* 701	*CTH* 690	*CTH* 705
CTH 700	*CTH* 714	*CTH* 691	*CTH* 706
CTH 711	*CTH* 715	*CTH* 692	*CTH* 720
CTH 712	*CTH* 721	*CTH* 693	
CTH 713		*CTH* 694	
CTH 719		*CTH* 770	
CTH 722		*CTH* 771	
		CTH 772	
		CTH 773	

Table 3. Schematic division of the Hurrian and Luwian festival traditions based on geographic or cultural internal evidence (following Trameri 2020; Görke 2022; Giusfredi and Pisaniello in Giusfredi et al. 2023: 259–83; Yakubovich in Giusfredi et al. 2023: 284–312; Bastici 2024 and literature cited therein).

Table 3 is a very schematic summarization of previous attribution in research of these *CTH* festival groups into four general geographic and cultural spheres: two Hurrian traditions, that of Kizzuwatna-Lower Land and that of Syro-Mesopotamia, a more distinct Luwian group, and one which has mixed cultic elements. To be clear, there are more ways to organise these groups, for example, linguistically or according to cult administration. Fig. 4 combines the scatter plot of the Hurrian-Luwian festival constellations with the schematic categorization of Table 3. While the Luwian texts are very clearly situated in the middle constellation (constellation **M**), the two Hurrian groups are mixed between the left and right constellations (constellations **L** and **R**, respectively).

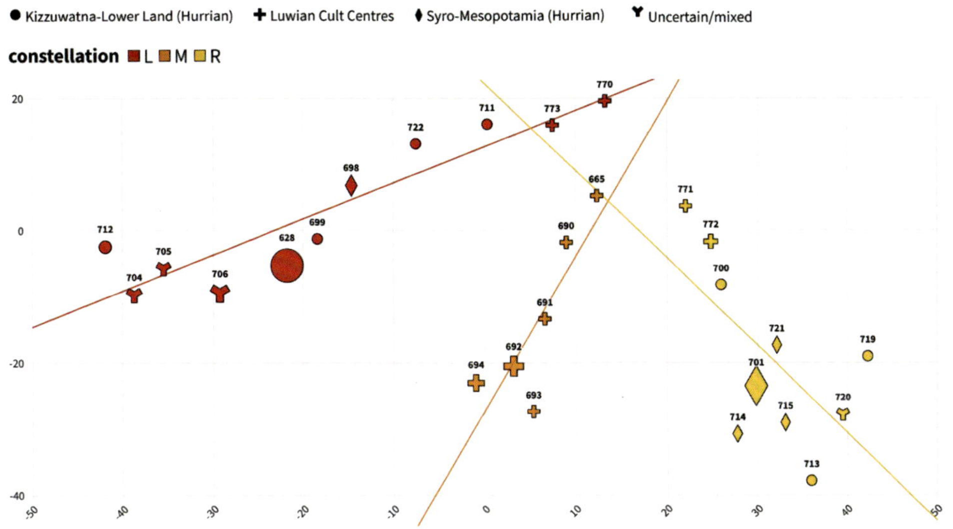

Fig. 4. The same constellations shown in Fig. 1, here shaped according to a schematic overview of previous literature (see Table 3).

To offer a new way to assess the coherence of groups of *CTH* numbers provided by previous research (Table 3), and the coherence of the constellations created based on word similarity, we employ basic counting methods. We measure coherence by checking how many tokens (i. e. how many words) are shared among all the *CTH* numbers in each overarching group. An overarching group includes all the *CTH* manuscripts under a certain constellation, or under one of the groups defined in Table 3. That is to say, we assume that overarching groups that have more shared tokens that are used in all or most of its *CTH* numbers, make for a more holistically defined overarching group.

In Fig. 5, the y-axis is the number of shared tokens. The x-axis represents a percentage threshold of how many of the *CTH* numbers need to contain a given token for it to be counted as a shared token in the overarching group. At 1, i. e. 100%, a given token must be attested in each of the *CTH* numbers under an overarching group for it to be counted as a shared token of that group. Namely, if the same word appears at least once in each of the *CTH* numbers of an overarching group, it is a shared token. At 0.5, i. e. 50%, a token must be attested in half of the *CTH* numbers of an overarching group for it to be counted as a shared token, and so forth. At 0, i. e. 0%, if the token appears in just one *CTH* number of a given overarching group, it is counted as a shared token. Thus, at threshold 0 all groups go back to the maximum number of unique tokens in the corpus (not counting multiple occurrences of the same word), around 14,000.

All groups follow a similar trajectory of rapidly sinking down from threshold 0 to 1. Only a limited number of tokens are shared by an entire group, 100 words or less. Unfortunately, the 'Uncertain/mixed' group is the one that has the most shared tokens in all of its *CTH* manuscripts. Many of the shared tokens remaining at threshold 1 are extremely common words that are not indicative of style.

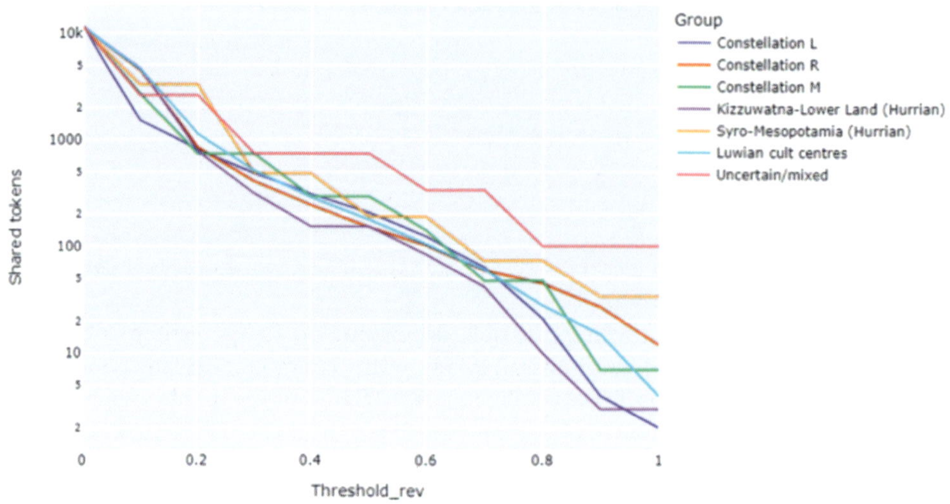

Fig. 5. Number of shared tokens (y-axis) versus the percentage of how many of the *CTH* numbers share them (x-axis). The 1-point is when 100% of the texts share all the tokens, and the 0-point is where there is no limitation as to the number of texts that need to share the tokens.

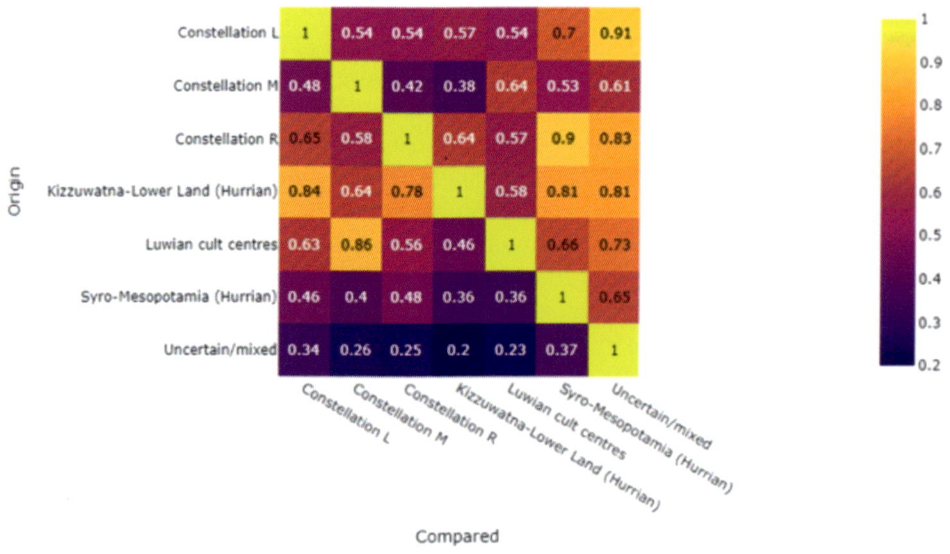

Fig. 6. Heatmap showing the percentage of shared tokens between each overarching groups (both those divided according to cultural and geographical background and the *CTH* constellations). The tokens of each overarching group are those which appear in at least 60% of its *CTH* numbers.

Therefore, we decided to examine this issue with a different lens. We thought of another way to measure coherence: how many of each overarching group's shared tokens are also shared with the other overarching groups? That is to say, we assume that overarching groups that have more shared tokens with other overarching groups are more dependent on those overarching groups, and less coherent as their own overarching group. For this additional test, we needed to decide at which threshold on the x-axis of Fig. 5 we should measure the shared tokens across the overarching groups. As the number of shared tokens amongst all the *CTH* numbers in all the overarching groups is rather low, we decided to test the shared tokens which appear in at least 60% of the texts of each overarching group.

Fig. 6 shows a heatmap of these possible dependencies. The percentage of shared tokens is relative to the number of overall tokens of the overarching groups on the left side of the graph. This means, for example, that 66% of most of the words which appear in the Luwian cult centre texts also appear in the Syro-Mesopotamia Hurrian corpus. However, only 36% of the common tokens in the Syro-Mesopotamia Hurrian corpus also appear in the Luwian cult centre texts. Also striking are the 81% of words in the Kizzuwatna-Lower Land Hurrian group that also appear in the Syro-Mesopotamia corpus and the Uncertain/mixed corpus. However, the flip side is that the Syro-Mesopotamia corpus only shares 36% of its tokens with the Kizzuwatna-Lower Land group. In fact, the **Kizzuwatna-Lower Land group** seems to be overall the most influential source for almost all text groups, except the Luwian cult centre group (compare these results to Trameri 2024: 184, 453f.). Note that it would make sense to consider the state of preservation for the different text fragments in each *CTH* number as another variable alongside the frequency of shared vocabulary.

Can this evidence be indicative of style transfer resulting from scribal practice in Ḫattuša's scholarly circles of copying, editing, and sourcing different manuscripts, some older, others younger, as part of Kizzuwatnean cultic traditions fusing into one another as well as into local Ḫattušan traditions (see already Miller 2004: 256)? In his monograph Trameri (2024: Ch. 8.5.2) brings together all relevant strands of evidence on this editorial process, analysing primarily the "Kizzuwatna rituals" group, dating the initial phase of this scholarly work to the early 14th century BCE (under Tudḫaliya I). Similarly, the quantitative shared tokens within the festival corpus in Fig. 6 agrees with a lack of mixed Hurrian-Luwian linguistic background in Kizzuwatna itself, rather suggesting that this mixed environment were the *scriptoria* of Ḫattuša in the Early Empire period.

Once measured at scale, we can move to observe these scribal practices and larger editorial patterns even closer, as if each case study, each text, was placed under a microscope.

4. Constellation R: A statistical close reading

We use *CTH* 701 as a case study for a microscopic look at shared tokens. At the epicentre of constellation **R** (Fig. 1) stands *CTH* 701, a conglomerate of compositions, primar-

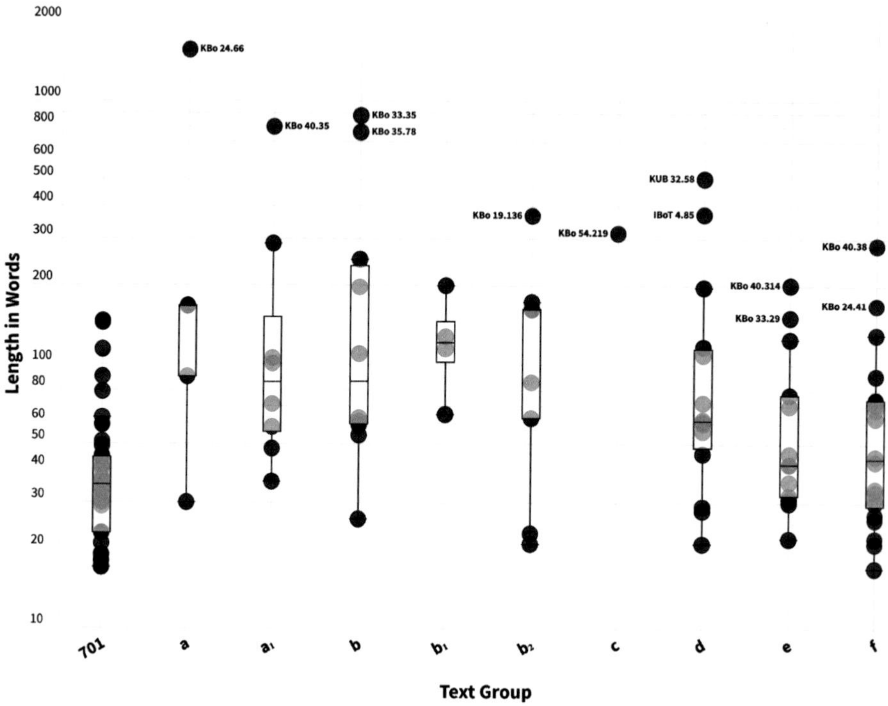

Fig. 7. Distribution of word length in text fragments of each text group in *CTH* 701 (publication names appear only for longer outliers in each group).

ily united through the agency of the performing AZU priest – equivalent of the Babylonian *āšipu* "exorcist" (magical expert). During their ritual performance the priests need to recite in Hurrian, and these recitations are shared in different formulae, either complete or abbreviated, across the different festival rituals (Bawanypeck and Görke 2007). The texts are catalogued in the online *CTH* under the cult of Teššub and Ḫebat. Close in their text similarity to *CTH* 701 are a group of texts related to the cult of Ištar/Šawuška from different cultural centres from Anatolia to Mesopotamia (Giusfredi et al. 2023; Bastici 2024): a MH ritual in Šamuḫa to the Ištar/Šawuška of Tamininga (*CTH* 713), Cilicia near the sea and Tuwanuwa (*CTH* 719),[3] the Amanus mountain range (*CTH* 721), the city of Nineveh (*CTH* 714–715), and many related fragments of the Ištar/Šawuška cult (*CTH* 720).

4.1 CTH 701: Corpus statistics and text groups

The *editio princeps* of Mirjo Salvini and Ilse Wegner identified 105 text fragments, dividing them into six groups marked with the letters *a* to *f*, including sub-numbered letters for hard to classify parallel fragments (Salvini and Wegner 1986):

- *a*: Offering to the throne of Ḫebat
- a_1: Parallel texts to *a*

3 Identified with classical Tyana near Niğde: https://pleiades.stoa.org/places/648801.

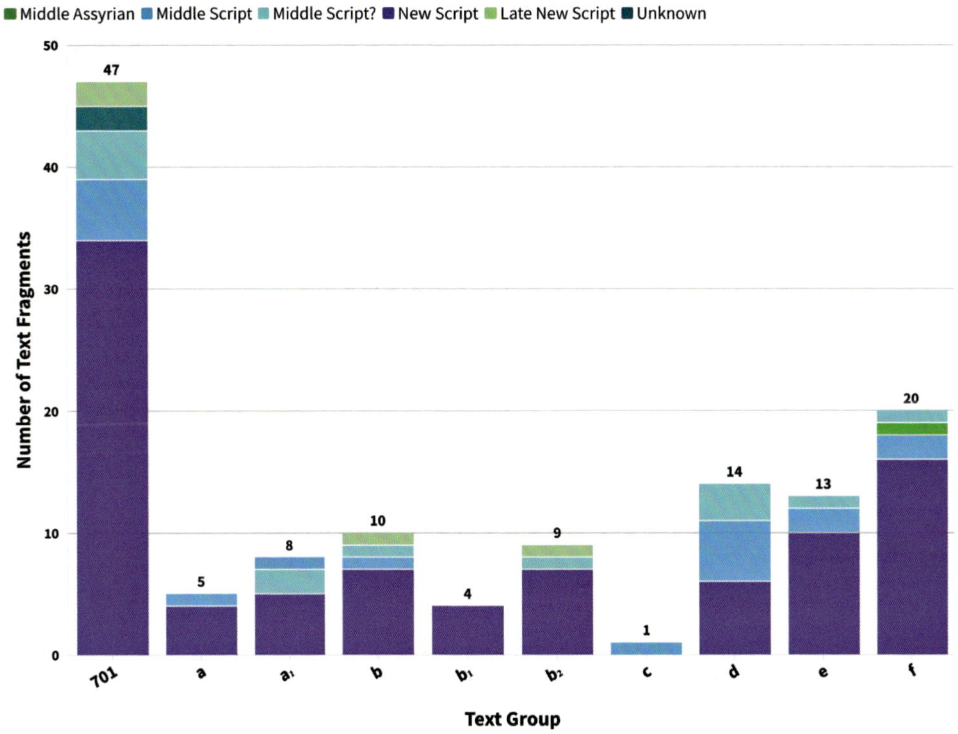

Fig. 8. Corpus statistics for *CTH* 701: number of text fragments in each text group divided according to script.

- *b*: The *šarra* ritual
- b_1: Close parallel to *b*
- b_2: Parallels to *b* and b_1
- *c*: The *allanuwašši* ritual
- *d*: Rituals for Teššub and Šawuška
- *e*: Likely belonging to one of the above-mentioned rituals
- *f*: Uncertain AZU rituals

The updated HFR Basic Corpus identifies 167 texts under *CTH* 701 (HFR-Team 2021). The classification into six groups was kept, adding a general designation for unspecified fragments simply as *CTH* 701. We selected texts that have more than 17 words, which brought down that total number of fragments to 131; a distribution of word length in the remaining fragments can be seen in Fig. 7. About a quarter of the corpus is written in Middle Hittite Script, spread relatively evenly across the text groups. The majority of text fragments, however, are written in New Script (Fig. 8).

4.2 CTH 701 and its shared tokens under the microscope

***CTH* 701.*a* and related texts (word tokens).** Fig. 9 uses the same *tf-idf* and t-SNE methods described above, but on each of the manuscripts of the *CTH* numbers under

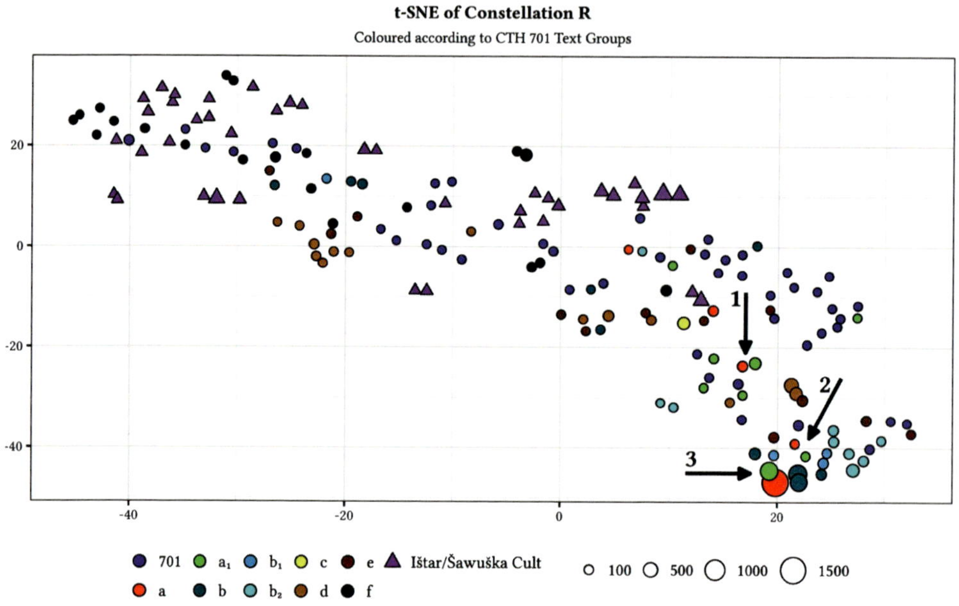

Fig. 9. Degree of similarity within constellation **R** on the word level. The arrows mark the three instances where texts of group *a* are relatively close to a_1 texts.

constellation **R**, which includes *CTH* 701 and the Ištar/Šawuška cult. It reveals a general pattern: most identifiable text groups of *CTH* 701 cluster on the bottom right section of the plot (groups *a–e*), whereas the uncertain group *f* (black circles) together with unclassified 701 fragments (dark purple circles) and Ištar/Šawuška cult texts (purple triangles) cluster on the upper sections of the graph. Let us focus on the bottom right section, and specifically on the manuscripts of group *a* (red circles).

a_1 texts (green circles) are considered by Salvini and Wegner parallel texts that are close to texts of group *a* based on some parallel lines, but cannot be considered content-wise an explicit part of the libation ritual to the throne of Ḫebat (Salvini and Wegner 1986: 7). This is also made apparent by the relatively close proximity of three out of the five fragments of *a* and other a_1 fragments indicating their textual similarity (marked with numbered black arrows in Fig. 9). It should be noted, however, that there seems to be more coherent proximities between the different *b*, b_1, and b_2 fragments, for example. Is it possible then to better define the alleged textual similarity between *a* and a_1 without it being primarily based on the Hurrian recitations (for the recitations of *a* see also Bawanypeck and Görke 2007)?

KBo 23.44 (*CTH* 701.a.B) vs KBo 38.281+ (*CTH* 701.a_1.3): Let us place one case study marked by black arrow 1 in Fig. 9 under the microscope. This textual similarity is interesting for two reasons. First, it posits an Empire period fragment against a text written in MS (KBo 38.281+). Second, the Empire period text has one of the colophons which identifies the title of this part of the festival as the "second tablet of the second day, not finished, when someone libates to the throne of Ḫebat".

Agent	DN	Function word	Hurrian	Realia	Verb
{LÚ}AZU-*ma*	{D}ḫepat	*natšan*	kunzip	{GIŠ}EREN	*pai*
{LÚ}AZU	DINGIR-*LIM*	*nat*	zuzzumakip	I.GIŠ	*šunnai*
{LÚ}AZU-*ya*		*arā*		GEŠTIN	*memai*
BE-EL		*parā*		NINDA.SIG{ḪI.A}	*memiškezzi*
		kuiš		{GIŠ}BANŠUR	*memišket*
		naškan		{DUG}GAL	*šipanti*
		nammaššan		AD.KID	*UŠ-KE-EN*
		nuza		SISKUR	*dai*
		kinunnaškan			
		našta			
		anda			
		peran			
		arḫa			
		maḫḫan			
		QA-TAM-MA			
		ŠA			
		ḫantezzia			
		A-NA			
		PA-NI			

Table 4. Shared word tokens between KBo 23.44 (*CTH* 701.a.B) and KBo 38.281+ (*CTH* 701.a_1.3).

It further carries the signature of the copyist Nananza, son of Adda, who wrote it under the supervision of Anuwanza. Anuwanza was a scribe, eunuch, and lord of the city Nerik during the reigns of Ḫattušili III and Tudḫaliya IV. He supervised at least 19 scribes. Some of the projects undertaken by his scribes directly relate to the Kizzuwatnean Hurrian-Luwian ritual and festival traditions. Examples include the AN.DAḪ.ŠUM^{SAR} festival, texts regarding the cult of the Goddess of the Night, the rituals of the old woman Maštigga, the *dupaduparša* Luwian ritual, and even the enthronement ritual of Tudḫaliya I (Gordin 2015: 166–78). Anuwanza and his scribes clearly had an intensive interest, or royal requirement, to study and copy texts related to the earlier MH wave of Hurrian-Luwian traditions. In my opinion, it is very likely that this scribal group was entrusted with this scholarly tradition through its links to the older Early Empire Ḫattuša scriptorium (on these links see Gordin 2014).

We can look through the microscope at the similarity between these texts by extracting the tokens they share. We further divided the tokens into six categories (Table 4): agents, divine names (DN), function words, Hurrian words, words representing realia, and verbs.

Attempting to separate cultic terminology from a stylistic scribal habit forces us to focus on the function words and verbs. In this regard, the shared Akkadograms attested as function words and verbs are indicative of a possible writing habit. This might even uncover the process by which a scribe like Nananza takes and adapts earlier MS sources in his work, which should be investigated further.

5. Next steps and some preliminary conclusions

The next steps in our project are to run additional experiments to assess the significance of different groups of words in the relationship between the texts. For example, how much will the constellations in our Hurrian-Luwian festival galaxy shift if we remove from the corpus all the Hurrian words, remove all the function words, or remove all the Sumerograms and Akkadograms? How much will the coherence of the groups described above change? To answer these questions, we are in the process of creating additional word level annotations that will allow for quicker filtering of relevant terms. Thus, we can test hypotheses as to which words are the most significant in defining one group of festivals or another.

The HFR and the new comprehensive TLH^{dig} are the result of enormous community efforts, interdisciplinary collaboration on a scale that is rare in ancient studies, including many other modern text-based disciplines in the Humanities. The next generation of students in the field can now combine more than a century of studies in the field of Hittitology with methods from data science.

This paper provides an overview of some of the methods that can be used for exploring this corpus computationally, which we hope will be the first of many such studies. There are many ways to count our texts, to measure relationships between texts, or to quantify assumptions. These methods can be seen as complementary to philological research, providing a different, external view to how we usually see or think of texts. Most importantly, it furnishes us with new tools to test our hypotheses on style and authorship on a large and small scale.

Bibliography

Bastici, Fabio

2024 *Philologische Untersuchungen zu den hurro-hethitischen Festritualen: ein Beitrag zum hethitisch-hurritischen Sprach- und Kulturkontakt.* THeth 34. Heidelberg: Winter.

Bawanypeck, Daliah and Susanne Görke

2007 Einige Bemerkungen zu den Hurritischen Sprüchen des Giziya-Rituals. In: Detlev Groddek and Maria Zorman (eds.), *Tabularia Hethaeorum: Hethitologische Beiträge. Silvin Kosak zum 65. Geburtstag.* DBH 25. Wiesbaden: Harrassowitz, 59–68.

Dardano, Paola

2006 *Die Hethitischen Tontafelkataloge aus Ḫattuša (CTH 276–282).* StBoT 47. Wiesbaden: Harrassowitz.

Eder, Maciej

2015 Does Size Matter? Authorship Attribution, Small Samples, Big Problem. *Digital Scholarship in the Humanities* 30 (2): 167–82. https://doi.org/10.1093/llc/fqt066.

Foster, Benjamin R.
1991 On Authorship in Akkadian Literature. *AION* 51: 17–32.
2019 Authorship in Cuneiform Literature. In: Ingo Berensmeyer, Gert Buelens, and Marysa Demoor (eds.), *The Cambridge Handbook of Literary Authorship*. Cambridge: Cambridge University Press, 13–26.

Gilan, Amir
2019 Religious Convergence in Hittite Anatolia: The Case of Kizzuwatna. In: Sandra Blakely and Billie Jean Collins (eds.), *Religious Convergence in the Ancient Mediterranean*. SAMR 2. Atlanta: Lockwood, 173–90.

Giusfredi, Federico, Valerio Pisaniello, and Alvise Matessi
2023 *Contacts of Languages and Peoples in the Hittite and Post-Hittite World: Volume 1, The Bronze Age and Hatti*. Ancient Languages and Civilizations 4. Leiden: Brill.

Gordin, Shai
2014 The Socio-Historical Setting of the Hittite Schools of Writing as Reflected in Scribal Habits. In: Shai Gordin (ed.), *Visualizing Knowledge and Creating Meaning in Ancient Writing Systems. Proceedings of the International Workshop of the Research Group "Notational Iconicity", 24–25 Sep. 2010*. BBVO 23. Gladbeck: PeWe.
2015 *Hittite Scribal Circles: Scholarly Tradition and Writing Habits*. StBoT 59. Wiesbaden: Harrassowitz.

Görke, Susanne
2022 Hurrian and Luwian Elements in the Kizzuwatna Religious Texts. *AoF* 49: 148–57.

Hay, Julien, Bich-Lien Doan, Fabrice Popineau, and Ouassim Ait Elhara
2020 Representation Learning of Writing Style. In: Wei Xu, Alan Ritter, Tim Baldwin, and Afshin Rahimi (eds.), *Proceedings of the Sixth Workshop on Noisy User-Generated Text (W-NUT 2020)*. Online: Association for Computational Linguistics, 232–43. https://doi.org/10.18653/v1/2020.wnut-1.30.

Helle, Sophus
2019 A Literary Heritage: Authorship in the Neo-Assyrian Period. *Kaskal* 16: 349–71.

HFR-Team
2021 Texte in CTH 701. hethiter.net/: HFR-Basiscorpus. 2021. https://www.hethport.uni-wuerzburg.de/HFR/bascorp_idx2.php?t=CTH%20701 – last accessed 01.05.2024.

Juola, Patrick
2008 Authorship Attribution. *Foundations and Trends in Information Retrieval* 1 (3): 233–334. https://doi.org/10.1561/1500000005.

Kaynar, Fatma
2019 Kizzuwatnean Rituals Under the Influence of the Luwian and Hurrian Cultures. *Olba* 27: 97–114.

Klinger, Jörg
2001 Die hurritische Tradition in Ḫattuša und das Corpus hurritischer Texte. In: Thomas Richter, Doris Prechel, and Jörg Klinger (eds.), *Kulturgeschichten. Altorientalische Studien für Volkert Haas zum 65. Geburtstag*. Saarbrücken: Saarbrücker Verlag, 197–208.

Košak, Silvin, Gerfrid G.W. Müller, Susanne Görke, and Charles W. Steitler
2022 Catalog der Texte der Hethiter (*CTH*). hethiter.net/: *CTH*. 2022. https://www.hethport.uni-wuerzburg.de/CTH/ – last accessed 01.05.2024.

Leclercq, Eveline and Mike Kestemont
2021 Advances in Distant Diplomatics: A Stylometric Approach to Medieval Charters. *Interfaces: A Journal of Medieval European Literatures* 8: 214–44. https://doi.org/10.54103/interfaces-08-10.

Michel, Jean-Baptiste, Yuan Kui Shen, Aviva Presser Aiden, Adrian Veres, Matthew K. Gray, The Google Books Team, Joseph P. Pickett, Dale Hoiberg, Dan Clancy, Peter Norvig, Jon Orwant, Steven Pinker, Martin A. Nowak, and Erez Lieberman Aiden
2011 Quantitative Analysis of Culture Using Millions of Digitized Books. *Science* 331: 176–82. https://doi.org/10.1126/science.1199644.

Miller, Jared
2004 *Studies in the Origins, Development and Interpretation of the Kizzuwatna Rituals*. StBoT 46. Wiesbaden: Harrassowitz.
2006 Von Syrien durch Kizzuwatna nach Ḫatti: Die Rituale der Allaituraḫḫi und Giziya. In: Doris Prechel (ed.), *Motivation und Mechanismen des Kulturkontaktes in der Späten Bronzezeit*. Eothen 13. Firenze: LoGisma, 129–44.

Moretti, Franco
2013 "Operationalizing". *New Left Review* 84: 103–19.

Piasecki, Maciej, Tomasz Walkowiak, and Maciej Eder
2018 Open Stylometric System WebSty: Integrated Language Processing, Analysis and Visualisation. *Computational Methods in Science and Technology* 24 (1): 43–58. https://doi.org/10.12921/CMST.2018.0000007.

Salvini, Mirjo and Ilse Wegner
1986 *Die Rituale des AZU-Priesters*. ChS I/2. Roma: Multigrafica Editrice.

Trameri, Andrea
2020 *The Land of Kizzuwatna. History of Cilicia in the Second Millennium BCE until the Hittite Conquest (ca. 2000–1350)*. PhD Dissertation, University of New York.
2024 *Kizzuwatna: History of Cilicia in the Middle and Late Bronze Age (ca. 2000–1200 BC)*. HbOr 1/185. Leiden: Brill.

Yakubovich, Ilya and Alice Mouton
2023 *Luwili. Hittite-Luwian Ritual Texts Attributed to Puriyanni, Kuwattalla and Šilalluḫḫi (CTH 758–763). Volume II: Discussion and Glossary*. StBoT 72,2. Wiesbaden: Harrassowitz.

Yavasan, Emma and Shai Gordin
2024 Glossed Hittite Texts with German Translation for Machine Learning (1.0) [Data set]. Zenodo. https://doi.org/10.5281/zenodo.14266302.

OF SCRIBES AND HANDS

The Palaeography of the Outline Tablets of the *nuntarriyašḫa-* Festival

Adam Kryszeń
Philipps-Universität Marburg / University of Warsaw

Abstract

The paper provides a palaeographic analysis of the re-evaluated corpus of the outline tablets of the *nuntarriyašḫa-* festival. Since the outline tablets, which provide an overview of the entire festival, are most likely all original compositions, and not copies, a palaeographic analysis of those texts could reveal their relative chronology and contribute to our understanding of the history of the festival. The investigation of the script of the outline tablets focuses both on the dating as well as on the handwriting, the latter in order to verify whether multiple outlines of the *nuntarriyašḫa-* festival could have been written by the same person. The handwriting-analysis proposes a structural approach and puts forth that certain groups of signs have common sets of wedges that always show the same manner of execution by individual scribes. As a result, it is argued that the last three outline tablets of the *nuntarriyašḫa-* festival were written by the same person.

Introduction

The ever-growing corpus of the *nuntarriyašḫa-* festival, for which an online edition is in preparation within the framework of the HFR project, encompasses currently over 200 texts. This includes not only tablets that have been attributed to *CTH* 626, but also (at least partly) texts describing local autumn festivals, like the ones in Zippalanda (*CTH* 592) or Matilla (*CTH* 596).

A palaeographic analysis of such a large group would certainly provide interesting results, such as how many and what kind of tablets were written by the same scribes. However, such an investigation is hardly feasible for one person, unless we find a way to automatise the entire mechanical aspect of the process of sign selection and form identification. For now, a more doable task of analysing smaller groups remains. This paper presents the palaeographic analysis of the outline tablets of the *nuntarriyašḫa-* festival, which promises new observations about these texts.

In a recent reassessment of this group of texts, I have argued that they all constitute unique manuscripts, i. e. none was copied from another.[1] Each outline tablet shows a distinct numbering of days that is different from the others, and originally each outline seems to have had a different set of days comprising the festival. In other words, it

1 The paper "The Outline Tablets of the *nuntarriyašḫa-* Festival. A Reappraisal." was presented at the 12th International Congress of Hittitology, Istanbul 04.–09.09.2023. See Kryszeń in press.

seems that each of the currently identified 17 outline tablets (see Table 1) presents a different version of the *nuntarriyašḫa-* festival.

Since no copies of the outlines are available, it is quite likely that those tablets were indeed never copied.[2] If so, it follows that they were all written at the time of their composition or redaction. Therefore, if one could establish a relative chronology of those texts, one could get a grasp of how the *nuntarriyašḫa-* festival changed over time.[3] Since historical data in the outline tablets are scarce, palaeography seems to offer the best available tool for that task.

While a good number of day tablets currently identified as belonging or pertaining to the *nuntarriyašḫa-* festival date to the Late New Hittite period, this is not the case for the outline tablets. All the outlines of the *nuntarriyašḫa-* festival are written in New Script (NS) and none shows the latest (IIIc) sign forms (see below). This paper, therefore, also deals with the handwriting of the scribes, rather than just the dating. Not only can such an investigation provide arguments for a chronological ordering of the texts, but it would also prove useful for verification of the previously assumed joins. Finally, it will also allow us to compare the hands of the scribes that wrote the outlines of the *nuntarriyašḫa-* festival with those responsible for the respective outline tablets of the AN.DAḪ.ŠUM festival, the second of the great Hittite *Reisefeste*.

Corpus

For the present analysis, 17 outline tablets of the *nuntarriyašḫa-* festival, joined from over 30 individual fragments, were investigated (see Table 1).[4] Certain texts had to be excluded from the analysis, due to either their state of preservation,[5] or the fact that they remain unpublished.

Due to the limited availability of photographs and 3D scans of tablets in previous decades, certain joins proposed in earlier studies seem to have been made based solely on the basis of hand copies of the tablets, which could not properly reflect sign shapes or the overall aspect of the script. For that reason, in the current investigation each fragment was analyzed separately, regardless of the (im)plausibility of existing join proposals.

This proved particularly useful in case of the fragments belonging to Outline.2, whose analysis showed that one piece, IBoT 4.81, previously assumed to form the part of the beginning of this outline (Nakamura 2002: 15, ÜT 1.B), cannot belong to this tablet. Despite being small, IBoT 4.81 contains enough characteristic sign shapes to

2 This would place the *nuntarriyašḫa-* outline tablets in Waal's 'semi-current records' (Waal 2015: 173–75) and van den Hout's 'short-term texts' category (van den Hout 2020: 239).

3 Although, due to the (very) fragmentary nature of some of the fragments, such a reconstruction will hardly prove entirely satisfactory, it can nevertheless provide interesting results.

4 The differences in the arrangement of texts in comparison to Nakamura 2002: 15 or Corti 2007 are due to the identification of new fragments and the reassessment of some proposed joins between the fragments (see Kryszeń in press).

5 This concerns the badly abraded Outline.4 (KBo 39.67+).

Outline	Manuscript	Dating	Findspot
Outline.1	KUB 9.16	NH	Ḫattuša
	+ IBoT 4.71	NH	Ḫattuša
Outline.2	KBo 39.63	NH	HaH
	+ KBo 56.75	NH	HaH
	+ KUB 10.48	NH	HaH
	+ KBo 3.25	NH	HaH
	+ Bo 9159	NH	HaH*
Outline.3	IBoT 4.72	NH	Ḫattuša
	+ DBH 46.2/31	NH	Ḫattuša
Outline.4	KBo 39.67	NH	T.I
	+ KBo 22.228	NH	T.I
Outline.5	KUB 51.15	NH	Ḫattuša
Outline.6	KBo 14.76	NH	Bk. G
Outline.7	KUB 55.5	NH	Ḫattuša
	+ IBoT 4.70	NH	Ḫattuša
Outline.8	KUB 59.2	NH	Ḫattuša
	(+) IBoT 2.8	NH	Ḫattuša
Outline.9	KBo 43.115	NH	Bk. A
Outline.10	KBo 52.114	NH	T.I
	+ Bo 7689	NH	T.I
Outline.11	KBo 51.130	NH	T.I
	+ CHDS 5.8	NH	T.I
	+ Bo 4097	NH	T.I*
	+ UBT 104	NH	T.I*
	+ Bo 7474	NH	T.I*
	+ Bo 3893	NH	T.I
	+ CHDS 2.115	NH	T.I*
Outline.12	KBo 13.257	NH	HaH
Outline.13	KBo 42.47	NH	Büyükkaya
Outline.14	KBo 58.112	NH	T.I
Outline.15	CHDS 5.43	NH	Ḫattuša
Outline.16	KBo 58.175	NH	T.I
Outline.17	IBoT 4.81	NH	Ḫattuša

Table 1. The outline tablets of the *nuntarriyašḫa-* festival. Findspots marked with an asterisk were established through new joins.

show that it was written by a different person than the remaining fragments of Outline.2 (see Fig. 1).[6] Apart from a clearly different NA, one sees that the scribe of IBoT 4.81 (1) did not allow the horizontal in AR to cross the verticals, which is the case in Outline.2, (2) used the older IIc form of SAR with both verticals tall and of equal length, and (3) wrote the middle verticals in É very low, quite in contrast to the scribe of the Outline.2. Therefore, IBoT 4.81 is to be treated as a distinct outline of the *nuntarriyašḫa-* festival (Outline.17).

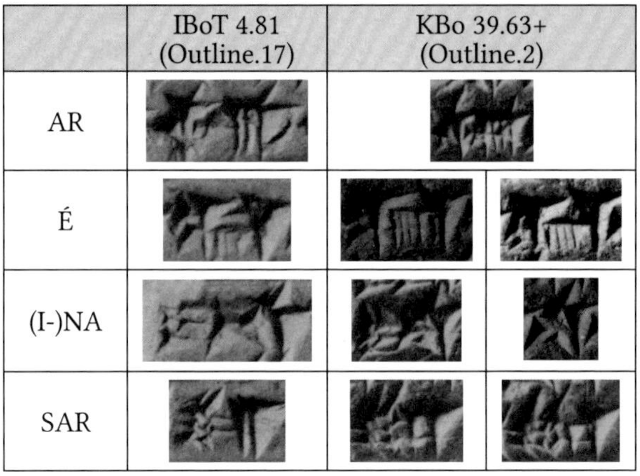

Fig. 1. The comparison of characteristic sign forms and sign types in IBoT 4.81 and Outline.2.

Methodology

Differently than for the dating of texts,[7] cuneiform palaeography has not yet developed a proper methodology for analyzing the handwriting of the scribes, although valuable comments have been made by scholars on many occasions.[8] In order to compare the handwriting on various tablets, one still has to look at all the signs, as has been carried out in a recent edition of the Luwian rituals by Yakubovich and Mouton (2023: 29–46). The present investigation of the handwriting of the outline tablets of the *nuntarriyašḫa-* festival included both the sign forms and sign types (personal ductus).[9] In addition, the position of the sign within the word was noted, whether at the beginning, the end, or in the middle.[10] Finally, the spatial relation between paragraph di-

6 Outline.2 presents a particularly characteristic script. Its scribe wrote GIŠ and MA with the horizontals crossing the vertical, Ú with the lower horizontal written under the verticals, and RA+A as a ligature.

7 For useful overviews see Weeden 2011: 42–52 and Gordin 2015: 83–90.

8 See, e. g. Weeden 2011, Cammarosano et al. 2014, Gordin 2015, Müller 2020, Steitler 2020, Klinger 2022.

9 For the terminology, see Gordin 2015: 83.

10 While this particular examination brought only negative results, the idea is not entirely off-mark. See Susanne Görke's contribution to this symposium, where a curious example of a tablet is described, on

viders and adjacent lines of texts (i. e. the first and the last lines in a paragraph) was examined.

A close analysis of the entire inventory of signs used in a text reveals that the sign forms relevant for the dating are not necessarily the same as those significant for identifying the handwriting. One of the goals of the present study was therefore to establish a representative selection of signs or groups of signs through which an individual scribal hand could be recognized.

Naturally, since handwriting is by definition an individual matter, one cannot expect such a selection to be a closed set. Each scribe had particular tendencies and idiosyncrasies. This is clearly visible in case of the outlines of the *nuntarriyašḫa-* festival (see n. 6). Nevertheless, handwriting can also be studied systematically and it is important to note that, while the signs relevant for dating can show multiple variants on the same tablet (quite frequently URU, or LI), this seems hardly to be the case for the signs relevant for handwriting.

Table 2 presents the comparison of signs that are considered diagnostic for the dating of the text and the signs that proved relevant for the identification of distinct handwriting in the present study. Naturally, those groups should never be treated exclusively, since signs considered diagnostic for dating purposes can often serve to verify an assumed similarity of the script on various tablets, or scribal tendencies in different periods.[11]

Further, in search of an efficient way to produce meaningful results, I tried to systematize and streamline the criteria according to which sign shapes can be described and distinguished. This approach is based on the assumption that certain writing habits are not sign-specific, but can be seen in structurally similar elements shared by multiple signs, such as pairs of horizontals or verticals, or specific wedge-compositions.[12] If one can correctly recognise such elements, instead of individual signs, groups of signs can be analysed, which would in turn improve our chances for identifying the same scribal hand, especially on smaller fragments.

The main premise is that sign shapes in such groups are distinguishable by only one feature and thus produce as few variants as possible. To give an example, the sign GA can be analyzed together with the signs GU_4, ŠA and TA according to the relative position of the (middle) vertical(s) and horizontals, with one variant having the verticals starting above the upper horizontal, and the second variant with the verticals starting together with or below the upper horizontal.

which two distinct forms of the sign NA are found: one only in the word *A-NA*, the other in all remaining instances. This is never the case in any of the outline tablets analyzed here. Outline.1 also seems have the sign LUGAL written differently at the beginning of the tablet (I thank Charles Steitler for drawing my attention to this possibility). Also, the colophons may contain other sign variants than the main body of the text.

11 See n. 10 for one outlier to this rule.

12 Thus, what is called 'element' here, i. e. a set sequence of wedges, is frequently called 'group' (e. g. a ŠE-group) in the literature. In the method proposed in this paper, however, the term 'group' refers to a group of signs sharing the same element.

SIGN(s)	Relevant for dating	Relevant for the study of handwriting
AḪ	X	
AG	X	
AL	X	
AN		X
AR	X	X
AZ	X	
BI		X
DA	X	X
DI	X	
DU	X	
DÙ		X
E	X	X
É		X
EN	X	X
GA		X
GI	X	
GAD	X	
GU_4		X
ḪA	X	X
ḪAR	X	X
ID	X	X
IG	X	
IN	X	X
IR		X
KA		X
KÁN		X
KI	X	X
KÙ	X	
LI	X	X
LÚ		X
LUGAL		X
MA		X
MEŠ	X	X
NA		X
NI	X	X
PA		X
RA		X
-ra-a	X	X
ŠA		X
SAR	X	X
SÌLA	X	
TA		X
TAR	X	
TE	X	
TU		X
UD		X
UN	X	
UG	X	
URU	X	X
ZI		X
ZU		X

Table 2. Comparison of signs relevant for the dating of the text with those relevant for identifying the handwriting of the scribe.

For the present analysis five such groups have been proposed (for the criteria within each group see below):[13]

1. the NI-group: the signs DÙ, IN, IR and NI, which share the NI-element;
2. the GU_4-group: the signs GA, GU_4, ŠA, TA, which share the GU_4-element;[14]
3. the GIŠ/PA-group: signs, which begin with two vertically aligned horizontals;
4. the LÚ/LUGAL-group: sign which share the LÚ element;
5. and the AN/AR-group: the signs AN, AR, RI and ZI, where the (broken) horizontal may or may not cross the subsequent verticals.

13 See James Burgin's contribution to this volume, where he discusses an UD-group (i. e. signs NA, WA, NA_4).

14 One could also consider the sign UL as belonging to this group, as hinted at in Tim Leonard's contribution to this volume.

However, as signs can usually be distinguished by more than one feature, they can appear in multiple groups created according to different criteria. Thus, the GU_4-group can also be analyzed together with a large number of other signs that all begin with a pair of horizontals, like GIŠ, PA etc. In this group, the decisive feature is the relative position of these horizontals: whether the upper is protruding, indented, or both begin at the same level.

Naturally, signs also exist that do not fit in any of these groups and have to be investigated on their own terms. The signs BI, EN, ḪA, GAD, KÁN, NA, RA (RA+A), SAR, UD, URU and ZU proved particularly telling for the study of the handwriting.

The following list presents variants of the sign shapes that were identified in the outline tablets of the *nuntarriyašḫa-* festival:[15]

AN, AR, RI, ZI (the AN/AR-group)
(1) with the (broken) horizontal ending with the vertical(s)
(2) with the (broken) horizontal crossing the vertical(s)
BI (1) with protruding upper horizontal
(2) with both horizontals beginning at the same level
(3) with indented upper horizontal
DA/ID (1) with protruding upper horizontal
(2) with all horizontals beginning at the same level
DÙ, IN, IR, NI (the NI-group)
(1) with the upper wedge in the NI-element significantly shorter and merging before the end of the lower wedge
(2) with the upper wedge in the NI-element clearly separated and both wedges meeting at their tips
(3) with the wedges in the NI-element never touching
É (1) with the middle verticals significantly smaller and beginning on the level of the upper horizontals
(2) with the middle verticals significantly smaller and beginning below the level of the upper horizontals
EN (1) with the wedges below the verticals written as *Winkelhaken* with a subscribed vertical
(2) with the wedges below the verticals written as horizontals and no subscribed vertical
(3) with the wedges below the verticals written as horizontals with a subscribed vertical
GA, GU_4, ŠA, TA (the GU_4-group)
(1) with the (middle) vertical(s) starting above the upper horizontal
(2) with the (middle) vertical(s) starting below the lower horizontal
GIŠ/PA et al. (the GIŠ/PA-group)
(1) with the protruding upper horizontal
(2) with both horizontals beginning at the same level
ḪA (1) with the first *Winkelhaken* in the upper half of the sign
(2) with the first *Winkelhaken* in the lower half of the sign
KA (1) the UŠ×PA variant
(2) a quasi UŠ×PA variant with the first vertical missing
KÁN (1) with the verticals positioned close to the head of the lower vertical
(2) with the verticals beginning to the right of the head of the upper vertical
KI (1) with a ŠU sign

15 For the sake of coherence, the lower values are assigned to the following characteristics: protruding upper horizontals in signs like BI, PA etc.; tall verticals crossing horizontals in signs like GA, ŠA, TA, GU_4; tall verticals in signs like RA; horizontals ending with verticals and not crossing them in signs like AN, ZI, AR or RI.

(2) with a KU sign

LI (1) late form with the rightmost *Winkelhaken* written over the head of the first vertical
(2) late form with the rightmost *Winkelhaken* written before the head of the first vertical
(3) late form with the rightmost *Winkelhaken* written between the verticals
(4) early form

LÚ/LUGAL (the LÚ/LUGAL-group)
(1) with the 'base' written as a horizontal or only slightly pointing upwards
(2) with the 'base' written as a diagonal

NA (1) written with the *Winkelhaken* aligned diagonally
(2) written with the *Winkelhaken* aligned vertically

RA (1) with tall verticals reaching above the upper horizontal
(2) with short verticals reaching the level of the upper horizontal
(3) with additional small horizontal above the left vertical, and the latter significantly smaller than the right vertical

-RA-A (1) written separately
(2) written as ligature

SAL (1) with the upper *Winkelhaken* protruding
(2) with both *Winkelhaken* beginning at the same level
(3) with the lower *Winkelhaken* protruding

SAR (1) with two verticals, both starting at the same level
(2) with two verticals, the first being smaller (slightly smaller or much smaller, depending on the example)
(3) with one vertical (the old form)

TU (1) with long horizontals
(2) with significantly contracted horizontals

UD (1) with the *Winkelhaken* high up and aligned almost horizontally
(2) with the *Winkelhaken* low and aligned horizontally
(3) with the *Winkelhaken* aligned diagonally
(4) with the *Winkelhaken* aligned vertically

URU (1) late form with the protruding middle horizontal and the first vertical at times slightly shorter than the second vertical
(2) MH form with all horizontals in alignment

ZU (1) with two lines of horizontals
(2) with three lines of horizontals

Analysis

Table 3 presents all the discussed variants in the analysed outlines, represented by numeric values. While a general overview of such a large dataset is difficult, one can quickly recognize that within the proposed groups the tablets show relative coherence in how the signs are executed (with the exception of the AN/AR-group).

The NI-group shows great consistency, demonstrating that the Hittite scribes considered the four signs DÙ, IN, IR and NI to be structurally similar (Fig. 2). On each tablet, the NI-element is written exactly the same: either (1) the upper wedge is much shorter and immediately merges with the lower edge, as in Outline.1, 11, and 8; (2) the two wedges are written separately and meet only at the end of the sign, like in Outline.13; or (3) the two wedges never meet and are almost drawn parallel to each other, like in Outline.2.

	Ou 1	Ou 11	Ou 8	Ou 13	Ou 12	Ou 17	Ou 5	Ou 6	Ou 7	Ou 9	Ou 10	Ou 15	Ou 3	Ou 2
AN	2	2	2	1	1		1/2	1	2	2	?	2	1	2
AR	2		2			1			2					2
RI	1	1	1	1	1						1			2
ZI	1	1	1	?	1	1	2	1	2	2	1?	1	1?	2
BI	3	3	3	1/2					3		2	1		3
DA/ID	1	1	1/2				2							2
DÚ		1	1	2										
IN			1	2					2			1?		3
IR	1								2					3
NI	1	1	1	2					2					3
É	2	2	2	2		2	1		1			2	2	1
EN			2	3							1			3
GA	1	1					2		1				2	
GU_4		1	1						1					2
ŠA	1	1	1		2				1					2
TA	1	1	1						1	2				2
GIŠ	1	1	1	1			2	1	1				2	1
PA	1	1	1	1			2	1	1			1		1
ŠA (2)	1	1	1		2				1					2
TA (2)	1	1	1						1					2
É	1	1	1										2	
ḪA	1	1	1	1?				2	1		2	2	2	1/2
KA	1								2					1
KÁN	1	1	1	1			1		2					1
KI	1	1	1						2		2			1
LI	1	1	1	1?	3		4		1		4			3
LÚ		1	1		1		1		2		1	1		1
LUGAL	1	1	1		1		1		2				1/2	1
MEŠ	2	2	2	2	1				1	1	1	1		1
NA	1	1	1	2		1	1							2
RA	3	3	3				1	1	2					1
-RA-A	1						1	2						2
SAR	2	2	2	3?		1			3					2
TU	1	1	1		2				1		2			2
UD	1	1	1		1			3	3	1		3		4
URU	1	1	1	2			1			1	2			1
ZU	1	1	1	1										2

Table 3. Variants of sign shapes in individual outline tablets of the *nuntarriyašḫa-* festival. Groups of signs analysed according to the same criterion are put in thick frames. The GIŠ/PA group includes only a selection of all possible signs.

	Outline.1	Outline.11	Outline.8	Outline.13	Outline.7	Outline.2
DÙ	n.a.			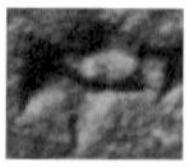	n.a.	n.a.
IN	n.a.	n.a.				n.a.
IR		n.a.	n.a.	n.a.		
NI			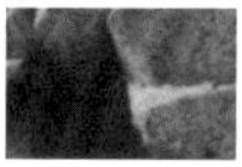			

Fig. 2. Comparison of the NI-group signs in individual outline tablets of the *nuntarriyašḫa*-festival.

	Outline.1	Outline.11	Outline.8	Outline.7	Outline.2
GA			n.a.		n.a.
GU_4	n.a.				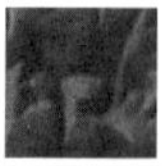
ŠA					
TA					

Fig. 3. Comparison of the GU_4-group signs in individual outline tablets of the *nuntarriyašḫa*-festival.

The same consistency can be noted in how the scribes wrote the signs in the GU_4-group (Fig. 3). In each tablet the position of the head(s) of the middle vertical(s) is the same for each sign, either above (Outline.1, 11, 8 and 7) or at the same level as/slightly below the upper horizontal (Outline.2).

Also, a large group of signs with a pair of initial horizontals (the GIŠ/PA group)[16] demonstrate a general consistency with regard to whether the upper is protruding (variant 1) or both horizontals are in alignment (variant 2). Consider the signs in Fig. 3 (this time looking at the initial horizontals) and Fig. 4. While outliers exist, most scribes of the *nuntarriyašḫa-* outline tablets wrote the two initial horizontals in the same manner: Outline.1, 11, 8, 7, and 13 all show variant 1; while Outline.3 and 5 show variant 2.

16 Virtually every sign that begins with two vertically aligned horizontals (apart from BI), such as all the signs of the GU_4-group, but also E, É, AD, LA, AZ, UK, UN, IŠ, UŠ etc., can belong to this group.

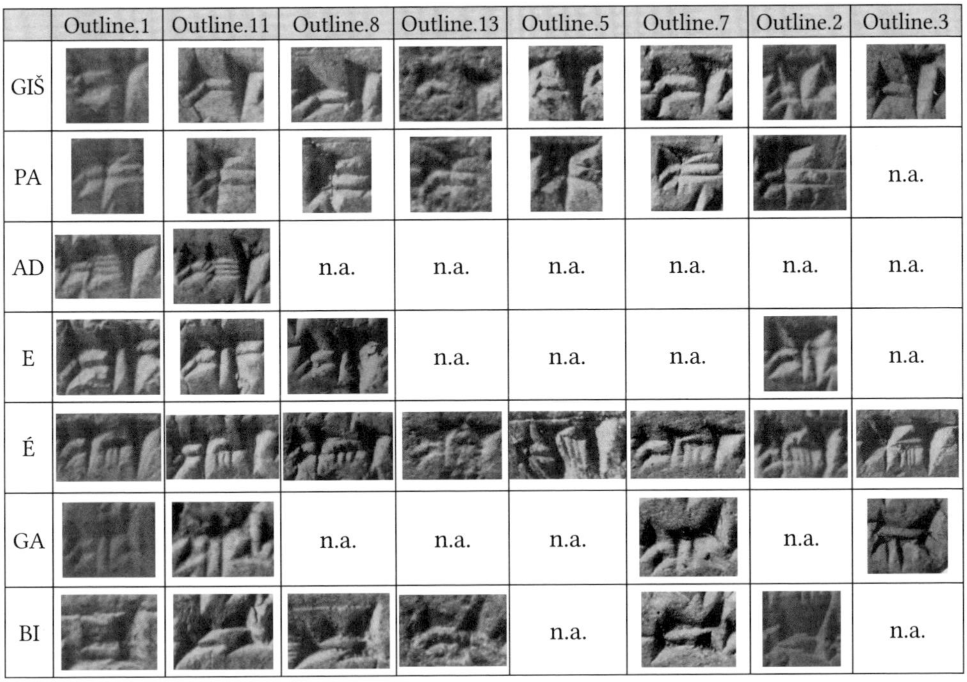

Fig. 4. Comparison of the GIŠ/PA-group signs in individual outline tablets of the *nuntarriyašḫa*-festival and the sign BI (last row).

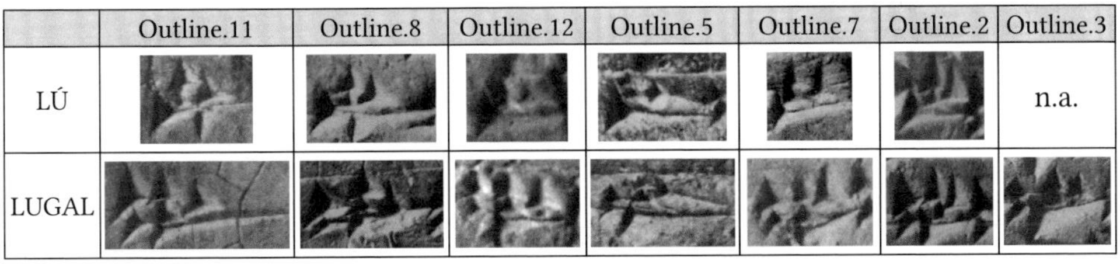

Fig. 5. Comparison of the LÚ/LUGAL-group signs in individual outline tablets of the *nuntarriyašḫa*-festival.

The only inconsistent scribe in this regard was that of Outline.2, as his sign GIŠ shows variant 1, but his sign PA shows variant 2.

Quite remarkably, the sign BI is entirely independent of this group and, more often than not, is written with the upper horizontal indented (the last row in Fig. 4).

With regard to the LÚ/LUGAL group (Fig. 5), the scribes are consistent in keeping the lower horizontal (the second one in case of LUGAL) that forms the 'base' of the sign in the same position. The more frequent variant is one where the sign is rather flat (Outline.11, 8, 5, 12, and 2), while the variant with a clearly diagonal 'base' wedge appears only in Outline.7. The case of Outline.3 is unclear. The additional subscribed ver-

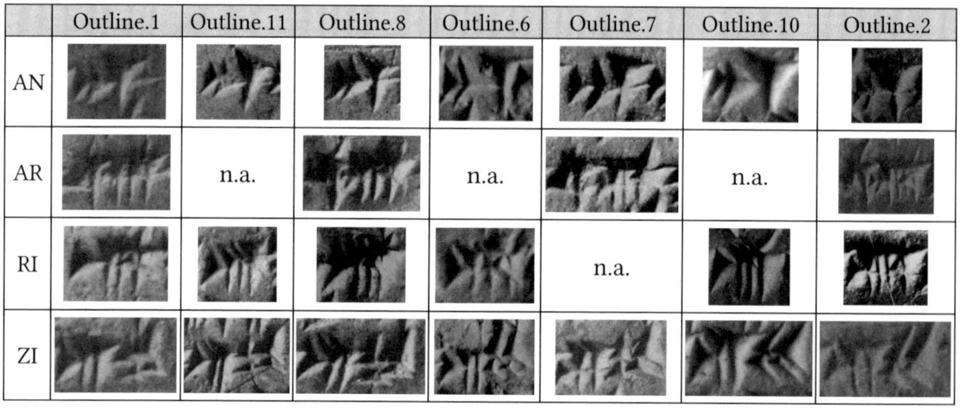

Fig. 6. Comparison of the AN/AR-group signs in individual outline tablets of the *nuntarriyašḫa*-festival.

tical appears to be less significant, as it can appear in LÚs but not LUGALs (Outline.11; see also below).[17]

Significantly less coherent is the last group, comprising the signs AN, AR, RI, ZI (Fig. 6). Those signs were analysed together in order to verify if the (broken) horizontals crossing the vertical(s) are systematic or random. While the group lacks consistency as a whole, the nature of the inconsistency is quite peculiar. First, in all tablets when the scribe crossed the vertical in the AN sign, he did so also in the AR sign (either only the first two verticals, or the entire row; see Outline.1, 8, 7 and 2). Second, this tendency does not include the RI sign, save in Outline.2. Third, the verticals in the ZI sign are crossed only in those tablets that also show the crossed AN sign (Outline.7 and 2).

In sum, four of the five groups display general coherence of sign shapes in each tablet. In addition, three tablets: Outline.1, 8 and 11, present identical variants throughout all five groups. A further examination of the remaining signs in those tablets (Fig. 7) leaves little doubt that all three texts were written by the same person. Note in particular the BI with an indented upper horizontal, KÁN with the verticals close to the head of the lower horizontal, or a characteristic form of RA with the additional small horizontal above the remaining horizontals.

Further, one could point to some common features of the script in two other texts, IBoT 4.71+ (Outline.3) and IBoT 4.81 (Outline.17). Note the similarity of É, NA, NU and the general manner in which the verticals are written on both tablets (Fig. 8). While there is not enough evidence to be certain, it is at least plausible that both outlines were written by the same person, or even belong to the same tablet.

Thus, it seems that the currently identified 17 outline tablets of the *nuntarriyašḫa*-festival were written by at least 14 scribes: one wrote Outline.1, 8 and 11, possibly one wrote Outline.3 and 17, whereas each of the remaining 12 outlines seems to have been written by a different person.

17 Outline.1 seems to write the two first instances of LUGAL (obv. i 1 and 8) with the additional verticals.

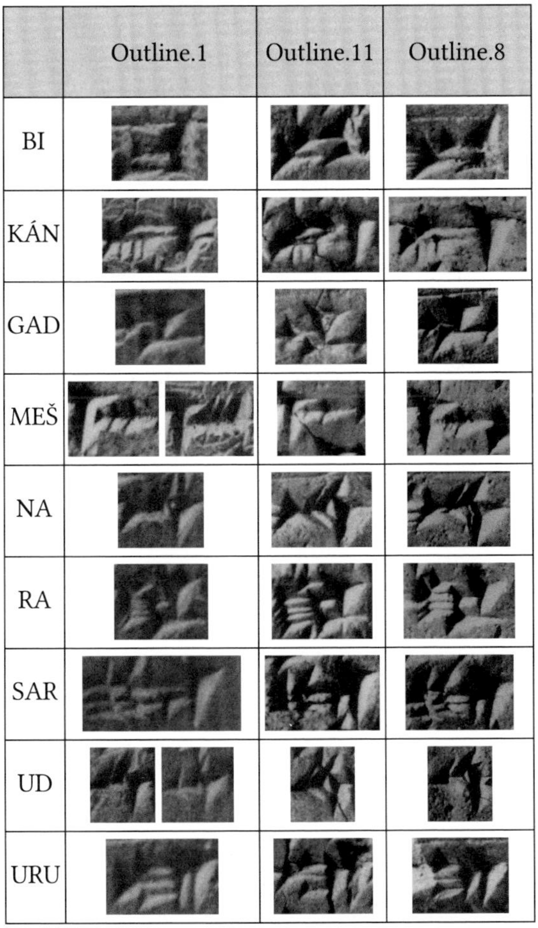

Fig. 7. Individual signs representative of the handwriting of Outline.1, 11 and 8 of the *nuntarriyašḫa-* festival.

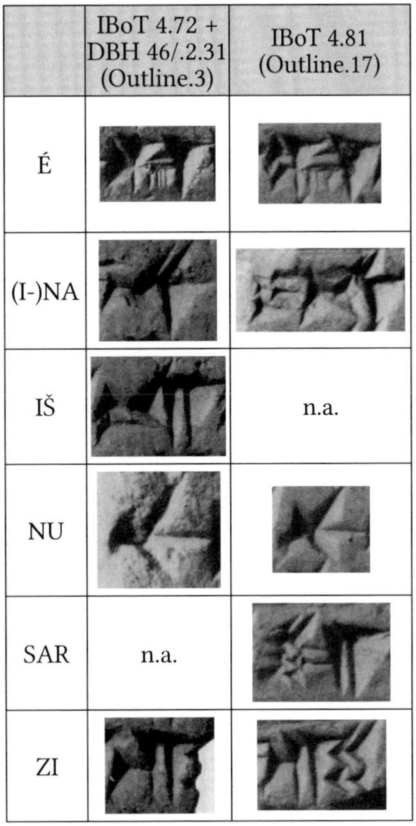

Fig. 8. Individual sign shapes in Outline.17, and 3 of the *nuntarriyašḫa-* festival.

Interestingly enough, a cursory comparative palaeographic investigation of the outline tablets of the AN.DAḪ.ŠUM festival brought only negative results. There seems to be no overlap between the scribes of the outlines of the respective festivals.

Dating of the outline tablets of the *nuntarriyašḫa-* festival

A palaeographic investigation with regard to the dating also brings interesting results. As stated at the beginning of this paper, all the preserved outline tablets of the *nuntarriyašḫa-* festival date to the New Hittite period. Indeed, a closer investigation demonstrates that they all seem to have been written in a relatively short time span, as they share an impressive number of palaeographic features relevant for dating: (1) all the

URU		Outline.7, 10, 13	RA+A		Outline.2
IG		Outline.1	AL		Outline.7
KÙ	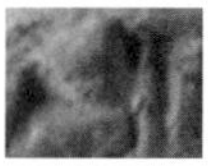	Outline.10	SAR		Outline.7, 13
GI	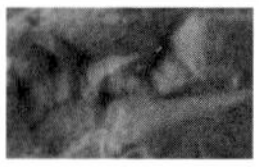	Outline.10, 12	GAD	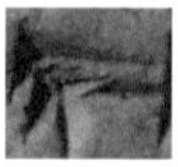	Outline.2, 3

Fig. 9. Pre-NS sign forms and features in the outline tablets of the *nuntarriyašḫa-* festival.

outline tablets have subscribed AZ/UG;[18] (2) virtually identical post-MS TAR forms with the broken horizontal and a diagonal underneath; (3) a simpler form of NI with no verticals; (4) DA/ID only with broken horizontals and with all the horizontals almost always of equal length (no 'stepped' variant);[19] (5) and DU with the upper horizontal instead of a *Winkelhaken*. Together, these features place the tablets firmly in the post-MS period.

Pre-NS forms and features are not infrequent, however (see Fig. 9): URU with equal horizontals (Outline. 10 and 13, with Outline.7 having mixed forms); older forms of IG (Outline.1), KÙ (Outline.10) and GI (Outline.10 and 12); AL with a flat bottom and an empty space between the verticals (Outline.7); GAD with the vertical crossing the lower horizontal (Outline.2 and 3) and SAR with one vertical (Outline.7 and 13) or two tall verticals of equal length (Outline.17). The ligature writing (RA+A) is found only in Outline.2.

On the other hand, apart from one instance of the latest form of EN with no vertical (Outline.8), there is not a single example of a IIIc form, i. e. all examples of DI, ḪA, KI, SAR, SÌLA or UN show variants that are older.[20]

The attested IIIb forms are AG, IG (only one example each), LI, MEŠ, SAR and URU (see Fig. 10).[21] With the exception of Outline.7, which shows both the older and the younger variant of LI and URU, each outline consequently uses only one shape of the listed signs.

Most tablets use IIIb forms only occasionally, but two extremes can easily be pointed out. Outline.1, 8 and 11, written by the same scribe, show the IIIb variants for all

18 While this is usually considered to be a feature of NS, these variants are already found in MS, see Weeden 2011: 44.

19 The sometimes protruding upper horizontal (e. g. in Outline.1, 8 and 11) seems to be a feature of individual handwriting.

20 Therefore, the assumption by van de Peut (2022: 22 with n. 87) that the variant of BI with an indented upper horizontal counts as a IIIc form does not find support in the outline tablets of the *nuntarriyašḫa-* festival.

21 But see Weeden 2011: 50f.

	Outline.1, 8 & 11	Outline.5	Outline.13	Outline.7	Outline.10	Outline.2
IG		n.a.	n.a.	n.a.	n.a.	
LI			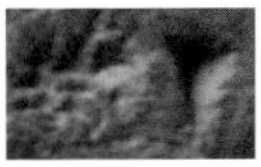	 		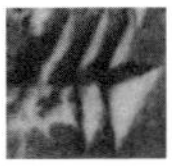
MEŠ		n.a.	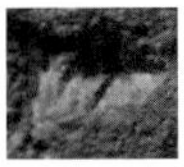			
SAR		n.a.			n.a.	
URU				 		

Fig. 10. Comparison of the pre-IIIb and IIIb sign forms in the outline tablets of the *nuntarriyašḫa*-festival.

the listed signs apart from IG,[22] while Outline.10 shows exclusively older variants of the signs in question.

In sum, virtually all the sign forms fall into the IIb–IIIb spectrum, with the extremes represented rarely. The predominance of IIIa (or at least pre-IIIb) variants suggests that the tablets were written sometime during the period between the reigns of Muršili II and Ḫattušili III. With very small differences between the texts, establishing the relative chronology of the tablets based on the palaeography could hardly be convincing, especially in case of smaller pieces. Nevertheless, if the sign forms shown in Fig. 10 are reliable, Outline.10 would represent the earliest available version of the *nuntarriyašḫa*- festival, which was written in early NS. This goes well with the idea that the festival originated during the reigns of Šuppiluliuma I or Muršili II. Given that Šuppiluliuma I was considered by the later rulers to be notoriously neglectful of satisfying the gods, Muršili II seems to be a more plausible candidate to have created the multi-day *nuntarriyašḫa*-.

If Outline.10 is the oldest, Outline.1, 8 and 11 have to be considered the youngest versions of the festival. Interestingly, the content of Outline.1 provides a rare historical piece of information: it mentions ᴰUTU-*ŠI* ᵐ*mur-ši*-DINGIR-*LIM*, "His Majesty, Muršili" (KUB 9.16 rev. 5′) in the last paragraph of the text before the colophon, seemingly in the section about the origins of the festival (or this particular version?). In the light of the presumably late dating of the text, one should ask, whether the use of the title

22 In addition, the only instance of the IG sign is in the theonym ᴰNIR.GÁL, which might be of relevance.

DUTU-*ŠI*, usually associated with the currently reigning king, should mean that it is Muršili III who is meant in this text? Or should one keep to the traditional interpretation of the king in question being Muršili II? In that case one could understand that particular section of the text as a fragment inserted in every outline tablet, in a fashion similar to the colophons of the *ḫišuwa-* festival (*CTH* 628) which mention Puduḫepa ordering Walwaziti to look for the necessary texts of the festival.

Nevertheless, the lack of *nuntarriyašḫa-* outline tablets that could clearly be dated to the reign of Tudḫaliya IV is remarkable and stands in clear contrast with a number of day tablets of the festival dating to his rule,[23] as well as with several outline tablets of the AN.DAḪ.ŠUM[24] festival which show clear IIIc sign variants, like, e. g. VSNF 12.1. Whether this discrepancy is due to the state of the preservation of the sources or other circumstances must remain an open question for the time being.

Bibliography

Cammarosano, Michele, Gerfrid G.W. Müller, Denis Fisseler, and Frank Weichert

2014 Schriftmetrologie des Keils. *WdO* 44: 2–36.

Corti, Carlo

2007 Notes Regarding Days 12, 13 and 14 of the *nuntarriyašḫaš* Festival According to the Second Outline Source. In: Detlev Groddek and Marina Zorman (eds.), *Tabularia Hethaeorum. Hethitologische Beiträge Silvin Košak zum 65. Geburtstag*. DBH 25. Wiesbaden: Harrassowitz, 163–74.

Gordin, Shai

2015 *Hittite Scribal Circles: Scholarly Tradition and Writing Habits*. StBoT 59. Wiesbaden: Harrassowitz.

Haas, Volkert

1994 *Geschichte der hethitischen Religion*. HbOr 1/15. Leiden / New York / Köln: Brill.

Klinger, Jörg

2022 Zu den Anfängen der hethitischen Überlieferung überhaupt und zur Methode der paläographischen Textdatierung. In: Eva Cancik-Kirschbaum and Ingo Schrakamp (eds.), *Transfer, Adaption und Neukonfiguration von Schrift- und Sprachwissen im Alten Orient*. Episteme in Bewegung 25. Wiesbaden: Harrassowitz, 255–340.

Kryszeń, Adam

in press The Outline Tablets of the *nuntarriyašḫa-* Festival. A Reappraisal.

23 See, e. g. KUB 44.8+, KUB 25.10, KBo 11.30+ or KBo 30.77, whose dating rests on palaeographic (IIIc sign forms), metatextual, and prosopographic arguments.

24 I would like to thank Charles Steitler for pointing that out to me.

Müller, Gerfrid G.W.
2020 Intra- und Inter-Schreiber-Variation: Zur Unterscheidung ähnlicher Schriften mittels häufiger Keilschriftzeichen auf 3D-Modellen. In: Walter Sommerfeld (ed.), *Dealing with Antiquity: Past, Present & Future: 63. Rencontre Assyriologique Internationale, Marburg*. AOAT 460. Münster: Ugarit Verlag, 361–79.

Nakamura, Mitsuo
2002 *Das hethitische* nuntarriyašḫa-*Fest*. PIHANS 94. Leiden: Nederlands Instituut voor het Nabije Oosten.

Steitler, Charles
2020 Festival Tablets from the Final Decades of the Hittite Empire: Scribes and Writing Conventions. In: Stefano de Martino and Elena Devecchi (eds.), *Anatolia between the 13th and the 12th Century BCE*. Eothen 23. Torino: Logisma, 411–55.

Taracha, Piotr
2009 *Religions of Second Millennium Anatolia*. DBH 27. Wiesbaden: Harrassowitz.

van de Peut, Lidewij E.
2022 *Persuading the Divine: On the Composition of Hittite Prayers*. StBoT 69. Wiesbaden: Harrassowitz.

van den Hout, Theo P.J.
2020 *A History of Hittite Literacy. Writing and Reading in Late Bronze-Age Anatolia (1650–1200 BC)*. Cambridge: Cambridge University Press.

Waal, Willemijn
2015 *Hittite Diplomatics. Studies in Ancient Document Format and Record Management*. StBoT 57. Wiesbaden: Harrassowitz.

Weeden, Mark
2011 *Hittite Logograms and Hittite Scholarship*. StBoT 54. Wiesbaden: Harrassowitz.

Yakubovich, Ilya and Alice Mouton
2023 *Luwili. Hittite-Luwian Ritual Texts Attributed to Puriyanni, Kuwattalla and Šilalluḫi (CTH 758–763), Volume II: Discussion and Glossary*. StBoT 72,2. Wiesbaden: Harrassowitz.

SOME OBSERVATIONS ON THE PALEOGRAPHY OF THE TEXTS FROM MAŞAT HÖYÜK

*Timothy D. Leonard**
Ann Arbor, Michigan

Abstract

The Hittite texts from Maşat Höyük comprise the letters and administrative documents sent between the Hittite king or members of the royal administration and the local officials residing at that site. This paper analyzes the paleography of the Maşat Höyük texts based on a data set of photographs and 3D scans of thirty-six of these tablets. The scholarly consensus is that the script of the Maşat Höyük tablets is MS, but this study concludes that these tablets also contain some features that are typically identified as early NS. In addition, this study attempts to describe the salient features of the handwriting of three scribes attested in this data set, viz. Tarḫunmiya, Mār-ešrē, and Ḫašammili, but refrains from ascribing anonymous tablets to any particular scribe on the basis of macroscopic analysis due to the limited number of texts available for study.

1. Hittite texts from Maşat Höyük

The texts from Maşat Höyük are a valuable source of information about Hittite provincial administration during the first half of the fourteenth century BCE. The letters discovered at this site provide a rare glimpse of the agricultural and military affairs taking place outside of the capital city of Ḫattuša, as well as the amusing exchanges of Hittite scribes writing to one another. These tablets are also of special interest for paleographical analysis in that they feature a variety of Hittite cuneiform sign-forms, and the script they bear seems to reflect a transitional period between MS and NS.

The corpus of texts from Maşat Höyük comprises the one hundred and sixteen tablets and fragments unearthed during the archaeological excavations that took place 1973–1981, as well as one tablet that was found on the surface (ABoT 1.65). This corpus includes ninety-eight pieces of correspondence between the Hittite king and the local officials residing at Tapikka (i. e. Maşat Höyük), seventeen administrative documents, and one oracular text.[1] All of the tablets found during the course of the excavations were published in handcopy by Alp (1991b). The *communis opinio* is that the script of

* I would like to thank Daniel Schwemer for inviting me to participate in this symposium. This research relies on the 3D scans and photographs of a selection of the Maşat Höyük tablets that were produced by Gerfrid G.W. Müller and Michele Cammarosano. I thank them, as well as Charles Steitler, for graciously making these resources available to me. I am also grateful to Gary Beckman, Susanne Görke, and Adam Kryszeń for their helpful suggestions and corrections on earlier drafts of this paper.

1 See van den Hout 2007. Editions of the letters have been published by Alp (1991a) and Hoffner (2009), and the administrative records were published by del Monte (1995). HKM 86a + HKM 86b was recently

the Maşat Höyük corpus can be identified as solidly MS (excepting HKM 116), but the recent availability of new photographs and 3D scans of thirty-six of these tablets allows for a reevaluation of this assessment.[2]

2. The scribes of the Maşat Höyük tablets

The content of these letters reflects a period when the Hittite state was resisting incursions from the Kaška on its northern frontier. While the letters themselves are not dated, they seem to cover a relatively short period of time, since the names of the officials mentioned in them remain the same throughout the corpus (Beckman 1995: 23). Two tablets from Maşat Höyük bear the seal impressions of Tudḫaliya III, which suggests that the bulk of the corpus can be dated to his reign (Alp 1991a: 109–12). However, Klinger has demonstrated (1995) that numerous officials mentioned in these texts are already attested during the reign of Arnuwanda I, which admits the possibility of a slightly earlier date for some of these texts (de Martino 2005: 313–18). It is difficult to assign a date to this corpus with any greater specificity, and the current scholarly consensus is that occurrences mentioned in the letters cannot be reliably connected to other events documented in the Ḫattuša archive (van den Hout 2007: 387).

Twenty-one of the thirty-six tablets in this data set can be attributed to particular scribes. Since the scribes did not sign their letters, we are only aware of their names because of the personal messages they appended to their official missives (the so-called "piggyback" letters). The eight scribes who are attested in this data set are Ḫašammili, Mār-ešrē (written ^{m}*ma-re-eš-re-e* and ^{m}DUMU.UD.20.KAM), Šanda, Šuriḫili, Tarḫunmiya (written ^{m}*tar-ḫu-un-mi-ia*, $^{m.D}$IŠKUR-*mi-ia*, and $^{m.D}$10-*mi-ia*), Ilī-kakkab (written ^{m}DINGIR-*LIM*.MUL), Ḫattušili (written $^{m.GIŠ}$GIDRU-DINGIR-*LIM*), and Adad-bēlī (written $^{m.D}$10-*BE-LÍ*). Ḫašammili wrote four of these letters,[3] Mār-ešrē wrote six of these letters,[4] and Tarḫunmiya wrote at least six of them.[5] Šuriḫili wrote two letters (HKM 2, HKM 3), and Šanda, Adad-bēlī, and Ilī-kakkab wrote one letter each.[6] This corpus consists of letters that arrived in Tapikka, so these scribes most likely resided in Ḫattuša, or possibly in Šapinuwa (see Hoffner 2009: 49, 52f., 92f.).

republished in Gander 2022: 323–25. A transliteration and translation of HKM 47 is available in Sakuma 2009: 638–46.

2 This data set consists of the following texts: HKM 2, HKM 3, HKM 10, HKM 17, HKM 19, HKM 20, HKM 21, HKM 22, HKM 23, HKM 26, HKM 29, HKM 30, HKM 31, HKM 32, HKM 33, HKM 36, HKM 45, HKM 46, HKM 47, HKM 52, HKM 53, HKM 56, HKM 62, HKM 67, HKM 69, HKM 71, HKM 73, HKM 76, HKM 81, HKM 82, HKM 86a + HKM 86b, HKM 93, HKM 95, HKM 99, HKM 114, HKM 115. Of these texts, HKM 19, HKM 22, HKM 23, HKM 32, HKM 45, HKM 67, HKM 86a + HKM 86b, HKM 93, and HKM 99 were only available as 3D scans, and HKM 69 and HKM 76 were only available as photographs.

3 HKM 17, HKM 19, HKM 30, HKM 36.

4 HKM 22, HKM 31, HKM 33, HKM 53, HKM 73, HKM 82.

5 HKM 29, HKM 52, HKM 56, HKM 62, HKM 71, HKM 81. Alp identified Tarḫunmiya as the scribe of HKM 10 and HKM 26 on the basis of handwriting (Alp 1991a: 132 n. 42, Taf. 8–9), even though HKM 10 contains a piggyback letter from the chief scribe Ḫattušili. For discussions of this Ḫattušili and the office of chief scribe, see Alp 1991a: 58f. and Bilgin 2018: 245–48, 265–71.

6 HKM 21 (Šanda), HKM 46 (Adad-bēlī), HKM 95 (Ilī-kakkab). HKM 46 does not include a piggyback letter, and Adad-bēlī is both scribe and sender of this missive (Alp 1991a: 52f., Taf. 10).

Because there are a few scribes to whom multiple tablets from this data set can be ascribed, this corpus presents the opportunity to identify the specific handwritings of the individual scribes. Through quantitative analysis Cammarosano has already identified subtle differences in the way Tarḫunmiya and Šuriḫili wrote the sign NA (2015: 163–66), viz. in the respective angles of the two *Winkelhaken* in this sign relative to the following vertical. The prospect of achieving similar results through simple macroscopic analysis is distinctly less promising. There is sometimes significant variation apparent in the ductus and sign-forms used not only within a tablet, but also between tablets written by the same scribe. For example, HKM 52 and HKM 71 were both written by Tarḫunmiya, but the former is lightly inscribed with relatively thin, elegant wedges and even lines of writing, whereas the latter is written more deeply, with thicker, more widely-spaced wedges and lines of writing slanting upwards. In HKM 71 lo.e. 17 the sign ḪU appears with the horizontal well below the point of the *Winkelhaken*, close to the tip of the tail of the first vertical, but in rev. 28 and rev. 30 of the same tablet, ḪU is written with the horizontal even with the point of the *Winkelhaken*. Elsewhere (e. g. HKM 29: 7′, HKM 56 obv. 1) Tarḫunmiya sometimes writes ḪU with the *Winkelhaken* placed lower than the horizontal. Some of the features apparent in HKM 71 most likely reflect the circumstances of this tablet's composition rather than characteristics of Tarḫunmiya's unique scribal hand, and the content of this letter further suggests that it was written in haste.

Alp (1991a: 98) described Tarḫunmiya as "ein Schreiber mit einer sehr eleganten und zierlichen Handschrift." Tarḫunmiya's handwriting features signs with very regular placement of wedges, with sequences of verticals or stacked horizontals of even lengths, and with the groups of *Winkelhaken* in signs like IT, ŠEŠ, and ḪI appearing to have been written at precisely the same angle (cf. Cammarosano 2015: 164). In HKM 52 obv. 10, for example, the upper *Winkelhaken* in the sign BI is set in line with the angle of the lower *Winkelhaken*, rather than being placed directly above it. The lines of text in Tarḫunmiya's shorter letters (HKM 56, HKM 71) tend to slope slightly upwards. The scribes of the Maşat Höyük corpus never justified the final sign in a line, as is typical in texts from Boğazköy, but Tarḫunmiya occasionally wrote the final sign of a line in the center of the column when it was the last line of a paragraph and it consisted of only a single word (HKM 62 obv. 11, HKM 71 rev. 34).

Mār-ešrē's lines of writing, on the other hand, never slope across the column, but remains steady even in short letters. Mār-ešrē sometimes wrote the final sign of a paragraph slightly to the right (HKM 53 obv. 11, HKM 56 obv. 3, HKM 73 rev. 18). Mār-ešrē's signs with prominent horizontals seem somewhat elongated in contrast to Tarḫunmiya's evenly spaced signs, and the *Winkelhaken* in Mār-ešrē's signs are not always placed as neatly as Tarḫunmiya's.

Ḫašammili's writing tends to be somewhat compact, with smaller signs overall and signs written more closely together, and his wedges tend to be thicker and shorter than Tarḫunmiya's. Ḫašammili often wrote the ḪI-group in signs like IT with the three smaller upper *Winkelhaken* directly in a line, but with the lower *Winkelhaken* set off, usually a bit lower, and somewhat elongated. HKM 19 provides a clear example of Ḫašammili's cursive script, with the lines of writing slanting upwards and vertical wedges leaning to the left. However, there is considerable variation in the ductus even within the four tablets that can be ascribed to Ḫašammili. Therefore, these observations must be taken as merely a general impression of the available texts in this data set, and not as accurately describing every instance of a particular sign written by these scribes.

Tarḫunmiya	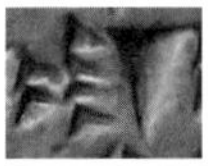			
Mār-ešrē	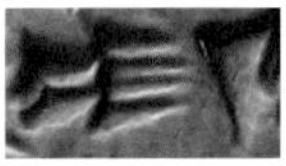		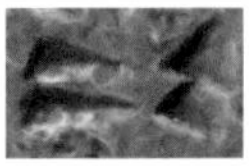	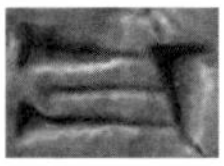
Ḫašammili		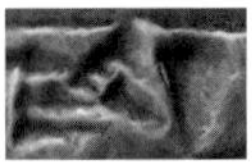	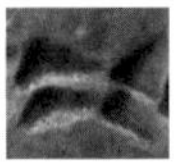	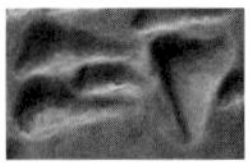

Table 1. A comparison of Tarḫunmiya's, Mār-ešrē's, and Ḫašammili's handwriting.

The tablets from Maşat Höyük frequently exhibit a cursive script, indicating that they were written relatively quickly, which stands in contrast to the library script that was used for the majority of the tablets of the Boğazköy corpus. Characteristics of cursive writing include a higher placement of *Winkelhaken* at the ends of signs, oblique wedges appearing nearly parallel to horizontals, horizontal wedges appearing without clear heads when written after verticals, slanted writing with verticals leaning to the left and horizontals sloping downwards, and the use of simplified signs with a reduced number of wedges.[7] All of these features are apparent in these tablets to some extent, but the use of simplified signs and signs written with relatively high *Winkelhaken* are the most salient cursive features in this data set (*infra*). Simplified sign variants occur frequently in HKM 10, HKM 47, HKM 52, and HKM 81. If Alp (1991a: 132 n. 42) was correct in suggesting that HKM 10 was written by Tarḫunmiya rather than the sender named in its piggyback letter, viz. Ḫattušili, then the use of simplified signs would seem to be a characteristic of the former's handwriting. Tarḫunmiya occasionally used these variants in other letters of his (e. g. HKM 29, HKM 62), but they also appear in texts that Mār-ešrē wrote (e. g. HKM 31, HKM 73). Due to the paucity of available data and the variability of handwriting in extant tablets with known authors, we should exercise caution in assigning texts to particular scribes on the basis of macroscopic analysis alone.

3. Paleography

The ephemeral nature of epistolary documents guarantees that the sign-forms present in our data set reflect the moment of their composition, rather than characteristics of writing that had been copied over from an older document. No such assurance can be made against archaic features in a given scribe's handwriting. Alp provided a synopsis of the sign-forms present in the Maşat texts in Alp 1991a: 113–19 and photographs of

7 Cammarosano 2021: 15–18; see also his contribution in this volume.

a few tablets as examples of handwriting in Alp 1991a: Tafeln 6–13. The paleographic studies of Starke (1985: 21–27) and Klinger (1996: 32–39) have come to define the discipline in the years since their publication. These studies advocate for the division of OS, MS, and NS into the subdivisions Ia–b, IIa–c, and IIIa–b (Starke) or IIIa–c (Klinger).[8] The following discussion employs the numbering system of the HZL. Particular cuneiform signs that are generally accepted as diagnostic either occur in older and later variants, differing in the number and type of their wedges (e. g. 343/A and 343/B), or they occur in approximately the same form and differ only in the relative size or placement of specific constituent wedges (e. g. 187/A and 187/B). Differences in sign shape provide more secure criteria for text dating than differences in the relative size or position of individual wedges.

3.1. Signs that are written fairly consistently

TAR is almost always written in this data set in its MS form (7/B), which consists of a broken downward-sloping diagonal wedge with a small vertical wedge beneath it. The OS form of TAR (7/A), which is written with a broken horizontal wedge and a small vertical beneath it, appears in this set of tablets twice (HKM 19 obv. 14, HKM 45 lo.e. 17′). The NS form of TAR (7/C), with a small downward-sloping diagonal beneath a broken horizontal, is wholly absent from the Maşat Höyük tablets (Alp 1991a: 113).

QA is consistently written in its older form (21/A), which is composed of a single horizontal wedge terminating in a single vertical wedge. This sign occurs fifteen times in the collection of tablets available for this study.[9]

TAR	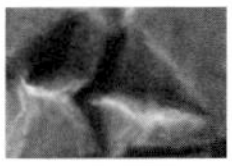	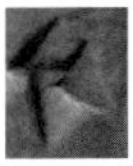	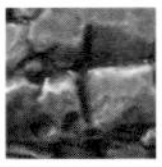	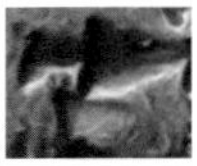
QA	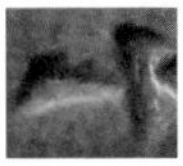		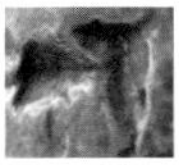	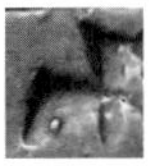

Table 2. TAR and QA.

GI only appears in this data set four times (HKM 17 obv. 10, HKM 26 obv. 7, HKM 71 l.e. 1, l.e. 2), and it is consistently written in its older *Leitzeichen* (30/A). This sign consists of a horizontal wedge followed by two verticals, then an upward-slanting diagonal with three *Winkelhaken* above it. The later form (30/B), which replaces the diagonal and *Winkelhaken* with the ḪI-group, does not seem to be present in the tablets from Maşat Höyük (Alp 1991a: 114).

EN appears in its oldest form (40/A) in almost every instance. This *Leitzeichen* has a small vertical wedge hanging from the horizontal in front of the two larger vertical wedges. There is only one occurrence of the MS version of EN (40/B), in which the small vertical is written directly below the two large verticals (HKM 19 rev. 23).

8 For a history of Hittite paleography and a discussion of current issues, see van den Hout 2009. Recent summaries of the topic are also presented in Gordin 2015: 83–94 and van de Peut 2022: 15–29.

9 HKM 2 rev. 17, l.e. 4, HKM 17 obv. 6 (twice), obv. 21, l.e. 5, HKM 19 obv. 7 (twice), HKM 36 l.e. 4, HKM 46 u.e. 26, l.e. 2, HKM 47 obv. 14, HKM 62 obv. 13, HKM 73 rev. 30, HKM 99 obv. 2.

GI	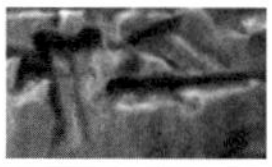		
EN	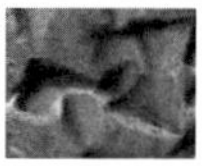	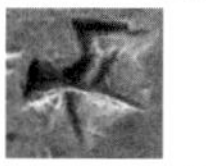	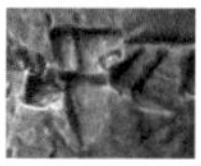

Table 3. GI and EN.

RU most frequently occurs in the older *Leitzeichen* 43/A, in which the middle vertical is written lower than the first and third verticals. In six texts the three verticals in RU are of even or nearly even height (43/B).[10] This development parallels that in the sign EL. According to Starke (1985: 24), RU and EL are first written with even verticals in the period IIIa. It should be noted that some tablets in this data set exhibit both 43/A and 43/B (e. g. HKM 36 rev. 41, l.e. 1). This data set contains two other variants of the sign RU. In HKM 56 rev. 25 RU appears with the first two verticals of even height and the third vertical slightly taller (43/4). In HKM 53 rev. 15 the heads of the three verticals in RU are stepped (43/8–9). It is unlikely that these two variant forms are of any paleographic significance.

IK is always written in its older form (67/A), which consists of one horizontal wedge with three or four stacked horizontals on top of it. These three stacked horizontals run into a single *Winkelhaken*, which is followed by a vertical wedge. The sign terminates in two stacked *Winkelhaken*. The later form (67/B), which has a vertical wedge before the single *Winkelhaken* instead of the stacked horizontals, does not appear in these texts. According to Klinger the form 67/B already appears in MS texts (1996: 35), but it is usually associated with NS (Starke 1985: 25).

RU	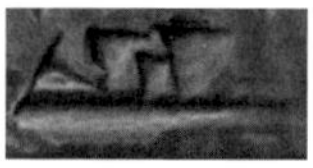	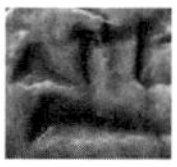	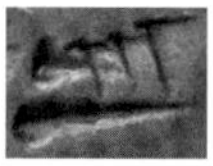	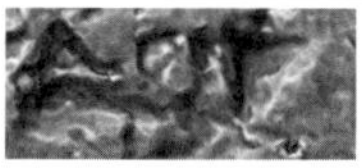
IK				

Table 4. RU and IK.

KÙ only appears once in this data set (HKM 26 obv. 7), and it appears in the older form (69/A), which resembles the sign ŠU with an additional broken vertical. As is to be expected, the late form of KÙ (69/B) does not appear in the texts from Maşat Höyük (Alp 1991a: 113).

AK always appears in its older sign-form (81/A) in the tablets from Maşat Höyük (Alp 1991a: 113). This form of AK consists of a single initial horizontal wedge followed by a long, low horizontal wedge. On top of the low horizontal there are two sets of three stacked horizontal wedges that abut a single vertical wedge. Following the vertical are two horizontals, one above the other. The later form of AK (81/B), which in-

10 HKM 2 u.e. 22, HKM 10 obv. 6, HKM 31 rev. 24, HKM 36 rev. 41, HKM 71 u.e. 37, HKM 73 rev. 23.

cludes two verticals and a broken horizontal instead of the two sets of three stacked horizontals, is wholly absent from these tablets (Alp 1991a: 113).

AZ (92/A) and UK (93/A) frequently appear without subscripts. AZ is written with a subscripted ZA (92/B) in HKM 2 u.e. 21 and HKM 53 rev. 16. UK appears in the form with a subscripted UD (93/B) in HKM 2 rev. 17, HKM 17 obv. 9, HKM 21 u.e. 24, and HKM 29: 4′, 6′. The use of subscripts is not always consistent within a single tablet. HKM 17 contains the sign UK with a subscript in obv. 9 but the sign AZ without a subscript in rev. 43, and HKM 53 contains the sign AZ without a subscript in obv. 7 but with a subscript in rev. 16. Starke asserts that the versions of AZ and UK with subscripts first appear in IIb (1985: 24).

KÙ	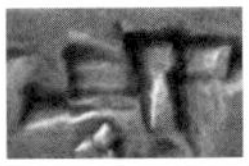	AK	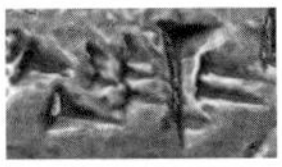	
AZ/UK	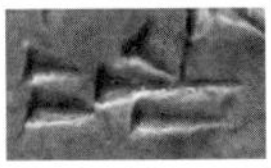	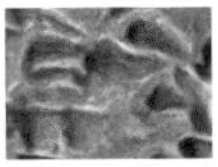		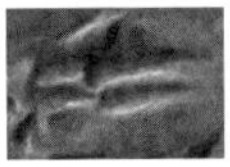

Table 5. KÙ, AK, and AZ/UK.

BI (153) is written with the heads of the two horizontals even in almost every instance. Van de Peut (2022: 24) proposes that BI with an indented upper horizontal is characteristic of the final NS stage (IIIc). This development would therefore be anachronistic for the majority of the tablets from Maşat Höyük, and so it is not strictly relevant to the texts at hand. There is one instance of BI written with the upper horizontal extending out in front of the lower horizontal (HKM 33 rev. 30′), which is the opposite of the expected chronological development for BI and of the similar trend towards indented horizontals in the MS stepped signs. This sign is in all likelihood an isolated and accidental variation, and not connected to other historical developments in signs beginning with stacked horizontal wedges.

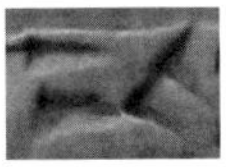	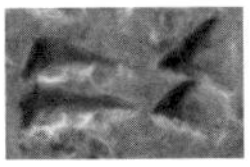	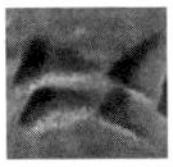	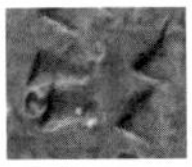

Table 6. BI.

ŠA appears with remarkable consistency either with the head of its internal vertical positioned between the two horizontals (158/A) or hanging from the upper horizontal (158/1). In a very few cases ŠA is written with the internal vertical hanging from the lower horizontal or positioned slightly above the upper horizontal. There are no examples of ŠA with its initial vertical extending prominently above the uppermost horizontal in this data set. According to Starke (1985: 24), the internal vertical in ŠA begins moving upwards during the period IIc and extends above the upper horizontal in the period IIIa. The sign GA (159) is typically written in this data set with its internal verticals within the same approximate range as those in ŠA, as are those in GU_4 (157) and UL (275),[11] although the latter two signs are not usually considered to be paleographically diagnostic.

TA also appears in this data set with its internal verticals within the same approximate range in height as those in the sign ŠA, either positioned directly between the two horizontals (160/B) or hanging from the upper horizontal (160/6–8). TA rarely appears with its internal verticals hanging from the lower horizontal or jutting slightly above the upper horizontal, and there is only one attestation of TA with the first two verticals inscribed at an equal height to the final vertical (HKM 71 u.e. 37). Forms of TA with the internal verticals written even with the upper horizontal appear already in OS (Weeden 2011: 44 n. 192) and is noticeable in IIa (Starke 1985: 23). The validity of the height of the internal verticals as a diagnostic feature was already called into question by Wilhelm, who observed that the "so stark betonte Kriterium der Länge der 'eingeschriebenen' senkrechten Keile bei dem Zeichen TA ist zweifellos wichtig, allerdings nicht unproblematisch" (apud Seeher 2005: 77 n. 18).

ŠA	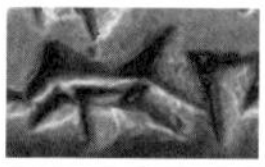	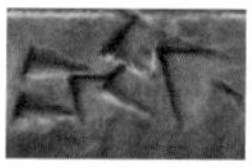	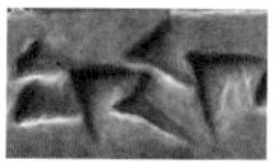	
GA	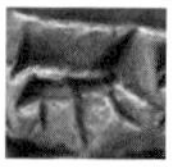	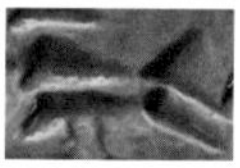		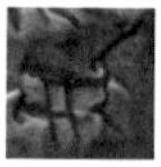
TA		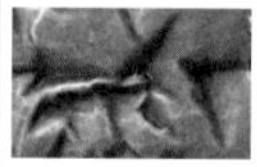	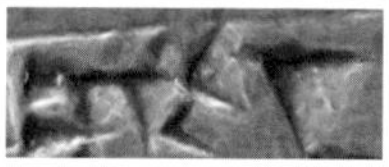	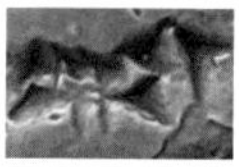

Table 7. ŠA, GA, and TA.

KAT is consistently written in its older *Leitzeichen* (173/A) with the head of the vertical wedge below the upper horizontal wedge (Alp 1991a: 113). In a few instances this sign is written with the vertical hanging from the lower horizontal (e. g. HKM 31 rev. 22, HKM 36 obv. 4).

AL typically appears without an internal *Winkelhaken* (183/A) in this data set, although Alp includes examples with an internal *Winkelhaken* in his presentation of the signs from the Maşat Höyük tablets (1991a: 115). There are only two instances of AL with an internal *Winkelhaken* (183/B) in the scans and photos (HKM 45 obv. 8′, HKM 73 obv. 12), but in both of these cases the signs in question are damaged. AL is regularly written with a flat bottom (183/5), which Weeden (2011: 44) identifies as a IIc form.

KAT			AL	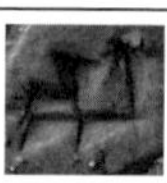

Table 8. KAT and AL.

11 Note, e. g. GU_4 in HKM 10 rev. 37, HKM 31 rev. 24, and HKM 46 u.e. 26, and UL in HKM 46 rev. 17, HKM 47 obv. 5 (twice), HKM 67 rev. 4′, HKM 71 obv. 9, obv. 14f., rev. 20, HKM 82 lo.e. 9, and HKM 86b rev. 13′.

E is generally written in this data set either with the head of its initial vertical positioned between the two horizontals (187/A) or with the initial vertical hanging from the upper horizontal (187/3). There are at least seven attestations of this sign with the initial vertical jutting above the upper horizontal but not quite even with the broken vertical (187/1, 7–8),[12] and there are at least eight attestations of the later form of E (187/B) with even verticals.[13] Starke (1985: 24) describes the upward movement of the initial vertical in E as coterminous with the one in ŠA, viz. beginning in the period IIc and first appearing above the upper horizontal in IIIa. The position of the initial vertical in the sign UN (197) in this data set closely resembles the initial vertical in E. It generally appears either between the two horizontals (197/1) or hanging from the upper horizontal (197/2), but occasionally will be written above the upper horizontal (197/B). E also occasionally appears in this data set with two unbroken verticals (187/10), e. g. in HKM 52 obv. 16.

E	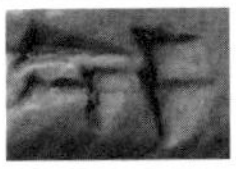			
UN	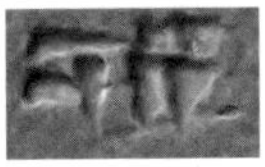	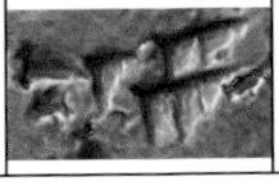		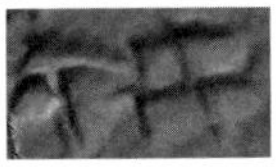

Table 9. E and UN.

SAG is only attested in two tablets in this data set. In both of these tablets this sign appears in its older variant (192/A), with the head of the initial vertical wedge below the upper horizontal. In one of the two tablets, SAG is written three times with space between the head of the initial vertical and the upper horizontal (HKM 46 obv. 8, rev. 20, rev. 23). In the other tablet, SAG is written with the initial vertical hanging from the upper horizontal (192/1, HKM 71 lo.e. 18).

KU (206) always appears in the same form in this data set, with three horizontal wedges and only one vertical wedge. Van de Peut (2022: 25) posits that the addition of a vertical wedge at the beginning of this sign (206/4–8) parallels the similar developments in the signs DI (312) and KI (313), although this sign is not usually considered to be diagnostic in other discussions of Hittite paleography.

Ù appears with some variation in this data set, but never in the form with a vertical wedge immediately after the initial *Winkelhaken* but before the first horizontal (265/B). In six instances[14] Ù is written in its oldest *Leitzeichen* (265/A), without an internal *Winkelhaken*. In HKM 21 rev. 18 this sign is clearly written with a second *Winkelhaken*. The traces apparent in the 3D scan suggest an internal *Winkelhaken* in the sign Ù in HKM 19 obv. 3, but this is not reflected in Alp's handcopy (Alp 1991b: 20). Starke claims that this form, "deren hinterer Teil dem alten IK ähnlich ist," first appears in the IIIa script (1985: 25). A deviating form of Ù appears in HKM 3 u.e. 22, which resembles

12 HKM 46 obv. 9, rev. 21, HKM 47 obv. 8, HKM 52 obv. 6, obv. 12, obv. 16, rev. 2.

13 HKM 29: 2′, HKM 52 obv. 3, rev. 27f., rev. 33, HKM 62 obv. 7, obv. 14, HKM 81 obv. 4.

14 HKM 17 obv. 2, HKM 23 obv. 2, HKM 67 obv. 2, HKM 69 obv. 2, HKM 81 obv. 1, HKM 82 obv. 3.

265/A, but begins with the sign MUNUS rather than a large *Winkelhaken* followed by a horizontal wedge.[15]

SAG	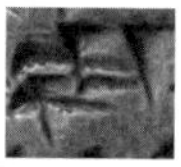	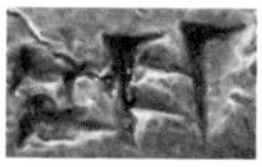	KU	
Ù	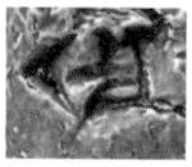	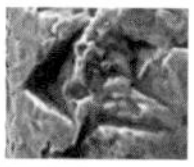	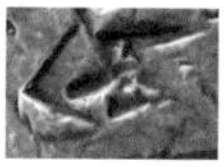	

Table 10. SAG, KU, and Ù.

AR is written with a broken horizontal in the majority of instances in this data set. However, AR appears with an unbroken horizontal (289/6) in HKM 31 rev. 28, HKM 47 obv. 33, lo.e. 38, and HKM 73 rev. 29. AR with an unbroken horizontal has been identified as a IIb feature by Miller (2004: 40f.) and Weeden (2011: 44). Alp (1991a: 117) presents two variants of AR, one with a twice-broken horizontal and one without a horizontal altogether. Neither of these forms occur in the tablets scanned by Müller and Cammarosano, nor are they presented in the HZL.

EL is only attested in nine texts in this data set.[16] In the majority of cases, EL appears with the middle vertical written lower than the first and third verticals (307/1–2). Although the HZL only presents one *Leitzeichen* for EL (307), Starke saw a parallel development in the increasing height of the verticals in EL and RU (43), dating the appearance of these signs with even verticals as IIIa (1985: 24). There are only two instances of EL with even verticals in this data set (HKM 56 obv. 7, lo.e. 14), both of which occur in a tablet that also contains the earlier form of this sign with an indented middle vertical (HKM 56 rev. 28).

AR	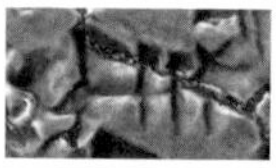	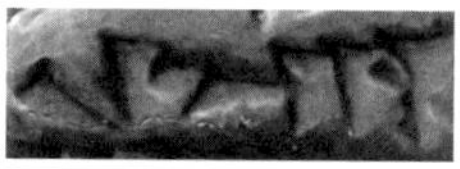	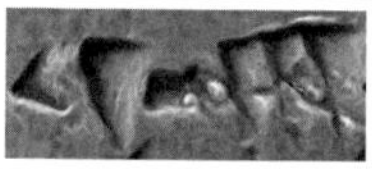
EL		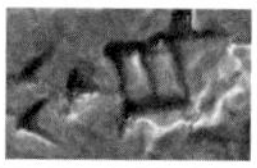	

Table 11. AR and EL.

DI is given in two *Leitzeichen* in the HZL, one with a large prominent *Winkelhaken* (312/A) and another with a smaller raised *Winkelhaken* (312/B). However, the presence or absence of an additional vertical before the horizontals is the diagnostic feature in this sign (Weeden 2011: 44), rather than the size and position of the initial *Winkelhaken*. DI is consistently written with only a single vertical throughout this data set.

15 This sign is transliterated "*ŠAL-MA*" by Alp (1991a: 122); cf. 1991b: 3; Hoffner 2009: 101.

16 HKM 3 obv. 7, HKM 10 rev. 47, HKM 19 rev. 13, u.e. 29, HKM 21 rev. 20, HKM 22 rev. 13, HKM 29: 8′, HKM 36 rev. 44, HKM 52 obv. 6, rev. 26, HKM 56 obv. 7, rev. 28, lo.e. 14.

The chronological development in DI parallels that in KI and KU, with the earliest forms containing only a single vertical, and the later forms with an additional vertical placed at the beginning of the sign before the horizontal wedges.

KI, like DI, is always written in this data set without an additional vertical directly after the initial *Winkelhaken.* The version of KI with two verticals (313/19–25) was identified as appearing in the latest stage of this sign's development by both Starke (1985: 25) and Klinger (1996: 38). However, several tablets (HKM 10, HKM 47, HKM 52, HKM 62, HKM 73, HKM 81) exhibit a variant of the sign KI with only two horizontals (313/12). These tablets reveal a tendency on the part of the scribe to write simplified sign-forms, which is also apparent in the variant of A with two unbroken verticals (364/4) and E with an unbroken second vertical (187/10).[17]

DI	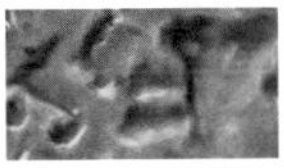	KI		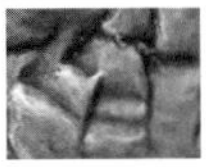

Table 12. DI and KI.

UZ appears with an unbroken horizontal (340/A, 340/C) twelve times in this data set,[18] and it is written with a broken horizontal (340/B) twice (HKM 19 rev. 27, HKM 22 lo.e. 10). UZ with a broken horizontal has been identified as a diagnostic sign for the period IIb (Gordin 2015: 90).

LI is always written in its distinctive older *Leitzeichen* (343/A) in the tablets from Maşat Höyük (see Alp 1991a: 118). This well-known sign is composed of the ŠE-group of four *Winkelhaken*, followed by two sets of two horizontals and a single vertical. The later form of LI (343/B), consisting of five *Winkelhaken* and two uprights, was not introduced until the period IIIb (Weeden 2011: 44).

SAR only occurs four times in this data set. It is written three times in the older *Leitzeichen* (HKM 47 obv. 2, HKM 52 obv. 13, HKM 86a rev. 13′), which contains only a single vertical wedge (353/A). SAR appears once in this data set with two verticals, the first of which is written below the upper horizontal (353/5). In this attestation (HKM 52 obv. 11) the initial vertical is very light, and the tablet is cracked at this point, but it does appear in the handcopy (Alp 1991b: 55). Starke (1985: 24) dates the appearance of SAR with two verticals to the period IIc, with no reference to the relative height of the verticals.

UZ		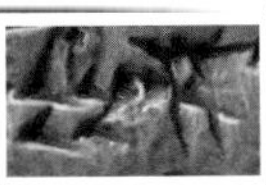	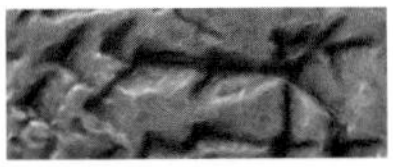	
LI	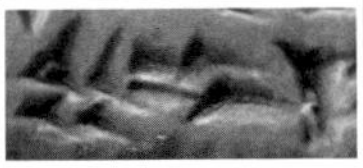	SAR		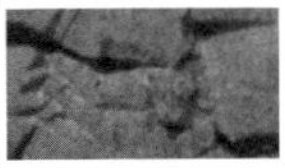

Table 13. UZ, LI, and SAR.

17 Note also "GIŠ" for MA (208/9) in HKM 73 rev. 19.

18 HKM 2 rev. 14, HKM 3 rev. 14, HKM 17 l.e. 1, HKM 21 rev. 16, HKM 31 rev. 21, HKM 33 rev. 34′, HKM 52 rev. 35, rev. 37, HKM 53 obv. 2, HKM 71 rev. 33, HKM 73 lo.e. 16, HKM 81 rev. 26.

MEŠ appears exclusively in its older *Leitzeichen* in this data set (360/A), which consists of a single vertical followed by three *Winkelhaken*. This set of tablets contains neither the later *Leitzeichen* (360/B), in which a doubly broken horizontal replaces the three *Winkelhaken*, nor the characteristically OS linked form ME+EŠ (360/1–4).

Ḫ̮A is consistently written in its older form (367/A), which includes two *Winkelhaken*. Even in cases where only a single *Winkelhaken* is clearly visible, close examination of the 3D scans reveals the second *Winkelhaken*. In HKM 53 obv. 6, for example, the first *Winkelhaken* is inscribed on top of the lower head of the second broken vertical. Similarly, in HKM 26 obv. 8, the first *Winkelhaken* is written between the two lower heads of the broken verticals. These examples serve to demonstrate that Ḫ̮A was regularly written with two *Winkelhaken*, even when the handcopies fail to depict them (cf. Alp 1991b: 29). Another variation of Ḫ̮A is apparent in these tablets that is not presented in the HZL, viz. Ḫ̮A with both *Winkelhaken* inscribed to the right of the second broken vertical (HKM 10, HKM 26, HKM 52, and HKM 81, passim). The first three of these tablets exhibit sign variants that appear simplified, such as KI with two horizontals (313/12) and A with two unbroken verticals (364/4).

MEŠ		Ḫ̮A		

Table 14. MEŠ and Ḫ̮A.

3.2. Signs that exhibit considerable variation

DU is written in three different ways in this data set. Of the fifty-six attestations of the sign DU that are clearly legible, forty of them are written with a diagonal as the uppermost wedge (128/2–3). Nine of these attestations present the sign in its oldest form, which features a *Winkelhaken* above the two stacked horizontals (128/A). Seven of these signs are written with the uppermost wedge as a horizontal (128/B). The contemporaneity of these sign-forms complicates the description of their relationship as a process of chronological development. According to Starke (1985: 24f.), the *Winkelhaken* first appears as a diagonal wedge in the earliest period of NS (IIIa).

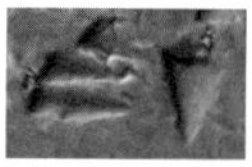	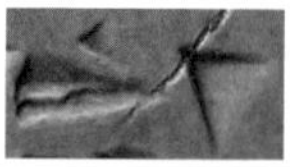	
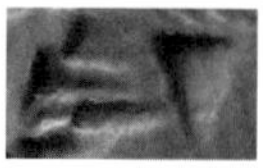	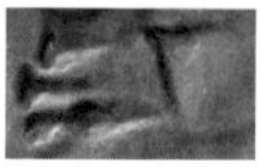	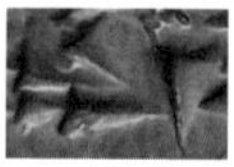

Table 15. DU.

ZU (209) appears in three forms in this data set. The most common variant comprises three horizontals, with the middle horizontal slightly indented, and the two vertical wedges of even or nearly even height (209/2–4). This sign can be found in ten texts that are part of this data set.[19] Starke (1985: 24) claims that this version of ZU first appears in the period IIIa. Two texts attest an older variant of ZU (209/1) in which the initial vertical is written at the level of the uppermost horizontal (HKM 30 lo.e. 11, HKM 73 lo.e. 16). Five texts have another variant of ZU (209/B), which consists of a broken horizontal above an unbroken horizontal terminating in two verticals.[20] HKM 2 contains both ZU with three unbroken horizontals and even verticals (rev. 14) and ZU with a broken horizontal (u.e. 21).

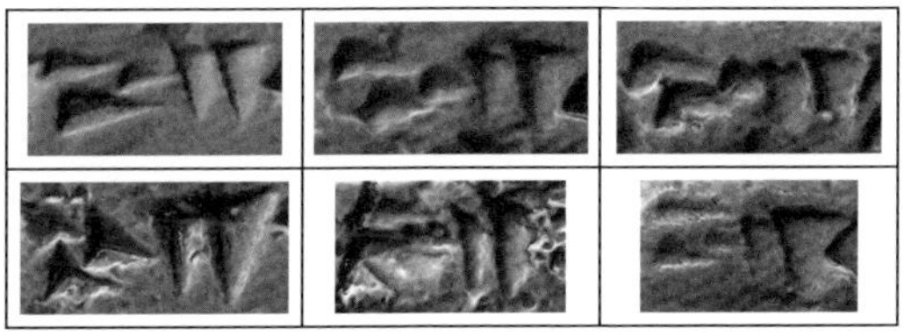

Table 16. ZU.

DA appears in several variations throughout these tablets. The strongest tendency apparent in this data set is for the *Winkelhaken* in DA to be set high, with its point approaching or even placed over the uppermost horizontal (214/6–7). This tendency to write a *Winkelhaken* higher than normal is also apparent in a few other signs throughout the Maşat Höyük tablets.[21] As noted *supra*, this feature is characteristic of cursive writing (Cammarosano 2021: 15f.). There are numerous attestations of the sign DA with a high *Winkelhaken* in this data set, and in the majority of these the internal horizontal is broken. The sign DA frequently appears in its oldest *Leitzeichen* (214/A), which has a broken internal horizontal and the heads of all of the stacked horizontals even. There are several attestations of the sign DA with an unbroken internal horizontal (214/C), a form which is typically associated with LNS (Klinger 1996: 37f.). However, the appearance of these signs could be the result of accidental causes, such as constrictions of space, an effect of writing quickly, or the broken horizontal simply being too lightly inscribed to be visible. There only one tablet attesting the MS stepped DA (214/B, HKM 19 obv. 12, rev. 24, l.e. 2), and there is one occurrence of DA with the middle horizontal protruding out ahead of the other two horizontals (HKM 36 obv. 11). In HKM 73 rev. 23, DA is written "reverse-stepped," with the uppermost horizontal extending out the farthest, and the unbroken middle horizontal extending out before the lowest horizontal.

IT appears in this data set in all three *Leitzeichen* that are given in the HZL. The oldest form of IT (215/A) is by far the most common, with at least thirty-three attestations. This version of the sign comprises three stacked horizontals with even heads, the middle of which is broken, followed by the ḪI-group and one vertical wedge. The latest form of this sign (215/C), in which the middle horizontal is unbroken, occurs at least

19 HKM 2 rev. 14, HKM 3 rev. 14, HKM 10 obv. 14, HKM 17 obv. 14, HKM 19 rev. 27, HKM 22 lo.e. 14, HKM 33 rev. 34′, HKM 46 rev. 19, HKM 53 obv. 10, HKM 81 rev. 26.

20 HKM 2 u.e. 21, HKM 31 rev. 21, HKM 71 rev. 33, HKM 95 rev. 6′, HKM 99 obv. 4, obv. 6, rev. 14.

21 For example, note GIGIR in HKM 52 rev. 42, and UTU in HKM 26 and HKM 46 (passim).

nine times in this data set. In a number of instances, it is difficult to make a determination about whether the internal horizontal is broken, due to damage on the tablet or the sign being very lightly written. IT appears in the MS stepped form (215/B) five times in this data set (HKM 10 lo.e. 27, HKM 17 obv. 13, lo.e. 24, l.e. 4, HKM 19 obv. 4). According to Starke (1985: 24), the signs IT and DA with extended lower horizontals are characteristic of the IIb–IIc script.

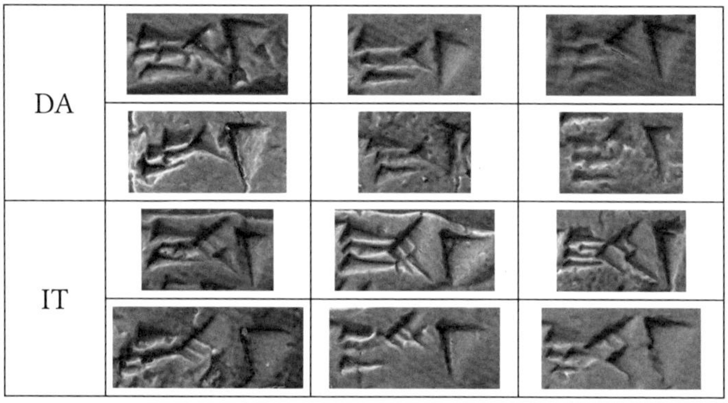

Table 17. DA and IT.

URU is attested in several variants in this data set. In the most frequently occurring form of URU the initial vertical extends above the uppermost horizontal and is even or nearly even with the second vertical (229/1). Somewhat less frequently attested is URU with the initial vertical below or hanging from the uppermost horizontal (229/2, 4). There is one attestation of URU with the initial vertical even with the second highest horizontal (HKM 32 obv. 7), and one attestation of the late form of URU (229/B), with the middle horizontal protruding out in front of the upper and lower horizontals (HKM 47 obv. 3). The form of URU with the initial vertical extending above the uppermost horizontal can be dated to the period IIc (Starke 1985: 25). URU with an extended middle horizontal appears in the latest phase of NS according to Starke (1985: 25) or IIIb according to Klinger (1996: 38).

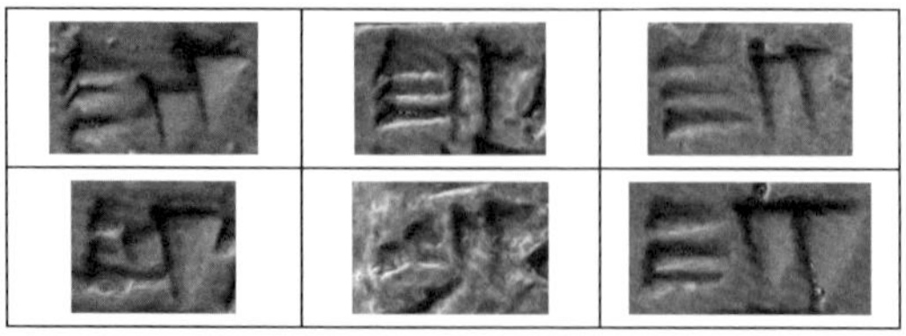

Table 18. URU.

AḪ is listed with two *Leitzeichen* in the HZL, viz. the older form (332/A), in which the horizontal wedge is written entirely within the triangle made by the three *Winkelhaken*, and the later form (332/B), in which the horizontal is placed outside of the three

Winkelhaken. In this data set a middle form can be identified (332/4), in which the horizontal is written in the mouth of the triangle, directly between the upper and lower *Winkelhaken*. Of the ninety-two attestations of AḪ that are written clearly in this data set, fifty-eight of them are late forms (332/B), twenty-three of them are middle forms (332/4), and ten of them are old forms (332/A). Starke first discerns the middle form of AḪ in the period IIc (Starke 1985: 24, cf. Weeden 2011: 44).

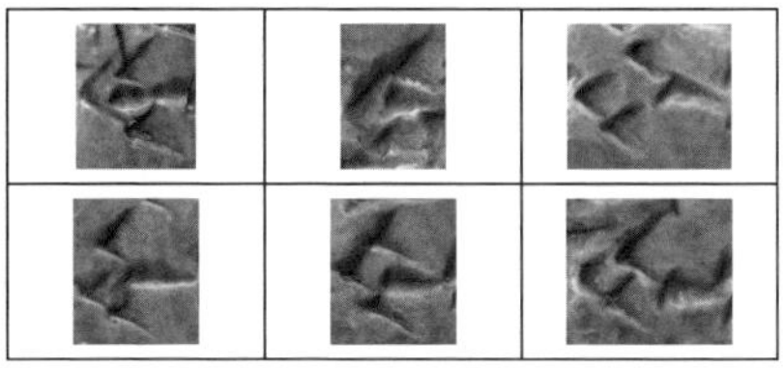

Table 19. AḪ.

ḪAR exhibits a parallel development to the sign AḪ, and is also presented in two *Leitzeichen* in the HZL. As in AḪ, the older form of ḪAR is written with three horizontals wholly within the triangle of *Winkelhaken* (333/A), and the three horizontals are outside of the triangle of *Winkelhaken* in the later form (333/B). A middle form of ḪAR (333/4) is also apparent in this data set. The late form of ḪAR (333/B) is attested twenty-six times in this data set, and the middle form (333/4) appears eleven times, but the old form of ḪAR (333/B) only appears once (HKM 21 rev. 18).

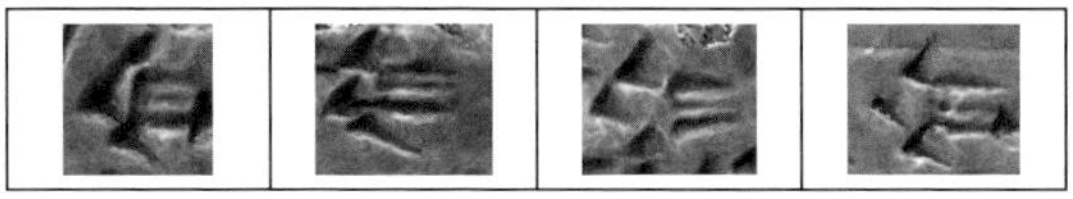

Table 20. ḪAR.

3.3. Ligatures

Ligatures occur frequently in the texts from Maşat Höyük. In the context of this paper, a ligature is understood as a sequence of two signs written without conspicuous interposing space, as if they were a single sign. This definition thus includes cases in which two signs are linked by one or more constituent wedges (e. g. *A+NA*), as well as cases in which there is markedly less space between the wedges of two sequential signs than there is between the other signs in the same line of text (e. g. KA+A). In ligatures containing the sign A (viz. *A+NA*, KA+A, RA+A, and MA+A), A is frequently written as two unbroken verticals (364/4), identical to the sign MIN (361). According to Starke (1985: 23), ligatures are characteristic of OS, but Miller (2004: 40 n. 73) has recognized their presence in MS texts.

The ligature *A+NA* is extremely common in this data set, occurring thirty-two times out of the fifty instances of the Akkadogram *ANA* that are clearly legible. The ligature *A+NA* therefore appears more often than the sequence *A-NA* written as separate signs. In this ligature A generally appears as two unbroken verticals (364/4), and the head of the horizontal is written on top of the second vertical. This ligature can be considered a characteristic of MS texts (van de Peut 2022: 29).

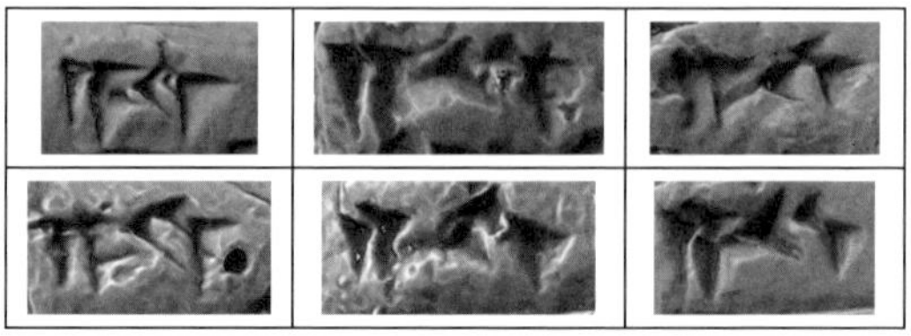

Table 21. A+NA.

The ligature KA+A is also very common in this data set. In this ligature the sign A (frequently 364/4, cf. Miller 2004: 41) is written directly after the final vertical in KA with no intervening space. In some instances, the horizontal(s) in KA reach(es) or extend(s) below the verticals of A (e. g. HKM 36 l.e. 3, HKM 56 obv. 11). The ligature KA+A occurs twenty times in this data set, whereas the signs KA-A are written separately fifteen times.

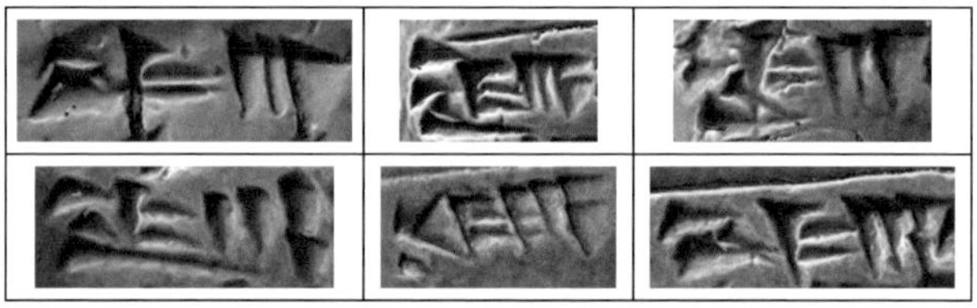

Table 22. KA+A.

A similar ligature is MA+A, in which the verticals in A (often 364/4) are written directly after the final vertical of MA with no intervening space, as if they were one sign. The ligature MA+A occurs eight times in this data set,[22] and there are an equal number of instances of the writing MA-A without ligature.[23]

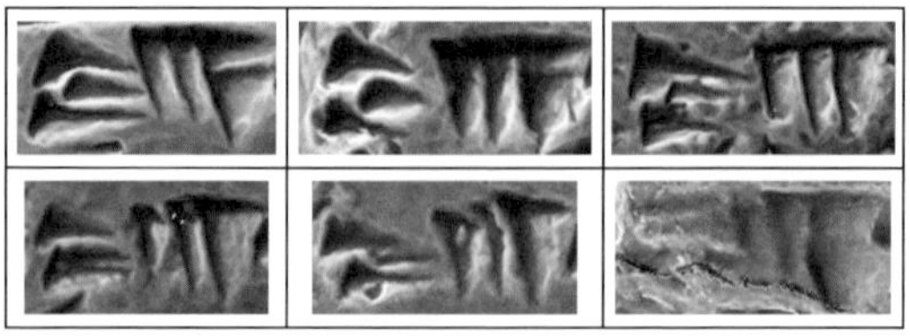

Table 23. MA+A.

Ligatures with the sign RA are relatively less common in this data set. The ligature RA+A occurs eleven times in these tablets, and the sequence RA-A occurs without lig-

22 HKM 17 obv. 22, HKM 30 l.e. 3, HKM 46 obv. 8, obv. 10, HKM 71 obv. 16, HKM 95 rev. 4′, rev. 8′f.
23 HKM 36 rev. 49f., HKM 47 rev. 51, rev. 54, HKM 52 obv. 17, rev. 39, HKM 73 obv. 11, obv. 14.

ature sixty-six times. The ligatures RA+AŠ and RA+AN are only present in a single text (HKM 47 obv. 23, obv. 27, obv. 32f.).

Ligatures with the sign KAT also occur in this data set. The ligature *kat+ti* occurs six times throughout these tablets,[24] and the sequence without ligature *kat-ti* only occurs four times.[25] The ligature *kat+ta*, however, only occurs once (HKM 30 obv. 9), whereas the sequence *kat-ta* appears in this data set five times.[26] The unique ligature KAT+DU can be found in HKM 46 obv. 8 (written on the reverse).

RA+A	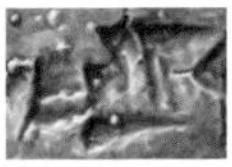	RA+AŠ	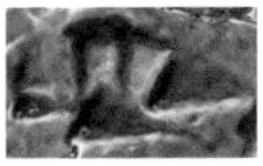
kad+du		*kat+ta*	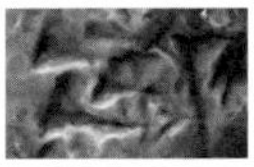
kat+ti	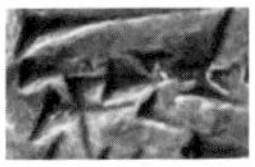	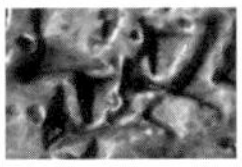	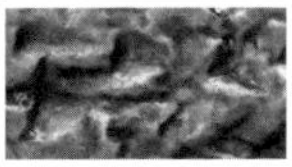

Table 24. Ligatures with RA and KAT.

4. Conclusions

Numerous paleographic features in these texts indicate that the designation MS is appropriate for the tablets from Maşat Höyük. The complete absence of the late forms of TAR (7/C), QA (21/B), GI (30/B), EN (40/C), IK (67/B), KÙ (69/B), AK (81/B), KAT (173/B), and LI (343/B) suggests a date for this corpus before NS, while the presence of the middle forms of TAR (7/B) and EN (40/B) requires a date after OS. The ligature *A+NA* is also characteristic of MS. The occurrence of the signs AZ and UK with subscripts (92/B and 93/B) suggests a date for these tablets of no earlier than IIb, and the rare occurrence of stepped IT (215/B) and DA (214/B) suggests a date of IIb–IIc. AR with an unbroken horizontal (289/6) and UZ with a broken horizontal (340/B) have been interpreted as IIb forms. AL with a flat bottom (183/5), on the other hand, suggests a IIc date for this corpus. The form of URU with its initial vertical extending above the upper horizontal or equal to the second vertical also suggests a dating of IIc. The latest form of URU (229/B) is characteristic of LNS, but it only occurs once in this corpus, and therefore it is most likely an accidental variation. Thus, the general appearance of this script is IIc, with some vestigial IIb sign-forms.

However, several other paleographic features suggest a general dating of these tablets to the earliest stage of NS (IIIa). The signs RU and EL occasionally appear in their later forms (43/B and 307/1–2), with all three verticals of equal height. DU with its uppermost wedge as a diagonal (128/2–3) has been interpreted as a IIIa sign-form.

24 HKM 3 rev. 17, HKM 10 rev. 44, HKM 21 rev. 17, HKM 30 rev. 22, HKM 31 rev. 22, HKM 52 obv. 3.

25 HKM 2 rev. 17, HKM 56 rev. 23, HKM 73 obv. 15, rev. 19.

26 HKM 10 rev. 36, HKM 31 rev. 19, HKM 36 obv. 4, HKM 46 u.e. 26, HKM 47 obv. 15.

The occurrence of the signs E (187/B) and ZU (209/2–4) with even verticals also suggest the dating IIIa. Ù with an internal *Winkelhaken* has been interpreted as IIIa, although this sign-form only occurs once or twice in this data set. While the middle forms of AḪ (332/4) and ḪAR (333/4) would suggest a date of IIc, the later forms 332/B and 333/B are attested more frequently than the middle forms of these respective signs. The signs ŠA and GA frequently appear with their internal vertical(s) hanging from the upper horizontal, which is indicative of IIc script, but occasionally these verticals protrude slightly above the upper horizontal.

The difference between the IIc and IIIa forms of E, UN, ŠA, and GA is one of the heights of their inscribed verticals, and the difference between the IIc and IIIa forms of AḪ and ḪAR is a matter of the slight outward placement of the horizontal(s). The distinction between the older form of DU and the IIIa DU is a slight elongation of the lower side of a wedge, resulting in a downward-sloping diagonal rather than a *Winkelhaken*. Such minor differences seem like tenuous grounds for meaningful argumentation. It could be the case that the tablets from Maşat Höyük depict a transitional phase between MS and NS, or it could be the case that the upward movement of the inscribed verticals in these signs began earlier than has previously been claimed.[27] A third option would be to dismiss such features as the height of the verticals as diagnostic criteria altogether. The range of the heights of these inscribed verticals that is apparent within a given tablet – or even within a given line – implies that the Hittite scribes paid far less attention to such details than Hittitologists do.

While it remains difficult to definitively describe the handwriting of individual scribes, some limited observations are nevertheless possible. Šanda, Šuriḫili, Ḫašammili, Mār-ešrē, and Tarḫunmiya all wrote the signs UK or AZ with a subscript in at least one instance, and all of these scribes except Šanda wrote texts containing the later variant of the sign RU (43/B). The use of these sign-forms can therefore be said to characterize the script of the texts from Maşat Höyük in general, and was not typical of any one scribe. Nor are ligatures a practical metric for identifying a particular scribal hand, since every known scribe in this data set except Ilī-kakkab employed both linked and non-linked forms.[28] The prevalence of ligatures is thus a common feature of this corpus, especially the ligatures of KA+A and *A+NA*, which are both attested more frequently than non-linked sequences of the same signs.

Similarly, the use of cursive can be understood as a general tendency in this corpus, and not as something that is a distinctive trait of any particular scribe. One remarkable cursive feature is the predilection for writing with simplified signs, especially KI with only two horizontals (313/12), A with two unbroken verticals (364/4), even outside of

27 The paleographic dating of this data set corresponds to the results of the orthographic and grammatical assessment of the texts from Maşat Höyük in Hoffner 2010: 139, which concluded that "the Maşat corpus of letters and administrative texts shows a stage of Hittite that, while it is certainly pre-NH, is already accepting innovations that we have come to think of as typically New Hittite." To Hoffner's collected observations can be added the typically NH use of the sign TÉN for the act. pret./imp. pl. 2 ending (HKM 17 obv. 4, obv. 13, obv. 21, rev. 43, l.e. 4, HKM 20 obv. 9, lo.e. 12, HKM 33 rev. 24′, HKM 36 obv. 8, HKM 45 lo.e. 16′, HKM 86b rev. 13′) and the OH spelling *e-eš-tu* (HKM 2 rev. 19, HKM 3 lo.e. 10, rev. 13, HKM 95 rev. 9′).

28 Ilī-kakkab is only known to have written one tablet in this data set, HKM 95, which preserves only sixteen lines of text, but contains three instances of the ligature MA+A.

a ligature, and E with an unbroken second vertical (187/10). As noted *supra*, these simplified signs frequently appear in texts written by Tarḫunmiya, but are also present in at least two of Mār-ešrē's texts, and therefore cannot be identified exclusively as a characteristic of the former scribe. The use of these simplified sign-forms is one element of an epistolary style of Hittite cuneiform, perhaps one specifically developed for hasty writing, as opposed to the library style that is apparent in the lengthier documents of the Boğazköy corpus.

Certain observations can also be made about the orthographic habits of individual scribes. Ḫašammili wrote one of the two tablets preserving the OS variant of TAR (HKM 19 obv. 14). Apart from this one sign, Ḫašammili's handwriting appears characteristically MS. He wrote all but one of the attestations of stepped IT (HKM 17 obv. 13, lo.e. 24, l.e. 4, HKM 19 obv. 4) and all attestations of stepped DA (HKM 19 obv. 12, rev. 24, l.e. 2) in this data set. Ḫašammili also wrote the only attestation of MS EN that is preserved in this data set (HKM 19 rev. 23), and he wrote one of the two attestations of UZ with a broken horizontal (HKM 19 rev. 27), the other of which was written by Mār-ešrē (HKM 22 lo.e. 10).

Mār-ešrē was the only identifiable scribe in this data set to write the sign AR with an unbroken horizontal (HKM 31 rev. 28, HKM 73 rev. 29). Mār-ešrē also wrote the "reverse-stepped" DA (HKM 73 rev. 23) and the sign BI with its upper horizontal extending out before its lower horizontal (HKM 33 rev. 30′), both of which involve a rightward movement of the stylus while writing a sequence of stacked horizontals. Mār-ešrē writes the sign DU with a diagonal (128/2–3) with remarkable regularity, although this form of DU is far more common in this data set than either DU with a *Winkelhaken* (128/A) or DU with an uppermost horizontal (128/B), so this might be better understood as a general trend in the Maşat Höyük corpus.

In addition to the preference for simplified sign-forms already discussed, the handwriting of Tarḫunmiya is characterized by the frequent writing of the sign E with tall verticals (HKM 29: 2′, HKM 52 passim, HKM 62 obv. 7, obv. 14, HKM 81 obv. 4) and by the sign ḪA written with both *Winkelhaken* to the right of the second broken vertical (HKM 52 and HKM 81, passim). The latter trait is also visible in HKM 10 and HKM 26, which Alp (1991a: 132 n. 42, Taf. 8–9) attributed to Tarḫunmiya on the basis of handwriting. Tarḫunmiya also wrote both examples of the sign EL with even verticals in this data set (HKM 56 obv. 7, lo.e. 14).

Due to the limited number of tablets that belong to named scribes in this data set, this study refrains from assigning anonymous tablets to known scribes on the basis of a macroscopic analysis of handwriting alone. While it is possible to propose some general remarks on the orthographic tendencies of a few scribes of the Maşat Höyük corpus, these results must be regarded as tentative on account of the paucity of sources available for this study and the variation in script and ductus apparent therein. With access to the entire collection of tablets from Maşat Höyük, Alp was able to identify the handwriting of particular scribes, and to ascribe some of the unsigned tablets to those scribes on the basis of script alone.[29] However, the prospect of identifying the authors of other anonymous tablets must remain, for the time being, a desideratum

29 See section 2 above; cf. also Alp 1991a: 52f., 57–62, 65, 78f., 91, 94, 96–98, Taf. 6–13.

for future studies, which could be facilitated by the further digitalization of this collection of tablets, or through the improved capability and application of computer analysis.

Bibliography

Alp, Sedat

1991a *Hethitische Briefe aus Maşat-Höyük.* TTKY VI/6. Ankara: Türk Tarih Kurumu Basımevi.

1991b *Hethitische Keilschrifttafeln aus Maşat-Höyük.* TTKY VI/34. Ankara: Türk Tarih Kurumu Basımevi.

Beckman, Gary

1995 Hittite Provincial Administration in Anatolia and Syria: the View from Maşat and Emar. In: Onofrio Carruba, Mauro Giorgieri, and Clelia Mora (eds.), *Atti del II Congresso internazionale di Hittologia.* Pavia: Gianni Iuculano, 19–37.

Bilgin, Tayfun

2018 *Officials and Administration in the Hittite World.* SANER 21. Berlin / Boston: de Gruyter.

Cammarosano, Michele

2015 3D-Joins und Schriftmetrologie. A Quantitative Approach to Cuneiform Palaeography. In: Elena Devecchi, Gerfrid G.W. Müller, and Jana Mynářová (eds.), *Current Research in Cuneiform Palaeography. Proceedings of the Workshop organised at the 60th Rencontre Assyriologique Internationale, Warsaw 2004.* Gladbeck: PeWe, 145–86.

2021 *At the Interface of Religion and Administration: The Hittite Cult Inventories. With a contribution by Adam Kryszeń.* StBoT 68. Wiesbaden: Harrassowitz.

de Martino, Stefano

2005 Hittite Letters from the Time of Tutḫaliya I/II, Arnuwanda I and Tutḫaliya III. *AoF* 32: 291–321.

del Monte, Giuseppe F.

1995 I testi amministrativi da Maşat Höyük/Tapika. *OAM* 2: 89–138.

Gander, Max

2022 *Geschichte und Geographie Westkleinasiens in der Hethiterzeit.* THeth 33. Heidelberg: Winter.

Gordin, Shai

2015 *Hittite Scribal Circles: Scholarly Tradition and Writing Habits.* StBoT 59. Wiesbaden: Harrassowitz.

Hoffner, Harry A., Jr.

2009 *Letters from the Hittite Kingdom.* WAW 15. Atlanta, Georgia: Society of Biblical Literature.

2010 A Grammatical Profile of the Middle Hittite Maşat Texts. In: Jörg Klinger, Elisabeth Rieken, and Christel Rüster (eds.), *Investigationes Anatolicae. Gedenkschrift für Erich Neu.* StBoT 52. Wiesbaden: Harrassowitz, 111–41.

Klinger, Jörg

1995 Das Corpus der Maşat-Briefe und seine Beziehungen zu den Texten aus Ḫattuša. *ZA* 85: 74–108.

1996 *Untersuchungen zur Rekonstruktion der hattischen Kultschicht.* StBoT 37. Wiesbaden: Harrassowitz.

Miller, Jared L.

2004 *Studies in the Origins, Development and Interpretation of the Kizzuwatna Rituals.* StBoT 46. Wiesbaden: Harrassowitz.

Sakuma, Yasuhiko

2009 *Hethitische Vogelorakeltexte. Teil 2: Bearbeitung.* Ph.D. dissertation, Universität Würzburg.

Seeher, Jürgen

2005 Die Ausgrabungen in Boğazköy-Ḫattuša 2004 mit Beiträgen von Rainer Pasternak und Gernot Wilhelm. *AA*: 63–80.

Starke, Frank

1985 *Die keilschrift-luwischen Texte in Umschrift.* StBoT 30. Wiesbaden: Harrassowitz.

van den Hout, Theo P.J.

2007 Some observations on the tablet collection from Maşat Höyük. In: Alfonso Archi and Rita Francia (eds.), *VI Congresso Internazionale di Ittitologia Roma, 5–9 settembre 2005. SMEA* 49, 387–98.

2009 A Century of Hittite Text Dating and the Origins of the Hittite Cuneiform Script. *Incontri Linguistici* 32: 11–35.

van de Peut, Lidewij E.

2022 *Persuading the Divine: On the Composition of Hittite Prayers.* StBoT 69. Wiesbaden: Harrassowitz.

Weeden, Mark

2011 *Hittite Logograms and Hittite Scholarship.* StBoT 54. Wiesbaden: Harrassowitz.

THE TEXTS FROM THE KAYALIPINAR 'ARCHIVE EXCAVATION' AND THEIR SCRIBES

Jürgen Lorenz and Elisabeth Rieken
Philipps-Universität Marburg

Abstract

The present article presents a paleographic investigation on the limited corpus of the 121 fragments from the 'archive excavation' in Kayalıpınar. Special focus is laid on identification of scribal hands by the visual appearance of the sign forms. As a result, several new direct and indirect joins are suggested (Section 2). Furthermore, the findspots of the fragments and the size of the joined tablets are taken into account to draw conclusions on the original conditions of the tablet storage (Section 3). The final section offers a short evaluation of the success of the paleographic method applied here (Section 4).

1. Introduction

Recently, Yakubovich and Mouton (2023: 29–239) presented a large-scale investigation on the paleography of the manuscripts belonging to the Puriyanni ritual (*CTH* 758) and those of the Kuwattalla tradition (*CTH* 760–763). The authors claim that, by way of identifying scribal hands and combining this information with other criteria traditionally used (e. g. content, peculiar expressions and spellings), they were able to propose new direct and indirect joins and dispute several of those suggested in previous scholarship. The key element of their paleographic analysis is the observation of individual sign forms (termed *ductus* in van den Hout 2012: 152f.). In addition, the general aspect of the script (slanted verticals, length of horizontals, position of the signs with regard to the virtual middle line, etc.) and the tablet as a whole (e. g. width and depth of the column divider) is taken into consideration. Yakubovich and Mouton (2023: 30) stress the relevance of their approach for the treatment of other corpora of Hittite texts:

> The proposed analysis arguably represents an approach whose significance goes beyond the Luwili Project. Indeed, there is no reason why it cannot be undertaken with respect to other groups of Boğazköy texts featuring numerous copies and/or parallel versions, with similar results for the improvement of their classification.

The present contribution wants to test the method regarding its feasibility and the validity of its results. On account of their limited number and dispersion, the finds from the so-called 'archive excavation' in Kayalıpınar offer a suitable test case, constituting a corpus of 121 fragments of clay tablets from an area of ca. 8.3–12.2 × 29.2 m^2 plus another smaller area of 3.3 × 10.0 m^2. Fig. 1 shows a concentration of tablet finds in an area of 5 × 6.7 m^2 in the center of the trench. The excavators interpret the situation as the result of the destruction by fire of an archive in the upper story of a building (Müller-Karpe and Müller-Karpe 2019: 7):

> Die Grabungen zeigten, dass sämtliche Stücke ursprünglich zu einem gemeinsamen Fundkomplex gehörten, der lediglich durch den Pflug auseinander gerissen worden war. Allerdings ist die Fundstelle auch nicht mit dem ehemaligen Aufbewahrungsort identisch. Wie bereits bei den Tafelfunden aus der Palastanlage Gebäude A und B erläutert, dürfte auch in diesem Fall von einer Aufbewahrung im Obergeschoss eines Gebäudes auszugehen sein, von dem sie dann verstürzten.

If the paleographic analysis as applied by Yakubovich and Mouton yields the expected results, answers to the following questions about the assumed archive should be possible:

- Is it possible to join the tablet fragments on the basis of the paleographic analysis and the outer appearance?
- Do the finds come from a unified archive?
- What was the archive's function?
- How many scribes worked for the archive?

The article is organized as follows: in Section 2, the corpus as presented in the principal edition DAAM 1 will be scrutinized for indications that two or more fragments were written by the same scribe. Based on the results of this investigation, new joins will be suggested and checked against clay quality, form, and content. Section 3 is devoted to further observations on the find situation of individual tablets whose reconstruction was considerably improved by the work presented in the preceding section. It will be shown that the assumption of a unified archive is less certain than at first sight, and it is doubtful that we are dealing with an archive at all. Section 4 presents an evaluation of the method of identifying scribal hands as suggested by Yakubovich and Mouton.

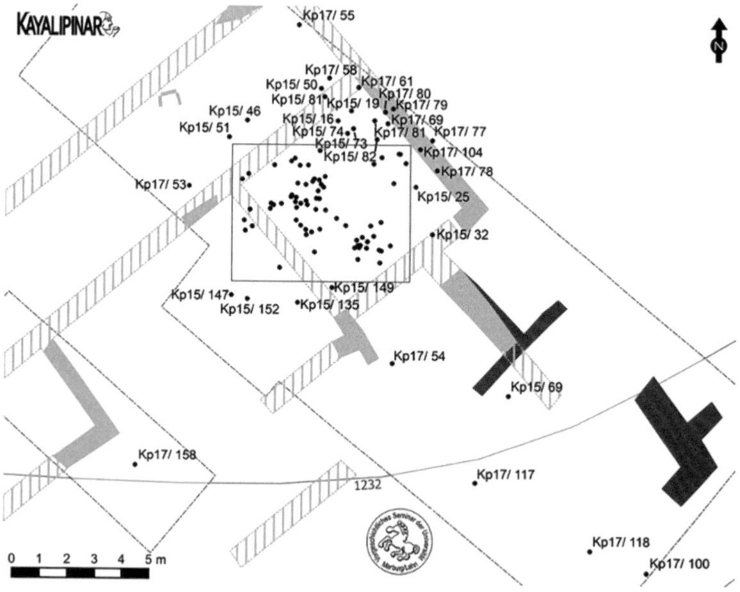

Fig. 1. Area of the 'archive excavation' in Kayalıpınar–Šamuḫa with the distribution of the tablet finds 2014–2017 (cited from Müller-Karpe and Müller-Karpe 2019: 4).

2. The corpus

With the exception of some tablets that are heavily burnt and difficult to read, the 121[1] fragments of the corpus under investigation have been published in DAAM 1 as numbers 34 and 36–100. At the time of their publication, roughly one half of the fragments (57) were directly joined with at least one other fragment, forming 13 separate texts. In addition, several indirect joins were proposed by the authors of DAAM 1. In general, the manuscripts feature New or Late New Script. Although not all fragments can be dated due to their small size and a lack of telltale signs, there is nothing that would suggest that any of them were written in an earlier period.

Reinvestigating the corpus and adopting the paleographic analysis of scribal hands as proposed by Yakubovich and Mouton (2023: 29–239), the reconstruction of the texts yielded a more accurate and clear-cut picture of the material. In the remainder of this section, we will focus on the texts resulting from the joins that emerged after the fragments were organised according to the scribal hands.

2.1 Cult inventories

DAAM 1.36, the so-called 'Šamuḫa Tablet', consists of eleven fragments, ten direct joins and one indirect join. Cammarosano (2019: 51, 60–62) already listed DAAM 1.37 and DAAM 1.38 as likely indirect joins with DAAM 1.36. In addition, DAAM 1.47 is written by the same scribe, as can be seen from the sign forms of ITU, ḪA, UP, NU, ZI, and GAG (cf. Table 1).[2] Also, its content fits well with DAAM 1.36, although a direct join seems to be impossible.

Thus, the tablet consists of ten fragments joining directly and four indirect joins – in sum, 14 fragments. It likely contained about 200 lines, of which 170 lines are fully or partly preserved.

DAAM 1.39 is another cult inventory. It consists of eight fragments joining directly. In his treatment, Cammarosano (2019: 83) already noticed that DAAM 1.39, 1.40 and 1.41 were written by the same scribe. Moreover, for DAAM 1.42, he considered the possibility that it belongs to DAAM 1.41 (2019: 91).

Based on the conclusions that Cammarosano drew from the paleographic analysis, Lorenz was able to confirm the suggested join between DAAM 1.41 and 1.42 by piecing them together as seen in the photo join in Fig. 2 (cf. Lorenz in the *Konkordanz*; Košak 2002–). Moreover, the question of the exact placement of DAAM 1.40 is sufficiently answered by the column divider, the empty line in the left column line 3′, and the erased line ibid. 7′. Thus, *contra* the edition, the obverse and reverse must be inverted. Conclusive support comes from the textual evidence, because the line ends in DAAM 1.40 and the beginnings in 1.39 yield coherent sequences:

1 Including the finds made by the guard of the excavation Vedat Erdoğan in 2014 (Kp 14/95 and Kp 14/125).

2 In most cases, the form of MA in DAAM 1.36 features a long upmost horizontal imprint, whereas the two lower ones begin further to the right and are shorter (e. g. ii 8). However, in ii 7, the two upper horizontals are longer and contrast with the lowest one, and in ii 4 all three horizontals have almost the same length, which makes the sign similar to one in DAAM 1.47: 3′.

	DAAM 1.47	DAAM 1.36
ITU	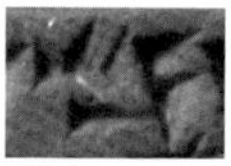	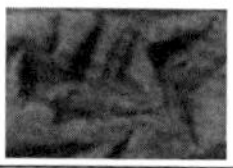
ḪA	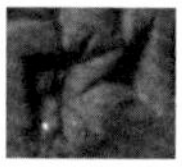	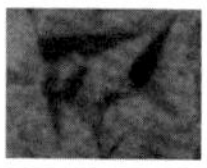
UP		
NU	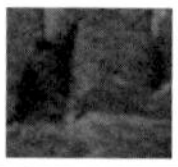	
ZI		
GAG		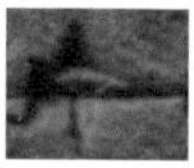

Table 1. Comparison of sign forms in DAAM 1.47 and 1.36.

DAAM 1.40 + 1.39:

$^{\text{1.40 i! 6′}}$ ^{LÚ}NAR *ḫ*]*a-at-ti-li* NU.GÁ[L] $^{\text{1.39 i 35}}$ ^{LÚ}NAR ^{URU}*ka-ni-i*[*š*

…

$^{\text{1.40 i! 10′}}$]x GU$_4$.MAḪ NIGA $^{\text{1.39 i 38}}$ $^{\text{GU}_4}$ÁB NIGA *i-ia-an-za*

$^{\text{1.40 i! 11′}}$ *-m*]*a-aš* AMAR$^{\text{ḪI.A}}$ $^{\text{1.39 i 39}}$ *ma-ak-la-an-te-eš* [

DAAM 1.51 represents yet another fragment with two empty lines before a paragraph ruler, which may therefore belong to the tablet DAAM 1.39. After the ruler, the text in DAAM 1.51: 6″ conforms well with the beginning of the line in DAAM 1.39 i 31: $^{\text{1.39 i 31}}$ 3 ⌜É⌝ [DINGIR-*LIM ŠA*] $^{\text{1.51: 6″}}$ ⌜^{D}⌝10 KARAŠ["3 temp[les: of] the Storm-god of the Army […]". In the following line DAAM 1.51: 7″, the dative *pá*]*r-ni* ^{D}KAL "to the [temp]le$^{?}$ of the Stag-god" fits perfectly with the line end in DAAM 1.40 i$^{!}$ 5′]UDU *pé-eš-kán-*[*zi*] "they give a sheep" producing a coherent sentence. As a consequence, the obverse and reverse of DAAM 1.40 must be exchanged *vis-à-vis* the labels in the edition. Regarding the sign forms, the few identifiable signs on this tiny fragment fit into the picture of DAAM 1.39, so that the overall evidence speaks strongly for the indirect join of DAAM 1.51 with 1.39

Finally, there is evidence beyond the sign forms that also DAAM 1.41 + 1.42 belong to the same tablet. First of all, the labels of the obv. i and rev. iv have to be switched as can be told from the *Randleiste* seen on the lower edge of obv. i. Thus, column rev. iii of DAAM 1.39 ending with a list of existing temples (Ì.GÁL) immediately precedes rev. iv$^{!}$ of DAAM 1.41 + 1.42 (labeled as obv. i in the edition), which begins with the statement that 16 temples are not established (NU.GÁL). This is followed by lists of $^{\text{NA}_4}$ZI.KIN stelae, stones, mountains, and springs. Thus, the entire text consists of a coherent sequence of

Fig. 2. Photojoin DAAM 1.41 + 1.42.

	DAAM 1.51	DAAM 1.39
NA		
IR		
Ú		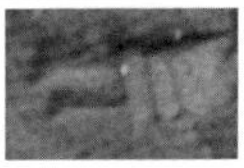
TE		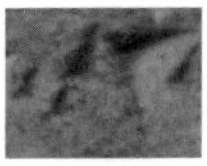
ZA		
KI	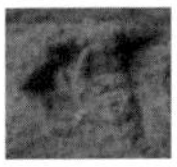	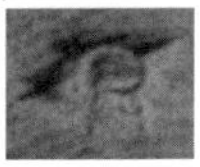

Table 2. Comparison of sign forms in DAAM 1.51 and 1.39.

extant temples, lacking temples, extant stelae, stones, mountains, and springs, and their respective cult activities.

In sum, the tablet DAAM 1.39(++) consists of 16 fragments with all possible direct and indirect joins.[3] Its column length can only be approximated from the preserved part of the left edge. The left edge is inscribed and is remarkable for its column divider located at roughly the thickest part of the tablet dividing the left edge into two columns and thus indicating its middle line. As the preserved upper part of col. i and the lower part of col. iv consist of 35 and 33 lines respectively, the columns should have had twice the number of lines, i. e. about 66 to 70 lines. Accordingly, the total number of lines on the tablet, including those on the lower edge and the left edge, amounts to 270–290. If it were possible to establish the exact position of the sandwich join suggested for between DAAM 1.39(++) and DAAM 1.41, these approximations could be verified. However, as it stands, about 190 of the estimated 270–290 lines are preserved at least partly.

Kp 15/45a is the third cult inventory of larger size. It features a script that differs only slightly from that of DAAM 1.39(++) (e. g. the form of BI), so that nothing stands against the assumption that it was written by the same scribe. Support comes from the

3 Cammarosano (2019: 86) considered another indirect join of DAAM 1.43 with DAAM 1.39(++). However, the similarity of sign forms, on which the suggestion is based, is only apparent. The drawing of EŠ with four wedges in the handcopy of DAAM 1.39(++) is mistaken, while IR, ID, KU and RA are quite different in DAAM 1.43.

Fig. 3. Photojoin between DAAM 1.39 (+) 1.40 (+) 1.51 (+) 1.41 (+) 1.42, obv.

subject matters of both texts. DAAM 1.39(++) describes mainly the administrative aspects of the cultic activities, while Kp 15/45a lists the worshiped deities with their respective cult objects (*Bildbeschreibungen*) of exactly the same cultic activities.

The remains of about 120 lines of the tablet are visible. Its edges are burnt heavily so that it is not possible to suggest any joins. The fragment having a width of 18.5 cm and being 5.9 cm thick permits an estimate of the original measurements of the tablet, which would have been approximately the same as those of DAAM 1.39(++). If this is correct and the illegible parts are taken into account as well, more than 40% of the tablet are preserved.

2.2 Oracle reports

The oracle report **DAAM 1.56** consists of eleven fragments. Miller (2019: 113 n. 1) joins DAAM 1.71 directly to the tablet, and proposes that DAAM 1.68 represents another fragment indirectly joining to DAAM 1.56 rev. iii (2019: 154). Thus, the text consists of twelve fragments joining directly and one fragment joining indirectly, altogether 13 fragments. The tablet had about 310 lines, of which approximately 260 are at least partly preserved.

As for **DAAM 1.58** and 1.59, Miller (2019: 141) assumes that they were written by the same scribe. Regarding DAAM 1.57 (Kp 15/28 + Kp 15/41), the same assumption seems to be more problematic; cf. Miller (2019: 139):

Fig. 4. Photojoin between DAAM 1.58 and 1.61.

> If it were not for the fact that this fragment consistently shows the KI with the additional vertical and the MEŠ with wedges rather than horizontals I would have assumed that it was written by the same scribe as that of KpT 1.58 [= DAAM 1.58, E.R.] and/or belongs to the same tablet.

However, in the meantime, Sakuma was able to join the fragments DAAM 1.58 and 1.61 (see *Konkordanz* and Fig. 4).

As a result, the number of signs available for comparison has increased. Since DAAM 1.61 ii$^{?}$ 6′ and iii$^{?}$ 6′ feature the same forms of KI and MEŠ as DAAM 1.57 (see Table 3), Miller's own objections are no longer valid. This suggests that DAAM 1.57 (consisting of two frag ments), DAAM 1.58 + 1.61 and DAAM 1.59, which, in addition, share the exceptional abbreviation MUŠEN *ḪUR*, were written by the same scribe. In sum, another five fragments can be assembled into one tablet.

	DAAM 1.58 + 1.61		DAAM 1.57
KI			
MEŠ			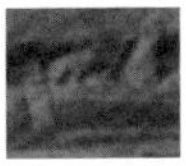

Table 3. Comparison of sign forms in DAAM 1.58 + 1.61 and 1.57.

	DAAM 1.64	DAAM 1.65
TU		
NU		
KIN		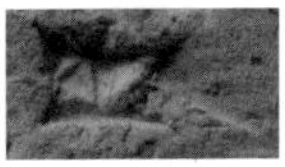

Table 4. Comparison of sign forms in DAAM 1.64 and 1.65.

Two other fragments were already joined as **DAAM 1.60** in the publication volume.

Isolated fragments: Regarding DAAM 1.64 and 1.65, Miller (2019: 151) considered that they might belong to the same tablet. However, the fragments are too small for a certain identification, and the conceived similarity of the sign forms of TU, NU, and KIN is less than obvious (see Table 4). The same is true for DAAM 1.92 and 1.93. Therefore, these fragments are regarded here as isolated.

In DAAM 1 (p. XVI), an indirect join between **DAAM 1.89** (consisting of two fragments) and DAAM 1.99 was proposed. Later, Lorenz suggested a direct join between the two pieces, which yields a text consisting of three fragments (see Fig. 5).

The join can be further confirmed by the composition of the two 3D-scans of the fragments (courtesy Gerfrid G.W. Müller), which shows that also the surfaces of the inside conform to each other (see Fig. 6).

Fig. 5. Photojoin between DAAM 1.89 and 1.99.

Fig. 6. 3D-join between DAAM 1.89 and 1.99 (courtesy Gerfrid G. W. Müller).

2.3 Festival texts

DAAM 1.72 represents a version of ***CTH* 645 "Fragments of festivals for the Netherworld Deities"** and consists of four fragments. On account of its content and the specific forms of RA shared with DAAM 1.73, the latter can be added to this text as an indirect join (see Soysal 2019: 158, 169f. with the respective figures).

Taken together, DAAM 1.72 (+) 1.73 includes four direct and one indirect join. It is one of the larger texts in the extant corpus, being a single column tablet with ca. 40 lines partly preserved on each side of DAAM 1.72, plus 8 more lines from DAAM 1.73. Unfortunately, the lower part of the tablet is broken off. However, the curvature of the remaining part permits an estimate that the 43 lines preserved on the reverse make up ca. 60 percent of the length of the tablet.[4]

***CTH* 712 "Festival for Ištar of Šamuḫa"** is best represented by DAAM 1.74, consisting of four directly joining fragments, and its indirect join DAAM 1.86. It is the only text reconstructed from more than two fragments that feature New Script (and not Late New Script). Remarkably, the columns i and iv of DAAM 1.74 seem to show a handwriting different from the colums ii and iii of the same text.

Other fragments that Soysal (2019: 179) claims belong to the same text group and even to same tablet probably do not show the same handwritings as DAAM 1.74 (+) 1.86 and must therefore be assigned to different tablets:

- DAAM 1.75: on account of the divergent sign forms, the date of the manuscript (LNS), and divergent paragraph rulers.

4 The duplicate text from Boğazköy, KUB 57.110(+), also a single column tablet, is damaged in a similar way and therefore does not provide any additional information as to the size of the text.

– DAAM 1.76: on account of the divergent handwriting and paragraph rulers. DAAM 1.45, which may belong to *CTH* 712 as well, was possibly written by the same scribe as DAAM 1.76; cf. Table 5.

	DAAM 1.76	DAAM 1.45
PA		
AN	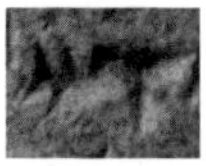	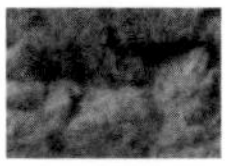
ZI	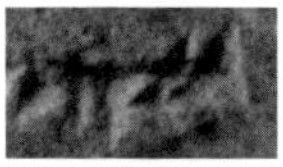	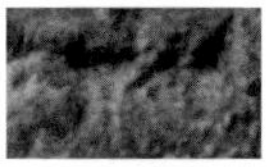
ŠI	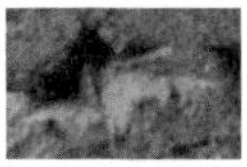	
BI		

Table 5. Comparison of sign forms in DAAM 1.76 and 1.45.

– DAAM 1.77: on account of a few divergent sign forms. However, the beginnings of several lines in column iii are preserved and permit the assignment to *CTH* 712 following Soysal 2019: 184.

Two more unpublished fragments, Kp 15/45d and Kp 15/45e, can be assigned to *CTH* 712 only by their content.

– Kp 15/45d: This fragment and DAAM 1.74 have in common that the verticals on the left columns are slanting slightly to the left, whereas the orientation of the verticals on the right column is upright. It is not clear how this feature emerges. It may simply result from the table being concave. Therefore, it seems advisable not to conclude too rashly that the tablets were written by the same scribe. Moreover, Kp 15/45d shows a form of LI with the verticals at a relatively wide distance, different from the LI at DAAM 1.74 iv 5′.
– Kp 15/45e: No conclusions can be drawn from the few signs visible on the fragment.

Kp 15/45d and Kp 15/45e are important because both of them contain parts of a colophon. Kp 15/45e: 6′ reads DUB 4[^{KAM}. If, then, more than one tablet of *CTH* 712 was stored in Kayalıpınar, perhaps DAAM 1.75, 1.76, 1.77, Kp 15/45d and Kp 15/45e, all of which show the damage from intensive burning, belong to the same series of at least four tablets.[5]

5 Cf. Soysal 2019: 171, also assuming a series for *CTH* 712, but for different reasons.

Differently, **DAAM 1.74 (+) 1.86**, which belongs to a different tablet, was not destroyed by any fire, but since its colophon is not preserved, its tablet number within the series remains unclear. A rough estimate based on the curvature of the tablet suggests that it contained about 200 lines, of which 65 (ca. 30 percent) are wholly or partly preserved.

2.4 A Hurrian offering list

DAAM 1.78 (*CTH* 787) consists of three joining fragments that constitute approximately three quarters of the tablet, with all lines at least partly preserved.

2.5 Letters

One of the two letters from the 'archive excavation', **DAAM 1.53**, is made of two fragments joining directly.

2.6. Preliminary results

A combination of paleographical evidence and considerations of content led to several direct and indirect joins between the fragments. DAAM 1.39(++) and Kp 15/45a seem to be the only two tablets that were most likely written by the same scribe.[6] They are both cult inventories and their content suggests that they were written as part of the same administrative process. So far, no duplicate fragments among the texts from the 'archive excavation' have been recovered. With the exception of the festival texts, this is to be expected for the texts from the other genres, since they all belong to the group of disposable and semi-current records, as defined by Waal 2015: 173–75 (corresponding to the group of short-term texts in van den Hout 2020: 239).

3. Find-situation of the material and possible conclusions

Based on the re-grouping of the tablet fragments of the 'archive excavation' suggested in Section 2, several observations can be made regarding the corpus:

- It is striking that, on the one hand, there are three very large tablets reconstructable to a substantial amount and, on the other hand, a large number of isolated fragments. The latter belong to several different text types and thus form only small groups. This makes a comparison of the handwritings within the groups relatively easy, so that the claim that almost all joins possible in the corpus have now been recovered is not over-optimistic. The uneven preservation of the texts is remarkable, since random distribution would, in all likelyhood, have produced a higher number of texts consisting of two to five fragments and at least some texts made of 6–12 fragments; cf. Fig. 7.
- The fragments of the three tablets with more than twelve fragments accumulate in the same relatively small area; cf. Fig. 8–10.

6 For another possible instance of two tablets written by the same scribe, cf. the remarks on *CTH* 712, DAAM 1.76.

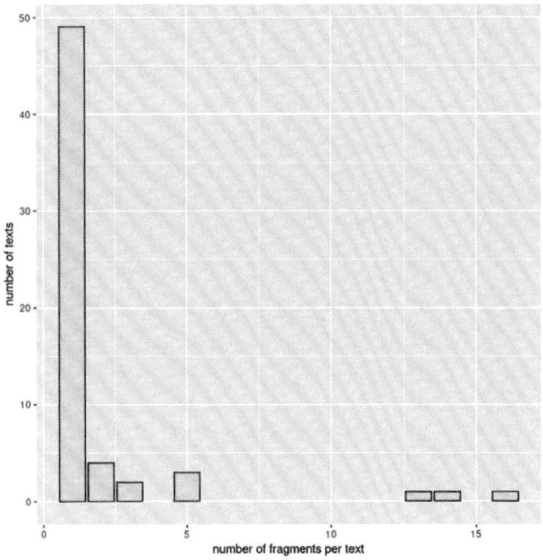

Fig. 7. Distribution of number of fragments per text.

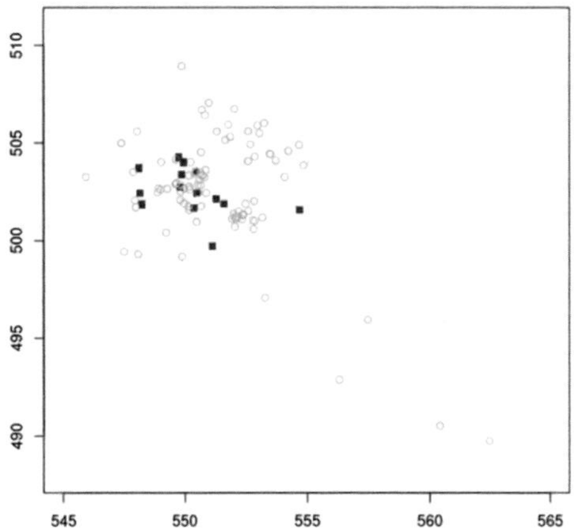

Fig. 8. Distribution of the fragments of 'new' DAAM 1.36(++).

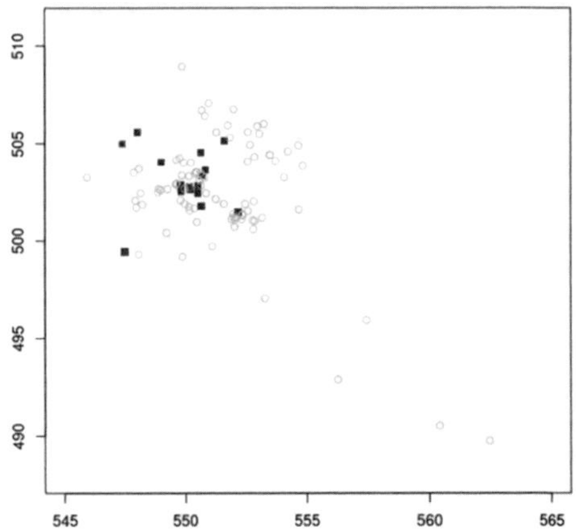

Fig. 9. Distribution of the fragment of 'new' DAAM 1.39(++).

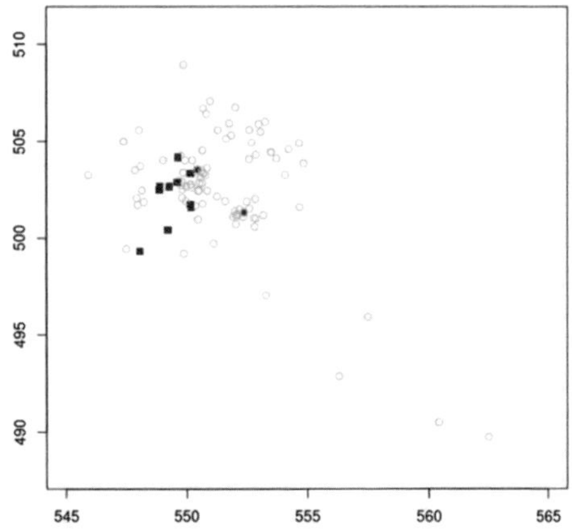

Fig. 10. Distribution of the fragments of 'new' DAAM 1.56++.

- Independent of the number of fragments, even the seven tablets with a preservation rate of more 40% show a similar pattern of dispersal. They center around a very small area (see Fig. 11). Most of the outliers are aligned with the two axes of a cross, meeting at the center of the highest tablet concentration and correlating with the two orthogonal directions of the recent plough activities (as indicated by the space between the lines in Fig. 11).
- In addition, there is a group of fragments from heavily burnt tablets. These tablets have their own center at a short distance of the main center (see Fig. 12), which accords well with their different and more damaging process of hardening by a destructive fire.

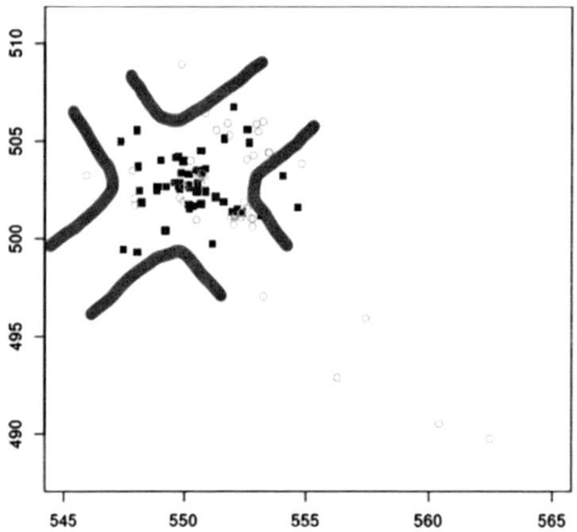

Fig. 11. Distribution of the fragments with a preservation rate of more than 40%.

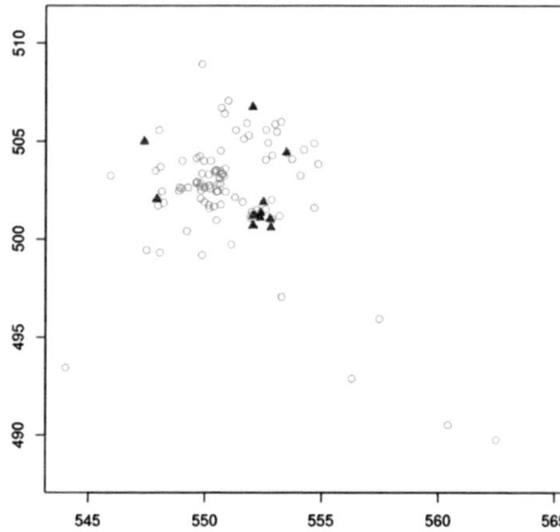

Fig. 12. Distribution of the heavily burnt fragments.

The largest piece of the heavily burnt tablets, Kp 15/45a, relates closely to the cult affairs of DAAM 1.39(++). Although it remained without joins, it represents almost half of the original tablet. Three of the four outliers in Fig. 12 (DAAM 1.45, 1.85, 1.76, 1.91) cannot have been transported by the plough in a single process to their respective findplaces and they are hence of tiny proportions.

Fig. 13. Kp 15/45a.

The evidence leads to the question of how the so-called 'archive' was organized. Four conclusions seem to be possible:

1) The twofold types of preservation represented in the statistics (unexpected from the point of view of random distribution) likely hint at two different origins for the fragments. Probably, one source was the area where the bigger parts of the three large tablets consisting of many fragments and the large Kp 15/45a tablet (heavily burnt) were found. Apparently, the tablets were destroyed only relatively recently, which is why their fragments were not widely dispersed, but shifted by the plough over only short distances. According to this hypothesis, a different source yielded the remaining isolated fragments in a context more heavily disturbed, and it is very well possible that they were shifted down the hill lying to the north-east of the trench.

The excavator Andreas Müller-Karpe points out that the current excavation did not uncover the whole building, but may be part of the larger complex that extends further to the north-east outside the trench (as indicated by the results of the geomagnetic survey performed in 2003). A possible scenario in line with the evidence could then be that, at the point of the destruction of the building, the well-preserved tablets lay in a room (or building) different from the one in which the archive proper was stored and were only secondarily mixed with the isolated fragments to form a single layer.[7]

2) The most solid information about the function of the building is provided by the three large tablets, i. e. three cult inventory texts about the cult of Šamuḫa (one listed according to the festivals, one listed according to the locations of the cult, and one listed according to the cult images, an oracle inquiry about the reasons for the anger of the Šawuška of Šamuḫa). Thus, everything points to a building that served the cult administration. Also, the five-piece festival text describing the cult of Netherworld Deities (*CTH* 645) found in this central area (with a single outlier) supports this assumption.

3) On account of the content of DAAM 1.39(++) and Kp 15/45a, a local cult inventory, it is very likely that the scribe was local. The same can be assumed for the other ephemeral texts found in the 'archive excavation'. In contrast, the scribes of the festival texts of *CTH* 712 and *CTH* 645 may very well have come from the chancery of the Hittite capital, although a comparison of DAAM 1.72 with its duplicate from Boğazköy KUB 57.110(+) shows a different handwriting.

4) Even if one does not follow the hypothesis of the two distinct origins of the tablets as suggested under 1), it is striking that there is only one instance in which the same scribe possibly wrote more than one tablet (DAAM 1.39(++) and Kp 15/45a), although the entire corpus was produced within a short span of time (LNS and possibly NS). Thus, the evidence permits the conclusion that there was not *the one* local scribe of Šamuḫa within a certain period who authored the main body of texts needed for the cult administration in the city, but instead a group of scribes.

7 Differently, Andreas Müller-Karpe emphasizes that most of the tablet fragments were found in very close vertical proximity to one another, i. e. they were found in a layer only about 20 cm thick at a relatively shallow depth below the present surface. Therefore, his conclusion is that all the pieces form a coherent find complex and, from an archaeological point of view, were all part of one and the same archive.

4. The pains and gains of examining scribal hands

The validity of the method of identifying scribal hands by the visual appearance of the sign forms was tested on a limited corpus of 121 fragments, a part of which was already joined. Even under these favorable conditions, it proved to be difficult to find identical forms (not sign forms) in small fragments that could be compared. Thus the frequent experience regarding the relevant signs for dating manuscripts was repeated here. Another problem, which verifiably occurred in the case of DAAM 1.57 and DAAM 1.58 (later joined to DAAM 1.61) as well as in DAAM 1.39(++) obv. as opposed to the rev., is the amount of variation in the forms of individual signs. It remained unclear which features are relevant for both the unification and the separation of tablets. Even such general features as the orientation of the heads of verticals may change between different columns of a tablet (cf. the case of DAAM 1.74).

In view of all these uncertainties, it is surprising that several direct joins could still be suggested based on the handwriting – and subsequently proved by clay quality, form and content of the fragments involved. The improved reconstruction of the tablets thus called into doubt the assumption of a single origin of the tablets.

The use of the method turned out to be an extremely time-consuming task. Its usefulness for larger corpora from the Hittite capital city is therefore limited. Probably one has to wait for photogrammetrical methods for the distinction of scribal hands to answer the question of whether local scribes wrote the festival texts found in the provincial centers or whether the tablets were produced in the capital and subsequently transfered to the local centers.

Bibliography

Cammarosano, Michele

2019 Kultinventare aus Kayalıpınar (Šamuḫa). In: Elisabeth Rieken (ed.), *Keilschrifttafeln aus Kayalıpınar 1. Textfunde aus den Jahren 1999–2017.* DAAM 1. Wiesbaden: Harrassowitz, 47–110.

Košak, Silvin

2002– *Konkordanz der hethitischen Keilschrifttafeln, Online-Datenbank Version.* hethiter.net/: hetkonk (v. 2.plus) – last accessed 14.04.2024.

Miller, Jared

2019 The oracular inquiries from the 2015 excavations at Kayalıpınar (Šamuḫa). In: Elisabeth Rieken (ed.), *Keilschrifttafeln aus Kayalıpınar 1. Textfunde aus den Jahren 1999–2017.* DAAM 1. Wiesbaden: Harrassowitz, 113–56.

Müller-Karpe, Andreas and Vuslat Müller-Karpe

2019 Die Fundsituation der Tontafelfunde in Kayalıpınar 1999–2017. In: Elisabeth Rieken (ed.), *Keilschrifttafeln aus Kayalıpınar 1. Textfunde aus den Jahren 1999–2017.* DAAM 1. Wiesbaden: Harrassowitz, 1–30.

Soysal, Oğuz

2019 Hethitische Festbeschreibungen aus den Grabungskampagnen 2015 und 2017. In: Elisabeth Rieken (ed.), *Keilschrifttafeln aus Kayalıpınar 1. Text-*

funde aus den Jahren 1999–2017. DAAM 1. Wiesbaden: Harrassowitz, 157–90.

van den Hout, Theo P.J.

2002 Another View of Hittite Literature. In: Stefano de Martino and Franca Pecchioli Daddi (eds.), *Anatolia antica. Studi in memoria di Fiorella Imparati.* Eothen 11 Tomo II. Firenze: LoGisma, 857–78.

2012 The Ductus of the Alalaḫ VII Texts and the Origin of Hittite Cuneiform. In: Elena Devecchi (ed.), *Palaeography and Scribal Practices in Syro-Palestine and Anatolia in the Late Bronze Age. Papers Read at a Symposium in Leiden, 17–18 December 2009.* PIHANS 119. Leiden: Nederlands Instituut voor het Nabije Oosten, 147–70.

2020 *A History of Hittite Literacy. Writing and Reading in Late Bronze-Age Anatolia (1650–1200 BC).* Cambridge: Cambridge University Press.

Waal, Willemijn

2015 *Hittite Diplomatics. Studies in Ancient Document Format and Record Management.* StBoT 57. Wiesbaden: Harrassowitz.

Yakubovich, Ilya and Alice Mouton

2023 *Luwili. Hittite-Luwian Ritual Texts Attributed to Puriyanni, Kuwattalla and Šilalluḫi (CTH 758–763). Volume II: Discussion and Glossary.* StBoT 72,2. Wiesbaden: Harrassowitz.

DIGITAL PALEOGRAPHY: AIMS, METHODS, AND TOOLS

Gerfrid G.W. Müller
Julius-Maximilians-Universität Würzburg
Akademie der Wissenschaften und der Literatur | Mainz

Abstract

In the last 20 years, the perception of Hittite cuneiform texts has changed considerably. During this time, tens of thousands of photographs and thousands of 3D models of cuneiform texts have been published on the *Hethitologie Portal Mainz*. These not only facilitate collations in philological work, but are also a stimulus for paleographic work, as there is now an image for almost every text. The symposium has shown that these large amounts of data raise new questions and require completely new digital tools to convert the media into machine-readable data. This entails description, classification, as well as comparative and contrastive visualization for a plausible comprehensibility of the results. The article first discusses aspects of the analysis of statistics generated from 3D data. The focus is on the identification or separation of fragments with a small number of comparable characters. In addition, tools for density and distance measurements are presented. The second part is dedicated to the new cuneiform character recognition tool and the prospects for the paleography's database currently being implemented.

Interest in ancient forms of writing is almost as old as writing itself. Paleographic lists can already be found in the ancient Near East. Collections of characters have been compiled ever since as deciphering aids, teaching materials, ornamental gimmicks, or even for the purpose of forgery. The most recent examples of this tradition are our cuneiform sign lists such as the *Hethitisches Zeichenlexikon* (HZL; Rüster and Neu 1989). What is compiled in such 'paleographies'? First and foremost, the various common forms of written characters, so that the user can get an idea of the diversity of forms, i. e. a cognitive concept that is not tied to a rigid form ('pixels'). In addition, special, rare, or singular forms are included for the sake of curiosity. Apart from the latter, the countless forms of characters found in texts have to be abstracted into form types and, in the best case, organized chronologically so that they can be presented in a clear and manageable way in a paleographic work.

What information can we gain from a handwritten text beyond the content of the text itself? An important issue is dating, and this appears to be all the more important because there is no actual dating in Hittite texts themselves. Probably even more important is the comparison of handwriting on fragments in order to join them, which was the origin of my efforts. The evaluation of both aspects is influenced by the development of writing traditions. These in turn characterize and influence schools of writing as quasi-personified traditions. And then, of course, there is the question of individual manuscripts and their characteristics, the identification of which can help to assign written documents to specific individuals. This in turn gives rise to the desire to compile dossiers to shed light on relationships, areas of activity and careers.

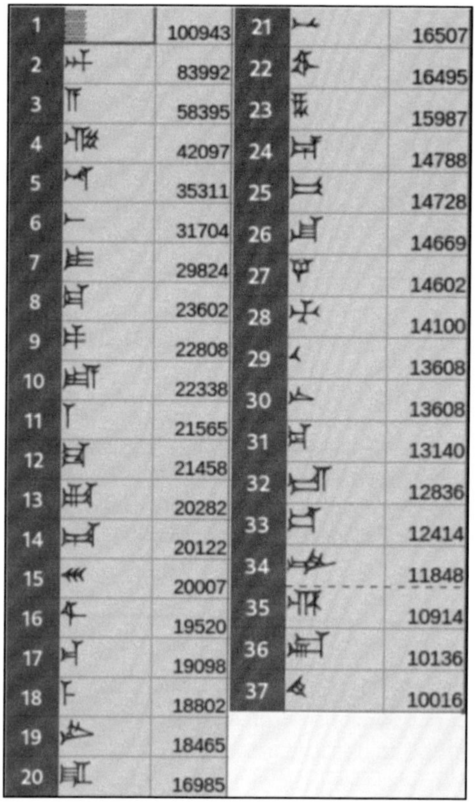

1	100943	21	16507
2	83992	22	16495
3	58395	23	15987
4	42097	24	14788
5	35311	25	14728
6	31704	26	14669
7	29824	27	14602
8	23602	28	14100
9	22808	29	13608
10	22338	30	13608
11	21565	31	13140
12	21458	32	12836
13	20282	33	12414
14	20122	34	11848
15	20007	35	10914
16	19520	36	10136
17	19098	37	10016
18	18802		
19	18465		
20	16985		

Fig. 1. Frequency of signs in the HFR corpus.

nu	6454
tai	6381
NINDA.GUR4.RA	4608
LUGALuš	3902
paršia	3857
GAL	3713
LUGALi	2471
šipanti	2419
anta	2400
peran	2317
SÌR-RU	2284
para	2218
ekuzi	2163
1-ŠU	2129
tianzi	2029
pai	2002
UDU	1867
NINDA.SIG	1804

Fig. 2. Frequency of words in the HFR corpus (automated transcription).

To give an idea of the magnitude, we are dealing with almost 10,000 fragments which, according to the files of the HFR Basic Corpus, contain over 300,000 words. And after the export of the cuneiform notations, there are over 1.1 million cuneiform characters (excluding the hundreds of thousands of illegible symbols ▒ – see Fig. 1). Therefore, it is advisable to use technical aids to deal with this mass of information. Thanks to the cooperation of many museums, we now have around 3,000 tablets and fragments available as 3D objects, including almost all fragments containing a scribe's name and many of the larger tablets describing festival rituals. In addition, tens of thousands of photos are on hand. For script comparisons on a larger scale, it makes sense to choose the most common signs (Fig. 1), as they appear on more tablets and in greater numbers, making the scribe's ideal form of the sign clearer. The same applies to frequently occurring words that are representative for the use of space and the sequence of characters (Fig. 2).

Text clusters based on the geometry of cuneiform characters

The geometries of the wedges can be measured on the 3D models without the presence of shadows that can distort the analysis. The CuneiformAnalyser program (Müller et al. 2015) automatically searches for all impressions on the tablet surface. The inner surfaces of the impressions are clustered, i. e. merged into point groups, in which the program attempts to find wedge impressions with three edges and three lateral surfaces. All wedges are numbered consecutively and can therefore be referenced. At the same time, the geometry is calculated automatically, such as the length of the edges, their angles to one another and their angles to the tablet surface. Only the recognition of the wedge type (horizontal, vertical, *Winkelhaken* or oblique wedge) requires the writing direction to be manually marked (black-to-white line above the 3rd cuneiform line in Fig. 3), as this is often not recognizable from the geometry alone. For cuneiform signs, the individual wedges are registered in lists so that the geometries can be evaluated in a consistent order. The example shows the sign MA with No. 833 for the vertical following the three horizontals No. 2304, 8070, 1992 (Fig. 3 – lower right).

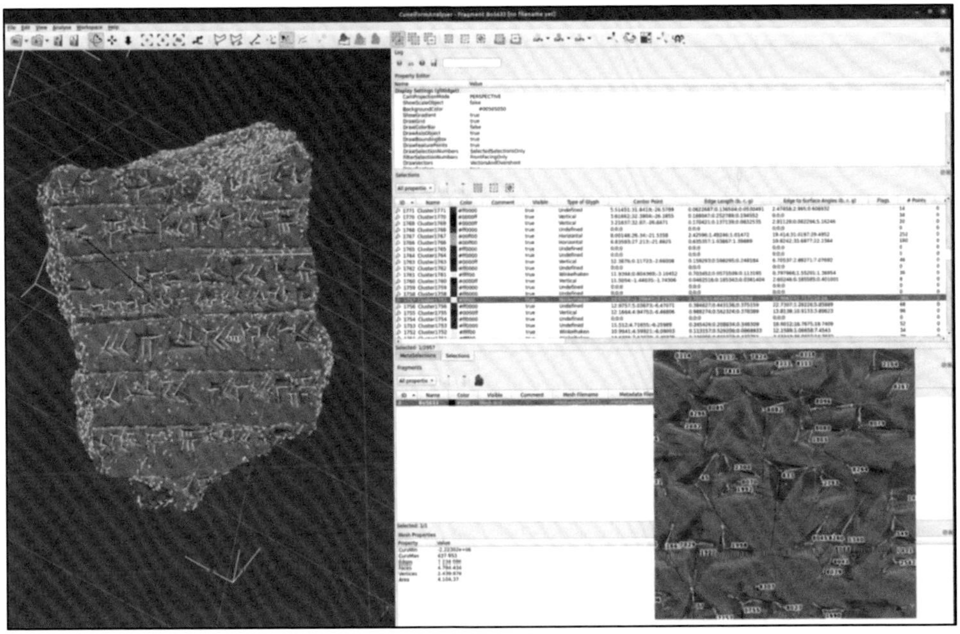

Fig. 3. Exploration of wedge geometry and character configuration.

Compiling the wedge numbers for individual characters is a time-consuming task, but it provides us with the data for a statistical analysis. We use a hierarchical cluster analysis method that creates a hierarchical tree or dendrogram of the objects to be clustered. The relationship between the objects is expressed by their distance to each other in the tree, with the objects grouped into clusters at different levels.

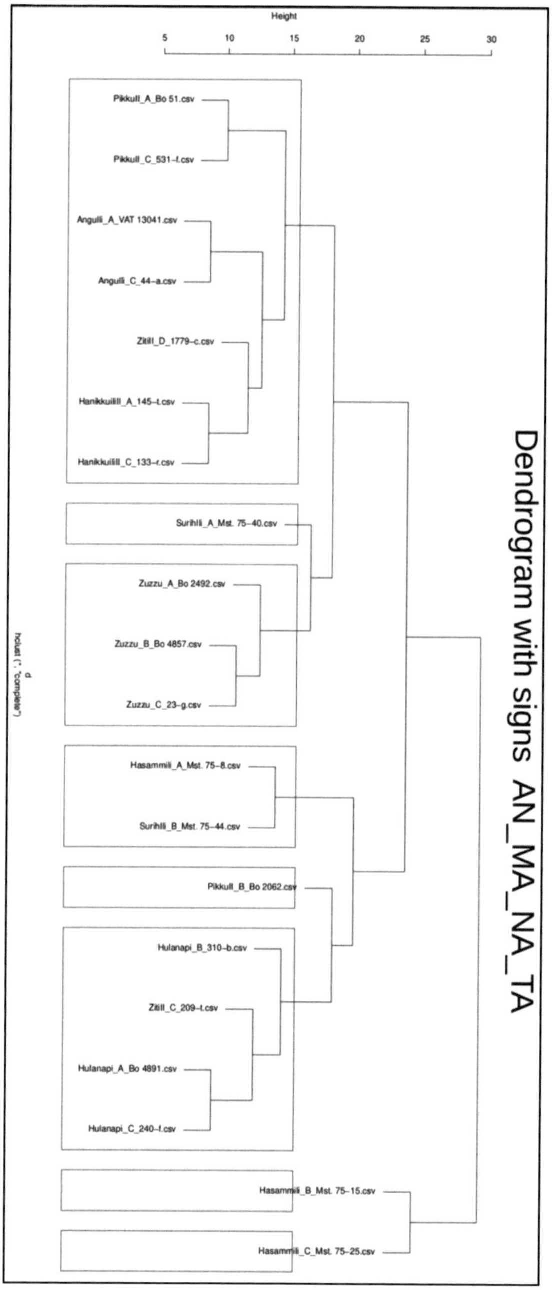

Fig. 4. Dendrogram of AN and MA.

To do this, we first have to calculate the distance matrix. For simple relationships, such as the distance between the lowest points of two wedge impressions, this can easily be illustrated by shifting the first lowest point to the zero point of a coordinate system and the second to the point in the coordinate system corrected by this shift. In this case, the distance would also be measured in millimeters. However, as more characteristics of a cuneiform character are measured and more dimensions are added, the *distance* becomes an *abstract value.*

Each object is initially considered as a separate cluster. In the distance matrix, the distances from one cluster to another cluster are calculated. Now the clusters (in the first round of objects) can be merged into clusters. The distances between the clusters are recalculated and the next clusters are merged again, and this process is repeated until all objects are united in a tree. The hierarchical clustering in a dendrogram with the simply structured characters AN and MA (Fig. 4) already provides a clear classification; the Empire period scribes Zuzzu, Pikku, Angulli, Ziti, and Ḫanikuili as well as Ḫulanapi are each grouped with two or three of their texts next to each other. Only the Middle Hittite scribe Šuriḫilu from Maşat appears once in between. The other Maşat scribes (recognizable by the Mst. text number) are all in the lower section of the diagram. In all clusterings, only signs that are used at least three times in a text are taken into account. Characters with unusual geometries are automatically eliminated.

When four different signs (AN, MA, NA, TA) are used, numerous Maşat texts are isolated (Fig. 5), because they do not fulfill the condition of three attestations for each sign. Šuriḫilu's Mst. 75.40 is isolated, while the remaining Maşat texts stand together if one flips the group of two texts of Ḫašammili and Šuriḫilu to the bottom of the second branch. One Pikku text (B) stands apart, while Ziti's texts are completely separated.

These experiments are carried on texts whose scribes are identified with certainty in order to test the method. One approach for further work is to compare the sign forms on individual tablets with groups of known scribes. A text by the scribe Ḫillu serves is a good example. This scribe belongs to the residual group, which cannot be affiliated with other scribes (cf. Gordin 2015: 226). The signs AN, NA, and ZI from his tablets are probed against the same signs in tablets of a group of known scribes of the Empire period. This time we use a multidimensionally scaled plot (MDS), that arranges the objects spatially so that the amount of distance between the objects represents the dissimilarities or similarities identified. The further apart the objects are, the greater the dissimilarity, the closer they are, the greater the similarity. The MDS shows a large statistical (i. e. abstract, see above) distance and dissimilarity of Ḫillu's writing (Fig. 6).

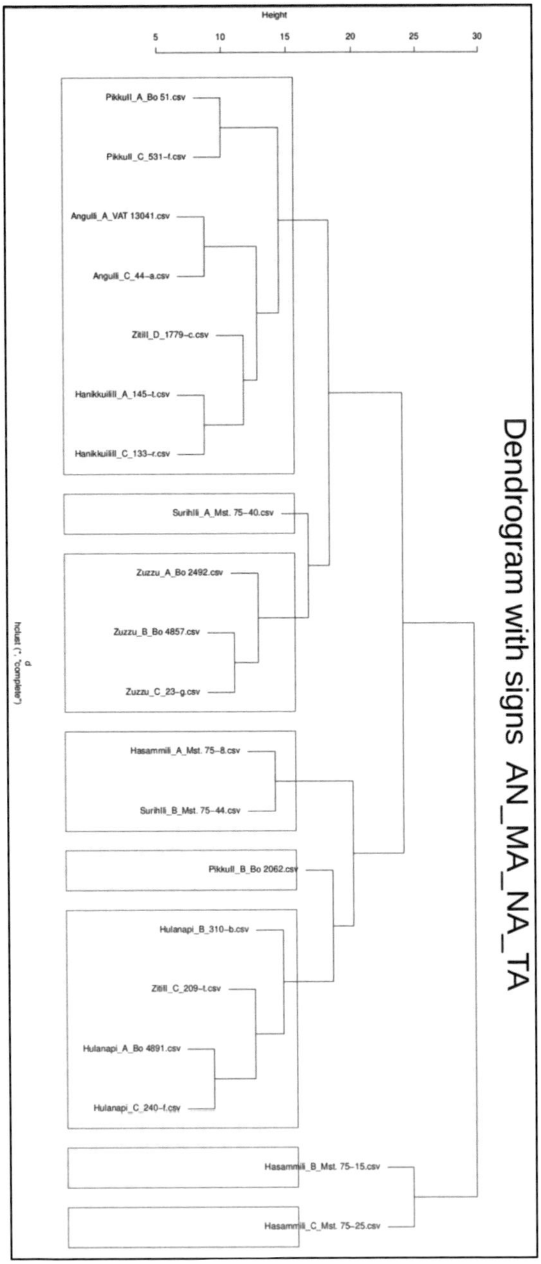

Fig. 5. Dendrogram (AN, MA, NA, TA).

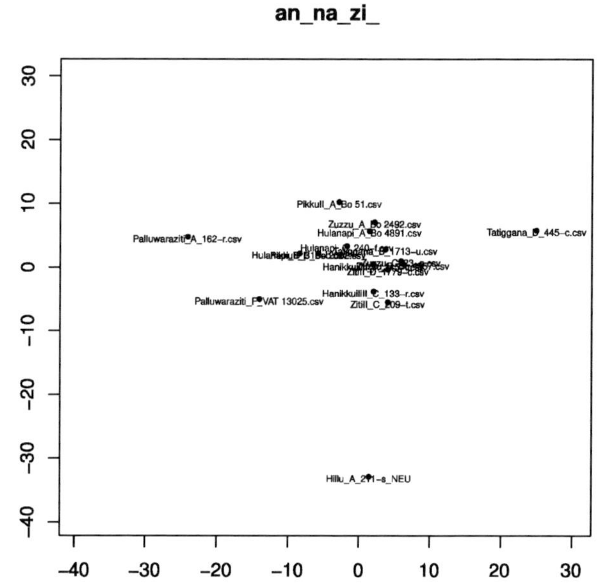

Fig. 6. The distance between the scribe Ḫillu and other scribes.

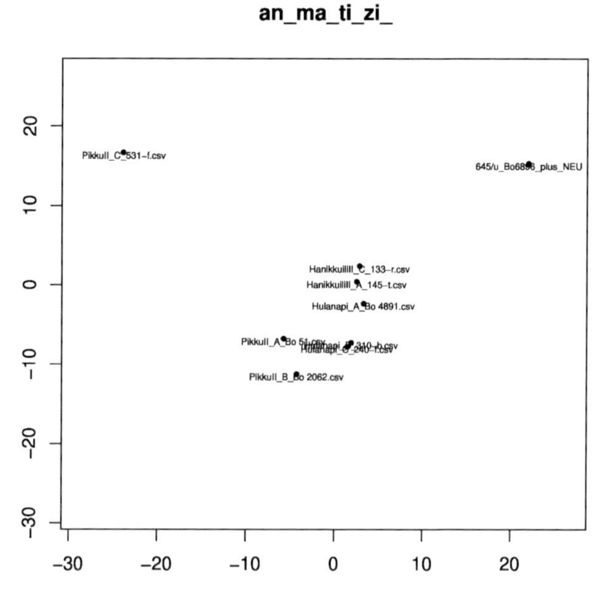

Fig. 7. Multidimensionally scaled (MDS) plot with AN, MA, TI, and ZI.

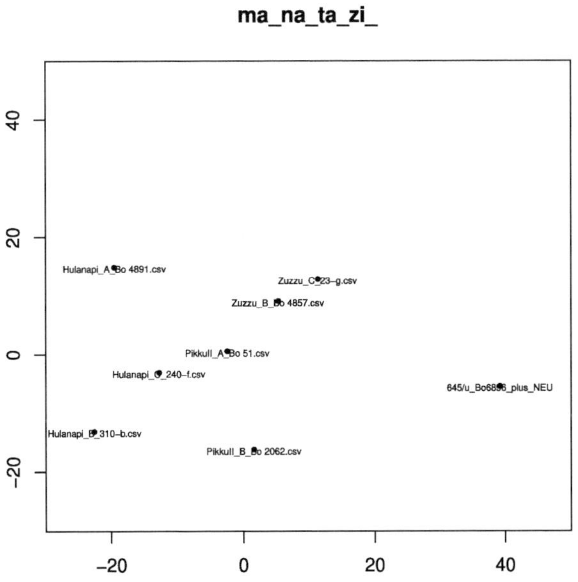

Fig. 8. Multidimensionally scaled (MDS) plot with MA, NA, TA, and ZI.

In the search for the scribe of the randomly picked fragment 645/u+, whose scribe is yet unknown, we analyzed AN, MA, TI, and ZI as well MA, NA, TA, and ZI; both times there is a clear distance in the plot, which indicates dissimilarity (Figs. 7 and 8). Clearly this fragment does not belong to this group of texts.

With AN, MA, NA, and TI (Fig. 9) and even more so with 6 characters (AN, MA, NA, ŠA, TA, ZI in Fig. 10), the distance is even greater. The use of alternating combinations of characters serves to exclude misdiagnoses due to outliers.

Let us try the same with texts from Pikku. Pikku B (Bo 2062; chiffres after Gordin 2015) was once scanned in parts because of its size. This raises the question of how, for example, the first, upper part of the tablet from the older 3D scan collection differs from the newer, second part of the obverse. With the characters AN, MA, NA, ŠA, and TA, both halves are close to each other in the MDS plot (Fig. 11). The two other Pikku texts, which we know to have been written by Pikku, are loosely grouped together, although they have already moved away from Bo 2062. The groups of texts by Ḫulanapi and Zuzzu are grouped together.

However, if we exchange some of the characters for AN, MA, NA, TA, TI, Pikku's texts appear even more scattered and visually are less distinguishable from Ḫanikku-ili's (Fig. 12). The group AN, MA, NA, ŠA, TA on Fig. 11 should be noted due to the arrangement of the texts.

We use the signs AN, MA, NA, ŠA, TA again (Fig. 13), but this time we cluster the old stock against a second scan of Ḫulanapi B (310/b). Now the tablets of all three scribes

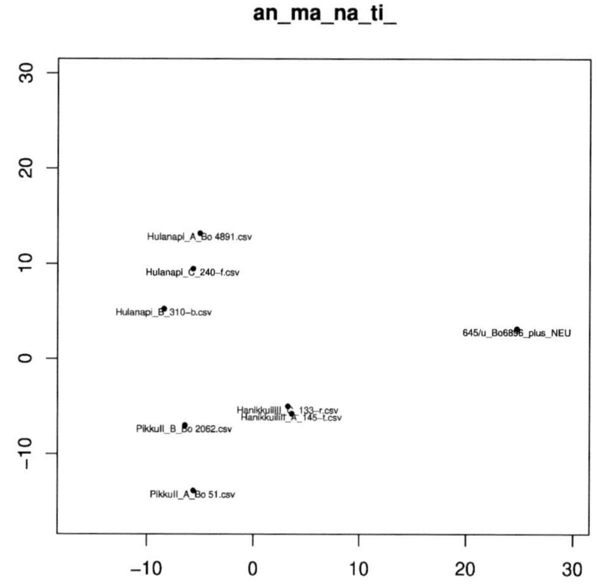

Fig. 9. Multidimensionally scaled (MDS) plot with AN, MA, NA, and TI.

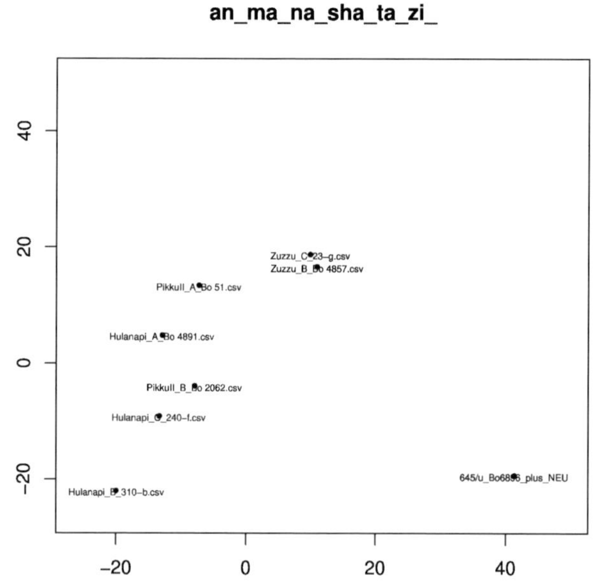

Fig. 10. Multidimensionally scaled (MDS) plot with AN, MA, NA, SHA (for the sign ŠA), TA, ZI.

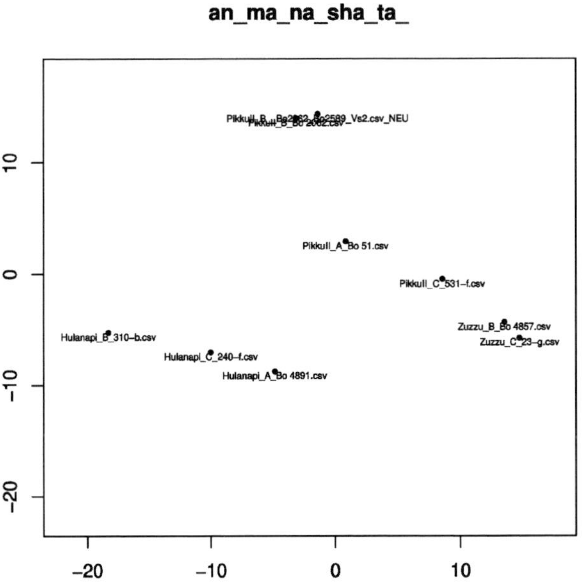

Fig. 11. AN, MA, NA, ŠA, and TA of Pikku compared.

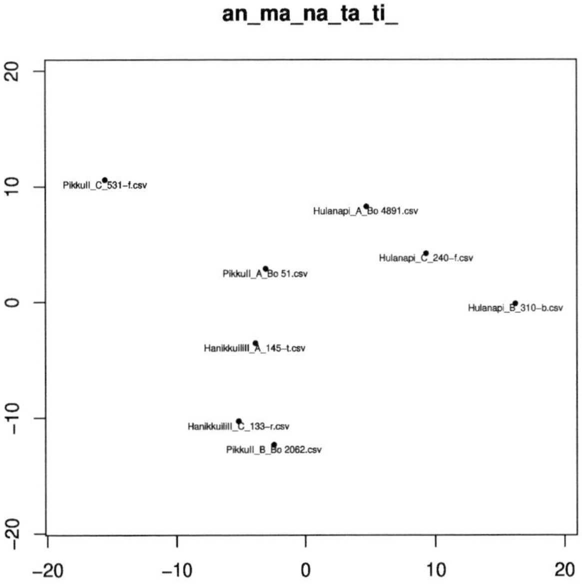

Fig. 12. AN, MA, NA, TA, TI of Pikku compared.

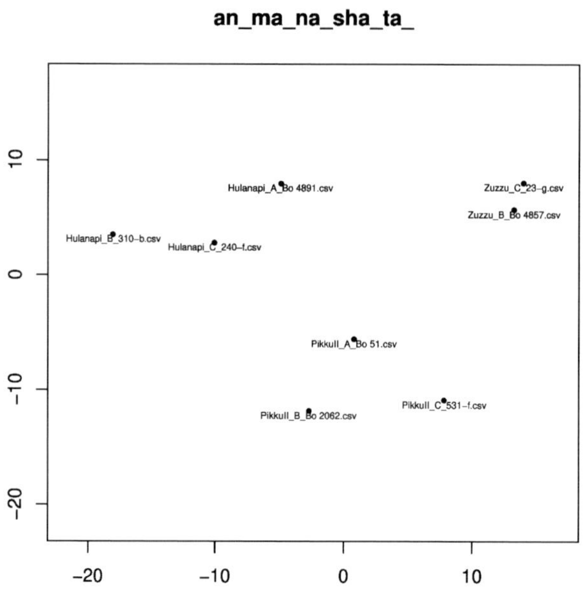

Fig. 13. AN, MA, NA, ŠA, TA and Ḫulanapi.

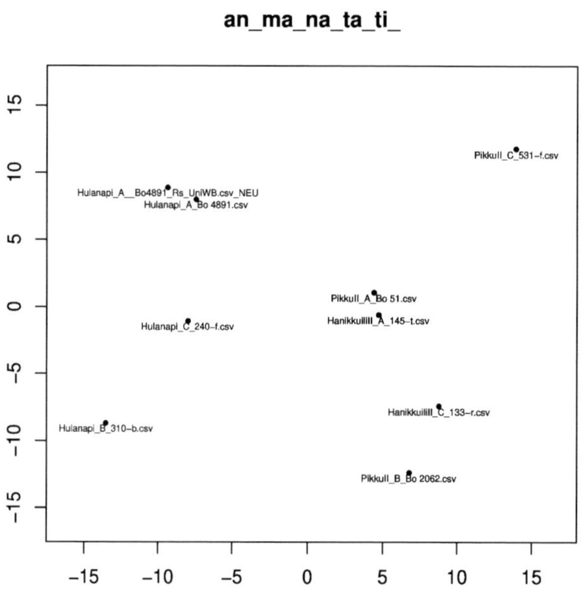

Fig. 14. AN, MA, NA, TA, TI and Ḫulanapi.

are positioned close to each other. However, if we again take the characters AN, MA, NA, TA, and TI, the texts of Pikku and Ḫanikkuili are no longer distinguishable (Fig. 14).

At this point, we must leave behind the visually accessible graphics and delve into the more daunting underlying figures. The table Fig. 15 shows the distances (dissimilarities) between the compared tablets and the newly added fragment Ḫulanapi B (310/b). We have to keep in mind that the 'distance' is an abstracted figure calculated from a larger set of (dis)similarities in properties of wedges and their positions in cuneiform signs. There is a certain distance between the two scans of the same text, but this distance value is usually less than 0.05. An exception is the combination AN, MA, NA, TI (row 8) with a distance above 0.1 in the copy and Ḫulanapi C. The deviation from the texts of Ḫanikkuili and Pikku is clearly higher, ranging from 0.28 to over 0.5.

In the case of the combination AN, NA, TI, ZI (Fig. 15 row 7), however, the distance from Ḫulanapi B to Pikku B (Bo 2062) is smaller than to his own text, Ḫulanapi A (Bo 4891). For the combination AN, MA, NA, TA (row 15) the distance from Ḫulanapi A also appears large at 0.2, but the other scribes show over 0.3 or 0.4. When using 6 characters (AN, MA, NA, ŠA, TA, ZI, row 16) and considering the average distances, the distance between Ḫulanapi and the other scribes is also clear and distinct.

In the table for the Pikku text (Fig. 16), the distance between the upper and lower parts of Bo 2062 is usually 0.3 or 0.4. Only in the character combination AN, MA, NA, TA (third data row) is the distance above 0.5, which is greater than the distance to the tablets of other scribes. There is obviously an error here. The average is strongly distorted by this error. In order to exclude these excessively high values from the evaluation, the distance values are arranged in groups according to their size, known as quantiles. The most common division is four quantiles (called, in this case, quartiles). The first quartile comprises all values that are less than a quarter of all values. In this first quantile the distance value to own texts is about 0.38, to the texts of other scribes 0.68 or over 1. This means that the texts of Pikku can be distinguished by using different groups of characters and excluding extreme values.

Cross-checking the abstract clustering results

The problem now lies in deciding when a tablet belongs to a group of texts written by one and the same scribe. If there are one or more comparison tablets by the same scribe in the sample, the close relationship can be made plausible by changing combinations of signs. It can also be expected that as the number of sign forms used increases, the distance will increase again. For fragments with few sign forms, however, we have to rely on this method.

Finally, some of the sign forms are used in the synopsis. As soon as the characters are registered in the CuneiformAnalyser using their wedge numbers, an image can be automatically generated from them in different representations and colors. At first glance, the forms of the sign TI appear to be similar despite all the variations. However, Pikku (Fig. 17) shows a tendency to point the lower *Winkelhaken* more downwards,

	A	B	C	D	G	I	J	K	L	M	N	O	P
1	Hulanapi_B_310-b_UniWB_NEU		Hulanapi_B_310-b	Hulanapi_C_240-f.csv	Hulanapi_A_Bo 4891	Zitill_D_1779-c	Hanikkuilill_A_145-t	Pikkull_B_Bo 2062	Hanikkuilill_C_133-	Zuzzu_B_Bo 4857	Pikkull_A_Bo 51	Zuzzu_C_23-g	Pikkull_C_531-f.csv
2	an_ma_na_zi_	0	0,0809	0,0677	0,1361	0,2006	0,1630	0,1996	0,1531	0,2385	0,3075	0,2918	NA
3	an_na_sha_ta_	0	0,0537	0,1149	0,1642	NA	NA	0,2770	NA	0,2977	0,2869	0,2748	NA
4	an_na_ta_zi_	0	0,0614	0,0673	0,1410	NA	NA	0,2623	NA	0,2040	0,2788	0,2314	NA
5	ma_na_ta_zi_	0	0,0495	0,0791	0,1666	NA	NA	0,2529	NA	0,1905	0,2364	0,2327	NA
6	an_ma_ta_zi_	0	0,0598	0,0781	0,1393	NA	NA	0,2480	NA	0,1842	0,2740	0,2397	NA
7	an_na_ti_zi_	0	0,0369	0,0307	0,0789	NA	0,0917	0,0594	0,0835	NA	0,0958	NA	NA
8	an_ma_na_ti_	0	0,1219	0,1312	0,0920	NA	0,3628	0,2860	0,4455	NA	0,5083	NA	NA
9	an_ma_sha_zi_	0	0,0369	0,0620	0,0860	NA	NA	0,0745	NA	0,1903	0,1390	0,2196	0,2883
10	ma_na_sha_ta_	0	0,0437	0,1451	0,1960	NA	NA	0,2526	NA	0,2969	0,2126	0,3002	NA
11	ma_na_sha_zi_	0	0,0402	0,0693	0,1192	NA	NA	0,1868	NA	0,2497	0,1718	0,2705	NA
12	an_sha_ta_zi_	0	0,0506	0,0812	0,1219	NA	NA	0,2160	NA	0,2121	0,2060	0,2267	NA
13	an_na_sha_zi_	0	0,0510	0,0590	0,1074	NA	NA	0,2138	NA	0,2515	0,2204	0,2665	NA
14	an_ma_sha_ta_	0	0,0528	0,1265	0,1625	NA	NA	0,2654	NA	0,2875	0,2677	0,2857	NA
15	an_ma_na_ta_	0	0,0795	0,1283	0,2066	NA	NA	0,3528	NA	0,3174	0,4117	0,3431	NA
16	an_ma_na_sha_ta_zi_	0	0,0414	0,0693	0,1158	NA	NA	0,2003	NA	0,2026	0,2036	0,2095	NA
17	an_ma_ti_zi_	0	0,0682	0,0624	0,0718	NA	0,1880	0,1024	0,2255	NA	0,1762	NA	0,3000
18	ma_na_ti_zi_	0	0,0444	0,0895	0,1976	NA	0,1983	0,2104	0,1870	NA	0,2488	NA	NA
19	na_sha_ta_zi_	0	0,0403	0,0917	0,1435	NA	NA	0,2082	NA	0,2185	0,1730	0,2324	NA
20	Mean	0	0,0563	0,0863	0,1359	0,2006	0,2008	0,2149	0,2189	0,2387	0,2455	0,2589	0,2941
21	First_Quantil	0	0,0420	0,0674	0,1095	0,2006	0,1630	0,1998	0,1531	0,2030	0,1831	0,2317	0,2912

Fig. 15. Distances from Ḫulanapi.

Pikkull_B__Bo2062_Bo2589_Vs2.csv_NEU		Hulanapi_A_Bo 4891.csv	Pikkull_C_531-f.csv	Zuzzu_B_Bo 4857.csv	Pikkull_B_Bo 2062.csv	Zuzzu_C_23-g.csv	Hulanapi_B_310-b.csv	Hulanapi_C_240-f.csv
an_ma_na_sha_	0	0,6898	0,3862	0,6800	0,3822	0,8229	1,1807	1,3414
an_ma_na_sha_ta_	0	0,6898	0,3862	0,6800	0,3822	0,8229	1,1807	1,3414
an_ma_na_ta_	0	1,5121	2,8544	4,1222	5,1427	4,6136	4,1837	3,7335
an_na_sha_ta_	0	0,6494	0,1819	0,7082	0,3141	0,6944	1,0896	1,1360
ma_na_sha_ta_	0	0,6811	0,8482	0,3316	0,4392	0,1784	1,0104	1,2103
Mean	0	0,8445	0,9314	1,3044	1,3321	1,4264	1,7290	1,7525
First_Quantil	0	0,6811	0,3862	0,6800	0,3822	0,6944	1,0896	1,2103

Fig. 16. Distances to Pikku's added text.

while Ḫulanapi (Fig. 18) writes the tips of the rear *Winkelhaken* pointing sharply upwards; these appear strangely rounded in Pikku.

In MA, the upper horizontal of Ḫulanapi (Fig. 19) is usually more pronounced than those of Pikku (Fig. 20) and appears to be set at a slight angle running down from above. The list of further examples of these minimal differences could continue.

When analyzing the characters, most of the basic graphic features are recorded implicitly, such as the depth of the impressions and their variation, the different pressure distribution on the individual wedges of a character, the height-width ratio of the characters, etc. But the spacing between words, lines and margins as well as the ratio of line height to *interlineum* and other tablet features are not measured or classified. Also, the regularity of the writing is not explicitly classified. Strong variation complicates the statistical evaluation, which uses averages and deviation measures. After clustering, such observations, which I can only briefly discuss here, should be made, as far as possible, metrically, otherwise ordinally according to degrees of expression. The writing density can be measured in various ways. The easiest way seems to be to measure the ratio of the written surface to the unwritten. In the 3D viewer (Fig. 21), one can create a contrast between the surface and indentations, which is then reduced to two colors (Fig. 22), and the percentage of coverage is calculated (Figs. 23–25). The result depends on the selection of areas. Comparisons of 2–3 lines up to the paragraph ruling are more meaningful.

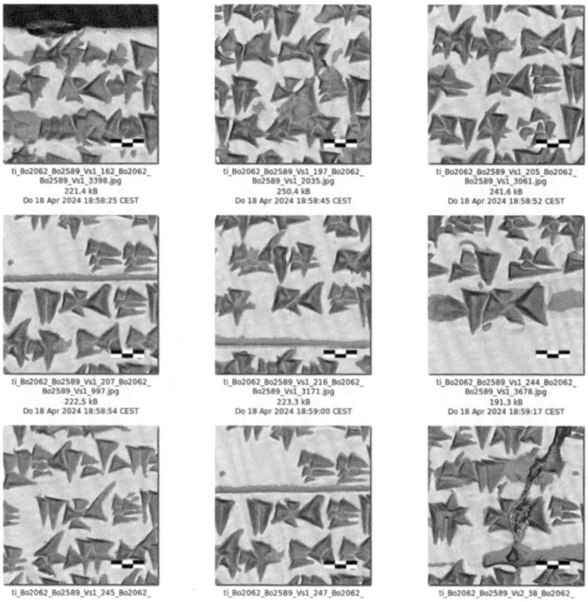

Fig. 17. TI of Pikku.

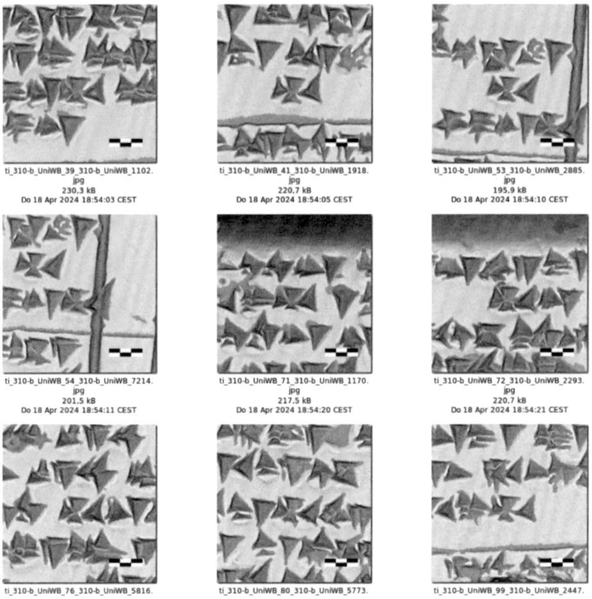

Fig. 18. TI of Ḫulanapi.

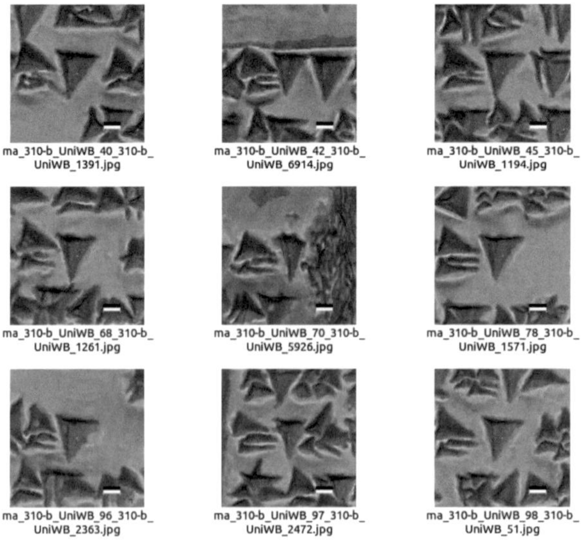

Fig. 19. MA of Ḫulanapi.

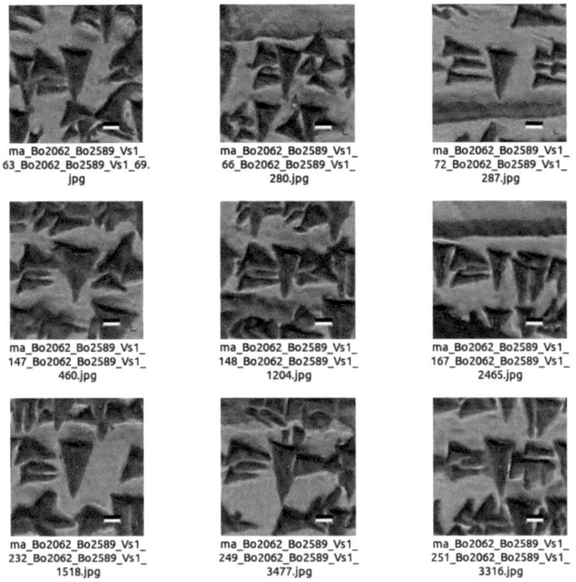

Fig. 20. MA of Pikku.

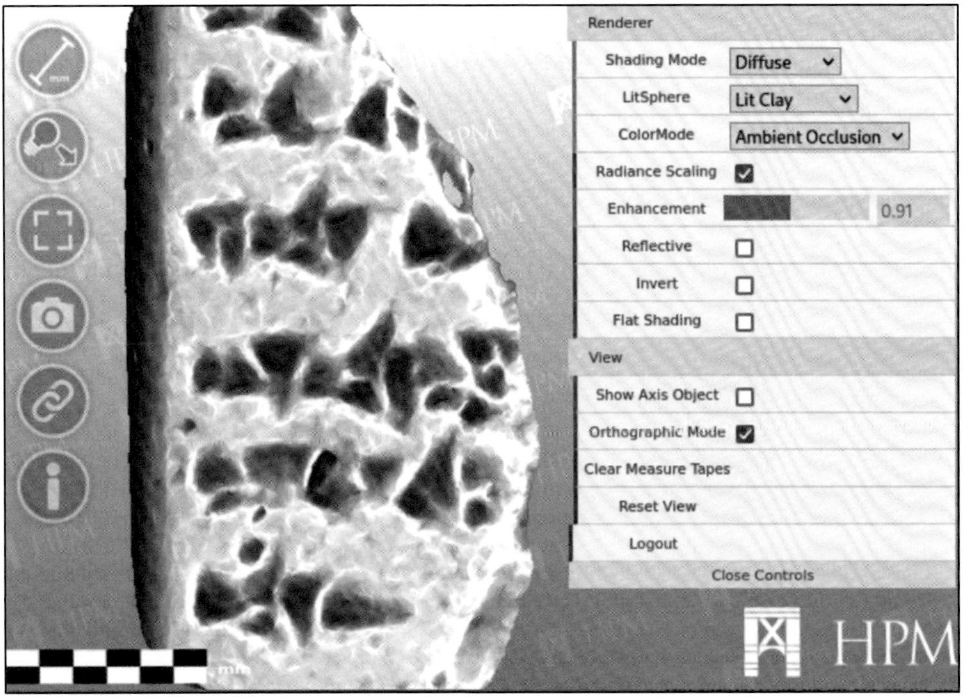

Fig. 21. Preparation of a screenshot for density measuring.

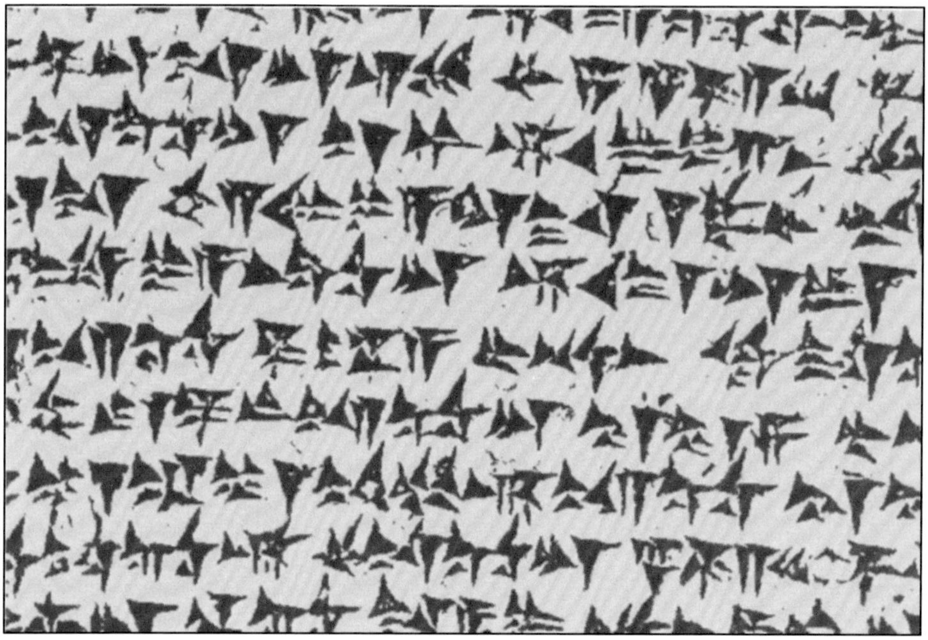

Fig. 22. Reduced colors.

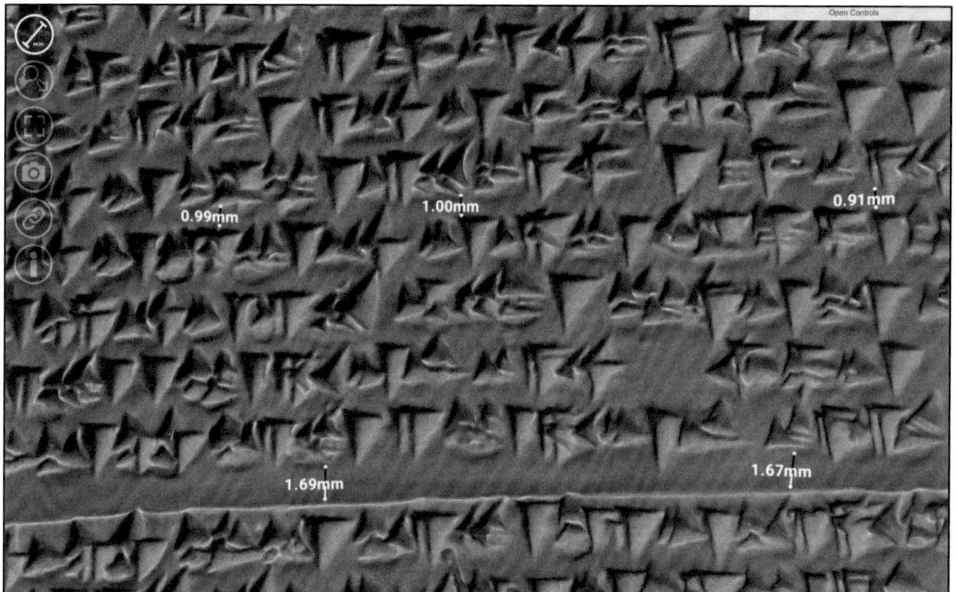

Fig. 26. Measuring Ḫulanapi's spacing.

Fig. 23. 27.46% / 24.28% / 26.04% / 27.05% / 29.33% of surface covered by impression on Bo 51 (Pikku; average 26.83%).

Fig. 24. 28.55% / 29.67% / 26.37% / 31.24% / 31.61% of surface covered by impression on Bo 2062 (Pikku; average 29.48%).

Fig. 25. 30.12% / 29.52% / 31.30% / 27.50% / 30.74% of surface covered by impression on 310/b (Ḫulanapi; average 29.83%).

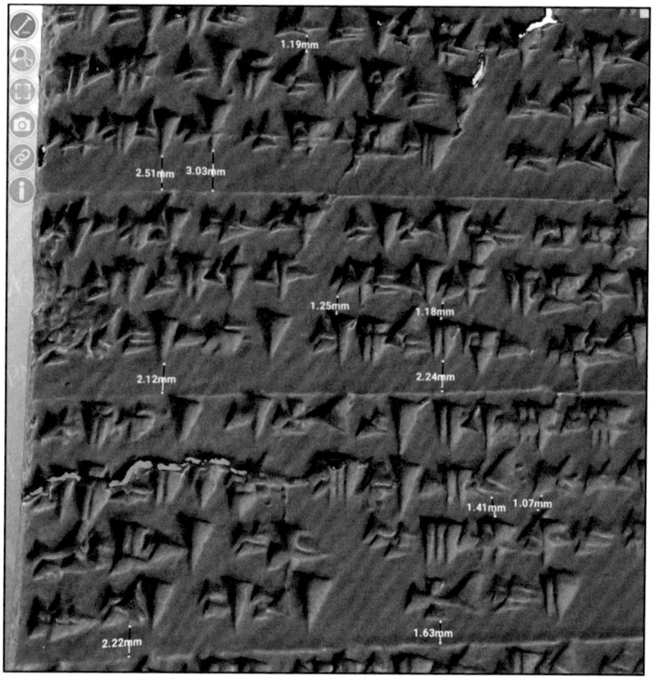

Fig. 27. Measuring Pikku's spacing.

In addition, the spacing between the characters mentioned are easily measurable in the 3D viewer (Fig. 26–27). The lines in Ḫulanapi's text 310/b are more even and straighter than in Pikku's Bo 51. The distances between the lines and the distance to the paragraph rulings are smaller.

Why have not more tablets been systematically compared and more characters used? We have registered thousands of characters, but some data are still missing because wedges are not recognized. For example, the broken middle horizontal in DA (Fig. 28) is not clustered as a wedge. By edge skeletonization (Fig. 29), we see that there is a depression with edges, but not three edges as in a wedge head. Therefore, there is no registration as a wedge with a number, instead the results of the skeletonization have to be made usable for the clustering. With characters such as NU, one of the

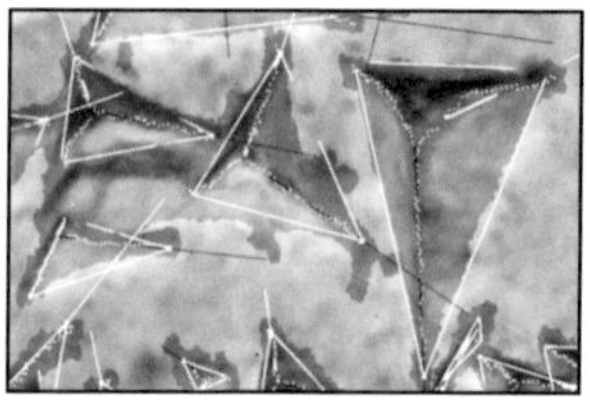

Fig. 28. DA with unclustered broken middle horizontal.

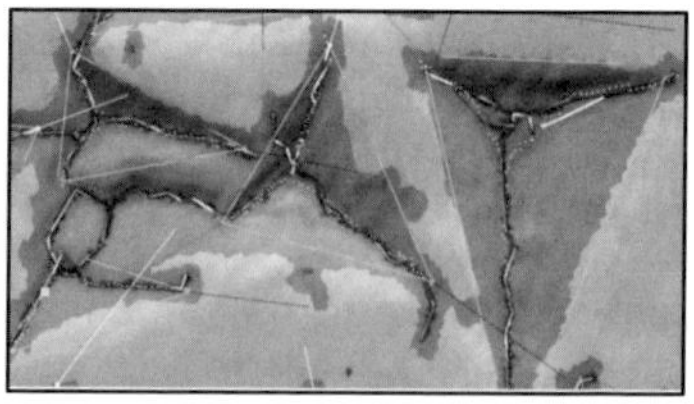

Fig. 29. DA with edge skeletonization.

Fig. 30. Semi-clustered NU.

wedges is regularly not recognized because it is incomplete (Fig. 30). Also, registering the characters is very time-consuming. If we define the cuneiform character as an area of the surface on a tablet, all clustered depressions (colored darker) and their geometric properties could be captured together, whereas manual marking of hundreds of thousands of cuneiform signs is of course illusory, prone to errors and no longer an up-to-date technique.

Recognizing cuneiform characters on photographs and 3D models

The aim of this approach is to identify and record all characters of a cuneiform tablet as completely as possible in order to achieve truly reliable classifications. To this end, the CuKa project (funded by the DFG)[1] in cooperation with the Technical University of Dortmund and Turna Somel has developed the prototype of a program, CuKa AI, that delineates these cuneiform character areas on optical 2D and 3D representations (Rusakov et al. 2021; Rest et al. 2022). This will allow for the addition of a new tool to the currently most widely used paleographic toolbox, the *Mainz Photo Archive.*

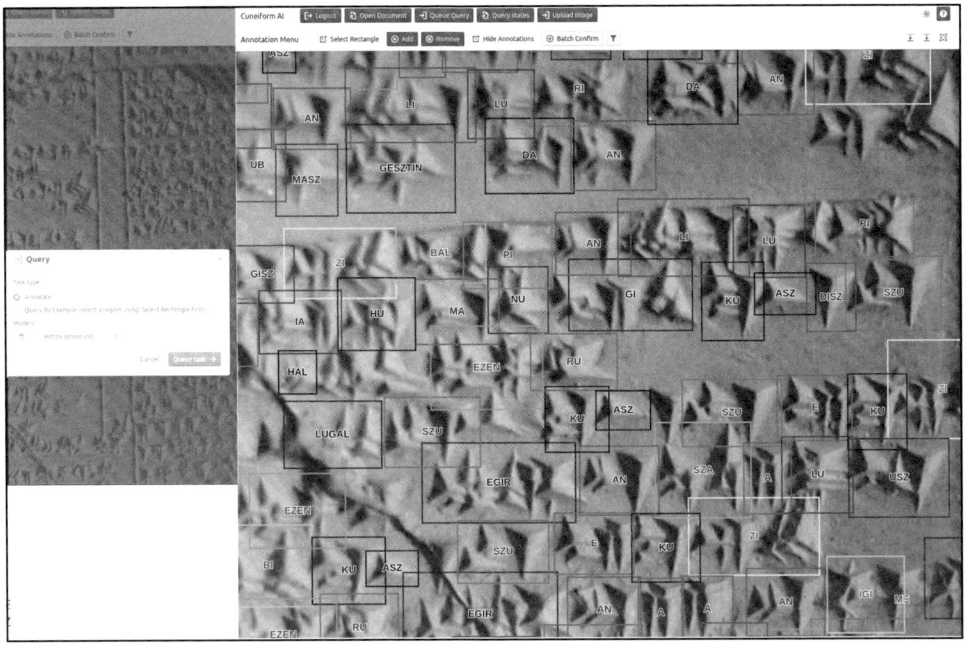

Fig. 31. Starting annotation query within the CuKa prototype.

1 CuKa – Computer-aided cuneiform analysis. Deutsche Forschungsgemeinschaft (DFG) – Project number 405966540. PIs: Gernot A. Fink, Gerfrid G.W. Müller, and Frank Weichert; team members: Christopher Rest, Eugen Rusakov, Turna Somel.

In the prototype, a photo can be uploaded via the browser window and an annotation task can be triggered. Though imperfect, the annotation results are quite satisfactory (Fig. 31), with success rates measured at around 80%.

The cuneiform characters found are stored both as reference coordinates on the respective photo or 3D image and as small photo snippets. Since artificial intelligence is essentially a statistical process that operates with probabilities, a confidence value is also stored.

Fig. 32. Spotting EGIR as an example.

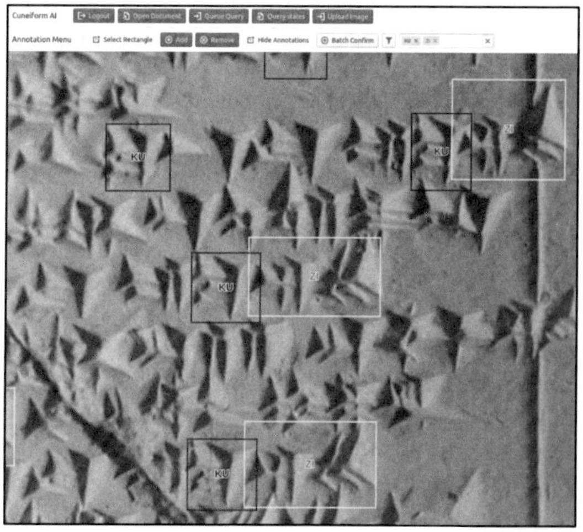

Fig. 33. Spotting KU and ZI.

A useful feature for everyday work is the search for one or more characters on the photo. The examples show searches for EGIR (Fig. 32), KU and ZI (Fig. 33), and A and NA (Fig. 34). Within the comparative sign table (Fig. 35), one can search for a selected sample section of an image (usually a cuneiform sign) in several photographs whose numbers are to be chosen. The sample is shown on the left together with a bigger section showing the surrounding. A different technique is used for this 'query by example', where a cuneiform sign can be selected by a bounding box to be searched for in the same and other selected images. Tests have shown a success rate of 70%–90% for the tool, depending on the frequency of the character. The number of characters displayed can be adjusted. Confidence is displayed to the right of the suggested excerpts. The character name is taken from the annotation table from the previous annotation procedure. In the example, the compared photograph

Fig. 34. Spotting A and NA.

Fig. 35. Comparative sign table.

```
N03882_HA_139,1676,248,1794,0.00000,0.00000,0.00000,1.00000,0.000
N03882_HA_1933,2329,2048,2435,0.00000,0.00000,0.00000,1.00000,0.0
W_BoFN03221_HA_1429,649,1557,758,0.00000,0.00000,0.00000,1.00000,
W_BoFN03221_HA_1558,995,1680,1114,0.00000,0.00000,0.00000,1.00000
W_BoFN04755_HA_1063,2082,1161,2153,0.00000,0.00000,0.00000,1.0000
W_BoFN04755_HA_1497,425,1609,517,0.00000,0.00000,0.00000,1.00000,
```

Fig. 36. The heads of the feature vectors to describe the cuneiform character on the image.

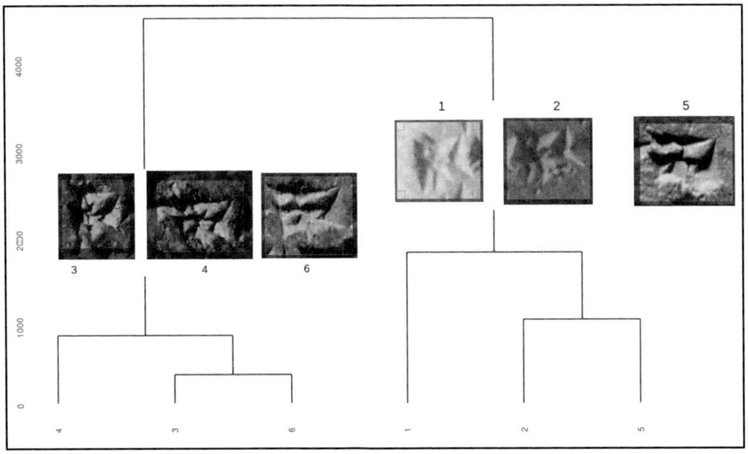

Fig. 37. Nr. 1–2: Bo 4891 (KUB 12.12 – *CTH* 628): scribe Ḫulanapi (N03882); Nr. 3–4: 101/b (KBo 15.10 – *CTH* 443): scribe ŠUKUR-*anza* (BoFN03221); Nr. 5–6: 403/b (KBo 15.10 – *CTH* 443): scribe ŠUKUR-*anza* (BoFN04755).

has only three ZI signs. The next similar sign is MEŠ, which is marked in a darker shade of grey as dissimilar and with a very low confidence value.

To determine the character class, our AI generates image-describing vectors with over 250 values, which are assigned an image number, character class, and image coordinates (Fig. 36). With these vectors, obviously one can attempt to cluster directly. The sample uses the sign ḪA (Fig. 37). Ḫulanapi consistently places the *Winkelhaken* in the sign ḪA (samples no. 1 and 2) higher than does the scribe ŠUKUR-*anza* (samples no. 4–6). Yet example no. 5 in the dendrogram is grouped with Ḫulanapi. The vectors for finding ḪA contain brightness values and are not trained for in-class classification. Thus the AI requires further adaptation.

A cuneiform search has already been implemented in the TLH^{dig} Corpus (Fig. 38). The phonetic value entered is automatically converted into cuneiform signs according to the Unicode standard and searches the cuneiform text attribute in the database. This makes it easy to find text passages with alternative phonetic values (Fig. 39). Certain limitations do exist, as shown by an example kindly provided by Charles Steitler: The cuneiform characters are systematically generated from the transcription according to the sign list (HZL). In the example (Fig. 40), the Sumerogram SAGI$^{!}$ is marked with an exclamation mark because it does not conform to the standard; this must be ignored by the computer program without a processing

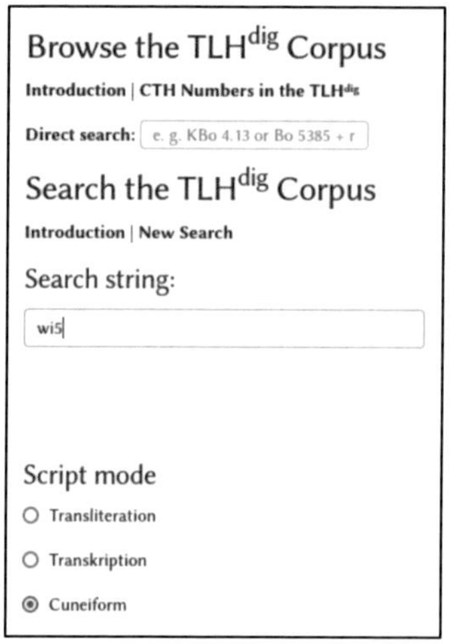

Fig. 38. Cuneiform search mask on TLH^{dig}.

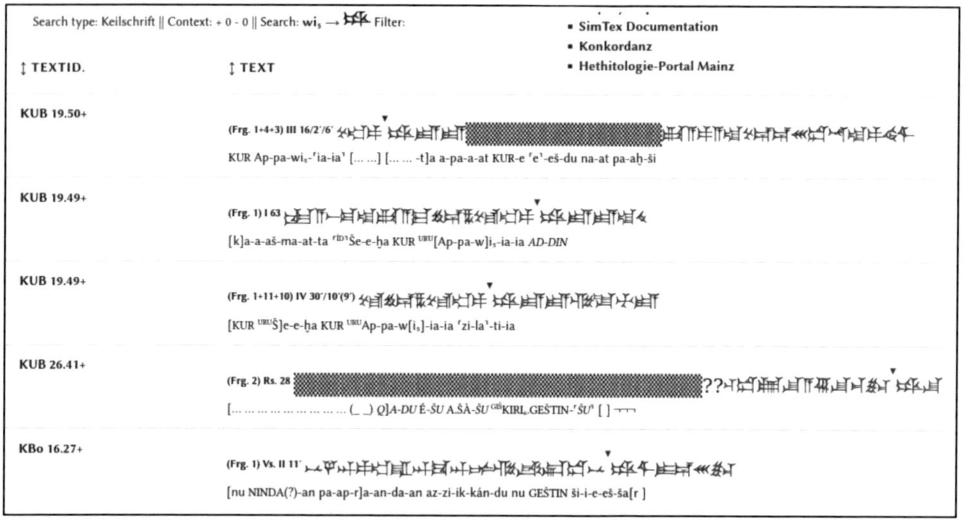

Fig. 39. Cuneiform search result showing logographic and syllabic use.

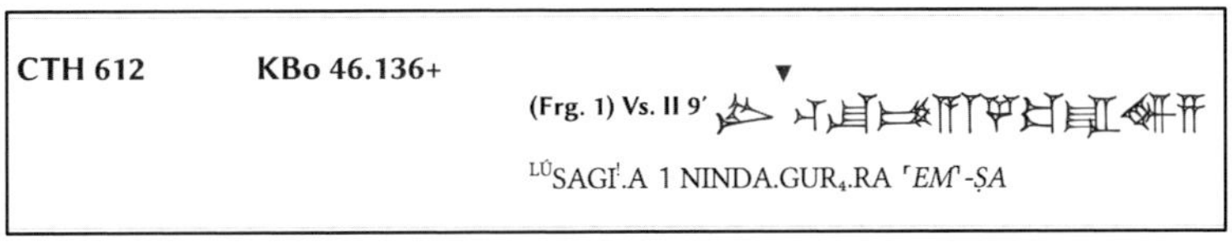

Fig. 40. SAGI$^{!}$.A in generated cuneiform string.

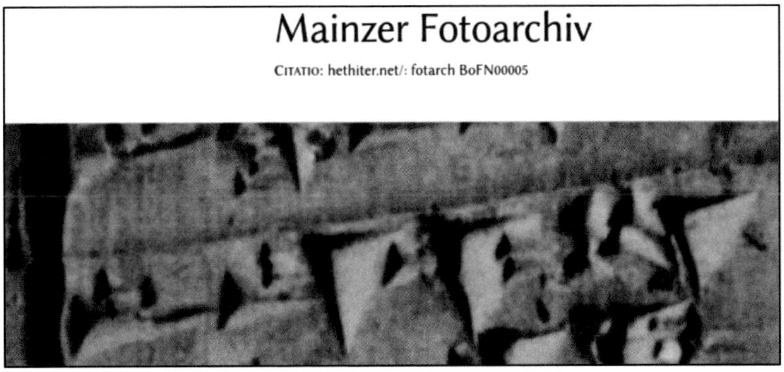

Fig. 41. SAGI!.A on photograph with inverted order of the elements.

Fig. 42. SAGI.A in normal order on the same tablet.

instruction. The character rearrangement ŠU SÌLA instead of SÌLA ŠU cannot be found in this way, but can only be seen on the photograph of the tablet KBo 46.136+ (Fig. 41). Elsewhere on this tablet the scribe uses the normal order (e. g. Fig. 42).

There is a good chance, however, that such exceptional cases can be found in the sign database in the future. In the aforementioned case, we looked at data that are still in progress. The new CuKa AI analyzed the photos of the two fragments of the festival ritual and localized the signs. The individual elements of the composite Sumerogram SAGI.A were found. The output consists of two result images that provide an overview of the recognized signs (Fig. 43). In the case of contradictory results, the hits with the higher probability score are shown in the first image and the second image shows possible alternatives (Fig. 44). As can be seen in the image sections, a supposed occurrence of TE was given a higher score than the correct reading, GAB, which was marked on the second image.

The database, which is currently being implemented, will allow for quick initial handwriting comparisons on photos. It can be used to create both a list of all characters on one photo (Fig. 45; taken from fragment 23/q shown above) or a list in which the same cuneiform sign on different photos or tablets can be inspected side by side (Fig. 46). This website could become an invaluable tool for paleographic and philological work.

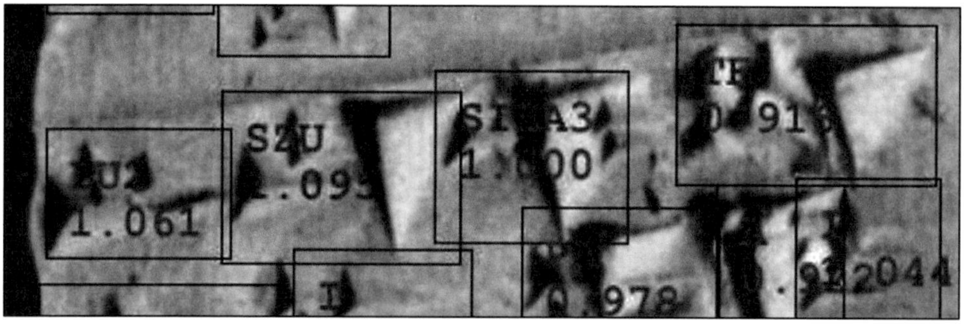

Fig. 43. AI results with higher probability.

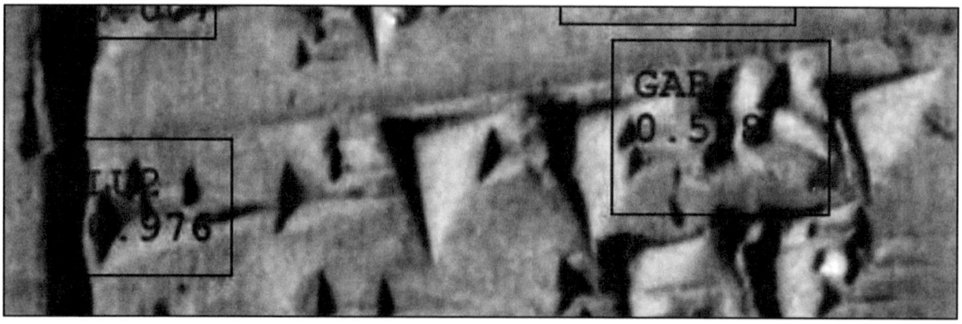

Fig. 44. Alternative AI sign interpretations with lower confidence.

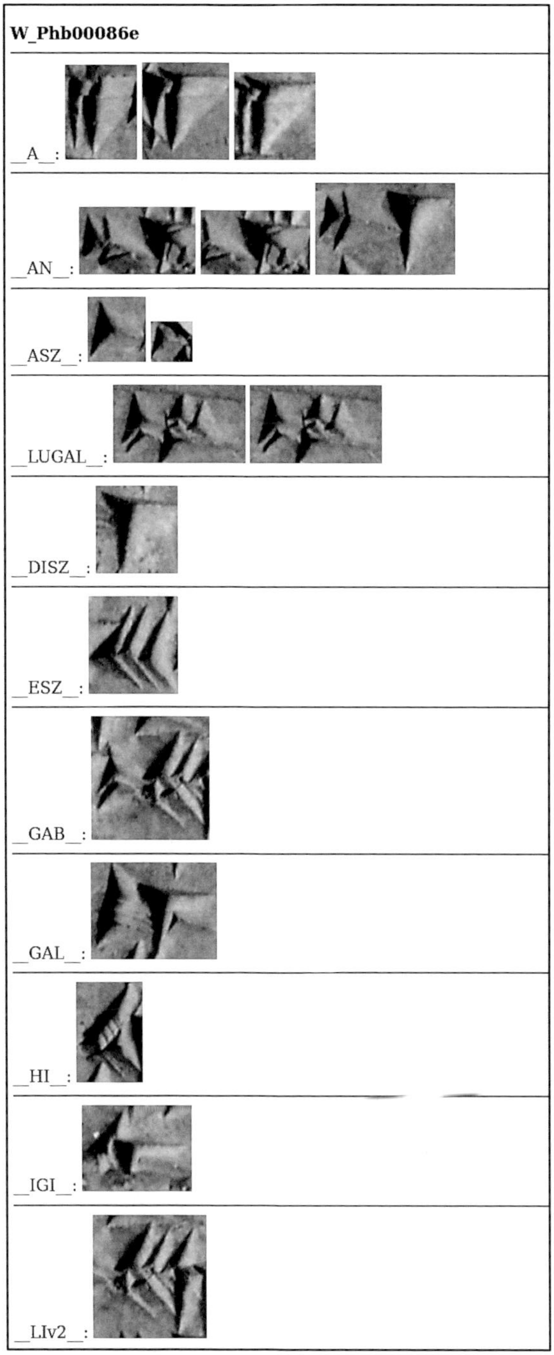

Fig. 45. Beginning of the sign list of fragment 23/q (photograph Phb00086e).

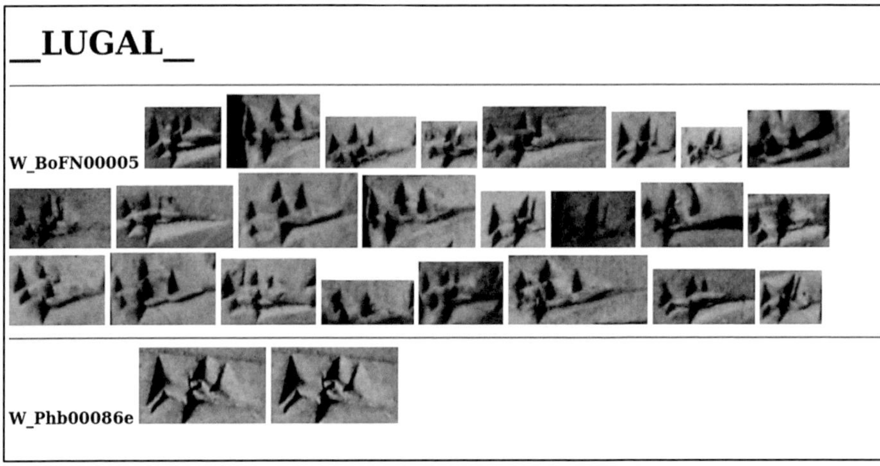

Fig. 46. Comparing LUGAL on two fragments of KBo 46.136+.

Bibliography

Gordin, Shai

2015 *Hittite Scribal Circles. Scholarly Tradition and Writing Habits.* StBoT 59. Wiesbaden: Harrassowitz.

Müller, Gerfrid, Denis Fisseler, and Frank Weichert

2015 3D-Joins und Schriftmetrologie. Die Entwicklung des "CuneiformAnalyser" zur Computer-unterstützten Visualisierung, Analyse und Rekonstruktion von Keilschrifttafeln. In: Elena Devecchi, Gerfrid Müller, and Jana Mynářová (eds.), *Current Research in Cuneiform Palaeography. Proceedings of the Workshop Organised at the 60th Rencontre Assyriologique Internationale, Warsaw 2014.* Gladbeck: PeWe, 129–44.

Rest, Christopher, Denis Fisseler, Frank Weichert, Turna Somel, and Gerfrid G.W. Müller

2022 Illumination-based Augmentation for Cuneiform Deep Neural Sign Classification. *Journal on Computing and Cultural Heritage* 15, Issue 3, Article 50. https://doi.org/10.1145/3495263.

Rusakov, Eugen, Turna Somel, Gerfrid G.W. Müller, and Gernot A. Fink

2021 Embedded Attributes for Cuneiform Sign Spotting. In: Josep Lladós, Daniel Lopresti, and Seiichi Uchida (eds.), *Document Analysis and Recognition – ICDAR 2021.* 16th International Conference Document Analysis and Recgonition 2021. Lecture Notes in Computer Science, vol. 12822. Cham: Springer. https://doi.org/10.1007/978-3-030-86331-9_19.

Rüster, Christel and Erich Neu

1989 *Hethitisches Zeichenlexikon. Inventar und Interpretation der Keilschriftzeichen aus den Boğazköy-Texten.* StBoTB 2. Wiesbaden: Harrassowitz.

THE SCRIBES OF PUDUḪEPA

Scribal Practice Reflected in Hittite Votive Texts

Daniel Schwemer
Julius-Maximilians-Universität Würzburg

Abstract

The extant Hittite votive texts were produced by the Hittite royal administration during a well-defined historical period spanning the reign of Ḫattušili III and, to a lesser extent, the reigns of his immediate predecessor and successor, Muršili III respectively Tutḫaliya IV; many of the surviving tablets and fragments are closely connected to queen Puduḫepa. The article investigates how and to what extent a macroscopic palaeographic analysis of the extant cuneiform manuscripts of such a historically homogeneous text group may contribute to a reconstruction of the underlying administrative processes. A macroscopic palaeographic survey not supported by digital metrical methods indicates that the votive texts despite their historical homogeneity reflect a great diversity of scribal hands. This leads to the provisional conclusion that almost all of the surviving tablets are semi-current records written by scribes who did not belong to a group of officials specifically concerned with the royal votive practice, but rather served as clerks at the royal court with a variety of scribal tasks.

1. Puduḫepa and her scribes

Puduḫepa, daughter of Pentipšarri, a priest of Ištar of Lawazantiya, rose to power together with her husband Ḫattušili, son of Muršili II and king of Ḫakpiš in the north of the empire during the reigns of his brother Muwattalli II and his nephew Muršili III (Urḫiteššup). With Ḫattušili's seizure of power and accession to the throne of the Great King, Puduḫepa became queen of the Hittite empire and one of the most influential royal women of antiquity. Numerous texts bear witness to Puduḫepa's enterprises and interests as a ruling queen, caring wife, and ambitious mother not only to many princesses, but also to her husband's successor Tutḫaliya during whose reign she remained active after her husband's death.[1] The tablets and fragments associated with Puduḫepa include her letters, in particular those in the context of the diplomatic negotiations with Ramesses II, the prayers *CTH* 383 (with Ḫattušili) and *CTH* 384, royal edicts and legal disputes, oracle reports, and festival texts, in particular manuscripts of the *ḫišuwa-* festival, a ceremony from her native Kizzuwatna, the reorganization and

1 For Puduḫepa, see Ünal 1974; Otten 1975; Klengel 1999: 235–97; Bryce 2005: 286–89; Frantz-Szabó and Ünal 2006.

documentation of which she personally commissioned to the chief scribe Walwaziti and his team.[2]

However, the most extensive group of texts directly connected to Puduḫepa is represented by records of vows she made to various deities, many of them for her husband's health and longevity, but also for her own and other family members' well-being, for military success, a rich harvest, and other concerns that were dependent on divine favour.[3] The vows are often prompted by (or even made during) dreams of the queen, whose content is recorded in the votive texts and sometimes clarified by oracle investigation. Therefore, the votive texts are closely connected to other texts that served the communication with the gods, especially oracle reports and prayers from the time of Puduḫepa.[4] Nevertheless, the votive texts form a clearly distinct type of text that provides insight not only into the personal piety of the Hittite royal family, but also into the mechanics of administrating the royal gift regime between the palace treasure houses and the divine beneficiaries and their temples.

It is recognized today that the vast majority of the extant votive texts should be dated to the time of Ḫattušili and Puduḫepa, with only a few texts clearly datable to their predecessor Muršili III and their successor Tutḫaliya IV.[5] None of the votive texts bears a scribal colophon, and their scribes therefore remain entirely anonymous. The texts show that a high official named Katapaili was tasked with the administration of Puduḫepa's votive gifts, but there is no indication in the available evidence that he himself wrote any of the votive texts.[6] With the exception of the multi-year vow of Puduḫepa to Lelwani (*CTH* 585), all votive texts are attested in only one copy. Following the terminology developed by Willemijn Waal and Theo van den Hout they represent "semi-current records",[7] tablets that were not written to be disposed of immediately after their use, but stored for a a certain time as administrative records without the need to produce new copies and thereby establish a lasting textual tradition.[8]

2 For a convenient overview of these texts, see Klengel 1999: 237–52. For a discussion of the scribes of the *ḫišuwa-* festival, see Gordin 2015: 255–80.

3 The tablets and fragments are collected as *CTH* 583, 584, 585, and 590. A comprehensive edition of the text in *CTH* 583, 584, and 590 was offered by de Roos (2007), who could include many fragments that had not been published yet at the time. Many texts are also treated by Mouton (2007), with a special focus on the (many) dream-related votive texts. *CTH* 585 was edited by Otten and Souček (1965). For a discussion of the text group, see Burgin and van den Hout 2016, Burgin 2020: 229–95.

4 See de Roos 2007: 3–17; the final section in Puduḫepa's prayer to the Sun-goddess of Arinna consists of vows to deities that are asked to convey Puduḫepa's message to the main addressee of the prayer (lines 116–63 in Rieken et al. 2016).

5 For the dating of the votive texts, see Burgin 2020: 229–41, with previous literature. The *Konkordanz* (Košak 2002–) records a few fragments among the votive texts that predate the empire period palaeographically: *CTH* 586: KBo 19.42 (MS?); *CTH* 590: KBo 47.279 (MS?); KUB 57.30 (MS). None of these fragments is a typical votive text, though KBo 47.279 certainly mentions votive gifts.

6 For Katapaili, see *infra*, section 3.3.

7 See Waal 2015: 173f. and van den Hout 2020: 236–41.

8 There is no indication in the extant sources that Puduḫepa herself would have written any of the tablets associated with or authored by her. As the offspring of a priestly family, Puduḫepa certainly would have acquired a significant amount of religious and ritual knowledge, but this does not necessarily include scribal training or more than rudimentary passive literacy (whether in the cuneiform or hieroglyphic

Since the votive texts can all be dated to the mid-thirteenth century and their tablets were neither copied from older manuscripts nor reproduced by later scribes, they form a homogeneous cache of scribal products with a shared and well-defined administrative and socio-historical context. Nevertheless, almost nothing is known about the scribes who wrote the votive texts.[9] Should we imagine them as clerks who produced the texts (besides many other tablets) at the behest of the officials who were in charge of the votive practice and liaised between the queen, oracle experts, and treasurers? Or are the votive texts the product of a small circle of specialists who themselves controlled the fulfilment of the royal vows and were trusted not only with the precious materials to be gifted to the gods, but also with the queen's dreams and worries?[10] The following is an attempt at approaching these questions through a study of the form and execution of the cuneiform signs in the manuscripts of the votive texts. How homogeneous and consistent are the scribal products within this well-defined text group, and can the writing preserved on the tablets and fragments as such teach us anything about the *modus operandi* of the votive practice in the times of Puduḫepa?

2. Surveyed text corpus and methodology

The following analyses are based on the tablets and fragments of the *CTH* groups 583 ('Dreams of the king'), 584 ('Dreams of the queen'), and 590 ('Fragments of dream and vow texts'), with a separate section devoted to *CTH* 585 ('Vow of Puduḫepa'). In short, the body of texts surveyed here is to a large extent identical to that edited by Johan de Roos in his *Hittite Votive Texts* (2007) with the addition of *CTH* 585. The investigation of the script and handwriting on the tablets and fragments is generally based on the photographs available online through the *Mainzer Fotoarchiv*, though a number of fragments in the Ankara Anadolu Medeniyetleri Müzesi could be studied in the original.[11] The documentation of the script and handwriting of selected tablets and fragments in

script). Van den Hout (2020: 244f.) discusses passages that suggest that scribes would read out prayer texts on behalf of the king and queen, concluding that scribes would serve "literally as the mouthpiece for the royal couple" (p. 245). Nevertheless, the possibility of Puduḫepa having acquired (some degree of) literacy should not be dismissed out of hand.

9 This applies by and large also to *CTH* 585, because the scribes produced the multiple copies in the context of the administration of the fulfilment of a single vow over several years (see *infra*, section 3.5).

10 One may point to the characteristic, readily recognizable format and writing of the Sargonid oracle queries that seem to reflect the writing conventions of a particular group of professionals at the courts of Esarhaddon and Ashurbanipal. Starr (1990: xiii) notes: "The tablets on which the queries were written are characterized by their large, coarse appearance, and by the equally large, coarse shape of their cuneiform writing, which usually runs broadside, across the rectangular tablets." However, the tablets and fragments of Hittite votive texts certainly do not represent a similarly distinct and easily identifiable group of manuscripts.

11 Thanks are due to the Turkish authorities for the permission to study tablets at the Ankara Museum in 2023, and I am very grateful to museum director Yusuf Kıraç and his team for their support during my stay.

the following is based exclusively on macroscopic scrutiny, employing neither a microscopic study of the impressions of the stylus nor digital metrological methods.[12]

Studies of tablets whose scribes can be identified by colophons have demonstrated that manuscripts produced by Hittite scribes generally exhibit sufficient idiosyncratic writing features to permit in principle a differentiated handwriting analysis, despite the non-cursive character of the cuneiform script.[13] In these studies it has also become apparent that the internal variability of an individual scribe's handwriting reduces the significance of analyses based on small fragments quite dramatically. This adds to the constraints of the present investigation, since the vast majority of the votive texts are preserved in small fragments of originally mostly two-column, sometimes single-column tablets in larger formats. The quality of the available data is further limited by some of the larger fragments having an abraded surface that obscures sign forms and handwriting (e. g. KUB 56.19).

Variation of palaeographically significant sign forms within one manuscript are routinely explained in Hittitology as due to scribes adopting older sign forms from the original and mixing them with sign forms more current in their own period. While this is a valid scenario, it should be noted that also tablets that were produced afresh and do not represent copies of earlier manuscripts occasionally exhibit, despite general consistency, a certain amount of variation in the form and execution of the cuneiform signs.[14] Thus in the corpus surveyed here, different forms of AG, DA and ID, GI, ḪA, KI, KÙ, LI, LU, LÚ, MEŠ, RA, and URU are attested within one and the same manuscript, as are more slight variations like the arrangement of the three *Winkelhaken* in AḪ and ḪAR, the writing of ḪI with three or four small *Winkelhaken*, the arrangement of the two *Winkelhaken* in NA, and the writing of Ú with three or four verticals.[15] There are, however, signs that show a remarkable consistency and may serve as criteria for assembling smaller groups of manuscripts, in particular the sign BI, which scribes in the corpus surveyed here either write with an indented lower or an indented upper hori-

12 For this approach, which would have to be employed to further refine and test results yielded here, see Cammarosano 2014; Cammarosano et al. 2014; Müller et al. 2015; Müller 2016a; Müller et al. 2017; all with further references.

13 See Cammarosano 2015; Müller 2016b; Müller and Pirngruber 2019. For the possibility that also specific local scribal traditions may be identified, see Miller 2012.

14 This is not particularly surprising and has been shown to be the case also in other groups of cuneiform texts; Wagensonner (2019: 43–47) compared the alternation between more archaic and modern sign variants in manuscripts from Old Babylonian Larsa to linguistic code-switching.

15 For manuscript-internal variation in the sources of *CTH* 585, see *infra*, section 3.5, n. 55. Forms of DA and/or ID with both broken and single middle horizontal can be found in KUB 15.8, 15.14 (+) 21, and 15.19. For GI in KUB 15.11+, see *infra*, section 3.3, and cf. also KUB 15.19. ḪA occurs in the standard and late variants in KUB 56.19. For KI and LI, see KUB 15.5+, *infra*, section 3.1. For RA, see KUB 15.1+, *infra*, section 3.2. The interchange of old and young KÙ is quite common, sometimes even on the same line (thus in KBo 9.96 obv. ii 7′ and in *CTH* 585.A, see Fig. 1 and cf. n. 55). Also the use of old and late URU in the same manuscript is attested more than once, cf. KUB 15.18, 15.22, 56.24+, and *CTH* 585.A (see n. 55). With regard to the slight variations, it is worth noting that in ranks of parallel wedges the actual number of impressed wedges is often difficult to determine, certainly on photographs, but occasionally also on the original fragment.

zontal, never both forms interchangeably. Some sign forms are, on the whole, surprisingly rare in the votive texts, in particular the old forms of IG and LI.[16]

Fig. 1. Variation of KÙ in KBo 9.96 obv. ii 7′ (left) and of KÙ and GI in CTH 585, ms. A, KUB 31.61 obv. i 6f. (right).

In the following pilot study, the cuneiform scripts on four of the best-preserved manuscripts of votive texts are characterized and systematically compared to the rest of the tablets and fragments in *CTH* 583, 584, and 590. In doing so, other manuscripts that were probably or possibly written by the same scribe should be identifiable if scribal hands can indeed be identified at all with the methods employed here. The following tablets will serve as lead manuscripts: KUB 15.5+ (*CTH* 383, section 3.1); KUB 15.1+ (*CTH* 584, section 3.2); KUB 15.11+ (*CTH* 584, section 3.3); KUB 48.123 (*CTH* 590, section 3.4). The manuscripts of Puduḫepa's multi-year vow to Lelwani (*CTH* 585) will be treated separately in section 3.5.

3. Case studies

3.1 Ḫepapiya demands ex-votos for the Great Deity (KUB 15.5+; CTH 583)

KUB 15.5 + KUB 43.66 + KUB 48.122[17] is a collection of demands for votive gifts stated by a certain Ḫepapiya in response to dreams of the king and a few other persons. The beneficiary of the votive gifts is exclusively the Great Deity (*A-NA* DINGIR-*LIM* GAL), and many of the ex-votos are reassigned from other deities or people who were their original recipients. Some entries include information on whether the vow was already (*karū*) or not yet (*nawi*) fulfilled. A subscript, which consists only of a single word, characterizes the contents of the tablet summarily as *wekuwar* "demand". This subscript is as unique in the corpus of the vow texts as the contents of the tablet itself, though Ḫepapiya is mentioned in one other small fragment[18] and also a votive gift to

16 Old LI is attested only in KUB 15.5+ (*infra*, section 3.1) and in several manuscripts of *CTH* 585 (mss. B, D, G+I, M, T, AA; mss. P and R exhibit both forms; see n. 55). Old IG occurs only in KUB 48.123 (see section 3.4), KUB 56.31, KBo 64.338, as well as *CTH* 585, ms. R.

17 Bo 1248 + 2157 + 4950 + 4953 + 1653 + 85/f; Büyükkale, building E; ed. de Roos 2007: 71–88; cf. also Mouton 2007: 244–55, n. 93.

18 Merzifon 3 (ed. de Roos 1998a: 160f.; 2007: 289f.). Unfortunately, the fragment's location is currently unknown; de Roos (1998a: 160) considered a join of the fragment to KUB 15.5+ impossible because of the vow *A-NA* DINGIR-*LIM* (not *A-NA* DINGIR-*LIM* GAL), as did H. G. Güterbock in his letter to Robert S. Hardy ("I tried whether the fragment might fit into one of the gaps of that text, but could not place"; 16.x.1988). Hardy's hand copy of Merzifon 3 shows the sign UM in its classical Hittite form (HZL 98/2), whereas KUB 15.5+ consistently writes the sign in the more ceremonial form with three inscribed verticals (HZL

the Great Deity occurs in one further text.[19] The carefully shaped, two-column tablet with slightly rounded edges and *Randleiste* is almost completely preserved. The scribe usually leaves some uninscribed space before the paragraph ruling and only rarely continues his lines on the right-hand edge; as to be expected the lower edge is uninscribed. Overall, the script with a line height of approximately three lines to the centimetre looks very neat and carefully impressed. The sign 'forms' and 'types'[20] employed show a high consistency, though two different forms occur with some signs (ḪI, KI, KÙ, LI):

AG	Shows the late form, the two horizontals start in the first vertical with aligned heads, only the upper one is broken.	cf. HZL 81/14
AḪ	Written with an initial 'KUR' group and the horizontal not inscribed into, but closely attached to the right wedges of the 'KUR' group.	cf. HZL 332/B
AL	Not attested in the extant portions of the tablet.	
AZ	Written with subscript ZA.	HZL 92/B
BI	The upper horizontal is far retracted.	HZL 153/2
DA	Written with three horizontals stacked from bottom to top with the heads moving slightly to the left. The middle horizontal is broken.	HZL 214/8
EN	With the subscript vertical; the two *Winkelhaken* are impressed side by side.	HZL 40/3
GAD	Written with high closing vertical and outdented upper horizontal.	HZL 173/9
GAL	With four initial horizontals stacked from bottom to top with the uppermost outdented.	cf. HZL 242/1
GI	Shows the later, 'Assyrian' form with *Winkelhaken*, not oblique wedge, underneath a rank of three small wedges in the 'ḪI' group.	HZL 30/B
GIM	With the two verticals in right half, the first of which is preceded and partly overwritten by the 'GAM' group.	cf. HZL 165/10
GÍN	With the fronted upper horizontal (late form).	HZL 209/B
ḪA	With two *Winkelhaken*, the first of which is placed in the first broken vertical, the second after the second broken vertical.	HZL 367/3
ḪAR	With four horizontals and an initial 'KUR' group.	not in HZL 333
ḪI	Mostly written with three, sometimes with four small wedges.	HZL 335/A and 2; HZL 335/4 and 6

98/11). Therefore a join is excluded also on formal grounds. I thank Theo van den Hout for providing me with a copy of Güterbock's and Hardy's correspondence and of Hardy's hand copies of the fragments.

19 KUB 56.30 obv. i 12′; since the text has *A-NA* DINGIR GAL (not *A-NA* DINGIR-*LIM* GAL), it cannot be excluded that the scribe actually intended *A-NA* ^{D}NIN.GAL (cf. obv. i 19′). The mention of the queen, the king, and Tutḫaliya dates the fragment safely to Puduḫepa during the reign of her husband Ḫattušili III as great king.

20 Terminology following Gordin 2015: 83–85.

ID	With three horizontals stacked from bottom to top with the heads moving slightly to the left. The middle horizontal is broken.	HZL 215/10
IG	Late, 'Assyrian' form.	HZL 67/B
IN	Standard Hittite form without inscribed verticals.	HZL 354/1
KA	The heads of the final two horizontals are set into the first vertical; their tails extend beyond the second vertical.	HZL 133/7
KI	Shows the form with two *Winkelhaken*; the bottom horizontal is slightly accentuated and outdented. In KBo 43.66+ obv. 7′ the 'Assyrian' form with one *Winkelhaken* and vertical is attested.	cf. HZL 313/B and, once, 23
KIŠ	Not attested in the extant portions of the tablet.	
KÙ	Usually shows the later, 'Assyrian' form; the oblique wedge is slanting moderately downwards with a long tail that connects it to following UD and GI. In obv. ii 37′ the older form is used.	HZL 69/11 and, once, A
LI	Standard late form (obv. ii 9′, rev. iii 52′) and old form (rev. iii 7).	HZL 343/B and, once, A
LU	Mostly with retracted middle horizontal and the first vertical close to the heads of the horizontals.	HZL 210/1
MEŠ	Written in the late form with a triple horizontal.	HZL 360/B
NA	The two *Winkelhaken* are set with their heads' upper edge almost in line.	cf. HZL 15/1
RA	Starts with four horizontals, the uppermost of which is usually slightly outdented; the verticals are set on the same height.	cf. HZL 233/4 and 6
RU	The three verticals have their head on the same height; the initial *Winkelhaken* precedes the horizontal.	HZL 43/8 and 9
SÌLA	Hittite form, written without the *Winkelhaken*.	HZL 21/A
SU	Not attested in the extant portions of the tablet.	
TAR	With oblique lower wedge and the broken wedge horizontal.	HZL 7/C
TI	The bottom *Winkelhaken* is not aligned with the closing *Winkelhaken*, but tends to appear as a horizontal.	cf. HZL 37/5
Ú	With three verticals; the two initial horizontals mostly have relatively long tails, which are not overwritten by the following verticals.	HZL 195/A
Ù	Shows the 'U.DAR' form, with a rank of four final horizontals, the upper one of which is slightly outdented.	not in HZL 265
UG	Not attested in the extant portions of the tablet.	

UM	Consistently in the form with three inscribed verticals, which is clearly distinct from the standard form in Hittite cuneiform.	HZL 98/11
URU	Shows the classical late form with three horizontals, the middle of which forms an outdented initial.	HZL 229/B
ZU	With the fronted upper horizontal (late form).	HZL 209/B

Among the tablets and fragments in the corpus surveyed here, I cannot name a single piece that shares all the characteristics of the script and handwriting on KUB 15.5+. This is not entirely surprising, since KUB 15.5+ is one of the few manuscripts of votive texts that certainly do not date to the period of the reign of Ḫattušili III and Puduḫepa. The role of Ḫepapiya is unique to this text and the small fragment Merzifon 3, setting them apart from all other votive texts. Based on prosopographical arguments and the theology evident in the exclusive preference for the Great Deity, de Roos considered a dating of the text in the reign of Muršili III (Urḫiteššup) most likely, and other scholars revisiting the same evidence have rightly followed his lead.[21] It should be noted, however, that also Merzifon 3, which in all probability belongs in the same historical context as KUB 15.5+, seems not to have been written by the same scribe.

3.2 Dreams and vows of Puduḫepa and Ḫattušili III (KUB 15.1+; CTH 584)

KUB 15.1 + DBH 43/2.14 + CHDS 2.145[22] represents a collection of mostly dream-related vows of the queen (Puduḫepa) for the health of her husband Ḫattušili III; in addition, the tablet contains vows of the king and queen for the safety of the town of Ankuwa as well as vows concerning Kelušḫepa and her son in fragmentary context. This Kelušḫepa was probably a daughter of the royal couple and given in dynastic marriage to a king of Išuwa, with her son being a grandchild of the Hittite royal couple and crown prince of Išuwa.[23] The fragments preserve a substantial part of a two-column tablet with a flat obverse and a moderately convex reverse. The left, right, top, and bottom sides are slightly rounded with the transition to the front and back surfaces forming a clearly pronounced edge. The column dividing lines are significantly deeper and wider than the paragraph rulings; the latter seem to have been impressed with the long side of the cuneiform stylus or a similar tool, though sometimes the straight impressed lines are accompanied by more wavy, drawn lines. Groups of paragraphs are set off by double lines, as is the end of the text in column iv. The Randleiste is preserved at the beginning and end of the reverse; as usual, there is no Randleiste at the beginning of the obverse. There is no scribal colophon. Overall, the script with a

21 See de Roos 2007: 33–36; cf. also Houwink ten Cate 1994: 253f.; Mouton 2007: 24–26; Cammarosano 2010: 59f.; Burgin 2022: 239.

22 Bo 2573 + 8282 + 9705; no findspot; ed. de Roos 2007: 88–105; cf. also Mouton 2007: 260–66, n. 98; for the passages treated in Burgin 2022, see there, p. 664.

23 For Kelušḫepa and her family relations, see Glocker 2011: 271–73 with previous literature; Glocker argues convincingly that Kelušḫepa was married to Ališarrumma of Išuwa and that Arišarrumma, with whom she shares a seal (Korucutepe bullae), is their son and the son of the king of Išuwa mentioned in the votive texts.

line height of approximately three lines to the centimetre looks very neat, though the scribe, as is the rule in Hittite scribal practice, made ample use of the right edge. The sign forms and types employed show a high consistency and may be characterized as follows:

AG	Not attested in the extant portions of the tablet.	
AḪ	Written with an initial 'TIN' group and the horizontal not inscribed into, but closely attached to the right wedges of the 'TIN' group.	HZL 332/4
AL	Written without the inscribed *Winkelhaken* and a slightly downwards slanting lower horizontal.	HZL 184/4
AZ	Written with subscript ZA.	HZL 92/B
BI	The upper horizontal is written on top of the lower and slightly outdented.	HZL 153/A
DA	Written with three horizontals stacked from bottom to top with the heads moving slightly to the left. The middle horizontal is not broken.	HZL 214/C
DUB	Not attested in the extant portions of the tablet.	
EN	With the subscript vertical; the two *Winkelhaken* are impressed side by side, the second slightly lower.	HZL 40/3 and 4
GAD	Not attested in the extant portions of the tablet. In KBo 55.208: With inscribed vertical and outdented upper horizontal.	[HZL 173/3]
GAL	Not attested in the extant portions of the tablet. In KUB 15.3: With four initial horizontals stacked from bottom to top.	[HZL 242/A]
GI	Shows the later, 'Assyrian' form with *Winkelhaken*, not oblique wedge, underneath a rank of three, sometimes four small wedges in the 'ḪI' group.	HZL 30/B and 5
GIM	With a centrally positioned first vertical, which is preceded and partly overwritten by the 'GAM' group.	HZL 165/7
GÍN	With the fronted upper horizontal (late form).	HZL 209/B
ḪA	With two *Winkelhaken* as a 'MAN' group starting in the second broken vertical.	HZL 367/9
ḪAR	With four horizontals and an initial 'TIN' group.	HZL 333/7
ḪI	Partly written with three, partly with four small wedges.	HZL 335/A and 2; HZL 335/4 and 6
ID	With three horizontals stacked from bottom to top with the heads moving slightly to the left. The middle horizontal is not broken.	HZL 215/15
IG	Late, 'Assyrian' form.	HZL 67/B
IN	Standard Hittite form without inscribed verticals.	HZL 354/1

KA	The heads of the final two horizontals are set into the first vertical; their tails extend beyond the second vertical.	HZL 133/7
KI	Shows the form with two *Winkelhaken*. The bottom horizontal is slightly accentuated and outdented and the initial *Winkelhaken* large.	cf. HZL 313/5
KIŠ	With a 'MAN' group followed by a pair of horizontals with inscribed 'EŠ' group.	HZL 273/3
KÙ	Shows the later, 'Assyrian' form; the oblique wedge is slanting moderately downwards.	HZL 69/11
LI	Standard late form.	HZL 343/B
LU	Mostly with retracted middle horizontal and the first vertical close to the heads of the horizontals.	HZL 210/1
MEŠ	Written in the late form with a triple horizontal.	HZL 360/B
NA	Shows the 'BAD+LIŠ' form.	HZL 15/4
RA	Starts with four horizontals, the uppermost of which is usually accentuated; the first vertical is set slightly lower than the second. In obv. i 6 a different form with a retracted uppermost horizontal above the head of the first vertical occurs (not in HZL 233).	HZL 233/4
RU	The three verticals have their head on the same height; the initial *Winkelhaken* precedes the horizontal.	HZL 43/8 and 9
SAR	Not attested in the extant portions of the tablet.	
SÌLA	Hittite form, written without the *Winkelhaken*.	HZL 21/A
SU	Not attested in the extant portions of the tablet.	
TAR	With a vertical lower wedge and the broken wedge horizontal.	HZL 7/3
TI	The bottom *Winkelhaken* is not aligned with the closing *Winkelhaken*, but tends to appear as a horizontal.	cf. HZL 37/5
Ú	With three verticals; the two initial horizontals mostly have relatively long tails, which are not overwritten by the following verticals.	HZL 195/A
Ù	Shows the 'U.DAR' form, with a rank of usually four final horizontals, the bottom of which is slightly outdented.	HZL 265/12
UG	Not attested in the extant portions of the tablet.	
UM	Not attested in the extant portions of the tablet.	
URU	Shows the classical late form with three horizontals, the middle of which forms an outdented initial.	HZL 229/B
ZU	With the fronted upper horizontal (late form).	HZL 209/B

A small group of fragments can be distinguished by a script (sign 'forms') and handwriting (sign execution: 'types' or 'variants') that share all features of the writing on KUB 15.1+ so that they may be considered to have been written by the same scribe. It is unclear whether these fragments come from one or more tablets:

The fragment KUB 15.3[24] comes from a two-column tablet that in format and script is so similar to KUB 15.1+ that one can conclude with great confidence that the tablet was written by the same scribe as KUB 15.1+. Since KUB 15.3 rev. iv preserves vows by Puduḫepa related to Kelušḫepa and her son, the tablet was probably written at about the same time as KUB 15.1+. Like KUB 15.1+, the text on the tablet ended in rev. iv with a double ruling that is not followed by any subscript or scribal colophon.

The small fragment KUB 15.9,[25] which probably belonged to a two-column tablet, shares with KUB 15.1+ and 15.3 the conspicuous writing of TAR with a vertical wedge. Since the other extant sign forms and types also agree with the evidence from KUB 15.1+ and KUB 15.3, the fragment is likely to have been written by the same person. Within the corpus surveyed for the present contribution, there is no other tablet or fragment that exclusively employs TAR in this specific form.[26]

The group KUB 15.1+, 15.3, and 15.9 consistently uses the sign BI with a slightly outdented upper horizontal that was impressed after the lower horizontal. The fragment KBo 55.208[27] preserves two inscribed sides from the left edge of a probably two-column tablet with substantial fragmentary text passages on each side; the extant text shows that it comes from a tablet with a collection of typical Puduḫepa vows for the health of her husband. The script is characterized by the BI form typical of the KUB 15.1+ group, and all other preserved diagnostic signs also agree with the script and handwriting of that group. KBo 55.208 therefore likely was produced by the same scribe as KUB 15.1+, 15.3, and 15.9. In the surveyed corpus no other fragment preserving this characteristic form of BI can be assigned to the present group.[28]

24 Bo 2312; no findspot; ed. de Roos 2007: 105–8.

25 Bo 3945; no findspot; ed. de Roos 2007: 163–65.

26 Attention should be drawn to KUB 31.71 +? 60.97 (Bo 83 +? 1728, ed. Mouton 2007: 272–78, n. 102), the large fragment of a two?-column tablet whose scribe writes TAR sometimes with an oblique (Bo 83 obv. ii? 2′, 14′) and sometimes with a vertical wedge (Bo 83 obv. ii? 9′, 24′). There are a number of differences between the handwriting of KUB 15.1+ and KUB 15.3 on the one hand, and that of KUB 31.71+ on the other: Note, in particular, the writing of DA and ÍD with a broken horizontal, the consistent use of 'Assyrian' SÌLA (obv. ii? 20′, 21′, 25′, rev. iii? 9, 12, 23), and the tendency to write the initial *Winkelhaken* of AḪ and ḪAR with a 'KUR' rather than a 'TIN' group. Overall, it seems excluded that KUB 31.71+ was written by the same scribe as KUB 15.1+, 15.3, and 15.9. Since KUB 31.71+ does not represent a typical Puduḫepa vow text, there are also no content-related reasons to associate KUB 31.71+ with these fragments. The *Joinskizze* in *Konkordanz* (accessed 8.iii.2024) shows the two fragments as joining directly, and a mounting of the photos of the two fragments, which are housed in different museums, lends plausibility to a direct join. Note, however, that Otten's assumption in KUB 31 that the fragment Bo 83 originally belonged to a three-column tablet was not unfounded (cf. the trajectory of the extant *Randleiste*). An indirect join can therefore not be entirely ruled out, even though the text portions preserved in the overlapping lines of the two fragments fit well together.

27 183/u; Lower City, Temple I area (L/19); ed. de Roos 2007: 293f.

28 AAA3, n. 2 (Liv. 49-47-42, ed. de Roos 1977–78; 2007: 288f.) is a small fragment of a typical Puduḫepa vow text. While most extant sign forms, including BI, agree with the group constituted by KUB 15.1+,

A survey based on the characteristic form of KIŠ with an initial 'MAN' group shows that all other fragments within the corpus under investigation that also employ this form of KIŠ include, at the same time, at least one sign that is written in a form significantly different from the form employed in the present group.

While it may not be excluded that some smaller fragments may still be assigned to the KUB 15.1+ group, the surveys based on TAR, BI, and KIŠ demonstrate that the scribe of KUB 15.1+ did not write a large proportion of the extant fragments of the Puduḫepa vow texts. If one further takes into account that KUB 15.9 and KBo 55.208 cannot be excluded to have belonged to the same tablet as KUB 15.3, the limited size of this manuscript group becomes even more pronounced.

3.3 Vows of Puduḫepa, fulfilled and unfulfilled (KUB 15.11+; CTH 584)

KUB 15.11 + KBo 60.99[29] is a large fragment from a record of vows of queen Puduḫepa to various deities and in various locations. The queen's concerns in the extant portions of text include the health of the king, the success of a military campaign, and the growth of cereal crops in the fields. The text specifies whether votive gifts have already been fulfilled or not and mentions in this context Katapaili, a high-ranking official who is attested in a number of other texts from the reigns of Ḫattušili III and Tutḫaliya IV. An oracle inquiry dating to the reign of Tutḫaliya confirms that the administration of votive gifts (*piyannaš uttar* "the matter of giving") was a regular part of Katapaili's brief,[30] and this role is further illustrated by a small fragment of an administrative or votive text where he is said to deliver a propitiatory gift in fulfilment of (royal) vows.[31] Since KUB 15.11+ mentions a vow concerned with kingship and a royal journey of the king and queen to Kummani, van den Hout argues that it should probably be dated in the transition period between the reigns of Ḫattušili III and his son and successor Tutḫaliya.[32] The fragment itself belonged to a two-column tablet with a line height of approximately three lines to the centimetre. The *Randleiste* is preserved at the bottom of rev. iii, whereas the text at the top of the obverse begins, as to be expected, without this ornamental border ruling. The script on KUB 15.11+ is characterized by the following sign forms:

15.3, and 15.9, the shape of KIŠ with only one initial *Winkelhaken* (HZL 273/1; lines 7′ and 8′, photo: de Roos 1977–78, pl. XII) shows that the fragment should not be assigned to the same scribe.

29 Bo 2732 + 1158/z; Lower City, Temple I area (Mag. 12); ed. de Roos 2007: 109–14; for the passages treated in Burgin 2022, see there, p. 664.

30 KBo 2.2 rev. iv 22–33, ed. van den Hout 1998: 136f.; cf. also de Roos 1998b: 492.

31 KUB 57.113 obv. i 5f. (mentioned already by de Roos 1998b: 492; for a slightly different transliteration, see Tischler 2016: 263f.): (5) *A-NA IK-RI-BI*$^{\text{ḪI.A}}$ *še-er maš-kán* ⸢*A*$^{?}$⸣-[*NA*$^{?}$ É^{MEŠ} DINGIR^{MEŠ}(?)] (6) ^{m}*ka-ta-pa-i-li-iš pé-e-da-i* […] "Regarding the vows Katapaili will take propitiatory gift(s) *t*[*o the temples;* …]" (cf. also obv. 12). The tentative restoration at the end of obv. 5 is based on the following quote in obv. i 7f. that may represent an assurance by Katapaili to personally take care of the temples (É^{MEŠ} DINGIR^{MEŠ}). All extant paragraphs of the text seem to deal with votive gifts and offerings, but the typical phrases related to the actual making of a vow are absent.

32 See van den Hout 1998: 69, and ibid., 67–70 for a comprehensive discussion of the attestations for Katapaili.

AG	Shows the late form; the upper of the pair of horizontals is not broken and starts to the right of the lower horizontal.	HZL 81/16
AḪ	Written with an initial 'TIN' group and the horizontal not inscribed into, but closely attached to the right wedges of the 'TIN' group.	HZL 332/4
AL	Written with the inscribed *Winkelhaken*, which sometimes is realized almost as a horizontal.	HZL 183/10
AZ	Written with subscript ZA.	HZL 92/B
BI	The upper horizontal is retracted.	HZL 153/A
DA	Written with three horizontals stacked from bottom to top with the heads moving slightly to the left. The middle horizontal is not broken, the uppermost accentuated by being slightly deeper impressed.	HZL 214/C
DUB	Not attested in the extant portions of the tablet.	
EN	Not attested in the extant portions of the tablet.	
GAD	Not attested in the extant portions of the tablet.	
GAL	Not attested in the extant portions of the tablet.	
GI	Shows both the later, 'Assyrian' form with *Winkelhaken* (obv. ii 22, rev. iii 23′), as well as the traditional form with an oblique wedge underneath a rank of three small wedges in the 'ḪI' group (rev. iii 4′, 18′).	HZL 30/A and B
GIM	With a centrally positioned first vertical, which is preceded and partly overwritten by the 'GAM' group.	HZL 165/7
GÌN	Not attested in the extant portions of the tablet.	
ḪA	With two *Winkelhaken*, the first of which is placed between the lower verticals, whereas the second *Winkelhaken* follows the second broken vertical in a slightly higher position.	not in HZL 367
ḪAR	With four horizontals (top accentuated) and an initial 'TIN' group.	HZL 333/7
ḪI	Partly written with four small wedges (top accentuated).	HZL 335/6
ID	With three horizontals stacked from bottom to top with the heads moving slightly to the left. The middle horizontal is not broken, the uppermost accentuated by a slightly deeper impression. The 'ḪI' group is written with four small wedges (top accentuated).	HZL 215/16
IG	Late, 'Assyrian' form.	HZL 67/B
IN	Standard Hittite form without inscribed verticals.	HZL 354/1
KA	The heads of the final two horizontals follow the first vertical; their tails extend beyond the second vertical.	HZL 133/B
IN	Standard Hittite form without inscribed verticals.	HZL 354/1

KA	The heads of the final two horizontals follow the first vertical; their tails extend beyond the second vertical.	HZL 133/B
KI	Shows the form with two *Winkelhaken* and four horizontals, the lowest of which is sometimes slightly accentuated and outdented.	cf. HZL 313/B
KIŠ	Not attested in the extant portions of the tablet.	
KÙ	Shows the later, 'Assyrian' form (the oblique wedge is slanting moderately downwards with a long tail that connects it to following UD and GI) and also, apparently more rarely, the traditional form (rev. iii 23′, combined with late form of GI).	HZL 69/11 and A
LI	Standard late form.	HZL 343/B
LU	With retracted middle horizontal and the first vertical close to the heads of the horizontals.	HZL 210/1
MEŠ	Written in the traditional form with a triple *Winkelhaken.*	HZL 360/A
NA	Shows the 'BAD+LIŠ' form.	HZL 15/4
RA	Starts with four, sometimes three stacked horizontals, the uppermost of which is slightly accentuated; the two verticals are at the same height.	HZL 233/A
RU	The head of the middle vertical is lower; the initial *Winkelhaken* precedes the horizontal.	HZL 43/3
SAR	Not attested in the extant portions of the tablet.	
SÌLA	Not attested in the extant portions of the tablet.	
SU	Not attested in the extant portions of the tablet.	
TAR	Not attested in the extant portions of the tablet. In KUB 15.4: With an oblique, almost horizontal lower wedge and the broken wedge horizontal.	[HZL 7/C and cf. 10]
TI	The bottom *Winkelhaken* is aligned with the closing *Winkelhaken.*	HZL 37/A
Ú	With four verticals; the two initial horizontals mostly have relatively long tails, which are not overwritten by the following verticals.	cf. HZL 195/10
Ù	Shows the 'U.DAR' form, with a rank of usually four final horizontals, the top and bottom of which are slightly outdented.	HZL 265/10
UG	Written with subscript UD.	HZL 93/B
UM	Not attested in the extant portions of the tablet.	
URU	Shows the classical late form with three horizontals, the middle of which forms an outdented initial.	HZL 229/B
ZU	Not attested in the extant portions of the tablet.	

Even though the inventory of signs attested in KUB 15.11+ is less than complete, a few fragments of votive texts that share a significant number of its script and handwriting characteristics may be identified. Since all of these fragments are comparatively small, a final decision on whether they reflect the same scribal hand as KUB 15.11+ is not possible even when there is a high level of agreement between the sign forms and types on the respective fragments.

KUB 15.4[33] is a small, one-sided fragment of a two-column tablet, which, based on the few extant lines, contained a collection of vows, probably of Puduḫepa. All sign forms preserved[34] are identical to those on KUB 15.11+, as is the size of the script with approximately three lines to the centimetre. It is therefore possible that KUB 15.4 reflects the same scribal hand as KUB 15.11+; at the same time, it cannot be excluded that the two fragments originally belonged to the same tablet.

KUB 15.19[35] probably comes from a single-column tablet with long lines whose height allows 3 to 3.5 lines to the centimetre. The vows of a queen on behalf of the king with notes on their fulfilment firmly place the text in the corpus of Puduḫepa votive texts. The sign forms are the same as found in KUB 15.11+, including the usage of both forms of GI (obv. 5′ and 13′). As in KUB 15.11+, the DA and ID signs are usually written with a single middle horizontal, though ID with a broken middle horizontal occurs once (obv. 4′; cf. KUB 15.8). As in KUB 15.8, EN (attested once) is written with the subscript vertical, but the *Winkelhaken* show a 'GAM' rather than a 'MAN' arrangement. It seems possible that KUB 15.19 and 15.11+ were produced by the same scribe, though as with KBo 27.60 (see *infra*), the inscribed verticals in ŠA and TA tend to be set slightly higher than in KUB 15.11+; also note that RU in KUB 15.19 shows the first two verticals in a slightly lower position than the third, rather than only the middle vertical as in KUB 15.11+.

The mention of Zamuwatti[36] securely identifies the fragment KUB 15.8[37] as a votive text of Puduḫepa. The forms of the extant signs on the small piece, which originally belonged to a two-column tablet, generally agree with KUB 15.11+, though it should be noted that besides the form of DA with the single middle horizontal (obv. i 3′) also the form with a broken middle horizontal occurs (rev. iv 2′). Also the fact that GI is written with a rank of four rather than three wedges in the 'ḪI' group cautions against assuming that the fragment comes from the same tablet as KUB 15.11+ or was written by the same scribe. EN, which is not attested on KUB 15.11+, occurs once and is written with the subscript vertical and the two *Winkelhaken* almost at the same level ('MAN' arrangement).

KUB 15.22[38], the fragment of a single-column tablet with long lines and comparatively small script (approximately 4.5 lines to the centimetre), at first glance seems to

33 Bo 4427; no findspot.
34 This includes TAR with broken horizontal and oblique wedge; in the extant portions of KUB 15.11+ no TAR is preserved.
35 Bo 3200; no findspot.
36 For the attestations of this woman, which all date to the time of Puduḫepa, see Zehnder 2010: 316f.
37 Bo 4532; no findspot.
38 Bo 3986; no findspot.

belong to the group of fragments with a script very similar to that of KUB 15.11+, but the consistent writing of LU with four verticals sets it apart from the other manuscripts discussed here, as does the use of late ḪA with only one *Winkelhaken* (line 9′). The fragment is also noteworthy because of its concomitant use of MEŠ with three *Winkelhaken* (lines 6′, 9′) and with three horizontals (line 12′) as well as URU with the outdented initial horizontal (lines 5′, 6′, 9′, 12′) and without (lines 3′, 8′).

KBo 27.60[39] is a small, one-sided fragment from a collection of vows in the preserved section of the queen on behalf of the king's health and therefore certainly dating to the reign of Ḫattušili and Puduḫepa. The extant sign forms agree with KUB 15.11+, but there are slight differences that militate against the assumption of the same scribal hand: The inscribed verticals in ŠA and TA tend to be set slightly higher than in KUB 15.11+, and Ù (preserved once) seems to be written with a rank of three rather than four horizontals. The other extant signs in KBo 27.60 that can serve as indicators of a specific handwriting are, unfortunately, not preserved in KUB 15.11+.[40] The line height on KUB 27.60 is about 3.5 lines to the centimetre and the writing therefore slightly smaller than on KUB 15.11+.

KBo 41.59[41] is a one-sided fragment of a two-column tablet with a line height of three lines to the centimetre. The formatting of the tablet clearly shows that the fragment comes from a different tablet than KUB 15.11+, even though the sign forms employed are the same. It should be noted, however, that NA in KBo 41.59 shows a tendency to arrange the two *Winkelhaken* at two different heights or even on top of each other, whereas KUB 15.11+ places them approximately on one line ('BAD+LIŠ' form).

KBo 55.221 and KBo 55.223[42] are one-sided fragments with comparatively large script (2.5 lines to the centimetre); both fragments certainly belonged to Puduḫepa-period votive texts, probably two-column tablets, perhaps even the same tablet. The extant sign forms agree with KUB 15.11+, but overall on neither of the two fragments is enough text preserved to arrive at any firm conclusion. Further fragments of probably Puduḫepa-period votive texts that share basic sign forms with KUB 15.11+, but seem to be set apart by writing ranks of parallel wedges with sets of four or even five impressions are KUB 44.27, KUB 56.21, KBo 55.219, KBo 55.226, and HT 33.

Overall, the examination of those fragments that show, on the whole, the same sign forms as KUB 15.11+ leaves only KUB 15.4 and KUB 15.19 as (more or less) plausible candidates for manuscripts written by the same hand.

3.4 Vows of Puduḫepa to Ištar of Lawazantiya (KUB 48.123; CTH 590)

KUB 48.123[43] contains records of vows by Puduḫepa apparently mostly to Ištar of Lawazantiya, her personal goddess, on behalf of her husband's health, the army on campaign, and other matters whose details remain undetermined due to the frag-

---

39 Bo 75/112; Lower City, in secondary context.

40 EN with subscript vertical; SÌLA without *Winkelhaken*; TAR with broken horizontal and oblique wedge.

41 2189/c; Büyükkale, building E.

42 1133/u and 410/u; both Lower City, Temple I area (L/19).

43 Bo 2753 (original collated); no findspot; ed. de Roos 2007: 215–24; cf. also Burgin 2022: 248f., 258f., 267, 271, 278.

mentary state of the text. The mention of high-ranking members of the royal family like Ḫešni and Urḫiteššup confirms the dating of the text to the time of Ḫattušili's reign as great king. The large fragment comes from the bottom of a two-column tablet with *Randleiste*, which is inscribed in a comparatively small script with four lines to the centimetre. The script on KUB 48.123 is characterized by the following sign forms:

AG	Shows the late form; the upper of the pair of horizontals is broken and starts like the bottom horizontal with its head in the first vertical.	cf. HZL 81/14
AḪ	Written with an initial 'TIN' or 'KUR' group and the horizontal not inscribed into, but closely attached to the right wedges of the initial group.	HZL 332/4
AL	Written with and without the inscribed *Winkelhaken*.	HZL 183/9 and 12
AZ	Written with subscript ZA.	HZL 92/B
BI	The upper horizontal is retracted.	HZL 153/A
DA	Written with three horizontals stacked from bottom to top with the heads moving slightly to the left. The middle horizontal seems not to be broken (well preserved in rev. iv 17; copy incorrect).	HZL 214/C
DUB	Not attested in the extant portions of the tablet.	
EN	Without the subscript vertical; the *Winkelhaken* show 'GAM' arrangement.	HZL 40/11
GAD	Not attested in the extant portions of the tablet.	
GAL	Not attested in the extant portions of the tablet.	
GI	Later, 'Assyrian' form with *Winkelhaken* underneath a rank of three or two small wedges in the 'ḪI' group.	HZL 30/B
GIM	Not attested in the extant portions of the tablet.	
GÍN	With the fronted upper horizontal (late form).	HZL 209/B
ḪA	With two *Winkelhaken*, the first of which is placed between the lower verticals, whereas the second *Winkelhaken* follows the second broken vertical at the same level.	HZL 367/2
ḪAR	Not attested in the extant portions of the tablet.	
ḪI	Written with only two small top wedges.	HZL 335/8
ID	With three horizontals stacked from bottom to top with the heads moving to the left. The middle horizontal seems to be broken in obv. i 8′, but elsewhere the sign is not well enough preserved.	HZL 215/15
IG	Traditional Hittite form, but with a rank of only three initial horizontals.	HZL 67/3
IN	Standard Hittite form without inscribed verticals.	HZL 354/1

KA	The heads of the final two horizontals follow the first vertical; their tails extend beyond the second vertical; the lower of the first two horizontals is retracted.	cf. HZL 133/8
KI	Shows the form with two *Winkelhaken* and four horizontals, the lowest of which is accentuated and outdented.	cf. HZL 313/B
KIŠ	With the two initial *Winkelhaken* on top of each other followed by a pair of horizontals with inscribed 'MAN' group.	HZL 273/13
KÙ	Shows the later, 'Assyrian' form (the oblique wedge is slanting moderately downwards with a long tail that connects it to following UD and GI).	HZL 69/11
LI	Standard late form.	HZL 343/B
LU	With retracted middle horizontal and the first vertical close to the heads of the horizontals.	HZL 210/1
MEŠ	Written in the late form with a triple horizontal (value *eš*$_{17}$ in rev. iii 12 and iv 8).	HZL 360/B
NA	Shows the 'BAD+LIŠ' form with a comparatively high final vertical.	HZL 15/2
RA	Starts with four horizontals, the uppermost of which is indented, whereas the second from the top is outdented and accentuated; the first vertical is set lower than the second, with its head beneath the uppermost horizontal.	not in HZL 233
RU	Written with two or three verticals on the same height; the initial *Winkelhaken* precedes the horizontal.	cf. HZL 43/18
SAR	Not attested in the extant portions of the tablet.	
SÌLA	Not attested in the extant portions of the tablet.	
SU	Not attested in the extant portions of the tablet.	
TAR	With an oblique lower wedge and the broken wedge horizontal.	HZL 7/C
TI	The bottom *Winkelhaken* is not aligned with the closing *Winkelhaken*, but tends to appear as a horizontal.	cf. HZL 37/5
Ú	With three verticals; the lower horizontal is slightly indented.	cf. HZL 195/A
Ù	Shows the 'U.DAR' form, with a rank of usually three final horizontals.	HZL 265/16
UG	Not attested in the extant portions of the tablet.	
UM	Shows the standard Hittite form, with the upper horizontals beginning slightly to the left of the lower horizontals.	HZL 98/5
URU	Shows the late form with three horizontals, the middle one forming an outdented initial; the head of the first vertical is beneath the uppermost horizontal's tail.	HZL 229/7
ZU	With the fronted upper horizontal (late form).	HZL 209/B

Whereas the contents of KUB 48.123 is very similar to that found in so many of the Puduḫepa-period votive texts, the script and handwriting are not only set apart by their small size, but also by the use of the traditional form of the sign IG. The sign is frequently attested in the fragments surveyed here, but there are only two other fragments that do not employ late IG: KBo 64.338 and KUB 56.31.

The small fragment KBo 64.338[44] shares, indeed, a number of peculiar sign forms with KUB 48.123 and only deviates from the signs preserved in KUB 48.123 in minor details. The very similar signs are BI, KI, KIŠ, MEŠ, RA, TAR, TI, and URU; also the very low first vertical in UN and the high initial vertical(s) in ŠA and TA are features shared between the two fragments. Differences are apparent in the following signs: ID shows a clear broken horizontal in KBo 64.338; RU is written with three verticals in KBo 64.338 (one occurrence), whereas it has two or three verticals in KUB 48.123; in GÁN the three verticals are placed below the lower horizontal in KBo 64.338 (one occurrence), whereas in KUB 48.123 the heads of the three and (sometimes) two verticals are placed on the lower horizontal. Nevertheless, it seems possible that KUB 48.123 and KBo 64.338 were written by the same scribe. It is worth noting, however, that the extant portions of KBo 64.338, like KUB 48.123, preserve vows to Ištar of Lawazantiya. It is therefore entirely possible that the two fragments originally belonged to the same tablet, with the obverse of KBo 64.338 representing the beginning of obv. i, which is not preserved in KUB 48.123, whereas the uninscribed reverse would preserve the bottom of rev. iv.[45] KBo 64.338 is only known from the photo Phb00897 in the *Mainzer Fotoarchiv*, which, unfortunately, is without a scale. However, Heinrich Otten, who copied the fragment, explicitly noted the "kleine Schrift" on the fragment (see KBo 64, p. XI), which would fit well with the small script size of KUB 48.123.

In contrast, KUB 56.31,[46] while also characterized by a small script with approximately four lines to the centimetre, cannot have belonged to the same tablet as KUB 48.123, since its intercolumnium is significantly narrower than that on KUB 48.123. At the same time, the signs AL, BI, GI, KIŠ, KÙ, NA, RA, ŠA, TA, UN, and URU seem to show the same form and kind of execution as in KUB 48.123, though the surface of KUB 56.31 is not well preserved and the exact sign forms are, occasionally, not recognizable on the photo (especially DA and ID). Nevertheless, KUB 56.31, which records vows of Puduḫepa to various deities, among them various Ištar figures, should certainly be considered as possibly having been written by the same scribe as KUB 48.123.

The fragment KUB 15.28 + IBoT 3.125 mentions the same *auli-* matter in the town of Zitḫara that is also subject of a vow in KUB 48.123.[47] The hypothesis that KUB 15.28+ formed part of the same tablet as KUB 48.123 was already rejected by de Roos,[48] and

44 Privat 73; unprovenanced; current location unknown ("Privatbesitz Mainz").

45 The lower part of rev. iv often remained uninscribed in the manuscripts of votive texts, which never bear a scribal colophon.

46 Bo 6656; no findspot; ed. de Roos 2007: 279–83.

47 Cf. Burgin 2022: 233 with n. 646.

48 See de Roos 2007: 192, n. 447; de Roos generally showed a healthy scepticism regarding indirect joins, but it should be noted that his doubts about the assumption that KUB 15.14 and 15.21 originally belonged to the same tablet (de Roos 2007: 170, n. 377) seem too cautious in light of the identical script on both fragments.

the significantly larger size of the script on KUB 15.28+ rules out any possibility of a join. Also the sign forms attested in KUB 48.123 are all so different from those on KUB 15.28+ that the two fragments cannot be assigned to the same scribe. This shows that two different scribes dealt with two vows relating to the same concern, probably because they were not made at exactly the same time or because two different deities were addressed in the same affair, in this case Ištar of Lawazantiya (KUB 48.123 obv. i 8′–11′) and, possibly, Ištar of Šamuḫa (no divine name is preserved in KUB 15.28+ obv. 2′–5′, but the following vows are addressed to that goddess).

3.5 The multi-year vow of Puduḫepa to Lelwani (CTH 585)

From a certain point during the reign of Ḫattušili III, the netherworld goddess Lelwani received extensive annual votive gifts from Puduḫepa in the form of precious materials, animals, and people. The vow, by which Lelwani was asked to grant Ḫattušili a long life, is set apart from all other attested vows of Puduḫepa (or any other person) by its extent over several years, the sheer volume of the annual offerings, and the inclusion of significant numbers of personnel in the votive gifts. The extraordinary nature of the vow is reflected in its administration by the Hittite officials and scribes: Whereas records of other vows are known only from single manuscripts that usually assemble a number of separate vows in one document, the complex Lelwani vow was recorded every year in several copies.[49] The exact administrative purpose of the multiple copies, most fragments of which were found in the Temple I area,[50] is difficult to determine, but as of now the *Konkordanz* registers 40 distinct manuscripts that certainly represent the same votive text.[51] This number may be reduced by indirect joins, but may also rise if indirect joins currently recognized by the *Konkordanz* are found to be doubtful.[52] The best preserved manuscripts have up to 20 duplicate fragments,[53] a number that may be

49 See Otten and Souček 1965: 1–14; Burgin 2022: 284–87; cf. also Hutter-Braunsar 2019 and van den Hout 2020: 156.

50 Otten and Souček (1965: 4) concluded that “alle bisher bekannten Texte des Gelübdes … stammen … aus den Ostmagazinen des Großen Tempels”; with the notable exception of KBo 71.150, which was found in 2023 on Büyükkale, this statement is still valid today, but may be of very limited significance (cf. van den Hout 2020: 276).

51 Currently, the *Konkordanz* records 45 manuscripts comprising 79 individual fragments. Of these KUB 48.115 (ms. U), KBo 39.57, 57.136, 57.137, and 58.97 cannot be assigned to *CTH* 585 with certainty. The remaining 41 manuscripts are (indirect joins indicated as in *Konkordanz*, 24.iii.2024; sigla as in Otten and Souček 1965 and *Konkordanz*): KUB 15.17+ (ms. A); KUB 15.16 (ms. B); KUB 31.52+ (ms. C); KUB 31.51+ (ms. D); KBo 3.39+ (ms. E); KUB 26.64 (+) KBo 55.271 (+) Bo 9100 (ms. F); KUB 31.53+ (ms. G+I); KUB 31.50 (ms. H); KUB 31.58 (+) KUB 31.75 (ms. J); KUB 26.60 (ms. K); VBoT 71 (ms. L); KUB 26.63+ (ms. M); KUB 31.56 (ms. N); KUB 31.54 (ms. O); KUB 31.56 (ms. P); KUB 56.7 (ms. Q); KUB 56.2+ (ms. R); KUB 56.1 (ms. S); KUB 48.116 (ms. T); KUB 56.5 (ms. V); 1421/u (ms. AA); 1384/u (ms. BB); KBo 51.122 (ms. CC); 1409/u (ms. DD); KBo 52.108 (+) 60.111 (+) KUB 56.11 (ms. EE); 1407/u (ms. FF); KBo 52.107a (+) 52.107b (+) 1638/u (mss. GG and HH); KBo 48.122 (ms. II); 1381/u (ms. JJ); KBo 19.34; 51.105; 55.92; 55.209; 60.103; 61.106; 64.268; 68.54; 68.153; 71.150; ABoT 2.362.

52 Corti, KBo 52, p. VIII, excludes the indirect join KBo 52.108 (+) KUB 56.11 (ms. EE). Furthermore, the following indirect joins are problematic: KUB 31.58 (+) KUB 31.75 (ms. J, see *infra*, n. 58); KBo 52.107a (+) 1638/u (mss. GG and HH, see *infra*, n. 59); KUB 26.64 (+) KBo 55.271 (ms. F, see *infra*, n. 65).

53 KUB 15.17+ (ms. A) overlaps with mss. B, C, G+I, H, J, K, L, M, R, T, V, AA, BB, CC, DD, as well as KBo 71.150 and ABoT 2.362. KUB 31.58 (+) KUB 31.75 (ms. J) overlaps with mss. A, D, G+I, H, K, L, M, Q, R,

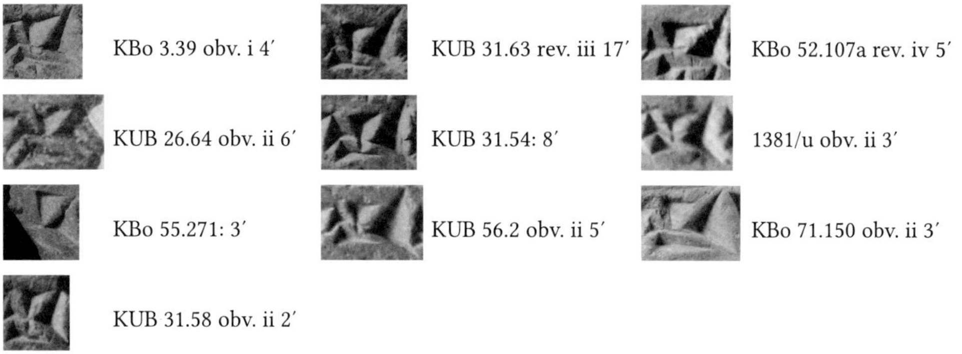

Fig. 2. The sign TI in the HZL 37/6 form.

reduced in the future by indirect joins among the duplicates, but the attestation of some text passages in six, seven, and up to nine duplicates[54] shows that the large number of fragments indeed bears witness to the production of multiple manuscripts of the same text, some of which differ in the extent to which they include the whole text or only parts of it.

None of the extant manuscripts includes a scribal colophon, and the fact that the majority of the known text witnesses are actually small fragments hampers all attempts at reconstructing groups of manuscripts that may have been written by the same scribe, not least because here, as elsewhere, variation in the use of specific sign forms can be observed within individual manuscripts.[55] Some of the manuscripts show peculiarities in the formatting of the tablet that are not found in other votive texts, such as the use of a left *Randleiste*, a top *Randleiste* on the obverse,[56] and the marking of double rulings with small pairs of *Winkelhaken*.[57] Nine sources are remarkable for their use of a specific form of the sign TI: The lower *Winkelhaken* is written as an oblique, sometimes almost horizontal wedge whose head is not far to the right of the head of the initial horizontal ('late GAD+U', HZL 37/6, cf. Fig. 2):

S, V, CC, EE, II, as well as KBo 19.34, 55.92, 60.103, 64.268, 71.150, and ABoT 2.362; but note that the indirect join of ms. J is uncertain.

54 Thus the paragraph in col. iii 40–45 (Otten and Souček 1965: 30f.) is attested in mss. D, J, M, S, EE, II, KBo 19.34, 55.92, and 60.103, the paragraph in col. i 64f. (Otten and Souček 1965: 22f.) in mss. A, G+I, J, K, L, and KBo 71.150.

55 KUB 15.17+ (ms. A) is particularly rich in that regard, using different forms of GI (cf. KUB 31.61 obv. i 6 vs. 7), ḪA (KUB 31. 61 obv. i 4 vs. ii 1), KÙ (KUB 31.61, both within obv. i 7), LU (KUB 15.17 obv. i 5 vs. 9), and URU (KUB 31.61 obv. i 1 vs. ii 13). Two different forms of signs are also found in KUB 31.52+ (ms. C): AG (KUB 31.52 obv. i 8′ vs. 11′); KUB 31.56 (ms. N): Ú (lines 2′ vs. 9′); KUB 4.33+ (ms. P): LI (KUB 56.10 obv. ii 4′, rev. iii 4 vs. rev. iii 6); KUB 56.2+ (ms. R): LI (rev. iii 7′ vs. 9′); KUB 56.1 (ms. S): LÚ (obv. i 1, 4, 5, 12, 15, 18, 21, 24 vs. 10, 11, 14, 26); KBo 52.108 (ms. EE): LÚ (lines 5′ vs. 7′); KBo 52.107a(+) (ms. GG): MEŠ (both within line 3′).

56 KUB 15.16 (ms. B): top and left *Randleiste* preserved; KUB 31.52 (ms. C): left *Randleiste* preserved on obverse and reverse; top of obverse not preserved; 1320/u (ms. G+I): left *Randleiste* only on reverse; cf. also KUB 48.115 (ms. U, but possibly not belonging to *CTH* 585): left *Randleiste* preserved on reverse[?]. For a discussion of this format, see Waal 2015: 106–8.

57 KUB 4.33 + 56.10 (ms. P); see Waal 2015: 114f.

- KBo 3.39 + KUB 56.6 (ms. E)
- KUB 26.64, KBo 55.271 (fragments assigned to ms. F)
- KUB 31.58 (m. J)[58]
- KUB 26.63 + 31.63 + 31.73 + 56.9 + KBo 51.121 + 55.211 + 68.53 (ms. M)
- KUB 31.54 (ms. O)
- KUB 56.2 + KBo 51.123 (ms. R)
- KBo 52.107a (+) 107b (ms. GG)[59]
- 1381/u (ms. JJ)
- KBo 71.150

Among these fragments, KBo 52.107a(+) stands out by using DU with a *Winkelhaken* (see *infra*) and a rare form of MEŠ with a rank of oblique three or four wedges (HZL 360/13), whereas all others share several characteristic features:

- earlier form of AG (attested in mss. E, J, R)
- BI with indented lower horizontal (attested in mss. J, M, O, R, JJ)
- DA and ID with broken middle horizontal (attested in all manuscripts but ms. R)
- ḪA in its traditional form with two *Winkelhaken* (attested in mss. J, M, R, KBo 71.150)
- LÚ without an inscribed vertical (attested in mss. M, R, KBo 71.150)
- MEŠ with a set of three *Winkelhaken* (attested in mss. J, M, O, R, KBo 71.150)
- SAR with only one vertical (attested in ms. M and KBo 71.150)
- ŠA and TA with high vertical(s) before the *Winkelhaken* (attested in all manuscripts but mss. E and F)
- Ú with three verticals (attested in all manuscripts but ms. J)

A certain variation can be observed in the use of the early and late form of LI,[60] early and late URU,[61] and the positioning of the *Winkelhaken* in NA.[62] Nevertheless, this is a group of fragments that show specific similarities in their handwriting, and indirect joins are excluded among most of them.[63] However, the extent to which they (or some of them) were actually written by one and the same scribe will have to be examined by using more sophisticated analytical tools than those employed here.

Several fragments are set apart from all other manuscripts by using DU with a *Winkelhaken* preceding the final vertical. In doing so, VBoT 71 (ms. L) 7′ shows the

58 The indirect join between KUB 31.58 and KUB 31.75 suggested by Otten and Souček (1965: 8) seems doubtful to me: Note the consistently different form of É between the two fragments (31.58 rev. iii 5′, 12′ vs. 31.75 rev. iii 2′, 4′, 8′) as well as the use of late AG in 31.75 rev. iii 9′ and early AG in 31.58 rev. iii 2′.

59 1638/u (ms. HH in Otten and Souček 1965: 12) is currently assigned to ms. GG by the *Konkordanz* (proposal Detlev Groddek, 16.ix.2009), but in light of the different forms of DU employed in 1638/u on the one hand, and in KBo 52.107a (+) 107b on the other, this seems uncertain to me.

60 Early LI: ms. M; late LI: mss. E, F, GG; both: ms. R.

61 Early URU: ms. R, KBo 71.150; late URU: mss. F, GG.

62 The 'BAD+LIŠ' form is found in mss. E, J, M, R, GG, sometimes varying with a form that sets the two *Winkelhaken* in a line (mss. E, J, M; for this form, see also mss. JJ, OO); ms. F and KBo 71.150 place the lower *Winkelhaken* slightly to the right of the upper one.

63 Ms. E overlaps with mss. F and M; ms. J overlaps with mss. M, R, and KBo 71.150; ms. M overlaps with mss. E, J, and R; ms. O overlaps with ms. GG; ms. R overlaps with mss. J, M, and KBo 71.150.

form that is typical for the earlier DU in Hittitological palaeographic terms, with the *Winkelhaken* above the upper horizontal (HZL 128/A), whereas the other fragments have an 'Assyrian' DU with the *Winkelhaken* inserted between the upper horizontal and vertical (not in HZL 128, see Fig. 3). In KUB 4.33 + 56.10 (ms. P), both the 'Assyrian' DU and the typical later Hittite DU are found;[64] like VBoT 71 (ms. L), KUB 4.33+ is further characterized by the use of MEŠ in the form 'ME+EŠ' (HZL 360/3), but the evidence for mss. L and P having been written by the same scribe (or even forming an indirect join) remains inconclusive. The other fragments showing 'Assyrian' DU are the following:

- KUB 26.64 (ms. F)[65] obv. ii 6′
- KUB 56.1 (ms. S) obv. i 2
- 1384/u (ms. BB) line 2′
- KBo 52.107a (+) 107b (ms. GG)[66] line 5′

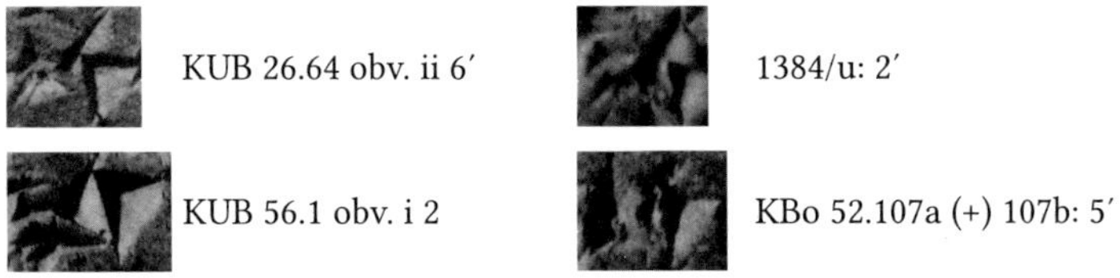

Fig. 3. The 'Assyrian' DU in some of the manuscripts of *CTH* 585.

Among these five fragments, KBo 52.107a(+) stands out by its use of MEŠ with a rank of oblique wedges (HZL 360/13) and the form of TI discussed above. The same form of MEŠ is also found in 1384/u (no TI extant) so that ms. BB and ms. GG may well have been written by the same scribe. Since there is no textual overlap between the fragments, an indirect join between 1384/u and KBo 52.107a (+) 107b cannot, however, be excluded. Two other manuscripts show this specific form of MEŠ, KUB 26.60 (ms. K) and ABoT 2.362; the latter preserves a classical later Hittite DU and therefore should provisionally be kept separate, the former preserves a LÚ with an inscribed vertical, whereas KBo 52.107a shows the more common LÚ without this inscription. The form of LÚ with the vertical is attested in a number of manuscripts of *CTH* 585,[67] but is a weak indicator as two fragments show the variant with and without the vertical side by side.[68]

Two manuscripts stand out by their tendency to write groups of parallel wedges with four or more instead of three members: KUB 31.53+ (ms. G+I) and KUB 56.1 (ms. S). Otten and Souček already noted that the two fragments are similar "in der Größe und Klarheit der Schrift", and wondered whether ms. S, whose text begins with

64 KUB 4.33 obv. ii 1′, KUB 56.10 obv. ii 3′, 7′ vs. KUB 56.10 rev. iii 3, 4, 6.

65 The indirect join of KUB 26.64 to KBo 55.271 should be treated with caution because the DU partially preserved in KBo 55.271: 4′ according the photo (*Mainzer Fotoarchiv*, fotarch E-1723) looks more like a typical late Hittite DU.

66 1638/u, ms. HH in Otten and Souček 1965: 12 and currently assigned to ms. GG by the *Konkordanz*, shows the standard later Hittite DU.

67 KUB 15.17+ (ms. A); KUB 26.60 (ms. K); KUB 56.5 (ms. V); KBo 51.105; KBo 68.54.

68 KUB 56.1 (ms. S) and KBo 52.108 (ms. EE).

the fifth year, may have been "die fortführende zweite Tafel" of ms. G+I (Otten and Souček 1965: 10). It seems indeed entirely possible that the two manuscripts were actually written by the same person.

It is finally worth noting that KUB 15.17+ (ms. A) is so far the only manuscript of *CTH* 585 that writes BI with an indented upper horizontal, whereas all other fragments that include an attestation of BI show the variant with the indented lower horizontal. Since a variation of the forms BI is very rarely found within one and the same manuscript, this is a comparatively strong indicator that sets ms. A apart from the rest of the transmission of *CTH* 585. Otten and Souček argued that ms. A probably contained the whole text, but represented a "spätere Abschrift", as shown by the inadvertent omission of a paragraph of text in the second column (Otten and Souček 1965: 5, 13f.). The hypothesis of a later copy would agree well with the distinct handwriting of the tablet[69] and the unusually frequent variation of different sign forms found in it (see n. 55), but it remains unclear whether this later copy was produced at a time when the votive obligations were still being fulfilled or at a later point, possibly even after the death of Ḫattušili III.

4. The scribes of the votive texts: provisional conclusions

The survey of the tablets and fragments of the votive texts led to the identification of small groups of tablets and fragments that may be argued to have been written by the same scribes in the service of the royal court during the reign of Ḫattušili III, whereas the scribe of KUB 15.5+ from the reign of Muršili III seems to be entirely isolated among the votive texts. However, the manuscripts that are dated to the time of Ḫattušili III and Puduḫepa also do not appear to form a homogeneous group that would have been written by a small circle scribes concerned with recording votive texts. For such an assumption, far too few fragments can be associated with the well-preserved lead manuscripts treated here in sections 3.2–3.4, and also the range of scribes producing the many copies of *CTH* 585 (section 3.5) seems too varied for such a hypothesis. Furthermore, the heterogeneous mixture of fragments that has come down to us is well illustrated by a survey of those fragments within *CTH* 583, 584, and 590 that show late ḪA with only one *Winkelhaken*: A comparison of the fifteen fragments and fragment groups with this marker[70] shows almost all of them to belong to different tablets written by different scribes. Only KUB 48.118[71] and KUB 56.20[72] seem to show a script and handwriting so similar that they may well have been written by

69 Cf. also TUR with a vertical and the addition of an extra initial vertical to É in KUB 15.17 obv. i 20.

70 KBo 8.63; KBo 9.96 (+) 41.60; KBo 33.216; KUB 15.14 (+) 15.21; KUB 15.22; KUB 15.30; KUB 31.69; KUB 48.118; KUB 50.47 + 52.90 + 56.24 + Bo 7832; KUB 56.12; KUB 56.14; KUB 56.19; KUB 56.20; KUB 56.25 + 60.118; KUB 60.60.

71 Bo 5454; no findspot; ed. de Roos 2007: 123–25 and Mouton 2007: 270–72. The fragment comes from the top left of a two-column tablet with *Randleiste* and a script size of approximately three lines to the centimetre. The fragment preserves the beginning of obv. i and the uninscribed bottom of rev. iv. There is no colophon.

72 Bo 5048 (collated); no findspot; ed. de Roos 2007: 255–57. The fragment comes from the top or bottom left of a one- or two-column tablet, thus preserving either the beginning of obv. (i) or rev. (iv). The curvature of the tablet surface indicates that the preserved side belongs to the reverse rather than the ob-

Fig. 4. VAT 13058 = KUB 15.23 (composite of the photographs Vorderasiatisches Museum, BoFN01669a, 01670a, 01671a, 01672b).

Fig. 5. 458/s = KBo 13.72 (composite of the photographs Hethitologie-Archiv B0153a, 0153b, 02024a).

the same scribe. As in other cases of this kind, however, the fragments are so small that it cannot be ruled out that they originally belonged to one and the same tablet. The assumption of an indirect join gains some support from the fact that both fragments deal with royal vows in the town of Uššа, though KUB 48.118 preserves vows concerning dreams of Puduḫepa, whereas KUB 56.20 contains vows of Ḫattušili for Puduḫepa's welfare, and therefore no direct connection between the extant text on the two fragments is apparent.[73] Also the shape of KUB 56.20 (see n. 72) cautions against assuming an indirect join too rashly.

Due to the methodological constraints described above in section 2, any general conclusions based on the above data are provisional in nature, but the most likely scenario at present seems to be that that the scribes who wrote the votive texts were clerks who wrote texts for the royal administration. They were probably not specifically concerned with the royal votive practice nor did their work demand any particular proximity to the queen. The officials who directly recorded the queen's and king's dreams and vows and who travelled with the royal couple were probably accompanied by a secretary who prepared the necessary records on small, single-column tablets like

verse and to a one- rather than a two-column tablet; however, a definitive decision on this point seems not possible to me. The script size is approximately three lines to the centimetre.

73 Cf. de Roos 2007: 256, n. 670 ("There would seem to be no connection"), but he seems to be referring only to contents, not to script and handwriting.

KUB 15.23 and KBo 13.72 (see Figs. 4–5). In the absence of a secretary scribe they were certainly able to prepare such records themselves. Whether Puduḫepa and Ḫattušili ever 'put stylus to tablet' when waking from a concerning dream is unknown, but the evidence currently available does not suggest this kind of routine literacy for this royal couple or any of the other Hittite kings and queens.[74] The standard two-column tablets that record many vows (see Fig. 6) were probably prepared in Ḫattuša by scribal administrators who then discarded the primary records on the smaller tablets, of which only the named two (KUB 15.23 and KBo 13.72) have come down to us because they were, in the terminology of Waal and van den Hout, "temporary or disposable records".[75] If this scenario is close to the administrative reality of the mid-thirteenth century Hittite royal court, attempts to identify specific scribal hands can be based only to a very limited extent on smaller groups of texts of the same type or with similar contents. It rather seems that the same anonymous clerk who wrote a two-column record of royal vows in the morning may have been charged with writing up the minutes of an oracle investigation at midday. The apparent diversity of scribal hands in the votive texts may also be taken as an indication that the total number of scribes employed by the royal court in the heyday of the empire should not be underestimated.

Fig. 6. Bo 2573 + 8282 + 9705 = KUB 15.1 + DBH 43/2.14 + CHDS 2.145 (composite of the photographs Vorderasiatisches Museum BoFN00566, 12705b, 13140f).

74 See Bryce 2002: 60–62; van den Hout 2020: 244f. (cf. also *supra*, n. 8).

75 Waal 2015: 173f.; van den Hout 2020: 240.

5. Tables of the sign forms in the lead manuscripts of sections 3.1–3.4

	KUB 15.5+	KUB 15.1+	KUB 15.11+	KUB 48.123
AG	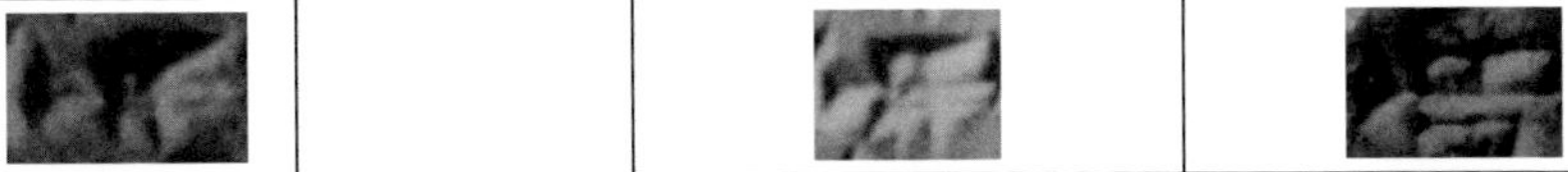			
AḪ	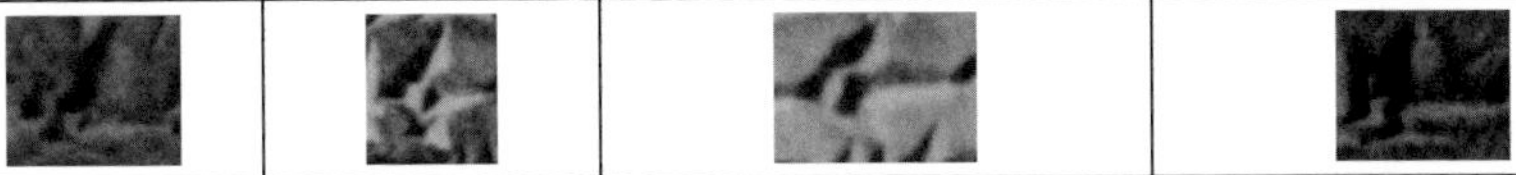			
AL				
AZ	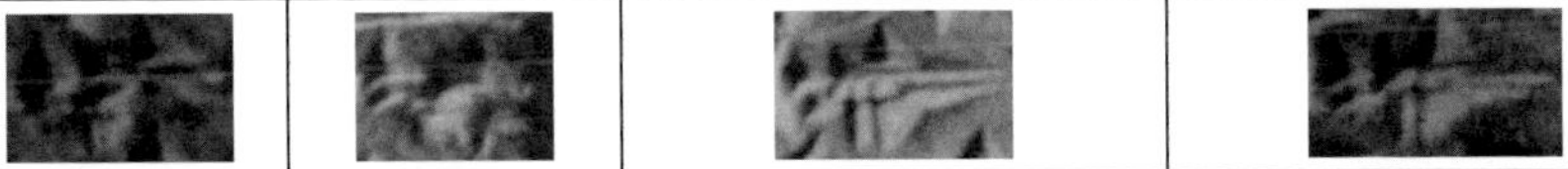			
BI	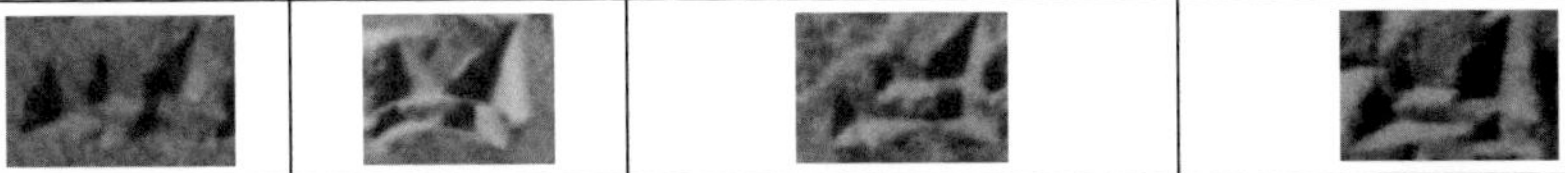			
DA	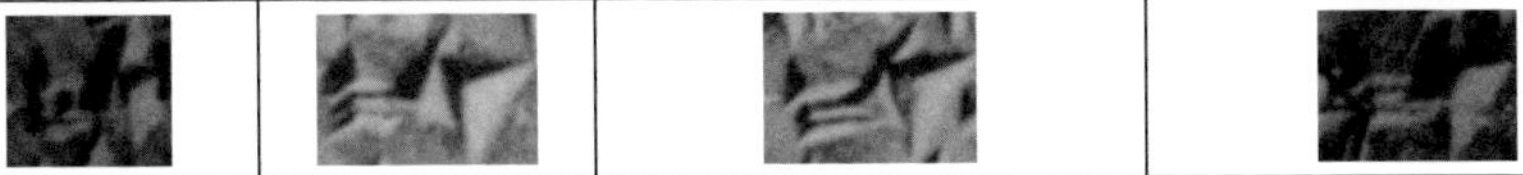			
EN				
GAD				
GAL	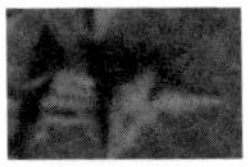			
GI	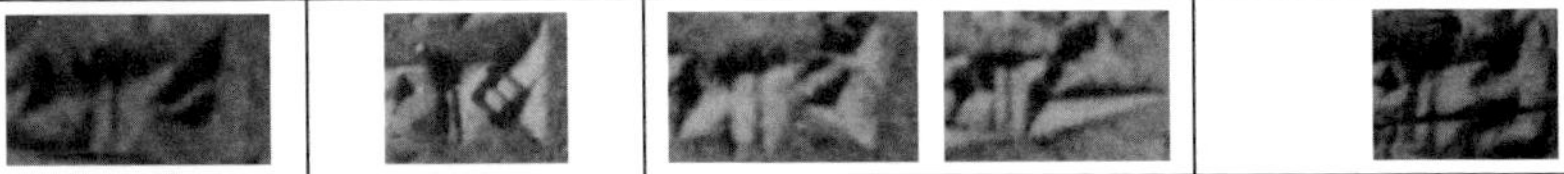			
GIM				
GÍN				
ḪA				
ḪAR	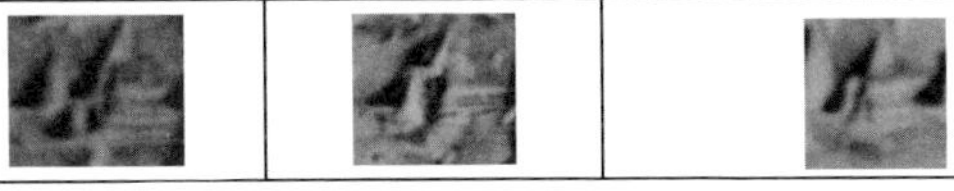			

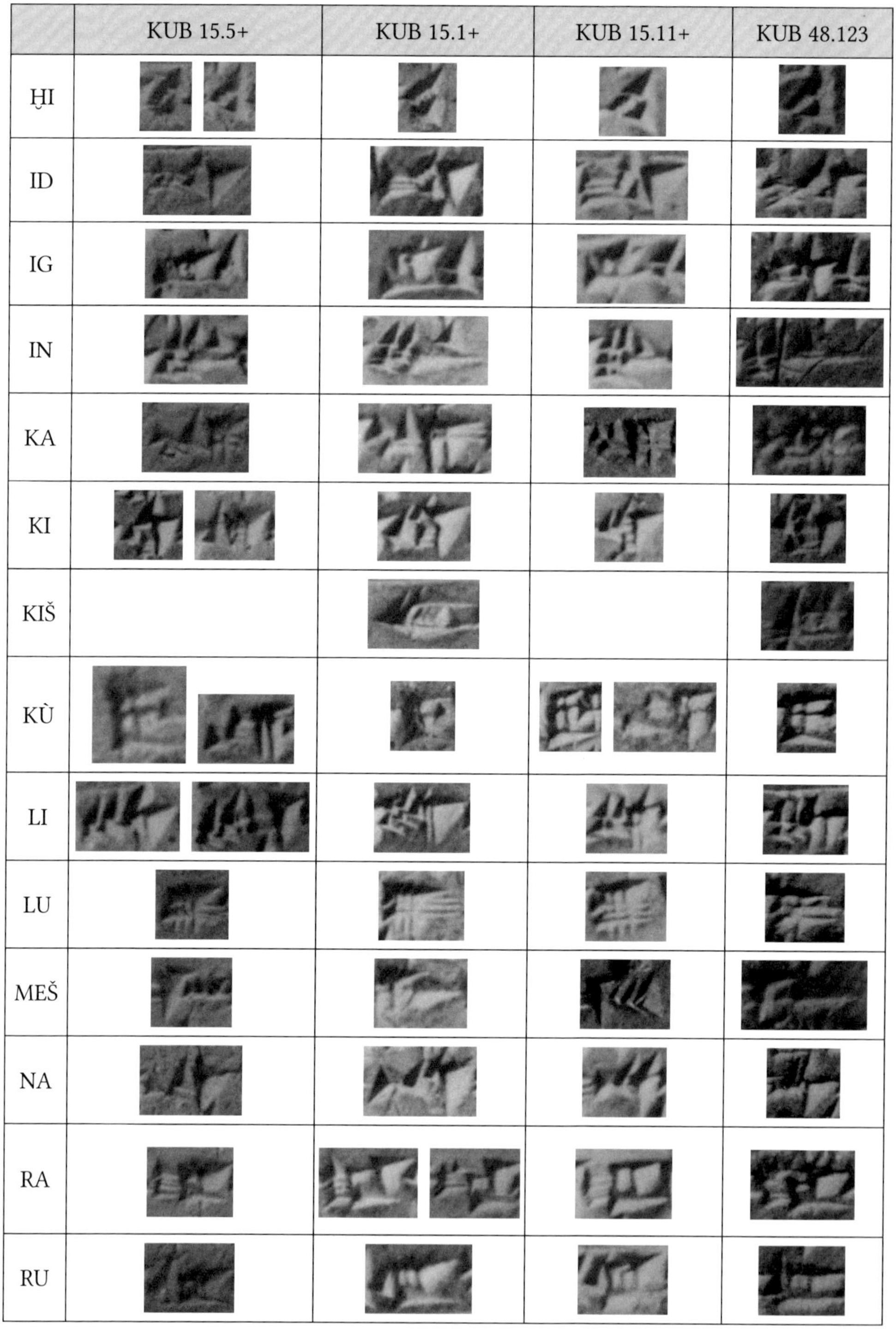
KUB 15.5+
KUB 15.1+
KUB 15.11+
KUB 48.123
ḪI
ID
IG
IN
KA
KI
KIŠ
KÙ
LI
LU
MEŠ
NA
RA
RU

	KUB 15.5+	KUB 15.1+	KUB 15.11+	KUB 48.123
SÌLA	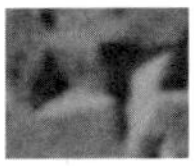			
TAR	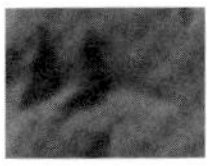			
TI	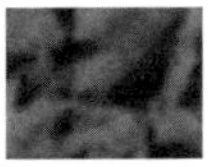			
Ú			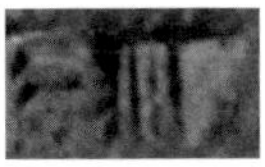	
Ù				
UG				
UM	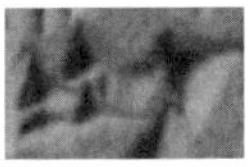			
URU	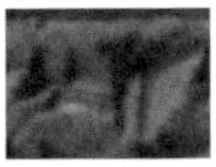			
ZU				

Bibliography

Bryce, Trevor

2002 *Life and Society in the Hittite World.* Oxford: Oxford University Press.

2005 *The Kingdom of the Hittites.* New Edition. Oxford: Oxford University Press.

Burgin, James M.

2022 *Studies in Hittite Economic Administration. A New Edition of the Hittite Palace-Temple Administrative Corpus and Research on Allied Texts Found at Ḫattuša. Volume I: Background, Corpus Overview, Case Studies, Lexical Commentary, and Glossary.* StBoT 70. Wiesbaden: Harrassowitz.

Burgin, James M. and Theo P.J. van den Hout

2016 Weihgabe. B. Bei den Hethitern. In: *RlA* 15: 32b–35a.

Cammarosano, Michele

2010 Tanuḫepa: a Hittite Queen in Troubled Times. *Mesopotamia* 45: 47–64.

2014 The Cuneiform Stylus. *Mesopotamia* 49: 53–90, Pl. 1.

2015 3D-Joins und Schriftmetrologie. A Quantitative Approach to Cuneiform Palaeography. In: Elena Devecchi, Gerfrid G.W. Müller, and Jana Mynářová (eds.), *Current Research in Cuneiform Palaeography. Proceedings of the Workshop held at the 60th Rencontre Assyriologique Internationale, Warsaw 2014.* Gladbeck: PeWe, 145–86.

Cammarosano, Michele, Gerfrid G.W. Müller, Denis Fisseler, and Frank Weichert

2014 Schriftmetrologie des Keils. Dreidimensionale Analyse von Keileindrücken und Handschriften. *WdO* 44: 2–36.

de Roos, Johan

1977–78 A Hittite Tablet in Liverpool Museum. *JEOL* 25: 67–74.

1998a A Few Missing Hittite Tablets. *AoF* 25: 158–62.

1998b Hittite Votive Texts. In: Sedat Alp and Aygül Süel (eds.), *III. Uluslararası Hititoloji Kongresi Bildirileri, Çorum 16–22 Eylül 1996 (Acts of the IIIrd International Congress of Hittitology, Çorum, September 16–22, 1996).* Ankara: Uyum Ajans, 491–95.

2007 *Hittite Votive Texts.* PIHANS 109. Leiden: Nederlands Instituut voor het Nabije Oosten.

Frantz-Szabó, Gabriella and Ahmet Ünal

2006 Puduḫepa. A. In: *RlA* 11: 106b–8b.

Glocker, Jürgen

2011 Urhi-Tessub Ališarruma, König von Išuwa. *AoF* 38: 254–76.

Gordin, Shai

2015 *Hittite Scribal Circles. Scholarly Tradition and Writing Habits.* StBoT 59. Wiesbaden: Harrassowitz.

Houwink ten Cate, Philo H.J.

1994 Urhi-Tessub Revisited. *BiOr* 51: 233–59.

Hutter-Braunsar, Sylvia

2019 Hethitische „Krankenkassenbeiträge". Die Gelübde Puduhepas für Leben und Gesundheit Hattusilis. In: Manfred Hutter and Sylvia Hutter-Braunsar (eds.), *Economy of Religions in Anatolia. From the Early Second to the Middle of the First Millennium* BCE. AOAT 467. Münster: Ugarit-Verlag, 49–59.

Klengel, Horst

1999 *Geschichte des hethitischen Reiches.* HbOr 1/34. Leiden / Boston / Köln: Brill.

Košak, Silvin

2002– *Konkordanz der hethitischen Keilschrifttafeln, Online-Datenbank Version.* hethiter.net/: hethkonk (2.plus) – last accessed 24.03.2024

Miller, Jared L.

2012 The Palaeography and Orthography of Six Rituals 'Redacted' in the Manner of Arusna. In: Elena Devecchi (ed.), *Palaeography and Scribal Practices in Syro-Palestine and Anatolia in the Late Bronze Age. Papers Read at a Symposium in Leiden, 17–18 December 2009.* PIHANS 119. Leiden: Nederlands Instituut voor het Nabije Oosten, 95–110.

Mouton, Alice

2007 *Rêves hittites. Contributions à une histoire et une anthropologie du rêve en Anatolie ancienne.* CHANE 28. Leiden / Boston: Brill.

Müller, Gerfrid G.W.

2016a Auf der Suche nach dem Schreiberprofil. In: Šárka Velhartická (ed.), *Audias fabulas veteres. Anatolian Studies in Honor of Jana Součková-Siegelová.* CHANE 79. Leiden: Brill, 257–75.

2016b Tausend Teile: Technische Mittel zur Rekonstruktion der Festrituale. In: Gerfrid G.W. Müller (ed.), *Liturgie oder Literatur? Die Kultrituale der Hethiter.* StBoT 60. Wiesbaden: Harrassowitz, 181–203.

Müller, Gerfrid G.W. and Reinhard Pirngruber

2019 Identifying Cuneiform Handwritings: a Case Study from the Late Babylonian Eanna Archive from Uruk. In: Elena Devecchi, Gerfrid G.W. Müller, and Jana Mynářová (eds.), *Current Research in Cuneiform Palaeography 2. Proceedings of the Workshop organised at the 64th Rencontre Assyriologique Internationale, Innsbruck 2018.* Gladbeck: PeWe, 177–210.

Müller, Gerfrid G.W., Denis Fisseler, and Frank Weichert

2015 3D-Joins und Schriftmetrologie. Die Entwicklung des „CuneiformAnalyser" zur Computer-unterstützten Visualisierung, Analyse und Rekonstruktion von Keilschrifttafeln. In: Elena Devecchi, Gerfrid G.W. Müller, and Jana Mynářová (eds.), *Current Research in Cuneiform Palaeography. Proceedings of the Workshop organised at the 60th Rencontre Assyriologique Internationale, Warsaw 2014.* Gladbeck: PeWe, 129–44.

2017 Web-Based Scientific Exploration and Analysis of 3D Scanned Cuneiform Datasets for Collaborative Research. *Informatics* 4/4, 1–16.

Otten, Heinrich

1975 *Puduḫepa. Eine hethitische Königin in ihren Textzeugnissen.* Akademie der Wissenschaften und der Literatur Mainz, Abhandlungen der Geistes- und Sozialwissenschaftlichen Klasse 1975/1. Wiesbaden: Steiner.

Otten, Heinrich and Vladimir Souček

1965 *Das Gelübde der Königin Puduḫepa an die Göttin Lelwani.* StBoT 1. Wiesbaden: Harrassowitz.

Rieken, Elisabeth, Jürgen Lorenz, and Alexandra Daues (eds.)

2016 Gebet der Puduḫepa an die Sonnengöttin von Arinna (*CTH* 384.1). hethiter.net/: *CTH* 384.1 (INTR 2016-01-18) – last accessed 24.03.2024.

Starr, Ivan

1990 *Queries to the Sungod. Divination and Politics in Sargonid Assyria.* SAA 4. Helsinki: Helsinki University Press.

Tischler, Johann

2016 *Hethitische Texte in Transkription. KUB 56 und KUB 57.* DBH 49. Wiesbaden: Harrassowitz.

Ünal, Ahmet

1974 *Ḫattušili III. Teil I. Ḫattušili bis zu seiner Thronbesteigung. Band 1: Historischer Abriß.* THeth 3. Heidelberg: Winter.

van den Hout, Theo P.J.

1998 *The Purity of Kingship. An Edition of CTH 569 and Related Hittite Oracle Inquiries of Tuthaliya IV.* DMOA 25. Leiden et al.: Brill.

2020 *A History of Hittite Literacy. Writing and Reading in Late Bronze-Age Anatolia (1650–1200 BC).* Cambridge: Cambridge University Press.

Waal, Willemijn

2015 *Hittite Diplomatics. Studies in Ancient Document Format and Record Management.* StBoT 57. Wiesbaden: Harrassowitz.

Wagensonner, Klaus

2019 Larsa Schools: A Palaeographic Journey. In: Elena Devecchi, Gerfrid G.W. Müller, and Jana Mynářová (eds.), *Current Research in Cuneiform Palaeography 2. Proceedings of the Workshop organised at the 64th Rencontre Assyriologique Internationale, Innsbruck 2018.* Gladbeck: PeWe, 41–86.

Zehnder, Thomas

2010 *Die hethitischen Frauennamen. Katalog und Interpretation.* DBH 29. Wiesbaden: Harrassowitz.

STADTBELAGERUNG, BÄRENJAGD UND TEXTDATIERUNG

Bemerkungen zum sogenannten „Zukraši-Text" im Hinblick auf eine Problematik in der Hethitologie

Oğuz Soysal
Philipps-Universität Marburg

Abstract

The present contribution discusses the tablet known in Hittitology as the Zukraši-Text, which was the starting point for dating Old Hittite texts from Boğazköy and generally for the topic of text dating in Hittitology. Firstly, this study focuses on the interpretation of the first paragraph of the Zukraši-Text in light of new philological studies. The subject here is the description of a military maneuver by a Hittite king (probably Ḫattušili I) against the city of Ḫaššu(wa) which is under Hittite siege and threatened with smoke or dust attacks. Secondly, the clay tablet of the Zukraši-Text is examined with respect to dating, i. e. whether it is an Old or Middle Hittite product. Although the cuneiform signs are not very helpful for dating the Zukraši-Text, one may claim without hesitation that it is an original Old Hittite document, based on the predominant *schwerer Duktus*, the not yet fully developed features of the writing technique, as well as on the layout of the tablet.

Einleitung

Obwohl das Hauptaugenmerk dieses Beitrags die zu diskutierende Thematik der hethitischen Keilschriftpaläographie sein soll, möchte ich zunächst meine Gedanken zur Datierung hethitischer Tontafeln innerhalb einer breiteren und allgemeinen Perspektive darlegen und dabei auch einige persönliche Erinnerungen kurz erwähnen. Aus diesem Grund ist es zunächst angebracht, die in der Hethitologie als „Zukraši-Text" bezeichnete Tafel ihrem Inhalt nach etwas genauer im Lichte neuer philologischer Erkenntnisse zu besprechen (Abb. 1).

In seinem Boğazköy-Tafelfundbericht 1953 legte Heinrich Otten die 1952 ausgegrabene Tafel 29/k mit ihren bemerkenswerten Schrift- und altertümlichen Sprachmerkmalen der wissenschaftlichen Welt vor, deren Inhalt für die althethitische Geschichte von besonderem Interesse war (Otten 1953; Abb. 2). Das betreffende Fragment wurde 1954 als KBo 7.14 veröffentlicht und später durch einen direkten Anschluss an 530/f (= KUB 36.100) aus den früheren Ausgrabungen von 1936 inhaltlich erweitert.[1] Der

1 Es sind noch zwei jh. Kopien KUB 36.101 und KUB 36.102 überliefert, die sich untereinander und KBo 7.14+ duplizieren. Als weiteres Duplikat kommt die wiederum jh. Kopie KUB 36.126 hinzu; vgl. Houwink ten Cate 1983: 108 Anm. 33; 1984: 76 Anm. 15, 81 Anm. 67. Ich zögere allerdings zuzustimmen, dass die Kompositionen *CTH* 14 und 15 (insgesamt 18 Tafeln, 24 Fragmente) in der Konkordanz zusammen behandelt werden.

Fundort des Fragments wurde von Kurt Bittel (1953: 6f.), Rudolf Naumann (1953: 21f.) und Heinrich Otten (1953: 59) als althethitische Schicht datiert. Später, im Jahr 1978, beschrieb auch Hans Gustav Güterbock, der bei der Ausgrabung 1952 in Boğazköy anwesend war, die seine Aufmerksamkeit erregenden, archaischen Merkmale der Zukraši-Tafel in Form eines Memoires in einem Artikel (Güterbock 1978; Abb. 3). In den 1960er und 1970er Jahren wurde dieses Dokument zum Ausgangspunkt der Etablierung einer ältesten Phase der hethitischen Keilschrift aus Boğazköy und stand im Mittelpunkt des damals heftig diskutierten Themas „Textdatierung in der Hethitologie". In den späten 1970er Jahren hatte ich als junger Student die Gelegenheit, diese Tafel im Anadolu Medeniyetleri Müzesi Ankara zu untersuchen. Sie war die erste hethitische Tafel, die ich jemals in den Händen hielt, und auch Gegenstand meines ersten wissenschaftlichen Versuchs, veröffentlicht Anfang der 1980er Jahre (Soysal 1981; Abb. 4).

Bemerkungen zum besseren Verständnis des ersten Paragraphen des Zukraši-Textes

Nach der oben erwähnten Veröffentlichung von Heinrich Otten und den darauffolgenden vollständigen oder partiellen Textbearbeitungen großer Anzahl[2] haben zwei Studien von Alwin Kloekhorst (2008 und 2016) wesentlich zum Verständnis des ersten Paragraphen des Zukraši-Textes beigetragen. Basierend auf den Ergebnissen dieser Studien und den von mir im Museum Ankara durchgeführten Tafelkollationen in den letzten Jahren möchte ich hier die aktuelle Transliteration und Übersetzung des ersten Paragraphen des Textes mit einigen neuen Lesungsvorschlägen vorlegen. Der Anfang der Tafel scheint formal und inhaltlich nicht den einleitenden Zeilen eines historischen Textes zu entsprechen. Daher kann diese Tafel ursprünglich zweikolumnig gestaltet gewesen sein. Für weitere Erklärungsversuche könnte man auch spekulieren, dass der besser erhaltene Teil von KBo 7.14+ entgegen dem Editionsband entweder die Tafelrückseite darstellt oder KBo 7.14+ als Ganzes die zweite Tafel einer Serie bildet. Erstgenannte Möglichkeit scheint mir weniger wahrscheinlich zu sein. Gegen die angebliche Rückseite werde ich später argumentieren. Eine Serie aus mehreren Tafeln einer historischen Komposition aus der althethitischen Zeit lässt sich zwar bisher nicht belegen, kann aber nicht ausgeschlossen werden.

Neue Lesungsvorschläge zu den ersten sechs Zeilen von KBo 7.14+ möchte ich wie folgt resümieren:

Die von Starke (1977: 162) vorgeschlagene Lesung 2 LÚ$^{\text{MEŠ URU}}$*ZA-AL-*[*PA*] für die Zeile 1 wird in der Sekundärliteratur allgemein akzeptiert und auch ohne weitere Diskussion wiederholt.[3] Ein neuer Vorschlag, und zwar 2 $^{\text{LÚ.MEŠ}}$*MU-UN-*⸢*NAB*⸣*-T*[*U*] „zwei

---

2 Otten 1953: 59–63; Werner 1956: 168f.; Soysal 1981: 24–33, 35f.; Kempinski 1983: 43–46; de Martino 2003: 110–21.

3 Wie z. B. Kempinski 1983: 44: „2 LÚ^{MEŠ} [^{URU}]*Za-al-*[*pa*]"; de Martino 2003: 110 mit Anm. 297: „2 LÚ⸤^{MEŠ}⸥ ⸤^{URU}⸥*Za-al-pa*⸥(-)*x-x*(?)". Ein anderer Vorschlag „2 $^{\text{LÚ.MEŠ}}$⸢*zi*$^{?}$⸣*-za-al*$^{?}$-⸢*le*$^{?}$*-eš*$^{?}$⸣" wurde von Soysal 1981: 25, 55 Anm. 53 übernommen, der einer mündlichen Mitteilung von Annelies Kammenhuber (wohl aus den Vorarbeiten von HW^{2} stammend) im Juni 1980 folgt.

F[lü]chtlin[g]e“ basiert auf der neuen Lesung der vier Zeichen nach „LÚ.MEŠ“, die nach Kollation der Originaltafel 2020 im Museum Ankara erzielt wurde. Die Zeichenreste von MU können mit der vollständig erhaltenen Form dieses Zeichens in Vs. II? 33 (URU*Ḫé-e-mu-wa*) verglichen werden. Für eine ähnliche Szene mit Nennung von „Flüchtling“ und einer belagerten Stadt s. unten Anm. 7.

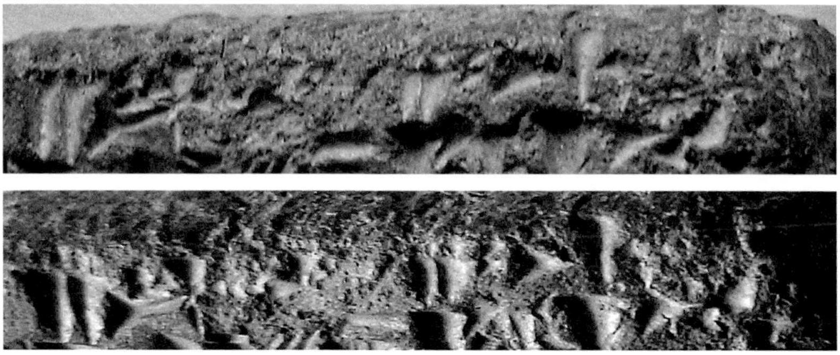

Fig. 1. KBo 7.14 + KUB 36.100 Vs. II? 1: 2 LÚ.MEŠ*MU-UN-*⌈*NAB*⌉*-T*[*U*] ⌈*x*?⌉.

Fig. 2. KBo 7.14 + KUB 36.100 Vs. II? 33: URU*Ḫe-é-mu-wa.*

Zu Beginn der abgebrochenen Zeile 6 gibt es Raum für knapp 2–3 Zeichen. Das erste, nur teilweise erhaltene Zeichen endet mit einem Senkrechten und kleinen oberen Winkelhaken und kann daher nur ḪU, RI, oder UZ, AR sein. Für diese Stelle wäre damit die Ergänzung [*ša-ak-ku*?*-r*]*i-iš-ki-mi* von Otten 1958: 82 (Anm. 24) die beste Lösung, die auch inhaltlich mit der Erzählung in KBo 10.2 II 18–21 (s. unten) mit Beschreibung wohl desselben historischen Ereignisses gut harmonieren kann.[4] In KBo 10.2 II 19 erscheint das Verb (*arḫa*) *šakkuriya-* eigentlich als Akt eines Raubtiers (Löwe). Dasselbe Verb betrifft im Zukraši-Text einen Menschen (Agens: König), der das gegen ein anderes Raubtier (Patiens: Bär) verübt. Dieser Sachverhalt erscheint als eine logische Inkompatibilität von Agens – Patiens und verursacht demzufolge inhaltliche Schwierigkeiten bei der Textinterpretation. Daher wäre, zusätzlich zu den Kommentaren von Kloekhorst 2008: 887f. und 2016: 171f., eine hypothetische Ergänzung [*tu-uḫ-ḫ*]*u-iš-ki-mi* „ich [räuch]ere aus > [überfal]le [mit Rauc]h“ für den abgebrochenen Anfang der Zeile 6

4 Zum Verb *(arḫa) šak(k)uriya-* „überwältigen, niederstrecken“ s. CHD Š 79f. Aus Raumgründen wäre die Ergänzung [*ša-ku-r*]*i-iš-ki-mi* ohne Geminierung °*-ak-ku-*° für KBo 7.14+ Vs. II? 6 vorzuziehen. Weitere Ergänzungsvorschläge sind aus Raumgründen und wegen der vorhandenen Reste der Keilschriftzeichen weniger wahrscheinlich, wie z. B.: CHD L–N 145: [*an*(?)*-da*(?) *š*]*i-iš-ki-mi*; Soysal 1981: 25, 56 Anm. 56: [GÌRḪI.A*-it*(?) *ša-ak-ku-r*]*i*(?)*-iš-ki-mi*; Kempinski 1983: 44: [*ú-i-šu-r*]*i-iš-ki-mi*; de Martino 2003: 110 mit Anm. 300: [*ši-ya-tal-l*]*i-iš-ki-mi.*

vorzuschlagen. Das bislang nicht belegte Verb **tuḫḫu(wa)i-* „ausräuchern; mit Rauch überfallen / angreifen“ (Iterativ **tuḫḫuišk-*; nach Muster *laḫḫu(wa)i-* mit der Iterativform *laḫḫu(i)šk-*) kann sehr wohl mit dem nominalen *tuḫḫu(wa)i-* „Rauch, Qualm“ und verbalen *tuḫḫiškiuwan dai-/tiya-* „beginnen, Qualm zu pusten“ verwandt sein.[5]

Fig. 3. KBo 7.14 + KUB 36.100 Vs. II$^?$ 6: [*ša-ku-r*]*i-iš-ki-mi* oder [*tu-uḫ-ḫ*]*u-iš-ki-mi*.

Im Lichte dieser Bemerkungen lautet der erste Paragraph des Zukraši-Textes in Umschrift und Übersetzung wie folgt:

KBo 7.14+ Vs. II$^?$:

1]-*x* 2 $^{\text{LÚ.MEŠ}}$*MU-UN-*⸢*NAB*⸣*-T*[*U*] ⸢*x*$^?$⸣
2]-⸢*x*⸣ *pé-ra-an e-eš-kán-ta-ti*
3]-*da i-it-te-en A-NA*(-)LÚ ^{URU}*Ḫa-aš-ši te-et-te-en*
4]-⸢*x*⸣ [...$^?$ *ka*]*t*$^?$*-ta pa-i-mi nu*(-)*me-na-aḫ-ḫa-an-da e-ḫu*
5 [*ták-ku*(?) *n*]*a-at-ta-ma ú-wa-ši nu-ut-ta ḫar-ták-kán ma-a-an*
6 [*tu-uḫ-ḫ*]*u-iš-ki-mi nu*(-)*tu-uḫ-ḫi-ia-at-ti-it a-ak-ti*

[...] zwei F[lü]chtlin[g]e [...] saßen vor [dem König$^?$, der sagte:] ‚Geht [... gegenübe]r$^?$ (und) sagt dem Mann von Ḫaššu. [Siehe$^?$,] ich gehe [aus$^?$ ... hina]b$^?$. Nun komm (mir) gegenüber. [Wenn] du aber [n]icht kommst, [überfal]le ich dich wie einen Bären [mit Rauc]h und (so) stirbst du durch Ersticken/Atemnot.‘

Fig. 4. KBo 7.14 + KUB 36.100 Vs. II$^?$, erster Paragraph.

5 Bereits von Roider 1981: 105–7 als „anfangen, Feuer zu speien“ interpretiert; vgl. auch Popko 1986: 559f. mit Anm. 1. Man möchte auch unter Berücksichtigung des möglicherweise verwandten verbalen *tuḫḫiški=uwan dai- / tiya-* und nominalen *tuḫḫiyatt-* im Zukraši-Text die lautliche Schwierigkeit nicht verschweigen, dass hier die Form [*tu-uḫ-ḫ*]*u-iš-ki-mi* vorliegt und nicht etwa *[*tu-uḫ-ḫ*]*i-iš-ki-mi*. Ob man allerdings tatsächlich in KUB 33.120 II 35 ein Prädikat *túḫ*$^?$*-ḫu-iš-ki-iz-zi* erkennen kann (HEG D, T 407), das formal mit dem postulierten Beleg im Zukraši-Text übereinstimmt, sei dahingestellt.

Wie aus dem zweiten Paragraphen der Tafel besser verständlich wird, handelt es sich um die Beschreibung eines Militärmanövers eines hethitischen Königs gegen die Stadt Ḫaššu(wa). Es wird allgemein angenommen, dass besagter König der hethitische König Ḫattušili I. war.[6] Denn eine Ḫaššuwa-Expedition wird in den Annalen dieses Königs häufig erwähnt. Laut der Erzählung im ersten Paragraphen von KBo 7.14+ sendet er an den Mann von Ḫaššu mit zwei Flüchtlingen[7] eine Nachricht und fordert ihn zum Krieg heraus. Andernfalls werde er seinen Feind mit einem Einkesselungsmanöver beseitigen. Die Interpretation der Zeilen 5 und 6, in denen dieser Umstand zum Ausdruck kommt und die aufgrund einiger Bruchstellen nicht klar verständlich sind, ist seit Jahren umstritten. Diese Textpassage enthält auch das Motiv der „Analogie mit der Tierwelt", das Ḫattušili I. in seinen schriftlichen Dokumenten häufig verwendete.[8] Die Aktion, durch die der hethitische Herrscher den Mann von Ḫaššu wie einen „Bären" erlegt, ist mit Rauch oder einem ähnlichen Stoff verbunden und führt zum Ersticken des Bären. Diese Situation erinnert uns an die typische Jägertaktik, vor den Höhlen von Wildtieren, die sich in ihren Höhlen verstecken oder dort überwintern, ein Feuer anzuzünden und sie durch den ins Innere geleiteten Rauch zur Flucht aus ihren Höhlen zu zwingen.[9] Hier droht der hethitische König seinem Gegner, der in der belagerten Stadt Ḫaššu(wa) umzingelt ist, mit einer ähnlichen Aktion.

Im weiteren Verlauf der Erzählung des zweiten Paragraphen wird der Mann von Ḫaššu erwähnt, der schließlich seine Stadt verließ und dem hethitischen König zum Kampf entgegenkam.[10] Die Streitkräfte von Ḫaššu(wa) aber, die Widerstand leisteten, wurden von der hethitischen Armee in mehreren Orten festgesetzt und dadurch aus dem Kampf genommen. Dann lesen wir, dass nach dem Sieg über Ḫaššu mehrere Anführer der hethitischen Armee anscheinend mit *ubati*-Land- und Lehensgut belohnt wurden. Im dritten Paragraphen wird wieder ein militärischer Konflikt geschildert, diesmal zwischen der hethitischen Armee und Ḫaluti,[11] dem Kommandeur der *Manda*-Soldaten, den der König von Ḫalap zur Unterstützung von Ḫaššu entsandt hatte, und Zukraši, dem Anführer der schwer bewaffneten Soldaten. Zukraši, der Heerführer der

6 Es ist jedoch nicht auszuschließen, den hethitischen Herrscher im Zukraši-Text mit Muršili I. zu identifizieren. Für Ḫattušili I. sprechen hauptsächlich die Angaben der Annalen dieses Königs bezüglich der militärischen Unternehmen gegen Ḫaššu(wa); s. unten.

7 Inhaltlich ebenso auf die Regierungszeit Ḫattušilis I. zurückweisend berichtet der Text der Belagerung von Uršu KBo 1.11 Rs.$^{!}$ 27–32, dass ein Flüchtling ($^{\text{LÚ.MEŠ}}$*MU-UN-NA-AB-*TU_4) aus der belagerten Stadt herauskommt und den hethitischen König über die aktuelle Situation in der Stadt während des Kriegs informiert; zuletzt Gilan 2015: 285.

8 KUB 1.16+ I 10, II 10, 20: MUŠ „Schlange", I 14f., II 15: GU_4 „Rind", II 39: UR.MAḪ „Löwe"; KBo 3.27+ Vs. 15′: UR.BAR.RA „Wolf"; Tikunani-Brief Vs. 10: UR.GI_7 „Hund", Vs. 16, Rs. 34: UR.MAḪ „Löwe", Rs. 33: *rīmu* „Bulle", Rs. 35: *šēlabu* „Fuchs"; vgl. Collins 1998: 15–17, 20.

9 Das folgende YouTube-Link kann einen Einblick geben, wie diese Jägertaktik praktiziert wird. In der Darstellung leidet kein Tier: https://www.youtube.com/watch?v=KkmL9Oz700c (Smoking a Bear's Den | Yukon Men).

10 In der Erzählung des Zukraši-Textes (Anfang der Zeile Vs. II$^{?}$ 7) bleibt unklar, ob die Drohung von Ḫattušili I. inzwischen in die Tat umgesetzt wurde, oder ob der König von Ḫaššu vor einer eventuellen Aktion des Hethiterkönigs seine Stadt für eine Schlacht verlassen hat.

11 Statt „Zaluti", der falschen Lesung des Eigennamens in der früheren Fachliteratur; zur revidierten Lesung s. Hoffner 1997: 107 und Soysal 2005: 143.

Yamḫad-Streitkräfte, kam während der Auseinandersetzungen ums Leben. Was hier beschrieben wird, deckt sich ungefähr mit den Berichten über den Ḫaššu(wa)-Feldzug in den Annalen von Ḫattušili I., darunter auch die militärische Unterstützung für Ḫaššu(wa) durch Yamḫad. Zusätzlich liefern die Annalen die Nachricht, dass nach der Einnahme von Ḫaššuwa dessen König von Ḫattušili I. zusammen mit dem König von Ḫaḫḫa vor einen Lastwagen gespannt wurde. Einige Einzelheiten in den Annalen betreffen möglicherweise die Episode „den Feind mit Rauch oder Staub bzw. Qualmwolke bedrohen" im Zukraši-Text. Tatsächlich berichten die Annalen, dass die Taktik der „Heranführung" von Asche gegen die militärisch anvisierten Städte nicht selten angewendet wurde. Die militärische Aktion gegen Zippašna verläuft zum Beispiel wie folgt:

KBo 10.2 II:[12]

49 *nu-kán* ^{URU}*Zi-ip-pa-aš-na-an* GE$_6$-*az-pát*
50 *ša-ra-a pa-a-un nu-uš-ma-aš* MÈ-*ia*
51 *an-da ti-ia-nu-un nu-uš-ma-aš* SAḪAR$^{\text{ḪI.A}}$-*iš*$^{(!)}$
52 *še-er ar-nu-nu-un*

Die Stadt Zippašna bestieg ich gerade in der Nacht. Ich trat gegen sie (Pl.) zum Kampf und brachte Aschen gegen sie heran.[13]

Gestützt auf diesen Textabschnitt lässt sich die folgende Passage der Annalen über die militärische Aktion gegen Ḫaššuwa dementsprechend ergänzen, die für unser Thema von besonderem Interesse sein könnte:

KBo 10.2 II:

18 *nu* KUR ^{URU}*Ḫa-aš-šu-wa* UR.MAḪ GIM-*an*
19 GÌR$^{\text{ḪI.A}}$-*i*[*t a*]*r-ḫa ša-ak-ku-ri-ia-nu-un*
20 ˹*nu-za*˺-[*an*$^{?}$ *ma-a*]*ḫ-ḫa-an wa-al-ḫu-un*
21 [*nu-uš-ši* (oder: *nu-uš-ma-aš*) SAḪAR$^{\text{ḪI.A}}$-*u*]*š še-er ar-nu-nu-un*

Das Land Ḫaššuwa [ü]berwältigte ich wie ein Löwe m[it] den Pranken. [A]ls ich [es$^{?}$] überfiel, brachte ich [die Asche]n gegen [es / sie (Pl.)] heran.[14]

Die akkadische Übersetzung davon ist sicher korrupt und weicht ab:

KBo 10.1 Vs.:

35 ^{URU}*Ḫa-aš-šu-wa ki-i-ma* UR.MAḪ *i-na ri-it-ti-šu iš-ta*$^{!}$*-pá-ak-šu ep-ra-am*
36 *a-na mu-ḫi-šu iš-ta*$^{!}$*-pá-ak-šu*

Die Stadt Ḫaššuwa zersprengte er (oder: machte er ohnmächtig) wie ein Löwe mit seinen Pranken. Die Erde schüttete er auf sie.

Dieser Textabschnitt ist mit einigen Unsicherheiten verbunden, wie durch den zweimaligen Gebrauch des Verbums *šapāku* angesichts seiner Semantik (CHD Š 79) und Tempus (entstanden wohl lediglich aus Zeichenvertauschung ŠA und TA) deutlich

12 Offensichtlich gibt es keine akkadische Entsprechung des letzten Satzes.
13 Wörtlich: „Ich führte die Aschen auf sie (Pl.)".
14 Wörtlich: „Ich führte [die Asche]n auf [es / sie (Pl.)]".

wird. Das Idiom *epram šapāku* „Erde aufhäufen“ ist in den mesopotamischen Dokumenten reichlich bezeugt (CAD Š/I 413f.) und erscheint auch im Text der Belagerung von Uršu aus Boğazköy KBo 1.11 Vs.$^{!}$ 16′f., 19′, in dem es wohl als *terminus technicus* der Kriegskunst „einen Belagerungshügel errichten“ bedeutet (Gilan 2015: 280, 292; Lorenz und Schrakamp 2014: 50). Die Entsprechung von akk. *epru* in KBo 10.2 ist logographisch geschriebenes SAḪAR, das ein breites Bedeutungsspektrum „Staub, Asche, Schmutz“ und sogar „Schmutz der menschlichen Genitalien“ (Soysal 2016: 418) besitzt. Die hethitische Lesung von SAḪAR wurde als *ḫaš(š)*- c. (Ünal 1990: 216–18) vorgeschlagen und wird nunmehr durch die Duplikatsangabe *ḫa-aš-šu-uš* (CHDS 6.28 + KBo 60.30 IV$^{?}$ 5′) // SAḪAR$^{\mathrm{ḪI.A}}$-*uš* (KBo 54.36 II 19) bestätigt. In jedem Fall liegt in KBo 10.1 Vs. 35f. ein Übersetzungsfehler aus dem Hethitischem ins Akkadische vor. Dass die Entsprechung von akk. *epram šapāku* (KBo 10.1 Vs. 35f.) im Hethitischen nicht SAḪAR$^{\mathrm{ḪI.A}}$-*uš šer arnu*- (KBo 10.2 II 21), sondern *ḫaššuš išḫuwai*- lauten sollte, wird aus den folgenden zwei Textstellen ersichtlich:

KUB 31.100 IV$^{?}$:

9′ [*nam-m*]*a-kán* ^{URU}*Ḫa-at-tu-ši še-er ḫa-aš-šu-uš le-e i*[*š-ḫu-wa-an-zi*]

10′ *na-aš-ta* [*ḫa-aš*]-*šu-uš kat-ta šal-la-a-i ḫu-uš-ši-li-pát* [...$^{?}$ *iš-ḫu-wa-an-du*]

[Ferne]r [soll man] die Asche(n) nicht in Ḫattuša aufs[chütten]; man soll die [Asc]hen nur in die große Abfallgrube hinab[schütten].

Die hier vorgeschlagene Ergänzung des Verbums mit *išḫuwa*- „schütten“ basiert auf dem ganz ähnlichen Kontext eines anderen Dokuments und kann daher als sicher gelten:

KBo 23.42 + KBo 35.76 I (mit Duplikat KBo 24.57+ I 8):

8 *nu ḫa-aš-šu-uš* I-*NA* AŠ-*RI* *ḫ*[(*u-uš-šu-ul-li*)] *iš-ḫu-wa-an-zi*

Und man schüttet die Aschen in den Ort der Abfallgrube.

Außerdem berichtet die Darstellung in KBo 10.2 III 37–40 – kombiniert mit der besser erhaltenen, aber teilweise korrupten, akkadischen Version KBo 10.1 Rs. 22–24 – im Zusammenhang mit der Eroberung zweier Städte Ḫaššuwa und Ḫaḫḫa Folgendes:

> [Ich], der Großkönig Tabarna, zerst[örte] Ḫ[aššuwa] und Ḫaḫḫa (akk. Version fälschlicherweise: die Könige$^{!}$ von Ḫaššu und Ḫaḫḫu) und [brannte] sie mit Feuer nieder. Den Rauch [zeigte ich dem Sonnengott des] Him[mels und dem Wettergott].

Diese Schilderung soll wohl eher den Schlussakt der Niederbrennung einer Stadt wiedergeben als einen Teil der Kriegsmanöver Ḫattušilis I., zeigt aber deutlich, dass gegen feindliche Städte – darunter das auch im Zukraši-Text behandelte Ḫaššuwa – gerichtete Eroberungsaktionen des Hethiterkönigs mit wie Luftverschmutzung wirkenden Mitteln, wie Feuer (heth. *paḫḫur* / sumerogr. IZI / akk. *išātu*), Rauch (heth. *tuḫḫu(wa)i*- / akk. *qutru*) und Asche(wolken) (heth. *ḫaš(š)*- / sumerogr. SAḪAR / akk. *ep(e)ru*), eng verbunden waren.[15]

15 Zu möglichen materiellen Spuren der Brandsetzung von Ḫaḫḫa durch Ḫattušili I. s. Liverani 1988. Das Thema von „Brandsetzung“ und „Rauch“ im Rahmen militärischer Operationen ist auch im vorhethitischen Anumḫirbi-Brief (Rs. 27–29) behandelt: *ú ma-tí-i iš-ta-ra-áp ú qú-ut-ra-am ub-ta-i-iš* „Er (der

Bemerkungen zur Datierung des Zukraši-Textes

Nach den inhaltlich-historischen Bemerkungen zum Zukraši-Text in Auswahl seien nun einige Kommentare zu Schrifteigenheiten der Tafel erlaubt. Zu diesem Thema wurden in den letzten Jahren mehrere und eingehende Studien vorgelegt,[16] deswegen möchte ich meine Ausführungen hier kurz und zusammenfassend darstellen.

Es ist zunächst festzustellen, dass die Keilschriftzeichen im vorliegenden Text keine markanten Merkmale aufweisen, die sich deutlich von ihren mittelhethitischen Formen unterscheiden. Unter den relevanten Zeichen erweist sich nur AK als typisch althethitisch. Es ist auffällig, dass die älteste Form dieses Zeichens als Datierungskriterium auch für die ebenso häufig diskutierte Tafel KBo 18.151 entscheidend zu sein scheint.[17]

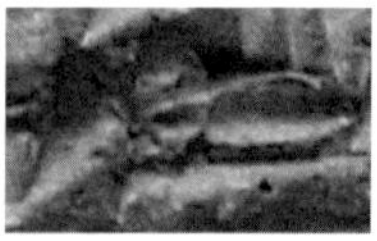

Fig. 5. Zeichen AK in KBo 7.14 + KUB 36.100 Vs. II? 6.

Fig. 6. Zeichen AK in KBo 7.14+ (Zeichnung nach Chr. Rüster).

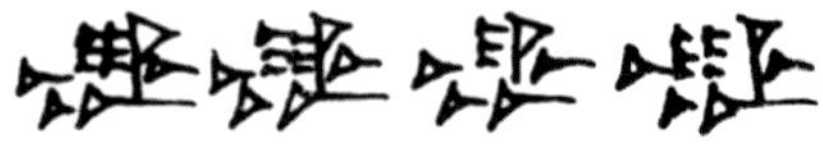

Fig. 7. Zeichen AK in KBo 18.151 (Zeichnung nach H. G. Güterbock).

Ferner sind die folgenden althethitischen Formen von AK zu notieren:

Fig. 8. Zeichen AK in der İnandık-Urkunde (Zeichnung nach K. Balkan).

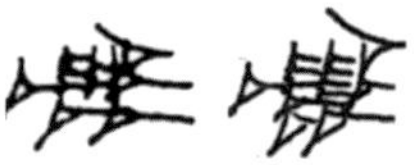

Fig. 9. Zeichen AK in KBo 22.1 (Zeichnung nach H. Otten).

Fig. 10. *na-AK-ki-it* in KBo 3.22 (Zeichnung nach H. H. Figulla).

Mann von Taišama) hat mein Land in Brand gesteckt und es nach Rauch riechen lassen“ (Balkan 1957: 7f., 16). Der wenngleich nicht ganz klare Ausdruck könnte sich auf eine negative Situation durch den Rauch beziehen, die aus dem Niederbrennen des Landes resultiert, und dies gilt auch für das Beispiel der Annalen von Ḫattušili I. um die beiden Städte Ḫaššuwa und Ḫaḫḫa. Es bleibt festzustellen, dass in den bisherigen Studien zu „Warfare“ bei den Hethitern (Ünal 1983 und 1984; Houwink ten Cate 1984; Lorenz und Schrakamp 2011 und 2014) der Einfluss von Rauch, Asche und Staub im Krieg abgesehen von der häufig diskutierten „Niederbrennung einer Stadt“ keine Erwähnung fand. Ünal 1984: 74 Anm. 9 spricht in Bezug auf die beiden Textstellen der Annalen von Ḫattušili I. von einer „Aschewolke als Folge der totalen Einäscherung der Stadt“. Ich kann im Rahmen dieser Arbeit kein einleuchtendes Beispiel zu einer mittels Rauchs und Asche ausgeführten Kriegsaktion in der Militärgeschichte bieten. Das wäre mit Dankbarkeit den Historikern mit breiterer Kenntnis zu diesem Thema zu überlassen. Es sei indes das folgende historische Ereignis angemerkt: Über die Eroberung der Stadt Maarat an-Numan im „Ersten Kreuzzug“ im Jahre 1098 schreibt Raimond d'Aguilers, *Historia Francorum qui ceperunt Iherusalem*, dass die Sarazenen und Muslime sich in den unterirdischen Höhlen versteckten, und die christlichen Krieger sie zwangen herauszukommen, indem sie Feuer anzündeten und Schwefelrauch benutzten.

16 Zuletzt Klinger 2022a mit sämtlicher Literatur.

17 Soysal 2000: 109. KBo 18.151 übermittelt keinen gewöhnlichen Text, sondern einen Orakel-Bericht in Briefformat. Eine elegante Kanzleischrift lässt sich deswegen hierfür nicht erwarten. Zur Diskussion, ob KBo 18.151 als alt- oder mittelhethitisch zu datieren ist, s. Soysal 2000: 108 mit Anm. 45 und 46.

Abgesehen von einzelnen Keilschriftformen fallen in der Zukraši-Tafel die folgenden Merkmale auf, die man in Bezug auf eine Datierung in Betracht ziehen möchte:

1) Die Keilschriftzeichen sind manchmal nicht ganz fest in den Ton eingedrückt, deshalb wirken sie unscharf. Dabei könnte die Qualität des Tons der Tafel oder des Schreibgriffels eine entscheidende Rolle spielen.

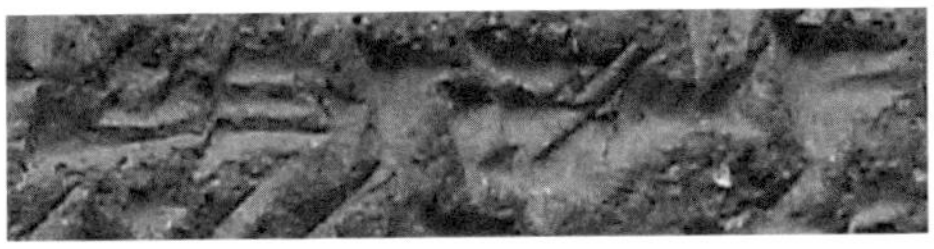

Fig. 11. KBo 7.14 + KUB 36.100 Vs. II$^{?}$ 26: LÚ ^{URU}*Ḫa-aš-ši.*

2) Die inneren und kleineren Waagerechten haben meistens keinen Keilkopf. Als Ursache dafür kann man die obengenannte Vermutung geltend machen.

Fig. 12. KBo 7.14 + KUB 36.100 Vs. II$^{?}$ 6: Zeichen KI.

Fig. 13. KBo 7.14 + KUB 36.100 Vs. II$^{?}$ 6: Zeichen TU.

3) Dagegen sind die Keilköpfe der senkrechten Zeichen übermäßig groß, so dass das Zeichen manchmal nur wie ein Keilkopf aussieht. Die senkrechten Keile sind am Ende des Wortes wohl als „Stopmerkmal" fest eingedrückt. Das entspricht genau dem Schriftbild des sogenannten „schweren Duktus", in dem die senkrechten Keile breite, nach rechts geneigte Köpfe besitzen.

Fig. 14. KBo 7.14 + KUB 36.100 Vs. II? 9: Zeichen UŠ.

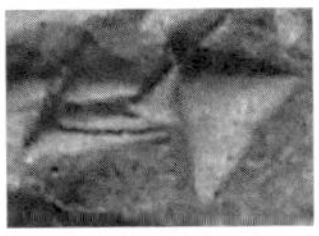

Fig. 15. KBo 7.14 + KUB 36.100 Vs. II$^{?}$ 4: Zeichen DA.

4) Insgesamt kann man sagen, dass die Schrift der Zukraši-Tafel ziemlich groß und nicht besonders elegant wirkt, wie es etwa für mittel- und junghethitische Niederschriften typisch sein kann. Eine sehr kleine, aber meist elegante Schrift beginnt erst mit der mittelhethitischen Schreibtradition.

Als Schreibgewohnheiten im Bezug auf Orthographie der Zukraši-Tafel wird man auch die folgenden Punkte notieren:

1) Spatia zwischen Worten sind unregelmäßig gesetzt, wobei die Zeichen innerhalb eines Wortes eng geschrieben sind. Ein Spatium zwischen der Konjunktion *nu* und dem

folgenden Wort fehlt, wie seit langem bekannt. Dieses Merkmal wird auch einmal nach dem als Ligatur geschriebenen Akkadogram *A+NA* beobachtet:

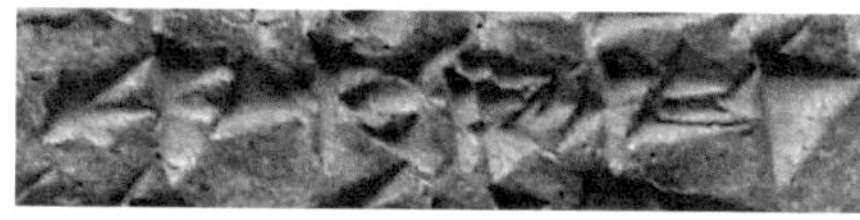

Fig. 16. KBo 7.14 + KUB 36.100 Vs. II? 4: *nu*(-)*me-na-aḫ-ḫa-an-da.*

Fig. 17. KBo 7.14 + KUB 36.100 Vs. II? 4: *nu*(-)*tu-uḫ-ḫi-ia-at-ti-it.*

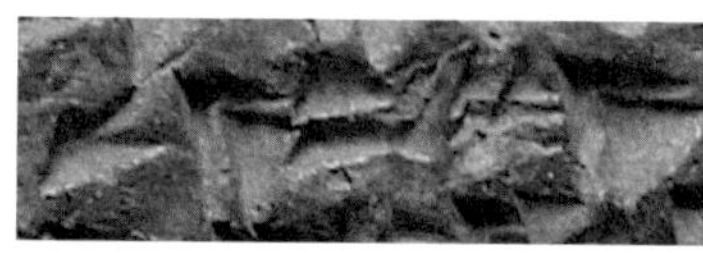

Fig. 18. KBo 7.14 + KUB 36.100 Vs. II? 8: *nu*(-)*a-pí-ia.*

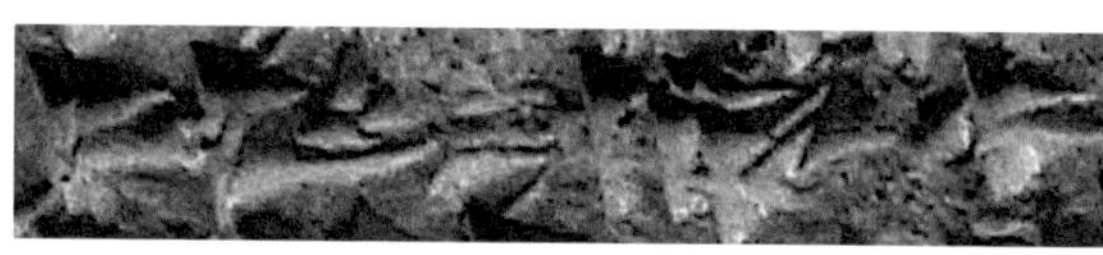

Fig. 19. KBo 7.14 + KUB 36.100 Vs. II? 3: *A+NA*(-)LÚ URU*Ḫa-aš-ši.*

2) Manchmal gibt es lange Abstände zwischen den Wörtern, wobei auch die Wortverteilung in einer Zeile nicht immer geglückt ist. Das könnte auf eine Unsicherheit bei der Nutzung der Tafelfläche, also technische Schwächen des Schreibers oder der dahinterstehenden Schreiberschule, hindeuten.

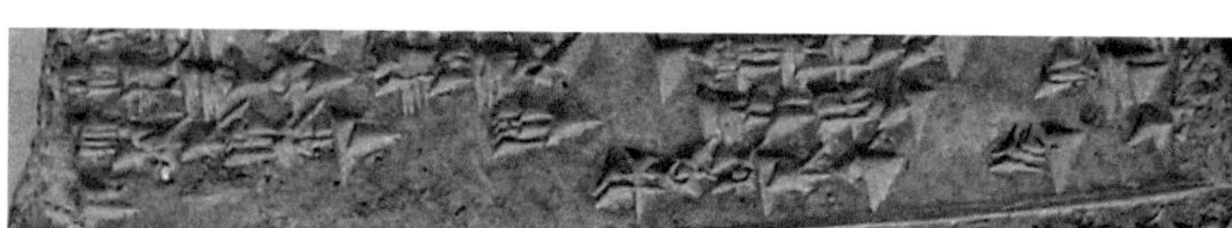

Fig. 20. Unregelmäßige Wortverteilung in KBo 7.14 + KUB 36.100 Vs. II? 13.

Bei dieser Gelegenheit bietet es sich an, kurz auf die äußeren Merkmale, das Layout der Zukraši-Tafel einzugehen. Die Tafel hat im erhaltenen oberen Teil keine Randleiste, und der Text beginnt unmittelbar nach dem oberen Randbereich, was auf die althethitische Tradition zurückgeht, aber auch in der mittelhethitischen Zeit fortgesetzt wurde. Wie oben angedeutet, lässt der Inhalt des ersten Paragraphen der besser erhaltenen Seite des Zukraši-Textes vermuten, dass es sich nicht um den Beginn des Textes einer dann einkolumnigen Tafel handelt. Da der obere Rand nicht beschriftet ist, kommt hierfür auch eine Rückseite nicht in Frage, wie wir es in den einkolumnigen Tafeln aus der ah., aber auch der mh. Zeit sehen. Daher können wir auch davon ausgehen, dass die Zukraši-Tafel ursprünglich zweikolumnig gestaltet war,[18] wie es auch beim Ritualtext KBo 17.1+ mit althethitischem Duktus zu beobachten ist.

Wenngleich die Zeichenformen für die Datierung der Zukraši-Tafel nicht ganz eindeutig sind, handelt es sich wohl um ein althethitisches Produkt, basierend auf dem vorherrschenden schweren Duktus und den nicht ganz entwickelten Merkmalen der Schreibtechnik, aber auch dem Layout der Tontafel.

Es war für die Hethitologie eine Überraschung, dass die Zukraši-Tafel, die seit Langem als ein Ausgangspunkt für die Datierung althethitischer Texte gilt, in rezenter Zeit als ein Produkt der mittelhethitischen Zeit klassifiziert wurde. Der eminente polnische Hethitologe Maciej Popko (2007) plädierte nämlich für eine mittelhethitische Datierung dieses Dokuments, basierend auf den Zeichenformen DA und IT mit vorgezogenem unteren Waagerechten, und dies scheint auch in der *Konkordanz* vorsichtig angenommen zu werden.[19] Der wichtigste Kritikpunkt dagegen besteht darin, dass bei der Textdatierung nur Zeichenformen – und zwar nur zwei davon – berücksichtigt wurden, und weitere kritische Zeichen wie zum Beispiel AK (s. oben) außer Acht gelassen wurden. Darüber hinaus sind die Zeichen DA und IT mit vorgezogenem unterem Waagerechten nicht nur im mittelhethitischen Schriftsystem zu finden, sondern auch in Tafeln mit typisch altem Duktus wie KBo 3.22 und KBo 22.1. Es ist weiterhin zu notieren, dass die oben genannte „Althethitische Fundschicht" der Tafel KBo 7.14 + KUB 36.100 von Maciej Popko ohne vernünftige Begründung abgelehnt wurde.[20] Daher möchten wir im folgenden Abschnitt die schon gut bekannten, aber immer noch zu berücksichtigenden Punkte bei der Datierung hethitischer Tafeln erneut resümieren.

Weitere Kriterien zur Datierung der althethitischen Texte

Bei der Frage der Datierung einer hethitischen Tafel – im Falle des Zukraši-Textes also, ob er in der althethitischen Zeit niedergeschrieben wurde – sollte neben Zeichenformen, Duktus und Orthographie auch ein weiterer, entscheidender Punkt berücksichtigt werden, und zwar der der Tafelstruktur bzw. des Tafelformats (Layout). Es handelt sich um folgende Aspekte:

1) Einkolumnig geschriebene Tontafeln sind schmal und lang. KBo 3.22 (der Anitta-Text) und KBo 22.1 (die sozial-humanitären Anweisungen eines althethitischen Königs, wohl Muršilis I.), die als typisch althethitisch anzusehen sind, gehören zu dieser Gruppe, und beide sind auch auf ihren unteren Rändern beschriftet. Auch die Tafel KBo 22.2 (der Zalpa-Text), die ebenfalls typisch althethitisch ist, wurde einkolumnig gestaltet, ist aber nicht so schmal wie KBo 22.1. Diese als „kissenförmig" bezeichneten drei Tonta-

18 Das jüngere Duplikat KUB 36.102 ist sicher zweikolumnig. Für die Möglichkeit einer Serie aus mehreren einkolumnigen Tafeln s. oben.

19 Vgl. die in der *Konkordanz* (Košak 2002–) angegebene, alternierende Datierung von KBo 7.14+ als „ah.?/mh.?".

20 Eine ausführliche und berechtigte Kritik an Popko findet sich jetzt bei Klinger 2022a: 273–85 und (kurzgefasst) 2022b: 112f. Anm. 67.

feln und zusätzlich KBo 20.33+ sind von Alwin Kloekhorst und Willemijn Waal (2019) aufgrund ihrer physischen Strukturen und inhaltlichen Einzelheiten eingehend untersucht worden. Eine nähere Überprüfung der paläographischen Eigenschaften der Tafeln KBo 3.22 und KBo 22.1 kam zu dem weiterführenden Ergebnis, dass beide Tafeln neben der Layoutähnlichkeit auch sehr ähnliche, ja sogar fast identische Keilschriftzeichen enthalten und demnach wohl Produkte eines und desselben, bisher anonym verbleibenden Schreibers aus der althethitischen Zeit gewesen sind (Abb. 5). Weitere Untersuchungen dazu sollen erfolgen.

2) Zweikolumnig gestaltete Tontafeln haben ungewöhnlich schmale Kolumnentrenner, wie man sie bei der althethitischen Ritualtafel KBo 17.1+ beobachtet.

3) Oberer und unterer Rand der einkolumnigen Tontafeln besitzen keine Randleisten und sind beschriftet, so dass der Text durchgängig läuft. Diese Eigenschaft gibt es aber auch in der mittelhethitischen Periode: Im Mittelhethitischen beginnt man nämlich mit der Beschriftung der Tafeln auf dem oberen Rand.

4) In alt- und mittelhethitischer Zeit ist die Herstellung sechskolumniger Tontafeln nicht üblich. Einzige Ausnahme scheint die Tafel KBo 20.10+ zu bilden, deren exakte Datierung nicht möglich ist, deren Duktus aber nach Neu (1980: 130) in den Grenzbereich der Duktustypen I/II gehört.

5) Insbesondere die historischen Kompositionen zeigen einen sehr knappen Kolophonraum, der schlicht die schriftliche Eintragung „vollendet“ enthält. Die althethitischen Tafeln KBo 22.2 (der Zalpa-Text) und KUB 36.104 (die Anekdotensammlung) zeigen beispielsweise ein blosses TIL.LA (statt jüngerem *QA-TI*). Auch KBo 3.67+, eine junghethitische Abschrift des Telipinu-Erlasses, bietet nur „Die erste Tafel von Telipinu. Vollendet“, ohne weitere bzw. präzise Angaben zum Inhalt der Komposition.

Unter Berücksichtigung nicht nur der hier besprochenen Arbeit von Maciej Popko, sondern auch weiterer Studien seit den Neunzigerjahren gewinnt man den Eindruck, dass die mittelhethitische Datierung der hethitischen Schriftdokumente insgesamt überschätzt und überstrapaziert wurde. In diesem Zusammenhang lässt sich auch anhand des bisherigen statistischen Textbefunds – aber mit allem Vorbehalt – vermuten, dass die Bestimmung einer Tafel historischen Inhalts als etwa „althethitische Komposition in mittelhethitischer Abschrift“ wohl nicht für alle Fälle geltend gemacht werden kann. Beispielsweise – und statistisch gesehen – sind bisher keine mittelhethitischen Kopien der historischen Texte aus althethitischer Zeit verfügbar, die auf Grund ihrer Niederschrift mit Sicherheit datiert werden können (s. Anhang). Es entzieht sich unserer Kenntnis, in welcher Situation die wenigen Abschriften von historischen Textgruppen während des mittelhethitischen Reiches überhaupt angefertigt wurden. Dies war vielleicht mit den ernsthaften militärisch-politischen Schwierigkeiten und den darauffolgenden wirtschaftlichen Auswirkungen verbunden, die insbesondere während der Herrschaft von Arnuwanda I. und seines Nachfolgers Tutḫaliya II./III. spürbar waren. Es ist aber ersichtlich, dass mit der intensiven Reproduktion historischer Kompositionen aus dem Alten Reich erst ab der junghethitischen Zeit begonnen wurde.

In den letzten fünfzig Jahren hat der Terminus „Duktus“ in der Hethitologie gravierende Veränderungen erfahren. Beginnend ab Heinrich Otten mit seiner Terminologie bezüglich der Alter des Duktus wie typisch alt, alt, alt-elegant, älter, ältlich, jung verzeichnete man ständig geänderte und präziser – aber gleichwohl komplizierter – gewordene Terminologien, wie Ah. I und II (Neu 1980: XVff.), I a-b, II a-c, III a-b (Starke 1985: 27), Ah. I und II, Mh. und Jh. A-C (Klinger 1996: 32ff.). Weil in diesem Fall eine Neuetickettierung fast jedes Jahrzehnt stattfindet, fragt man sich, ob es sich wirklich lohnt, die ständig revidierte Terminologie unkritisch zu übernehmen. Die Erkennung der Keilschriftzeichen und Handschriften in den hethitischen Schriftdokumenten, die sich im Laufe der Zeit nach Schreiberschulen, Schreibern selbst und sogar nach persönlicher Karriere jeweiliger Schreiber ständig geändert haben sollen, stellt sich als eine schwierige Aufgabe der Hethitologie dar. Hinzu kommen noch die kontroversen Ergebnisse der zu diesem Thema gewidmeten Studien in beachtlicher Zahl in den letzten Jahren. Daher hat man insgesamt den Eindruck, dass diese Aufgabe die individuellen Leistungen der Hethitologen übersteigt und daher zukünftig den Arbeiten von 3D-Scannern und Computer-Analysen im Rahmen der digitalen Forschung überlassen werden sollte.

Abschließend wäre zu betonen, dass die Bemühungen zur Datierung einer Keilschrifttafel als alt- oder mittelhethitische Niederschrift nicht nur auf einzelne Keilschriftzeichen, Handschrift, Paläographie und Duktus konzentriert und beschränkt werden sollten. Auch die anderen oben genannten Faktoren, insbesondere aber das Layout einer Tontafel, sollten für die Datierungsproblematik gleichermaßen berücksichtigt werden (Abb. 6). Kritisch ist hier anzumerken, dass sich die Keilschriftkopien, von denen in den Anfangsjahren der Hethitologie viele leider nur ungenau gemacht wurden, alte Schwarz-Weiß-Fotos und sogar hoch entwickelte digitale Fotos für die Textdatierung manchmal als unzureichend herausstellen. In diesem Sinne erweist sich die Museumsarbeit als unverzichtbar, die physische Untersuchungen am Originalmaterial ermöglicht, um die äußeren Merkmale wie Format und Layout einer Tafel festzustellen.

Bibliographie

Balkan, Kemal

1957 *Letter of King Anum-Hirbi of Mama to King Warshama of Kanish.* TTKY VII/31a. Ankara: Türk Tarih Kurumu Basımevi.

Bittel, Kurt

1953 Einleitung. *MDOG* 86: 3–8.

Collins, Billie Jean

1998 Ḫattušili I, the Lion King. *JCS* 50: 15–20.

de Martino, Stefano

2003 *Annali e Res Gestae antico ittiti.* StMed 12. Pavia: Italian University Press.

Gilan, Amir

2015 *Formen und Inhalte althethitischer historischer Literatur.* THeth 29. Heidelberg: Winter.

Güterbock, Hans Gustav
1978 Some Aspects of Hittite Prayers. In: Torgny Segerstedt (Hg.), *The Frontiers of Human Knowledge*. Uppsala: Almqvist & Wiksell, 125–39.

Hoffner, Harry A., Jr.
1997 Review of Otten and Rüster, *KBo 40*. *JCS* 49: 103–8.

Houwink ten Cate, Philo H. J.
1983 The History of Warfare according to Hittite Sources: The Annals of Hattusilis I. *Anatolica* 10: 91–109.
1984 The History of Warfare according to Hittite Sources: The Annals of Hattusilis I (Part II). *Anatolica* 11: 47–83.

Kempinski, Aharon
1983 *Syrien und Palästina (Kanaan) in der letzten Phase der Mittelbronze IIB-Zeit*. ÄAT 4. Wiesbaden: Harrassowitz.

Klinger, Jörg
1996 *Untersuchungen zur Rekonstruktion der hattischen Kultschicht*. StBoT 37. Wiesbaden: Harrassowitz.
2022a Zu den Anfängen der hethitischen Überlieferung überhaupt und zur Methode der paläographischen Textdatierung. In: Eva Cancik-Kirschbaum und Ingo Schrakamp (Hg.), *Transfer, Adaption und Neukonfiguration von Schrift- und Sprachwissen im Alten Orient*. Episteme in Bewegung 25. Wiesbaden: Harrassowitz, 255–340.
2022b The Hittite Writing Traditions of Cuneiform Documents. In: Stefano de Martino (Hg.), *Handbook Hittite Empire. Power Structures*. Empires through the Ages in Global Perspective 1. Berlin / Boston: de Gruyter Oldenburg, 93–155.

Kloekhorst, Alwin
2008 *Etymological Dictionary of the Hittite Inherited Lexicon*. Leiden / Boston: Brill.
2016 The Story of Wāšitta and Kumarbi. In: Šárka Velhartická (Hg.), *Audias fabulas veteres. Anatolian Studies in Honor of Jana Součková-Siegelová*. CHANE 79. Leiden / Boston: Brill, 165–77.

Košak, Silvin
2002 *Konkordanz der hethitischen Keilschrifttafeln, Online-Datenbank Version* hethiter.net/: hethkonk (2.plus) – last accessed 08.2024.

Kloekhorst, Alwin und Willemijn Waal
2019 A Hittite Scribal Tradition Predating the Tablet Collections of Ḫattuša? The origin of the 'cushion-shaped' tablets KBo 3.22, KBo 17.21+, KBo 22.1, and KBo 22.2. *ZA* 109: 189–203.

Liverani, Mario
1988 The Fire of Ḫaḫḫum. *OA* 27: 165–72.

Lorenz, Jürgen und Ingo Schrakamp
2011 Hittite Military and Warfare. In: Hermann Genz und Dirk P. Mielke (Hg.), *Insights into Hittite History and Archaeology*. CollAnat 22. Leuven et al.: Peeters, 125–51.

2014 „Our Master! Do not destroy us!“ The Fate and Role of Non-Combatants in the Wars of the Hittites. In: Davide Nadali und Jordi Vidal (Hg.), *The Other Face of the Battle. The Impact of War on Civilians in the Ancient Near East.* AOAT 413. Münster: Ugarit-Verlag, 37–64.

Naumann, Rudolf

1953 Die Grabung auf Büyükkale. *MDOG* 86: 9–23.

Neu, Erich

1980 *Althethitische Ritualtexte in Umschrift.* StBoT 25. Wiesbaden: Harrassowitz.

Otten, Heinrich

1953 Die inschriftlichen Funde. *MDOG* 86: 59–64.

1958 Keilschrifttexte. *MDOG* 91: 73–84.

Popko, Maciej

1986 Rezension zu G. Beckman, *Hittite Birth Rituals. 2nd Ed.* StBoT 29. Wiesbaden: Harrassowitz (1983). *OLZ* 81: 559–61.

2007 Althethitisch? Zu den Datierungsfragen in der Hethitologie. In: Detlev Groddek und Marina Zorman (Hg.), *Tabularia Hethaeorum. Hethitologische Beiträge Silvin Košak zum 65. Geburtstag.* DBH 25. Wiesbaden: Harrassowitz, 575–81.

Roider, Ulrike

1981 Griech. *θυμός* „Mut“ – ai. *dhūmáhò* „Rauch“. *ZVS* 95: 99–109.

Soysal, Oğuz

1981 Zukraši Metni ve Diğer Tarihsel Konulu Boğazköy Tabletleri Işığında MÖ 16. YY. Ḫalap-Ḫaššu(u̯a) ile Hitit Siyasal İlişkileri. *Fırat Üniversitesi Edebiyat Fakültesi Dergisi* I/2: 15–64.

2000 Analysis of a Hittite Oracular Document. *ZA* 90: 85–122.

2005 Beiträge zur althethitischen Geschichte (III). Kleine Fragmente historischen Inhalts. *ZA* 95: 121–44.

2016 On Recent Cuneiform Editions of Hittite Fragments (III). *JAOS* 136: 417–38.

Starke, Frank

1977 *Die Funktionen der dimensionalen Kasus und Adverbien im Althethitischen.* StBoT 23. Wiesbaden: Harrassowitz.

1985 *Die keilschrift-luwischen Texte in Umschrift.* StBoT 30. Wiesbaden: Harrassowitz.

Ünal, Ahmet

1983 Untersuchungen zur Terminologie der hethitischen Kriegsführung I. „Verbrennen, in Brand stecken“ als Kriegstechnik. *OrNS* 52: 164–80.

1984 Studien über das hethitische Kriegswesen II: Verba delendi *ḫarnink-*/*ḫarganu-* „vernichten, zugrunde richten“. *SMEA* 24: 71–85.

1990 Hititler devri Anadolu’sunda temizlikle ilgili araştırmalar: Çivi yazılı metinler ve arkeolojik verilere göre kentlerde halk sağlığı ve temizlikle ilgili yapılar /Ritual Purity versus Physical Impurity in Hittite Anatolia: Public Health and Structures for Sanitation according to Cuneiform Texts and

Archaeological Remains. In: Mustafa Yıldırım (Hg.), *1. IKH. Uluslararası 1. Hititoloji Kongresi Bildirileri (19–21 Temmuz 1990) Çorum*. Ankara: Ünal Offset, 186–207, 208–23.

Werner, Rudolf
1956 Rezension zu H. Otten, *KBo 7*. Berlin: Mann (1954). *OrNS* 25: 167–72.

Abb. 1. Die Zukraši-Tafel KBo 7.14 + KUB 36.100 Vs. II?.

DEZEMBER 1953 Nr. 8

Mitteilungen

der

Deutschen Orient-Gesellschaft

zu Berlin

Vorläufiger Bericht

über die Ausgrabungen in Boğazköy

im Jahre 1952

60

eine nähere Zeitbestimmung möglich wäre[1]). Die Schrift ist eng gesetzt, entspricht aber in ihrem Duktus völlig den neuhethitischen Formen (s. Abb. 28). Als auffällige Eigentümlichkeit wäre die Zusammenschreibung des satzeinleitenden *nu* mit dem folgenden Wort zu nennen[2]).

Abb. 28 Vorderseite der Tafel 29/k

Inhaltlich bietet die Tafel eine historische Erzählung, die in ihren besser erhaltenen Abschnitten wie folgt lautet:

(II 1) „Zwei . . . Männer [ ] vor saßen sie [:] Geht! Dem Manne von Ḫaššu sagt: Ich werde [ge]gen [dich] ziehen, wohlan, komm du ⟨mir⟩ entgegen! [Wenn] du aber nicht kommst, werde ich dich

[1]) Graphik *a-ak-ti* (Alterskriterium nach Sommer-Falkenstein, Heth. Akkad. Bilingue, München 1938, 151 Anm. 5), die Verbalform *e-eš-kán-ta-ti* (neben 2 BoTU 12 A III 15, dazu Bechtel, Verbs in -šk- 78, 92!), vergleichendes *ma-a-an* (Alterskriterium nach HAB 42 m. Anm. 2); Asyndese, Fehlen jeglicher Partikel *-za* und *-kán* (in Übereinstimmung mit der Inschrift des Anitta); für's Lexikon *ták-ka-li-it* (nur in älterer Sprache bezeugt nach HAB 33 ff.: 2 BoTU 4 B III 22).

[2]) 29/k II 4 *nu-!me-na-aḫ-ḫa-an-da*, 6 *nu-!tu-uḫ-ḫi-ia-at-ti-it*, 8 *nu-!a-pí-ia*. Die gleiche Graphik findet sich wieder in 2 BoTU 10 β Z. 16, wo auch E. Forrer *nu-!ku-i-e-ia* umschreibt, aber auch 2 BoTU 10 γ Z. 10 *nu-!ša-a-ku-ua-at-te-et* nach Ausweis der Photographie BoFN 6608; beide Texte gehören der Zeit Ḫattušili's I. an, vgl. Sommer-Falkenstein HAB 211 f.

Abb. 2. Publikation von H. Otten 1953.

Reprint from

The Frontiers of Human Knowledge

Skrifter rörande Uppsala universitet, C: 38

Acta Universitatis Upsaliensis

Uppsala 1978

Some Aspects of Hittite Prayers

Hans G. Güterbock

Professor of Hittitology

University of Chicago, USA

To be here and to have this opportunity of talking to you is not only a great pleasure but has a very special meaning for me. While expressing my thanks to the colleagues who arranged this visit, foremost among them Professor Nils Simonsson and Folke Josephson, I also want to mention my lasting gratitude to the University for having invited me as a guest lecturer in 1948 when I was forced, as it were, to emigrate a second time. It was the late Axel Persson who arranged that invitation and also personally helped us no end in getting used to the new environment. It was a great experience to teach here and to meet the colleagues, and it is a special pleasure for me to see quite a few of them still around now. It was from here that I was called to the University of Chicago, and now this invitation—not to speak of the great honor your University is bestowing on me—comes shortly after my retirement from teaching, symbolically closing the circle.

Twenty-eight years is a long time, and it would be sad if Hittitology had not progressed during that period. The field has gained a great number of workers in many countries, and they all have made their contributions. These include a large amount of tablets excavated and made available in cuneiform copies, a significant number of new editions (or "Bearbeitungen") of Hittite texts, and many penetrating studies of various aspects of Hittite language and civilization.

Permit me to continue for a moment with my personal reminiscenses. In 1952, only three years after I left Uppsala, Prof. Bittel resumed the excavations at Boğazköy and invited me to join his expedition again. Thus I had the privilege of being present when one of the most important finds was made. I was in the house one day when a messenger brought a piece of a tablet from the excavation with a note from Prof. Naumann saying that this had been found in an old level, and could I tell what it said. It was what is now known as the Zukraši text,[1] i.e., part of an account of Hattušili I (about 1620 or so)

[1] Hittite texts are quoted here by reference to numbers in E. Laroche, *Catalogue des textes hittites* (Paris, Klincksieck, 1971), abbreviated CTH. Other abbreviations are: ANET = J. B. Pritchard, ed., *Ancient Near Eastern Texts Relating to the Old Testament* (Princeton Univ. Press, [1]1950, [3]1969); JAOS = *Journal of the American Oriental Society;* JNES = *Journal of Near Eastern Studies;* KBo = *Keilschrifttexte aus Boghazköi;* KUB = *Keilschrifturkunden aus Boghazköi;* StBoT = *Studien zu den Boğazköy-Texten* (Wiesbaden, Harrassowitz).—The text here mentioned is CTH 15, A.

Abb. 3. Publikation von H.G. Güterbock 1978.

Fırat Üniversitesi

EDEBİYAT FAKÜLTESİ DERGİSİ

I. Cilt, 2. Sayı'dan Ayrı Basım

Elazığ, Edebiyat Fakültesi Basımevi, 1981

Abb. 4. Publikation von O. Soysal 1981.

Abb. 5a-b. KBo 22.1 „Erlaß für die Adligen“ Vs. und Rs.

Abb. 5c-d. KBo 3.22 „Der Anitta-Text“ Vs. und Rs.

Abb. 6. Ausgewählte Beispiele von althethitischen Tontafeln verschiedener Textgenres.
1. KBo 8.27+ (Landschenkungsurkunde; gehört in den Grenzbereich des Alt- und Mittelhethitischen)
2. KBo 22.2 (Der Zalpa-Text)
3. KBo 22.1 (Ein Erlass für die Adligen)
4. KBo 7.14 + KUB 36.100 (Der Zukraši-Text)
5. KBo 18.151 (Bericht von einem Losorakel im Briefformat)
6. KBo 37.3 + (Hattisch-hethitisches Bauritual; mit einer nicht-elegant wirkenden Schrift).

Anhang

CTH 1 (Anitta)	ah. Niederschrift KBo 3.22 + mehrere jh. Abschriften Nach *Konkordanz*: 6 Tafeln, 10 Fragmente
CTH 2 (Anumḫirbi)	ah. Niederschrift KUB 36.99 + zwei jh. und sjh. Fragmente Nach *Konkordanz*: 3 Tafeln, 3 Fragmente
CTH 3 (Ḫattušili I. oder Muršili I.)	ah. Niederschrift KBo 22.2 + mehrere jh. und sjh. Abschriften Nach *Konkordanz*: 14 Tafeln, 18 Fragmente
CTH 4 (Ḫattušili I.)	jh. und sjh. Abschriften Nach *Konkordanz*: 9 Tafeln, 15 Fragmente
CTH 5 (Ḫattušili I.)	jh. Abschriften Nach *Konkordanz*: 1 Tafel, 7 Fragmente
CTH 6 (Ḫattušili I.)	jh. Abschrift Nach *Konkordanz*: 1 Tafel, 2 Fragmente
CTH 7 (Ḫattušili I.)	Akkadischer Text KBo 1.11 ist aufgrund von Schrift und Duktus der Tafel nicht relevant.
CTH 8 (Ḫattušili I. / Muršili I.)	ah. Niederschrift KUB 36.104 + mehrere jh. und sjh. Fragmente Nach *Konkordanz*: 11 Tafeln, 15 Fragmente
CTH 9 (Ḫattušili I. / Muršili I.)	ah. Niederschrift KBo 8.42 + mehrere jh. und sjh. Fragmente Die (ah.?/**mh.**?) Datierung von KUB 36.105 in der *Konkordanz* gilt nur als Alternative. Nach *Konkordanz*: 8 Tafeln, 9 Fragmente
CTH 10 (Ḫantili I.)	jh. Abschriften Nach *Konkordanz*: 3 Tafeln, 4 Fragmente
CTH 11 (Ḫantili I.)	jh. Abschriften Nach *Konkordanz*: 2 Tafeln, 2 Fragmente
CTH 12 (Muršili I. oder Ḫantili I.)	ah. Niederschrift KBo 13.52 + mehrere jh. Fragmente Nach *Konkordanz*: 5 Tafeln, 11 Fragmente
CTH 13 (Muršili I.)	jh. Abschriften Nach *Konkordanz*: 4 Tafeln, 7 Fragmente
CTH 14 (Ḫattušili I.)	ah. Niederschrift KBo 7.14 + KUB 36.100 + zwei jh. Fragmente (KUB 36.101 und 102) Die (ah.?/**mh.**?) Datierung von KBo 7.14 + KUB 36.100 in der *Konkordanz* gilt nur als Alternative. Nach *Konkordanz*: 18 Tafeln, 24 Fragmente
CTH 15 (Ḫattušili I.)	jh. und sjh. Abschriften bzw. Fragmente (siehe *CTH* 14)
CTH 16 (Ḫattušili I.)	jh. Abschriften Nach *Konkordanz*: 6 Tafeln, 13 Fragmente

CTH 17 (Ḫattušili I.)	jh. Abschrift(en) Nach *Konkordanz*: 2 Tafeln, 2 Fragmente
CTH 18 (Ammuna)	jh. Abschriften Nach *Konkordanz*: 2 Tafeln, 5 Fragmente
CTH 19 (Telipinu)	jh. und sjh. Abschriften Die (**mh.**?) Datierung von KBo 7.15 + KBo 12.4 und KBo 19.96 + KUB 11.1 in der *Konkordanz* kann nicht als sicher gelten. Nach *Konkordanz*: 11 Tafeln, 25 Fragmente
CTH 20 (Telipinu)	jh. und sjh. Abschriften Nach *Konkordanz*: 2 Tafeln, 2 Fragmente
CTH 21 (Telipinu)	ah. Niederschrift KUB 31.81 + zwei jh. Fragmente Die (**mh.**) Datierung zweier Fragmente der akkadischen Version KUB 31.82 (+) KUB 4.76 in der *Konkordanz* ist nicht beweiskräftig. Nach *Konkordanz*: 4 Tafeln, 5 Fragmente
CTH 22 (Telipinu)	jh. Abschrift Nach *Konkordanz*: 1 Tafel, 1 Fragment
CTH 24 (Pimpira)	jh. Abschriften bzw. Fragmente Die (**mh.**) Datierung von KBo 3.23 in der *Konkordanz* ist nicht beweiskräftig. Nach *Konkordanz*: 7 Tafeln, 12 Fragmente
CTH 27 (Ḫattušili I. oder Muršili I.)	ah. Niederschrift KUB 36.106 (+) KBo 9.73 Die Datierung (ah.?/**mh.**?) in der *Konkordanz* gilt nur als Alternative. Nach *Konkordanz*: 1 Tafel, 3 Fragmente
CTH 39 (Diversa)	ah. und jh. Fragmente Das einzige Fragment mit (**mh.**?) Datierung ist CHDS 5.47 (so nach *Konkordanz*; kann nicht als sicher gelten). Nach *Konkordanz*: 13 Tafeln, 13 Fragmente
CTH 272 (Muršili I.?)	ah. Niederschrift KBo 22.1 Nach *Konkordanz*: 1 Tafel, 1 Fragment
CTH 310 (Sargon)	jh. und sjh. Abschriften Nach *Konkordanz*: 7 Tafeln, 10 Fragmente
CTH 311 (Naramsin)	jh. und sjh. Abschriften Nach *Konkordanz*: 6 Tafeln, 15 Fragmente

Tabelle 1. Datierung der Nieder- und Abschriften der althethitischen historischen Texte.

Unter 148 Tafeln und 234 Fragmenten findet man in der Konkordanz insgesamt 7 Eintragungen, die als „mh." datiert oder als alternativ vorgeschlagen worden:

3 x (ah.?/mh.?)	mit alternativer Datierung, daher entfallen sie als sichere Belege
2 x (mh.?)	fraglich, daher entfallen sie als sichere Belege
2 x (mh.)	Duktus, Keilschriftformen und Paläographie sind weiter zu überprüfen

Abgesehen von den in der Konkordanz als alternativ oder fraglich ah.?/mh.? oder mh.? datierten Fragmenten bleiben nur zwei anscheinend „mh." Schriftdokumente übrig, und diese sind KUB 31.82 (+) KUB 4.76 (*CTH* 21.I; akkadische Version des Vertrags von Telipinu mit Išputaḫšu von Kizzuwatna) und KBo 3.23 (*CTH* 24.I.A; Erlass von Pimpira). Es scheint einmalig und merkwürdig, warum die akkadische Version eines Vertrags ausgerechnet in mh. Abschrift vorhanden sein soll, während die hethitische Version desselben Vertrags in einer ah. Ausfertigung vorliegt. Daher es ist denkbar, dass auch KUB 31.82(+), wie die hethitische Version KUB 31.81, eine zeitgenössische Urkunde aus der Regierungsperiode von Telipinu ist. Auch der zweitgenannte Text KBo 3.23 weist meines Erachtens weder schriftlich noch sprachlich auffällige mittelhethitische Merkmale auf. Diese Problematik wäre jedoch weiterhin zu diskutieren.

THE TABLETS OF THE 16TH DAY OF AN.DAḪ.ŠUM

A Palaeographic Analysis

Charles W. Steitler
Akademie der Wissenschaften und der Literatur | Mainz

Abstract

Among the texts describing the 16th day of the AN.DAḪ.ŠUM festival, a group of texts refer to the prince as the celebrant, whereas the other texts attribute this role to the king. This raises the question, under what circumstances did the prince take on this role? A palaeographic analysis of the texts attributes individual sign forms, rather than entire tablets, to palaeographic categories such as I, II, IIIa, IIIb or IIIc, in order to propose a relative chronology of the texts. This reveals that the earliest and the latest texts describe the king as celebrating the festival, while in an intermediate group of texts, the prince is the celebrant. In a second step, the same palaeographic analysis is applied to two outline tablets of the AN.DAḪ.ŠUM festival and a prayer of Muwatalli II, serving as comparanda in order to propose an absolute dating for those texts describing the prince as celebrant.

Introduction

The texts currently attributed to the 16th day of AN.DAḪ.ŠUM (*CTH* 612) offer sufficient material with regard to both the quantity of tablets/fragments and the heterogeneity of their content and palaeographic dating as to make them a promising object of a palaeographic analysis. The philological basis for this study is provided by the author's critical edition of the relevant texts, which makes use of newly identified joins and text fragments and reconstructs various text versions describing the festival proceedings. This critical edition is being prepared within the auspices of the project *Das Corpus der hethitischen Festrituale.*

The objective of this paper is threefold: 1) to identify the palaeographic strata represented in the texts describing the 16th day of AN.DAḪ.ŠUM;[1] 2) to compare the relative dating of the texts describing the 16th day of AN.DAḪ.ŠUM with texts that may

1 The "16th day of AN.DAḪ.ŠUM" refers to the events summarized in the best-preserved outline tablet of the AN.DAḪ.ŠUM festival, KBo 10.20 obv. II 32–39. Although the day number is not explicitly mentioned there, this can be derived from the explicit numbering of day 10 in obv. II 10. After this, the text continues uninterrupted up to line 32, and the beginning of each day is clearly indicated by *lukkatti=ma*, allowing for a reliable day count. The numbering of days of the AN.DAḪ.ŠUM festival, however, does vary between the preserved outline tablets. In VSNF 12.1, for example, the very poorly preserved entry in obv. 20′f. most likely would have described a 16th day of the festival. However, we cannot be certain whether this entry referred to the same festival events known from KBo 10.20 II 32–39. If so, then VSNF 12.1 gave a much more abbreviated description of this day than did KBo 10.20.

help to establish an absolute dating; and 3) to draw conclusions based on the relative and absolute datings with regard to the evolution of this festival over time in the context of the Hittite Empire period. The palaeographic analysis is based on the diagnostic sign forms widely recognized by Hittitologists (see the summaries in Weeden 2011: 42–52 and Gordin 2015: 90f.). Caution must be exercised in assigning entire fragments or tablets wholesale to a particular palaeographical category. Instead, preference is given to identifying categories of particular sign forms, such as IIIa, IIIb and IIIc, and then comparing the distribution of sign forms from these categories on individual tablets.

The earliest manuscript in the analyzed text sample is dated by the *Konkordanz* as "mh."; the palaeographic scope of this study is limited to MS and later texts. Three groups of diagnostic sign forms are employed for NS texts, IIIa, IIIb or IIIc, each of which consists of innovative sign forms that should be understood in contrast to their older conservative counterparts. IIIa forms are identified for the signs TAR, AZ, UG,[2] AL, E, URU, DI, KI, AḪ, ḪAR and SAR, IIIb forms for GI, IG, KÙ, AG, DU, GAD, AL, DA, ID, URU, TE, DI, KI, LI and SAR, and IIIc forms for SÌLA, EN, UN, DI, KI, SAR and ḪA. The palaeographic analysis of the tablets of AN.DAḪ.ŠUM day 16 will be compared with a corresponding analysis of the two best-preserved outline tablets of the AN.DAḪ.ŠUM festival and a tablet of the prayer of Muwatalli II to the assembly of the gods (*CTH* 381).

1. Texts of AN.DAḪ.ŠUM Day 16

The 16th day of the Hittite AN.DAḪ.ŠUM festival has received substantial attention, for example, in the excellent translation by Goetze (1950: 358–61) or the edition of some of the best-preserved texts by Badalì et al. (1994), and Haas (1994: 797–803) provided *verbatim* renderings of extensive portions of texts describing day 16. The most recent translation was given by Klinger (2008: 196–202). However, all of the aforementioned publications focus primarily on the well-preserved tablets KBo 4.9 and KBo 13.222 + KUB 11.29 + KUB 41.52 + IBoT 4.183, which are both identified in their respective colophons as the "second tablet", as well as KUB 2.5 and KUB 25.1, which partially overlap with the aforementioned "second tablet", but are identified by their respective colophons as the "third tablet". In the colophon of KUB 25.1, the statement "not complete" (*Ú-UL QA-TI*, rev. VI 46) confirms that in the series to which KUB 25.1 belonged, at least one more tablet must have followed.

In contrast, very little work has been done to reconstruct and understand the contents of the "first tablet", which describes the beginning of the festival in the temple of Zababa. In KBo 20.77, which was included in the edition of Badalì et al. (1994: 18–21), the colophon clearly identifies this fragment as a "first tablet". However, KBo 20.77 only preserves 14 lines of obv. I and the colophon of the reverse. Further fragments can now be identified as descriptions of the beginning of the festival in the temple of Za-

2 While it is true that AZ and UK with subscripted ZA respectively UD already occur in MS texts (see Weeden 2011: 44), these signs have nevertheless been considered diagnostic as part of the cumulative evidence pointing toward earlier or later datings of the manuscripts.

baba: these include a MS text, KBo 41.82 + KBo 40.61 + KBo 24.74 + KBo 20.38 (see Akdoğan 2012), and DBH 46/2.111 (see Akdoğan 2013: 7–9). Akdoğan attributed both texts to *CTH* 660, "offerings to royal images". The content of the recently joined fragments of KUB 10.7 + IBoT 1.4 + CHDS 4.224 correspond to that of the "first tablet" of AN.DAḪ.ŠUM day 16. Though the contents of a reconstructed "first tablet" are still incomplete, when the aforementioned fragments are considered together, they provide us with substantial and coherent sections of text. The resulting text reconstruction includes a sequence of ritual activities involving a drinking rite for the goddess NIN.É.GAL and Zababa, followed by repeated drinking rites for a deity Ḫataurit, each time accompanied by the performance of songs of or for NIN.É.GAL or Zababa.

Such content is unique in the corpus of Hittite festivals. The name *ḫadauri(t)-* is normally used as a specification of a type of festival, and it only occurs in the first tablet of AN.DAḪ.ŠUM day 16 as the name of a deity receiving a drinking rite.[3] This alongside the songs of NIN.É.GAL and Zababa are known not only from the aforementioned texts, but also from two further fragmentary festival texts, which I propose should also be identified as descriptions of the 16th day of AN.DAḪ.ŠUM. VSNF 12.13 + KUB 2.14 + VSNF 12.12 and KBo 45.72 + KBo 45.71 were formerly assigned to *CTH* 647, because they describe a festival performed by the prince. The contents of these two texts closely correspond with the contents of the other fragments of a "first tablet" of AN.DAḪ.ŠUM day 16. Moreover, the description of day 16 in the outline tablet KBo 10.20 allows for the interpretation that the festival in the temple of Zababa may have been performed by the prince:

KBo 10.20 obv. II

32 *lu-⸢uk⸣-kat-ti-ma* LUGAL ⸢MUNUS⸣.LUGAL *I-NA* É ^{D}10 *pa-a-an-zi*
33 *nu šal-li a-še-eš-š[ar]* ⸢*I*⸣*-NA* É ^{D}*ZA-BA$_4$-BA$_4$-ma* ⸢EZEN$_4$⸣ *ḫ[a-ta-ú-ri*$^{(?)}$]^{4}
34 ⸢*i-ia*⸣*-an-zi* …

On the next day, the king (and) the queen go to the temple of the Storm-god, and the great assembly (takes place), but in the temple of Zababa they celebrate the *ḫ[adauri-* festival]. …

This outline tablet implies that the primary festival of the 16th day was the "great assembly" since this is mentioned first and took place in the temple of the Storm-god in Ḫattuša (most likely the Great Temple of the lower city) and since the royal couple was present at this festival. I suggest that the *ḫadauri-* festival in the temple of Zababa took place at the same time as the "great assembly" in the Storm-god's temple. Since the king and queen were busy celebrating the latter, someone else must have celebrated

3 *ḫadauri(t)-* may be related to the divine name *tauri(t)-*, who is frequently attested as the recipient of drinking rites.

4 This restoration follows Güterbock 1960: 82 n. 20, who despite a possible reading as EZEN$_4$^{Ḫ}[$^{I.A}$] also notes that the parallel outline tablet of KUB 25.27 obv. I 9f. should be restored with [*ḫa-da*]*-ú-ri*. A recent photo of KBo 10.20 confirms that the sign following EZEN$_4$ is ḪA, with the *Winkelhaken* written on top of the lower half of the first broken vertical, as is also the case with other ḪA signs on this tablet, including that in EZEN$_4$ *ḫa-da-ú-ri* in obv. II 17.

the *ḫadauri-* festival in the temple of Zababa. The celebrant's identity is suggested by the next entry in the same outline tablet, describing day 17:

KBo 10.20 obv. II

40 *lu-uk-kat-ti-ma* LUGAL MUNUS.LUGAL *I-NA* É ^{D}*ḫa-an-nu pa-a-an-z*[*i*]
41 *nu* ⸢*šal*⸣*-li a-še-eš-šar* *I-NA* É ^{D}10-*ma* DUMU.LUGAL
42 *IŠ-TU* É.GAL-*LIM u-i-ia-an-zi nu* EZEN$_4$ *ḫa-*⸢*ta*⸣*-ú-ri*
43 *i-ia-zi* …

On the next day, the king (and) the queen go to the temple of Ḫannu, and the great assembly takes place. But they send the prince to the temple of the Storm-god from the palace, and he celebrates the *ḫadauri-* festival.

Other instances of celebrating the *ḫadauri-* festival are usually expressed with the impersonal 3.pl. verb *iyanzi* "they celebrate". While this impersonal verb conceals who the celebrant was, in each case where the context is sufficiently preserved, the king can always be excluded, since the context always indicates his occupation with a different festival. Although the texts do not normally tell us who the celebrant of the *ḫadauri-* festival was, the prince is a likely candidate. There are numerous fragmentary festival texts in which the prince plays a prominent role, whereas the king is absent (e. g. in many texts of *CTH* 647). Furthermore, like the outline tablet description of day 17 of AN.DAḪ.ŠUM, one of the *nuntarriyašḫa-* outline tablets also connects the prince with the celebration of a *ḫadauri-* festival in the temple of the Storm-god that occurs simultaneously with a festival celebrated by the king in the temple of Ḫannu:

KBo 14.76 obv. I:

5′ [*lu-uk-kat-ti-ma* LUGAL-*uš I-NA* É] ⸢^{m}⸣*ḫa-an-nu pa-iz-zi*
6′ [-*i*]*a-zi nu* EZ[EN$_4$]-⸢*ŠU*⸣ *šal-li ḫal-z*[*i-ia*]
7′ [*I-NA* É ^{D}10-*ma* LUGAL-*uš m*]*a-a-an* DUMU.LU[GAL *m*]*a-a-an* ⸢^{LÚ}*ME*⸣*-ŠE-DI*
8′ [*u-i-ia-zi nu* EZEN$_4$ *ḫa-t*]*a-ú-r*[*i i-ia-z*]*i*[5]

[On the next day the king] goes [to the temple] of Ḫannu. [… he …]-s. His (the god's) fest[ival] takes place. The great (assembly) is call[ed out. The king sends e]ither the prin[ce o]r the bodyguard [to the temple of the Storm-god. He then celebrate]s [the *ḫad*]*aur*[*i-* festival].

Here, the option is given to designate either the prince or the bodyguard as the celebrant of the *ḫadauri-* festival.[6] The evidence thus points to a similar scenario for day 16 of AN.DAḪ.ŠUM, suggesting that VSNF 12.13+ and KBo 45.72+ describe a *ḫadauri-* festival celebrated by the prince in the temple of Zababa.[7] In light of all the other texts

5 The reconstruction of these lines is based in part on the parallel texts of KBo 22.228+: 8′–10′ and KBo 3.25+: 10′–12′, thus the text edition by Kryszeń forthc.

6 The parallel outline tablets, KBo 3.25+: 8′–12′ and KBo 22.228+: 7′–12′, provide a slightly different description of the events, beginning with the visit of the supervising palace servant (DUMU.É.GAL ^{LÚ}*parā uwanza*) to the temple of Ziparwa, but without mention of a festival in the temple of Ḫannu; see Kryszeń forthc.

7 If VSNF 12.13+ and KBo 45.72+ are indeed descriptions of the *ḫadauri-* festival referred to in KBo 10.20 obv. II 33′f., one might also ask if the name of this festival relates to the drinking rites performed for

describing the festival performed by the king in the temple of Zababa on day 16, the performance by the prince seems to represent an important development in the evolution of the AN.DAḪ.ŠUM festival. The palaeographic analysis of the texts will shed light on this subject.

2. Palaeographic analysis

Before presenting the palaeographic analysis of the tablets describing the 16th day of AN.DAḪ.ŠUM, it should be noted that the following texts currently identified in the *Konkordanz* as AN.DAḪ.ŠUM day 16 (*CTH* 612) were excluded from the palaeographic analysis: 1) texts whose identification relies solely on their similarity to descriptions of the "great assembly", which could equally be attributed to other festivals in which the "great assembly" occurred;[8] 2) unpublished texts;[9] and 3) fragments that do not allow for meaningful conclusions about palaeographic questions due to their small size or lack of sufficient diagnostic signs.[10] The following discussion focuses on better-preserved tablets and larger fragments that are listed in Table 1.

Textpublication	Version	Find Spot	Date (*Konkordanz*)	Discussed in Section
KBo 41.82+	*CTH* 612.a.B	Büyukkale Building A	mh.	2.1
KBo 20.77	*CTH* 612.a.A	Büyukkale Building A	jh.	2.2
KUB 25.1	*CTH* 612.b.C	Ḫattuša	jh.	2.2
KBo 13.222+	*CTH* 612.b.B	House on the Slope	jh.	2.2
KBo 11.51	*CTH* 612.c.A	Büyukkale Building K	jh.	2.2
DBH 46/2.111	*CTH* 612.m.A	Ḫattuša	jh.	2.2
KBo 4.9	*CTH* 612.b.A	Ḫattuša	sjh.	2.3
KUB 2.5	*CTH* 612.b.D	Ḫattuša	sjh.	2.3
KUB 10.7+	*CTH* 612.n.A	Ḫattuša	sjh.	2.3
VSNF 12.13+	*CTH* 612.q.A	Ḫattuša	jh.	2.4
KBo 45.72+	*CTH* 612.r.A	House on the Slope	jh.	2.4

Table 1. Texts included in the palaeographical analysis of AN.DAḪ.ŠUM day 16.

the deity named *Ḫadauri(t)*. However, drinking rites for *Ḫadauri(t)* are also found in the fragments of a "1st tablet" in which the king, and not the prince, is the celebrant. Such texts should be considered descriptions of a normal festival celebrated by the king, not the *ḫadauri-* festival celebrated by the prince. This distinction does not preclude the possibility that the *ḫadauri-* festival was substantially identical with the festival celebrated by the king – that is in fact our working hypothesis. The primary difference between the two seems to have been the celebrant.

8 Texts excluded on these grounds are Bo 7212, IBoT 3.56, IBoT 4.76, IBoT 4.77, KBo 3.12, KBo 11.59, KBo 31.170, KBo 45.23, KBo 46.137, KBo 47.94, KBo 54.209, KBo 56.69, KBo 58.113, KBo 69.21, KUB 10.12, KUB 20.36, KUB 57.96, UBT 29, and VSNF 12.6.

9 Unpublished texts include Bo 6709 and Bo 6785 + Bo 9375.

10 Texts excluded on these grounds are CHDS 4.22, CHDS 5.165, IBoT 1.20, IBoT 4.186, KBo 9.121, KBo 14.35, KBo 23.77, KBo 44.120, KBo 46.89, KBo 59.89+, KUB 46.9, VBoT 34, VBoT 35, and VSNF 12.3.

Each tablet/fragment will be discussed individually, giving attention to its format and size (if known or estimable) and the palaeographic types of signs attested on each.

2.1 A Middle Script tablet

The earliest known text describing the 16th day of AN.DAḪ.ŠUM is KBo 41.82+. It consists of four directly adjoining fragments that were discovered in rooms 5 and 6 of Building A on Büyükkale and belonged to a two-columned tablet, which is a typical format for MS festival texts (Waal 2015: 86). The width of the intercolumnium, 0.57 cm, is also very close to the average for MS two-columned tablets (Waal 2015: 92).[11] The upper and lower edges as well as the right edge of the tablet are completely missing. The colophon follows a double paragraph marker and an empty space equivalent to about two lines of text. Enough uninscribed space remains after the three-lined colophon to suggest that no scribal signature followed (in contrast to the colophon of the duplicate text, KBo 20.77 rev. 4′f.; see below).

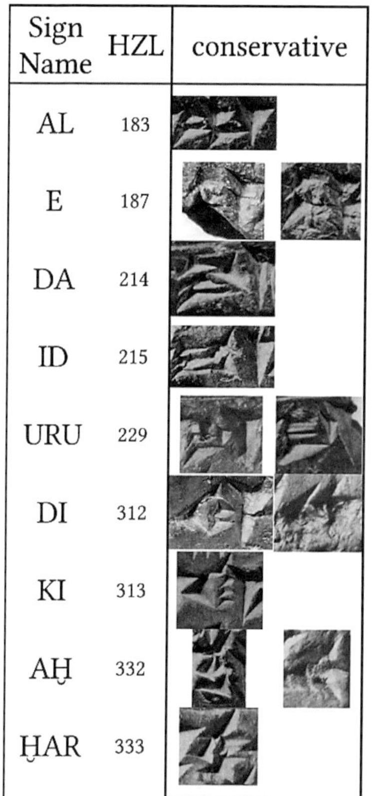

Fig. 1. Conservative sign forms in KBo 41.82+.

The distinctly conservative sign forms (contrasting with the IIIa sign forms) preserved on this tablet and shown in Fig. 1 include E and URU each with a lowered first vertical, KI and DI with prominent front *Winkelhaken*, and ḪAR and AḪ with the horizontal(s) positioned between the upper and lower *Winkelhaken*. The only IIIa sign forms identifiable on this tablet are DA and ID. Finally, the sign SAR, although damaged, seems to have a trace of a small lowered vertical before the final vertical to the right, thus corresponding to the IIIa sign form (see Excursus: Forms of SAR).

2.2 Earlier New Script tablets

2.2.1 KBo 20.77

The only tablet of the 16th day of AN.DAḪ.ŠUM preserving a colophon with the scribe's name is KBo 20.77, which was written by Karunu under the supervision of Šipaziti (see Gordin 2015: 191–94). The text preserved on this tablet duplicates KBo 41.82+ exactly,

11 Unless otherwise noted, the measurements given for the tablets and fragments are based on digital(ized) photos of the fragments including a scale, and in some cases combined into a photomontage. The measurements of KBo 41.82+ given by Akdoğan 2012: 21 as 24 cm height × 13.7 cm width × 3.8 cm thickness correspond closely to the estimates based on the photos.

including most of the line breaks. The only significant difference between the two is the lack of a scribal signature in KBo 41.82+. Originally, the first column (obv. I) of KBo 20.77 must have been at least 1 cm wider than the fragment's current remaining width (8.3 cm),[12] suggesting that KBo 20.77 was also a two-columned tablet like KBo 41.82+. In addition to the aforementioned similarities between them, the fact that both KBo 20.77 and KBo 41.82+ were found in Building A on Büyükkale raises the possibility that KBo 41.82+ may have been the *Vorlage* for KBo 20.77. A possible indirect join with DBH 46/2.111 is discussed below (see section 3).

Unlike KBo 41.82+, there are no conservative diagnostic sign forms earlier than IIIa on KBo 20.77, with the possible exception of ḪAR. The IIIa form of AZ is used. Only DA occurs in its IIIb form. The conservative forms of ḪA and EN are used (as opposed to their IIIc counterparts).

Sign Name	HZL	conser-vative	IIIa
AZ	92		
ḪAR	333		

Fig. 2. Conservative vs IIIa sign forms in KBo 20.77.

Sign Name	HZL	conser-vative	IIIb
DA	214		
TE	249		
LI	343		

Fig. 3. Conservative vs IIIb sign forms in KBo 20.77.

Sign Name	HZL	conser-vative
EN	40	
ḪA	367	

Fig. 4. Conservative vs IIIc sign forms in KBo 20.77.

2.2.2 KUB 25.1

Much of the four edges of this three-columned tablet are preserved, although large sections of text from both sides of the tablet are missing. The colophon is completely preserved, including the remark *A-NA* GIŠ.ḪUR-*kan ḫandan* (rev. VI 47f.). Only parts of the unwritten surface following the colophon at the end of rev. VI are missing. The double paragraph marker is decorated with two pairs of *Winkelhaken* toward the right end of the lines (Fig. 5); for various interpretations of this ornamentation, see Gordin (2015: 309f.).

Fig. 5. Double paragraph marker decorated with *Winkelhaken* in KUB 25.1.

12 This is based upon KBo 20.77 obv. 1, the final word of which must be restored as ⌜*ḫa-aš*⌝-[*ša-an-zi*]; if written as normal, the final three missing signs would have required a little more than 1 cm of space beyond the broken edge of the fragment.

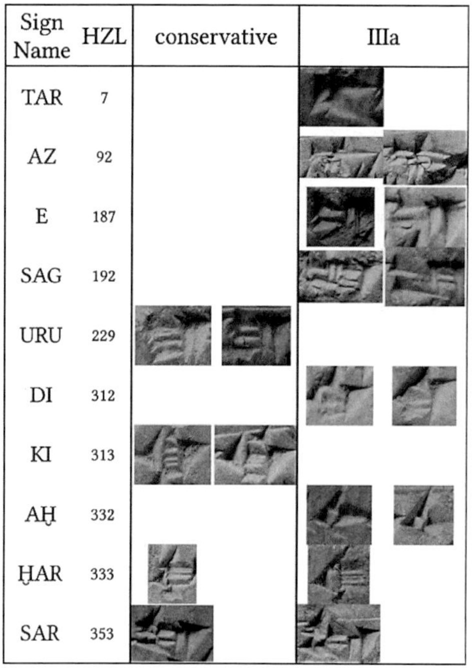

Fig. 6. Conservative vs IIIa sign forms in KUB 25.1.

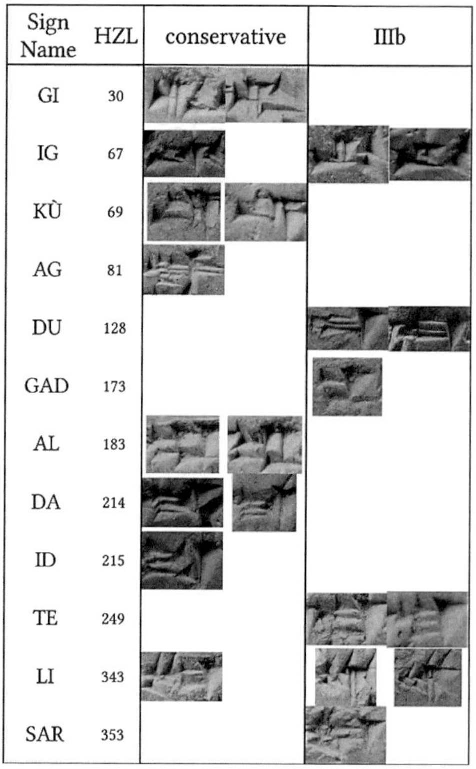

Fig. 7. Conservative vs IIIb sign forms in KUB 25.1.

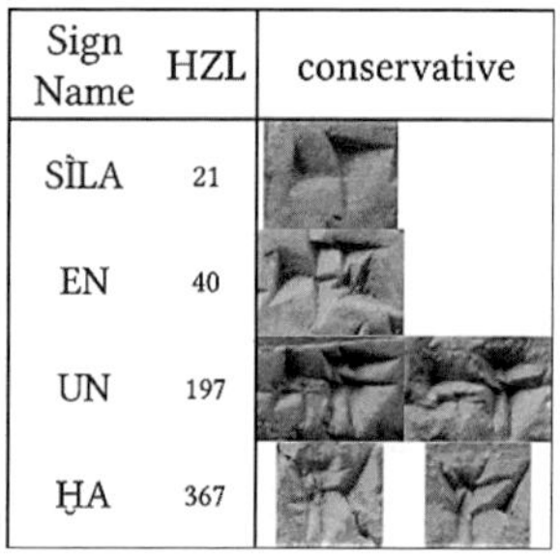

Fig. 8. Conservative vs IIIc sign forms in KUB 25.1.

Palaeographically, KUB 25.1 makes use of numerous conservative sign forms but also IIIb forms. The conservative forms of URU, KI, ḪAR and SAR occur rather than their IIIa counterparts. The conservative form of SAR appears alongside its later IIIa and IIIb forms (see Excursus: Forms of SAR). The conservative forms of GI, IG, KÙ, AG, AL, DA, ID and LI occur frequently (Fig. 7). Both the conservative and IIIb forms of IG and LI occur. In addition to IG and LI, other IIIb sign forms include DU, GAD and TE. Only the conservative sign forms of ḪA, EN, QA and UN, never their IIIc counterparts, are used (Fig. 8).

2.2.3 KBo 13.222+

Only the upper portion of this three-columned tablet is preserved, including parts of the first two lines of the colophon on the rev. VI. The horizontally adjoining fragments, including pieces of the left and right edges, allow in some sections for a full reconstruction of the tablet's width. The conservative forms of AZ and ḪAR occur (Fig. 9), although these are frequently present on later tablets as well (including those analyzed

Sign Name	HZL	conservative	IIIa
TAR	7		
AZ	92		
E	187		
AḪ	332		
ḪAR	333		

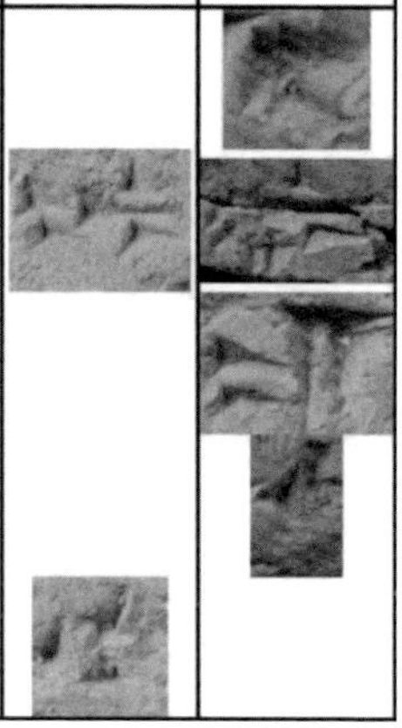

Fig. 9. Conservative vs IIIa sign forms in KBo 13.222+.

Sign Name	HZL	conservative	IIIb
GI	30		
KÙ	69		
GAD	173		
DA	214		
ID	215		
TE	249		
DI	312		
KI	313		

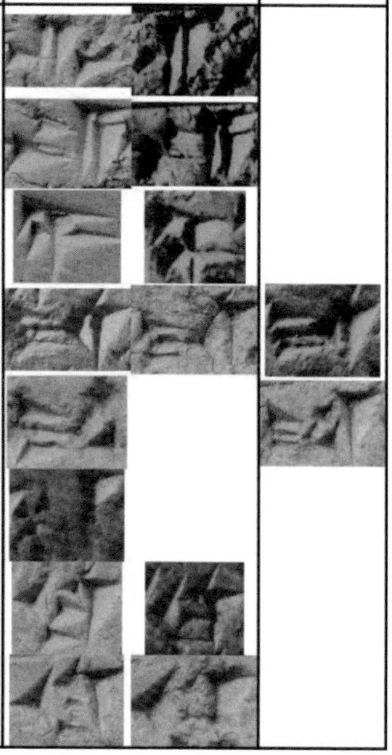

Fig. 10. Conservative vs IIIb sign forms in KBo 13.222+.

by the present study). Palaeographically, the tablet is dominated by a preference for conservative over IIIb sign forms (Fig. 10). Noteworthy is the use of both the conservative and the IIIb forms of DA and ID (Fig. 10). No IIIc sign forms are preserved.

2.2.4 KBo 11.51

This fragment stems from the lower right corner of what was most likely a two-columned tablet. The obv. preserves the right column in its entire width, 7.8 cm, including a portion of the intercolumnium. Since the right columns of three-columned tablets are typically narrower than both the middle and the left columns, it is hardly likely that this was a three-columned tablet. Thus, the full width of the tablet may have been about 17 cm, slightly less than the average of 18.7 cm for (L)NS two-columned tablets. This fragment contains a mixture of conservative (AZ, GI, KÙ, DU, GAD, DA, ID) as well as IIIa (TAR, ḪAR, SAR) and IIIb sign forms (IG, AG, URU, DI, KI) (Figs. 11–12). The sign LI appears in both the conservative and IIIb forms. ḪA (with a single *Winkelhaken*) is the only IIIc sign form attested, while SÌLA and UN only occur in their conservative forms (Fig. 13).

Sign Name	HZL	conservative	IIIa
TAR	7		
AZ	92		
ḪAR	333		
SAR	353		

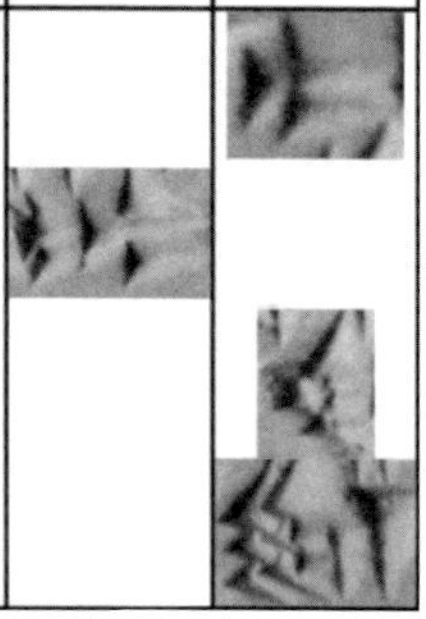

Fig. 11. Conservative vs IIIa sign forms in KBo 11.51.

Sign Name	HZL	conservative	IIIb
GI	30		
IG	67		
KÙ	69		
AG	81		
DU	128		
GAD	173		
SAG	192		
DA	214		
ID	215		
URU	229		
DI	312		
KI	313		
LI	343		

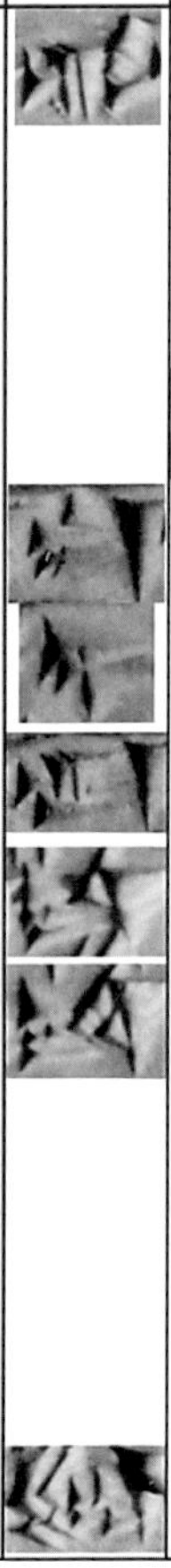
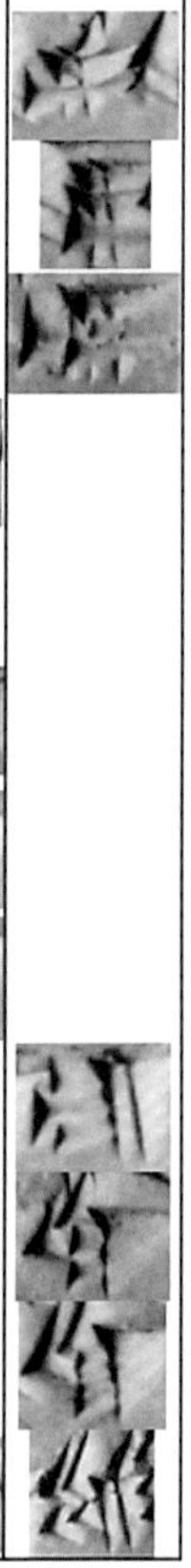

Fig. 12. Conservative vs IIIb sign forms in KBo 11.51.

Sign Name	HZL	conservative	IIIc
SÌLA	21		
UN	197		
ḪA	367		

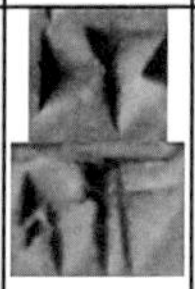
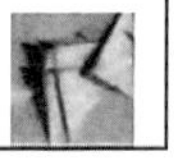

Fig. 13. Conservative vs IIIc sign forms in KBo 11.51.

Sign Name	HZL	conservative
DA	214	
ID	215	
Ù	265	

Fig. 14. Conservative vs IIIb sign forms on DBH 46/2.111.

Sign Name	HZL	conservative
SÌLA	21	
UN	197	
ḪA	367	

Fig. 15. Conservative vs IIIc sign forms on DBH 46/2.111.

2.2.5 DBH 46/2.111

Portions of the right column of the obv. and rev. are preserved on this fragment. The width of the column can be estimated at about 8–9 cm, indicating that this must have been a two-columned tablet. A possible indirect join with KBo 20.77 is discussed below (see section 3). Only a few diagnostic signs occur on this fragment: three conservative rather than IIIb signs forms (Fig. 14) and three conservative rather than IIIc sign forms (Fig. 15).

2.3 Late(r) New Script tablets

2.3.1 KBo 4.9

This very well-preserved tablet is only missing pieces of the upper edge of the right column and of the lower right corner of the tablet. Palaeographically, KBo 4.9 is quite heterogeneous in the sign forms used, ranging from MS (IIc) to IIIc. The conservative forms of AZ and ḪAR stand in contrast to the IIIa forms of TAR, AZ, UG, and AḪ (Fig. 16). SAR occurs in both the conservative (IIc) and the IIIa (or perhaps IIIb) forms. Many conservative sign forms are used consistently throughout, such as GI, DU, DA, ID, TE and LI (Fig. 17). The sign KÙ occurs in both the conservative and IIIb forms, while for the signs IG, AG, GAD, AL, URU, DI and KI only the IIIb forms are employed. The conservative form of UN stands in contrast to the IIIc forms of EN and ḪA (Fig. 18). SÌLA occurs once in its IIIc form, but is otherwise written in the conservative form.

Sign Name	HZL	conservative	IIIa
TAR	7		
AZ	92		
UG	93		
AḪ	332		
ḪAR	333		
SAR	353		

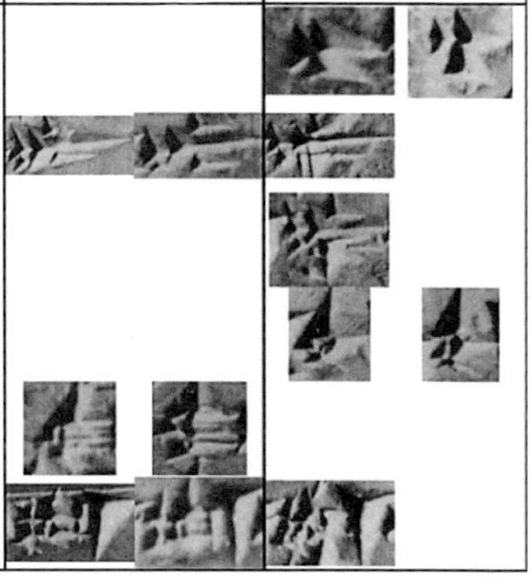

Fig. 16. Conservative vs IIIa sign forms in KBo 4.9.

Sign Name	HZL	conservative	IIIc
SÌLA	21		
EN	40		
UN	197		
ḪA	367		

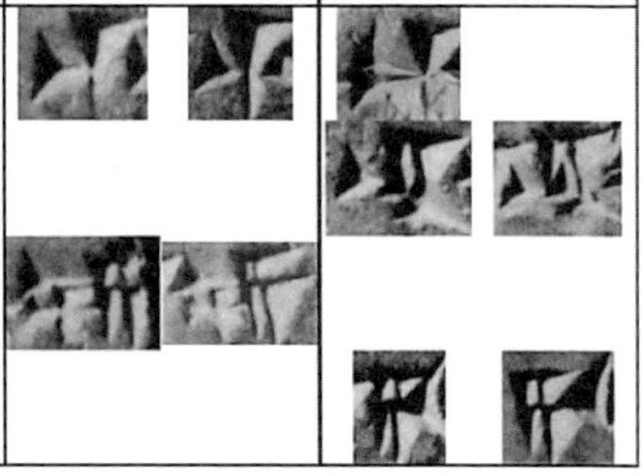

Fig. 18. Conservative vs IIIc sign forms in KBo 4.9.

Sign Name	HZL	conservative	IIIb
GI	30		
IG	67		
KÙ	69		
AG	81		
DU	128		
GAD	173		
AL	183		
DA	214		
ID	215		
URU	229		
TE	249		
DI	312		
KI	313		
LI	343		

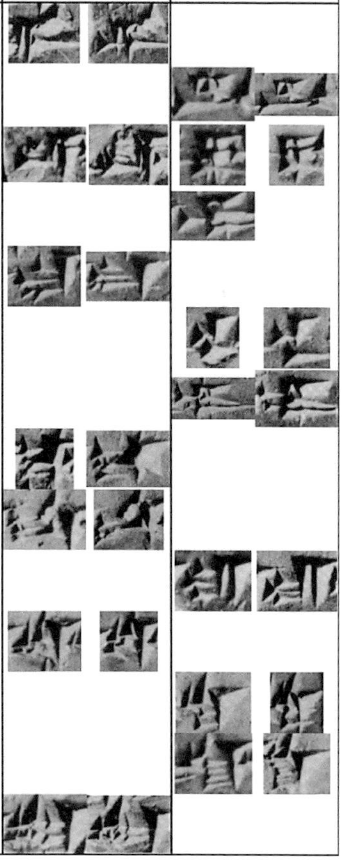

Fig. 17. Conservative vs IIIb sign forms in KBo 4.9.

2.3.2 KUB 2.5

Although the core of the tablet of KUB 2.5 is very well preserved, larger sections of text, especially on the rev., are badly damaged or lost. Like KBo 4.9, KUB 2.5 also uses sign forms ranging from MS (IIc) to IIIc. KUB 2.5 uses the same conservative sign forms contrasting with IIIa sign forms that are found on KBo 4.9: AZ, ḪAR[13] and SAR, although IIIa AZ is also used in KUB 2.5 (Fig. 19). The conservative sign forms contrasting with IIIb sign forms in KUB 2.5 also conform broadly to those of KBo 4.9:

13 The only preserved occurrence of the sign ḪAR occurs in rev. IV 45″ and is slightly damaged. Enough can be seen on the photo to confirm that the *Winkelhaken* are spread out vertically, allowing for the horizontals to be placed in between them, rather than separated to the right of the horizontals.

GI, KÙ, DU, DA, ID, TE, LI (Fig. 20). Note, however, that KÙ, DA, ID and LI are attested in both the conservative and IIIb forms, while IG, GAD, URU, DI and KI only occur in the IIIb forms, similar to KBo 4.9. Finally, the distribution of conservative vs IIIc sign forms conforms almost exactly to that of KBo 4.9: conservative UN, IIIc EN and ḪA, and both forms of SÌLA (Fig. 21).

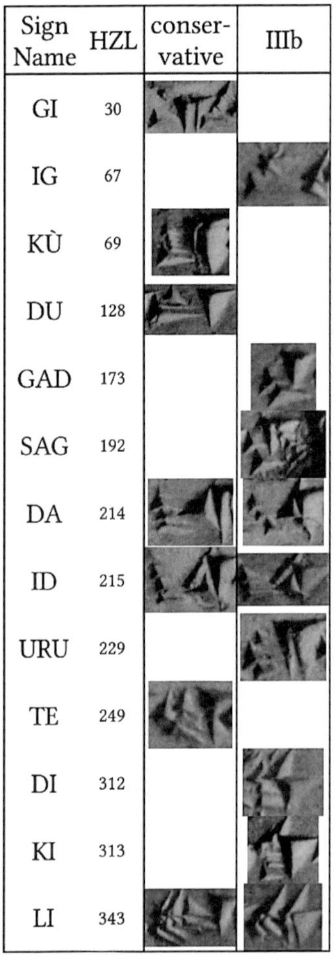

Fig. 20. Conservative vs IIIb sign forms in KUB 2.5.

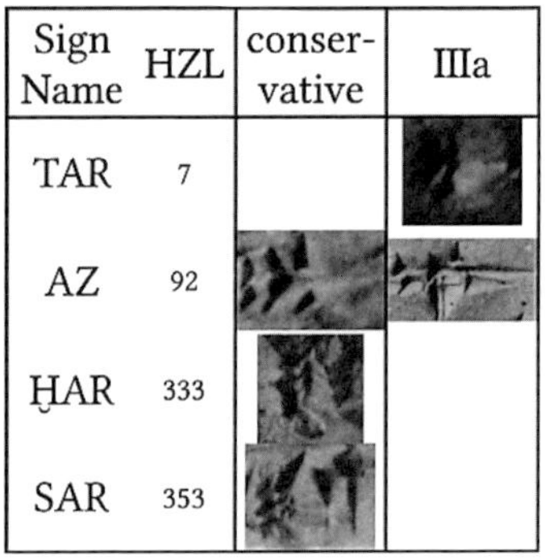

Fig. 19. Conservative vs IIIa sign forms in KUB 2.5.

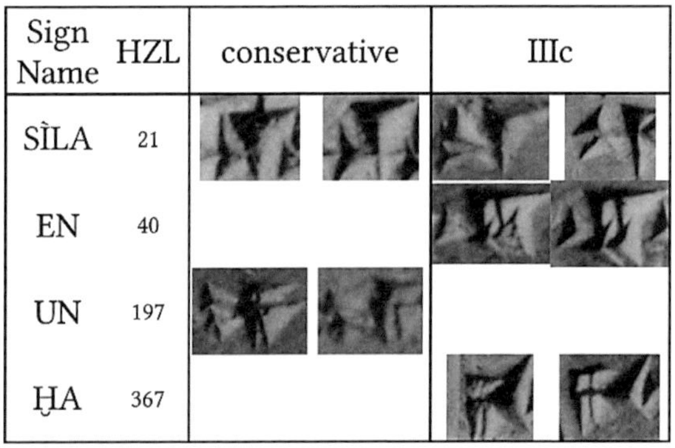

Fig. 21. Conservative vs IIIc sign forms in KUB 2.5.

A particularly unusual feature of this tablet is the insertion of LIŠ between DUḪ and A in the Sumerograms SAGI.LIŠ.A and IGI.DU$_8$.LIŠ.A. There are only a handful of other occurrences of this phenomenon in other texts: SAGI.LIŠ.A: IBoT 4.159 (NS, *CTH* 670) obv. 6′, KBo 46.136 (LNS, *CTH* 612) obv.[?] 6′ and KUB 39.4 + KUB 30.25+ (LNS, *CTH* 450.I.7e.A) obv. 27′ and 32′;[14] IGI.DU$_8$.LIŠ.A: HKM 90 (MS, *CTH* 190) obv. 3′ and 4′ (both partially reconstructed). There is no clear explanation for this sign variation, and it occurs in different time periods and text genres, as the cited occurrences demonstrate.

14 In both cases in KUB 39.4+, the sign form varies slightly from the form in KUB 2.5 in that the additional LIŠ is written without the *Winkelhaken* (see Kassian et al. 2002: 324 n. i), but since this stands in such close proximity to the immediately preceding group of *Winkelhaken* in the sign DUḪ, this may be insignificant.

It seems to have been conditioned by the group of *Winkelhaken* followed by verticals (in this case, the sign A), so that the sign cluster is visually similar to the late forms of LI as well as SAR (Fig. 22).

Fig. 22. Sumerograms with superfluous LIŠ in KUB 2.5: left: ^{LÚ}SAGI.LIŠ.A (obv. II 38′); right: IGI.DU$_8$.LIŠ.A (obv. II 20′).

2.3.3 IBoT 1.4 + KUB 10.7 + CHDS 4.224

The joins between IBoT 1.4, KUB 10.7 and CHDS 4.224 discovered in the preparation of this study were identified based on the similarity of the handwriting as well as the contents of these fragments. They belonged to a three-columned tablet whose width can be estimated at about 18 cm: the preserved width of the rev. of the adjoining fragments (spanning from the right edge of the tablet up to and including the left intercolumnium) measures 12.6 cm, and the width of rev. VI can be estimated at 5–6 cm. Judging from the few diagnostic sign forms preserved, IBoT 1.4+ is palaeographically quite homogeneous, using IIIb sign forms throughout, such as DA, ID, TE, DI and LI (Fig. 23), but the conservative rather than IIIc forms of SÌLA, EN, and UN (Fig. 24). Only ḪA appears in the IIIc form.

Sign Name	HZL	IIIb
DA	214	
ID	215	
TE	249	
DI	312	
LI	343	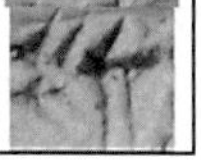

Fig. 23. IIIb sign forms on IBoT 1.4+.

Sign Name	HZL	conservative	IIIc
SÌLA	21		
EN	40		
UN	197		
ḪA	367		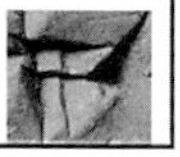

Fig. 24. Conservative vs IIIc sign forms on IBoT 1.4+.

2.4 Texts referring to the prince

The connection between VSNF 12.13+ and KBo 45.72+ with other texts representing the "first tablet" of the description of the 16th day of the AN.DAḪ.ŠUM festival was explained above (see section 1). Although the handwriting of VSNF 12.13+ and KBo 45.72+ is very similar, or even identical (Fig. 42), these fragments do not belong to the same tablet. The contents of KBo 45.72+ left column (obv. I or, less likely, rev. IV/VI) correspond to obv. II of the reconstructed tablet VSNF 12.13+, making it impossible for

Fig. 25. Reconstruction of VSNF 12.13+ (left) and KBo 45.72+ (right) with corresponding text passages highlighted.

these fragments to be positioned in a single tablet. They may, however, have been written by the same scribe.

2.4.1 VSNF 12.13+

VSNF 12.13+ belonged to a three-columned tablet, as evidenced by preserved portions of all three columns on the obverse. Portions of the upper and left edges of the tablet are preserved by VSNF 12.12, which does not join the other two fragments directly. Nevertheless, the dividing lines of the *intercolumnium* on VSNF 12.12 can be aligned with those of VSNF 12.13, which in turn directly joins KUB 2.14. The sparsely preserved lines of text from obv. II can only be understood in connection with the parallel texts of DBH 46/2.111 rev. III and CHDS 4.224 + KUB 10.7+ rev. V, which describe drinking rites for NIN.É.GAL, Zababa and Ḫatauri(t), followed by songs of/for NIN.É.GAL and Zababa.

The tablet only has one occurrence of a MS sign form, URU, but employs the IIIa signs AḪ and SAR (Fig. 26). Other conservative signs include GAD, DA, ID, TE and LI, but IIIb signs are also well represented: GI, IG, DU, AL, DI and KI (Fig. 27). Both the conservative and IIIb forms of NI occur. The conservative forms SÌLA and EN contrast only with IIIc ḪA (Fig. 28).

Sign Name	HZL	conser-vative	IIIa
URU	229		
AḪ	332		
SAR	353		

Fig. 26. Conservative vs IIIa sign forms in VSNF 12.13+.

Sign Name	HZL	conser vative	IIIc
SÌLA	21		
EN	40		
ḪA	367		

Fig. 28. Conservative vs IIIc sign forms in VSNF 12.13+.

Sign Name	HZL	IIIa
SAR	353	

Fig. 29. Conservative vs IIIa sign forms in KBo 45.72+.

Sign Name	HZL	conser-vative
GAD	173	
DA	214	
ID	215	
LI	343	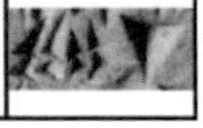

Fig. 30. Conservative vs IIIb sign forms in KBo 45.72+.

Sign Name	HZL	conservative	IIIb
GI	30		
IG	67		
NI	72		
DU	128		
GAD	173		
AL	183		
DA	214	 	
ID	215		
TE	249	 	
DI	312		
KI	313		
LI	343	 	

Fig. 27. Conservative vs IIIb sign forms in VSNF 12.13+.

2.4.2 KBo 45.72+

It is unclear whether KBo 45.72+ belonged to a two- or three-columned tablet. Since its contents correspond to KBo 41.82+ rev. IV, DBH 46/2.111 rev. III and IBoT 1.4+ rev. V, it seems more probable that KBo 45.72+ represents the reverse of the tablet (column IV or VI) if the text was distributed similarly in the tablet series to which it belonged. Although very few diagnostic signs are preserved, including IIIa SAR (Fig. 29) and conservative GAD, DA, ID and LI (Fig. 30), the sign forms used closely align with the sign forms of VSNF 12.13+.

2.5 Comparanda

Three texts will be used as palaeographic *comparanda* to the texts that have just been described. Two of them are the best-preserved outline tablets of the AN.DAḪ.ŠUM festival: KBo 10.20 and KUB 30.39 + KBo 24.112 + KBo 23.80.[15] As was already mentioned, the only description of day 16 preserved in the outline tablets is found in KBo 10.20, which regulates the festival in the temple of Zababa as a *ḫadauri-* festival, possibly celebrated by the prince. This would correspond well with the two fragments of day tablets, VSNF 12.13+ and KBo 45.72+, in which the prince is the celebrant of the festival. A palaeographic comparison might offer some insight into whether KBo 10.20 and the day tablets referring to the prince might have been produced in the same era. The other outline tablet, KUB 30.39+, is the earliest known outline tablet of the AN.DAḪ.ŠUM festival, making it suitable for comparison with the earliest day tablets describing day 16.

Sign Name	HZL	conservative	IIIa
TAR	7		
AZ	92		
UG	93		
AḪ	332		
ḪAR	333		
SAR	353		

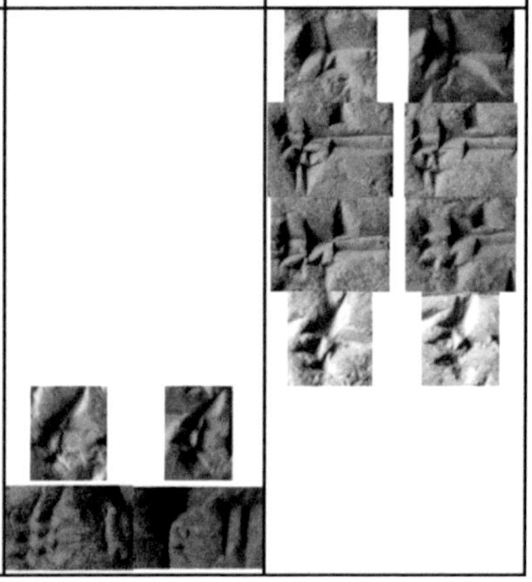

Fig. 31. Conservative vs IIIa sign forms in KBo 10.20.

2.5.1 KBo 10.20

The diagnostic sign forms used in KBo 10.20 are somewhat heterogeneous, but nevertheless there is an overall tendency towards the use of IIIb and occasionally even IIIc sign forms (Figs. 32–33). Surprisingly, the older forms of ḪAR and SAR also appear (Fig. 31), but these contrast with the younger forms of AḪ and SAR (Figs. 31 and 33) on the same tablet. Notably, both instances of the conservative (MS) SAR form occur in the colophon of the tablet, whereas elsewhere the scribe employed the latest (IIIc) form of SAR (see Excursus: Forms of SAR).

The signs DU and LI occur in both their conservative and IIIb forms (Fig. 32). The TE sign is written at least once with horizontals instead of obliques (IIIb form), but elsewhere on this tablet TE employs clearly angled oblique wedges. Aside from these signs and the conservative forms of GAD, the tablet consistently employs IIIb sign forms of IG, KÙ, DA, ID, URU and KI. The only IIIc sign forms attested are one occurrence of SÌLA as well as a very late form of SAR, in which the two verticals stand close together immediately after the *Winkelhaken* with two very short horizontals placed at the top and bottom between them (Fig. 33). This form of SAR does not occur in any of the day tablets describing day 16 discussed above (see Excursus: Forms of SAR).

15 An indirect join of these fragments with KBo 47.242 is probable on the basis of the handwriting of the fragments, size of the handwriting, the one-columned format of the tablet to which it belonged, as well as the find spot of the fragment on the western slope of Büyükkale, so that it may have originated in building A of Büyükkale, where KUB 30.39 and KBo 24.112 were both found (KBo 23.80 stems from Büyükkale v/17 "im Schutt").

Sign Name	HZL	conservative	IIIb
IG	67		
KÙ	69		
DU	128		
GAD	173		
DA	214		
ID	215		
URU	229		
TE	249		
KI	313		
LI	343		

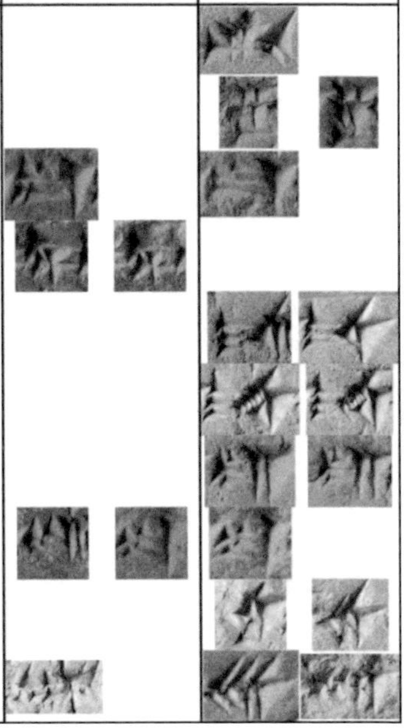

Fig. 32. Conservative vs IIIb sign forms in KBo 10.20.

Sign Name	HZL	conservative	IIIc
SÌLA	21		
EN	40		
DI	312		
KI	313		
SAR	353		
ḪA	367		

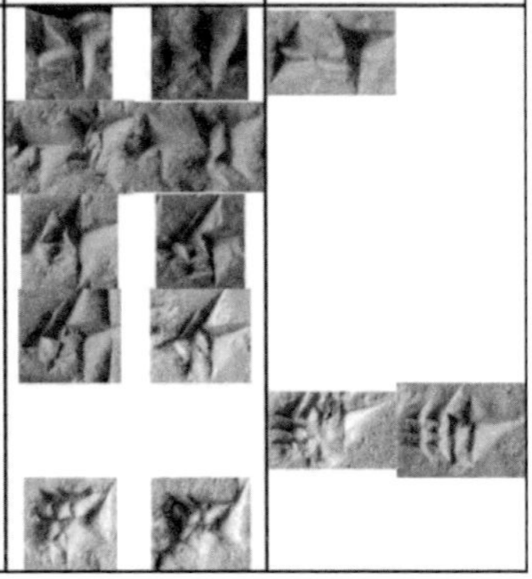

Fig. 33. Conservative vs IIIc sign forms in KBo 10.20.

2.5.2 KUB 30.39+

In contrast to KBo 10.20, KUB 30.39+ frequently employs the conservative sign forms of GI, GAD, DA, ID and LI (Fig. 35), and even some MS sign forms, such as those of TAR, URU, ḪAR and SAR (Fig. 34). No IIIc sign forms are attested (Fig. 36).

Sign Name	HZL	conservative	IIIa
TAR	7		
AZ	92		
UG	93		
URU	229		
AḪ	332		
ḪAR	333		
SAR	353		

Fig. 34. Conservative vs IIIa sign forms in KUB 30.39+.

Sign Name	HZL	conser-vative
GI	30	
GAD	173	
DA	214	
ID	215	
TE	249	
KI	313	
LI	343	

Fig. 35. Conservative vs IIIb sign forms in KUB 30.39+.

Sign Name	HZL	conser-vative
SÌLA	21	
EN	40	
UN	197	
ḪA	367	

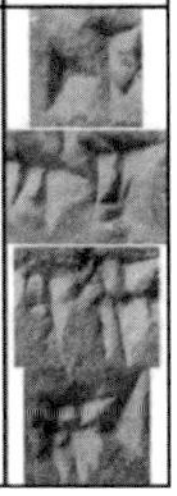

Fig. 36. Conservative vs IIIc sign forms in KUB 30.39+.

Sign Name	HZL	conser-vative	IIIa
TAR	7		
AZ	92		
UG	93		
ZU	209		
SAR	353		

Fig. 37. Conservative vs IIIa sign forms in KBo 57.18+.

Sign Name	HZL	conser-vative	IIIc
SÌLA	21		
EN	40		
UN	197		
DI	312		
KI	313		
ḪA	367		

Fig. 39. Conservative vs IIIc sign forms in KBo 57.18+.

Sign Name	HZL	conser-vative	IIIb
GI	30		
IG	67		
KÙ	69		
AG	81		
DU	128		
GAD	173		
AL	183		
DA	214		
ID	215		
URU	229		
TE	249		
LI	343		

Fig. 38. Conservative vs IIIb sign forms in KBo 57.18+.

2.5.3 KBo 57.18+

The third *comparandum* is one of the tablets on which Muwatalli's prayer to the assembly of the gods was written: KBo 57.18 + KUB 30.14 + KUB 6.45 (*CTH* 381.A). The diagnostic sign forms have already been identified by Singer (1996: 124f.), which served as a basis for the selection of signs shown in Figs. 37–39. Summing up the results, the tablet generally tends toward the use of IIIb signs, used consistently for GI, IG, DU, AL, DA, ID, TE and LI, while there are splits between the use of conservative and IIIb sign forms of KÙ and AG (Fig. 38). Notably, the MS sign form of TAR is used, and the SAR sign form is always written (a total of seven times) with one vertical, which is typical for OS, as opposed to the MS form with two verticals (Fig. 37). The only attested IIIc sign form is SÌLA (Fig. 39), which is used in the colophon (in *QA-TI*). This is a very common scribal practice, occurring even when no other signs, including SÌLA in other parts of the tablet, employ the IIIc form.

3. Proposed datings of the texts

3.1 Relative dating

The preceding palaeographic analysis of individual fragments and tablets has been synthesized in Table 2. For each text, the number of tokens of sign forms is entered in the relevant column for a category of diagnostic signs. Thus, for KBo 41.82+, the token number 7 in the column labeled "MS (or earlier)" refers to the presence of the 7 MS sign forms of E, URU, DI, KI, AḪ, ḪAR and LI, regardless of how often any one sign form occurred on the fragment (multiple occurrences of MS forms of E, URU and DI are not reflected by the token count of 7). The occurrence of different forms, i. e. conservative and innovative, of the same sign is reflected by treating the distinct sign forms as separate tokens, each of which is counted in the relevant palaeographic category. The contrasting categories of conservative and innovative sign forms have been placed between the heavy vertical lines. With respect to these contrasting categories, a clear tendency toward conservative or innovative sign forms has been indicated by bold font and gray shading of the higher token number. The three *comparanda* are highlighted by placing all values in italics. Texts referring to the prince as celebrant of the festivals are marked by an asterisk. The far right column summarizes the general palaeographic tendency of a particular tablet on the basis of the number of tokens represented for each palaeographic category.

Text		MS (or earlier)	IIIa	conservative	IIIb	conservative	IIIc	tendency
KBo 41.82+		**7**	--	**4**	--	**3**	--	IIc
KUB 30.39+		***4***	*3*	***7***	--	***4***	--	
KBo 20.77	indir. join?	1	1	**2**	1	**2**	--	IIIa
DBH 46/2.111		--	--	**3**	--	**3**	--	
KBo 13.222+		2	**4**	**8**	2	**3**	--	
KUB 25.1		4	**8**	**8**	6	**4**	--	IIIa/b
KBo 11.51		1	**3**	**7**	6	**2**	1	
KUB 10.7+		--	--	--	**5**	**3**	1	IIIb
VSNF 12.13+*	same scribe	2	2	6	**7**	**2**	1	
KBo 45.72+*		--	1	4	--	--	--	
KBo 10.20		*2*	***4***	*4*	***9***	***5***	*2*	
KBo 57.18+		*3*	*3*	*5*	***11***	***6***	*1*	
KBo 4.9		3	**5**	7	**8**	2	**3**	IIIc
KUB 2.5		**3**	2	7	**9**	2	**3**	

Table 2. Distribution of sign forms in palaeographic categories and resulting relative dating of the texts.

The earliest texts of the analyzed sample, grouped under IIc, are the outline tablet KUB 30.39+ and the day tablet KBo 41.82+. The latter especially makes use of MS sign forms, whereas the innovative sign forms of the categories IIIa, IIIb and IIIc are completely absent. KUB 30.39+ generally employs conservative sign forms, including some MS sign forms (more so than KBo 10.20 and KBo 57.18+) alongside IIIa sign forms, but uses no IIIb or IIIc sign forms at all.

The next group of texts, IIIa, can be distinguished from the IIc texts by the increased use of IIIa instead of MS sign forms. This is more obvious in KBo 13.222+ than in KBo 20.77 and DBH 46/2.111, as the latter two texts lack the diagnostic signs for the contrasting categories MS and IIIa. There are occasional occurrences of IIIb sign forms, but still no IIIc sign forms attested. The two IIIa/b texts are characterized by a marked

Sign Name	HZL	DBH 46/2.111	KBo 20.77
RU	43		
IB	44		
LUGAL	115		
UŠ	132		
TA	160		
E	187		
Ú	195		
É	199		
DA	214		
IGI	288		
ḪA	367		

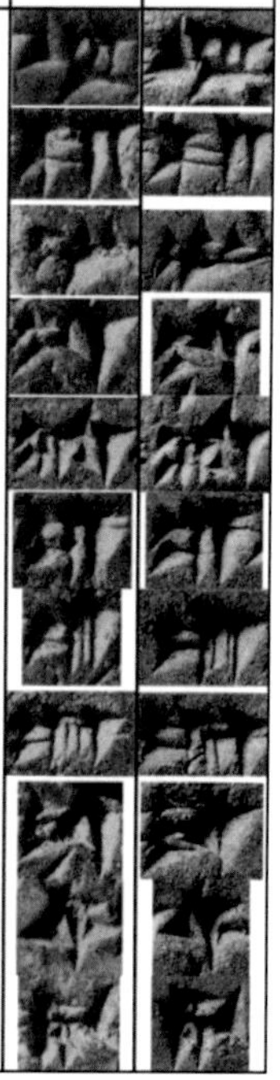

Fig. 40. Handwriting comparison of KBo 20.77 and DBH 46/2.111.

increase in the use of IIIb sign forms, but these are still outweighed by their conservative counterparts. The IIIc sign forms remain almost non-existent in this category.

The handwriting in KBo 20.77 and DBH 46/2.111 is identical (Fig. 40), and the size and format of both fragments allows them to be positioned as part of the same two-columned tablet (Fig. 41). The contents of KBo 20.77 and DBH 46/2.111, which clearly allow for their identification with the "1st tablet" of day 16 of AN.DAḪ.ŠUM, also make it highly probable that they belonged to the same tablet.

The IIIb texts include the day tablets referring to the prince as celebrant, the outline tablet KBo 10.20, and the prayer of Muwatalli. In these tablets, the IIIb sign forms occur more frequently than their conservative counterparts, although the latter continue to be well represented. The use of IIIc sign forms remains very minimal. It is also notable that, while KBo 10.20 also employs the latest (IIIc) sign form of SAR, it also uses the MS form of this sign, which can be compared to the use of the OS form of SAR in KBo 57.18+. The palaeographic proximity of KBo 10.20 and KBo 57.18+ to the texts VSNF 12.13+ and KBo 45.72+ in which the prince celebrates the festival in the temple of Zababa is less clear. This is due to the frequent use of IIIa conservative signs in both VSNF 12.13+ and KBo 45.72+. However, the conservative sign forms of GAD, TE and LI

Fig. 41. Proposed positions of KBo 20.77 and DBH 46/2.111 as part of the same tablet.

that appear in VSNF 12.13+ and KBo 45.72+ are also used in KBo 10.20, and two of them (GAD and LI) also occur in KBo 57.18+. Furthermore, VSNF 12.13+ makes equal use of IIIb sign forms and, except for a IIIc ḪA, does not otherwise employ IIIc signs forms. In sum, the palaeographic characteristics suggest that VSNF 12.13+, KBo 10.20 and KBo 57.18+ might stem from the same period.

One must be cautious about drawing conclusions from KBo 45.72+, which preserves very few of the diagnostic signs at all, and the fact that most of these are conservative may be due purely to chance. If the IIIb sign forms preserved in VSNF 12.13+ (GI, IG, NI, DU, AL, DI, KI) had also been preserved in KBo 45.72+ (they are in fact all absent), the results may have looked quite different. Furthermore, the handwriting on VSNF 12.13+ and KBo 45.72+ looks so similar, that they could indeed have been written by the same scribe (Fig. 42). While the contents of each does not allow for VSNF 12.13+ and KBo 45.72+ to be positioned together in a single tablet (see section 2.4 and Fig. 25), it is still possible that these fragments belonged to two separate tablets written by one and the same scribe. There is no reason to exclude the palaeographic similarity of KBo 45.72+ with VSNF 12.13+, KBo 10.20 and KBo 57.18+.

Sign Name	HZL	VSNF 12.13+	KBo 45.72+
GAD	173		
GAD	173		
Ú	195		
É	199		
UZU	203		
DA	214		
ID	215		
TUR	237		
LI	343		
SAR	353		
ḪA	367		

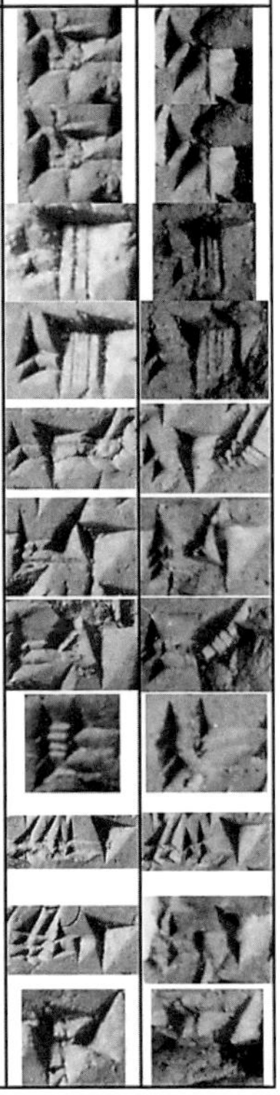

Fig. 42. Handwriting comparison of VSNF 12.13+ and KBo 45.72+.

The final group, IIIc, continues to make occasional use of MS sign forms and has a mixture of conservative and IIIb sign forms, though the latter are in the majority. Unlike the IIIb texts, the use of IIIc signs outweighs the use of their conservative counterparts. However, some signs continue to occur frequently or exclusively in their conservative rather than IIIc forms, namely, SÌLA and UN.

3.2 Absolute dating

The earliest text, KBo 41.82+, can possibly be dated to the reign of Šuppiluliuma I when multiple individual festivals were probably first organized into the extensive, month-long conglomerate AN.DAḪ.ŠUM festival described in the outline tablets. Since KBo 41.82+ and KBo 20.77 were both found in Building A on Büyükkale, KBo 41.82+ may even have served as the *Vorlage* for KBo 20.77, written down perhaps a century or so later. KUB 30.39+ is the earliest preserved outline tablet of AN.DAḪ.ŠUM and perhaps one of the first outline tablets of AN.DAḪ.ŠUM that were ever recorded. The IIIa and IIIa/b texts were written down in the decades following, but their date of origin cannot be pinpointed specifically.

The IIIb texts were probably written down during the time of Muwatalli II. With the exception of KUB 10.7+, these texts attest to the celebration of the festival in Zababa's temple by the prince instead of the king. Contemporary with these texts was the prayer of Muwatalli, KBo 57.18+. Since the entries for days 10–31 preserved on KBo 10.20 are missing from the outline tablet of KUB 30.39+, we cannot know whether the latter described the festival in the temple of Zababa performed by the king or as a *ḫadauri*-festival celebrated by the prince (or someone else). In light of the earlier texts, it seems more likely that the outline tablet of KUB 30.39+ would have named the king as the celebrant. Furthermore, the festival for the Storm-god of lightning on day 18 would not have been included in the itinerary of the AN.DAḪ.ŠUM festival described by KUB 30.39+. The total number of days of the AN.DAḪ.ŠUM festival was 35 according to KUB 30.39+ rev. 5′, while KBo 10.20 rev. IV 21′ gives the total as 38 days. The additional three days of KBo 10.20 implies that some of the festivities described in this outline tablet were not yet included in the outline tablet of KUB 30.39+.

Remarkably, the IIIc texts do not designate the prince, but rather the king, as celebrating the festival in the temple of Zababa. These were likely written down in the years after the death of Muwatalli II, thus the celebration in the temple of Zababa seems to have reverted to its former state, that is, with the king as celebrant, and no longer the prince.

As far as the relative palaeographic and absolute dating are concerned, KBo 20.77, written by the scribe Karunu and possibly belonging to the same tablet as DBH 46/2.111, is an outlier. Gordin (2015: 240) has dated the scribe Karunu on prosopographical grounds to the end of the reign of Ḫattušili III or the beginning of the reign of Tudḫaliya IV. However, KBo 20.77 and DBH 46/2.111, surprisingly, not only lack the characteristic IIIc sign forms that could be expected for this period but also the IIIb sign forms as well. If the prosopographical dating of Karunu is correct, then he seems to have employed conservative sign forms in a period when the use of IIIb and IIIc sign forms had already become widespread.[16] However, it should be noted that KBo 20.77 and DBH 46/2.111 contain relatively few diagnostic signs, making palaeographic conclusions about these fragments uncertain. We therefore cannot know whether KBo 20.77 and DBH 46/2.111 were written earlier than, later than or around the same time as the IIIc texts KBo 4.9 and KUB 2.5.

4. Conclusions

The palaeographic analysis of the texts describing the 16th day of the AN.DAḪ.ŠUM festival, two of the AN.DAḪ.ŠUM outline tablets, and the prayer of Muwatalli (KBo 57.18+) offers further evidence that the reign of Muwatalli II was a watershed moment for the introduction of new sign forms that gradually displaced older ones. The IIIb texts likely stem from this period and employ very heterogeneous sign forms. The fre-

16 Compare KBo 30.165 (*CTH* 634), also written by Karunu but under the supervision of Anuwanza (see Gordin 2015: 192), whose career began prior to Šipaziti's.

<table>
<tr><th colspan="2">Text</th><th>tendency</th><th>Absolute Date</th></tr>
<tr><td colspan="2">KBo 41.82+</td><td rowspan="2">IIc</td><td rowspan="2">(Šuppiluliuma I?)</td></tr>
<tr><td colspan="2">KUB 30.39+</td></tr>
<tr><td colspan="2">KBo 13.222+</td><td>IIIa</td><td rowspan="3">?</td></tr>
<tr><td colspan="2">KUB 25.1</td><td rowspan="2">IIIa/b</td></tr>
<tr><td colspan="2">KBo 11.51</td></tr>
<tr><td colspan="2">KUB 10.7+</td><td rowspan="5">IIIb</td><td rowspan="5">Muwatalli II</td></tr>
<tr><td>VSNF 12.13+*</td><td rowspan="2">same scribe</td></tr>
<tr><td>KBo 45.72+*</td></tr>
<tr><td colspan="2">KBo 10.20</td></tr>
<tr><td colspan="2">KBo 57.18+</td></tr>
<tr><td colspan="2">KBo 4.9</td><td rowspan="2">IIIc</td><td rowspan="2">?</td></tr>
<tr><td colspan="2">KUB 2.5</td></tr>
<tr><td>KBo 20.77</td><td rowspan="2">indir. join?</td><td rowspan="2">IIIa!</td><td rowspan="2">Ḫattušili III / Tutḫaliya IV</td></tr>
<tr><td>DBH 46/2.111</td></tr>
</table>

Table 3. Absolute dating of the texts of the palaeographical analysis.

quency of IIIb signs forms stands out, but the continued use of the contrasting conservative sign forms is made clear by their frequent presence in the relevant texts. Significantly, the same texts show a clear tendency to continue the use of MS sign forms, while rarely employing IIIc sign forms. In most cases, the only IIIc form used is ḪA. These texts can be clearly distinguished from the IIIa group, which rarely uses IIIb sign forms and almost never uses IIIc sign forms. In our text sample, the IIIc group continues to employ more conservative (MS and IIIa) sign forms, while at the same time giving slight preference to IIIb sign forms. The presence of multiple IIIc sign forms is the critical factor that distinguishes these texts from those of the IIIb group.

The reign of Muwatalli II may have introduced temporary changes to the itinerary of the AN.DAḪ.ŠUM festival. If our dating of KBo 10.20, VSNF 12.13+ and KBo 45.72+ to the reign of Muwatalli II is correct,[17] then the changes reflected in them could be explained by the political and religious developments that occurred under this ruler. The IIc, IIIa and IIIa/b groups clearly testify that the king performed the festival in the temple of Zababa on day 16 of AN.DAH.ŠUM. What changes would have made it necessary for the king to be present at the "great assembly" in the temple of the Storm-god rather than at the festival in Zababa's temple, as reflected by KBo 10.20? It is helpful to note what celebrations for or in a sanctuary of the Storm-god took place at all in the entire course of the AN.DAḪ.ŠUM festival as described by KBo 10.20 (which preserves at least partial descriptions of all 38 days). If we exclude sanctuaries of secondary hypostases of the Storm-god, such as the Storm-god of Zippalanda, of Aleppo, or of lightning, as well as the rites such as of "opening the pithos" of a Storm-god or the invocation (*mūga-*) of the Storm-god, we are left with the following events:

17 This assumes the possibility of attributing KBo 45.72+ to the IIIb rather than the IIIa group (see above).

- day 14: a rite at the cult stela of the Storm-god in the boxwood grove, possibly in preparation for day 15 (KBo 10.20 obv. II 29, partially damaged)
- day 15: the slaughtering of sheep and cattle at the cult stela of the Storm-god in the boxwood grove (obv. II 30f.)
- day 16: the great assembly in the temple of the Storm-god (obv. II 32f.)
- day 17: the prince's celebration of the *ḫadauri-* festival in the temple of the Storm-god (obv. II 41–43)

Days 14 and 15 pertain to a natural cult sanctuary, likely outside of Ḫattuša and not within a monumental temple. They also do not refer to a "festival" (EZEN$_4$) or "great assembly" (*šalli ašeššar*) *per se*. Therefore, the events of days 14 and 15 may not have carried the same significance as a festival or great assembly in the temple of the deity. According to KBo 10.20, day 16 was the only day on which the king performed a celebration in the temple of the main Storm-god (presumably Temple I of Ḫattuša). Obviously, a festival in the largest temple of Ḫattuša for arguably the most significant deity of the state pantheon could not have been left out of the extensive AN.DAḪ.ŠUM festival. It is possible, however, that in the decades prior to the reign of Muwatalli II and the writing down of KBo 10.20, this festival in the temple of the Storm-god might have taken place on a different day.

Although the description of numerous days is missing in KUB 30.39+, it is certain that this MS or early NS tablet would not have included a celebration for the Storm-god of lightning, who is only known from a later period as the personal deity of Muwatalli II. This is supported by the fewer number of days of the AN.DAḪ.ŠUM festival, 35, as recorded in KUB 30.39+ in contrast to the total of 38 days according to KBo 10.20. This also implies that, in addition to the festival for the Storm-god of lightning on day 18, at least two other festivals (or days) described in KBo 10.20 were not included in the outline tablet of KUB 30.39+. If KBo 10.20 presents us with an expanded itinerary for the AN.DAḪ.ŠUM festival from the time of Muwatalli II, then perhaps KUB 30.39+ reflects an itinerary from years prior that was less dense, allowing the king to perform more or all of the festivals personally, including the celebration in the temple of Zababa. This is confirmed by most day tablets describing the celebration of this festival by the king. Since the king is also the celebrant in the IIIc texts of KBo 4.9 and KUB 2.5, which were presumably written after the reign of Muwatalli II, this suggests more changes occurred following the period in which the prince celebrated the *ḫadauri-* festival in the temple of Zababa. A festival such as that for the Storm-god of lightning on day 18 may have been abandoned after the death of Muwatalli II. This could have freed up a day in the itinerary of the AN.DAḪ.ŠUM festival, giving the king once again enough time to perform the festival in the temple of Zababa personally, thus reverting back to the standard practice of prior generations.

Excursus: Forms of SAR

The different forms of the sign SAR have been mentioned several times in the above discussion. These are presented together in Fig. 43 in order to highlight the chronologi-

Text	I	IIc	IIIa	IIIb	IIIc
KBo 41.82+ (IIc)					
KUB 30.39+ (IIc/IIIa)					
KBo 45.72+ (IIIa?)					
KBo 11.51 (IIIa/b)					
KUB 25.1 (IIIa/b)					
VSNF 12.13+ (IIIb)					
KBo 10.20 (IIIb)					
KBo 10.20 (IIIb)		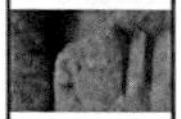			
KBo 57.18+ (IIIb)					
KBo 4.9 (IIIc)					
KUB 2.5 (IIIc)					

Fig. 43. Overview of the various forms of SAR.

cal development of this sign. The oldest form (I), known already from OS texts, is characterized by the use of the single (rather than double) vertical. It is not surprising to find this form in KBo 41.82+, which generally uses IIc sign forms. It is, however, perplexing that KBo 57.18+ (the prayer of Muwatalli), which belongs to the IIIb group (see Table 2), would repeatedly and consistently used this same archaic form of SAR. The next development is the use of a second vertical, resulting in the IIc (or MS) form of SAR. This form continued to be used in later periods, but often occurs alongside of further developed forms of SAR (e. g. in KUB 25.1, KBo 10.20 and KBo 4.9). It should be noted that KBo 10.20 employs the IIc form of SAR in the colophon only (occurring there two times), while using the IIIc form elsewhere. The form identified here as IIIa deviates only slightly from the IIc form in that it lowers the first of the two verticals, which generally remain positioned close to one another. The IIIb form, however, separates the verticals and moves the lowered first vertical significantly to the left, just after the *Winkelhaken*. This seems to have led to the form of SAR where the verticals and horizontals form a box after the *Winkelhaken*, which does not occur in our text sample (compare HZL Nr. 353/13–14). The latest form, IIIc, retains this box shape, but significantly reduces its width. The resulting sign form looks quite similar to the late form of LI, with the verticals aligned at the same height and immediately following the *Winkelhaken*. The narrow box is enclosed at the top and bottom by very short horizontals that appear to be squeezed in between the two closely set verticals.

Bibliography

Akdoğan, Rukiye

2012 Neue Textzusammenschlüsse zu dem Text eines Opferrituals für die Statuen der Könige (KBo 41.82 + KBo 20.38 + KBo 25.74 + KBo 40.61) (*CTH* 660). *NABU* 2012/1: 20–26.

2013 Zu einigen unveröffentlichten Bo-Tafeln. *AoF* 40: 1–19.

Badalì, Enrico, Christian Zinko, and Michaela Ofitsch

1994 *Der 16. Tag des AN.TAḪ.ŠUM-Festes. Text, Übersetzung, Glossar.* 2nd ed. Scientia 20. Graz: Institut für Sprachwissenschaft.

Goetze, Albrecht

1950 Hittite Rituals, Incantations, and Description of Festivals. In: James B. Pritchard (ed.), *Ancient Near Eastern Texts Relating to the Old Testament.* Princeton: Princeton University, 346–61.

Gordin, Shai

2015 *Hittite Scribal Circles: Scholarly Tradition and Writing Habits.* StBoT 59. Wiesbaden: Harrassowitz.

Güterbock, Hans Gustav

1960 An Outline of the Hittite AN.TAḪ.ŠUM Festival. *JNES* 19: 80–89.

Haas, Volkert

1994 *Geschichte der Hethitischen Religion.* HbOr 1/15. Leiden; New York; Köln: Brill.

Kassian, Alexei S., Andrej Korolëv, and Andrej Sidel'tsev

2002 *Hittite Funerary Ritual šalliš waštaiš.* AOAT 288. Münster: Ugarit.

Klinger, Jörg

2008 Texte der Hethiter. Rituale. In: Bernd Janowski and Gernot Wilhelm (eds.), *Omina, Orakel, Rituale und Beschwörungen.* TUAT NF 4. Gütersloh: Gütersloher Verlag, 187–206.

Kryszeń, Adam

forthc. *A Critical Edition of the nuntarriyašḫa- Festival.* Das Corpus der hethitischen Festrituale. Hethitologie-Portal Mainz.

Singer, Itamar

1996 *Muwatalli's Prayer to the Assembly of Gods Through the Storm-God of Lightning (CTH 381).* Atlanta, Georgia: Scholars Press.

Waal, Willemijn

2015 *Hittite Diplomatics. Studies in Ancient Document Format and Record Management.* StBoT 57. Wiesbaden: Harrassowitz.

Weeden, Mark

2011 *Hittite Logograms and Hittite Scholarship.* StBoT 54. Wiesbaden: Harrassowitz.

WRITING PRACTICES AND SCRIBAL CUSTOMS IN HITTITE DIVINATION TEXTS

Andrea Trameri
Julius-Maximilians-Universität Würzburg

Abstract

Hittite tablets of oracular content exhibit a range of features unique or particularly distinctive to this genre. The article discusses these features as a source of information on oracular practice in the Hittite context, on the textualisation of divination, and within a broader scope of the study of Hittite writing traditions. The topics covered include the use of different scripts in oracle tablets and the reasons for this practice (§3.1); the presence of blank spaces and paragraphs in oracle tablets, with an analysis of selected documents (§3.2); the use of abbreviations across the various divination genres, and the reasons behind these writing habits (§3.3); and the purpose and scope of the usage of tablets of small and special format for oracular writing (§3.4).

1. Introduction

This article discusses distinctive writing and scribal practices in tablets of oracular content within the Hittite corpus. While not all of these features and scribal habits are necessarily unique to oracle texts, they appear to be common in this genre and, to some extent, differentiate these texts from other types. Due to the high number of oracular tablets and fragments, a complete examination and evaluation of the characteristics of oracular writing would only be possible after a comprehensive study of the corpus. This is one of the tasks of the project, *The Hittite Corpus of Divinatory Texts: Digital Edition and Cultural Historical Analysis* (*HDivT*), initiated in 2022, whose primary goal is the publication of a fully annotated, open-access corpus of the Hittite divinatory texts, along with other selected texts related to divination.[1] This article's content derives from ongoing research and preparatory work for the text editions within the project and from an initial study of the many fragments with oracular content catalogued under *CTH* 582.

As will be shown in this article, the analysis of writing habits in oracular tablets provides essential information for the broader investigation of scribal practices in Hittite Anatolia. Additionally, it elucidates aspects of the logic behind text composition and organization, the relationship between the texts and the activities of oracular in-

1 The texts discussed in this article will be available in the online editions of the project and some will be discussed in additional publications by the present author and B. Christiansen (Universität München). Excerpts from original texts and translations derive from editions in preparation by the present author unless otherwise specified.

quiry, and the interaction between scribes and divination professionals. Some distinctive writing practices recurring in oracular texts, which will be discussed here, are (1) the use of multiple scripts in the same tablet; (2) special writing layouts, paragraphing, and spacing, notably the presence of blank paragraphs in the tablets; (3) the use of abbreviations within the technical lexicon and cases of 'cursive' scripts; and (4) the use of 'micro tablets' for oracular writing, with some rare examples of perforated tablets.

Due to the absence of an original 'theoretical' literature of oracular inquiry from the Hittite archives and the fact that the texts focus on oracle results, few details on the procedures are known. How divination was carried out can thus be approached primarily on the basis of limited data: results, descriptions of oracular observations, and the experts' interpretation of the signs observed. Specific writing habits, scribal conventions, and formal aspects of oracular tablets are potential sources of information on the performance of the oracles and are among the few tools available for research.

While introducing the discussion on oracular writing, it is helpful to refer to the distinction between 'permanent' and 'ephemeral' texts primarily reflected by the existence of texts with duplicates versus texts that exist only in one copy.[2] Hittite oracles typically belong to the second category. This distribution reflects, again, the lack of a substantial corpus of oracular 'theory' (such as omen collections) and the focus of scribal activity on oracular 'practice' (oracles).[3]

Apart from the large groups catalogued primarily by oracle techniques,[4] the corpus of minor oracle fragments collected under *CTH* 582 includes several texts that have not been previously edited or studied in detail. Some of these documents are of interest for the study of writing features and have been selectively discussed in this article.

2. Chronology of the Hittite oracular corpus and palaeography

The features of oracular writing discussed in this article are not strictly related to Hittite palaeography as the term is often intended in Hittitology, i. e. as the study of sign forms and variants, aiming at text-dating or the individuation of scribal handwritings, but are concerned with palaeography in a less restrictive meaning, i. e. general aspects of epigraphic interest, which are potentially informative for the study of these texts and Hittite writing customs.

2 See in particular van den Hout 1998: 10–32; 2002: 864f.; also Waal 2015: 12f., and 20–39 for the terminology 'permanent' vs 'ephemeral', and on tablet formats.

3 For an orientation on the research terminology and divination in Mesopotamia, see Maul 2003: 45–88; among the Hittites, Beal 2002 and van den Hout 2003a; 2003b. This article will not consider the omen texts since these belong primarily to series in Akkadian and of Mesopotamian derivation (*CTH* 531–560), although translations and versions in Hittite also exist.

4 Together with the texts catalogued by Laroche on the basis of topics or the deities involved (*CTH* 561–569), the primary groups are: KIN oracles (*CTH* 572), augury (*CTH* 573) – both practices original to Anatolia –, *ḪURRI*-bird oracles (*CTH* 574; to be distinguished from augury, and whose origins and exact modes of practice remain unclear), and extispicy (*CTH* 570–571), a type of inquiry of Mesopotamian derivation. Several oracle reports include multiple types at once, with various combinations (hence the 'mixed' groups *CTH* 577–580). Other oracle types exist, but with few examples (clinomancy, snake oracles, etc.). For useful overviews of Hittite divination, see Beal 2002 and Haas 2008.

Apart from one report in Old Script (KBo 18.151), the earliest documents are Middle Script and can be assigned historically to the beginning of the New Kingdom (Early New Kingdom, ca. 1425–1350 BC), i. e. the reigns of Tudḫaliya I, Arnuwanda I and Tudḫaliya II/III (with a majority, most likely, dating to the reign of the latter). Among the earliest documents, several belong to the local corpora from outside the capital archives. From Tapikka (Maşat Höyük) comes an important corpus of letters from the Early New Kingdom, some with oracular content (augury, KIN oracles). Šamuḫa (Kayalıpınar) yielded two early letters with oracular content (DAAM 1.21, 1.31). In Šarišša (Kuşaklı), a few KIN oracles and bird oracles were found, notably two letters with bird/KIN and bird oracles of early date.[5] Šapinuwa (Ortaköy) provided several early bird oracles and extispicy reports, still unpublished, but apparently no KIN oracles.[6] A letter with bird oracles from Büklükale also dates to this period or shortly after (BKT 19).[7]

From a purely palaeographic perspective, based on the ongoing work on groups of texts currently being edited for the *HDivT* project, it is not possible to establish conclusively whether certain scribal groups wrote mainly or only oracle texts and whether within the corpus one can observe palaeographic differences and standards. At least preliminarily, these answers may be answered negatively. The texts do not display clear palaeographic differentiation from other Hittite tablets. Thus, it does not seem that certain scribes or groups of scribes were specifically trained for and assigned the task of writing only oracular texts. Neither does it appear that different scribal "schools" or groups were responsible for distinct types of oracle texts, although there are differences across individual types in certain writing practices (§3.3 infra).

However, some general scribal habits and peculiar usages of oracular writing can be outlined, which appear to be primarily bound to the texts' nature, content, and practical purposes.

3. Aspects of Hittite oracular writing and oracle tablets

3.1 Tablets with multiple scripts

Some tablets of oracular content contain sections of text written in different cuneiform scripts. Most of the examples of tablets with multiple scripts[8] discussed in previous literature belong to oracles; thus, relative to other genres, this phenomenon appears to be more common in this type of text. On the other hand, in absolute terms, only a handful of examples stand out within the large number of texts in the corpus. In most cases, a different script (in size, handwriting, or both) within one text typically belongs to portions of texts written later than the rest, usually as a separate paragraph. There

5 Published in Wilhelm 1998. The other oracle reports from Šarišša which can be dated palaeographically are all of late date (published in KuSa 1/1 = Wilhelm 1997).

6 Information courtesy of A. Süel and D. Schwemer.

7 See the contribution of Mark Weeden in this volume.

8 I will use 'script' to recognize specific characteristics distinguishing cuneiform writings, including the size of writing, sign forms/variants, ductus, and any other salient visual element. For a discussion of the terminology, see van den Hout 2012: 152f.; Gordin 2015: 15–17; Cammarosano 2015: 170–72.

are cases of distinct scripts within the same paragraph as well. These tablets raise a number of questions, such as: (1) whether the distribution of writing on the tablet corresponds to differences in content; (2) whether the writing belongs to the same or a different scribal hand; and (3) whether the whole text was written on one or several occasions, which might explain the different appearance of a script.[9] Although most of the texts are fragmentary, several provide hints on the background of the text composition and the writing process.

A few examples of tablets with different scripts were listed by Berman (1982: 94 n. 5) and will also be discussed here in more detail. More recently, three documents were considered in a discussion on the writing organization of KIN oracles in Warbinek 2019: 147–49 (KBo 18.142, KUB 49.39 and KUB 52.41). In the latter study, the analysis of these examples focused primarily on space management and in terms of writing within 'confined space', but in the following pages, it will be shown that space management does not seem to be a primary motive of the use of different scripts. For the scope of this study, I was able to identify other relevant fragments, including smaller and poorly preserved ones, which nonetheless contribute to the discussion of this topic.

KBo 18.142 (Fig. 1).[10] The tablet has been catalogued as a letter with oracles (*CTH* 581), but it is not a letter in the proper sense (van den Hout 2001: 432). It has no address formula or other epistolary features and contains the full report of an individual KIN oracular inquiry. The landscape format and the oval shape of the tablet are also more common to texts of oracular content.[11] On the other hand, it is possible that tablets of this kind were used in epistolary exchanges, for delivering oracle results over a distance, and as 'attachments' of a proper letter.[12]

The text concerns the potential predictive meaning of a dream of the queen, where she had seen "witchcraft" against the wife of a certain Ḫaranziti. The obverse contains the oracular question, which reaches the lower edge of the tablet. The oracle report, written on the reverse, established that the sign was not negative, thus excluding the possibility that the dream warned of mortal danger for the woman. The short text can be quoted in its entirety:

KBo 18.142

(script A) [obv. 1] UḪ$_7$-*za-kán ku-in* [2] Ù MUNUS.LUGAL [3] *A-NA* DAM ^{m}TI$_8$^{MUŠEN}-LÚ [4] *an-da I-MUR* [5] *[n]a-at-ši ma-a-an* [lo.e. 6] [S]AG.DU-*aš* ÚŠ-*an* [7] *nu* KIN NU.SIG$_5$-*du*
(script B) [rev. 8] ^{D}UTU AN-*E* GUB-*iš* [9] *ŠA* DAM ^{m}⸢TI$_8$⸣^{MUŠEN}-LÚ ZAG-*tar* ME-*aš* [10] *na-at pa-⸢an⸣-ga-u-i pa-iš* [11] *INA* UD 2^{KAM} SIG$_5$-*u-an-za* ZALAG.GA-*an* ME-[*aš*][12] *na-an*

9 Although clay may otherwise dry quickly, it is possible to keep a tablet suitable for writing virtually indefinitely if the material is kept sufficiently moist, such as by wrapping it in a wet cloth. It is also possible, in principle, to moisten a superficial layer of a dried tablet and write on it, although this method might be suboptimal for the writing results, and is more prone to ruin other previously written portions of text. Thus, different methods of writing and re-writing, and even small delays within the inscribing process, may have an impact on the aspect of the script.

10 See Mouton 2007a: 220f.; 2007b: 551–55; Warbinek 2020: 307f.

11 On this tablet type, Waal 2015: 35 (type catalogued 'type B III: Oval-shaped or rounded').

12 For this interpretation, see Soysal 2000: 85–89; one such example is the OS KIN oracle KBo 18.151.

Fig. 1. KBo 18.142 (obv. – rev.). Photos: hethiter.net/: fotarch B1133e; B1116a.

〈DINGIR〉.MAḪ-*ni pa-iš* [13] *INA* UD 3^{KAM} ^{D}10 GUB-*iš* [14] MU^{KAM}-*an* ME-*aš* [15] *nu-kán* ^{D}GUL-*še* [u.e. 16] DA.BI-*i*[13] ZI-*ni* SIG$_5$

(script A) [obv. 1–7] The dream which[14] the Queen saw concerning witchcraft against the wife of Ḫaranziti: If for her it is (like a) death sentence, let the KIN be unfavourable.
(script B) [rev. 8-16] The SUN GOD OF HEAVEN arose; he took the RIGHT(NESS) of the wife of Ḫaranziti and gave it to the ASSEMBLY. On the 'SECOND DAY': the GOOD took the LIGHT and gave it to ḪANNAḪANNA. On the 'THIRD DAY': the STORM GOD arose; he took the YEAR, (and gave it) to the WHOLE SOUL OF THE FATE DEITY. Favourable.

Remarkably, the obverse (the question) and the reverse (the report and answer) are written in distinct cuneiform scripts. Apparently, the reverse was written after some delay, as evidenced by the features of the script, written when the clay was much drier. Traces of fingerprints (in the bottom right part of the obverse) and surface depressions in correspondence to thick clusters of wedges (e. g. the sign MUR) indicate that the clay was quite soft and malleable when the obverse was written, whereas the appearance of the script in the reverse is easily explained by the significantly hardened surface at the time of writing.

Soysal (2000: 88f.) considered that the scripts probably belong to the same scribe, which is possible, even though this remains difficult to determine with certainty, given that the different writing conditions might have affected the appearance of the script. Differently, Mouton (2007b: 552f.) considered it more likely that the scripts belong to two distinct scribes. The script of the reverse has been characterized as "careless hand-

13 I follow Kloekhorst's convincing proposal (Kloekhorst 2022) that the Hitt. word *dapi(a)-* 'all' is a phantom word, and the sequence is to be read as a logogram representing Hitt. *ḫumant-* (see also n. 86 below).

14 Mouton 2007a: 221 translated "L'ensorcellement que la reine a vu dans un rêve ..." (also Warbinek 2020: 308 "La stregoneria che la regina in un sogno ... vide"). However, *alwanzatar* (UḪ$_7$) is neuter, so one expects *kuit* in agreement. With this reading, one also needs to interpret *=za* as chain particle, but its usage with the verb 'to see' is difficult to explain. Instead, the form must be the abl. *alwanzannaz, alwanzešnaz,* while the relative pronoun refers to 'the dream'. The resumption in the neuter *=at* in the next sentence is less problematic, referring back to the whole 'content' of the previous sentence.

writing" (Soysal 2000: 87), but its less legible form might likewise have been conditioned by the less-than-ideal state of the writing surface.

KUB 49.39 (Fig. 2). This fragment contains multiple oracle reports, presumably for a lengthy inquiry with several questions. The preserved reports are of two distinct types: KIN oracles and bird oracles (augury). On the obverse, two paragraphs were written in two scripts different from the one used throughout the rest of the tablet. On the reverse, one paragraph is also written in a different script. The scheme in Fig. 3 summarizes the content of the paragraphs and the different scripts employed.[15]

KUB 49.39

§1 $^{\text{obv. II 1'}}$ [...]x x[...] $^{2'}$ [... SI]G$_5$-*ru* $^{3'}$ [... -*a*]*n* NU.SIG$_5$ /

$^{\text{(obv. II 1'-3')}}$ [...] let [the KIN$^?$] be favourable. [...] ... Unfavourable.

§2 $^{4'}$ [...] *ar-ḫa tar-nu-um-ma-an-zi* SI×SÁ-*at* $^{5'}$ [... *d*]*a-ni-nu-ma-an-zi* ⌜SI⌝×SÁ-*an-ta-at* $^{6'}$ [...] *ku-in-ki ar-ḫa tar-na-an-zi* $^{7'}$ [...]x ⌜*da-a*⌝-*an nu-kán* DINGIR-*LIM*-*ni* DA.BI-*i* ZI-*ni* NU.SIG$_5$ /

$^{(4'-7')}$ [... *he did not grow rebellious*][16] it was confirmed to be released completely. [...] it was confirmed [...] to be set up. [...] they (will) release whichever [...] completely. [...] taken, (and given) to the WHOLE SOUL OF THE DEITY. Unfavourable.

§3 $^{8'}$ [...] ⌜*Ú*⌝-*UL ša-al-la-iš-ta ar-ḫa tar-nu-um-ma-an-zi* SI×SÁ-*at* [...] ^{D}10 ^{URU}*ne-ri-ik* DINGIR-*LUM* GAL ^{D}*ú-li-li-ia-aš-ši-*⌜*in*⌝ *na-aš-*⌜*za*$^?$⌝ [... *ki*]-*nu-un-ma-aš-kán a-ri-ia-še-eš-ni ku-it an-da Ú-UL píd-da-a-*⌜*i*⌝ [... *n*]*u* KIN NU.SIG$_5$-*du pa-an-ku-uš-za wa-aš-túl da-a-aš nu-kán* DINGIR^{MEŠ}-*aš* NU.SIG$_5$ /

$^{(8'-11')}$ [...] he did not grow *rebellious*:[17] it was confirmed to be released completely. [...] the Storm god of Nerik, the Great Deity (and$^?$) Uliliyašši; and he [...]. But now, *because* he does not *run to the oracle*[18] [...]. Let the KIN be unfavourable. The ASSEMBLY took SIN and (gave it) to THE GODS. Unfavourable.

§4 $^{12'}$ [...][19] *nu* KIN SIG$_5$-*ru* LUGAL-*uš-za* ZAG-*tar* ME-*aš nu-kán* ^{D}GUL-⌜*še*⌝[20] $^{13'}$ [...]x x *a-aš-šu* ME-*an na-at* DINGIR.MAḪ-*ni pa-iš* $^{14'}$ [...] ⌜^{D}⌝UTU AN GUB-*iš* NINDA.GUR$_4$.RA ME-*aš na-an pa-an.-u*$^?$-*i*$^?$ ⌜*pa*$^?$-*iš*$^{?!}$⌝[21] SIG$_5$[22] /

15 Previous studies have offered only partial editions (of the oracular response sections): Warbinek 2020: 441–43; Sakuma 2009: vol. II 330f. Transliteration in Tischler 2019: 63–65.

16 See obv. II 8'.

17 Lit. 'become/grow big(?)'; see CHD Š 83: "[...] did not grow big(?). It was determined for setting free". For the possible translation 'rebellious', 'arrogant' see, e. g. Hoffner 1975: 57 n. 69.

18 The meaning of this sentence remains difficult; translation follows CHD P 355 (*piddai-* A).

19 Probably to be restored with the standard formula: [*IŠ-TU* ^{MUNUS}ŠU.GI *ER-TUM QA-TAM-MA-pát n*]*u* ... (e. g. also Warbinek 2020: 442).

20 From photo collation; omitted in autography KUB 49.39 and Warbinek 2020: 442.

21 Warbinek 2020: 442 reads: ⌜*pa-an-ga-u-i pa-iš*⌝, but the sequence is dubious, based on photo collation. The present reading (*pa-an-u*$^?$-*i*$^?$) may be a different, abbreviated form of the same oracle 'symbol'.

22 From photo collation. Some traces were also copied in autography KUB 49.39, omitted in Warbinek 2020: 442. The sign is written, isolated, below line 14', overwriting the paragraph line.

(12′-14′) [*Through the Old Woman, the same question* ...] let the KIN be favourable: the KING took RIGHT(NESS), and (gave it) to the FATE DEITY. [*In the 'SECOND DAY'* ...] GOOD (was) taken, and [...] gave it to ḪANNAḪANNA. [...] the SUN GOD OF HEAVEN arose, he took the THICK BREAD and *gave it*? *to THE ASS*[*EMBLY*?]. Favourable.

§5 15′ [... *ku-i*]*t ŠA* DINGIR.MAḪ *da-li-ia-u-wa-ar* 16′ [...]-⌜*ú*⌝-*ul-la ar-ḫa tar-nu-um-ma-an-zi* SI×SÁ-*at* 17′ [...]x *ku-u-uš ku-i-e-eš* DINGIR.MAḪ$^{\text{ḪI.A}}$ ⌜*ki-nu-un*⌝ *da-n*[*i*?-*nu-* ...] 18′ [... SI×SÁ-*a*]*n-ta-at nu a-pé-e-el* ⌜*ŠA*⌝ DINGIR.MAḪ x x[...] 19′ [...]x-⌜*e-ek*⌝-*mi na-at-mu-kán pé-ra-an* x x[...]

(15′-19′) [...] *which* [...] the release of/from Ḫannaḫanna. [...] ... (it) was confirmed to be released completely. [...] these which Ḫannaḫanna, now ...[...] was confirmed. However, that [...] of Ḫannaḫanna [... ...] I [...], and for me it/they [...] before.

§6 rev. III 1 [...]x-*un-ma*-x x x x x x[...] 2 [...]-*an iš*-⌜*ḫi-ú-la-aḫ-ḫu-u-un*⌝ [...] 3 [...]-*an-ma* ⌜x x⌝ GÙB-*la-aḫ-ḫu-u*[*n* ...] 4 [... S]IG$_5$-*ru* /

(rev. III 1-4) [...]... [...]... I made swear an oath ...[...]... I made it unfavourable ...[...]... let [...] be favourable.

§7 5 [... -*i*]*t*? MUNUS.LUGAL 𒑱 *i-pár-wi*$_5$-*iš-ša-*[...] 6 [... *nu* MUŠEN$^{\text{ḪI.A}}$] SI×SÁ-*an-du* 2 *a-li-li-iš-k*[*án*[23] 7 [...-*a*]*n*? *ar-ḫa pa-a-er* TI$_8$^{MUŠEN}-*ma* [...] 8 [... *p*]*é.*?[24] *ar-ḫa pa-a-er* EGIR KASKAL-*NI* ⌜2⌝[...] 9 [...] ⌜*ú*⌝-*e-er na-at* 2-*an ar-ḫa* ⌜*pa-a*⌝-[*er*] 10 [*UM-MA* ... *ar-ḫ*]*a-wa pé-eš-šer* /

(5-10) [...]... the Queen(.) In the west [*a bird*? ...] [... Let the birds] confirm it. Two *ālili*- birds [... ...] they flew away. An eagle, however, [and a bird ... ...] they flew away [in fron]t. Behind the road: two [birds ... ...] came [...] and they flew away in the middle. [Thus (says) PN (the augur):] "they (i. e. the birds) excluded it".

§8 11 [*IŠ-TU* ^{MUNUS}ŠU.GI *ER-TUM* ... *QA-T*]*AM-MA-pát nu* KIN NU.⌜SIG$_5$⌝-*du* 12 [... DINGIR^{MEŠ}-*n*]*a*?-*aš-ša*[25] *mi-nu-mar da-a-er* 13 [... Z]I-*ni INA* UD 2^{KAM} ^{D}DAG-*iš* GUB-*iš* 14 [... *n*]*u-kán an-da* SIG$_5$-*u-i* 15 [... *in-na-r*]*a-wa-tar-ra da-a-aš* 16 [...] SIG$_5$ *⟨⟨SIG$_5$⟩⟩* /

(11-16) [Through the Old Woman,] the same [question]. Let the KIN be unfavourable. [...] and they gave KINDNESS *to* [*THE DEITIES*(?)] [... (gave it) to the WHOLE?] SOUL. In the 'SECOND DAY': the THRONE (GODDESS) arose, [...] and into GOOD. [In the 'THIRD DAY' ...] took VIGOUR [and ...]. Favourable.

The text's structure, organization and content make it evident that the writing in the two smaller scripts was added later than the inscription of the rest of the tablet. However, as summarized in the scheme in Fig. 3, the case of this tablet is not as simple as KBo 18.142 since the additional writing is added within a blank section in the continuous text. Most of the text in the oracle questions is poorly preserved and difficult to

23 For tentative restorations of the broken portion of the flight observation, see Sakuma 2009: vol. II 331.

24 Sakuma 2009: vol. II 331.

25 Tentative; the reading [^{D}GUL-*š*]*a*?-*aš-ša* (Warbinek 2020: 442) seems less likely based on visible traces.

Fig. 2. KUB 49.39 (obv. II – rev. III). Photos: BoFN11368; BoFN11364. Staatliche Museen zu Berlin – Vorderasiatisches Museum.

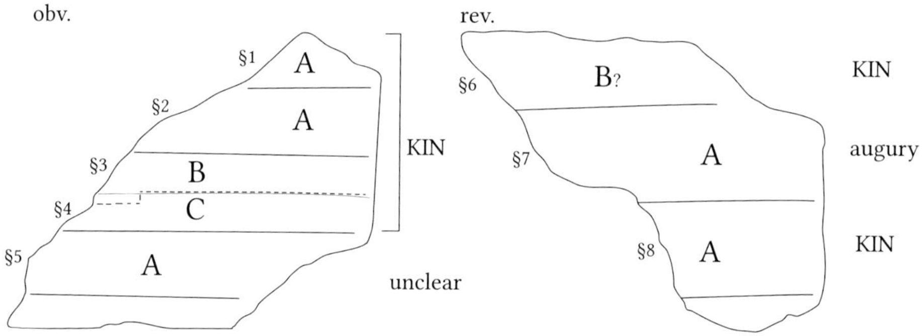

Fig. 3. KUB 49.39, distribution of different scripts (A–C) and content.

interpret; the reports are more intelligible thanks to the standard formulation. Even with these constraints, the text allows for an overall interpretation of the writing process:

- The paragraphs in script A were written first. On the obverse, one blank paragraph, approximately the same size as the others on the tablet, was necessarily left blank (between §2 and §5). Since the reverse begins with a paragraph written in a script closely recalling the script B on the obverse, it would appear this was also left blank before resuming the writing with §7.[26]
- The text written in script B was added into the blank paragraph of the obverse at a second moment, not necessarily after a long delay. Note that B continues for a half-line into the 4th paragraph before the text switches to script C. The paragraph line that separates the 3rd and 4th paragraphs is secondary and was added either while this second portion of the text was written, or, most likely, when the third portion (script C) was added. The scribe who added the text of B in the

26 Regardless of the exact determination of obv. and rev., which might be switched, this paragraph had been intentionally left blank at the beginning of a new column.

blank paragraph took care not to use up all the available space and employed a smaller, densely written script, which saved much space, with the awareness that yet additional text would have to be written afterwards – the oracular response.

– The text of B ends with an oracular question. The oracle report answering this question, script C, was added last. Similarly to the previous case of KBo 18.142, the last script (C) was written sometime after the former two. The script B is smaller than A, but overall, it is very similar to the previous text and is well-impressed into the clay. The text of C was impressed more superficially, and since the text was not very long, the scribe did not need to pay much attention to space management. Instead of writing a tightly packed script, he deliberately utilized all the available space. The result was a very loosely written text, whose characteristics might also suggest that the clay was drier at this point in time. The sign forms of the different scripts do not show significant differences, especially between scripts A and B, when a comparison is possible. Thus, it is likely that the same scribe was responsible for the additional text. As C is more poorly written, it is difficult to determine whether this was written by the same or another scribe.

The structure of these paragraphs can be summarized schematically as follows (see also Fig. 3):

obv.

§1	A	[oracular question] and oracle result (KIN)
§2	A	oracular question, with similarities to §3, and oracle result (KIN)
§3	B	additional oracular question, concerned with various deities, and oracle result (KIN)
§4	B	control/countercheck oracle question (KIN) in l. 12′, in §4
	C	control oracle result (KIN)
§5	A	text concerned with Ḫannaḫanna; apparently, no question

rev.

§6	B?	unclear content. The paragraph ends with an oracular question
§7	A	brief question and full bird oracle report, with augural response
§8	A	control/countercheck oracle of §7 (KIN)

The document contains both KIN oracles and augury, but the use of different scripts does not correlate with the switch of oracle technique.[27] Instead, it involves various steps within a series of inquiries on the same matter and using the same method (KIN). The paragraph with augury, on the reverse, was written in the same script as the rest of the tablet, thus during the primary inscription of the tablet. Therefore, adding new text did not depend on the use of different methods of inquiry but on the necessity to add further

27 *Pace* Warbinek 2019: 149, who determined that "the two central paragraphs [i. e. §3–4 on the obv.] are both KIN oracles in between two other paragraphs with augury divinations". The paragraphs here numbered as §§1–2 and §5 do not contain bird oracles, and the last lines of §1 suggest this is also a KIN oracle; obv. II 7′ also contains a KIN formula. Cf. also the discussion of selected extracts from the document, in Warbinek 2020: 441–43 (obv. II 11′–14′ and rev. III 11–16).

content within a previous section. The similarities between the text of the questions in §2 and §3 show that the second question is closely connected to the preceding one.

This document is important for the potential implications in the discussion of the relation between oracular practice and textualization. First, this tablet shows that a text that included different types of oracles at once and whose reports and results were written simultaneously, is not necessarily to be understood as a finished library copy or a *compendium* of several concluded procedures collected for a final report. At least in this case, one such 'mixed' oracle tablet was deemed not yet complete, and part of the procedure was still to be performed, and its results had to be added after the first writing phase. Content and text distribution suggest that the space for this addition was left blank on purpose. Second, the fact that the primary text (script A) already included, from the beginning, content deriving from oracular inquiries of different kinds (both KIN and augury) raises questions on how the various procedures were carried out and their results communicated for the production of the tablet. Another useful information provided by this tablet is that it demonstrates that scribes were responsible for writing oracle tablets, not the oracle experts. Although this can also be presumed based on the existence of many examples of mixed oracle tablets, in principle, those could be interpreted as final copies or archival summaries. This case shows that the production of such documents could also happen in several steps, that modifications and additions were sometimes necessary, and that the oracular procedures were not always complete when the 'final' tablets were written down.

While the blank paragraph on the obverse of this tablet was intentionally left empty by the scribes with the expectation of adding a new oracle at a later time, other oracle texts contain empty paragraphs and sections that were never filled (see §3.2 infra). Since there is no consistent pattern to explain all instances, we should contemplate the existence of a range of reasons for this practice. For example, it is difficult to explain the purpose of the blank paragraph at the beginning of the reverse of this tablet, corresponding with the beginning of a new column.

KUB 52.41 (Fig. 4).[28] This fragment with KIN oracle reports features two different scripts. As in KUB 49.39, the second script is smaller and might have been written some time after the rest of the text. The other side (obv.?) is almost entirely lost.

The question in §1, which has similarities with the better preserved §2, refers to a certain Ḫuzziya and oracular determinations about him.

KUB 52.41

§1 (script A) rev.? 1′ [...]-*ša-ma*[29] *e-ep-zi* NA₄ZI.K[IN][30] 2′ [... *ku*]-*wa-pí a-ri-iš-ket₉-ta-ri ma-a-an-ma-z*[*a*?] 3′ [... m*ḫu*]-⌜*uz*⌝-*zi-ia* DAB-*an-na ma-a-la-an ḫar-te-ni* [ ] 4′ [... *ku-it-k*]*i* ḪUŠ-*u-e-ni nu* KIN SIG₅-*ru pa-an-ku-uš-za* GÙB-*ta*[*r*] 5′ [... DMA]Ḫ-*ni*[31] *pa-iš* NU.SIG₅

28 See Marcuson 2016: 504; Warbinek 2020: 266f. Discussed also in van den Hout 1995: 106f.

29 Perhaps to be restored based on rev.? 8′: [*A-NA* GIŠKIRI₆ḪI.A *iš-ga-ra-an-ta-*]*ša-ma* (e. g. Warbinek 2020: 267), although this is tentative due to the large gaps in this paragraph.

30 The text probably breaks close to the edge of the tablet (see the end of lines rev.? 7′–9′); cf. the different distribution of the restorations in Warbinek 2020: 267.

31 Most likely reading, with Warbinek 2020: 267. Cf. Marcuson 2016: 504: ...]⌜D⌝U-*ni*.

Fig. 4. KUB 52.41 (rev.?). Photo: BoFN11313. Staatliche Museen zu Berlin – Vorderasiatisches Museum.

(<u>script A</u>) [...]... will take [...]. A cult stele [...]. [...] *as soon as* it will be determined by oracles: if [*you deities*] for Ḫuzziya you have approved [... *and*] we [have noth]ing to fear [...], let the KIN be favourable. The ASSEMBLY [*took*] SINISTERNESS [...] gave (it) to [ḪANNAḪ]ANNA. Unfavourable.

§2 (<u>script A</u>) 7′ [... ^{m}*ḫu-uz*]*-zi-ia-aš A-NA* ^{GIŠ}KIRI$_6$$^{\text{ḪI.A}}$ *iš-ga-ra-an-ta-aš-ma e-ep-zi* 8′ [*ma-a-an-ma-za*[32] DINGIR$^{\text{ME]Š?}}$ ^{GIŠ}KIRI$_6$$^{\text{ḪI.A}}$ ⸢*iš-ga*⸣*-ra-an-ta-aš A-NA* ^{m}*ḫu-uz-zi-ia* DAB-*an-*⸢*na*⸣ 9′ [*ma-a-la-an ḫar-te*]*-ni A-NA* SAG.[D]U-*ŠÚ* IGI [ ][33] ⸢*Ú*⸣*-UL ku-it-ki* ḪUŠ-*u-e-ni nu* KI[N ...]
(<u>script B</u>): 10′ [...]x x x ⸢*na*⸣*-at pa-an-ga-u-i pa-iš INA* UD 2^{KAM} ^{D}DAG GU[B]-⸢*iš*⸣ x x[...] 11′ [... DA.BI-*i*$^{(?)}$] ZI-*ni* ⸢*INA* UD⸣ 3^{KAM} DINGIR-*LUM-za* EGIR-*an a*[*r-ḫa kar-pí-in*] 12′ [...] SIG$_5$

(<u>script A</u>) [*If*] for Ḫuzziya, you [deitie]s have ap[proved] the gardens *planted in rows*?[34] [...] (and) for his life we have nothing to fear afterwards, let the KIN [be favourable/unfavourable].
(<u>script B</u>): [...] and gave it to the ASSEMBLY. On the 'SECOND DAY' the THRONE (GODDESS) arose ...[...] [...] to the [WHOLE] SOUL. On the 'THIRD DAY' the deity [took] the *HIDDEN* ANGER [...]. Favourable."

On this tablet as well, the text added later in the remaining space of §2 before the edge of the tablet is the answer to an oracular question.

32 See van den Hout 1995: 107.

33 There is probably no sign after IGI (cf. Marcuson 2016: 504; Warbinek 2020: 267).

34 For this meaning of ^{GIŠ}KIRI$_6$ *išgarantaš* see HW^2 IV I 182, with ref.

Warbinek (2019: 148) discussed the text written in a different, smaller script, primarily in reference to writing conditions under space constraints. Although also contemplating other options, such as later addition, he considered that the most likely explanation for this switch was that "while the scribe was writing, he noted the insufficient space and therefore decided to scale down his script". Based on several other parallels discussed here, it seems more likely that the KIN report was indeed written at a second time, after the Old Woman carried out the procedure. As for the identity of the scribe of the two parts, a close comparison of several signs suggests that the same scribe wrote this additional text. Apart from the size of the script and the shallower impression of the signs in the clay, there are no significant differences in individual sign forms. In my view, the differences in size of the script, or its appearance in general, in this and the other cases analyzed in this section, can also be explained through the usage of different writing instruments, e. g. a stylus of a different width. Although, in principle, a small sign can be written with a stylus of any size, a tool of smaller dimension facilitates writing on a smaller scale, not only for easier handling of the instrument but also because it actually prevents the impression of wedges wider than the tool's width.

It is possible that the scaling down of the script in this tablet also aimed to save space. In this respect, Warbinek (2019: 148) commented on the sparing use of abbreviations under these writing circumstances, which could have helped further to abbreviate the text: "(...) if the scribe wrote all six lines without a pause, why did he not use more abbreviations rather than reduce the script?" It will be discussed in §3.3 that abbreviations were not employed in oracle tablets primarily for saving space on the tablet but were a general feature of technical oracular writing, bound primarily to tradition and, probably, originating from the necessity to record the texts more swiftly.

KUB 18.44 (Fig. 5). Similar considerations apply to this fragment with two different scripts. The difference between the two scripts here is more subtle, also because there is no difference in size. The differences could be ascribed to two different handwritings, different styli, or both. A thinner stylus, for example, would explain the narrow width of the individual wedges, but differences between sign forms (notably NA) also point to a different handwriting.

KUB 18.44

// (script A) $^{\text{obv. II } 1'}$ [... EZEN$_4$ *te-e*]*t-ḫe-eš-na-aš ku-it* $^{2'}$[... -*a*]*n*$^{?}$-*za*[35] *nu* EZEN$_4$ *te-et-ḫe-eš-na-aš* $^{3'}$ [...]x GAM-*an-na za-an-ki-la-tar* $^{4'}$ [...]x 1 ^{DUG}*ḫu-up-pár* KAŠ[36] SUM-*an-zi* $^{5'}$ [...] ⸢SIG$_5$⸣-*ru* //

$^{6'}$ ⸢*IŠ-TU* ^{MUNUS}ŠU.GI *ER*⸣-*TUM QA-TAM-MA-pát nu* KIN SIG$_5$-*ru*

(script B) $^{7'}$ DINGIR^{MEŠ} GUB-*er* TI-*tar* ME-*er na-at pa-a*[*n*][37] SUM-*er* $^{8'}$ *INA* UD 2^{KAM} *a-aš-*⸢*šu*⸣ ME-*an na-at* DINGIR.MAḪ SUM-*an* $^{9'}$ *INA* UD 3⸢^{KAM}⸣ [x x M]E$^{?}$-⸢*an*⸣[38] *nu-kán an-da* SUD-*li*$_{12}$ SIG$_5$

35 Perhaps a participle, such as TUKU.TUKU-*a*]*n-za*.

36 Clear from photographs; cf. Warbinek 2020: 452: ^{DUG}*ḫu-up-pí* SUM-*an-zi*.

37 After photo collation; compare to AN in the two following lines. The autography of KUB 18.44 copies too many traces in this small break, from which the reading of Warbinek 2020: 452 (*pa*.-⸢*i*⸣) probably derives; the spelling must be a different abbreviation of *pa-an-ga-u-i* (see e. g. supra KUB 52.41 rev.? 10).

38 Warbinek 2020: 452 restores ⸢ḪUL-*lu*$^{?}$ ME-*an*⸣.

(script A) [...] which/concerning that [... the Festival of Th]under [... *a deity is anger*]*ed*$^{?}$, and the Festival of Thunder [...]. The penalty ... [...] they will offer one *ḫuppar-* vessel of beer [... let the KIN$^{?}$] be favourable/[un]favourable. //
Through the Old Woman, the same question. Let the KIN be favourable.
(script B) THE GODS arose, they took LIFE, and gave it to THE ASSEMBLY. On the 'SECOND DAY', GOOD was taken, and given to ḪANNAḪANNA. On the 'THIRD DAY' [*EVIL*$^{?}$] was taken, and (put) into EMPTINESS. Favourable.

(script A) $^{\text{rev. III 1}}$ [...]x *ke-e-el* MU-*aš kar-ša-an-za* ^{2} [... *-a*]*n*$^{?}$*-zi* ^{3} [...]x ^{4} [...] SUM-*an-zi* ^{5} [...]x ^{6} [...]x ME-*an* ^{7} [...]

[...] the 'cutting' of this year [...] they will [...]. [...] they will give [...]. [...] taken [...].

The first paragraph includes an oracular question concerning offerings due as atonements, likely for the neglect of cultic celebrations (ref. to the Festival of Thunder). Since at the end of l. 5′ some space was left blank, and the rest of the paragraph is empty, it appears that the response is missing. In the next paragraph, the first line was written in the same script and is a countercheck/control question: usually, this follows a previous response. It might be the case that the original answer was meant to be recorded in the remaining space of §1, but the oracle was not carried out or copied here. The second oracle, instead, is present (7′–9′), and it was recorded in a different script (B) than its question in l. 6′.

Fig. 5. KUB 18.44 (obv. II). Photo: BoFN00898c. Staatliche Museen zu Berlin – Vorderasiatisches Museum.

Some differences in sign forms may suggest that another scribe wrote the additional text at a later time. The form of NA is quite distinctive compared to the previous text.[39] I believe that the different configuration of wedges is a strong graphic marker of a different habit in writing this sign, which clearly distinguishes the two handwritings. Another diagnostic sign might be UD, and, more generally, the orientation of all the *Winkelhaken* (angular wedges), slightly tilted upwards, is a characteristic that broadly distinguishes the two scripts. Only NU makes an exception to this handwriting habit. Overall, these characteristics of the script may reflect two different scribal hands.

KBo 69.214 (Fig. 6). This small fragment displays at least two different scripts, although the poor state of preservation does not allow a reliable analysis of its content. The first portion is written in a smaller script, while the two last lines are much larger.

39 Not to be confused with the sequence *INA* UD.

Fig. 6. KBo 69.214. Photo: hethiter.net/: fotarch E-1533.

Fig. 7. KuSa 1/1.17 (KuT 26). Photo: hethiter.net/: fotarch KuT26_2.

Unfortunately, only a few signs are preserved in the latter, so differences in content are impossible to determine. The legible portion of the tablet includes KIN oracle reports in the first two paragraphs and extispicy in the third one. They seem to be written in the same script, although §3 is poorly preserved.

KBo 69.214

(script A) $^{\text{l. col. }1'}$ [...]x x[..] $^{2'}$ [...] ⸢DA⸣.BI-*i* ⸢ZI⸣-*ni* NU.SIG$_5$ $^{3'}$ [...] (*blank*) //
$^{4'}$ [...]x *a-pí-ia* EGIR-*pa* x x x[ ] $^{5'}$ [...]x-*i nu* KIN SIG$_5$-*ru* [ ] $^{6'}$ [... *n*]*a-at pa.-ga-u-i* [S]UM-*er* MUNUS.L[UGAL] //
$^{7'}$ [...] x x x x x x x EGIR(-)[ ] $^{8'}$ [... NU.SI]G$_5$-*du ni. ši.* GÙB-⸢*za*?⸣ R[A-*IṢ*(?)] $^{9'}$ [...]x //
(script B) $^{10'}$ [... -*z*]*i*? x $^{11'}$ [...]-*ik*?-*pát*

KuSa 1/1.17 (KuT 26; Fig. 7). As pointed out by Haas and Wegner (1996: 106) and Wilhelm (1997: 27), this small fragment of an oracular tablet from Šarišša (Kuşaklı) features two distinct scripts. The available photos are not of ideal quality but allow us to distinguish the script of ll. 1′–3′ and 6′ from ll. 4′f. and 7′.[40]

KuSa 1/1.17

§1 (script A) $^{1'}$ [...] IGI-*an*-⸢*da*⸣ EZEN$_4^{\text{ḪI.A}}$ 10 x[...] $^{2'}$ [...]-*an-za* ZAG?-*na peš-ši-at* DINGIR^{MEŠ} x[...]
$^{3'}$ [... *ŠA* ^{D}U]TU-*ŠI-ma-kán* TI-*an-ni UL ku-i*[*t-ki* ...]
(script B) $^{4'}$ [...] DA.BI-*an* ZI ^{D}NAM-*aš* T[I-...] $^{5'}$ [...] *na-aš pa.-i*[41] SUM-*za* LUGAL-*za* ZAG-*tar* MÈ(-)[... ME-*aš* ...] //

40 Previously Marcuson 2016: 515 and Warbinek 2020: 298f.
41 Abbreviation for Hitt. *pankui* (dat. of *pankuš*), one of the KIN 'symbols'.

§2 (script A) 6′ [...]x *A-NA* ᴰUTU-[*Š*]*I* ⸢*IT*⸣-*T*[*I* ...]
(script B) 7′ [...] GÙB-*tar* TI-[*tar* ...]

§1 (script A) [...] *before* [...] the festival ... [...] ... threw to the right. The gods [...]. [*If*] there is nothing [to fear] for the life of 'My Sun' [*let the* KIN *be favourable/ unfavourable*].
(script B) [...] the WHOLE SOUL, [LI]FE of? the (DEMON) NAM(TAR) [...] [...] and he/she was given to THE ASSEMBLY. The KING [took] for himself RIGHTNESS (and) BATTLE [...].
§2 (script A) [...] for 'My Sun', *with* [...]
(script B) [...] SINISTERNESS, (and) LIFE [...]

Some improvements from previous readings allow us to read to some extent the content of the lines written in the second script (ll. 4′f. and 7′), which contain KIN oracle reports. Both reports follow after text (a question?) written in a different cuneiform script, but a determination of their content is prevented by the poor state of preservation of the fragment.

Fig. 8. KBo 8.56. Photo: BoFN13657. Staatliche Museen zu Berlin – Vorderasiatisches Museum.

KBo 8.56 (Fig. 8).[42] This fragment is a peculiar case because the text appears to be primarily a cult inventory (ll. 1′–8′) "to which another scribe had added an oracle report" (Berman 1982: 94, credited to H. G. Güterbock). As Berman already discussed, lines 9′–12′ are written in a different, slightly smaller ("shallower handwriting") script.

KBo 8.56

9′ *ma-a-an ku-u-un* EZEN₄ *ša-ra-a t*[*i-ia-an-ta-an*[43] ...] 10′ *Ú-UL-kán ku-it-ki da-a-liš-kán-*[*zi* ...]
11′ ⸢SIG₅⸣ ME-*an* ⸢*na-at*(?) *A-NA*(?)⸣ [...] 12′ [...]x (erasure) NU.SIG₅

If [*they will perform*] this Festival in com[plete form, ... and] they will leave nothing [*out, let the* KIN be favourable/unfavourable].
[...] GOOD was taken, and [...] into? [...]. [...] Unfavourable.

The sentence with an oracular question has close parallels in at least one text, KBo 14.21 (ed. Marcuson 2016: 424–35), concerned with the investigation of cultic neglect for the god Pirwa, which permits the restoration of some of the missing text. It seems quite likely that the content of this part, which includes a conditional clause and a KIN oracle report, is directly related to the previous text, especially for the resumption of

42 For the online edition, see Cammarosano 2016–20.
43 For parallels, see KBo 14.21, obv. I 4′, 26′.

discourse through the demonstrative, which must refer to some content mentioned before. Cammarosano observed precisely that ll. 1′–9′ "preserve a festival description with the usual formulae of cult inventories" (Cammarosano 2016–20). Thus, the inquiry, subsequently added in the text, perhaps aimed at verifying whether the rites or a portion of the celebrations just described were complete and fulfilled the cultic requirements (l. 9′ *šarā t[iyantan]*).

In addition to these observations, I identify three rather than two distinct scripts in the added text. Apart from the 'inventory' portion of the text, ll. 9′f. look quite different and better written than the report itself (11′f.). The script in ll. 11′f. is misaligned with the previous text and slanted downwards, compared to the ordered writing before in the fragment; the final response, NU.SIG$_5$ in l. 12′, appears to be written somewhat hastily to the side of some erased text. Thus, the fragment shows not only that the oracular 'section' was added later but also that the question and answer within it were written in two distinct moments.

Fig. 9. KBo 23.110 (rev.). Photo: BoFN05895. Staatliche Museen zu Berlin – Vorderasiatisches Museum.

KBo 23.110 (Fig. 9). The bottom half of the better-preserved side of this tablet (rev.) is largely blank, apart from a few lines written sparsely with a script quite different from the text above. The fragment deals with some activities (whose nature is unclear) in certain towns, ^{URU}*Šapi*-[ ], Nerik, and Kummani. The presence in ll. 8′f. of the formula ŠE-*rù* ŠE "Let it be favourable: favourable", closing the two paragraphs, suggests that the text was concerned with oracular inquiries, and these lines only report the final result. The different script of lines 15′–18′ is quite difficult to read, but the only line which can be read to some extent contains terminology from KIN oracles (rev. 16′).

KBo 23.110

(script A) $^{\mathrm{rev.}\ 1'}$ [... $^{\mathrm{UR]U}}$PÚ-[*na*] $^{2'}$ [...]x KI.MIN S[IG$_5$$^{?}$] / $^{3'}$ [...]x ^{URU}*ša-pí-[nu-wa*$^{(?)}$] $^{4'}$ [...]x RA-*u-e-ni* $^{4\mathrm{bis}'}$ [...] (blank) /
$^{5'}$ [... GU]B-*ri* (erasure) *nu ku-it-ta* $^{6'}$ [...-*z*]*a* ⌜*UL*⌝ *ku-it-ki a-ra-a-ši* Š[E-*rù* ŠE] /
$^{7'}$ [...] *ku-wa-pí* DAB-*u-e-ni* $^{8'}$ [...]x x-*zi* ŠE-*rù* ŠE /
$^{9'}$ [...]-⌜*e*⌝-*ni* ŠE-*rù* ŠE /
$^{10'}$ [...]x ^{URU}*ne-ri-ik pé.-an ar-nu-ma-z[i]*[44] $^{11'}$ [...]x GUB-*ri nu kiš-an* DÙ-*u-ni* $^{12'}$ [...]x-*en* ⌜INIM⌝ *INA* ^{URU}*kum-man-ni pa-ra-a ne-an-zi* $^{13'}$ [...]x-*ru* DÙ-*zi nu an-ne-eš-kán-zi* $^{14'}$ [... *n*]*a-at INA* ^{URU}*kum-man-ni QA-TAM-MA pa-a-an-zi* /

44 Probably defective spelling for *arnumanzi* (inf.), thus HED A 166. See Hoffner and Melchert 2008: 46f. for the loss of /n/ before /ts/.

(rev. 1′–9′) [...] Arin[na ...]. The same: favo[urable].
[...] Šapi[nuwa? ...] we will vanquish.
[...] stands, and what [... *If*] you will not arise: let it be favourable. Favourable.
[...] anywhere/anything we will seize [...] ...: let it be favourable. Favourable.
[...] we will [...]: let it be favourable. Favourable.
(rev. 10′–14′) [...] to move (troops?) before Nerik. [...] stands, we will make as follows: [...] we [...]. We will dispatch a message to Kummani [...]. [...] ... he will make [...] and they will keep operating. [...] and they will likewise go to Kummani.

(script B) rev. 15′ [...]x x INIM? x x x x *šar* x *nu* 16′ [... -*z*]*i nu-za*(?) LUGAL-*aš*? ZAG-*tar* *A-DÁM-MA* ⸢*ŠA*⸣ LUGAL SILIM?-*an* ME-*aš* /

17′ [...]-*pát-ma ku-wa-ma*(?) (erasure) ŠE-*eš* ME-*aš* 17bis′ [...] /

18′] x x x x-*et*?

(rev. 15′–18′) [...] *unreadable* [...] and he took the RIGHT OF THE KING, BLOOD OF THE KING, and GOOD.
[...] *unclear*

One or more reports may have been written in these paragraphs, which are left blank otherwise.

KUB 49.33 (Fig. 10).[45] This fragment contains oracles of two different types: augury (on the obverse) and extispicy (on the reverse). The first paragraph on the obv. is divided into two parts: ll. 1–3, with the same script as the rest of the tablet, are an oracular question. The remainder (ll. 4–9) contains the augury report, written in a slightly smaller script and more superficially impressed. The same scribe seems responsible for this content, as there are no remarkable differences in individual sign forms and ductus.

Fig. 10. KUB 49.33 (obv. I). Photo: BoFN11127a. Staatliche Museen zu Berlin – Vorderasiatisches Museum.

45 Previous edition in Sakuma 2009: vol. II 320f.

KUB 49.33

(<u>script A</u>) $^{\text{obv. I 1}}$ DINGIR-*LIM*-⸢*tar*⸣ *ku-it pé.-an ti-an-na* SI×SÁ-*a*[*t* …] ^{2} *ku-i-e-eš ka-ru-ú še-ek-ku-u-e-ni* […] ^{3} *ku-iš-ki pé.-an ti-ia-at nu* MUŠEN$^{\text{ḪI.A}}$[$^{\text{I.A}}$ …]
<u>script B.</u> $^{\text{obv. I 4}}$ *ḫa-aš-ta-pí-eš-kán pé.-an ku-uš. ú-et n*[*a-aš*(-) …] ^{5} [*p*]*a-it* 2 *mar-ša-na-aš-ši-iš-ma-kán* ⸢EGIR⸣ x[…] ^{6} *na-at* 2-*an ar-ḫa pa-a-er ḫar-ra-ni-in-*[*ma*$^{?}$ … *NI-MUR*] ^{7} *na-aš* GUN-*liš* 2-*an ar-ḫa pa-it* EGI[R KASKAL-*NI* …] ^{8} *pé.-an ku-uš. ú-et na-aš-kán* EGIR ⸢GAM⸣ [*ku-uš. ú-et*][46]
$^{\text{obv. I 9}}$ [*na*]-*aš* 2-*an ar-ḫa pa-it* *UM-MA* ^{m}DINGIR.G[E$_{6}$-LÚ[47] *ar-ḫa-wa pé-eš-še-er*[48]]

(<u>script A</u>) $^{\text{(obv. I 1-3)}}$ Concerning the fact that it was confirmed for the 'divinity' *to step forward* […] (those) which we already know [… *If*] anyone will step forward, let the birds [confirm/exclude it].
(<u>script B</u>) $^{\text{(obv. I 4-9)}}$ A *ḫaštapi-* bird came in front from the unfavourable side, and i[t] flew […]. Two *maršanašši-* birds, however, [came] in the back […] and they flew away in the middle. [We saw] a *ḫarrani-* bird […] and it flew away GUN-*li-* in the middle. Behind the ro[ad: a bird …] came in front from the unfavourable side, (then) [it came] in the back down […] and it flew away in the middle. Thus (says) *Ar*[*ma-ziti*$^{?}$: "they excluded it"].

The rest of the fragment, including the reverse, is written in the 'regular' script. Thus, in this case as well, sufficient blank space was left for recording the oracle report. The surviving text in the reverse contains terms from extispicy, even though this part is less well preserved for a good understanding of the content.

KUB 49.100 (Fig. 11). This fragment with oracles about campaigns in the Kaškean regions (based on the toponyms in the text) is partially preserved for five paragraphs. Each paragraph includes an oracular question, but only in two of them the oracle report is present (§4 and §5). In §2 and §3, only a short question was written down, while the rest of the paragraph was left blank, perhaps implying that the reports were expected here: §2: "['My Sun'] will go on campaign this winter to the land of Iškuruḫ. If [the army …] will go out well and return well, let the KIN be fav[ourable]."; §3 "'My S[un'] will go on campaign this winter to the land of Išgamaḫ. If the army […] will go out well and return well, let the KIN be favourable."[49]

It is noteworthy that two reports in §4′ were clearly added later and are written in different scripts. Ll. 12′f. are a report of a KIN oracle, while l. 14′ is a report of extispicy, written in another script slightly smaller and even more loosely written than the former. The script of the KIN oracle is relatively close to that of the rest of the tablet and might have been written by the same scribe.[50]

46 Restoration according to Sakuma 2009: vol. II 320.

47 This is the preferred reading in Sakuma 2009: vol. II 320 and Tischler 2019: 56 (with n. 134). However, another possible reading is $^{\text{m.D}}$10-*p*[*í-ia*], *Tarḫuntapiya* (Sakuma 2009: vol. II 708–12). Augurs with these names are attested elsewhere.

48 The majority of movements from the unfavourable side (*ku-uš*, for *kuštayadi*, an augural technical term) suggest that the result was 'unfavourable' (see Sakuma 2009: vol. I 471).

49 For these oracular questions, see Beal 1992: 310 and n. 1181.

50 Transliteration adapted from Tischler 2019: 136f., based on photo collation.

Fig. 11. KUB 49.100 (rev.?). Photo: BoFN11014. Staatliche Museen zu Berlin – Vorderasiatisches Museum.

KUB 49.100

(script A) $^{rev.?\ 6'}$ [... ^{D}UTU]-*ŠI* ^{KUR}*iš-ka la-aḫ-ḫi-ia-zi* *INA* ^{KUR}*ḫar-pu-uš-ta* GAM *pa-iz-zi* [...]
7′ [... $^{KU]R}$*iš-ta-ḫar dam-ma-iš* IGI-*an-d*[*a*] x x GIM-*an-ma* *A-NA* ḪUR.SAG^{MEŠ} *a*-x[...]
8′ [... K]ARAŠ *ŠA A-BI* ^{D}UTU-⸢*ŠI*⸣-*ma* ZI ⸢*pé-ra-an*$^{(?)}$⸣ *INA* ^{KUR}*iš-ku an-da-an* ⸢*pa*⸣-[*iz-zi* ...]
9′ [... $^{K]UR}$*zu-un-ti ḫar*-⸢*ga*⸣-*nu-zi nu-kán* UGU *ú-ez-zi ma-a-an-ma ka-a-aš*(-)[...]
10′ [...]x *A-NA* KARAŠ$^{ḪI.A}$ 2-*an* 2-*an*-⸢*pát*⸣ *ma-la-a-an-za* ^{D}UTU-*ŠI pa-iz-z*[*i* ...]
11′ [...] *ú-ez-zi ar-ḫa-za mu-u-wa-an du-uš-ga-ra-at-tan*$_{x}$*-na ú-da*-⸢*i*⸣(-)[...]

(script A) $^{(rev.?\ I\ 6'-11')}$ [*If/when* ...] 'My Sun' will go on campaign against Iška(maḫ)[51]. He will go down in Ḫarpušta [... in$^{?}$] Ištaḫar a *second time* afterwards [he will ...]. However, when [...] to the mountains [...]. [... *in*] the encampment of the father of 'My Sun' ...[...] will go into Išku(ruḫ) [...] and destroy Zunti and he will *return* (lit. 'come up'). However, if *this/hereby* [...] it is approved (that) 'My Sun' goes to the encampments *two by two*$^{?}$[52] [...] and will return, and (that) he will obtain for himself power and happiness[53] [*let the* KIN *be favourable ... and the exta*[54] ...].

(script B) $^{rev.?\ 12'}$ [...] *in-na-ra-tar*[55] KASKAL ^{KUR}*ḪAT-TI* ME-*er na-aš-kán ANA* ⸢LÚ⸣^{MEŠ} *ḪAT-TI* x x[...]
13′ [... EGIR/*appan*] *ar-ḫa wa-aš-túl* ME-*aš a-ra-aš* MÈ DA.⸢BI⸣(-)[...]
(script C) $^{rev.?\ 14'}$ [...]x *ta. ke.* ^{GIŠ}TUKUL ZAG *ŠA* x-*at*$^{?}$-x[
15′ [...]x-*an*

---

51 A. Kryszeń kindly brought to my attention that this form might be interpreted as an abbreviation of the toponym in rev. 4′: (...) KUR *iš-ga-maḫ*. The same holds true for the toponym Išku in l. 8′ vs l. 2′ Iškuruḫ (KUR *iš-ku*-⸢*ru*⸣-*uḫ*).

52 Unclear: 2-*an* might have to be taken as 'together' or 'in the middle' (2-*an* = *takšan*), since a distributive form is expected to be 2-*at* 2-*at* (Hoffner and Melchert 2008: 156).

53 For parallels to this sentence, see KUB 5.1 III 54–57, also an oracle question, and KUB 16.47: 9f. (CHD L-N 314).

54 Tentative; based on the presence of a one-line extispicy report of l. 14′, after the KIN oracle.

55 Tischler 2019: 137, *in-na-ra-⟨wa⟩-tar*.

Fig. 12. KUB 50.81 (left edge). Photo: BoFN12556b. Staatliche Museen zu Berlin – Vorderasiatisches Museum.

Fig. 13. KBo 18.147. Photo: BoFN08169. Staatliche Museen zu Berlin – Vorderasiatisches Museum.

(script B) (rev.? 12´-13´) [...] they took VIGOUR, CAMPAIGN/ROAD IN ḪATTUŠA, and he [...] to the PEOPLE OF ḪATTUŠA [...]
(script C) (rev.? 14´) [...] he took *HIDDEN* SIN. FRIEND (IN) BATTLE, WHOLE [SOUL?...][56]
[...] *ta(nani) ke(ldi),* a weapon to the right ...[...]

§5 is too fragmentary for a meaningful analysis. Notable in this fragment are also traces of an impressed pattern interpreted as the impression of a textile (Tischler 2019: 136). One can speculate that such textile wrappings were used to preserve the tablet's clay from drying, as additional text had to be added later.

KUB 50.81 (Fig. 12).[57] The edge of this small fragment of KIN oracles preserves portions of four lines of text, three of which are in a much smaller script than the rest of the tablet.

KUB 50.81

(script A) l.e. 1 [...]x *i-ši-ia-aḫ-ta nu* [...]
(script B) l.e. 2 [...]x-*ma-aš*[58] *i-ši-ia-aḫ-ta nu* x[...]
l.e. [...]
l.e. 3 [...]x-*zi nu* DINGIR-*LUM a-pa-a-at i-ši-ia-aḫ-ta ki-*[...]
l.e. 4 [...]x *INA* UD 3^{KAM} ḪUL-*lu* ME-*an nu-kán an-da* SUD-*li_{12}* [...]

(script A) [...] it (was) foretold, and [...]
(script B) [...] ... foretold, and [...].
[...] he/she [...]. And the deity foretold that. *Th*[*is/thus*? ...].
[...] On the 'THIRD DAY': EVIL was taken, and (put) into EMPTINESS. [Favourable].[59]

56 The reading of this line is difficult, as the sequence syntax is not transparent.
57 See Marcuson 2016: 499; Warbinek 2020: 288f.
58 Or: ⸢É⸣.GAL?
59 Whenever the 'symbol' EMPTINESS (or VOID) appears, the result of a KIN oracle is favourable. Previously

The text of l. 2 apparently repeats or re-formulates a text similar to l. 1, but *išiyaḫḫ-* 'to predict; forecast' appears again in l. 3, clearly recalling the previous content. Only l. 4 is intelligible and contains the end of a KIN oracle report. As in the previous cases, it can be presumed that this additional determination was added later, after the rest of the tablet. However, the first line on the edge was written in a script consistent with the rest of the text; thus, in part, this section was already 'prepared' with the question or an anticipation of the oracle to be performed.

KBo 18.147 (Fig. 13). This fragment, catalogued as a letter with oracles due to its small size and one-columned format, is probably not a letter but a report of extispicy inquiries. Both parts, written in two (perhaps three) different scripts, contain formulae from extispicy reports but present several difficulties and unusual terminology.[60] The last three lines of the fragment stand out for their cursory script and l. 6′ appears to be even more poorly executed than ll. 7′f. The paragraph line separating them is irregular and somewhat follows the orientation of the script, as opposed to the other paragraph lines that are parallel and similarly traced. The paragraph line might have been added after the three lines of text were written.

KBo 18.147

(script A) / $^{2'}$ [... -*z*]*i*? NU.ŠE-*du* 8 [^{ŠÀ}*DIR* ...]
/ $^{3'}$ [...]x ^{LÚ}KÚR *a-ra-iz-zi* $^{4'}$ [... -*z*]*i* NU.ŠE-*du* ^{GIŠ}TUKUL-*kán* ZAG-*aš* $^{5'}$ [...]-*ka* x[...]-*ši-iš ar-ḫa* *x*-x-*it-ta* /

(*two blank lines*)

(script B) $^{6'}$ ...] AB.BA$^{(?)}$ *ni.* Ì.GÁL /
$^{7'}$... -*r*]*i*/*ḫu*?-*i-ma*(-)*da-aš* ZAG IGI DUMU?-*RU*-*wa-aš* x[...] $^{8'}$ [...] 6 ^{ŠA}*DIR* /

It appears that the last words of l. 5′ still belong to a description of the *exta*, which means that in this paragraph the result of the oracle was not provided. Since the text is technically not concluded, one wonders whether the following lines, added later, explain this oddity and belong to a continuation of the inquiry, completed at another time. Given the text conditions, any analysis of this fragment remains tentative.

KBo 24.131 (Fig. 14).[61] I would conclude this section with an example of a large fragment with bird oracle reports; it is, unfortunately, very fragmentary. The case of this tablet is even more remarkable than others previously discussed as, first of all, it shows macroscopic differences between the obverse and the reverse in terms of writing, which are easily visible when observing photos of both sides at once. In addition, one also finds evident differences across different paragraphs within the text on *both* sides. The paragraph obv. 16′–20′ is a block of text written in a densely packed, smaller script: the space occupied by these five lines corresponds to ca. 3.5 lines of the rest of the text

Archi 1974: 121f.; Beal 2002: 80.

60 For example, "six turns of the entrails" (l. 8′) is not an 'expected' number (usually eight, ten, twelve, rarely fourteen; Beal 2002: 62f.).

61 See Sakuma 2009: vol. II 433–40.

Fig. 14. KBo 24.131. Photos: BoFN08272, BoFN08273. Staatliche Museen zu Berlin – Vorderasiatisches Museum.

in the obverse. This section is preceded and followed by some blank lines and contains an oracle about an offering rite. One notes that there is no paragraph line incised before this section. Potentially, obv. 12′–14′ also appear somewhat different from the 'regular' text of the tablet (e. g. obv. 21′–32′), but this is difficult to establish from the photographs. The text distribution might suggest that the block of text in obv. 16′–20′ was written separately into a larger space that was previously left blank.

In the reverse, a portion of the second paragraph (rev. 6′–11′) does not recall any of the writings in the obverse and stands out when compared with the remainder of the reverse. It was more loosely written with a less deeply impressed script, whose features might suggest writing at a different moment than the rest, such as when the clay was drier, or on clay that was superficially moistened for re-writing (etc.). There are also some similarly loosely written signs in rev. 23′–27′, but it is difficult to get a good impression due to the limited extent of the preserved text. It seems significant that, in their respective paragraphs, these sections correspond with the observation of the flight, following the oracular question written in the 'regular' script. On the other hand, the central paragraph in the reverse (rev. 12′–20′) does not present such a difference.

The report in rev. 6′–11′ was authored by the augur Zapalli but, frustratingly, only this and the previous very fragmentary paragraph preserve the name of the augur (rev. 3′, 11′), while it is accidentally missing in all the others. With some more luck, we might have been able to verify at least whether the writing differences could correlate with oracles performed by different augurs, and inscribed on the tablet at different moments or by different individuals.

3.2 Special paragraphing: text insertions, blank lines, and blank paragraphs

A well-known characteristic of several oracular documents is the presence of blank spaces and even whole blank paragraphs within the text. A systematic study of this peculiar practice has yet to be undertaken, but some of the tablets discussed in the previous section provide hints on the possible reasons behind this scribal habit. A good example is KUB 49.100 (Fig. 11), with several extensive blank paragraphs and without the expected oracular report. Such cases, along with the examples of tablets presenting multiple scripts, support an interpretation of these spaces as sections left blank to be filled at a later moment.[62] However, these texts are not numerous, and in many other texts none of the 'expected' text is missing based on the content.

Only a systematic study of the tablets and their graphic features might verify whether any general pattern behind the practice can be identified. For this contribution, I selected two texts that allow some analysis in this regard, thanks to their excellent state of preservation and the possibility of establishing a direct link between content and specific aspects of writing layout, including the presence of blank sections in the tablet. In comparison with the cases previously discussed, the motivations for the presence of these features are quite different.

For the first example, KUB 22.70,[63] a long and well-preserved oracle text, a schematic representation of the tablet is suitable for highlighting the order in which the text was written down based on content, epigraphic features, and text distribution (Fig. 15–16).

From the point of view of scribal practice, one of the most striking features of this tablet is the fact that §12 (obv. 41–48), approximately in the middle of the obverse, originally had four lines (41–43 and part of 44); the additional lines, written by the same scribe in a much smaller script (obv. 44–48), had to be written in the rest of the available space before the paragraph line. These inserted lines occupy not only the available space in the paragraph but obv. 45 continues uninterrupted directly onto the tablet's edge and reverse (see [2] in Fig. 16). With respect to the orientation of writing, the tablet was flipped along the long edge so that, when the scribes wrote the actual reverse, the few lines carried over onto the reverse were upside down in relation to the rest of the text. Since on the obverse only one and a half lines could fit into the cramped space (which is probably the primary reason for the smaller size of the added writing), the scribe wrote a few more lines entirely on the reverse so that this became effectively a complete paragraph on its own with a total of five lines: one entirely on the obv. (44), a long line distributed between obv. and rev. (45), and three entirely on the reverse (46–48).

62 A special case is KBo 41.179, a bird oracle report in which some paragraphs, not fully inscribed, end with the sign PAB. In one case, the meaning of PAB is obvious: in fact, the paragraph contains only the oracular question but not the oracle report (rev. 12′). The scribe evidently marked that this was not (or could not be) copied on the tablet, or it had not been performed. The use of PAB in two other paragraphs, on the obverse, is less clear, since these are largely fragmentary; one has only a short text of one and a half lines, thus it might be likewise an incomplete oracle report (obv. 4′). A partial edition in Sakuma 2009: vol. II 463–66.

63 Edited in Ünal 1978; an updated edition and study of this text is in preparation by B. Christiansen. An English translation of obv. 1–60 is available in Beckman 2003: 204–6 and has been used here for reference.

As a mark of this special insertion, the new text is preceded by a single, oversized *Glossenkeil* (𒑱) in obv. 44. Another similar *Glossenkeil* also precedes l. 46, the first line entirely written on the reverse, apparently as a marker of the transition of the text onto the rev. with the last three lines.

Thanks to this text insertion, a reconstruction of the order of writing of the various sections can be established (n. [1] to [6] in the scheme), which is also supported by the text's content. This is relevant in the present discussion because it also explains the presence of an ample blank space on the reverse (n. [4]). It can be argued that the whole text of the obverse (n. [1]) was written originally *without* n. [2]. The paragraph divisions precisely match the written space; thus, these lines were added while writing this text without any substantial space left behind. The insertion of the additional lines of n. [2] as just described suggests that this was inserted afterwards, but also requires that the reverse, most likely, had not yet been written. It is implausible that the extra space necessary for the new section had been somehow left blank by pure chance, allowing precisely the inscription of n. [2] without overlaps to any text written in the reverse. It can also be demonstrated that the text of n. [5] was written after [2], thanks to details at the end of rev. 28: here, one or perhaps two signs are still visible but were then partially erased (Fig. 17). They were written slightly over the last sign belonging to obv. 44, IT,

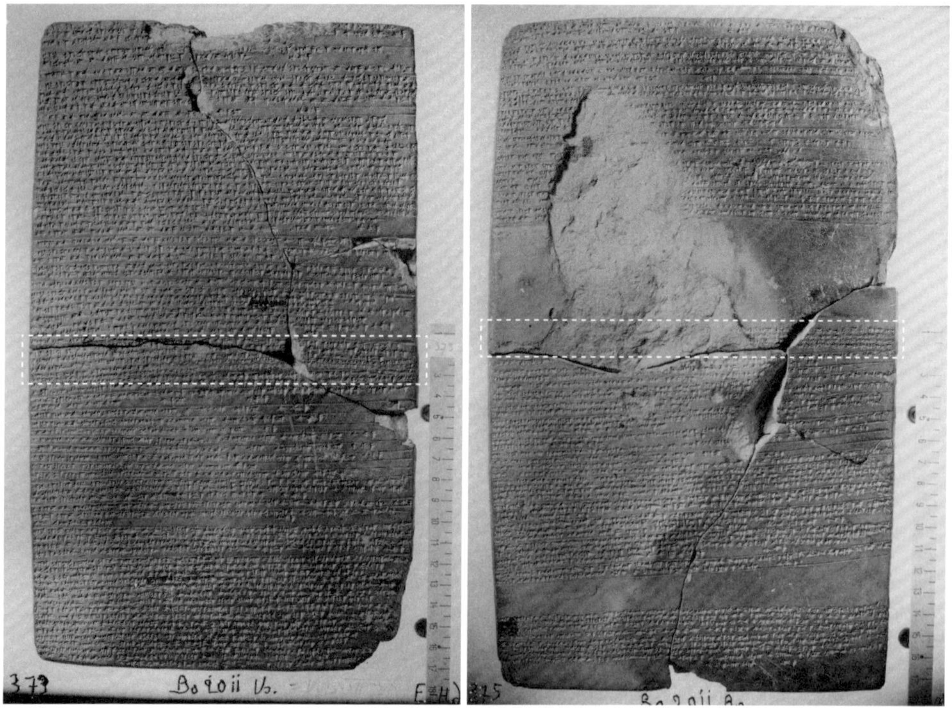

Fig. 15. KUB 22.70. Highlights of §12 (obv. 41–48; with added text, obv. 44f. and 45(cont.)–48, written on the reverse). Photos: BoFN20373; BoFN20375. Staatliche Museen zu Berlin – Vorderasiatisches Museum.

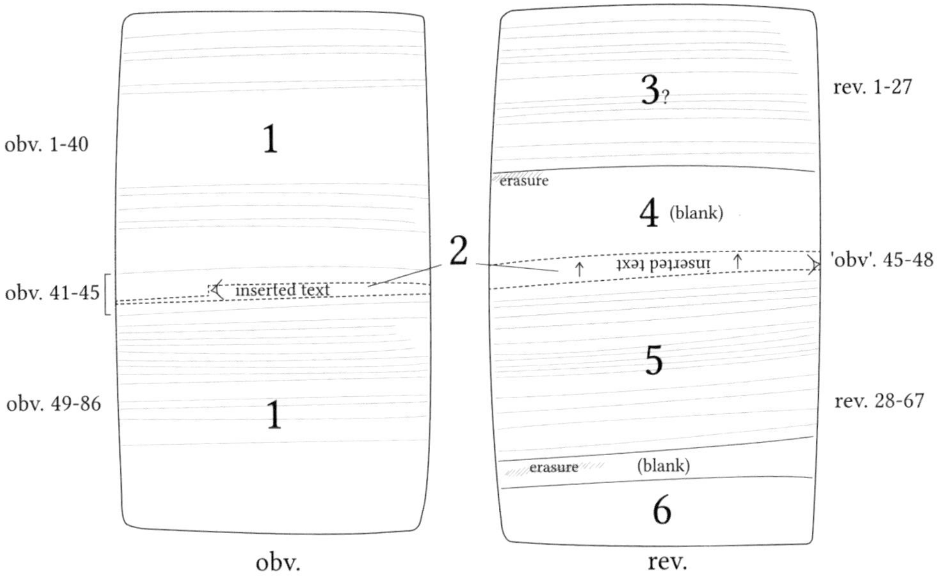

Fig. 16. KUB 22.70. Schematic representation of paragraphing and order of text composition (1–6).

which completes a word written on the edge of the tablet for the most part (*iš-ta-ta-a-et*), thus they are posterior.[64] More importantly, the fact that the text of n. [5], beginning with rev. 28, immediately follows the lines written upside down, and that these lines of text even follow the same orientation, slanting upwards – thus quite differently from the rest of the tablet, written orderly in horizontal lines – suggest that the scribe resumed the text at the earliest possible point after the gap (n. [4]) and the obverse *addendum.*

Fig. 17. KUB 22.70, detail of rev. 28, partially erased(?) signs after *še-er* and overwriting signs belonging to text of obv. 44. Photo: BoFN20375 (detail). Staatliche Museen zu Berlin – Vorderasiatisches Museum.

64 If one ignores the 'erased' sign in question, the text/content of rev. 28f. is complete, thus this can be considered a mistake.

Some doubt remains as to the exact position of n. [3], which might have been written immediately after [1]. Instead, it is highly likely that the exact extent of the large gap n. [4] was dictated by the presence of [2] and not the other way around. Since the text of n. [5] consisted of short one- to three-line paragraphs, in principle, several of them would fit into the space available above, right after [3]; a thorough erasure of several signs, visible at the beginning of the large blank area, shows that the scribe indeed began to write here. Nonetheless, he then decided to resume writing in the lower half of the tablet, potentially because all the following text was considered a distinct section of the composition.

A comment can also be made on the remaining blank space before [6]: the scribe was too scrupulous, and, in hindsight, he could have resumed the text of [5] leaving some space after the inserted lines from obv. 45–48. Towards the end of the tablet, being aware that the text was almost complete, he left a blank paragraph and continued to write with a more orderly horizontal orientation closer to the edge of the tablet, taking advantage of the available space. Another partially erased line within this blank paragraph probably shows his change of mind on where exactly to begin writing the last portion of the text.

The content of this long text, which cannot be discussed here extensively, generally supports this interpretation. A cursory analysis shows why n. [2] (obv. 44–48) was inserted later and likely does not belong to the first 'draft' of the text.

The text refers to an illness of the king, and the inception of the tablet shows that it was determined through oracles that the discontentment of an angry deity, the 'deity of Arušna', was probably the reason. The following series of inquiries delves into the exact reasons for the deity's anger. Various topics and people are brought up in the investigation. Before the passage of our interest, the text focuses on the mismanagement of items belonging to the temple of the deity and on the misbehaviour of some of its personnel (until obv. 33). The queen as well was accused of wrongdoing, based on accusations of a certain Mala, in particular for skimping on offers for the deity, and for the fact that some precious belongings of the temple went missing (obv. 12–27); apparently, these problems fell upon the king's shoulders, due to his proximity to these people.

The repeated negative results of the inquiry showed that there were yet more problems to be unveiled, and a new section of inquiries refers to accusations against another woman, Pattiya, who, we learn, was expelled from the palace and should be handed over (in service?) to the deity, without further details on the circumstances (obv. 34–40).

The section obv. 41–44 deals with a new topic: it is questioned whether a dream of the queen is a reason for concern as well. If we read only the main text, skipping the insertion of ll. 44–48, we can appreciate the thematic continuity:[65]

KUB 22.70

> (obv. 41–44) In regard to the fact that an omen of the deity of Arušna occurred once more, (is this) because the queen saw a dream? In the dream someone repeats:

65 Translation from Beckman 2003: 206, with minor additions for obv. 44 and obv. 48, summarized in his translation.

"Why will you give the furnishings which are in the mausoleum of the Tutelary Deity to the deity of Arušna? Leave something!" If this omen has occurred because of this, let the extispicy be unfavourable. The extispicy was favourable: but (there was) *zi.*, (and) *šuri-*: Unfavourable. ⧼ [*obv.* $44_{(cont.)}$*–48 inserted here*].
(obv. 49–50) In regard to the fact that it was once more unfavourable, (is it) because an offense remains in the mausoleum of the Tutelary Deity? We will make an oracular inquiry about it. Whatever is ascertained will be given to the deity. If you, O deity, have likewise approved, let the extispicy be favourable. The extispicy was unfavourable: but (there was) *zi.*, (and?) *šuri-*: Favourable.

As the text stands ignoring the insertion, the sequence deals with individuating what offended the Stag-god (or 'Tutelary' god) concerning his *ḫekur* sanctuary: the following passage, obv. 51ff., discusses, in fact, what kind of compensation, in the form of precious items, should be granted to the deity. The succession of these two paragraphs is logical, and this was probably the original order of the text.

The inserted text appears to go into several details regarding the issue involving Pattiya, only briefly mentioned a few lines before: Pattiya had "stayed too long up in the palace",[66] which was apparently wrongdoing. Perhaps she was an employee or a servant of the deity, who thus had been neglecting her duties. This paragraph also adds that two other women should be given to the deity as compensation, and further details about the dream of the queen, with the decision that some goods are to be left behind in the mausoleum of the Stag-god, while "Those of the royal household will be kept separate."[67] The ending of this paragraph insists that the matter involving Pattiya should not influence the rest of the inquiry, according to Beckman's interpretation of these difficult lines. Unfortunately, the end of this paragraph, written on the rev., is incomplete, so the result of this additional oracle is unclear.

It seems that the author(s) considered it essential to include this information in the text, even though they had already progressed with recording the investigation into the problems concerning the *ḫekur* of the Stag-god. The additional text provides more specific information about Pattiya, the resolution of a 'dispute' over previous items between the two temples, and the meaning of the queen's dream. Evidently, the matter required further scrutiny, or, more simply, this portion of the text was forgotten and not copied during the primary composition of the text. However, the latter option seems less likely, given the apparent continuity between obv. 44 (with the end of the oracle determination) and the follow-up in obv. 49. The additional paragraph is instead a digression into specific questions and concerns – perhaps initially overlooked – related to what was discussed in the preceding lines.

The rest of the obverse (obv. 61–86) and the first part of the reverse (rev. 1–27) return to some of the previous issues, referring again to the same people but also introducing new topics and problems. The text does not lead to a clear-cut resolution for each of them, with, on the contrary, a proliferation of problems discovered during the inquiry, and it opens several threads that remain in large part unresolved when the tablet ends.

66 Obv. 44: *ᶠPattiyaš=wa=kan kuit INA* É.GAL-*LIM arā itatāet.*

67 Following the general interpretation of Beckman (2003: 206), but with the *caveat* that these lines are partially fragmentary.

Compared with some of the other tablets discussed in the previous sections, the motivation for the presence of blank paragraphs in this tablet is very different. We have seen cases in which additional space was intentionally left for future writing, either with the expectation that further text *would* be added (such as a yet-to-be-performed oracle) or perhaps simply for the *possibility* that additional text could be added, even if this necessity might never arise. In KUB 22.70, no blank space was left by the scribe while writing the obverse, and the necessity to insert the additional text, probably realized not much later than the completion of this side, forced him to resort to a more creative solution. The text distribution in the reverse can be fully explained based on this circumstance.

We can compare this case to KUB 5.7+,[68] which presents a few similarities with the previous document: not only for its layout, as this is a very similar large one-columned tablet, but also for its content, the presence of later inserted text and distinctive paragraphing. Digitally composite images of the tablet aid in highlighting the text distribution and the presence of spacious blank sections (Fig. 18).

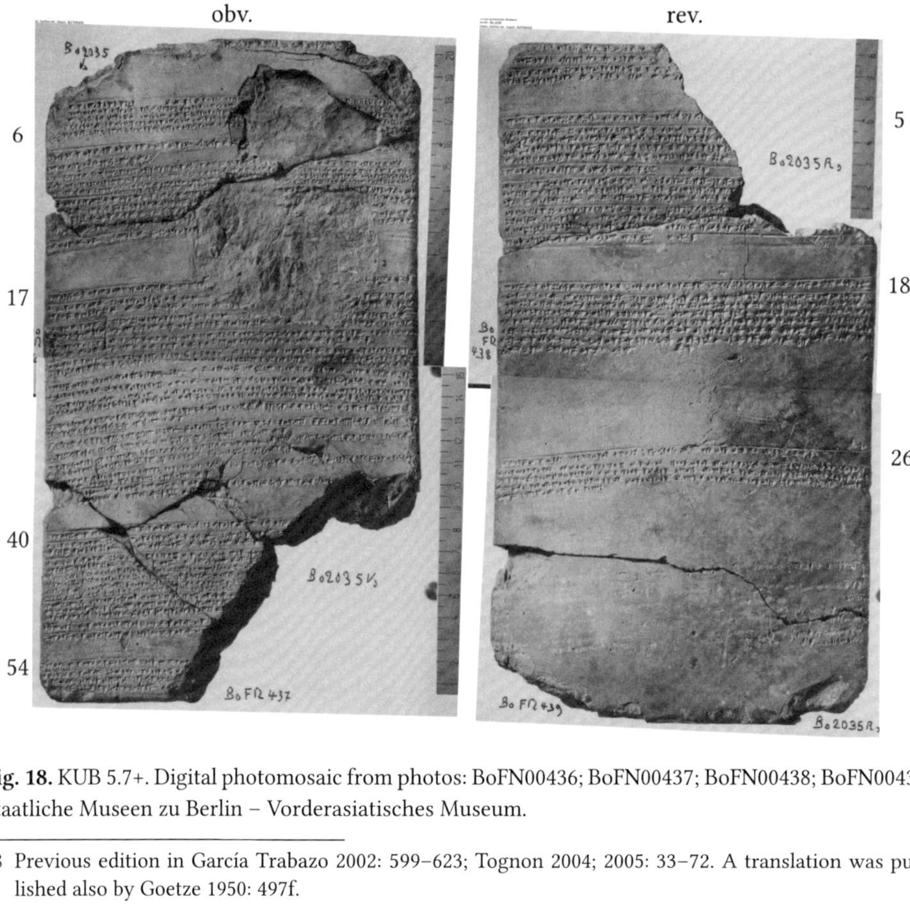

Fig. 18. KUB 5.7+. Digital photomosaic from photos: BoFN00436; BoFN00437; BoFN00438; BoFN00439. Staatliche Museen zu Berlin – Vorderasiatisches Museum.

68 Previous edition in García Trabazo 2002: 599–623; Tognon 2004; 2005: 33–72. A translation was published also by Goetze 1950: 497f.

This tablet deals likewise with dissatisfied deities. In this case, the matter was investigated chiefly through the technique of the *ḪURRI*-birds, perhaps a special type of extispicy with birds,[69] and control oracles were performed by means of extispicy.

The first few lines of text help frame the discussion:

KUB 5.7+ obv.

> [1] [ ]x MUŠEN *ḪUR-RI* NU.SIG$_5$ *kat-ta na-ú-i* [ ]
> (ca. six blank lines) /
> [2] [ŠÀ[?]][70] É ^{URU}*ki-iz-ma-ra* NU.SIG$_5$ LÚ^{MEŠ} É DINGIR-*L*[*IM pu-nu-u*]*š-šu-u-e-en*
> *nu* [*me-mi-er*[71] ^{DUG}*ḫa*]*r-ši-ia-al-li-wa-ká*[*n* UD] 9^{KAM} (...)
>
> [...] *ḪURRI*-bird (oracle), unfavourable. Not yet [ ] 'down'.[72]
> [The *sanctum*[?]] of the temple (institution) of Kizmara ⟨ ⟩; unfavourable. We [quest]ioned the men of the temple, and [they said: "the *ḫarš*]*iyalli*- vessels [... the ninth] day [...]".

I agree with Archi (1975: 135 n. 33) that the sentence in obv. 1 might be complete as such, and a verb is not necessarily expected in the lacuna, as also confirmed by another similar sentence briefly after and better preserved (obv. 6).[73] For an interpretation, two options are that the oracular inquiry had 'not yet' been performed or that the scribe had 'not yet' registered it.[74] It is possible that the verb *ariye/a-* 'to determine by oracle' is implied, as in the restoration suggested in HW^2 A 294 *katta nawi* [*a-ri-ia-u-en*].[75] If it is meant that the report was not yet *written* here, this might explain the blank paragraph right at the beginning of the composition. Likewise, after obv. 6 a blank line is left behind after *nawi*. On the space left in the middle of obv. 2, Goetze (1950: 497) wrote: "Apparently the scribe was unable to decipher this passage on the tablet from which he was copying", thus understanding these features primarily in terms of scribal transmission.

While this intra-linear gap is not self-explanatory, in the remainder of the tablet the distribution of blank spaces shows a coherent pattern: right after the first section of text (obv. 1–16), a whole blank paragraph of ca. six lines is followed by a new section of the inquiry, focusing on the anger of a god Ḫuriyanzipa, "within the temple" (obv. 17). The blank paragraph was not meant to contain additional content, but used to separate the first portion of text from the remainder, which constitutes a distinct textual macro-unit. In fact, the following blocks of text investigate whether some deities are

69 This interpretation remains tentative, due to the lack of any details provided in these essential reports, only stating whether the *ḪURRI*-birds were 'favourable' or 'unfavourable'; discussion in Beal 2002: 71f.; on this type of oracle see also the dissertation by Tognon 2005.

70 If the sentence structure is similar to KUB 5.7+ obv. 12, 17, 24, etc. However, [*I-NA*] is also possible.

71 Restorations based on obv. 9, 12, 17, 18, 24, etc.

72 For parallel uses of *nawi* in nominal sentences, see CHD L–N 424, although *katta* here is peculiar.

73 Cf. obv. 6 (...) *ma-a-*⌜*an*⌝ [*ki-pát*] KI.MIN N[U].ŠE-*du na-a-ú-i* "If [this] (matter) [alone], likewise let it be unfavourable. Not yet (done[?]/researched by oracle[?])"; see CHD L–N 424.

74 Thus also Tognon 2004: 71.

75 For a parallel see KUB 22.70 obv. 73: *n=an katta nawi ariyanzi.*

"not at all angry in the temple".[76] Each section refers to a different god, and at the end of each, some space, spanning a few lines, was left blank until the next entry (obv. 40, ^{D}x[…]; obv. 54, ^{D}10 ^{É}*ḫamri*; rev. 5, ^{D}*Ziparfaš*; rev. 18, ^{D}NISABA ^{URU}*ḪATTI*; rev. 26, ^{D}GÌR). On the reverse, the blank sections become progressively larger, and this is arguably a deliberate choice of the scribe, who was aware that the text was almost finished and decided to utilize the available space more freely.

In the ample empty space at the end of the reverse, traces of several deleted lines of an additional paragraph (at least eight) are visible. Few signs are preserved, confirming the oracular content, but for some reason the scribe decided to scrape all these lines off the text.

As in the case of KUB 22.70, far from being a 'final' copy of an oracular procedure, this tablet shows many traces of work in process, such as procedures which were not yet completed, additions, changes, and deletions. Some lines, added in constrained space into already completed paragraphs and marked with 𒑱, can be considered as later additions (e. g. obv. 11b, 25b).[77] We can conclude that several decisions concerning space management in KUB 5.7+, in particular the distribution of paragraphs and spacing, occurred during the inscribing of the tablet, including the drawing of the paragraph lines, since the close correspondence between exact content and paragraphs' layout excludes these could be drawn *before* the inscription of the text.

These two examples make it evident that the topic of blank paragraphing is quite complex. Its study requires a case-by-case analysis since, to some extent, these graphic characteristics also seem dependent on individual scribal choices and the circumstances of writing a specific document.[78] However, the recurring presence of blank paragraphs across oracular tablets also speaks for a trend or a habit connected closely with this type of documents.

The peculiar habit of leaving blank paragraphs in oracle tablets can become a valuable tool for identifying fragments and texts whose content is not immediately apparent. In this respect, it is worth mentioning two interesting texts with potentially oracular content: KBo 20.90 and KUB 31.122+. Previously classified as cult inventories of late date, they were convincingly re-dated to the Early New Kingdom Period by M. Cammarosano (2013: 84–87). They both refer to cult restorations in Kizzuwatna. KBo 20.90 discusses the reconstruction of temples which were previously destroyed:

KBo 20.90 rev.$^{?}$

> $^{1'}$ [*U*]*M-MA* ^{m}***tù-ud-ḫa-li-ia*** LUGAL.GAL LUGAL KUR $^{\mathrm{U[RU}}$*ḪA-AT-TI*$^{(?)}$ …] $^{2'}$ [*nu*] É^{MEŠ} DINGIR^{MEŠ} *ḫu-u-ma-an-du-uš wa-a*[*r-nu-e-er*$^{(?)}$ …] $^{3'}$ [É$^{?}$]^{MEŠ} DINGIR^{MEŠ} *ḫu-u-ma-an-du-uš* EGIR-*pa* […] $^{4'}$ […] *ú-et* ITU 3^{KAM} ^{URU}*zu-un-na-ḫ*[*a-ra* …] $^{5'}$ [… *a-r*]*i-eš-ke-nu-un*

76 The same formula, *mān=za=kan* ⟨deity⟩ *INA* ŠÀ É DINGIR-*LIM ŪL kuitki* TUKU.TUKU-*wanza*, introduces each new section.

77 The additional text, strongly indented, adds what compensations should be given, probably for cultic infractions verified in the oracle inquiry in the previous lines. Elsewhere in this text, the *Glossenkeil* is likewise used with indented text (e. g. obv. 25b), but other times, apparently, it is used as a section separator within a paragraph (obv. 23, 28, 29). For the use of *Glossenkeil* as a marker of indented lines, see Pisaniello 2020: 129–35.

78 For a discussion of some other examples see previously Warbinek 2019: 143–47.

nu-uš-ša-an x[...] $^{6'}$ [...]x É^{MEŠ} DINGIR^{MEŠ} *na-ak-ki-i-*⌈*e*⌉*-*[*eš* ...] $^{7'}$ [... *-r*]*a-aš a-ri-ia na-aš-*⟨*ta*⟩ *ú-wa-nu-*[*un* ...] $^{8'}$ [...]x*-an-te-eš* $^{\text{NA}_4}$*ḫu-wa-ši* [...] $^{9'}$ [...]x *nu-un* x[... (text after Cammarosano 2013: 85, with minor adaptations).

Thus (says) Tudḫaliya, Great King, King of the land [of Ḫattuša]: all the temples of the gods *they bur*[*ned down* ...] all [the temples] of the gods I *re*[*built/restored*]. [...] He proceeded to [...] in the third month/in three months, in Zunnaḫara [...] I kept consulting the oracles, and [...] the honoured temples of the gods [...] ... "make oracle inquiries!". Then I came [and ...] ... a stele [...] ... [...

The small fragment KUB 31.122+ is parallel – but not identical – to this text:

KUB 31.122+ obv.

^{1} [*UM*]*-MA* ^{m}*tù-ud-ḫa-li-ia* LUGAL.GAL LUG[AL KUR ^{URU}*ḪA-AT-TI*$^{(?)}$ ...] // ^{2} *ka-ru-ú ku-wa-pí* ^{URU}*kum-ma-an-ni* x[...] ^{3} *nu* É DINGIR^{MEŠ} ⌈*ḫu*⌉*-u-ma-an-du-uš* [...] ^{4} *nam-ma-mu ú-e-er* ⟨É^{MEŠ}⟩ DINGIR^{MEŠ} *na-ak-k*[*i-i-e-eš* ...] ^{5} *nu* É^{MEŠ} DINGIR^{MEŠ} *ḫu-ma-an-du-uš* x[...] ^{6} *I-NA* KUR ^{URU}*zu-na-ḫa-ra-ma* x[...] ^{7} ⌈MUŠEN *a-ra-a-an ḫar*⌉*-ta* ⌈*nu-mu*⌉ x[... (text after Cammarosano 2013: 86, with minor adaptations).

Thus (says) Tudḫaliya, Great King, *Ki*[*ng of the land of Ḫattuša*]. Formerly, when (in) Kummani [...] and [...] all the temples of the gods [...]. Then they proceeded to [*rebuild/restore*$^{?}$] to/for me the honoured ⟨temples of the⟩[79] gods [...]. All the temples of the gods [...] in the land of Zunnaḫara [...] a bird oracle had been taken,[80] and for me [...

Cammarosano (2013: 86f.) argued that this Tudḫaliya cannot be Tudḫaliya IV, to whom these texts were previously assigned, as both tablets are palaeographically early. He suggested that these fragments might belong to Annals of Tudḫaliya I/II (i. e. Tudḫaliya I), and refer to campaigns in Kizzuwatna, although an attribution to the later Tudḫaliya II/III (successor of Arnuwanda I) cannot be excluded.[81] Based on this finding, the two fragments have been now catalogued as belonging to historical texts in the HPM *Konkordanz* (Košak 2002–) (*CTH* 214). However, the formatting of the tablet KBo 20.90 is peculiar, and unusual for an annalistic text (Fig. 19).[82] The preserved paragraph is written right below a paragraph line, after a whole empty paragraph spanning some twelve lines. This feature reminds us of the ample blank paragraphs in oracular reports. In consideration of the content of the two fragments, both referring explicitly to oracles, and the similar wording of the two passages, I wonder whether these texts are to be interpreted as semi-parallel versions of oracular reports concerning destruction

79 For this emendation cf. KBo 20.90: 6′; also Cammarosano 2013: 86.

80 In a similar sentence from the Annals of Muršili (KBo 5.8 I 17, *nu=mu* MUŠEN *arān ḫarta*), Goetze 1933: 149 understood the participle *arān* as a form of *arai-* 'to arise' ("hatte sich ein (Orakel-)Vogel erhoben"; followed by Cammarosano 2013: 86). Differently, Haas 2008: 135 translated "... hatte ein Vogel mich angehalten". However, in oracular context, a form of *ariye/a-* 'to consult/determine by oracle' is a better choice (lit. a bird was 'oracled'); see the formula ... *kattan aran ḫarti* 'you determine ... (through oracle)', e. g. KBo 24.127: obv. 2.

81 A more detailed discussion in Trameri 2024: §8.5.1.

82 For this layout, KBo 20: IX considered that the text could be part of a colophon.

Fig. 19. KBo 20.90. Photo: BoFN07225. Staatliche Museen zu Berlin – Vorderasiatisches Museum.

events and reconstruction activities in Kizzuwatna. It can be expected that oracular inquiries would have been necessary after such events (of military nature?), especially as they involved temples.[83] On the other hand, the heading "Thus (says) Tudḫaliya ..." does not match any typical content of oracle texts and points to a very different kind of composition. Due to these unusual characteristics, these documents may pose a problem for an attribution to the canonical genres.

3.3 Abbreviations in technical lexicon and 'cursive' writing

The use of abbreviations is a well-known characteristic of Hittite oracular texts, although it might be misleading to characterize all oracular writing as rich in abbreviations. Certainly, compared with other text types, abbreviations are more common, and the same goes for other writing conventions that might be subsumed under this category. For example, KIN oracle reports frequently display the Akkadian prepositions *ana* and *ina* in their respective 'logographic' forms DIŠ and AŠ; this is not systematic, however, and in several documents both spellings appear. Similar in scope is the preference in these oracles for TA over *IŠ-TU* for ablatival/instrumental constructions.[84] Naturally, these choices might be seen as means to abbreviate the texts and align with the more general use of proper abbreviations of recurring terms.

All three main types of Hittite oracle texts (KIN, augury, extispicy) commonly use abbreviations, primarily in the technical lexicon and in the formulae and jargon distinctive of these divination practices. Still, their usage frequency and typology differ significantly in each oracular 'sub-genre'. Each of them displays characteristic choices and strategies towards conciseness for communicating the procedures and their results.

KIN oracle reports have recurrent abbreviations, particularly for the 'symbols' used in this divinatory system, whose exact modalities remain obscure.[85] The texts are con-

83 In a paper presented at a conference in Leiden in March 2023 ("Kizzuwatna à la fin du Bronze Récent. Troubles, incendies, morts, destructions... Que s'est-il passé?"), M.-C. Trémouille independently observed that the fragments might belong to oracular texts, although she maintained that the tablets date to the late Empire period, *contra* Cammarosano 2013. According to her interpretation, these destructions pertain the last decades of the Empire.

84 On these sentences, see Warbinek 2020: 60–63.

85 On the KIN oracles see in particular Archi 1974; Orlamünde 2001; Beal 2002: 76–80; Warbinek 2020. On the use of abbreviations in this type of oracles see a summary in Warbinek 2020: 73f.

cise, with fixed types of sentences referring to certain 'movements' and 'actions' of the symbols in the procedure: these sentences are also shortened with various methods. For the interests of this study, the extensive use of Sumerian logograms for the oracle 'symbols' stands out. Is this spelling convention to be understood, on its own, as a tendency to abbreviate? Since the KIN oracle technique is a native Anatolian tradition, the names of the 'symbols' also existed in Hittite – as demonstrated by cases of alternation, and the use of the Hittite variants in a few old documents, as opposed to the later preference for logograms. Thus, it can be argued that these spellings were chosen for conciseness. A tendency to use logographic writing can also be seen in the predominant usage of logograms in verbal forms. However, this trend might be skewed by the late date of most reports if it is true that an increase in the frequency of some logographic writings in Hittite cuneiform corresponds to a later writing habit.[86]

It must be stressed that a logographic spelling cannot always be seen as a valid, effective abbreviation; for example, SUM-*iš* can hardly be considered a good 'abbreviation' of *pa-iš*, being, on the contrary, a longer and more complex sign sequence. A similar case comes from the bird oracles, where one of the technical terms referring to a specific quality of birds' flight is GUN, a long, composite sign (= GÚ.UN), frequently considered as an 'abbreviation' of a complete form, yet unknown. The choice of this rare sign, and the fact that GUN itself is, arguably, a more complex sign combination than <*gu-un*>, seems to suggest that this was not chosen for its reading value <gun>, but rather for its semantic weight as a logogram, whatever its meaning in that context. In the case of GUN, the usage has to do with technical lexicon rather than with the practical goal of abbreviating the texts.

In the case of KIN oracles, there are only a few early documents as a term of comparison for analyzing the development of these choices, whereas in the case of augury, we can appreciate several differences existing between the earliest documents (Early New Kingdom; late 15th–early 14th c.) and the Empire Period/Late Empire Period reports. The later texts appear to be much more standardized and display a consolidated tradition of writing, with significantly less variation in both formulae and content. Still, the few early examples of KIN reports might show something similar: the KIN reports on the Old Script tablet KBo 18.151 have no logograms apart from LUGAL, MUNUS.LUGAL and DINGIR, thus providing potential evidence of changes in writing habits for this oracular genre through time. It has been observed that, in structure and content, this text also stands out with several divergencies from the typical KIN oracle of the Empire age.[87] The letter KuT 49 (MS), which contains a short report with typical terminology, also does not feature logographic spellings.[88]

86 Discussed in Weeden 2011: 35–38. As this finding is very recent, it is worth underlining that the spelling DA.BI for Hitt. *ḫūmant-* can also be regarded as logographic (see n. 13); note that this can be found in KIN oracles in shortened forms as well (DA-*an*; DA-*i*; DA-*az*; see also Kloekhorst 2022: 213 n. 73).

87 Text edition in Ünal and Kammenhuber 1974; recently Marcuson 2016: 166 and Warbinek 2020: 156, with previous literature. For the oracular content of a tablet from Uşaklı (KBo 52.280), also of early date, see Corti 2010: 198–206; in this case as well, several differences from the late reports have been pointed out.

88 See obv. 5–7: *nu=wa kē ūrkiēš kīšandati idāluwa dān nu=war=at=kan* EGIR-*pa* ^{D}*ḫalmaššuitti* "The following signs occurred: EVIL was taken, and (given) back to the THRONE (DEITY)."

Bird oracles look very different in terms of writing conventions, and logograms are quite rare, apart from common adverbs, such as EGIR, UGU, GAM, and the spelling SIG$_5$ for the 'favourable' side of flight.[89] Even its contrary, the 'negative side' was not NU.SIG$_5$, ubiquitous in all the other oracular types, but was always expressed with a Luwian word, *kuštayadi* (abl. of *kuštai-* or *kuštaya-*), whose exact meaning is unknown. This choice had to do with the local origins of this divinatory practice and, possibly, the fact that there were no exact 'Sumerographic'/logographic equivalents for most of the technical terms of this fully Anatolian tradition. Numerous names of birds, as well as other lexemes in the augural texts, also appear to be Luwian or of suspect Luwian origin, which points to a correlation between this practice and traditions transmitted in Luwian language.[90]

Bird oracles also contain abbreviations, but these are limited to selected and recurrent terms of the augural practice; as these are not numerous, they appear in almost every report.[91] Another way to abbreviate the texts, frequently attested in texts of both early and late date, is the omission of the forms of *uwa-* 'to come' (pret. 3sg. *uet;* 3pl. *uer*), referring to one of the two possible movements of birds.[92] However, several recurring terms, such as the names of birds, more than thirty of which are known, could well be abbreviated in some form but never were.[93]

In the extispicy texts, the brevity of the reports and the resort to abbreviations are particularly conspicuous compared to both previous techniques. The technical terms are almost all (and always) abbreviated, and as a result the texts are laconic. It would be difficult even to understand what is being described if it were not for our knowledge of the functioning of this divination technique, based on the parallel oracular systems of Mesopotamia, from which this tradition was imported into Anatolia. Abbreviations are indeed such a hallmark of this text type that Laroche catalogued the extispicy oracles separately in two groups: *CTH* 570 "Oracle hépatoscopiques" ('liver' oracles), and *CTH* 571 "Idem, rédaction non abrégée" (unabbreviated version) (Laroche 1971: 98); for

89 For the current interpretation of the mechanisms of bird flight observation, see Archi 1975; Beal 2002: 65–71; Haas 2008: 27–45; Sakuma 2009: vol. I; Sakuma 2013.

90 For preliminary observations on the Luwian linguistic characterization of bird oracles see van den Hout 2003: 120; Haas 2008: 32–34; Mouton and Rutherford: 2013: 332. For another term possibly of Luwian origin, *warā(i)-*, see Trameri 2023.

91 Abbreviated forms existed for Luw. *kuštayadi* (*ku., ku-uš.*, and even *ku.-za, ku-uš.-za*, with redundant Hittite abl. complementation), *zilawan* (*zi., zi.-an)* and *pariyawan* (*pa-ri., pa.-an,* rarely *pa-ri.-an*), *taruya(l)li-* (*tar.-li*$_{12}$, *tar-u.*) and perhaps GUN/GUN-*li*$_{12}$ (although it is not known what 'unabbreviated' form this would represent). Other than *kuštayadi,* all these forms are used as adjectives (at times adverbially) and are difficult to interpret and translate. In context, they refer to certain qualities of birds, their positions, or the kind of flight observed.

92 See, for example, the text of DAAM 1.31 infra, p. x. The other movement was (*arḫa*) *pai-* "to go (away)", but this verb, as a rule, was never omitted.

93 Some birds' names were spelled logographically, but their Hittite/Luwian equivalent is unknown; thus, whether these might be understood as 'abbreviated' spellings for their original correspondents cannot be determined. Notably, with the exception of a bird ḪAR.ḪAR (if this is the correct reading), these names are those of *other* animals: 'fox' (KA$_5$.A), 'mouse' (PÉŠ), 'snake/snake-bird' (MUŠEN.MUŠ) and, recently resurfaced, 'wolf' (UR.BAR.RA; in DAAM 1.21, obv. 9, 13; discussion in Trameri forthc.). On bird names in Hittite oracles, see Sakuma 2009: vol. I 334–411.

the latter type, only a handful of texts exists. The use of abbreviations in extispicy was, possibly, imported together with the technique from the south. Since many of the terms appear to be Hurrian, the precursor of Hittite extispicy is to be sought somewhere in northern Mesopotamia, in the Hurrian-speaking areas, or perhaps Kizzuwatna. The most frequent ones are *ni.* (*nipašuri-*), *ši.* (*šintaḫi-*), *ta.* (*tanani-*), *ke.* (*keldi-*), which refer to 'sectors' of the liver and appear, in this order, almost in any oracle report.[94] The 'turns' of the intestines, Akk. *tīrānu* were abbreviated as ^{ŠÀ}*DIR* or ^{ŠÀ}*TIR*. At times, the reports are so concise that one may find just a sequence *ni. ši. ta. ke.*, which seems to indicate that each item in this checklist was controlled, but there was nothing significant to be highlighted – typically a negative sign. The 'name' of this oracular practice was also abbreviated, since extispicy oracles are known as *TE*^{MEŠ} or SU^{MEŠ}, both standing for Akk. *terētu*.[95]

Thus, all the text types resorted to strategies for abbreviation, but their typology and the extent to which they were used are bound to the individual traditions. It is difficult to say whether some of these uses were handed down by the oracular experts – the 'Old Woman', the augurs, and the (extispicy) 'diviner' – as this would imply their involvement with the recordings and knowledge of writing. From a scribal perspective, each oracular tradition developed its own writing trends and standards, resulting in significant differences, ranging between the brevity of the extispicy reports and the relatively more verbose flight descriptions of the bird oracles. The physical evidence represented by the tablets themselves suggests, in my view, that the common thread among all these abbreviation strategies was not so much to improve the writing organization in terms of *space* on the tablets but rather the desire to save *time* for recording those reports. Several examples discussed in the previous sections illustrate this clearly, since the available space on the tablets is at times overabundant. Also, specific cases of space constraints and their respective solutions do not seem to have significantly impacted the language of texts – for example, leading the scribes to write using *more* abbreviations (Warbinek 2019: 147–50). The habit of leaving blank spaces within the text in several oracular documents, especially those recording multiple techniques simultaneously, also supports this view.

This pattern is seemingly very different from that of other writing contexts. If one were to draw an axis between prioritizing saving space or time at two opposite extremes, one would place the Hittite scribe, at least for oracles, almost at one end of the spectrum, where the worry about space seems minimal. Professionals of writing in other traditions stand at the opposite end, with a predominant concern for saving space. For example, for centuries Catholic monks of Medieval Europe performed work that required an enormous amount of time for each writing project and whose writing strategies, including the abundant use of abbreviations and ligatures, were also (or even primarily) aimed at a sparing use of the extremely costly writing material. These limitations determined context-specific strategies for space management and the de-

94 Other frequent abbreviations are: *ḫi-li*$_{8/13}$. *(ḫilipšiman), ir.-li*$_{12}$*/liš (irkipelli-), ma-zé.-(eš) (mazeri-), zi. (zizaḫi)*; an overview in Beal 2002: 59–64. Some remarks on the chronology of the development of the terminology and the usage of abbreviations in Schuol 1994: 98–101.

95 According to Beal 2002: 59, the frequent usage of SU might be erroneous, as opposed to the supposed original *TE*.

velopment of extensive tools of abbreviation and summarization. For the Hittite scribes, who could write on clay, the writing material and its availability were arguably a lesser concern. Thus, the development of abbreviation strategies, at least to some degree, happened within a different background.

Distinct approaches in the three main kinds of oracles in the Hittite context reveal the search for practical ways to hasten the recording of the texts, although an important component seems to be as well the weight of the previous tradition; especially in the case of extispicy, one wonders to what extent the recording systems followed previous models. A scenario in which the standardizations of the oracular language had a strong basis in tradition might explain why the oracles of Anatolian background are largely descriptive in comparison with the heavily condensed language of extispicy, whose features had, realistically, a well-established background in Mesopotamia.

In part connected with the issue of the usage of abbreviations and their purposes, another characteristic of oracular tablets has been precisely linked to time-saving efforts, namely the usage of scripts that have been characterized as 'cursive' but which might also be defined as 'cursory' writings. As we saw in the previous examples analyzed in §3.1, some of the tablets with multiple scripts present examples of hastily or less carefully written cuneiform, at times also more superficially impressed and showing less attention to regularity and readability. There are also whole tablets written with loose, relatively irregular and unevenly distributed writing, of much different appearance than the typical Hittite cuneiform. Some examples catalogued as fragments of oracle in the autography editions are shown in Fig. 20 (see also Fig. 2, 8, 9, 11, 13). It must be noted that these tablets remain particularly difficult to read, and their cataloguing as oracles appears to have been influenced precisely by their peculiar appearance. However, at scrutiny, their content does not always confirm that they are, in fact, oracle texts.[96]

Fig. 20. Examples of tablets with 'cursory' scripts (KBo 41.226; KUB 6.1; KUB 22.58). Photos: BoFN05941; BoFN00574a; BoFN01024b. Staatliche Museen zu Berlin – Vorderasiatisches Museum.

96 Of the three shown as examples in Fig. 20, only KUB 22.58 is clearly of oracular content (extispicy); the legible portions of KBo 41.226 and KUB 6.1 seem to be texts of different kinds, but their content cannot be determined due to their state of preservation and the difficult writing.

The concept that oracles would be hastily and carelessly written, as opposed to other text types, sometimes rehearsed or implied in the research literature, is probably misleading in the face of the reality of the sources. To offer one example, in *Religions of Asia Minor*, Popko stated: "Their language is sparing and simplified, the *writing itself hasty* and full of graphic abbreviations" (Popko 1995: 135; my emphasis). This characterization of oracular writing is somewhat unfair, particularly concerning the 'hastiness' of writing. As shown in the examples discussed in §3.1, occasionally, there are parts in oracular texts with scripts showing these characteristics. However, these cases are rare within texts otherwise displaying 'regular' cuneiform scripts. This distinction was acknowledged by Soysal, who noted: "In these tablets, the passages with the oracular questions were set down *in conventional handwriting*; however, the parts which contain the divination performances were *carelessly written, due to the stress involved in recording the procedures with haste*." (Soysal 2000: 88; my emphasis).

This is one possible interpretation of the reasons behind the addenda with 'cursory' writing. On the other hand, we also saw cases of added texts, which are generally well-readable and structured. Arguably, several of the smaller script insertions discussed in §3.1 require even more effort and care in writing to produce orderly text at a smaller size. Furthermore, the typical oracle tablets do not show significant divergences from other genres in terms of cuneiform writing.

Nonetheless, the analysis of the use of special or unusual scripts might be of interest to enhance our understanding of the process of oracular writing. For example, most examples of 'cursory' scripts are extispicy reports, thus text typology might be significant for contextualizing this phenomenon. Materials that include these peculiar scripts deserve attention as they might also be evidence of early layers in the textualization circuit of oracular practice, such as primary reports, drafts, or notes. The fact that there are relatively few examples is also potentially significant 'negative' evidence because it might suggest, for instance, that other methods of communicating oracle results were more common, such as oral transmission, but also the resort to perishable media that were typically discarded or destroyed.

3.4 'Micro tablets' and perforated tablets

Some oracle texts were written on tiny tablets (type B I–III in Waal 2015: 35–39), although this cannot be considered a typical format for all oracular writing, which in the majority of cases is found on larger size, one- or two-columned tablets.[97] The shapes of these small tablets vary, and there are rectangular ones in portrait or landscape orientation and oval-shaped ones, usually in landscape orientation.

Some of these 'micro tablets' were published in KBo 18 (KBo 18.138, 141–150), and other examples are KBo 43.59 (fragment of bird oracle), KBo 32.226 (mentioning Alašiya), KBo 41.215 (KIN oracle, about something done in a city URU*ta*-[ ]), in addition to those briefly discussed in this section.[98] Tablets of this type have also been called

97 For the potential diachronic relevance of different tablet formats in oracle tablets, see van den Hout 2001: 431–34. Although small, rounded tablets often contain oracle reports, they could also be used for other text types (a few cases of labels and economic inventories; Waal 2015: 35).

98 KBo 18.138 is a fragmentary mixed oracle report, with extispicy and augury; KBo 18.141 mentions Kizzuwatna, and the type of oracle recorded or mentioned is unclear; KBo 18.142 (see p. x); KBo 18.143

"Etikett-artige Orakeltexte" (van den Hout 2001: 432). It is to be noted, however, that several texts of this format, currently catalogued as tablets with oracle content, should be reassigned to other groups, as it is the case, for example, of three tablets catalogued as oracular fragments KBo 48.274–276 (MS?), that are almost complete texts and none of them with oracular content.

Due to their small size, some of these tablets have also been catalogued as letters, even if they do not show epistolary content (see, e. g. KBo 18.142, previously discussed). The texts which can be read to some extent show that small oracle tablets usually contained an individual oracle, with question and result, or, frequently, just one or the other. KBo 18.144 is a well-preserved example:

> (obv.) 'My Sun' and the Queen will go spend the winter in Ankuwa. Gods, if you have approved the city of Ankuwa for them (for wintering), (l.e./rev.) (and) for the safety of 'My Sun' and for the safety of the queen, and in all respects, everything will be good: let the KIN be favourable. Two.[99]

The ending of this tablet is quite puzzling, with the isolated numeral "two" written in the center of the last line. According to van den Hout (2001: 434), a few tablets which display such numbers could be meant as aids for those who would later compile individual oracular reports into larger tablets. These larger reports, such as compendia with sets of questions on the same matter, would bring together individual reports, and the number might have to do with organizing the preparatory materials.[100] A notable parallel is the small tablet HKM 115, also with oracular content (KIN) and with a numeral "two" in the last line.[101] In that case, likewise, the tablet ends with a question: "Let the KIN be unfavourable. Two", and the report is missing. Since the reverse is blank, this could accommodate a short response, but this was never inscribed. In both cases, apparently, the reports had to be recorded somewhere else. For a similar usage, the minuscule tablet KuT 39 (KuSa 1/1.29; ca. 2.5 × 2.5 cm) should also be mentioned, where the numeral "22" is found on the lower edge – although this is catalogued as a label and not an oracle report.[102] An alternative approach would be to interpret the number "2" (and possibly "22"?) as an abbreviation for KI.MIN ('the same'), intended as a confirmation of the positive or negative result anticipated in the oracle question.[103] However, there are

contains extispicy; KBo 18.144 (see *infra*); KBo 18.145 is catalogued as a letter concerning witchcraft and bloodshed in the "house of Šaušgatti", but it might be as well an oracle report; KBo 18.146 is catalogued as a letter, but might be an oracle report (thus de Martino 2005: 307); KBo 18.147 (see p. x); KBo 18.148 is very fragmentary (SIG_5-*ru* is visible); KBo 18.149 is a fragment of a letter or a report, but of unclear content; KBo 18.150 cannot be confidently catalogued as oracle text; KBo 18.151 (see p. x n. x).

99 My translation; cf. previously Warbinek 2020: 309.

100 The topic of interest of this oracle, the wintering of the king and queen at a certain location, is recurrent in other oracle texts; see e. g. the long composition KUB 5.4+, which is precisely one such 'compendium' of a series of detailed oracular inquiries on one topic. On this text see Christiansen forthc.

101 Discussed in van den Hout 2001: 425f., 433f.; text in Marcuson 2016: 514.

102 For a reading, see Wilhelm 2007: 30 (Notiz in der Form eines "Etiketts"). See also Haas 2008: 9: "Solche Täfelchen sprechen dafür, daß jeder einzelne Orakelgang sogleich notiert worden ist, um am Ende zu größeren Tafeln zusammengestellt zu werden. Dies würde auch die Zahlenangabe 2, in einer anderen Tafel sogar 22, erklären."

103 I owe this suggestion to Susanne Görke.

no clear parallels for this usage, as KI.MIN is frequently found in oracle questions, but for results either SIG$_5$ or NU.SIG$_5$ is typically repeated. Since so few examples of 'numbered' tablets exist, it remains difficult to find a pattern of this use and establish what exactly these numbers were used for.[104]

While small tablets with individual inquiries may represent prior steps in the preparation of complete, extensive oracle reports, individual reports of this kind might also have been used in epistolary exchanges to communicate oracle results to a distance – as is perhaps the case of KBo 18.142 (p. x, Fig. 1) and the Old Script tablet KBo 18.151 (Soysal 2000: 87–89).

In this respect, a few tablets within this corpus of 'micro tablets' are particularly interesting because they were also perforated and have a passing hole. It can be argued that the perforations drilled in the tablet's body were functional to or connected with the communication and delivery of oracles since they appear intentional and made before or during the tablet's writing. Two examples of perforated tablets were briefly discussed in Waal 2015: 55–57 (KBo 31.32, NS; and KUB 32.130, MS), and the recently published DAAM 1.31 (MS), from Šamuḫa can be added to this short list.

KBo 31.32 (Fig. 21) is catalogued as a 'label' (*CTH* 283); however, as Waal (2015: 55) pointed out, the content instead suggests that this is a small oracle report. In particular, the formula *kī kuit* ... "concerning the fact that" (l. 1) generally (re-)introduces the topic of investigation at the beginning of a new question. The rest of the tablet is difficult to read. As noted by Waal, the perforation seems to have interfered slightly with the writing, as visible from photographs of the reverse, thus it cannot be ruled out that the tablet was drilled after its inscription. However, the way the signs are laid out around the hole may suggest that these were arranged around it or even that the perforation, done when the clay was still soft, secondarily impacted the writing area, deforming the tablet and the original orientation of the signs.

Fig. 21. KBo 31.32 (rev.). Photo: BoFN05103a. Staatliche Museen zu Berlin – Vorderasiatisches Museum.

104 A single numeral "one" might be written in the last line of the tablet KBo 48.277, even smaller than any of those hereby discussed (ca. 1.5 × 1.5 cm). Its text, constituted by only two lines with two/three signs each, is largely illegible.

Fig. 22. KUB 32.130 (obv.), and detail from rev. 23. Photos: BoFN03471; BoFN03473 (detail). Staatliche Museen zu Berlin – Vorderasiatisches Museum.

KUB 32.130 (Fig. 22), a well-formed and carefully written rectangular tablet, shows that smaller tablets were not always more hastily or poorly executed.[105] The text describes how the king, currently away on a military campaign, ascertained through oracles that Šavoška of the (Battle)field of Šamuḫa was angry, apparently because of the neglect of her cult in her hometown. The text lists measures taken to appease the deity, particularly by restoring an appropriate daily regimen of offerings and celebrating festivals dedicated to her. The plan even included the transport of the statue of the goddess from Šamuḫa to the king after the campaign so that he could worship her in person. The text ends with a long question (ll. 25–32), in a format that typically introduces an oracle report; the oracle will determine whether these measures will please the goddess: "If this is good for (you) Šavoška of the (Battle)field of Šamuḫa: (…) Let the birds confirm it. These (are) the birds".

105 Previous editions: Lebrun, 1976: 167–71; Klinger 2010: 153–67; Beckman 2012. A new edition and discussion in Trameri 2024: §8.5.1. This tablet was previously dated to the Empire period, but convincing palaeographic, linguistic and historical-cultural arguments have been put forward for attributing it instead to the early New Kingdom, between Tudḫaliya I and Tudḫaliya II/III (on the dating see Klinger 2010: 162–67; also Beckman 2012: 2).

The final sentence of the tablet, "these are/were the birds", usually introduces the description of birds' flights with the response of the augurs. Since these parts are missing and could not possibly be added to this tablet (the last four lines are written on one of the short edges), these were expected on another tablet. The photos show that the hole did not affect the writing and that this was formed before the inscription: in the obverse, the sign PÁT in the word *pé-di-pát* (obv. 7) was written right above DI, relatively small, to avoid the hole; the following line is shorter so that the area in correspondence to the hole is left blank altogether. On the reverse, the scribe was writing (…) *I-NA* ^{URU}*ša-mu-ḫi* (rev. 23) when he realized that URU and the city name would be separated by the hole. Thus he decided to erase the determinative and write the whole toponym to the right of it (Fig. 22, detail). Therefore, the hole had already been drilled before or during the writing process, and this could have served the purpose of attaching the tablet to something – such as one or more tablets with the oracular report itself (e. g. Beckman 2012: 6).

Interestingly, the last example of similarly pierced tablets, DAAM 1.31, also dating to the Early New Kingdom (MS), only contains a birds' flight report, this time regarding the case of a little girl who had fallen sick. It is possible that KUB 32.130 was meant to be accompanied by such a report. Similar 'attachments' could be used in epistolary exchange: requests for inquiries might come with a letter, and the pierced tablet could be re-used for returning a response to court after the investigations, for example. The full context of the message in DAAM 1.31 remains unclear since the abrupt incipit is uncommon for a conventional letter, lacking epistolary headings and addressee formulae.

DAAM 1.31

obv. 1 ⸢*ki-i*⸣*-kán*[106] *ku-*⸢*it*⸣ 10 KA$_5$.⸢A⸣ 2 ÍD-*za ša-*⸢*ra*⸣*-a pé-ra-an* SIG$_5$-*za* 3 *nam-ma-za* EGIR-*pa da-a-aš* 4 *na-aš-kán pé-ra-an* ⸢*ku*⸣*-uš.* 5 *nu-za* EGIR-*pa da-a-*⸢*aš*⸣ *na-aš-*⸢*kán*⸣
6 *pé-ra-an* SIG$_5$-*za zi-la-wa-*⸢*an*⸣ SIG$_5$-*za* 7 *a-al-li-aš-ša-kán*[107] *ku-iš* 8 ⸢ḪUR⸣.SAG-*an pa-ri-ia-an* 9 *zi-la-wa-an ku-uš. pa-it* 10 *nu ku-it-ma-an* $^{\text{LÚ.MEŠ}}$MUŠEN.⸢DÙ⸣ lo.e. 11 *I-NA* ^{URU}*aš-ra-am-ma*
rev. 12 *a-ra-an-*⸢*zi*⸣ *ku-*⸢*it*⸣*-ma-na* 13 EGIR-*pa ú-wa-an-zi* 14 *nu ma-a-an A-NA* DUMU.MUNUS TUR 15 SAG.DU-*ni ta-pa-aš-ša-aš*[108] 16 *ud-da-na-za ap pé-ez-zi-ia-az* 17 *Ú-UL ku-it-ki* 18 *na-ḫu-wa-ni nu* MUŠEN$^{\text{ḪI.A}}$ 19 *ar-ḫa pé-eš-ši-an-du* //

(1-4) Concerning (the fact) that: ten 'fox'-birds, up from the river, (came) in front from the favourable side. Then, it[109] (i. e. the group?) turned back and (came) in front from the unfavourable side.

106 The reading ⸢*ki-i*⸣*-ma* in Rieken 2019: 268 is probably mistaken, as the sign copied in her autography is *-kán*, well visible in the photo.

107 *Pace* Rieken 2019: 268 *a-al-li-iš-ša-kán*.

108 The reading in Rieken 2019: 268 *ta-pa-aš-ši* seems unlikely from the photograph.

109 I. e. the group of birds? Resumption in the singular seems to refer to the ten birds as a group, moving together (thus also Rieken 2019: 268).

(5-9) It turned back (again), and it (came) in front from the favourable side, (and) *zilawan* from the favourable side. An *ālliya-* bird, which (was) across the mountain, flew *zilawan* from the unfavourable side.
(10-19) Until the augurs arrive at Ašramma, and until (later) they come back, if for the life of the little girl, for the matter of (her) fever, we have nothing to fear later on: let the birds exclude it.

In this letter, the hole, drilled almost in the middle of it, also belongs to the original making of the tablet (discussed in Rieken 2019: 270f.). Similarly to KUB 32.130, this tablet ends with an oracular question, making the text 'incomplete', albeit in a different way. In the text about the resolutions for Šavoška of Šamuḫa, the report is missing entirely and must be expected elsewhere. In DAAM 1.31, however, a report had already been compiled and is being delivered by the present message. The context might suggest that the addressees of this text were contacted for further consultation through a new oracle, anticipated in the final lines, and perhaps also for gathering their opinion on the results of the former. Both KUB 32.130 and DAAM 1.31 can thus be connected with correspondence – and oracle results and discussions are indeed well attested in other, full-fledged letters. Their possible nature of 'attachments' is also compatible with the interpretation that short oracular texts could be delivered accompanying epistolary exchanges.

4. Concluding remarks

An overview of salient aspects of writing in oracular tablets highlighted the potential wealth of information derived from the tablets' physical and graphic features, text distribution and organization, and writing standards and conventions. Their study helps elucidate the logic of the writing process as well as some of the mechanisms of the oracular practices in their background. Some peculiarities of oracle tablets and oracular writing stand out and are also of interest, on their own, for the broader study of Hittite writing traditions.

The analysis of several tablets displaying multiple scripts (§3.1), in some cases inserted into the text at a later time, shows that those sections written in different scripts, and arguably later insertions, reflect different moments of text composition and directly correlate with the performance and recording of the oracles. The habit of leaving blank spaces and entire paragraphs in tablets of oracular content sometimes responds to the same motivation. However, other examples discussed in the article show that this peculiar practice depends on numerous factors: the text's organization in oracle tablets was relatively flexible, bound to the individual document and depended on variable choices, taken also during the process of inscription, rather than following standardized scribal conventions and rules of 'pagination' (§3.2).

The relatively widespread use of abbreviations and the presence in the corpus of a few tablets featuring 'cursory' scripts are other features distinguishing Hittite oracular writing (§3.3). The discussion showed that each oracle technique and text type (e. g. the three main types: KIN oracles, augury, extispicy) displays distinct trends in the attempt to abbreviate the texts and the oracular formula, which speaks of different trajectories in the development of writing standards, probably bound to tradition and the lore of the oracle experts. But the texts have in common at least the aim of time-saving in the recording of the documents, whereas the preoccupation with space management on the tablet was, apparently, less relevant for the scribes – as it is also demonstrated by other characteristics of oracle tablets, such as the abundance of blank spaces and paragraphs. Although peculiar handwritings, less regular, loosely, and hastily written, are attested in oracle texts, they are a relatively rare occurrence in the corpus, which otherwise displays regular cuneiform scripts compatible with the other text genres produced by the Hittite scribal circles. Several examples of texts secondarily added within oracular inquiries also display carefully written scripts.

Finally, tablets with oracular content of minute size and distinctive formats are potentially representative of the early steps in the *chaîne opératoire* of Hittite oracular writing (§3.4). They contain brief oracle requests, results, and inquiries for further scrutiny and could be used for collecting information and compiling long and detailed complete oracle reports on larger tablets. A few perforated tablets of this kind might be interpreted as means for delivering results and oracle communications at a distance, in the form of attachment to letters or as epistolary means on their own, bundled with other reports or documents.

Bibliography

Archi, Alfonso

1974 Il sistema KIN della divinazione ittita. *OA* 13: 113–44.

1975 L'ornitomanzia ittita. *SMEA* 16: 119–80.

Beal, Richard H.

1992 *The Organization of the Hittite Military*. THeth 20. Heidelberg: Winter.

2002 Hittite Oracles. In: Leda Ciraolo and Jonathan Seidel (eds.), *Magic and Divination in the Ancient World*. AMD 2. Leiden: Brill / Styx, 57–81.

Beckman, Gary

2003 Excerpt from an Oracle Report. In: William W. Hallo and K. Lawson Younger, Jr. (eds.), *The Context of Scripture. Volume 1: Canonical Compositions from the Biblical World*. Leiden et al.: Brill, 204–6.

2012 An Irate Goddess (CTH 710). In: Behrad Aghaei and M. R. Ghanoonparvar (eds.), *Iranian Languages and Culture: Essays in Honor of Gernot Ludwig Windfuhr*. Costa Mesa, California: Mazda, 1–7.

Berman, Howard

1982 Some Hittite Oracle Fragments. *JCS* 34: 94–98.

Cammarosano, Michele

2013 Hittite Cult Inventories – Part One: The Hittite Cult Inventories as Textual Genre. *WdO* 43: 63–105.

2015 3D-Joins und Schriftmetrologie. A Quantitative Approach to Cuneiform Palaeography. In: Elena Devecchi, Gerfrid G.W. Müller, and Jana Mynářová (eds.), *Current Research in Cuneiform Palaeography. Proceedings of the Workshop organised at the 60th Rencontre Assyriologique Internationale, Warsaw 2014.* Gladbeck: PeWe, 145–86.

Cammarosano, Michele (ed.)

2016–20 Cult Inventory (CTH 528.15) hethiter.net/: CTH 528.15 (INTR 2020-04-07, TX 03.06.2016) – last accessed 1.8.2024.

Christiansen, Birgit

forthc. Oracular Procedures as a Strategy for Coping with Crises at the Hittite Royal Court. In: Marta Pallavidini, Constanza Coppini, and Johannes Bach (eds.), *Change, Order, Remembrance: Crisis and Religion in the Ancient Near East. Proceedings of the workshop held at the 18th EASR conference, Pisa, August 30th – September 3rd 2021.* Kasion 13. Münster: Zaphon.

Corti, Carlo

2010 The History of the Exploration of Uşaklı/Kuşaklı Höyük and the "Rediscovery" of a Middle-Hittite Tablet. *CollAnat* 9: 193–212.

de Martino, Stefano

2005 Hittite Letters from the Time of Tutḫaliya I/II, Arnuwanda I and Tutḫaliya III. *AoF* 32: 291–321.

García Trabazo, José Virgilio

2002 *Textos religiosos hititas. Mitos, plegarias y rituales.* Biblioteca de Ciencias Bíblicas y Orientales 6. Madrid: Trotta.

Goetze, Albrecht

1933 *Die Annalen des Muršiliš.* MVAeG 38. Leipzig: Hinrichs.

1950 Hittite Omen (Investigating the Anger of the Gods). In: James B. Pritchard (ed.), *Ancient Near Eastern Texts. Relating to the Old Testament.* Princeton, New Jersey: Princeton University Press, 497f.

Gordin, Shai

2015 *Hittite Scribal Circles. Scholarly Tradition and Writing Habits.* StBoT 59. Wiesbaden: Harrassowitz.

Haas, Volkert

2008 *Hethitische Orakel, Vorzeichen und Abwehrstrategien. Ein Beitrag zur hethitischen Kulturgeschichte.* Berlin / New York: de Gruyter.

Haas, Volkert and Ilse Wegner

1996 Orakelprotokolle aus Kuşaklı. *MDOG* 128: 105–20.

Hoffner, Harry A.

1975 Propaganda and Political Justification in Hittite Historiography. In: Hans Goedicke and Jimmy J.M. Roberts (eds.), *Unity and Diversity. Essays in the History, Literature, and Religion of the Ancient Near East.* Baltimore / London: Johns Hopkins University Press, 49–62.

Hoffner, Harry A. and H. Craig Melchert

2008 *A Grammar of the Hittite Language. Part 1: Reference Grammar.* Winona Lake, Indiana: Eisenbrauns.

Klinger, Jörg

2010 Der Kult der Ištar von Šamuḫa in mittelhethitischer Zeit. In: Jörg Klinger, Elisabeth Rieken, and Christel Rüster (eds.), *Investigationes Anatolicae: Gedenkschrift für Erich Neu.* StBoT 52. Wiesbaden: Harrassowitz, 153–67.

Kloekhorst, Alwin

2022 Hittite *dapi(a)-*, *dapit/d-*, *dapiant-* 'all, every, each; entire': a logographic interpretation. *Hungarian Assyriological Review* 3: 203–20.

Košak, Silvin

2002– *Konkordanz der hethitischen Keilschrifttafeln, Online-Datenbank Version.* hethiter.net/: hetkonk (2.plus) – last accessed 1.8.2024.

Laroche, Emmanuel

1971 *Catalogue des Textes Hittites.* Paris: Klincksieck.

Lebrun, Renée

1976 *Samuha, foyer religieux de l'Empire Hittite.* Louvain-la-Neuve: Institut Orientaliste.

Marcuson, Hannah

2016 *"Word of the Old Woman": Studies in Female Ritual Practice in Hittite Anatolia.* Ph.D. dissertation, University of Chicago.

Maul, Stefan M.

2003 Omina und Orakel. *RlA* 10: 45–88.

Mouton, Alice

2007a *Rêves hittites : contribution à une histoire et une anthropologie du rêve en Anatolie ancienne.* CHANE 28. Leiden / Boston: Brill.

2007b Au sujet du compte rendu oraculaire Hittite KBo 18.142. In: Detlev Groddek and Marina Zorman (eds.), *Tabularia Hethaeorum – Hethitologische Beiträge. Silvin Košak zum 65. Geburtstag.* DBH 25. Wiesbaden: Harrassowitz, 551–55

Mouton, Alice and Ian Rutherford

2013 Luwian Religion, a Research Project: The Case of "Hittite" Augury. In: Alice Mouton, Ian Rutherford, and Ilya Yakubovich (eds.), *Luwian Identities. Culture, Language and Religion Between Anatolia and the Aegean.* CHANE 64. Leiden / Boston: Brill, 329–43.

Orlamünde, Julia

2001 Überlegungen zum hethitischen KIN-Orakel. In: Thomas Richter, Doris Prechel and Jörg Klinger (eds.), *Kulturgeschichten. Altorientalische Studien für Volkert Haas zum 65. Geburtstag.* Saarbrücken: SDV, 295–311.

Pisaniello, Valerio

2020 Glossenkeil and Indentation on Hittite Tablets. *AoF* 47: 123–42.

Popko, Maciej

1995 *Religions of Asia Minor.* Warsaw: Dialog.

Rieken, Elisabeth

2019 Kp 14/03 – eine SMS aus der Hethiterzeit? In: Doris Prechel and Hans Neumann (eds.), *Beiträge zur Kenntnis und Deutung altorientalischer Archivalien. Festschrift für Helmut Freydank zum 80. Geburtstag.* Dubsar 6. Münster: Zaphon, 265–73.

Sakuma, Yasuhiko

2009 *Hethitische Vogelorakeltexte (I: Teil 1: Untersuchung; II: Teil 2: Bearbeitung).* Ph.D. dissertation, Universität Würzburg.

2013 *Terms of Ornithomancy in Hittite.* Tokyo University Linguistic Papers 33: 219–38.

Schuol, Monika

1994 Die Terminologie des hethitischen *SU*-Orakels. Eine Untersuchung auf der Grundlage des mittelhethitischen Textes KBo XVI 97 unter vergleichender Berücksichtigung akkadischer Orakeltexte und Lebermodelle. *AoF* 21: 73–124, 247–304.

Soysal, Oğuz

2000 Analysis of a Hittite Oracular Document. *ZA* 90: 85–122.

Tischler, Johann

2019 *Hethitische Texte in Transkription – KUB 49.* DBH 52. Wiesbaden: Harrassowitz.

Tognon, Rosanna

2004 Il testo oracolare ittita KUB V 7. *KASKAL* 1: 59–81.

2005 *Gli Oracoli* MUŠEN *ḪURRI: una Tecnica Divinatoria Ittita.* Ph.D. dissertation, Università degli Studi di Napoli L'Orientale.

Trameri, Andrea

2023 Hittite *warā(i)-*: '(bird) mate, companion'. *Hungarian Assyriological Review* 4: 23–35.

2024 *Kizzuwatna. History of Cilicia in the Middle and Late Bronze Age (ca. 2000–1200 BC).* HbOr 1/185. Leiden et al.: Brill.

forthc. *Capturing Birds for the King. On Fauna in a Hittite Letter from Tapikka* (HKM 48), *JCS* 77.

Ünal, Ahmed

1978 *Ein Orakeltext über die Intrigen am hethitischen Hof (KUB XXIII 70 = Bo 2011).* THeth 6. Heidelberg: Winter.

Ünal, Ahmed and Annelies Kammenhuber

1974 Das althethitische Losorakel KBo XVIII 151. *ZVS* 88: 157–80.

van den Hout, Theo P.J.

1995 *Der Ulmitešub-Vertrag. Eine prosopographische Untersuchung*. StBoT 38. Wiesbaden: Harrassowitz.

1998 *The Purity of Kingship. An Edition of CTH 569 and Related Hittite Oracle Inquiries of Tuthaliya IV*. Leiden et al.: Brill.

2001 Bemerkungen zu älteren hethitischen Orakeltexten. In: Thomas Richter, Doris Prechel, and Jörg Klinger (eds.), *Kulturgeschichten. Altorientalische Studien für Volkert Haas zum 65. Geburtstag*. Saarbrücken: SDV, 423–40.

2002 Another View of Hittite Literature. In: Stefano de Martino and Franca Pecchioli Daddi (eds.), *Anatolia antica. Studi in memoria di Fiorella Imparati*. Eothen 11. Firenze: LoGisma, 857–78.

2003a Omina (Omens). B. Bei den Hethitern. *RlA* 10: 88–90.

2003b Orakel (Oracle). B. Bei den Hethitern. *RlA* 10: 118–24.

2012 The Ductus of the Alalaḫ VII Texts and the Origin of Hittite Cuneiform. In: Elena Devecchi (ed.), *Palaeography and Scribal Practices in Syro-Palestine and Anatolia in the Late Bronze Age. Papers Read at a Symposium in Leiden, 17–18 December 2009*. PIHANS 119. Leiden: Peeters, 147–70.

Waal, Willemijn

2015 *Hittite Diplomatics. Studies in Ancient Document Format and Record Management*. StBoT 57. Wiesbaden: Harrassowitz.

Warbinek, Livio

2019 Abbreviations, Lines, and Clay Tablets: How to Write a KIN Oracle, How to Manage the Space. In: Elena Devecchi, Jana Mynářová, and Gerfrid G.W. Müller (eds.), *Current Research in Cuneiform Palaeography 2. Proceedings of the Workshop organised at the 64th Rencontre Assyriologique Internationale, Innsbruck 2018*. Gladbeck: PeWe, 137–55.

2020 *Il sistema mantico Ittita KIN*. Firenze: Firenze University Press.

Weeden, Mark

2011 *Hittite Logograms and Hittite Scholarship*. StBoT 54. Wiesbaden: Harrassowitz.

Wilhelm, Gernot

1997 *Keilschrifttexte aus Gebäude A*. Kuşaklı–Šarišša. Band 1/1. Rahden: Leidorf.

1998 Zwei mittelhethitische Briefe aus dem Gebäude C in Kuşaklı. *MDOG* 130: 175–87.

REFLECTIONS ON THE ORIGINS OF SOME HITTITE SCRIBAL PRACTICES

*Willemijn Waal**
Leiden University

Abstract

When the Hittites adopted the cuneiform writing system, they took over many of the existing scribal habits along with the script. Some Hittite scribal practices, however, differ from those found in Mesopotamian cuneiform traditions. This paper will explore the possible motives behind some of the adjustments made by the Hittite scribes. It will be proposed that they may be the result of interaction with the Anatolian hieroglyphic writing system that co-existed with the cuneiform script in Hittite Anatolia.

1. Introduction

It is generally assumed that the Hittites took over a variant of the Old Babylonian cuneiform script via northern Syria in the 17th century BCE, though earlier introduction dates have been suggested as well.[1] Little is known about the precise transmission and adaptation process; the first records of the Hittite tablet collections testify to an already well-established Hittite scribal tradition. The Hittites imported the cuneiform writing system together with its most important scribal conventions. Some Hittite scribal habits, however, are clearly different from those of the Mesopotamian cuneiform tradition. In this paper, I would like to look at some of these typically 'Hittite' features in relation to the other writing system that was in use in Anatolia, the Anatolian Hieroglyphs. When the interaction between these two writing systems is discussed, it is usually assumed that the Anatolian Hieroglyphs were influenced by Hittite cuneiform (recently, e. g. Payne 2017a; Rieken and Yakubovich 2023: 211–17). I would like to argue that some phenomena may in fact be better explained as influence in the opposite direction, that is, as influence of the Anatolian Hieroglyphs on the Hittite cuneiform. This scenario implies an earlier date of the Anatolian Hieroglyphs than is held by the *communis opinio,* which places the origins of this writing system in the 15th century BCE, so well after the introduction of the cuneiform script (e. g. Yakubovich 2010: 295–99; Payne 2015: 66–68; van den Hout 2020: 127–33; Mora 2022: 69–75). It is, however,

* This paper has benefitted much from the stimulating discussions during the second International HFR Symposium "The Tablets and Their Scribes" in Mainz. I would like to thank the organizers Susanne Görke, Adam Kryszeń, Gerfrid Müller, Elisabeth Rieken, Daniel Schwemer and Charles Steitler, and also Mark Weeden, Shai Gordin, Alwin Kloekhorst and Adam Kryszeń for their valuable comments. Needless to say, I alone remain responsible for the views expressed here.

1 See recently e. g. Wilhelmi 2016; Kloekhorst and Waal 2019; Klinger 2022.

in line with new insights and discoveries over the last decades, including a hieroglyphic graffito on an Old Hittite vessel,[2] which makes it exceedingly more likely that the Anatolian Hieroglyphs were already in use as a writing system from at least the Old Hittite period onwards (Simon 2020), and possibly earlier (Waal 2012; in press a; Waal and Kloekhorst in press).

2. Hittite sealing practices

In Mesopotamia and Syria, clay tablets were sealed by means of rolling a cylinder seal over the surface of a clay tablet. The cylinder seal is closely linked with cuneiform writing on clay; with the emergence of the cuneiform script at the end of the fourth millennium BCE, the cylinder seal quickly replaced the stamp seal, which was in use throughout the ancient Near East from the Neolithic period onwards. In the words of Dominique Collon (1987: 5): "Wherever cuneiform had spread, so had the cylinder seal and when cuneiform and clay tablets fell into disuse, so the cylinder seal was replaced by the stamp seal". Indeed, the role of stamp seals becomes marginal in regions where cuneiform was used, and they only make their comeback with the rise of alphabetic writing systems in the first millennium BCE.

In Anatolia, a very different situation presents itself. In this region, the introduction of the cuneiform script did not bring about a switch to cylinder seals, but the use of stamp seals continued.[3] These stamp seals were not gently rolled over the clay like cylinder seals, but impressed quite deeply into the clay. Moreover, the impression of a stamp seal was not the only means of certification. Almost all Hittite sealed tablets, which mainly consist of royal land deeds, have strings in their core, which protruded from a central point in the tablet's lower edge (Fig. 1).[4] The strings have not survived, but they did leave their marks in the soft clay on the inside of the tablet. Since in case of the land deed VAT 7436, which was accidentally broken in half, the number of string imprints corresponds to the number of witnesses mentioned at the end of the tablet, it has been suggested that to these strings, *bullae* or *cretulae* (i. e. lumps of clay impressed with a stamp seal) were originally attached with the seal impressions of the witnesses.[5] Though the original *bullae* belonging to the land deeds are missing, we do have ample evidence for their existence.[6] In the Hittite capital, clay *bullae* have been found in sub-

2 For this discovery, see Doğan-Alparslan and Alparslan apud Schachner 2023: 63.

3 Cylinder seals are dominant only during one chapter of Anatolian history: the Old Assyrian period (ca. 1950–1720 BCE). Their use was clearly connected to the Assyrian merchants, and as soon as their presence in Anatolia disappeared, the use of cylinder seals was virtually abandoned.

4 In addition to the land deeds, these include KBo 62.32, 230/f and KBo 44.7. There are three sealed Hittite tablets that certainly do not have such strings (see below n. 12), for most other sealed tablets, it cannot be determined whether or not strings were present in the tablet.

5 See Güterbock 1997: 30. Note that he leaves open the possibility that the bullae were sealed not by the witnesses only, but perhaps by a combination of witnesses, the scribe and the contracting parties. For the view that the bullae probably only contained the seals of the witnesses, see van den Hout 2020: 81f.

6 Intriguingly, the clay bullae discovered in the immediate vicinity of the land deeds stem from a different, later period, and they cannot be matched to these documents. For the view that these land deeds and bullae served as reference collections, see van den Hout 2020: 230.

Fig. 1. 3D model of Hittite land deed Bo 90/741 with a large stamp seal impression in the middle of the obverse and a hole for strings in the middle of the lower edge. Courtesy of Gerfrid Müller (Source: hethiter.net/:3DArchiv, Modellnr. Bo 90-751).

stantial numbers,[7] and recently a large collection of *bullae* was discovered at the Hittite town Kayalıpınar/Šamuḫa.[8]

The use of *bullae* and strings for sealing in itself is nothing remarkable. The practice of sealing doors, sacks, vessels, and other objects by means of string and lumps of clay is attested all over the ancient Near East (e. g. Moortgat-Correns 1957: 451–55; Otto

7 Most of the bullae are teardrop or cone-shaped pieces of clay with an impression of a stamp seal at the bottom; sometimes the sides of the cone could also be covered with (partial) seal impressions. They were formed around a knot of strings, protruding from the narrow end of the cone (Herbordt et al. 2011: 26). In the exceptional cases that the bullae are impressed with cylinder instead of stamp seals, they are stamped rather than rolled over the clay, demonstrating the tenacity of the stamping tradition (Boehmer and Güterbock 1987: 107; Dinçol and Dinçol 2018: 17, 60). For an edition of the bullae found in Ḫattuša, see Herbordt 2005; Herbordt et al. 2011.

8 See Müller-Karpe 2020: 194–214 and Müller-Karpe and Müller-Karpe 2020: 196–201.

2010: 469–72). However, it was *not* the regular way of sealing clay tablets. The sealing of clay tablets by means of stamp seals, strings and *bullae* seems to be a uniquely Anatolian feature. Before exploring the possible motives behind this practice, it is good to note that only a tiny percentage of Hittite tablets are sealed. Of the ca. 30,000 cuneiform clay tablets and fragments, only some 53 have a seal impression – or slightly more than 100, if one includes fragments that were in all likelihood sealed, but of which the sealing itself has not survived. As mentioned above, the sealed tablets are primarily royal land deeds,[9] and some ten tablets of other text genres (Balza 2012; Waal 2015: 44–50; in press b). This low number is hardly surprising; the Hittite cuneiform corpus predominantly consists of religious, historical and literary compositions – documents that one does not expect to be sealed. Document types that are usually sealed in Mesopotamia, such as legal contracts and receipts, are virtually absent. It has long been suggested that these kinds of records were written down on wood, and consequently did not survive. References in the Hittite cuneiform texts to wooden documents reveal that they included sale contracts and receipts, and in some cases, it is explicitly mentioned that they were sealed.[10] As it happens, these missing sealed wooden documents are key to understanding why the sealing practices in Anatolia are so different from those in other cuneiform traditions.

As I have recently argued elsewhere, the unusual Hittite sealing practices can be explained through the concept of anchoring innovation; the introduction of a new writing system (the cuneiform script) was integrated with the already existing sealing tradition of wooden documents (inscribed with Anatolian Hieroglyphs), of which the tying of strings was a crucial component (Waal in press a). I will briefly summarize the main argumentation below. As mentioned above, Hittite texts refer to wooden documents that could be sealed. The appearance and usage of these wooden documents are heavily debated.[11] Regardless of their precise physical characteristics, however, the sealing of these wooden documents would undoubtedly have involved strings that were tied around the document, and closed off by means of *bullae*. The use of strings is a very common element in the sealing of documents that are made of (relatively) perishable materials such as papyrus, leather, bark, leaves or wood (for examples, see Waal 2022). Wooden diptychs, for instance, could be sealed by means of tying strings around the closed diptych and attaching a *bulla* to the fastening knot (Herbordt 2005: 37f.; Cammarosano et al. 2019: 148). In a similar vein, strings could be tied around rolled

9 For the sake of convenience, I use the conventional term 'land deeds' though this term is not entirely adequate (cf. Rüster and Wilhelm 2012: 35).

10 For the use of (sealed) writing boards, see e. g. Symington 1991; Cammarosano et al. 2019: 136–41; van den Hout 2020: 184–217; Waal 2011; 2023a: 142–46.

11 The wooden documents are usually thought to have looked like the diptychs found in a shipwreck near Uluburun, dating to the 14th century BCE (see, e. g., Symington 1991; Herbordt 2005: 37; Cammarosano et al. 2019: 141–48), but it is very possible that their physical characteristics were quite different, especially if they were inscribed with Anatolian Hieroglyphs rather than cuneiform (for this ongoing debate, see recently e. g. Cammarosano et al. 2019; van den Hout 2020: 184–217; Waal 2022; Waal and Kloekhorst in press). Perhaps they were not diptychs, or at least not exclusively, but rather strips of wood or bark, on which the texts were carved or painted (Waal 2022).

strips or folded documents of wood or bark, which were subsequently sealed by means of *bullae*.

The Hittite verb used for sealing eloquently shows that the tying of strings was a crucial component of the Hittite sealing practice. The action of sealing is expressed by the verb *šai-/šiye-* (see CHD Š 16; HED 11, 49) of which the primary meaning is 'to tie', 'to fasten (by means of strings)' or 'to knot together' (Waal 2023b). The tying of the strings likely symbolized the 'binding' of the witnesses and/or contracting parties to the agreement that was made in the document.[12]

I would therefore like to suggest the following scenario: Hittite sealed documents were predominantly wooden records (including sale contracts and receipts) that were sealed by means of strings and *bullae*. Because the tying of strings was such a vital component of the sealing process, the use of strings was transferred to the sealing of clay tablets – on the rare occasions that transactions or agreements were recorded on clay (or metal),[13] and not on wood. For this reason, the Hittites did not adopt the stringless cylinder seal practice along with the cuneiform script, but instead found a way to creatively merge the sealing of clay tablets with their own sealing tradition, leading to the unique combination of strings, stamp seals, *bullae* and clay tablets. It may be added that the Hittite attachment to using strings in their sealing process is by no means exceptional; strings still feature in many official documents today, even though they no longer serve a practical function (Waal in press a).[14]

The above scenario would not only account for the curious presence of strings in Hittite tablets, but also explain why the stamp steal remained the preferred sealing tool in Anatolia, and why only so few Hittite tablets were sealed. Even after the arrival of the cuneiform script and the clay tablet, the most commonly sealed documents continued to be wooden records (sealed with strings and *bullae*), and sealed clay tablets remained the exception. This all implies that a writing tradition on wood already existed in Anatolia *before* the arrival of the cuneiform script.[15] After all, if there was no preexisting practice of document sealing, there would have been no pressing reason not to take over the Mesopotamian cylinder seal, and no incentive to invent the ingenious, yet cumbersome practice of inserting strings to the core of sealed clay tablets. The only logical candidate for the script used on these wooden records are the Anatolian Hieroglyphs. As mentioned in the introduction, there is growing evidence that this writing system was already in use before the arrival of the cuneiform script in Anatolia. The assumption that the Anatolian Hieroglyphs predate the Hittite cuneiform script, rather than the other way around, as is now usually assumed, may also explain some other characteristics of Hittite cuneiform, such as the prolific use of determinatives or classifiers.

12 Indirect confirmation hereof is the fact that the three sealed Hittite tablets that certainly do not have strings (KUB 25.32, HKM 4 and 14) do not involve any witnesses or contracting parties (Waal in press b).

13 For the sealing of metal tablets, see Waal in press b.

14 Note that the practice of tying of strings is also reflected in the terminology related to contracts and agreements in many languages ('tying the knot', 'obligation', 'binding', etc.).

15 For the evidence of use of bullae in the Old Assyrian period, see recently Strupler 2021 (with references).

3. Hittite use of classifiers

In Mesopotamian cuneiform, some logograms functioned as determinatives or classifiers,[16] identifying the following or preceding word as belonging to a certain semantic class. The use of classifiers has long been an understudied phenomenon in Hittitology and in cuneiform studies in general, but fortunately this is starting to change.[17] In a groundbreaking study on Hittite geographic classifiers, Adam Kryszeń (2019: 2) makes the following important observation:

> Whereas in texts from other cuneiform corpora a toponym is not always readily apparent and can be mistaken for, e. g., a personal name, Hittite scribes almost never allowed a controversy of this sort and consequently applied a geographic classifier to the name. Only 3.1% (611 instances) of all attestations have no classification at all.[18]

Not only is the Hittite usage of geographic classifiers extremely stable, but their inventory is also more varied and elaborate compared to the traditional geographic classifiers in cuneiform. Kryszeń (2019: 3f.) lists no less than 30 distinct kinds of geographic identification in Hittite texts, over 40 if one includes texts composed in other languages. He discerns a chronological development: the Hittite repertoire of geographic classifiers starts to expand from the Middle Hittite period onwards, reaching its peak in the New Hittite period (Kryszeń 2019: 3f.). An interesting innovation is the introduction of compound classifers, which can contain up to three elements (Kryszeń 2019: 3). Though exact numbers with respect to other types of classifiers are not available, it seems safe to say that the Hittite use of classifiers in general is more profuse than in other cuneiform traditions. For instance, Hittite seems to be the only cuneiform script in which MUŠ 'snake' is used as a determinative.[19]

In the Anatolian hieroglyphic script, the use of classifiers is well-established, and especially thanks to the recent studies of Annick Payne (2017a; 2017b; 2018) their usage is more and more understood. Payne (2017a; 2018) has demonstrated that the use of classifiers in Anatolian Hieroglyphs develops over time; classifiers are less common in the Hittite period than in the later Iron Age. As she observes, this may be due in part to the surviving material evidence: most of the Late Bronze Age hieroglyphic material consists of legends on seals and seal impressions that necessarily contain only limited and concise information, without a great need to use determinatives (Payne 2017a: 222).[20]

16 The term 'determinative' is still the most commonly used term in cuneiform studies for logograms in this function, but since the seminal study of Selz et al. 2017[2018] has shown that the term 'classifier' is more appropriate, I will use this term here.

17 See, e. g. the important studies of Selz et al. 2017[2018]; Kryszeń 2019, 2020 and the unpublished MPhil thesis of Eleanor Home, University of Oxford.

18 In Hittite compositions, the number of unclassified place names is even lower and comes down to 2.3% (Kryszeń 2019: 12).

19 As observed by Selz et al. 2017[2018]: 314 in the Sumerian system animals are classified mainly according to utilitarian and functional considerations; as a rule, snakes and worms are not classified.

20 An additional complication is that the only more substantial surviving texts from the Late Bronze Age are royal monumental inscriptions on stone. These kinds of texts, which were meant for public display, may have constituted a special category ('eine Sonderform', cf. Payne 2015: 65) and some of their features (e. g. a high level of iconicity and limited grammatical marking) may not be representative.

It is usually assumed that the Anatolian hieroglyphic classifiers were inspired by the cuneiform script, because most classifiers found in the earliest surviving hieroglyphic texts resemble those found in the cuneiform script. The table below, which is based on Payne 2017a: 224, shows that there is indeed a substantial overlap between Anatolian hieroglyphic and cuneiform classifiers in the Hittite period. However, there are also some striking differences. Most arresting are the two final signs listed in the table, *273 and *85.[21] They do not have a counterpart in cuneiform, as this script does not employ classifiers for verbs or for abstract concepts. The Sumerian system of classifiers has been identified as a 'noun classifier system' by Selz et al. 2017[2018]: 306–9. Within this system, they distinguish between 'sortal' classifiers, including animate (humans, deities, animals) and inanimate (vegetal, cloth/textiles, mineral, natural elements, spatial, time) classifiers, and 'mensural' classifiers (unitizers/plural, mensuratives, arrangements and containers). Classifiers for abstract concepts[22] and classifiers marking events (generally realized as verbs) that we do find in the Anatolian Hieroglyphs are missing in cuneiform. Another crucial difference is that the Anatolian Hieroglyphs lack grammatical classifiers indicating plural, which are omnipresent in cuneiform (notably ^{MEŠ} and $^{\text{ḪI.A}}$). The cuneiform and Anatolian hieroglyphic classifiers thus function in fundamentally different ways from early onwards.

Category	AH Classifier	AH Sign	Cuneiform Classifier
Country	– REGIO		– KI
City	– URBS		URU –
Mountain	MONS –		ḪUR.SAG –
Divinity	DEUS –		D –
Male person	VIR$_2$ –		LÚ –
Human being	ǀ –		M –
Strength	*273 –		–
'to kneel'	*85 –		–

Table 1. Empire/Early determinatives after Payne 2017a: 224 (table 3).

In addition to typological differences, there are also dissimilarities between some of the early hieroglyphic classifiers and their alleged cuneiform counterparts. The two first classifiers mentioned in Table 1, REGIO and URBS, have been regarded as examples of influence of the cuneiform script on the Anatolian Hieroglyphs. Like in cuneiform, in the Anatolian hieroglyphic script most classifiers are placed before the host word, but some are found in postposition. The latter applies to the classifiers REGIO and URBS. The sign REGIO ('land') has been identified with the cuneiform classifier ^{KI} ('place'),

21 Both classifiers are first attested in the Yalburt inscription; *273 is used in combination with the verb 'to conquer' (block 16 §2a) and *85 with the verb 'to kneel' (block 6 §1), translation following Hawkins 1995: 68–71, see also Payne 2017a: 225 with n. 14.

22 A possible exception may be the classifier GIG 'illness'. This classifier is listed by Selz et al. 2017[2018]: 308 in the category humans and deities, as it is perceived as the result of demonic forces (Selz et al. 2017[2018]: 312).

a geographic classifier that exceptionally occurs in postposition. Payne (2017a: 223) suggests that since the classifier ^{KI} in cuneiform may have been at the roots of the Anatolian hieroglyphic classifier REGIO, the latter is therefore placed in postposition. As for the sign URBS, which is also in postposition, whereas its cuneiform counterpart ^{URU} is always placed before the host word, she cautiously speculates that the iconic similarity between the signs URBS and REGIO (the latter is basically a reduplication of the former) may have led to its postpositioning. This suggestion is taken over by Rieken and Yakubovich (2023: 216f.), who see the unusual position of REGIO and URBS as an example of graphic interference of the cuneiform script with the Anatolian Hieroglyphs.

This scenario is not without problems. As shown by Kryszeń 2020, the cuneiform classifier ^{KI} is seldom used in Hittite cuneiform. Among the almost 20,000 attestations of place names in Hittite cuneiform, only about 120 are accompanied by the classifier ^{KI}. Moreover, most of its attestations are found in Sumerian or Akkadian compositions, or in texts that were translated from Akkadian or based on an Akkadian *Vorlage*. There are altogether only 14 attestations in Hittite compositions, which, even though they may be preserved in later copies, can all be traced back to the Old Hittite period. After this period, the classifier no longer seems to be productive in Hittite context (Kryszeń 2020: 215). Altogether, its highly specialized and restricted use make ^{KI} a very unlikely source of inspiration for the Anatolian hieroglyphic classifier REGIO.[23]

As for the Late Bronze Age Anatolian hieroglyphic classifiers that do have a cuneiform counterpart, since they mostly concern very generic and common terms, their correspondence does not necessarily point to a direct influence of one script upon the other.[24] In fact, the above-mentioned typological differences between the Anatolian Hieroglyphs and cuneiform classifier systems make a direct impact of the cuneiform script on the creation of the Anatolian hieroglyphic classifiers improbable. By contrast, we may perhaps see an influence in the opposite direction. The – in the words of Adam Kryszeń – 'overwhelming attachment to classify all geographic names' (2019: 13) and the abundant use of classifiers in Hittite cuneiform in general could be explained by the prominent role of classifiers in the Anatolian hieroglyphic script. Because the Hittite scribes were familiar with the rich and profuse Anatolian hieroglyphic classifier system, they were more inclined to modify, expand and develop the traditional use of classifiers in the cuneiform script.[25]

---

23 A much more likely equivalent of REGIO would be the (prepositioned) cuneiform classifier KUR ('land'), but considering that 'land' is a very general term, the correspondence between these two classifiers does not necessarily point to direct influence in one way or the other (see also below).

24 Unfortunately, a one-to-one comparison between the use of classifiers in Anatolian Hieroglyphs and cuneiform is seriously hindered by the very different nature of the text corpora of the two scripts. As pointed out by Payne (2017a: 224), there is, for example, no mention of textiles, reptiles or plants in the surviving Anatolian hieroglyphic texts, and consequently, also no classifiers for these words are attested.

25 A similar conclusion was independently reached by Eleanor Home in her MPhil thesis. I am grateful to her for generously sharing her work with me.

4. Hittite text subdivisions and word dividers

The layout of Hittite tablets is both very standardized and structured. Virtually all Hittite tablets containing more than a few lines of texts are subdivided by means of horizontal lines, which may best be described as paragraph dividers (Waal 2015: 107f.; Kitazumi 2019).[26] Larger tablets are usually split into vertical columns.[27] These columns are separated by means of an *intercolumnium* consisting of two vertical lines with about 1 cm blank space in between. Though these features develop over time, they are present from the Old Hittite period onwards, and they can be considered Hittite innovations.[28] In contemporary cuneiform traditions the tablets' surface is usually more densely written, and though subdivisions could be made in texts, this was not done on the same large scale and with the same rigidity.

Perhaps the most striking Hittite adjustment with respect to textual layout is the introduction of word space. Virtually without exception, Hittite scribes separated individual words by leaving a blank space in between. The amount of space between words increases over time; on Old Hittite tablets the distance is still quite small, but the practice of word spacing is already there from the start (van den Hout 2020: 106f.). This habit constitutes a break with the Mesopotamian and Syrian traditions, which do not separate words but are written in *scriptio continua* (van den Hout 2020: 106, 108f.).[29] Further, in the last line of a paragraph we may encounter the phenomenon of 'right justification'; the signs of the last word(s) are spread out over the line with longer spaces in between in order to avoid a blank space at the end. All these adjustments combined give Hittite tablets a distinct, orderly and spacious appearance (Fig. 2).

In the Anatolian hieroglyphic script, larger inscriptions are arranged in horizontal lines or registers that are subdivided by means of horizontal rulings. If an inscription is longer than one line, the writing direction changes with each line, this alternation is called *boustrophedon* ('as the ox ploughs'). Within the horizontal registers, the signs are written in vertical columns, usually consisting of 2–3 (sometimes 4) signs stacked on top of each other.[30] There seems to have been an overall preference to start a new word at the beginning of a new vertical column and inscriptions sometimes make use of word dividers, though not consistently (Fig. 3).[31] In addition, the scribes preferred to fill

26 Altogether, only six Hittite compositions of substantial length do not have any paragraph division, in three cases their aberrant layout may be explained by their *Vorlagen* (Waal 2015: 109–11).

27 In total, about 56% of the Hittite tablets have two columns per side, 15% have three, and 0.2% have four columns. The remaining 28.5% is single-columned, see Waal 2015: 85.

28 The space between column dividers (i. e. the width of the *intercolumnium*), for example, increases over time (Waal 2015: 92).

29 An exception is formed by some Old Assyrian texts from Anatolia that have short vertical strokes that can be used to separate words. They are, however, by no means used consistently and they do not strictly serve as word dividers, but may also have other functions (for discussion, see Adelholfer 2024: 173–80). Other, later cuneiform scripts that (inconsistently) use word dividers are Ugaritic (short vertical stroke) and Old Persian (oblique wedge or *Winkelhaken*); see Adelholfer 2024: 173 with n. 408. I thank Jan Gerrit Dercksen for this reference.

30 For the possible origins of this particular layout, see Waal 2022.

31 The appearance of a word divider in the middle of a column is quite rare, see Vertegaal 2017: 240.

Fig. 2. Standard layout of a Hittite two-columned tablet (KBo 2.3, reverse). Courtesy of the Museum of Anatolian Civilizations, Ankara.

the columns completely, without leaving any gaps at the bottom. They therefore played with the sign order or made use of so-called space fillers (Vertegaal 2017).

Anatolian hieroglyphic texts were thus subdivided in various ways, through horizontal registers, vertical columns and word dividers. It is perhaps worthwhile to consider the possibility that this may have instigated the Hittite scribes to apply subdivisions into the cuneiform texts. This was, of course, achieved in very different ways: words were separated by means of word spacing rather than word dividers and/or vertical columns, texts were structured by means of column division and paragraph lines rather than vertical columns and horizontal registers, and the *horror vacui* at the end of a line or column was resolved by right justification instead of space fillers. Moreover, the paragraph dividers in Hittite cuneiform are dictated by content; this is not the case for the horizontal registers in the Anatolian Hieroglyphs.[32] Though the textual subdivision obviously materialized in a very different manner, the very need to distinguish separate words and to divide up the texts into smaller units in Hittite cuneiform may have been prompted by the fact that the scribes were used to doing so in the hieroglyphic script.

32 As kindly pointed out to me by Alwin Kloekhorst, the only clear example of textual subdivision based on content in the hieroglyphic script are the vertical rulings in the Kululu lead strips (Hawkins 2002: 503).

Fig. 3. Typical layout of an Anatolian hieroglyphic inscription (part of Karatepe inscription). Courtesy of Tayfun Bilgin (Source: https://www.hittitemonuments.com/karatepe/karatepe34.jpg).

5. Hittite 'antipathy to polyvalence'

In Akkadian cuneiform, a single sign can not only be read both logographically and phonographically, but it can also have multiple sound values that have evolved historically. In Hittite cuneiform, this kind of polyphony is limited. Though it was no problem if signs had a different logographic and syllabic reading, the Hittite scribes preferred to keep the number of different phonographic readings restricted and we do not see the same development of polyvalence as we do in contemporary Mesopotamian cuneiform traditions (Weeden 2011: 2, 382f.; van den Hout 2020: 105f.). When signs in Hittite cuneiform do have more than one phonographic reading, they usually express similar sounds (e. g. the vowels *e* and *i* or voiced and voiceless consonants). The signs LI and BU, for example, could also be read as *le* and *pu*. However, entirely different, unrelated phonographic readings of the same sign, a well-known phenomenon in Akkadian cuneiform, are less common in Hittite cuneiform.

Similarly, polyphony is rare in the Anatolian Hieroglyphic script. Signs can have a distinct phonographic and logographic reading, but there are no signs that have two or more completely unrelated sound values. If they do have more than one phonetic value, it is only for closely related sounds, like in Hittite cuneiform. The Hittite "antipathy to polyvalence" (Weeden 2011: 383) may perhaps be attributed to influence of the Anatolian Hieroglyphs. Possibly, the Hittite cuneiform scribes were less inclined to attribute more sound values to a single sign than their Mesopotamian colleagues, because this phenomenon hardly existed in the Anatolian hieroglyphic writing system – though it is also conceivable that the need for simplicifation was an independent development.

To conclude, we may mention the Hittite use of the logogram GEŠTIN ('wine') to represent the syllabic value *wi*$_5$. The Hittite word for 'wine' was **wiyanaš*; we thus see an acrophonic principle at play here. Interestingly, in the Anatolian hieroglyphic script, where acrography is a well-established principle, the sign VITIS ('vine') is used to represent the syllabic value *wí*. Mark Weeden (2011: 375) therefore plausibly suggests that the fact that the sign GEŠTIN was used to represent the syllabic value *wi*$_5$ can be seen as an example of the cuneiform script being influenced by hieroglyphic writing. However, considering that acrophony is a rather universal phenomenon, it cannot be excluded that this correspondence is due to coincidence (cf. van den Hout 2020: 132).

6. Concluding remarks

In the above, it has been proposed that some of the adjustments and innovations made by the Hittites when they took over the cuneiform script may be the result of influence from the Anatolian Hieroglyphs. This holds especially true for the sealing practices, which can only be satisfactorily explained as the outcome of the creative incorporation of the sealing habits used for the wooden hieroglyphic documents into the sealing of clay tablets. The other discussed Hittite scribal features are more ambiguous; they may reflect hieroglyphic influence, but alternative explanations cannot be excluded.

Moreover, it is certainly not the case that the Hittites adjusted the cuneiform script to make it more compatible with the Anatolian Hieroglyphs in every respect. The essential characteristics of the cuneiform script were taken over without change and the frequent use of Sumerograms and Akkadograms, as well as the presence of Sumerian and Akkadian compositions in the Hittite tablet collections testify to the Hittite attachment to the Mesopotamian cuneiform tradition.

As the focus of this paper was on the possible influence of the Anatolian hieroglyphic script on the development of certain Hittite cuneiform scribal habits, the possible influence of the cuneiform script on the Anatolian Hieroglyphs has only been marginally addressed. Considering the fundamental differences between the two scripts, such as the writing direction (left to right, line by line vs *boustrophedon* in vertical columns), the syllabic sign system (CV, VC, CVC signs vs CV and CVC(V) signs), the classifier system (strictly noun classifiers vs noun and event classifiers), a direct impact of the cuneiform on the creation of the Anatolian Hieroglyphs seems unlikely. However, this does not mean that the cuneiform script could and did not interfere with the Anatolian Hieroglyphs at a later stage during their centuries-long co-existence.[33]

33 A possible example of influence of the cuneiform script on the Anatolian Hieroglyphs may be the personal marker (|), which, as Payne 2017a: 225 observes, may be either an abbreviated form of VIR$_2$, or it may have been formed after the cuneiform personal marker consisting of a single vertical wedge. It should be noted, however, that the Anatolian hieroglyphic personal marker is used for both male and

In the multilingual and bigraphic Hittite Empire, the interaction between the two writing systems was probably not a static and unilateral affair, but rather a dynamic, mutual and ongoing process. The chronological expansion of classifiers that we witness in both scripts, for example, may well have developed in tandem. Likewise, scribal interaction may have reinforced the repression of polyvalence and the practice to separate words in both scripts. The level of interference may for a large part have depended on the scribes and their level of familiarity with both writing systems.

Bibliography

Adelholfer, Matthias
2024 *Old Assyrian Epistolography. Materiality, Form, Rhetoric, Mentalities, and Norms.* Ph.D. dissertation, University of Vienna.

Balza, Maria Elena
2012 Sealed Tablets from Ḫattuša. In: Maria Elena Balza, Mauro Giorgieri, and Clelia Mora (eds.), *Archivi, depositi, magazzini presso gli Ittiti. Nuovi materiali e nuove ricerche/Archives, Depots and Storehouses in the Hittite World. New Evidence and New Research.* Genova: Italian University Press, 77–110.

Boehmer, Rainer M. and Hans G. Güterbock
1987 *Glyptik aus dem Stadtgebiet von Boğazköy: Grabungskampagnen 1931–1939, 1952–1978.* BoHa 14. Berlin: Gebr. Mann.

Cammarosano, Michele, Katja Weirauch, Feline Maruhn, Gert Jendritzki, and Patrick L. Kohl
2019 They Wrote in Wax. Wax Boards in the Ancient Near East. *Mesopotamia* 54: 121–80.

Collon, Dominique
1987 *First Impressions. Cylinder Seals in the Ancient Near East.* London: British Museum Publications.

Dinçol, Ali and Belkis Dinçol
2008 *Die Prinzen- und Beamtensiegel aus der Oberstadt von Boğazköy-Ḫattuša vom 16. Jahrhundert bis zum Ende der Grossreichszeit.* BoHa 22. Mainz am Rhein: von Zabern.

Güterbock, Hans G.
1997 Erinnerungen an das alte Boğazköy-Archiv und die Landschenkungsurkunde VAT 7436. *AoF* 24: 24–30.

female persons, in contrast to its cuneiform counterpart that is only used to identify male persons. In any case, if the Anatolian hieroglyphic personal marker was indeed inspired by the cuneiform script, this must have happened at a later stage, as initially only VIR_2 seems to have fulfilled this function (Payne 2017a: 225). Further, Rieken and Yakubovich (2023: 216) suggest that the occasional right-branching of divine epithets such as (DEUS) TONITRUS CAELUM in Anatolian Hieroglyphs was inspired by the word order of heterographic cuneiform combinations like ^{D}IŠKUR AN in Hittite cuneiform.

Hawkins, J. David

1995 *The Hieroglyphic Inscription of the Sacred Pool Complex at Hattusa (Südburg). With an Archaeological Introduction by Peter Neve.* StBoTB 3. Wiesbaden: Harrassowitz.

Herbordt, Suzanne

2005 *Die Prinzen- und Beamtensiegel der hethitischen Grossreichszeit auf Tonbullen aus dem Nişantepe-Archiv in Ḫattuša – mit Kommentaren zu den Siegelinschriften und Hieroglyphen von J. David Hawkins.* BoHa 19. Mainz am Rhein: von Zabern.

Herbordt, Suzanne, Daliah Bawanypeck, and J. David Hawkins

2011 *Die Siegel der Grosskönige und Grossköniginnen auf Tonbullen aus dem Nişantepe-Archiv in Ḫattuša.* BoHa 23. Mainz am Rhein: von Zabern.

Home, Eleanor

Classifiers in Hittite Cuneiform and Hittite Scribal Culture. Unpublished MPhil thesis, University of Oxford.

Kitazumi, Tomoki

2019 Typologies of Setting Paragraph Dividers in the Hittite Texts. In: Aygül Süel (ed.), *IX. Uluslararası Hititoloji Kongresi Bildirileri, Çorum 08–14 Eylül 2014 / Acts of the IXth International Congress of Hittitology, Çorum, September 08–14, 2014. Çorum.* Ankara: Baski, Dumat Ofset, 417–58.

Klinger, Jörg

2022 Zu den Anfängen der hethitischen Überlieferung überhaupt und zur Methode der paläographischen Textdatierung. In: Eva Cancik-Kirschbaum and Ingo Schrakamp (eds.), *Transfer, Adaption und Neukonfiguration von Schrift- und Sprachwissen im Alten Orient.* Episteme in Bewegung 25. Wiesbaden: Harrassowitz, 255–340.

Kloekhorst, Alwin and Willemijn Waal

2019 A scribal tradition predating the tablet collections of Ḫattuša? The origin of the 'cushion-shaped' tablets KBo 3.22, KBo 17.21+, KBo 22.1 and KBo 22.2. *ZA* 109: 189–203.

Kryszeń, Adam

2019 Hittite Toponymy. An Overview. *AoF* 46: 1–14.

2020 The Postdeterminative KI in the Hittite Cuneiform Corpus. *ZA* 110: 212–21.

Moortgat-Correns, Ursula

1957 Glyptik. *RlA* 3: 440–62.

Mora, Clelia

2022 Anatolian Hieroglyphic Documentation. In: Stefano de Martino (ed.), *Handbook Hittite Empire. Power Structures.* Empires through the Ages in Global Perspective 1. Berlin / Boston: de Gruyter Oldenburg, 45–91.

Müller-Karpe, Andreas

2020 Kulthandlungen und Kultpersonal in hethitischen Palästen. In: Susanne Görke and Charles W. Steitler (eds.), *Cult, Temple, Sacred Spaces. Cult*

Practices and Cult Spaces in Hittite Anatolia and Neighbouring Cultures. Proceedings of the First International HFR Symposium, Mainz, 3–5 June 2019. StBoT 66. Wiesbaden: Harrassowitz, 179–220.

Müller-Karpe, Andreas and Vuslat Müller-Karpe
2020 Untersuchungen in Kayalıpınar 2019. *MDOG* 152: 191–236.

Otto, Adelheid
2010 Siegelpraxis B. *RlA* 12: 469–74.

Payne, Annick
2015 *Schrift und Schriftlichkeit. Die anatolische Hieroglyphenschrift.* Wiesbaden: Harrassowitz.
2017a Determination in the Anatolian Hieroglyphic Script of the Empire and Transitional Period. *AoF* 44: 221–34.
2017b Determination in the Anatolian Hieroglyphic Script. *News from the Lands of the Hittites* 1: 101–12.
2018 Determination in the Anatolian Hieroglyphic Script: The Late 10th and Early 9th Centuries BC. *AoF* 45: 102–21.

Rieken, Elisabeth and Ilya Yakubovich
2023 Encounters between Scripts in Bronze Age Asia Minor. In: Ilona Zsolnay (ed.), *Seen not Heard. Composition, Iconicity, and the Classifier Systems of Logosyllabic Sripts. Papers from the Oriental Institute Seminar Held at the Oriental Institute of the University of Chicago March 1–2, 2017.* Chicago: Institute for the Study of Ancient Cultures of the University of Chicago, 205–35.

Rüster, Christel and Gernot Wilhelm
2012 *Landschenkungsurkunden hethitischer Könige.* StBoTB 4. Wiesbaden: Harrassowitz.

Schachner, Andreas
2023 Die Ausgrabungen in Boğazköy-Ḫattuša 2022. *AA* 2023: 1–210.

Selz, Gebhard J., Colette Grinevald, and Orly Goldwasser
2017[2018] The Question of Sumerian "Determinatives". Inventory, Classifier Analysis, and Comparison to Egyptian Classifiers from the Linguistic Perspective of Noun Classification. In: Daniel E. Werning (ed.), *Proceedings of the Fifth International Conference on Egyptian–Coptic Linguistics (Crossroads V), Berlin, February 17–20, 2016.* Lingua Aegyptia 25. Hamburg: Widmaier Verlag, 281–344.

Simon, Zsolt
2020 On the Origins of the Hieroglyphic Luwian Writing System: The Chronological Problem. *Chatreššar* 3: 42–56.

Strupler, Néhémie
2021 Overview of Sealing Practices at Kültepe during the Anatolian–Old Assyrian Trade Network Period. In: Fikri Kulakoğlu, Guido Kryszat and Cécile Michel (eds.), *Cultural Exchange and Current Research in Kültepe and*

its Surroundings: Kültpe, 1–4 August, 2019. Subartu 46. Turnhout: Brepols, 181–96.

Symington, Dorit

1991 Late Bronze Age Writing-Boards and Their Uses: Textual Evidence from Anatolia and Syria. *AnSt* 41: 111–23.

Vertegaal, Alexander

2017 Filling in the Facts. The Practice of Space-Filling in Hieroglyphic Luwian Inscriptions. *AoF* 44: 235–60.

van den Hout, Th. P. J.

2020 *A History of Hittite Literacy. Writing and Reading in Late Bronze-Age Anatolia.* Cambridge: Cambridge University Press.

Waal, Willemijn

2011 They wrote on wood. The case for a hieroglyphic scribal tradition on wooden writing boards in Hittite Anatolia. *AnSt* 61: 21–34.

2012 Writing in Anatolia. The Origins of Anatolian Hieroglyphs and the Introductions of the Cuneiform Script. *AoF* 39: 287–315.

2015 *Hittite Diplomatics. Studies in Ancient Document Format and Record Management.* StBot 57. Wiesbaden: Harrassowitz.

2022 Relations between script, writing material and layout: the case of the Anatolian Hieroglyphs. In: Philippa Steele and Philip Boyes (eds.), *Writing Around the Ancient Mediterranean. Practices and Adaptations.* Oxford / Philadelphia: Oxbow, 121–44.

2023a Sealed Breads and Tax-Free Canopies? Reflections on Non-Written Administrative Practices in Hittite Anatolia. In: Lucy E. Bennison-Chapman (ed.), *Bookkeeping Without Writing. Early Administrative Technologies in Context.* PIHANS 84. Leuven: Peeters, 137–59.

2023b Ties That Bind. A New Interpretation of the Hittite Verb *šai-/šiye–*. *Anatolica* 49: 187–205.

in press a Tying the New to the Old. The Introduction of the Cuneiform Script in Anatolia and Hittite Sealing Practices. In: Ineke Sluiter and Willemijn Waal (eds.), *Anchoring the Invention of Writing in Ancient Societies. A Global Comparative Approach*, Leiden: Brill.

in press b With Strings Attached. Document Sealing in Hittite Anatolia. In: Sarah J. Scott and Oya Topçuoğlu (eds.), *The Routledge Companion to Seals and Seal Studies in Antiquity: New Approaches to Mediterranean and West Asian Visual Culture.* London: Routledge.

Waal, Willemijn and Alwin Kloekhorst

in press The Use of the Anatolian Hieroglyphic Writing System in the Hittite Period, the Old Assyrian Period and Possibly Beyond (*to appear in a Festschrift*).

Weeden, Mark

2011 *Hittite Logograms and Hittite Scholarship.* StBoT 54. Wiesbaden: Harrassowitz.

Wilhelmi, Lisa
2016 Materiality and Presence of the Anitta Text in Original and Secondary Context: Considerations on the Original Nature of the Proclamation of Anitta (*CTH* 1) and Its Transmission as Part of Hittite Traditional Literature. In: Thomas E. Balke and Christina Tsouparopoulou (eds.), *Materiality of Writing in Early Mesopotamia*. MTK 13. Berlin: de Gruyter, 223–39.

Yakubovich, Ilya
2010 *Sociolinguistics of the Luvian Language*. BSIEL 2. Leiden / Boston: Brill.

THE PALAEOGRAPHY OF THE CUNEIFORM TABLETS FROM BÜKLÜKALE

Mark Weeden
University College London

Abstract

A small but important collection of cuneiform fragments has been excavated since 2009 by the Japanese Institute of Anatolian Archaeology at the site of Büklükale on the western Kızılırmak. Since 2019 these have surprisingly included Hurrian-language tablets. Most of these tablets are still in the process of publication and new finds continue to be made each year. Some methodological considerations on the differences between palaeography and material handwriting studies, as well as typological vs chronological research practices, preface an initial presentation of the palaeography of these mostly fragmentary finds. Although it is still too early to say for definite what is happening at Büklükale, it seems inescapable that this was a very significant site for the Hittite royal family. There is likely to have been some sort of archive there, and some of the tablets show traces of palaeographic and orthographic writing traditions that are different to the standard Hittite cuneiform practice known from royal residences such as Boğazköy and Ortaköy. The palaeographic study of the tablets from Büklükale may thus reveal evidence for more diverse cuneiform writing traditions in ancient Anatolia than previously thought likely.

1. Some key concepts of analysis

Cuneiform palaeography means studying the material traces of physical scribal activity performed by real individuals in concrete historical contexts. Identifying the way people physically wrote can tell us about the kinds of institutional contexts in which they were writing, and about contacts and influences that carried knowledge through space and time. There is a degree to which the material nature of palaeographic study lends an authority to arguments about knowledge transmission that can seem more trenchant and reliable than associations made between similarities of ideas, motifs or words across different cultures and epochs. At the same time the kind of resolution to big research questions that one gets when talking about palaeography is often rather general. In the absence of named scribes we tend to end up talking about general institutional entities or outlines and contacts with vague cultural-political areas from broad regions, even though palaeography offers us a window into the process of writing at the individual level.[1] Palaeography as done in Hittitology is also fiendishly difficult, and takes a long time to research.

1 For the scribal habits of named scribes and their palaeographic groupings at Ḫattuša, see Gordin 2015; Steitler 2020.

The urgent need for a palaeography of Hittite cuneiform tablets arises from the fact that there are very few independently datable Hittite tablets and none that are dated to the days and months of particular years, as frequently the case with tablets from ancient Iraq. Without entering into an exhaustive history of Hittite cuneiform palaeographic research I wish to make a couple of observations on methodology before starting.[2] One concerns the distinction between cuneiform palaeography and material handwriting studies, a general term which I use in preference to the word graphology, with its psycho-social associations, or cheirography, with its typically forensic background (Stratford 2015: 118–22). The other concerns the distinction between typology of script and chronology of script.

The primary function of Hittite cuneiform palaeography is the dating of tablets on the basis of their sign-forms. I avoid the word ductus to characterise the totality of sign-forms on a tablet in combination with other features such as crowding of the writing (Cammarosano 2015: 155f.). The word ductus is used in palaeography-related disciplines such as medieval manuscript studies to indicate the order of strokes that is employed to make a single character or letter.[3] These are areas of inquiry that need to be separated out. On the one hand we have research that involves identifying physical features of tablet construction using material clay analysis by pXRF or other methods through to the techniques of producing a tablet from clay by hand, and then the formatting of the text on the tablet, the depth and slant of stylus impressions and the crowdedness of the script, the size of the column divider, features that can be referred to as non-textual visual aspect.[4] All of these could be described as material considerations, and all of them are needed when trying to date a tablet, as well as to answer further questions about the world in which the tablet was produced. Recent research has made great advances in these fields, particularly due to the work of Sh. Gordin (2015) looking at the habits of writing of identified scribes, W. Waal (2015) looking at the shape, formatting and layout of tablets, and M. Cammarosano (2014; 2015; Cammarosano et al. 2014) looking at the handwriting of scribes and the materials of the scribal profession.

The development of the CuneiformAnalyser programme that enables the measurement of all surface features of 3-D photogrammetric images of cuneiform tablets has opened a whole new area of inquiry to Hittite handwriting studies (Müller et al. 2015). Strikingly, it is not the visibly different cuneiform sign-forms that might be used to identify the scribal hand of one tablet as being the same as that of another, it is features such as the statistical frequency of angles between uprights and *Winkelhaken* or horizontals which are not at all visible to the human eye which are helpful in this regard (Cammarosano et al. 2014; Müller 2018). As M. Cammarosano has demonstrated, such

2 For the history of Hittite cuneiform palaeography see van den Hout 2009: 11–28; Klinger 2022a: 255–302, with very different emphases.

3 The order of impression of wedges has been shown to be a significant field of study for cuneiform manuscripts: Taylor 2015.

4 Cammarosano (2015: 156) uses the term *equilibrium* (following Parkes 2008) to describe this kind of visual aspect especially with reference to the relationship between verticals and horizontals, while Parkes (2008: Glossary) uses the term *aspect* solely to refer to the impression made by a specimen of handwriting on a page "at first sight".

features as the ratio of the lengths of the spines of horizontals to verticals do seem to correspond to broad dating categories (Cammarosano 2015: 171–75). However, for the purposes of this contribution I would like to separate, albeit somewhat artificially, these rather handwriting and materials oriented approaches from what I would call Hittite cuneiform palaeography in the narrow sense, which concerns itself with the history of the introduction of sign-forms within the repertoires of the Hittite cuneiform scribes.

As far as this history is concerned, I would argue that there are two separate activities being pursued in modern scholarship, which are of necessity closely related, but should be kept distinct: typology and chronology. The first of these is the process of categorising tablets into groups which use particular sign-forms, an essentially typological exercise. This can be done for example using statistical methods, noting the proportions in which individual sign-forms occur on particular tablets. This has been alleged to be significant in studies of tablets of the Hittite Empire period, from around 1350 BC onwards, with the proportion of "late" forms increasing as time continues.[5] We will be asking below whether such methods are useful for evaluating the dating of some of the tablets from Büklükale which are likely to come from the end of the Middle Hittite period. Can we talk about a steady development of palaeographic features in one direction, or do clusters of palaeographic elements come, go and resurface over the history of the script after their introduction? I would argue that at this stage the process of categorising tablets according to the proportions of sign-forms that occur in them is something that should be kept methodologically separate from the dating of tablets. The prospects of machines being able to do this tedious work of typological classification for us using 3-D photogrammetric scans is something that I am looking forward to, because counting takes a long time and is boring.

The nowadays conventional chronological grouping of palaeographic features as manifested in sign-forms also uses categories: Old Script = Ia, b, Middle Script = IIa, b, c, New Script = IIIa, b, c, with each category corresponding to a particular time period. Precisely what those time periods are is a matter of some debate, with Old Script corresponding roughly to the Old Kingdom (ca. 1650–1500 BC) and/or shortly before (Kloekhorst and Waal 2019; Klinger 2022a) or thereafter (van den Hout 2009), the distinction between the early stages of Middle Script and Old Script being very difficult to define palaeographically, the continuation of Middle Script features into the New Kingdom period (ca. 1450–1180 BC), and the use of Late New Script (IIIc) features subsisting beside and at the same time as those of the category IIIb. These categories are defined mainly but not solely according to the appearance or more importantly non-appearance of particular sign-forms, which are introduced gradually throughout the history of Hittite cuneiform, or so the theory. Reference will be made below in particular to discussions of the dating of tendencies in the introduction of new sign-forms according to the defining discussions of F. Starke (1985: 21–27), J. Klinger (1996: 32–39) and J.L. Miller (2004: 40–51, 268–71).[6] But we will also need to ask to what extent these categories of the various chronologically sequential script stages are also themselves

5 Goedegebuure 2014: 9f. with reference to van den Hout 1989.

6 See also Gordin 2015: 83–93; van de Peut 2022: 15–29.

typological categories. Similarly to the previous paragraph, it appears to me that there has been an albeit necessary and unavoidable mixing of methodological procedures, which need to be separated out a little more stringently than they often are.[7] That does not alter the fact that the basis of this system is chronological and was set up to answer chronological questions, a fact that is hidden by using the categories I, II, III as if they were without chronological assessment. For this reason, I have preferred to use the designations OSa, b; MSa, b, c; NSa, b, c.

A word should be said about the notion of the diagnostic sign. The publication in 2012 of the Land Donation tablets by Chr. Rüster and G. Wilhelm has for the first time introduced a series of tablets dated to reigns of Hittite kings which can serve as an index of changes in the palaeographic repertoire from just before the reign of Telipinu up until just before the reign of Tudḫaliya I.[8] The previously available Land Donation tablet of Kuwatalla from the reign of Arnuwanda I, already served F. Starke as a key fixed point for the onset of his palaeographic category IIc, which encompasses the end of the Middle-Hittite period (Starke 1985: 26). How we use these data is key, and there is a tendency to abstract sign-forms from their contexts and call them diagnostic of a particular time-period. If a sign-form is really so unique and unparalleled in tablets from other periods, then this is a legitimate procedure, and this seems to be the case for the forms of DA and IT identified on the early Land Donation tablets by Rüster and Wilhelm (2012: 66f.; Klinger 2022a: 304f.). However, in general it is necessary to consider any individual sign-form in the context of the other sign-forms that appear on the tablet in a cumulative manner, as well as other features of the tablet's writing and layout, before moving to a dating. This is important because the majority of the cuneiform pieces from Büklükale are fragments, which would usually rightly be considered too small for any attempt at a palaeographic dating. When so-called diagnostic signs occur on them it is exciting, but we must face up to the fact that whatever implications we draw from their presence belong mainly in the realm of hypothesis, if not even imagination.

In the above I have explained how I approach cuneiform palaeography. On the one hand I see it as necessary to separate out the different fields of study: study of handwriting, study of sign-forms (Hittite cuneiform palaeography in the narrow sense) both typological and chronological, study of spelling, study of layout and format, study of tablet production and study of clay composition. The performance of these fields of study involves different techniques (and technologies), which often have different criteria of proof, suitability for different research questions, and varying likelihoods of reaching reliable conclusions, as well as requiring different skill-sets. On the other hand, it is necessary to employ all of these methods in as holistic a manner as possible

7 Similarly Gordin 2015 envisages different New Script palaeographic types being used concurrently, which assumes a use of palaeographic categories in a typological sense. Steitler 2020 has also correlated palaeographic categories with sign-formation techniques across different scribal groups operating broadly at the same time.

8 For the purposes of this contribution, the question of whether the Land Donation tablets define the beginning of a Hittite writing tradition as preserved at Ḫattuša (van den Hout 2009: 31), or whether there is a longer tradition of writing before that which is evidenced by a few tablets from Ḫattuša (Kloekhorst and Waal 2019; Klinger 2022a), is not relevant, as all of the fragments from Büklükale almost certainly come from after this period.

in order to assess not only the dating but also the wider historical, cultural and social implications of these material objects that contain writing. These were carriers not only of text, but objects in the world that played a role in peoples' lives. Clearly this investigation can only be pursued collectively, employing various skill-sets and disciplinary approaches, as well as taking a very long time to achieve reliable results. With the cuneiform remains from Büklükale we are only at the beginning of such a process.[9]

2. Variety: sites and contexts

Palaeographic research regarding the use of Hittite cuneiform has always been based on a very limited sample of tablet-producing sites compared to ancient Iraq, even if the number of sites available for study has increased somewhat in the last 20 years. Broadly the same criteria can be used to date tablets that write Hittite-language texts found at different sites within the Hittite area of influence as have been developed to date the many thousands which were found at Boğazköy-Ḫattuša (van den Hout 2020: 170, 315–22; Torri 2023: 26). This level of apparent standardisation indicates a well-disciplined cadre of scribes and a central education system based on imitation of the type that is commonly found in other imperial contexts, whether or not such education was carried on in the home or in an institutional context (Torri 2015; Gordin 2015; Klinger 2022b: 120).

The expansion of the number of sites where cuneiform is found in central Anatolia, however, is likely to lead to a re-evaluation of this paradigm, particularly after the discovery of over 100 tablets at Kayalıpınar. Some of the tablets excavated at Büklükale, particularly those from the 2023 season, present features which cannot be subsumed under the model of a centralised education system, and widen the parameters of the flexibility that was available to scribes even within the central Hittite area to be able to write in a fashion that could be understood by their peers. The following is an attempt to assess the contribution of the Büklükale tablets to Hittite palaeographic studies, with the proviso that the majority of them have not yet been published, and can thus only be presented here in limited scope using traditional sign-lists.[10]

The site of Büklükale is located 110 km to the southwest of the Hittite capital at Boğazköy-Ḫattuša. It is located at one of the main historical crossing-points of the Kızılırmak, on the far side of the river from the Hittite capital. After numerous surveys the site has been excavated by the Japanese Institute of Anatolian Archaeology under the direction of Dr. K. Matsumura every year since 2009 (Matsumura and Weeden 2019). Büklükale consists of a site of 34 hectares, which includes a rocky outcrop forming a citadel with public buildings that seem to have been built around 2000 BC and

9 The talk on which this chapter is based was delivered in early May 2024. Already by the end of June 2024, the author had managed to make joins between two tablet fragments excavated in 2023 and one excavated in 2024, which required some of the observations of this chapter to be modified. This should serve as a notice of the provisional nature of any conclusions reached here.

10 Thus far published are three tablets (Weeden 2013; 2016; 2017). The remaining tablets found from 2017 to 2023 will be published in copy, transliteration and photo in a forthcoming issue of the journal *Anatolian Archaeological Studies*, the house journal of the Japanese Institute of Anatolian Archaeology.

were finally destroyed and abandoned in the early 16th century BC. There is also a lower city enclosed by a wall with gates built in a typical Hittite casemate style, as revealed by geo-physical prospection, which are likely to date to a little later than the public buildings of the Middle Bronze Age. Excavation has revealed at least 8 Hittite-period, Late Bronze Age architectural layers on the citadel with a complex stratigraphy. Unfortunately, the Iron Age occupation of the site has destroyed most of the Late Bronze Age remains and Hittite period levels are only accessible at the edges of the rocky hill. That there must have been a major building on the top of the hill during the Hittite period is made very likely by the remains of a drainage system that must have led from it down the hill on the northern slope.

The proposals for the identity of the site of Büklükale in the Hittite period are varied: Waḫšušana, a site well attested in the Middle Bronze Age but less so during the LBA was proposed by G. Barjamovic (2010), Durḫumit/Turmitta was proposed by M. Forlanini (2008: 68–74), Šalatiwara according to Ö. Sir Gavaz (2019), and finally Nenašša was proposed by C. Corti (2017: 232 n. 144) and A. Kryszeń (2016: 376, Karakeçili), a site well attested in texts from the time of Kültepe level II and the Old Hittite period, but less well documented in texts from Kültepe level Ib and the Hittite Empire period. None of the tablet finds thus far has contributed decisively to answering the question concerning the identity of the site, but it is becoming clearer that whoever lived here had very close connections to the Hittite royal family, likely since the very inception of the Hittite state.

Fig. 1. Preliminary drawing of BK190186 by author. Reproduced with kind permission of K. Matsumura.

For example, a recently excavated seal-impression on a clay stopper (BK190186) refers to an individual called Kana(?), who is also attested on another sealing from Büklükale, as the *HATTUSA+li* CULTER, which might be interpreted as "Sword of Ḫattušili" (see Fig. 1).[11] What this means in concrete terms is open to interpretation. Later impressions are also found which belong to a cuneiform seal that has much in common with a seal used to make an impression at Kuşaklı-Šarišša, and could in fact have been made from the same seal.[12] As can be seen from the Kuşaklı example, this 15th or early 14th century cuneiform seal belongs to the Hittite Great Queen, even if this crucial part of the cuneiform ring is not preserved on the Büklükale exemplars.

11 For the seal of *kà-na* (BHS 5) see Weeden 2016: 98f. On BHS 5 there are no traces between the *kà* and the *na*, but on BK190186 (seal series number not yet assigned) there are some traces, which I am interpreting as damage for the moment.

12 BCS 1, at Weeden 2016: 82–86, comparing Ku 98/56, with further literature.

Thus far, 21 fragments of tablets have been found at the site, although three of them were joined to each other during the 2024 season. Only one of them (BKT 2) was found in a level which is likely to date to the Hittite period (Weeden 2016: 81). The others were all found in secondary locations, mostly having been discarded as rubbish during the Iron Age and thrown onto the slope outside an Iron Age fortification wall. Seven of the tablet-fragments are in or contain Hurrian language. The reasons for this might be varied. The presence of Hurrian-language texts at Büklükale might be explained by the afore-mentioned closeness to the royal family, in which Hurrian queens are attested from at least the reign of Tudḫaliya I in the second half of the 15th century (Campbell 2016). However, one might also argue that the presence of cuneiform in the first place is also to be explained in this manner (Weeden 2011a: 117f.; Torri 2023: 26). In the following we will look at the Hurrian and the Hittite material separately. There is no justification for treating these groups separately in terms of palaeography or handwriting studies alone. However, if we look at other writing habits such as spelling and sign-use there are in fact quite significant differences between the corpora.

3. BKT 1–4: (Late) Middle Hittite letters/diplomatic documents

The first tablet excavated at Büklükale in 2010 exhibits a palaeographic profile that overlaps well with some of the sign-forms found at Maşat Höyük, for which see Timothy Leonard's contribution to this volume.

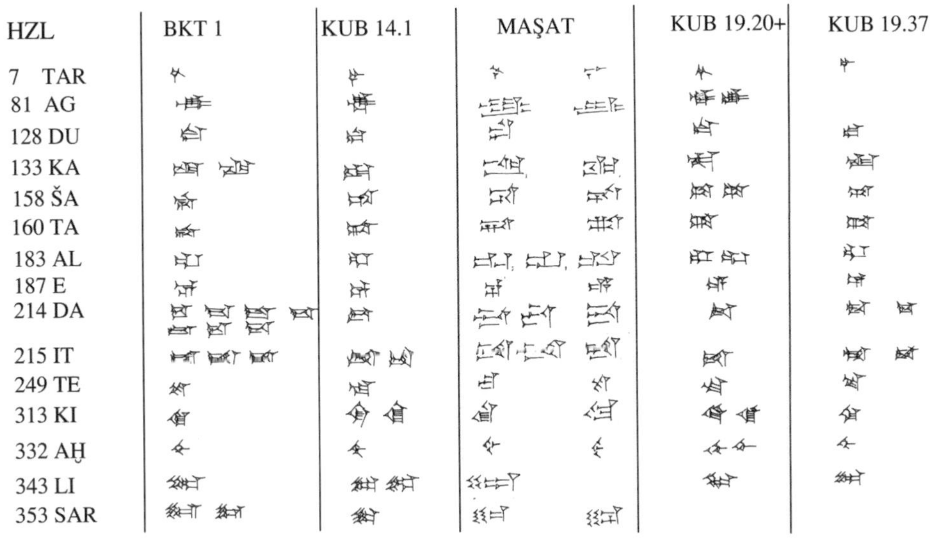

Fig. 2. Comparative sign-list for BKT 1, taken from Weeden 2013: Fig. 5. KUB 14.1 = Madduwatta Text, KUB 19.20+ draft letter of Šuppiluliuma I, KUB 19.37 Annals of Muršili II (*CTH* 61.II.9.A).

The tablet contains no content that would help us to date it apart from its palaeography as well as spellings and language that are also typical of earlier rather than later phases of Hittite writing: the use of the adversative particle in =*a* rather than =*ma* after a consonant, and the form *iššumeni*, which could have been predicted to be the expected earlier form of *išš(a)*- "to perform", parallel to the forms *tumeni* (from *dā*- "to take") and *tarnumeni* (from *tarna*- "to leave").[13] Some of the sign-forms (e. g. LI) occur in later texts despite being typical of the older types of writing, some (e. g. TAR) tend not to occur in later texts and to go out of fashion sometime after the end of the Middle Hittite period.[14] Sometime from the last quarter of the 15th century through to the end of the first half of the 14th century, i. e. from the reigns of Arnuwanda I through to the end of Tudḫaliya II is as specific as I would like to be for the dating of this tablet. The hypothesized content potentially regarding detention of messengers might also point to the kind of situation that may have arisen during a period of political fragmentation and invasion, such as the period of the so-called concentric invasions (Stavi 2015: 38–43).

Some of the variants that are used on this tablet fall into the category of handwriting analysis rather than palaeography, in that they are less specific sign-forms than they are variants of sign-forms.[15] Thus one has two-different sign-forms of the sign LI, one older, one later, and there are different variants of each of these.[16] As such, a variant of a sign-form, where for example a single horizontal is a little higher than another one, cannot be used on its own for dating purposes unless it is found as part of a cluster of features which might indicate a particular *community of practice* or school.[17]

Such is the case with a comparison of BKT 1 and BKT 3 (Fig. 3, Fig. 4). Both fragments have a very similar colour, and a comparative clay analysis would be welcome here. BKT 1 has the characteristic shape of a letter, but it is likely that BKT 3 belonged to a larger (possibly one-columned) tablet than is typical for a letter due to the curvature of its surface. Although very subjective, the signs LI and DA appear to be formed in similar ways. DA has reverse-stepped horizontals, where the upper horizontal is protruding further than the lower ones. LI has very small initial horizontals, that are raised a little above the level of the main bottom horizontal, although this is quite a normal variant of this sign-form, although this only pertains in one case of the two on BKT 3. The form of ŠA has a high upper *Winkelhaken* compared to the level of the upper horizontal in BKT 1. This is not so clearly visible on BKT 3, which is on the whole more carefully written, but the upper *Winkelhaken* of ŠA is larger than the lower one. The

13 Hoffner and Melchert 2008: 220f. §13.15.

14 See discussion at Weeden 2013: 29–32.

15 For the terminology of sign, sign-form, variant see Homan 2019: 21–24.

16 Separate sign-forms generally correspond to the *Leitzeichen* in HZL (e. g. old vs new LI = HZL 343A and 343B), while the variants are listed below (HZL 343/1, 2, 3 etc.). The distinction between a sign-form and a variant is essentially heuristic and can depend on a lot of factors, such as whether the form is palaeographically significant and could in combination with other features make a difference to the dating, or whether the form is used to distinguish this sign from a similar looking one on a particular tablet. Thus, the definition of sign-form and variant can theoretically change from tablet to tablet, even if we take as a rule the division as envisaged by Rüster and Neu in HZL.

17 On the other hand, it is precisely elements that have to do with the construction of signs and would usually be classified as variants possibly dependent on writing materials or mechanics of education that play a role in the dating criteria developed by Cammarosano 2015.

other palaeographically relevant features, i. e. sign-forms, are also almost identical: the forms of TAR, AL, E, AG, and IG. It is thus possible that these fragments belong to a similar writing context even if they might have belonged to different types of document: the one a letter, the other a larger tablet, but both with apparently diplomatic content.

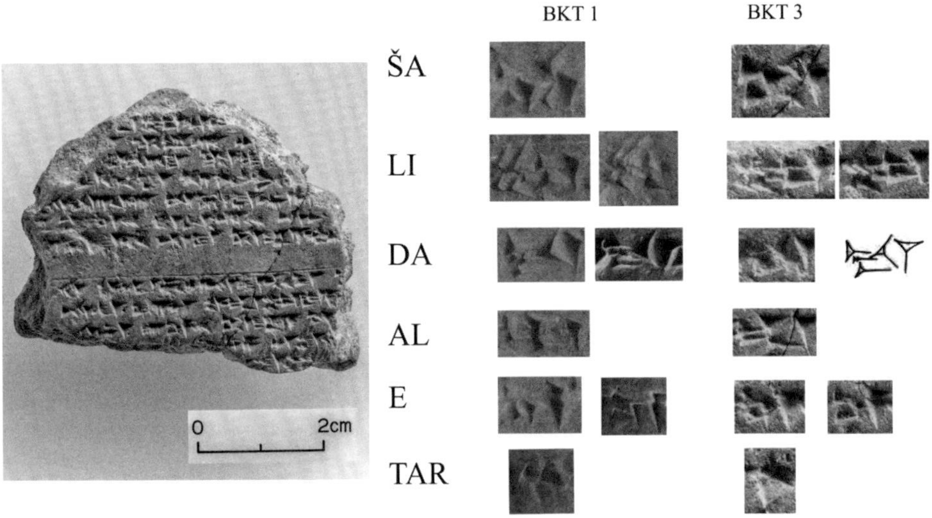

Fig. 3. BKT 3 (photo K. Matsumura © JIAA) compared with close-ups of a selection of signs on BKT 1 and BKT 3.

4. Incantations, omens and ritual fragments

The texts BKT 6, 7, 16, 18 are mostly very small fragments which have only a few signs on them. It is therefore very dangerous to rely on dating such fragments. However, they do seem to fit into certain patterns, when compared to the other tablet fragments, whether in Hurrian or Hittite, and it may be possible to establish certain provisional groups within the material (Fig. 4). Possibly the oldest is BKT 16, which seems to be a Hittite-language ritual text that includes the Hurrian term *keldi*, "well-being". This is a particularly interesting fragment because it mentions a fortress (URU.BÀD) and also something that is happening "in this? city", [*k*]*ēdani* URU-*ri*, presumably a ritual. The tablet is neatly written and shares a sign-form variant (EL, see fig. 4) with a Hurrian tablet-fragment, to be considered later, which also contains other old features.

On a further very small fragment (BKT 6), which probably contains part of a Hittite-language incantation, we see a combination of older and newer forms of the sign E. Probably the latest fragment of the group, at least according to sign-forms, is a more sizeable chunk of a letter including bird-oracles (BKT 18). This is a strangely shaped tablet, with almost square edges to the left side. The form of AZ with a subscript ZA and the form of E also show that this is a reasonably late tablet from this group, possibly

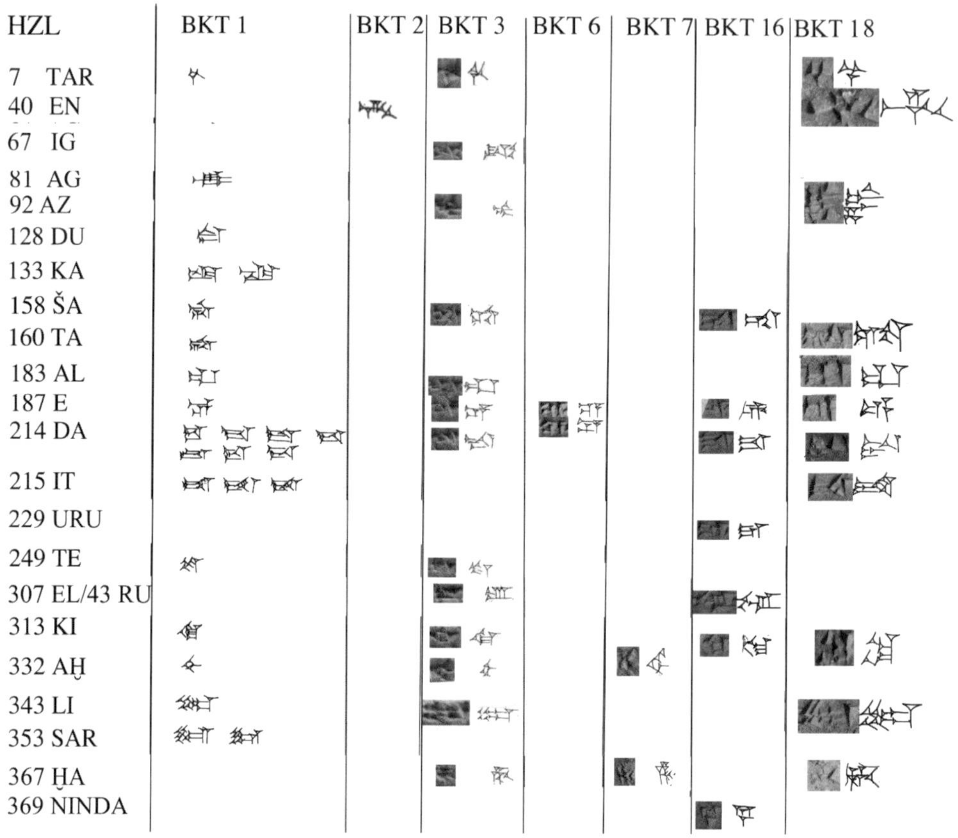

Fig. 4. The sign-forms from the main Hittite-language fragments from Büklükale.

even to be dated to the Early New Script (NSa = IIIa) category, or the transitional phase between MSc (= IIc) and this, thus sometime between the reigns of Tudḫaliya II, Šuppiluliuma I and Muršili II.[18] Some of the spellings on the tablet, such as *tar-u*, however, are typically associated with Middle Hittite bird-oracle reports (Sakuma 2009: vol. I 266).

5. The Hurrian fragments: maybe old, possibly late, definitely strange

The fact that Hurrian tablets were found at Büklükale at all came as a surprise. Either these tablets are to be considered part of the above-mentioned royal predilection for using Hurrian texts in cult, which we find at least from the reign of Arnuwanda I, or there is a special relationship of the settlement at Büklükale with Hurrian population elements. At the moment I incline towards the first explanation, but the second cannot be entirely excluded.[19]

18 For the significance of AZ with a subscript in the traditional dating scheme see Miller 2004: 40.

19 If Büklükale does turn out to be the city of Nenašša, then it may well have been involved in the rebellion against Ḫattušili I that was instigated by the Hurrian enemy (KBo 10.2 obv. i 24; de Martino 2003).

BKT 10 is the fragment which appears to be the oldest. It shares a number of properties with the group BKT 8–11, all of which have some old-looking sign-forms and all seem to be part of an *itkalzi* ritual of some kind, even if they are very fragmentary and one cannot say for sure. It is possible that these fragments belonged to the same tablet, but I am unable to see any direct joins, and the size of the signs is variable: BKT 10 has uprights measuring 2–3.5 mm, while on BKT 8 they are 3.5–4 mm high and on BKT 9 they are 3.5–4.5 mm. In 2009 the author conducted a survey of Old Script tablets in the Ankara Museum. A variation from 2–4.5 mm in the height of the uprights on one tablet would be unusual. It is thus possible that the fragment of BKT 10 comes from a tablet separate from the tablets BKT 8 and 9.

BKT 10 was from a multi-columned tablet, as was BKT 11 and BKT 9. Only in the case of BKT 9 and 11 is the column-divider preserved at its full width: 8mm. In all cases where the column-divider is preserved, the line-initial signs cut into it. This can be a sign of a tablet from the older period. However, the width of the column-divider on Old Script tablets is more regularly 4mm, rarely 6mm, hardly ever 8mm or more.[20] Thus it is possible that we have more than one multi-columned tablet with a script that uses older signs being kept at Büklükale. This means that the Büklükale collections are likely to have contained "library" tablets and points to the existence of an archive at the site. The width of the column-dividers on BKT 9 and 11 also means that even if the sign-forms on this group of tablets are old, then we are dealing with tablets written towards the end of the Old Script continuum or they are Middle Script tablets.

BKT 10, whose column-divider is not preserved to its full width, contains some very old sign-forms. The form of the sign ŠI is one such, with the head of its horizontal wedge tucked in to the left of the vertical. This form is listed as the earliest one under HZL 288. It is not among the earliest forms of the sign that is attested in the Land Donation tablets, appearing for the first time as far as can be seen in Rüster and Wilhelm 2012 no. 15 rev. 53′, possibly no. 22 rev. 63, no. 40 obv. 4 (in copy, not clear in photo).[21] Tablet no. 22 is to be dated to late Telipinu or Alluwamna, while no. 40 is dated to Ḫuzziya II (Rüster and Wilhelm 2012: 51, 55). Rüster 1972 no. 224 indicates that the Zukraši tablet KBo 7.14+ (e. g. obv. 5), the only Old Script tablet that was found in an Old Hittite archaeological context,[22] has a similar form of ŠI, and this is clearly visible on the photograph hethiter.net/: fotarch BoFN 13478a.

The fragment BKT 10 also has the form of the sign AḪ that is used on the Zukraši tablet (HZL 332/A). It is also the form that is used on the Land Donation tablets through to Muwattalli I (Rüster and Wilhelm 2012: 77, sign no. 332). The form of the

20 2117/g (KBo 37.26) is currently listed as "ah." by the *Konkordanz* (Košak 2002–); cf. Klinger 1996: 55 "Ah II"). The column-divider is over 8 mm wide, but the tablet also contains the NS sign-form of E, of TAR in l. 3′ and the later AḪ in l. 7′, as well as a form of ID with an unbroken horizontal in l. 5′ (although this is not a diagnostic sign-form unless it occurs together with other NSb features). The only available indications are that this fragment is from a NSa tablet, even if NSb or c are not to be excluded. It is not from an Old Script tablet. Bo 2416 (KBo 17.3+) does have consistently Old Script sign-forms, but also has a column-divider of 9 mm. This is the only case I saw in Ankara where an Old Script tablet has such a wide column-divider. See also Waal 2015: 92–94.

21 ŠI is not included in the chart at Rüster and Wilhelm 2012: 74–78.

22 KBo 7.14+, for which see Klinger 2022a: 263–65, 273–82; 2022b: 111.

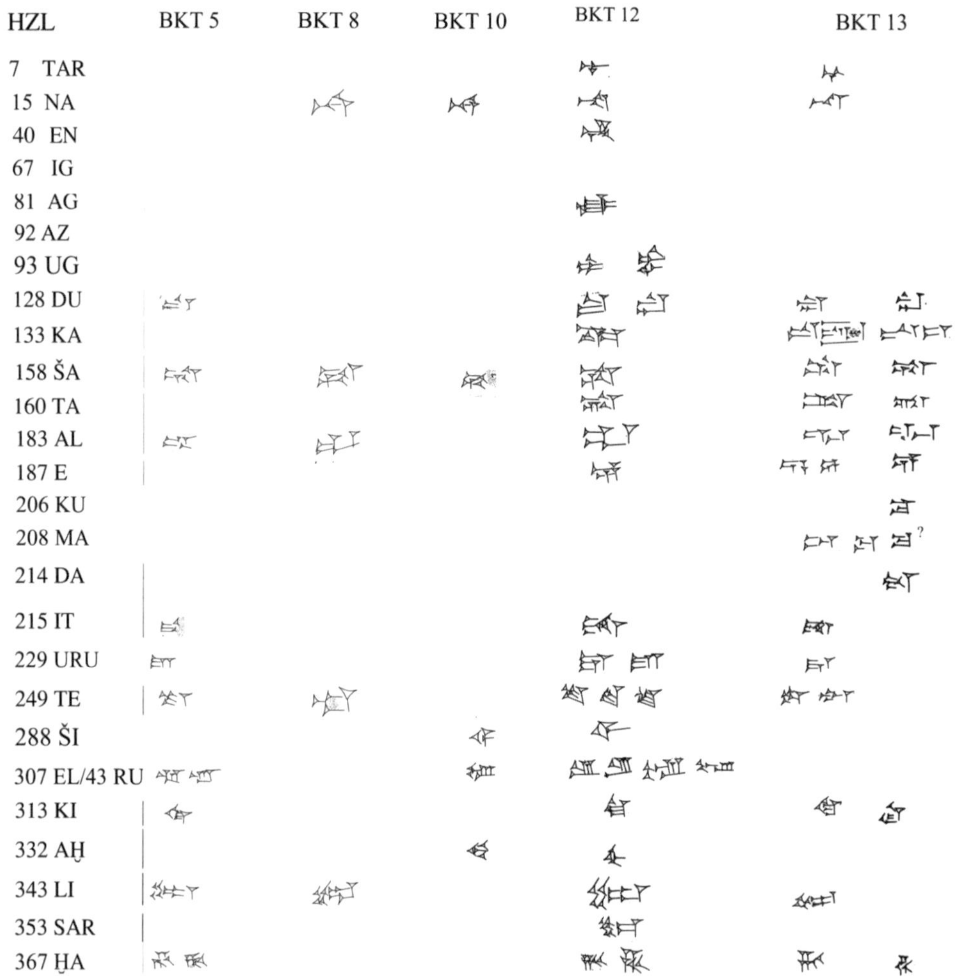

Fig. 5. The sign-forms of the Hurrian-language tablets from Büklükale.

sign NA found both on BKT 10 and BKT 8 seems particularly archaic, preserving a clear diamond shape where the *Winkelhaken* intersect with the upright, as in the classic third millennium BC form of the sign, and including a single horizontal stroke inside the diamond, which is the continuation of the sign's main horizontal. Similar forms are found on the Land Donation tablets from no. 11 (Telipinu) through to no. 46 (Muwattalli I – see Rüster and Wilhelm 2012: 74 no. 15). The form of EL on BKT 10, however, does not correspond to the typical Old Script form with the middle vertical lower than the outer two (HZL 307/1–3). Rather it looks rather similar to the form of the sign in the Hittite-language ritual text BKT 16.

Old Script Hurrian tablets from Boğazköy are few: KUB 47.93 (= ChS 1/7 no. 24), KUB 8.47 (= ChS 1/7 no. 6), KBo 62.54 (Wilhelm 2010: 623–35; 2018: 497–508). These are all omen tablets (*CTH* 774). KUB 47.93 and KBo 62.54 also both have the form of the signs DA and IT which have been identified by Rüster and Wilhelm as diagnostic for the earlier Land Donation tablets, thus tablets datable to the time of Telipinu and his immediate successors (Rüster and Wilhelm 2012: 65–67; type 1). KUB 8.47 has a similar form of DA to that found on the Zukraši tablet (Rüster and Wilhelm 2012: 65–67; type 2b). The Büklükale fragments BKT 8–11 do not have any examples of these signs, so we cannot know how they would have been written. It is of course very dangerous to date small fragments, but at Büklükale that is mostly all we have. The initial indications seem to be with this group that BKT 10 at least might date to anywhere in the period after Telipinu, possibly being datable as late as the time just before or early in the reign of Tudḫaliya I or even early Arnuwanda I, which is when we might expect Hurrian cult to be favoured at the imperial court, while the other *itkalzi* fragments from Büklükale may be a little later, mainly due to the width of the column-divider where it is preserved. But as above, this is highly tenuous given the size of the fragments.

At least one other Hurrian tablet from Boğazköy combines this early form of AḪ with sign-forms that are usually thought to be later: KUB 27.38 contains a Hurrian song in honour of royal ancestors, with Hittite instructions for performance, which has been ideologically compared with the Sumerian king-list (Bachvarova 2012). It also contains the later form of UG with subscript UD. Neither UG nor AZ appear with a subscript in the Land Donation tablets until the Kuwatalla Land Donation from the time of Arnuwanda I (Rüster and Wilhelm 2012: 75).[23] Starke set the beginning of the trend to write subscripts under these signs in his IIb category (MSb), which he dated to the end of the 15th century BC, while he put the Kuwatalla Land Donation into his IIc category (Starke 1985: 24, 26f.; = MSc).[24] So we have a parallel for this archaic-looking form of the sign AḪ continuing in use beside signs that are usually associated with later developments and it being used in a Hurrian text, which also includes some late features. Furthermore, KUB 27.38 also consistently uses the older forms of signs like EL (and RU), for which BKT 10 seems to use a less old variety. Another Hurrian fragment from Boğazköy, KBo 27.188, has the older forms of AḪ (l. 2′) and ḪAR (l. 8′), shows a typically Middle Hittite LU (HZL 210/1) but uses the late form of E (HZL 187B in 3′, 5′). Possibly the early form of AḪ continued longer in use in the writing of Hurrian tablets, although this seems at first to be a counter-intuitive position: the language scribes are writing in should not affect the sign-forms they use, although the models they are copying from might. Altogether this means that it is difficult to date the use of this sign-form any more closely than broadly to the 15th century BC, perhaps a little earlier, perhaps a little later, and even then this is tentative due to the paucity of the evidence. If we use only independently datable texts to fix its usage, then this sign-form is older (i. e. mid-to-late 15th century BC) rather than later (early-to-mid 14th century BC) within the historically acceptable time-frames for the use of Hurrian in royal cult.

23 UG with subscript at KBo 5.7 rev. 7, photo HW200583, but AZ without in KBo 5.7 rev. 52, 53 (twice).

24 UG and AZ with subscript occur in the Madduwatta Text KUB 14.1, for example, which Starke 1985: 24 n. 23 also attributes to his category IIb. KBo 1.5, the main tablet of the Šunaššura treaty (*CTH* 41) does not have the subscript on AZ apart from in unclear cases. See below for more on these tablets.

The possibly latest fragment we have is BKT 5, the first Hurrian tablet that was excavated at Büklükale in 2019, as with the others in secondary context. The fragment consists of one side with only traces of signs on three lines and another with the beginnings of 25 lines that must have belonged to the end of a text, quite possibly the end of a tablet. It is difficult to work out whether this would have been a multi-column or a single-column tablet, or even which is the obverse and which the reverse. I incline to the view that the preserved 25 lines are from the reverse, due to the fact that there is a little more curvature of the tablet and the writing is untidy, with lines beginning at irregular distances from the edge, which sometimes occurs towards the end of a tablet. The text seems to be a god-list for invocation purposes of a type that might be associated with the cult of Ištar-Šauška, even if the only individual deity mentioned by name is Ḫebat.[25] The fragment has the old form of LI and it has the "middle" form of URU (HZL 229/1), as opposed to the older one (HZL 229/2) which is found more consistently in BKT 12. Both of these sign-forms can be found in later tablets of the New script category, and are thus of little value for dating purposes.

Even in the limited number of signs available on this fragment, there are some strange ones. The forms of RU have in one case the lower central vertical that is meant to be characteristic of earlier tablets, in the other the front two verticals are level and the final one slightly higher. Compared to all examples of HZL 43 (with the exception of HZL 43/19) the initial *Winkelhaken* is a horizontal wedge rather than one impressed at an angle. It is unclear how seriously this can be taken as a separate variant.[26] However, there is also an unusual form of the sign SAG on this tablet (= SI+GIŠ), which also does not correspond to any listed under HZL 192 (the closest being HZL 192/10), although a vaguely similar one is found in KUB 26.80: 4′ (a fragment of *CTH* 83 which must be from the time of Ḫattušili III or after). While the aberration in the form of RU can perhaps be explained by the clearly hurried and untidy writing of the tablet, we are here dealing with a different sign-form, although its dating must hang in uncertainty.

Fig. 6. The forms of SAG (HZL 192) in BKT 5 and KUB 26.80.

It would be unwise to venture a dating on the basis of these scanty data, other than anything between the late 15th and the 13th centuries BC. However, we may have to do with a tablet that has been written using sign-forms which cannot be immediately slotted into the regular narrative of Hittite practice.

25 Similar listings of gods as part of invocations in the Hurrian language are to be found in *CTH* 615: KBo 11.20 (NSc, Wegner 1995: 141f. no. 32); KBo 46.102 (NSc, Wegner 1995: 138f. no. 31; Groddek 2015); VBoT 50 (NSb-c, Wegner 1995: 143 no. 33); and in *CTH* 712: KUB 27.1 (Bastici 2024: 217–85; Wegner 1995: 31–54 no. 1). They are all on manuscripts belonging to the 13th century BC.

26 There are also a couple of variants with a straight horizontal on RU in KBo 1.5.

6. BKT 12–13: Hurrian tablets with more text[27]

At this point we cannot do any more than hint at possibilities with these older-looking and potentially later-looking fragments. However, the 2023 season brought forth tablets with larger numbers of signs on them. BKT 12 is a small tablet shaped much like a letter, but it contains 71 lines of text. The writing is extremely small, with few signs on the obverse being higher than 2–3 mm. The reverse makes a more untidy impression and the signs are also slightly larger, although sign-size measured by the height of the uprights varies marginally over the whole tablet. The reverse also contains an extra line that seems to have been forgotten and squashed in very small writing between two other lines. The final line appears to have been erased. A total of 89 different signs are deployed throughout the tablet. The text consists of 6 lines of Hittite which instructs people who wish to invoke the gods of various cities and also of the land of Ḫattuša, to go to Katapa, prostrate themselves and recite a prayer in Hurrian. The 64-line Hurrian prayer addresses Teššob as king of the gods, mentions Kumarbi, Ani and other deities and the fact that Teššob rules them, talks about Teššob's power to ensure military victory and destroy cities, and mentions various historical personalities by name, some of whom are known from other texts and provide important dating anchors for the tablet. The text, written on a small, letter-shaped and thus practical tablet as opposed to a library or archival tablet, presents a clear example of the use of religion and mythology in a concrete political context. One suspects that something bad has happened at Katapa, and that Teššob and the other gods must be appeased by going there and performing the prayer.

From a palaeographic perspective all the sign-forms belong essentially to older types apart from two instances of UG on the reverse of the tablet (out of a total of twelve), which have the subscript UD (see discussion above). None of the fifteen cases of E has the initial vertical level with the broken vertical, but in a couple of cases this has happened for URU.[28] The horizontal wedge is not entirely surrounded by the *Winkelhaken* that make up the frame of the sign AḪ, it is pulled out to the right quite considerably, while the *Winkelhaken* are "flattened out" vertically rather than appearing in a classic "cluster" (HZL 332/7 perhaps comes closest). Both "older" and the "later" versions of the signs EL and RU are used, although there are not so many examples.

Some other features of the script may have to do with haste in writing: the fact that DU is frequently written with an unbroken bottom horizontal (HZL 128/9, 10) and elongated *Winkelhaken*, and other times written with a more standard form 128A, might be explained in this way. On the other hand, the fact that the form with the unbroken bottom horizontal usually has an elongated *Winkelhaken* should indicate that this is a separate sign-form, where the extension of the *Winkelhaken* compensates for

27 The two tablets dealt with in this section were the subject of an online reading group held from October through to January 2023–24, which helped greatly with the understanding of their problems. I would like to thank the following colleagues for giving their time so freely in helping me to work towards comprehending these texts: S. Fischer (Berlin), M. Giorgieri (Pavia), S. Görke (Marburg), T. Kitazumi (Berlin), J. Hazenbos (Berlin), H. Yamamoto (Yamaguchi), M. Bachvarova (Wilamette).

28 Starke 1985: 24 sees the completion of this step as a sign of his category IIc, the last stage of Middle Script (= MSc).

the loss of the broken horizontal, rather than being a tachygraphic variant. The late posting of the entry with the unbroken bottom horizontal in the series of variants listed in HZL may indicate that this is supposed to be a late variant. However, the reasonably clear dating of BKT 12 to the early 14th century shows it to be a sign-variant or sign-form that is an option from an earlier period.

The forms of the similarly constructed signs AB and UM are minimally but significantly differentiated. We can tell the difference between UM and AB in BKT 12 because the former has a second bottom horizontal which protrudes somewhat to the right (HZL 98/1, 6), whereas the first bottom horizontal can be a little higher than the second. There are forms of AB in other Hittite texts which can look like this, as booked at HZL 97/6. However, this seems to be the method that is used in this tablet to distinguish between them. The differentiation is thus tablet specific. A similar practice seems to obtain on KBo 1.5 (*CTH* 41.I, Šunaššura Treaty), where UM and AB are differentiated in precisely the same way. Quite the opposite seems to obtain on the very few samples of AB on the Madduwatta tablet, on the other hand.

		KUB 14.1+	KBo 1.5	KBo 5.7	BKT 12
AZ	with subscript	4	2?	1	0
	no subscript	1	18	1	0
UG	with subscript	4	1?	1	2
	no subscript	5	0	0	9
UM	HZL 98/1	0	26	0	3
	HZL 98/2	0	4	0	0
AB	HZL 97/6	1	0	0	0
	HZL 97/1	2	16	0	2
DUB	HZL 99/1	1?	2	2	0
	HZL 99/4		1		
DU	HZL 128/1-3	56	17	16	7
	HZL 128/4	0	1	0	0
	HZL 128/9	0	0	0	9
	HZL 128/10	0	0	0	1
RU	HZL 43/3	6	7	2	3
	HZL 43/4	1	7	1	2
	HZL 43/5	0	0	0	1
EL	HZL 307/1	10	1	2	1
	HZL 307/6	0	0	0	1
URU	HZL 229/1	2	4	7	2
	HZL 229/2	21	44	17	5
LU	HZL 210/1	6	25	9	1
	HZL 210/x	0	0	0	4

Table 1. The frequency of sign-forms that vary in BKT 12 in other MS tablets: Madduwatta, Šunaššura A, Kuwatalla Land Donation. Variants in HZL are given which are most similar to the forms identified on photos from the Mainz Fotoarchiv at www.hethiter.net.

The palaeographic comparison with KBo 1.5, KUB 14.1 and KBo 5.7 is quite instructive. The forms of E in KBo 1.5 include several that have level heads of verticals and in the majority form the initial horizontals always start below the level of the initial vertical.[29] In BKT 12, as in KUB 14.1+, the initial vertical is always below the level of the top horizontal. All the forms of AḪ are "earlier" (HZL 332/1–3) on all three of KBo 1.5 (×20), KUB 14.1 (×14) and KBo 5.7 (×5), while all the forms of AḪ in BKT 12 (×11) are "later" (HZL 332/6–7). A similar case can be made for ḪAR, although the Madduwatta text (KUB 14.1+) shares later forms of this sign with BKT 12 (HZL 333/4). The distribution of "older" and "later" forms of URU is roughly similar proportionally between the different tablets.

Even if we might want to call this script "majority IIb" using Starke's categories, the fact that historical personalities such as Tarḫuntaradu and "Kummanean" Pariyawatra are mentioned gives this tablet a secure dating in the early 14th century, likely during the reign of Tudḫaliya II. And these late features (essentially two cases of UG and all cases of AḪ) might fit well with a later dating than the end of the 15th century, even if traditional palaeographic accounts allow the former to become apparent as early as the IIb category. In terms of the proportions of the earlier vs the later sign-forms, there is little to tell between the different tablets compared above, with all of them showing consistencies of opposing later and earlier sign-forms for different signs. As we will see below when discussing BKT 13, there are other reasons for thinking that there might be some relationship between KBo 1.5 and the Büklükale tablets. But the method of statistical comparison allows us to come to no more than typological conclusions, identifying tablets that contain different combinations of sign-forms, and does not help with the dating in any shape or form. There is in my view no way to distinguish between tablets written in the reign of Arnuwanda I and those written in the reign of Tudḫaliya II on the basis of the proportional frequency of sign-forms occurring on a tablet.

The script of BKT 12 is neat and well executed, at least on the obverse. However, there are a couple of peculiarities in spelling conventions, some of which are typical of Hurrian texts found at Boğazköy, and some of which are less typical. Unusual from the perspective of Hittite (but not Hurrian) spelling, is that the sign LU, taking a form not found in HZL with two inset horizontals rather than one (Fig. 7), is used with the value *tip* in the word *tipšari* "words" and possibly one other case.[30] It is noteworthy that the attestations of this value cluster over a couple of lines (53–55).

Fig. 7. The forms of LU (HZL 210) on BKT 12 with line numbers.

29 Left vertical below top horizontal (HZL 187A, 187/2): KBo 1.5 obv. i 33, 41, ii 27, rev. iii 37, 41, 47, iv 25, 26, 28(?); Left vertical higher than top horizontal but lower than top of right broken vertical (HZL 187/B, 187/1): KBo 1.5 obv. i 10, 12, 13, 22, 43, 45, 50, 52, 56, ii 5, 15, 35, 41, 49, 56, 59, rev. iii 7, 11, 14 (twice), 16, 19, 29, 33, 40, 43, 46, iv 14, 17; Heads of uprights level (HZL 187/9): KBo 1.5 obv. i 29, 33, ii 1, rev. iii 16, 21, 45, 57, 60, iv 5, 35. Checked on photos hethiter.net/:fotarch B0560, N03568, N03561, N03559.

30 BKT 12 rev. 53 tip-ša-ri-ip "your words"; 54 tip-ša-[...]; 55 e-ia-am-tip$^{?}$-al "?". HZL 210 books this value as Hurrian. The probable attestation on line 55 is not included in Fig. 7 due to uncertainty of identification.

BKT 12 uses the signs wa_{a}, we_{e}, wu_{u}, $wu_{ú}$ as is perfectly regular for Hurrian texts from other Hittite sites as a means of specifying a change in vowel-quality for the essentially polyvalent cuneiform sign PI (= *wa, we, wi, wu*). In many cases in BKT 12 the upper horizontal under which the qualifying vowel sign is written is very high (Fig. 8), whereas the form of *wa* without subscript has a horizontal halfway up the vertical (except in one case). One of these types of signs is also attested in the *itkalzi*-group constituted by BKT 8–11.[31] However, very rare is the writing we_{er} which is used to write the phrase *evern(i)-a=m* "you (abs.) as king (ess.)" in the form e-we$_{\mathrm{er}}$-nam.[32] Using a subscript to turn a CV-sign into a CVC sign, rather than just altering the quality of the vowel is quite unusual. Rüster and Neu (1989) record only two signs that are comparable in that they contain a subscript that consists of a VC-sign: HZL 318 wa_{ap} and HZL 325 wi_{ip}. In the case of wa_{ap} the syllable has been supposed to be a writing of the syllable *af(f)*.[33] For HZL 325 wi_{ip} a similar explanation is imaginable, but the context in which it occurs is too fragmentary to be considered proof.[34] This explanation does not come into question here, where it is clear that a CVC sign with fixed vowel has been produced by addition of the subscript.

A similar phenomenon is attested on a further tablet from Büklükale: BKT 13 uses the regular signs wu_{u} and wa_{a} (BKT 13 obv. 32 wu$_{\mathrm{u}}$-u-ri, 33 [ke]-e-wa$_{\mathrm{a}}$-a-nu-du-u-wa$^{?}$), where in each case the subscript vowel is reproduced by the following vowel-sign, but also wu$_{\mathrm{u}}$-ri-ta(-)at (l. 26) where it is not. In a broken context in line 23, however, we also have the writing]-wa_{an}-*an*. Here the syllable -*wan* (or -*fan*, -*van*) has been written using both a subscript VC-sign and using a non-subscript sign to complete the syllable. This is structurally parallel to the writings -wa_{a}-*a*- and -wu_{u}-*u*- that we saw above, but in this case the sign-combination -wa_{an}- could theoretically have been used on its own to complete the syllable. We also see this happening in BKT 13, 29, where we find al-ki-ib-wa$_{\mathrm{an}}$.[35] In line 27 the same word written ending]-wa_{an}-*an* in line 23 is written -wa_{a}-*an*, so it may have been a facultative rather than a prescriptive writing. Structurally speaking, -wa_{an} in line 29 is also comparable to the use of zu-u-lu-u-tu-u-ub-wu$_{\mathrm{ú}}$ to end a word in line 28 of the same text. This is the only evidence we have thus far for this phenomenon and it is word-final, so we cannot say whether it is meant to be syllable-ending or word-ending.

Fig. 8. BKT 12 we$_{\mathrm{er}}$, BKT 13 wa$_{\mathrm{an}}$-an, BKT 13 wa$_{\mathrm{an}}$.

31 BKT 11: 5′ wa$_{\mathrm{a}}$-a-šu-l[i$^{?}$(-) for *fāž-ol-i*(-), antipassive with Root Complement of faž- "enter"?

32 BKT 12 obv. 12. I had thought this was completely unparalleled, but S. Fischer now alerts me by email to the existence of one possible, albeit broken, example from Boğazköy.

33 hi-il-la-wa$_{\mathrm{ap}}$ "I invoke" KUB 47.78 i 16′, 18′, 20′ (= ChS 1/8 no. 8, Thiel and Wegner 1983: 208), HZL 318.

34 ti-i-ši-wi$_{\mathrm{ib}}$-w[V] tīž(a)-iff[V(-)] "your heart"? KBo 33.61a obv.$^{?}$ 5′ (= ChS 1/6 no. 11, Thiel and Wegner 1983: 212).

35 The first part of this word was only identifiable after a join made in the 2024 season. The joins also enabled the identification of parallel texts from Boğazköy, ChS 1/5, no. 126–128, which clarified numerous lexical issues, but these will need to be explored in the publication of the tablet. The parallel texts from Boğazköy do not show any trace of this spelling convention.

This writing with a subscript AN is unknown to me from other Hurrian texts. Now that we know it is something they did, a careful scan of photographs of tablets may yet reveal cases where *-wa-an* has been transliterated and *-wa*$_{an}$ would in fact be more correct. Secure cases such as the *-wa*$_{an}$*-an* from BKT 13 are to my knowledge not attested at all at Ḫattuša or elsewhere. For the moment, this feature remains unique. The fact that we have two tablets containing this feature at Büklükale out of a very small number of fragments that have been excavated there so far might suggest that the Büklükale tablets are products of a special school with a community of practices that is in some respects different to those found at Ḫattuša, Šapinuwa and Šamuḫa. Whether the tablets were written at Büklükale or come from somewhere else is something that remains to be established using methods such as clay analysis, in as far as this can usefully bring about knowledge within the limitations of that form of inquiry.[36] But if they do come from somewhere else, it is currently unlikely to be Ḫattuša.[37]

Further evidence for an alterity among the Büklükale tablets when contrasted with those from Ḫattuša and Šapinuwa is witnessed by some further linguistic and graphic features of BKT 13. The tablet has one section written in Hittite and one in Hurrian, as well as a reverse which contains only fragmentary most likely Hittite but also unclear words, as well as an apparent drawing of a vessel, bag or container of some kind. Some elements of the language on the Hurrian part, such as optatives, may indicate that this is another example of a prayer or incantation, but the relationship between the two parts has yet to be clarified.[38]

Whoever wrote the Hittite parts of this tablet was not a first-language speaker of Hittite. The clearest indication of this is that they have problems with the enclitic chain, not understanding that *nu* elides its vowel when enclitic pronouns starting in *-a-* are added to it, and writing the enclitic pronouns as separate words, with a word-space between them and the *nu-*: l. 7 *nu at* Ú-UL *ḫal*$^{!}$*-za-a-i* "he does not call them/it"; l. 12 *nu aš-kán*. I can well imagine that for anyone who spoke a language that does not include fronting of pronouns in an enclitic chain, this must have been a very confusing feature of Hittite. The word-order implications of this seem to have been understood, but not the phonotactics or the phenomenon of enclisis, at least for the pronominal element of the chain. The particle *-kán* appears to be attached to the 3rd sg. nom. enclitic pronoun (-)*aš-* as if the latter were an independent pronoun. The writer of this Hittite part also had problems articulating double consonants, which are such an important part of

36 Methodologically speaking, clay analysis can only ever establish that two samples of clay are different, not that they are the same. The latter can only be established with varying grades of likelihood, not certainty.

37 A fragment found during the 2023 season at Boğazkale (KBo 71.166), which also contains a hymn to Teššob, has a shape and writing that looks very similar particularly to the bottom of BKT 12 and is also written in late Middle Hittite script. A similar looking tablet also with a prayer to Teššob was found at Ortaköy in 2022. These other tablets do not have these specific aberrant features which are found on the Büklükale tablets. I am grateful to Aygül Süel, Leila Murat-Karakurt and Daniel Schwemer for discussing these finds with me.

38 A join from the 2024 season reveals that the Hurrian text has a partial parallel in ChS 1/5, no. 126–128.

Hittite phonology:[39] l. 6 *ma-ḫa-an*, l. 7 LÚ-*at-tar*, possibly l. 6 *a-ni-i-ia-an*, for *maḫḫan*, *pešnatar* and *anniyan*.[40] In the word *me-ma-a-ta* it is unclear what is going on.

Against the background of these data it is worthy of note that the tablet also contains one sign and at least two sign-forms that are not otherwise attested at Ḫattuša or elsewhere in Anatolia as far as I am aware. A sign that is completely alien to Ḫattuša and other places is the one booked first in Fig. 5 in order to illustrate the form of KA.[41] The sign-form (UŠ+GIŠ) is unproblematic in this case, but the sign itself with its inscribed elements UŠ$^{\text{MEŠ?}}$ is unknown. It is quite normal for Hittite signs to be constructed using the box-like element of KA to insert elements which clarify the meaning or pronunciation in some way (Weeden 2011b: 32, 102, 261–63). Sometimes such constructions are not attested as yet anywhere else in the cuneiform world, e. g. KA×UD = ZU_9 = "tooth". That would also be the case here. As far as the meaning is concerned one can only guess.[42] However, the fact that this feature of Hittite cuneiform is being performed innovatively on this tablet fits with tendencies in Hittite scholarship more generally, even if it remains unique for the moment.

Particularly the sign-forms of MA (HZL 208) and TE (HZL 249) appear in forms that seem to have a parallel construction (Fig. 5): both consist of one upright to which a cluster of 3 or 4 horizontals/diagonals are attached by only one horizontal/diagonal, instead of (all) three of the horizontals/diagonals being attached or close to the vertical wedge. There are no forms booked in HZL which correspond to this. The shape of the tablet is consistent with that of a Hittite letter, just like BKT 12, although this one looks like it would have been slightly taller (9.5 cm compared to 9 cm) and thicker. From the perspective of shape, there is thus no reason to think that this tablet must have come from outside of Anatolia, although this is a fairly regular tablet shape throughout the cuneiform world.

A brief perusal of sign-forms from roughly contemporary Syrian sites (Ugarit, Emar, Qaṭna) does not give any immediate connections. The form of MA looks like it could have arisen in a number of ways: confusion with certain variants of BA

39 There is an extensive debate on the pronunciation of these double-consonants, for which I refer to Kloekhorst 2021 as a recent example of discussion that addresses various viewpoints.

40 Reading *-at-*, and *a-ni-i-* courtesy M. Giorgieri (pers. comm.). Originally (in June 2023), I had read ŠEŠ-*ma-tar* and NAM.MA.A.NI, the first because the initial horizontals of AT are not clear and the second because spelling of *anniyan* with one -n- is unusual. Giorgieri's proposals (from December 2023) fit the regular form of MA in this tablet much better, and add a further piece of evidence for the scribe's difficulties with double consonants.

41 There is possibly another example of KA being used for the logogram INIM "word" on the tablet in the same line which has the same form, but the reading is too insecure to serve as a piece of evidence. The sign-form would be the same, however, as in this case: UŠ+GIŠ.

42 The guess I currently favour for the interpretation of this sign is that the inscribed UŠ is a phonetic writing of ÚŠ (= BAD), and that this is an attempt to write the logogram UŠ_{11} (= KA×BAD) "(black) magic" which does not occur at Ḫattuša, where it has been replaced by the innovated logogram UḪ_7 (= *alwanzatar*, cf. Weeden 2011b: 68, 323). The MEŠ is unclear and reading it requires some of the apparent traces to be damage, but this is the best solution currently available. ÚŠ (= BAD) is spelled BA.UŠ in a phonetic writing of the logogram meaning "died" once at KBo 3.54: 8′ (Weeden 2011b: 35, 334). In BKT 13 the logogram KA×UŠ$^{\text{MEŠ?}}$-*i* would be a verb, "performs magic, conjures", presumably concerning an enemy.

(e. g. HZL 205/8), or out of writings of MA under pressurised circumstances, such as on the edge of the tablet, where the upright might become separated from the horizontals/diagonals. On KBo 1.5 (Šunaššura Treaty, *CTH* 41.I, tablet A), the regular form of MA has a good deal of distance between the upright and the horizontals, with the middle horizontal being set back from the upper and lower ones.[43] This technique differentiates the form of MA clearly from the form of KU on the tablet. It would only involve one step, pushing the central horizontal to the right until it touches the upright, before we had the form that is available in BKT 13 (see Fig. 9), and indeed one variant in BKT 13 may take a similar shape to that regularly found on KBo 1.5.[44] A similar form of MA to that in KBo 1.5 is also attested in BKT 18, the strangely shaped oracular letter excavated in 2022. Such speculative explanations mean that it is not impossible that these are sign-forms that developed in the central Hittite area as part of independent processes, but did not become regular at Ḫattuša.

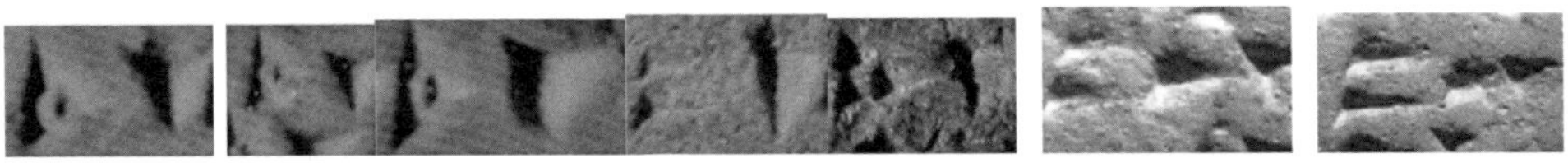

Fig. 9. Examples of MA from KBo 1.5 (on left) and BKT 18 (centre) that might be structurally comparable to MA on BKT 13 (right).

What is precisely to be inferred from this situation is unclear. Was the tablet of BKT 13 written at Büklükale or sent from somewhere else? In other words, is the fact that the author is apparently a second-language speaker of Hittite relevant for arguing that the tablet has been sent from somewhere else where Hittite was not primarily spoken, or is it more relevant for consideration of the significance of a multi-cultural court presence at Büklükale? Is this one of the "foreign experts" that some modern scholars credit with bringing new knowledge of cuneiform lore and new cuneiform writing techniques to the Hittite heartland, or is this a local person, or someone from the west or north, a non-Hittite speaker, who had trouble learning the conventions of writing Hittite in cuneiform?[45] Without further evidence it is difficult to answer these questions. It is to be hoped that a comprehensive clay analysis of the tablets using pXRF or other methods will bring further data that can contribute towards finding a solution.

43 See e. g. KBo 1.5 rev iii 51 the form of MA in *a-am-ma-an-ga*$_{14}$*-ar* and at iii 58 in *ap-pu-na-ma*, fotoarchiv B0560. In fact there are only three cases on the tablet-photos, as far as I can see, where the horizontals touch the vertical, the clearest being at iii 41, where the sign looks more like KU. For BA on the same tablet: KBo 1.5 obv. ii 11 (*ú-ba-ʾa-a-ma*, iii 34 *i-ba-ʾa-ar-šu-nu* where the BA also looks similar to the form of MA in BKT 13). BA has a bottom horizontal that is set slightly to the right of the top horizontal. Investigation of the differences between BA and MA on this tablet reveals a couple of cases where current readings are mistaken: obv. ii 18, 21, 23, 25, rev. iii 24, 27 each read *i-pá-aš-ša-ar* not *i-ma-aš-ša-ar* (Wilhelm 2014). It makes no difference to the meaning (CAD P 241f.).

44 This only became clear by collation during the 2024 season, but the attestation (BKT 13: 3, listed second under MA in Fig. 5) cannot be interpreted as completely secure.

45 One hypothesis for Büklükale's history, if it is to be equated with Nenašša, is that it may have been briefly occupied by or closely connected to the Kaška-people, if we believe that part of Ḫattušili III's narrative of the concentric invasions (Stavi 2015).

And what of the comparison to KBo 1.5? The fact that KBo 1.5 differentiates between UM and AB in a manner similar to BKT 12 is a matter for typological observation, that will only become significant once further examples of this practice have been identified. The fact that KBo 1.5 and BKT 18 differentiate MA and KU in a manner comparable to BKT 13, even if they are not using precisely the same sign-form of MA, is a peculiarity of handwriting which is to my mind striking enough to show that KBo 1.5 might have been written around the same time as BKT 13 or at least is part of a scribal tradition that may have been related to it. This would fit with some of the other "late" characteristics within the Middle Script category on KBo 1.5 (form of E), as well as on BKT 18. However, other examples of this phenomenon need to be found, and if a similar form of MA to that used on BKT 13 turns up anywhere, then this would make a much better comparison. For the moment MA and TE on BKT 13 remain unique, and considered in combination with the other features of the writing and language on the tablet, likely not to be from Ḫattuša.

7. Conclusions: Hypothetical timeline, ambiguity and alterity

If we want to construct a hypothetical timeline of the tablets from Büklükale we must be extremely cautious and remember the caveats of the introductory section concerning the dangers of relying on diagnostic signs and trying to date small fragments. However, the form of AḪ in BKT 10 really does seem to go out of fashion at least before the last phase of the Middle Hittite period: Examples on the Kuwatalla-Text (Arnuwanda I), the Madduwatta-Text (Arnuwanda I), and tablet A of the Šunaššura Treaty (late Middle Hittite copy of text originally from the time of Tudḫaliya I?)[46] are quite different, and this sign-form does not occur on any of them. On the other hand, at least one other Hurrian tablet (KUB 27.38) has this form, also exclusively, combining it with forms of UG and AZ that are supposed to start only sporadically in the IIb (MSb) period according to the traditional account. On this basis, in combination with consideration of the formatting of the columns cut by line-initial signs, and of all further due caveats, we might hypothesise that this is the earliest tablet we have, although it would be very rash to suggest a dating. The presence of this fragment and of other fragments from multi-columned tablets suggest that there were in fact longer-lasting tablet archives at Büklükale, which in turn suggests at least the possibility of a home-grown scribal tradition.

Then we have a cluster of fragments that may date from the time of Tudḫaliya II, but could also date from the time of Arnuwanda I, but which lack independent internal dating criteria: BKT 1 and 3, which seem to have a diplomatic context. They could have been sent from Ḫattuša, or wherever the king was resident at the time. BKT 13 is also

46 For a brief assessment of the palaeography of KBo 1.5 see Klinger 1998: 373 ("... ist zweifelsohne deutlich vor den späteren Verträgen, die von Šuppiluliuma I geschlossen wurden, anzusetzen"). This present article follows the conclusions of Klinger 1998 and 2003 and following research that the dating criteria for Hittite texts can by and large be used to date Akkadian tablets from Boğazköy.

MSb? Tudḫaliya I?	BKT 10	*itkalzi*
Tudḫaliya II	BKT 12	Hurrian prayer
MSb/c?	BKT 1, 3, 13	diplomatic, cultic/magical texts
MSc/NSa	BKT 18	bird oracle
Latest?	BKT 5	Hurrian invocation of deities

Table 2. A hypothetical chronology of the tablets from Büklükale.

probably to be included in this group, which cannot be fixed in time as easily as BKT 12 that is likely to be dated to the time of Tudḫaliya II.

The major question that can only be answered by further evidence is whether the majority context of almost all the tablets belongs to one particular point in time, possibly diplomatic activity leading up to or in the wake of a destruction event in the early 14th century BC, rather than being separated out chronologically in the manner imagined above. The alternative is that we have tablets from different periods, some of which may have been stored in an archive. Further evidence will make it clearer whether the isolated features that might be understandable in one way or another are in fact outliers or part of larger trends.

The overall assessment of the palaeography particularly of BKT 12, dated by the occurrence of historical personages to the reign of Tudḫaliya II, shows us that it is difficult to use statistical methods for the dating of sign-forms on tablets in this period with any clarity of result. Older sign forms and later sign-forms are used in waves of varying combinations, by different schools of scribal practice. How one ascribes palaeographic labels to tablets belonging to these waves is something that still needs to be worked out, noting that typological classifications and chronological ones do not necessarily overlap. There is no such thing as a tendential directional development in the frequency of use of particular sign-forms at this period. On the contrary, what we can still do is continue the traditional work of Hittite cuneiform palaeography, which has been to work out when sign-forms or remarkable variants start being used, but also importantly: when they stop being used.

Finally, the presence of unusual sign-forms among the tablets at Büklükale indicates that some of them (probably not the diplomatic texts) are the products of traditions of writing that are not entirely the same as those in use at Ḫattuša. Either these were developed locally, or the tablets have been sent from elsewhere, being somewhere that does not use the same conventions as Ḫattuša. The current evidence is insufficient to answer this. However, the number of idiosyncrasies present, particularly the use of VC-signs as subscripts in Hurrian texts to create CVC values, the invention of a logogram and the use of unique sign-forms that are likely to have developed within Central Anatolia, and have likely relationships with tendencies observable in Ḫattuša cuneiform, make me think initially that some of them at least may be products of a local scribal tradition, albeit one with close contacts to Ḫattuša, Šapinuwa and other royal centres. It thus seems that there is likely to be more variety and diversity in the cuneiform of Central Anatolia than previously thought by some scholars, including myself.

Bibliography

Bachvarova, Mary

2012 From "Kingship in Heaven" to King Lists: Syro-Anatolian Courts and the History of the World. *JANER* 12: 97–118.

Barjamovic, Gojko

2010 Sites, Routes and Historical Geography in Central Anatolia. In: Itamar Singer (ed.), *ipamati kistamati pari tumatimis – Luwian and Hittite Studies Presented to J. David Hawkins on the Occasion of His 70th Birthday.* Tel Aviv: Institute of Archaeology, 10–25.

Bastici, Fabio

2024 *Philologische Untersuchungen zu den hurro-hethitischen Festritualen. Ein Beitrag zum hethitisch-hurritischen Sprach- und Kulturkontakt.* THeth 34. Heidelberg: Winter.

Cammarosano, Michele

2014 The Cuneiform Stylus. *Mesopotamia* 49: 53–90.

2015 3-D Joins und Schriftmetrologie. A Quantitative Approach to Cuneiform Palaeography. In: Elena Devecchi, Gerfrid G.W. Müller, and Jana Mynářová (eds.), *Current Research in Cuneiform Palaeography. Proceedings of the Workshop organised at the 60th Rencontre Assyriologique Internationale, Warsaw 2014.* Gladbeck: PeWe, 145–86.

Cammarosano, Michele, Gerfrid Müller, Denis Fisseler, and Frank Weichert

2014 Schriftmetrologie des Keils. Dreidimensionale Analyse von Keileindrükken und Handschriften. *WdO* 44: 2–36.

Campbell, Denis

2016 The introduction of Hurrian religion into the Hittite empire. *Religion Compass* 2016; 10: 295–306.

Corti, Carlo

2017 The North: Hanhana, Hattena, Ištahara, Hakpiš, Nerik, Zalpuwa, Tummana, Pala and the Hulana River Land. In: Mark Weeden and Lee Ullmann (eds.), *Hittite Landscape and Geography.* HbOr 1/121. Leiden: Brill, 219–38.

de Martino, Stefano

2003 *Annali e res gestae antico ittiti.* StMed 12. Pavia: Italian University Road.

Forlanini, Massimo

2008 The Historical Geography of Anatolia and the Transition from the Kārum-Period to the Early Hittite Empire. In: J. G. Dercksen (ed.), *Anatolia and the Jazira during the Old Assyrian Period.* PIHANS 111. Leiden: Nederlands Instituut voor het Nabije Oosten, 57–86.

Goedegebuure, Petra

2014 *The Hittite Demonstratives: Studies in Deixis, Topics and Focus.* StBoT 55. Wiesbaden: Harrassowitz.

Gordin, Shai
2015 *Hittite Scribal Circles. Scholarly Tradition and Writing Habits.* StBoT 59. Wiesbaden: Harrassowitz.

Groddek, Detlev
2015 *Hethitische Texte in Transkription. KBo 46.* DBH 47. Wiesbaden: Harrassowitz.

Hoffner, Harry A. and H. Craig Melchert
2008 *A Grammar of the Hittite Language.* Winona Lake: Eisenbrauns.

Homan, Zenobia
2019 *Mittani Palaeography.* Leiden: Brill.

Klinger, Jörg
1996 *Untersuchungen zur Rekonstruktion des hattischen Kultschicht.* StBoT 37. Wiesbaden: Harrassowitz.
1998 "Wer lehrte die Hethiter das Schreiben?" Zur Paläographie früher Texte in akkadischer Sprache aus Boğazköy: Skizze einiger Überlegungen und vorläufiger Ergebnisse. In: Sedat Alp and Aygül Süel (eds.), *III. Uluslararası Hititoloji Kongresi Bildirileri, Çorum 16–22 Eylül 1996 – Acts of the IIIrd International Congress of Hittitology, Çorum, September 16–22, 1996.* Ankara: Uyum Ajans, 365–75.
2003 Zur Paläographie akkadischsprachiger Texte aus Ḫattuša. In: Gary M. Beckman, Richard H. Beal, and Gregory McMahon (eds.), *Hittite Studies in Honor of Harry A. Hoffner Jr. on the Occasion of His 65th Birthday.* Winona Lake: Eisenbrauns, 237–48.
2022a Zu den Anfängen der hethitischen Überlieferung überhaupt und zur Methode der paläographischen Textdatierung. In: Eva Cancik-Kirschbaum and Ingo Schrakamp (eds.), *Transfer, Adaption und Neukonfiguration von Schrift- und Sprachwissen im alten Orient.* Episteme in Bewegung 25. Wiesbaden: Harrassowitz, 255–340.
2022b The Hittite Writing Traditions of Cuneiform Documents. In: Stefano de Martino (ed.), *Handbook Hittite Empire. Power Structures.* Empires through the Ages in Global Perspective 1. Berlin / Boston: de Gruyter Oldenburg, 93–155.

Kloekhorst, Alwin
2021 The phonetics and phonology of Hittite intervocalic fortis and lenis stops. *BiOr* 78: 327–52.

Kloekhorst, Alwin and Willemijn Waal
2019 A Hittite Scribal Tradition Predating the Tablet Collections of Ḫattuša? The origin of the 'cushion-shaped' tablets KBo 3.22, KBo 17.21+, KBo 22.1, and KBo 22.2. *ZA* 109: 189–203.

Košak, Silvin
2002– *Konkordanz der hethitischen Keilschrifttafeln, Online-Datenbank Version* hethiter.net/: hethkonk (2.plus) – last accessed 10.04.2024.

Kryszeń, Adam

2016 *A Historical Geography of the Hittite Heartland.* AOAT 437. Münster: Ugarit.

Matsumura, Kimiyoshi and Mark Weeden

2019 Büklükale in the Hittite Period. In: Aygül Süel (ed.), *IX. Uluslararası Hititoloji Kongresi Bildirileri, Çorum 08–14 Eylül 2014 / Acts of the IXth International Congress of Hittitology, Çorum September 08–14, 2014, voll. I–II.* Çorum: Valilik, 533–66.

Miller, Jared L.

2004 *Studies in the Origins, Development and Interpretation of the Kizzuwatna Rituals.* StBoT 46. Wiesbaden: Harrassowitz.

Müller, Gerfrid

2018 Sign chains and writer identity. How to deal with intra- and inter-writer variations. *News from the Land of the Hittites* 2: 7–15.

Müller, Gerfrid, Denis Fisseler, and Frank Weichert

2015 3D-Joins und Schriftmetrologie. Die Entwicklung des "CuneiformAnalyser" zur Computer-unterstützten Visualisierung, Analyse und Rekonstruktion von Keilschrifttafeln. In: Elena Devecchi, Gerfrid Müller, and Jana Mynářová (eds.), *Current Research in Cuneiform Palaeography. Proceedings of the Workshop organised at the 60th Rencontre Assyriologique Internationale, Warsaw 2014.* Gladbeck: PeWe, 129–44.

Parkes, Malcom B.

2008 *Their Hands Before Our Eyes: A Closer Look at Scribes: The Lyell Lectures Delivered in the University of Oxford 1999.* Aldershot: Ashgate.

Rüster, Christel

1972 *Hethitische Keilschrift-Paläographie.* StBoT 20. Wiesbaden: Harrassowitz.

Rüster, Christel and Gernot Wilhelm

2012 *Landschenkungsurkunden hethitischer Könige.* StBoTB 4. Wiesbaden: Harrassowitz.

Sakuma, Yasuhiko

2009 *Hethitische Vogelorakeltexte. Teil 1: Untersuchung; Teil 2: Bearbeitung.* Dissertation, University of Würzburg.

Sir Gavaz, Özlem

2019 Büklükale'nin Hititler Dönemindeki Adı Üzerine Yeni Bir Değerlendirme (A New Evaluation of the Name of Büklükale in the Hittite Period). *TÜBA-AR* 25: 85–94.

Starke, Frank

1985 *Die keilschrift-luwischen Texte in Umschrift.* StBoT 30. Wiesbaden: Harrassowitz.

Stavi, Boaz

2015 *The Reign of Tudhaliya II and Šuppiluliuma I. The Contribution of the Hittite Documentation to a Reconstruction of the Amarna Age.* THeth 31. Heidelberg: Winter.

Steitler, Charles

2020 Festival Tablets from the Final Decades of the Hittite Empire: Scribes and Writing Conventions. In: Stefano de Martino and Elena Devecchi (eds.), *Anatolia between the 13th and the 12th century BCE.* Eothen 23. Firenze: LoGisma, 411–55.

Stratford, Edward

2015 Old Assyrian Literacy: Formulating a Method for Graphic Analysis and Some Initial Results. In: Fikri Kulakoğlu and Cécile Michel (eds.), *Proceedings of the 1st Kültepe International Meeting, Kültepe, 19–23 September 2013. Studies dedicated to Kutlu Emre. KIM 1 (Kültepe International Meetings 1).* Subartu 35. Turnhout: Brepols, 117–28.

Taylor, Jon

2015 Wedge Order in Cuneiform: a Preliminary Survey. In: Elena Devecchi, Gerfrid Müller, and Jana Mynářová (eds.), *Current Research in Cuneiform Palaeography. Proceedings of the Workshop organised at the 60th Rencontre Assyriologique Internationale, Warsaw 2014.* Gladbeck: PeWe, 1–30.

Thiel, Hans Jochen and Ilse Wegner

1983 Eine Anrufung an den Gott Teššup von Ḫalab in hurritischer Sprache. *SMEA* 24: 187–213.

Torri, Giulia

2015 Hereditary Transmission of Specialized Knowledge in Hittite Anatolia: The Case of the Scribal Families of the Empire Period. In: Alfonso Archi (ed.), *Tradition and Innovation in the Ancient Near East: Proceedings of the 57th Rencontre Assyriologique Internationale at Rome 4–8 July 2011.* CRRAI 57. Winona Lake: Eisenbrauns, 577–86.

2023 The Hittite King as Administrator of the Land. In: Giulia Torri and Clelia Mora (eds.), *Administrative Practices and Political Control in Anatolian and Syro-Anatolian Polities in the 2nd and 1st Millennium BCE.* StAs 13. Firenze: Firenze University Press, 25–36.

van den Hout, Theo P.J.

1989 *Studien zum Spätjunghethitischen: Texte der Zeit Tudhaliyas IV. KBo IV 10+ (CTH 106).* Unpublished Dissertation, Universiteit van Amsterdam.

2009 A Century of Hittite Text Dating and the Origins of the Hittite Cuneiform Script. *Incontri Linguistici* 32: 11–35.

2020 *A History of Hittite Literacy. Writing and Reading in Late Bronze-Age Anatolia (1650–1200 BC).* Cambridge: Cambridge University Press.

van de Peut, Lidewij E.
2022 *Persuading the Divine. On the Composition of Hittite Prayers.* StBoT 69. Wiesbaden: Harrassowitz.

Waal, Willemijn
2015 *Hittite Diplomatics. Studies in Ancient Document Format and Record Management.* StBoT 57. Wiesbaden: Harrassowitz.

Weeden, Mark
2011a Hittite Scribal Schools Outside of Hattusa? *AoF* 38: 116–34.
2011b *Hittite Logograms and Hittite Scholarship.* StBoT 54. Wiesbaden: Harrassowitz.
2013 A Hittite Tablet from Büklükale. *Anatolian Archaeological Studies* 18: 19–35.
2016 Hittite Epigraphic Finds from Büklükale, 2010–14. *Anatolian Archaeological Studies* 19: 81–104.
2017 A Cuneiform Fragment from the 2016 Season at Büklükale, BKT 3. Part of a Diplomatic Text? *Anatolian Archaeological Studies* 20: 17–21.

Wegner, Ilse
1995 *Hurritische Opferlisten aus hethitischen Festbeschreibungen, Teil 1: Texte für IŠTAR-Ša(w)uška.* ChS I/3–I. Roma: Bonsignori Editore.

Wilhelm, Gernot
2010 Ein Fragment mit hurritischen Gallenomina und der Beginn der hurritischen Überlieferung in Ḫattuša. In: Jörg Becker, Ralph Hempelmann, and Ellen Rehm (eds.), *Kulturlandschaft Syrien. Zentrum und Peripherie – Festschrift für Jan-Waalke Meyer.* AOAT 371. Münster: Ugarit, 623–35.
2014 Vertrag Tutḫaliyas I. mit Šunaššura von Kizzuwatna (akk. Fassung – *CTH* 41.I.2). hethiter.net/: *CTH* 41.I.2 (TX 19.02.2014, TRde 19.02.2014) – last accessed 10.04.2024.
2018 *Kleine Beiträge zum Hurritischen.* StBoT 64. Wiesbaden: Harrassowitz.